The Institute of Chartered Accountants in England and Wales

BUSINESS STRATEGY

For exams in 2016

Question Bank

www.icaew.com

Business Strategy
The Institute of Chartered Accountants in England and Wales

ISBN: 978-1-78363-213-8
Previous ISBN: 978-0-85760-993-9

First edition 2008
Ninth edition 2015

The content of this publication is intended to prepare students for the
ICAEW examinations, and should not be used as professional advice.

British Library Cataloguing-in-Publication Data
A catalogue record for this book is available from the British Library
Originally printed in the United Kingdom by Polestar Wheatons on
paper obtained from traceable, sustainable sources.

Polestar Wheatons
Hennock Road
Marsh Barton
Exeter
EX2 8RP

Contents

The following questions are exam-standard. Unless told otherwise, these questions are the style, content and format that you can expect in your exam.

The Study Manual reference column highlights where the questions in this Question Bank have been explicitly referred to in the Study Manual. The references in the Study Manual highlight how key business strategy concepts and theories have been examined in past exam questions. This should be used as a guide to help you with your studies and is not intended to provide any insight into those syllabus areas which may be examined in future sittings. The Sample Paper can also be found at the back of the Study Manual.

Title	Study Manual Reference	Marks	Time allocation Mins	Page Question	Page Answer
Business Strategy past exam questions					
March 2008 – December 2009					
1 DA plc (Mar 08)	Ch2/4/7/8	40	60	3	139
2 Kraftvagen Gmbh (Mar 08)		28	42	5	146
3 Campaign for Trading Equitably (Mar 08)	Ch3	32	48	7	155
4 Embury Ltd (Sept 08)	Ch15	42	63	9	162
5 DT Ltd (Sept 08)	Ch7/11/13	32	48	11	171
6 CWI International Ltd (Mar 09)	Ch12	20	30	13	177
7 Kemmex Ice Cream plc (Jun 09)	Ch12	43	64	15	183
8 Evara Electrical Engineers Ltd (Jun 09)	Ch9	32	48	18	191
9 Rugeley Tableware plc (Sept 09)	Sample paper	40	60	19	197
10 Pitstop Ltd (Sept 09)	Sample paper	27	40	21	205
11 Somborne Zoological Park Ltd (Sept 09)	Sample paper, Ch1/14	33	49	23	212
12 Green Cards Ltd (Dec 09)		43	64	25	220
13 Efficiency Systems Ltd (Dec 09)		32	48	27	228
14 Total Equipment Hire Ltd (Dec 09)		25	37	30	232
March 2010					
15 Blazing Bicycles Ltd	Ch5	42	63	32	236
16 Deeshire Council		36	54	35	244
17 NP Ltd	Ch8	22	33	36	253
June 2010					
18 Executive Travel Ltd	Ch16	42	63	37	258
19 Hutton Haulage plc		31	47	40	264
20 Cutting Edge Ltd		27	40	41	268
September 2010					
21 Supaspeed Ltd		43	64	42	272
22 e-Parts Ltd	Ch10	21	32	45	280
23 Marcham plc	Ch11	36	54	46	284

Title	Study Manual Reference	Marks	Time allocation Mins	Page Question	Answer
December 2010					
24 Quantum Agencies Ltd		44	66	47	291
25 SkinDeepe plc		33	50	50	297
26 Heaton Home		23	34	51	301
March 2011					
27 Family Entertainment Company plc	Ch10	45	67	53	304
28 MPW Ltd	Ch6	31	47	55	312
29 SPV plc		24	36	56	319
June 2011					
30 Cauldron Cereals plc		44	66	58	323
31 Henford plc	Ch9	34	51	60	330
32 Felan Fashions plc		22	33	62	336
December 2011					
33 KoganAir plc		43	64	63	340
34 Universal Office Supplies plc		33	50	65	348
35 Conchester Theatre		24	36	67	353
September 2012					
36 Bigville Council	Ch3	42	63	68	356
37 Beauty Soap Ltd		33	50	71	365
38 Maureen's Motors		25	37	73	371
December 2012					
39 Grassgrind Garden Mowers plc		45	67	74	375
40 Care 4U Ltd	Ch7	31	47	77	385
41 The Mealfest Corporation		24	36	79	390
March 2013					
42 Mayhews Ltd	Ch5	41	62	80	394
43 Cabezada Ltd		32	48	82	403
44 Chiba	Ch15	27	40	84	407
June 2013					
45 Hire Value Ltd	Ch16	45	67	85	413
46 Up 'n' Over plc	Ch10	30	45	87	420
47 Moogle plc	Ch4	25	38	88	423
December 2013					
48 The Contract Cleaning Corporation Ltd	Ch12	42	63	90	427
49 The Foto Phrame Company	Ch13	35	53	92	434
50 FeedAfrica		23	34	94	440

Title	Study Manual Reference	Marks	Time allocation Mins	Page Question	Page Answer
March 2014					
51 Emelius Ltd	Ch6/14	48	72	95	444
52 Boom plc		22	33	98	452
53 Tai Ltd and Jelk plc	Ch11	30	45	99	456
June 2014					
54 Albatross Golf Equipment plc		40	60	101	461
55 Best Fresh Bakeries Ltd	Ch9	28	42	103	469
56 ElectroInfo Ltd		32	48	104	474
September 2014					
57 Forsi Ltd	Ch14	45	68	106	480
58 ToyL Ltd	Ch13	30	45	108	489
59 Water On Tap	Ch16	25	37	110	494
December 2014					
60 Confo plc	Ch1/1112	46	69	111	498
61 Radar Traditional Radios Ltd	Ch1/5/6/8	31	47	114	506
62 The Norgate Bank plc	Ch1	23	34	116	512
March 2015					
63 Rocket Co	Ch12/16	46	69	117	515
64 The Scottish Woodlands Commission		34	51	119	522
65 WeDive Ltd		20	30	121	528
June 2015					
66 Reyel plc		42	63	122	531
67 Home of Leather plc		34	51	124	538
68 Zuccini plc		24	36	126	544
September 2015					
69 Kentish Fruit Farms		43	64	127	548
70 Premier Paper Products plc		30	45	129	555
71 Taxi Tracker		27	41	131	560

Question Bank

Your exam will consist of three questions   100 marks

Time available   2.5 hours

1 DA plc

DA plc (DA) is an information solutions company, listed on the London Stock Exchange.

Company background

DA began trading a number of years ago, providing credit reference services for business customers. Although this remains its primary activity, it has grown organically and now provides financial and statistical information to a variety of UK businesses to help them manage the risk of commercial and financial decisions.

The company is split into three divisions:

- Credit reference services – provides factual information to clients, via credit searches of an individual's financial history, to assist them to lend profitably or offer trade credit.

- Decision software – assists clients in improving the consistency and quality of business decisions in areas such as credit risk, fraud prevention and customer account management.

- Vehicle history – provides financial and statistical information to the automotive industry to help clients understand the risks associated with the purchase or sale of a particular second-hand vehicle.

A breakdown of key data, by division, for 20X7 is as follows:

	Credit reference services	Decision software	Vehicle history	Total
Sales (£m)	166	115	64	345
Operating profit (£m)	41	34	13	88
Growth in sales from 20X6	3%	15%	0%	6%
Number of employees	686	490	300	1,476

Credit reference services

Clients for credit reference services can be split into two groups:

(1) Banks, credit card companies and other financial services organisations which need help assessing the risk associated with lending decisions; and

(2) Commercial companies seeking credit references before supplying goods on credit to other businesses and private customers.

When an individual or business makes an application for credit, the lender or supplier usually asks a credit reference agency (CRA) for a credit search to check the applicant's identity and credit worthiness. The database system operated by a CRA enables different lenders, such as banks, to share information about their customers' credit accounts and repayment histories. Applicants have to give permission for their credit report information to be shared when they apply for credit.

Although a number of companies are currently licensed as CRAs in the UK, DA is the largest, with a 58% market share. DA has built its market position by compiling and managing the most comprehensive credit database in the UK. Communication and information technology are a core part of DA's business. Online systems allow lenders to update data directly, resulting in more accurate information and efficiency gains for DA.

DA's main competitor, CC Inc (CC) is an American-based business with an acknowledged expertise in credit scoring (a statistical technique that combines several financial characteristics to form a single score to represent a customer's creditworthiness). CC has recently announced that, as part of its global expansion strategy, it plans to increase its share of the UK credit market, which is currently 32%. CC intends to use low cost web-based systems to deliver online consumer credit scores directly to lenders and companies extending trade credit. In this way, it hopes to reduce DA's market dominance in the UK.

DA's strategic development

Decision software

Having created a reputation for holding the most comprehensive credit database in the UK, DA went on to develop analytical software to enable clients to process credit applications and manage customer credit accounts more efficiently.

The software takes data from DA's credit management database and other sources, such as the client's own customer account information, and uses analytical tools and scoring systems to provide decision support. Typical users of this product are banks, credit card companies, mortgage providers and other organisations that grant personal or trade credit. DA's software enables them to assess quickly and accurately whether to accept a new customer or extend credit arrangements for existing customers. It can also define the processes the businesses should adopt in managing an account that has fallen into arrears.

Vehicle history

Recognising that it had a core skill in the management of large databases for the financial services industry, DA also decided to provide similar services to the automotive industry. It compiles and manages data on the histories of 30 million vehicles and 25 million car insurance policies in the UK.

This data is used to provide vehicle history information to car dealers, finance providers and insurers. Fraudulent representation of used vehicles is a significant risk for private consumers and a potential financial liability for the businesses involved in the sale or purchase. The vehicle history can assist in establishing the market value of a vehicle; and whether a vehicle is registered as stolen or has outstanding finance.

Proposed diversification

Recently, DA has decided to target a new market, the individual consumer market, with a new online service: 'Checksta'.

Under current UK legislation, individuals have a legal right to see the information about them held by a CRA. In return for a statutory fee of £2, the CRA is legally obliged to provide a written copy of the information held on the individual's credit report. Instead of making a written application for a statutory credit report, individual consumers will be able to pay to subscribe to Checksta.

The Checksta service will allow individuals to check online that their credit report is accurate and up-to-date, as many times as they want. Checksta will send a text or email alert every time there is a significant change to the information held on an individual's credit report. This alert service assists in identifying identity fraud (where somebody applies for credit in another person's name). Individuals will also be able to order a credit score, based on their DA credit report, which will give them an idea of how a lender would view the information, if they were to apply for credit.

The introduction of Checksta is partly in response to the aggressive marketing stance currently being adopted by CC and also as a reaction to the following changes in the external environment:

- Changing attitudes to money and credit

    An increase in spending has led to an increase in demand for credit and it is very easy to apply now, both by telephone and online. This means that individuals are more likely to shop around for credit and lenders have to carry out more credit checks.

- Changes in legislation

    DA has to conform to the UK laws that govern the way it does business. Government concerns that debt levels are too high have caused a tightening of the legislation to give consumers better access to information held on them, more rights regarding disputes with lenders and more protection from rogue lenders. As a result, CRAs have had to implement a consumer education programme, working closely with consumer organisations to help consumers understand how credit referencing works.

- The growth of e-commerce (products bought online)

    This has necessitated more frequent and rapid credit checks and a subsequent upgrading of DA's information technology systems.

- An increase in identity fraud

    Identity criminals steal people's personal information and use these details to commit crimes, usually obtaining credit illegally.

Marketing

To date, DA has worked mainly with business clients, attracting business customers through personal selling and retaining them by developing strong client relationships. The sales director is aware that to succeed in the consumer market, DA will need to use a different marketing strategy for Checksta.

DA intends to use its knowledge of consumers who have applied for their statutory credit reports in the past, to build up a profile of the consumers it wants to target with its online service. Preliminary market research suggests that those most likely to be interested are people who are Internet users, credit users and those keen to manage their financial affairs effectively. Such people are likely to read the financial pages in newspapers or visit personal finance websites.

Requirements

1.1 Explain the factors that may have contributed to DA's competitive advantage. **(6 marks)**

1.2 Using relevant strategic models, analyse the ways in which DA has chosen to expand its business since it began trading, including its plans for Checksta. **(10 marks)**

1.3 Prepare a PESTEL analysis on the credit reference industry, clearly explaining the implications for DA's plans to implement the Checksta product. **(8 marks)**

1.4 Advise DA on an appropriate marketing strategy for Checksta. **(8 marks)**

1.5 Identify the strategic and operational risks arising from DA's use of Information Technology and Information Systems and outline the measures that can be implemented to deal with such risks. **(8 marks)**

Total: 40 marks

2 Kraftvagen Gmbh

The date is March 20X8.

Kraftvagen GmbH (KV) is a car manufacturer, based in Germany. It produces a range of luxury cars.

KV has production facilities in a number of continents, normally located where labour is cheap and it can take advantage of economies of scale, enabling costs of production and assembly to be minimised. KV cars are sold worldwide although its core markets are in the USA, Europe and Japan (see **Exhibit 1**).

Market development

KV has been attempting to identify a new sales market and has recently identified a potential opportunity in India. There is an increasing trend for organisations to outsource service provision to India because of the availability of a low cost but skilled workforce. In addition, rapid economic growth (9% per annum) is attracting investment from an increasing number of entrepreneurs and professionals such as investment bankers, accountants and software engineers, drawn by the prospect of significant returns. This has started to create demand for luxury cars, which currently represent less than one per cent of new car sales in India. The luxury sector in India is widely forecast by the automotive industry to grow significantly in the next ten years (see **Exhibit 2**).

The Indian government has allocated significant funding to improving the infrastructure of the country and in particular the national highways. It has a ten-year plan to improve and widen 25,000 kilometres of highway and to build a new motorway linking India's four largest cities. There is some concern however about the speed with which this may be achieved.

Last year KV decided to test the market by exporting a number of luxury cars to India. The trial was successful, resulting in the sale of 300 cars. KV's Chief Executive, Walter Bergen has decided that KV should actively pursue this business opportunity.

Walter Bergen commented: 'I am keen to pursue this venture as I believe there are significant growth opportunities for those who are first in the market place. This would give us the chance to establish our brand reputation, build market share, develop economies of scale and create barriers to entry. However, I am mindful that our experience in other emerging markets suggests that initial sales may be low and that it may take some time to recover the costs of our investment. Whatever we do, I am keen to minimise the downside risk.'

Plans for implementation

Options available for KV's planned sales expansion into the Indian market are as follows:

(1) Continue to export luxury cars to India, using KV's existing production operations.

(2) Set up an assembly-only plant in India. This plant will import the parts for the luxury cars in kit form from KV's existing production operations and then assemble the final car locally. The plant would occupy 7,500 square metres and could make 1,700 cars per year, on a single shift operation. The number of shifts, and therefore output, could be doubled if demand increased.

(3) Invest in a full scale production operation, which would build the cars in India. This would have an annual production capacity of 8,000 cars. Initially any spare capacity could be used to produce cars for export to KV's other markets.

The Indian government does not currently place restrictions on the level of imports. It has, however, recently announced that it is 'looking at this area, because it is keen to promote jobs for the local population and ensure spending contributes to the growth of the domestic economy'. One possibility being considered is the introduction of quotas restricting the volume of imports; another is an import tax, which would be levied on the value of any finished goods entering the country. There are currently no plans to impose similar restrictions or taxes on exports.

Expected competition

Two other car manufacturers, which both compete in KV's core luxury car market (see **Exhibit 3**), are also considering entering the Indian market:

- Lima plc (Lima) a UK company which produces a wide range of cars, has recently announced plans to create an assembly-only plant for its luxury car model.

- Durant Inc (Durant), an American company, primarily seen as a maker of mid-range cars in USA and Europe, but considered a luxury brand in India, is considering opening up a full production operation, with a complete range of cars.

Conrad SA (Conrad), a French manufacturer of luxury cars and the European market leader, currently has no plans to enter the Indian market.

Exhibit 1: Analysis of KV's 20X7 sales by location of market and also by location of production, (expressed in Euros)

Market	Sales revenue	Production (valued at selling price)
	€m	€m
USA	22.4	18.3
Europe	53.6	45.3
Japan	43.7	25.2
Other	9.5	40.4
Total	129.2	129.2

Exhibit 2: Indian domestic car sales volumes, 20X2 – 20Y7

Sales volumes '000 cars	20X2 actual	20X7 actual	20Y2 forecast	20Y7 forecast
Luxury cars	3	12	28	56
Total passenger cars	600	1,300	1,900	2,800

Exhibit 3: Extract of market information for volume of luxury car sales, 20X7

Number of cars sold	USA '000	Europe '000	Japan '000
KV	280	670	546
Lima	750	308	150
Durant	120	295	434
Conrad	405	714	240
Other manufacturers	765	233	190
Total luxury car sales	2,320	2,220	1,560

Average annual market growth

20X2-20X7 actual	0%	−4.6%	+5.5%
20X7-20Y2 forecast	−2.5%	−6.2%	+3.2%

As an external consultant, Walter Bergen has asked for your help in assessing the proposed development in India.

Requirements

2.1 Using the data provided, evaluate the relative product and market positioning of KV. Identify, with reasons, any other information that would be necessary to make a more complete assessment of KV's competitive position and performance. **(10 marks)**

2.2 Explain the possible reasons for targeting the emerging markets for sales expansion and the issues, including risk, that KV needs to take into account with this strategy. **(7 marks)**

2.3 Assuming that the decision is taken to develop the Indian market, prepare a report advising KV as to:

(a) The factors to consider in selecting the most appropriate of the three options for implementation; and

(b) Ways in which it could minimise the downside risks associated with each of the three options. **(11 marks)**

Total: 28 marks

3 Campaign for Trading Equitably

The Campaign for Trading Equitably (CTE) is a charity, registered in the UK.

Mission and founders

CTE's mission statement is 'to promote the relief of poverty and suffering arising in connection with the conduct of trade in any part of the world. This will be achieved by providing assistance to disadvantaged producers and workers in order to help improve their social and economic position.'

CTE was founded in 20X3 by a number of charitable bodies with an interest in the developing world. All the founder members have a strong interest in helping promote CTE and they contribute significant funds to the organisation.

Activities

CTE promotes fair trade by providing independent certification of the ethical nature of a product, via the 'CTE logo'. This acts as a consumer guarantee as to the adherence of standards by producers and traders. As such, consumers can be confident that in purchasing a product bearing the CTE logo, they are contributing to fairer trading terms for developing nation producers and their workers.

Currently the CTE logo applies to a range of products including food, wine, clothing, cosmetics and flowers. CTE receives a licence fee from companies whose products carry the CTE logo. In addition to the payment of the licence fee, those businesses adopting the CTE logo are required to offer overseas producers and farmers a guaranteed income, as well as a social premium to support local community projects.

In its Constitution, the charity's primary activities are listed as:

- Establishing and maintaining the CTE licence agreements, including the monitoring of adherence to standards and terms

- Assisting new producers and products to enter the supply chain for CTE certified products

- Activities to promote the knowledge and awareness of the CTE logo and the need for more equitable trade

- Fundraising, including the sale of promotional items to CTE supporters

Funding

In addition to the annual contributions of the founder members, the charity's major sources of funds are:

- Licence fees for the use of the CTE logo
- European Union grants and other grant funding
- Corporate sponsorship
- Donations and other miscellaneous income
- Sale of CTE merchandise

Medium-term priorities

As consumers become more supportive of ethical goods, the number of retailers keen to stock CTE certified products is increasing. Although retailers have to accept a lower margin on CTE goods, the volume of sales makes them more profitable overall. As a result of this trend, the work of the charity is increasing and it has recently appointed a new director, Ellen Bates. Ellen has a commercial background and has no previous experience of working in the charitable sector. Ellen has identified the charity's medium-term priorities as:

- To widen the range of products currently operating under the CTE logo;

- To ensure that the UK market for CTE certified goods delivers benefits to an increased number of producers and farmers; and

- To enhance the impact of CTE as an organisation.

This involves creating strategies for:

- Raising awareness so consumers can make more informed choices
- Influencing UK companies to develop better trading relations with overseas suppliers
- Persuading more companies to adopt the CTE logo and take up CTE licences

Governance issues

Ellen is concerned that, as CTE's activities become more prominent, the Board of Trustees should not do anything to create exposure to risk. In particular, she is aware that there has been much discussion among the founder members about:

- Spending money on promoting the CTE logo and CTE as an organisation, which might be seen as a waste of resources

- Offending the ethics of current and potential stakeholders, by accepting donations and corporate sponsorship from large multinationals that might be seen as having previously operated unfair trade practices

Requirements

3.1 Discuss the extent to which the objectives of the charity will differ from those of a typical profit focused organisation. **(4 marks)**

3.2 Critically evaluate the content of CTE's mission statement, making recommendations for any improvements. **(5 marks)**

3.3 Identify the key stakeholders of CTE, explain their interests and analyse the influence they are likely to have in their relationship with the charity. **(6 marks)**

3.4 With reference to the concerns of the founder members, advise Ellen on the specific governance issues facing the charity. **(5 marks)**

3.5 Explain how Ellen could measure the performance of CTE, suggesting appropriate key performance indicators. Describe the nature and sources of data or information that would assist Ellen in measuring CTE's performance. **(12 marks)**

Total: 32 marks

4 Embury Ltd

Extract taken from *The Digby Herald* newspaper, 5 September 20X8:

Local firm Embury Ltd (Embury), which manufactures garden equipment, plans to close its two factories in this area, and move all of its UK manufacturing operations to an extended factory at its main site in Birmingham. The Digby Herald discovered this shocking news when a copy of some recent board minutes was emailed to our news desk just hours before we went to press. Up to 400 jobs could be lost. The decision is being blamed on poor product sales which resulted from recent water shortages and the subsequent local government restrictions placed on the use of garden watering equipment such as hosepipes.

When asked to comment on the plans, the managing director of Embury said:

This proposal is part of an attempt to move to a flexible manufacturing strategy. This will allow the company to counter high UK production costs and the impact that these have had on our margins.

The rationalisation of our UK production under one roof will save overheads, reduce transportation and communication costs and improve cost effectiveness in our supply chain. In line with our European competitors, we also intend to outsource the manufacturing of selected product ranges to China, in the face of escalating raw material costs.

It is extremely regrettable that these measures will result in a reduction of up to 35% of the company's UK workforce. However we need to take this opportunity to consolidate so we can meet the challenges in our market.'

Company information

Embury is the UK's leading manufacturer of watering equipment such as hosepipes, water sprinklers and irrigation systems for use in domestic gardens. Embury's products are sold to consumers via retailers, such as supermarkets, home improvement superstores and garden centres and are also available through independent mail order catalogues and internet retail sites.

The major challenges currently facing Embury's business are three-fold:

(1) The availability of low cost products produced in China and other countries where labour costs are low;

(2) The difficulty of predicting demand; and

(3) Pressures as a result of environmental issues and the impact of changing weather patterns.

Industry information

The garden equipment industry is divided into four market segments:

- Hand-held garden tools
- Powered garden equipment
- Irrigation and watering equipment
- Garden pond and ornamental water features

There are a number of large, multinational manufacturers which produce a complete range of garden equipment across all four segments and sell to a variety of geographic markets. Most of these companies have large manufacturing facilities to take advantage of economies of scale, typically sited in areas where labour costs and other operating costs are low.

The European market leader, GartenZwerg Gmbh (GZ) is a German company which began as a manufacturer of small hand-held garden tools. By developing new products and extending existing product ranges, GZ has evolved from a small, family-run business to a multinational public company with a strong reputation for innovative garden products across all four market segments. In an attempt to expand into the UK market, GZ has recently signed a long-term contract with a major chain of UK garden centres, to stock its products on an exclusive basis, rather than those of other manufacturers, including Embury.

In addition to the large multinationals, there are a number of other smaller manufacturers, such as Embury, which have chosen to focus on individual segments of the market and/or domestic markets only. Embury's products also face competition from retailers' own brand products which are always competitively priced.

Factors affecting industry demand

Although there has been an increase in the number of households in the UK and hence the number of garden owners, sales of gardening equipment have remained static in value terms since 20X0, because of a trend towards smaller gardens.

A recent report from the UK Gardening Trade Association suggests that future prospects for the garden equipment industry depend on:

- The general level of economic wealth
- Personal disposable incomes
- The number of households and hence gardens
- The age distribution of the population
- Consumer attitudes to leisure and gardening

Historically, gardening has been seen as the preserve of the older generation but the industry has identified the need to appeal to new and younger target groups.

Recent market research now predicts an increasing interest in gardening across all age groups. This is a result of a desire for a better quality of life, a home environment that includes natural surroundings, an increased focus on leisure time, and the availability of a better climate to enjoy the outdoors. Thus gardening is widely expected to gain importance in the future, causing the market for gardening equipment products to expand at higher rates over the next few years.

Environmental issues

The garden equipment industry requires consumers to have access to adequate, reliable and secure water supplies.

Governments around the world are paying increasing attention to issues of water quality and quantity, as climate and lifestyle changes mean that water demand increasingly exceeds supply. Shortages of water have led to greater focus on the need for the sustainable use of resources in order to secure the water supply for current and future generations. As a result, in many countries, the national government sets water conservation regulations and standards and environmental groups promote the efficient use of water.

In recent years, environmental pressures have given rise to demands by the UK government and the water companies for households to reduce the pressure on limited water supplies by cutting their domestic water consumption. This has led to restrictions on the non-essential use of water during periods of extreme shortage.

Thus, for example, in dry summers, bans have been imposed on the use of hosepipes and water sprinklers in some areas of the UK. In other areas households have been encouraged to avoid washing their cars and to adopt other water conservation measures, such as the collection of rainwater for use on the garden and the installation of special irrigation systems that deliver only limited amounts of water directly to plants.

In addition to the scarcity of water supply, charges for water services across the UK (using water meters to determine charges according to the amount used) have increased significantly in the last decade and as a result more households are making attempts to conserve water to reduce their monthly running costs.

Changing weather patterns and the increased focus on water conservation have caused significant issues for Embury. Periods of warm spring weather cause a surge in demand for watering equipment, which puts enormous pressure on the business and creates problems in the supply chain for raw materials and components. Conversely restrictions on the use of water imposed in times of water shortage prevent consumers from using Embury's products. These factors, which give rise to varying seasonality of demand, have resulted in periods of both stock-outs and over-stocking.

Plans for product development

In response to the fluctuations in demand caused by the weather, the increasing pressure from the government and environmental groups, and the threat posed by GZ's expansion into the UK, Embury has decided to increase spending on research and development. It plans to develop a new water-efficient product range that will help conserve water usage.

New products currently under development include:

- An underground tank and pump which allows rainwater to be stored and used for various outdoor purposes thus avoiding the use of expensive drinking water;

- A garden irrigation system that waters plants directly from the underground water tank; and

- A watering device which allows household waste water to be pumped onto the garden.

Requirements

4.1 Prepare a PESTEL analysis on the garden equipment industry. **(8 marks)**

4.2 (a) Describe the issues facing Embury in respect of production capacity planning and procurement; and

(b) Explain how outsourcing elements of production might benefit Embury and describe the possible problems and risks associated with outsourcing. **(12 marks)**

4.3 Embury is considering introducing an ethical procurement policy. Explain the impact this could have on any outsourcing agreement. **(5 marks)**

4.4 Explain the change management problems that are likely to occur as a result of the newspaper article and the planned factory closures. Discuss how these problems might be addressed. **(11 marks)**

4.5 Discuss the advantages and disadvantages of Embury's plans for product development. **(6 marks)**

Total: 42 marks

5 DT Ltd

DT Ltd (DT) was established in 20X5 by David Thomas, a software specialist with a keen interest in driving cars. David owns 100% of the share capital and is the sole director. DT operates in the vehicle driver education industry, providing training for learner drivers, via a virtual reality driving simulator, similar to those used in airline pilot training. The simulator is used in addition to traditional road-based instruction and learning.

DT's mission is 'to provide high quality, convenient and comprehensive driver education courses at the lowest cost'.

Industry information

In the UK, all learner drivers are required to pass a driving test before they can obtain a full driving licence to drive a car. Most choose to prepare for the test by taking driving lessons provided by a self-employed driving instructor or driving school.

The driver education industry is fragmented into two different types of businesses. 55% of the market consists of self-employed driving instructors. There is significant variation in the cost of the driving education provided, the quality of instruction and the overall success rate of the learner.

The remaining 45% consists of a few national or international companies, known as driving schools. The driving schools are well funded, have excellent facilities and services and provide high quality tuition. However as a result they also adopt a premium pricing policy.

The industry is highly seasonal. Most learner drivers undertake lessons during spring or autumn, with numbers of learner drivers declining in the summer months due to holidays and falling even more substantially in winter when the daylight hours are short and road conditions are poor.

Barriers to entry are low. Anybody can set up as a driving instructor provided that they have a driving licence, access to a vehicle, and the necessary insurance. Most driver training providers obtain their clients through some form of referral and as a result of the large number of competitors, the industry is very price competitive.

DT's competitive position

Using his software expertise and driving knowledge, David spotted a gap in the market and developed a driving simulator to help new drivers prepare for the test to obtain a full driving licence. It is also used to help existing drivers prepare for high risk driving conditions including driving on busy roads and national highways, extreme weather such as ice and snow, and brake failure.

David identified the potential for DT to create a new low cost position, using modern training techniques, while still being able to compete with the larger companies on quality.

The use of a simulator reduces the total hours that a learner driver takes to become competent. If a learner driver uses a simulator, the total time spent altogether on the simulator and the road is less than 50% of the normal learning time required under the traditional model on a road only. Training in a safe environment reduces accidents and driver stress and it has also been shown to improve the success rate in passing the test to obtain a full driving licence.

In addition there are significant benefits for DT. As less time is spent on the road, there are reduced costs of fuel, vehicle acquisition and repair and since one driving instructor can control up to four simulators at a time, this training can be offered for a lower price than competitor driving schools which offer only on-road experience.

An added benefit is the positive effect on the environment as a result of reduced fuel consumption.

Although DT's core market is learner drivers wishing to acquire a full driving licence, there is also a market in existing drivers, who want to refresh or enhance their driving skills, and commercial drivers, who are required to undertake regular and rigorous training to maintain their licences.

Expansion

After early tests of the simulator concept had proved successful, David successfully applied for a software patent. The business grew much faster than David had originally anticipated and by mid-20X8 DT had developed a good reputation locally and expanded to five outlets based in and around the London area. To finance the growth David had reinvested the profits generated and personally borrowed considerable sums of money.

David now wants to increase the rate of growth but is unsure about the best way to do this:

'We are a small business and our financial and physical resources are limited. I believe the product has the potential to be successful on a national and international basis but I am not really sure what is the best way to go about expanding outside London. Also I think I will need help to sell the idea to prospective investors.'

David is currently considering two mutually exclusive proposals for expansion:

- DT could expand the network of outlets across the UK by offering franchise arrangements to individuals seeking to become driving instructors. This would give the franchisee the right to use the DT name and software. DT would receive an upfront capital payment and ongoing commission based on sales revenue generated.

- The International Motoring School (IMS) has approached DT. IMS currently operates a network of driving schools across Europe but has no UK presence. IMS would take up a one third share in DT by subscribing for new share capital. There would be an option for IMS to extend this to a 50% holding after five years. IMS would also provide significant loan finance at a commercial rate of interest and support with marketing activities and instructor training. In return, IMS would gain access to the simulator software for use in its existing driving schools.

Requirements

5.1 Prepare a SWOT analysis of the current strategic position of DT and clearly identify what you consider to be the major issues. **(8 marks)**

5.2 Evaluate the key factors to be considered with respect to the two proposals for expansion. Use the following headings:

    (a) Governance and control
    (b) Risks
    (c) Resource requirements **(12 marks)**

5.3 David has asked for your help in producing a business plan to attract potential franchisees.

    Write the sections of the plan which cover:

    (a) DT's business model
    (b) The basis of DT's competitive advantage
    (c) The benefits for a franchisee **(12 marks)**

Total: 32 marks

6 CWI International Ltd

CWI International Ltd (CWI), whose head office is in the UK, operates a chain of English language schools in a range of African, European and Asian countries.

Background information

CWI schools offer two types of English language course for students wanting to learn English. The majority of CWI students are aged 16-18 years and want qualifications to improve their employment prospects or to fulfill the English language entry requirements for higher education in the USA and the UK. In common with most language schools, CWI operates a selective entrance system where prospective students are required to attend an interview and undertake a skills assessment, based on their academic ability.

All CWI schools, irrespective of size, offer courses for the following two qualifications:

- **International Baccalaureate Diploma (IBD)**

  The IBD programme offered by CWI is a 12-month course of study that leads to an examination set by an external board, once a year. IBD holders are eligible for admission to premium universities throughout the world. The total course fee for the one year programme is £7,200. The course consists of nine weeks' tuition, comprising a three-week introductory course at the start of the programme, a five-week interim course and a one-week revision course before the IBD exam. Throughout the year students undertake home study in between the tuition phases, with tutorial support as required.

- **Test of English as a Foreign Language (TOEFL)**

  The TOEFL is a five-week course of study leading to a test, which is set by an external board, eight times a year. The test measures the ability of non-native speakers of English to use and understand English as it is read, spoken, written and heard in college and university settings. The course fee is £1,250.

All CWI schools are approved exam centres so the IBD exams and TOEFL tests are sat in school.

Each CWI school offers at least one course per exam/test sitting. The larger schools have the facility to offer up to five courses per sitting for each qualification. CWI primarily generates income by charging tuition fees but also receives some educational grants.

CWI has an outstanding academic record and achieves excellent results. Many CWI students progress to Higher Education, normally to their 'first choice' universities or colleges. To maintain the highest teaching standards CWI only employs tutors with specialist qualifications in English language teaching. It encourages tutors to improve their qualifications by providing them with financial support for further study and training, and all CWI schools offer regular training for tutorial staff.

Performance measurement

CWI has recently decided to apply for accreditation by the English Language Board (ELB). A wide range of schools offer English language courses and accreditation by the ELB is the main internationally recognised guarantee of quality. To be accredited CWI must demonstrate that it meets the ELB performance criteria in all of its schools. Every aspect of each school's English language provision will be scrutinised, based on stringent criteria covering tutors, results, class sizes, materials, management, student welfare and premises.

Currently the internal evaluation of performance at CWI schools derives mainly from annual results in the external examinations, IBD and TOEFL. These are monitored closely by reference to the average world-wide pass rate for the particular examination.

In order to receive accreditation from ELB, CWI's chief executive believes that it will need to introduce a more rigorous and wide-ranging system of performance measurement and has written to your firm asking for help. An extract from the letter is as follows:

'We need reliable information that will assist us in evaluating the profitability and performance of our schools. This should include financial analysis as well as providing us with other non-financial information in preparation for ELB accreditation and the subsequent two-yearly inspection that is a condition of retaining it. In addition, the market for English language courses is becoming more competitive due to the global economic downturn and I believe better performance information will help us to differentiate CWI when talking to prospective students. Finally, I believe that there is significant variation of performance between each CWI school and the different qualifications. I hope to use the measures from the new performance measurement system to increase consistency and to identify underperforming tutors and schools, and I would like some suggestions as to how to go about this.

I need to select a member of my staff to manage the implementation of this performance measurement project, but I need some advice on the project management skills they will need and the barriers to change that they are likely to face.

Exhibits 1 and 2 contain some data that I have collated for the last two years, which will help you.'

Requirements

As a consultant, prepare a report which:

6.1 Using the data provided, evaluates the financial and non-financial performance of CWI, providing supporting explanations of your data analysis. Identify and justify any additional information that you would require in order to assess the performance of the individual CWI schools. **(14 marks)**

6.2 Explains the barriers that may be encountered in implementing a new performance measurement system and indicates how these might be overcome. **(6 marks)**

Total: 20 marks

Note. **Exhibits 1 and 2** are below.

Exhibit 1: Financial performance data

Reporting period ending 31 December

	20X8 £'000	20X7 £'000
Income		
Tuition fees:		
IBD	3,600	2,304
TOEFL	3,840	3,360
Total tuition fees	7,440	5,664
Grants	600	560
Total income	8,040	6,224
Expenditure		
Tutor costs	3,250	2,240
Premises	1,525	1,260
Course and study materials	446	336
Marketing	745	392
Administration including support staff	1,050	840
Total expenditure by schools	7,016	5,068
Contribution	1,024	1,156
Head office costs	(450)	(420)
Profit before interest and tax	574	736

Exhibit 2: Other relevant data

		20X8	20X7
Number of schools		10	8
Number of tutors		145	104
Number of courses:	IBD	30	16
	TOEFL	240	224
Course fee per student:	IBD	£7,200	£7,200
	TOEFL	£1,250	£1,250

Pass rates	IBD		TOEFL	
	20X8 %	20X7 %	20X8 %	20X7 %
CWI pass rate	85	89	90	89
Worldwide pass rate	81	79	75	74

7 Kemmex Ice Cream plc

Ralph Reines is the recently appointed chief executive of Kemmex Ice Cream plc (KIC), which is a listed company manufacturing ice cream.

Company background

KIC was established a number of years ago. Its only factory is located within a reasonable distance of both London and the major seaports which serve France and other North European countries. The company produces low cost ice creams in the 'economy' sector of the industry. All its ice creams are for the 'take home' market, being sold in large containers of one litre or two litres in a range of flavours.

Manufacturing costs have been kept low due to the low cost of ingredients, the narrow product range and a basic production process. Distribution costs have been kept low by maintaining a customer base of ice cream retailers including small shops, cafés and low cost independent supermarkets, all located within 100 miles of the factory – an area that includes London. This has also enabled KIC to compete with larger ice cream manufacturers by offering a good level of service. In particular, the company's willingness to deliver small quantities at short notice appeals to many retailers.

Ralph Reines took over as chief executive from his father, David Reines, on 30 November 20X8. David had run the company for many years and, while there had been little expansion during this period, it had generated reasonably stable profits in its local market.

Falling profits at KIC

The management accounts for the quarter ended 30 May 20X9 (**Exhibit 1**) did not make pleasant reading when Ralph first saw them. He immediately called the finance director, Charlie Milton, and the marketing director, Jane Chang, into his office. Ralph was first to speak:

'Just look at the latest management accounts. They are a disaster. We have increased sales, but we are not making any profits.'

Charlie was quick to interrupt: 'Well, I told you so when we devised the strategy to cut prices, grow sales volumes and build market share. The board took too much notice of Jane and her marketing team. We took our eye off the bottom-line profit.'

Jane was not pleased with Charlie's remarks: 'That's just typical of accountants. You can't see beyond the next quarter's profit figures. We cannot stay where we are. We need to grow, or the company will stagnate.'

Ralph had indeed wanted to expand the company rapidly and had initially supported Jane Chang's plan to lower prices by 10% from 1 March 20X9 to encourage growth. The poor results for the quarter to 30 May 20X9, however, caused him real concern so he called a board meeting in early June 20X9 to review future strategy.

The ice cream industry and the UK market

The global ice cream manufacturing industry is dominated by two major international food and drinks companies which manufacture about 25% of the world's output of ice cream by value. There are a few other large manufacturers, but the remainder of the industry is highly segmented with many smaller manufacturers. In the UK alone, there are in total around 200 ice cream manufacturing companies.

Ice cream, in economy form, can be manufactured using a simple low-cost process, but large scale production or higher quality ice creams require significant capital investment.

The European ice cream market generates sales of about £13,000 million at retail selling prices, with the UK market making up about £1,000 million of that total. The ice cream consumer market can be divided into two separate sectors. First, there is the 'impulse' sector, which are ice creams bought for one person for immediate consumption, typically wrapped in bars, or being held on a stick or cone.

Second, there is the 'take-home' sector, which are purchases made in large units, typically at supermarkets or grocers, for consumption normally by a number of people some days or weeks after purchase. The 'take-home' market consists of large containers of ice cream (eg one or two litres) or multipacks (several individual wrapped bars, normally of the same type as sold individually as 'impulse' purchases). In the UK, the take-home sector makes up about 72% of the total market, but in many other European countries there are different tastes and there is a more equal split between the impulse and take-home sectors.

The global ice cream industry is segmented by price and quality as follows:

- **Economy**. At the lower end of the market is economy ice cream, produced using low cost ingredients, mainly by smaller manufacturers using basic processes. This is a large market, but is low value added and is price competitive. There is little branding other than supermarket 'own labels'. Distribution is to local markets to reduce transport costs. Retailers are small outlets or low cost supermarkets.

- **Regular**. Regular ice cream incorporates standard quality ingredients with some limited branding, normally being the manufacturer's name. It is a large market with moderate value added. It is mainly produced by larger manufacturers using capital intensive, large-scale production and it is distributed nationally and internationally to a wide range of retailers.

- **Premium branded**. Good quality ingredients with some branding of individual products and advertising to support the brand are found in the premium branded segment, which is a moderate, but growing, market with high value added. It is almost entirely produced by larger manufacturers using capital intensive, advanced technology processes and it is distributed nationally and internationally to a range of large and specialist retailers.

- **Superpremium branded**. Very high quality ingredients with significant dedicated branding of individual products and high spending on advertising to promote the brand are found in the superpremium branded segment. This is a small, but rapidly growing, market with high prices and very high value added. It is produced solely by larger manufacturers, using capital intensive processes and is distributed nationally and internationally to selected retailers. New product developments are constantly taking place.

There is some seasonality in the industry but this is less pronounced for the take-home market and for premium and superpremium products.

A key factor in the industry is distribution. This needs to be in chilled conditions for transport, but also the freezer space of retailers is a constraining factor on sales and storage.

The UK is a net importer of ice cream from the EU. There is limited trade outside the EU for UK manufactured ice creams due to transport costs.

Retailers impact on the industry significantly. Supermarket chains are significant buyers and they force down the prices that they pay to suppliers in all sectors of the market, but particularly at the lower end. Last summer, for instance, a large supermarket chain reduced ice cream prices in the 'regular' sector so significantly that they were below prices in much of the 'economy' sector. This price reduction was, however, only on a temporary basis.

Future strategy – board meeting

At the board meeting two mutually exclusive strategies were put forward.

Strategy 1 – Continue with the low price strategy. This strategy was suggested by Jane who argued that: 'The strategy adopted from 1 March 20X9 of reducing all our prices – to both existing and new customers – by 10% needs to be given time. Sales volumes will continue to increase as our pricing policy becomes better known. The number of existing customers and the quantity of ice cream sold to them has remained unchanged since the quarter to 28 February 20X9 despite the price reduction. This means that our sales volume growth has been entirely due to new customers.

In particular, we are now appealing to retailers well beyond the 100 mile limit in the UK that we used to have and this is where our new customers have arisen. We are beginning to have national UK coverage. I expect that revenues will improve, with sales volumes eventually growing 25% from that achieved in the quarter to 31 May 20X9, mainly from customers in the north of England up to 350 miles away.'

Strategy 2 – Enter the premium branded sector. The research department has developed a new high quality ice cream. The board has discussed a possible contract with a large, international confectionery manufacturer, Yocolate plc, which does not produce ice cream products. The agreement would be that the new ice cream could be branded to look like one of Yocolate plc's well-known chocolate bars, the 'Chocnut', and KIC would use the same name. Yocolate plc would require a fixed annual royalty of £1 million, plus 5p per item sold. The annual fixed costs of making 'Chocnut' ice creams would be £3 million and the variable production and distribution costs would be 20p per item. Typically, ice creams of this type produced by other manufacturers sell to retailers for around 50p per item. Sales of the 'Chocnut' ice cream would be through existing retailers to the 'take-home' market in multipacks and KIC would also attempt to enter the 'impulse' market, selling individual bars through the same retailers. It would also be necessary to sell the 'Chocnut' throughout the whole of the UK and in some other European countries in order to achieve an adequate sales volume. This strategy would require reversal of the 10% price reduction made on 1 March 20X9 for existing economy ice creams.

Requirements

7.1 Explain the barriers to entry that exist in the ice cream industry, identifying particular issues that affect the four separate industry segments. **(8 marks)**

7.2 Briefly evaluate KIC's current market share. Describe how KIC's 'market' should be defined most appropriately for the purpose of determining its market share. **(6 marks)**

7.3 Using the data in Exhibit 1 and the other information provided:

(a) Assess and explain the performance of KIC during the quarter ended 31 May 20X9. Provide appropriate data analysis to support your arguments.

(b) So far as the information permits, evaluate Strategy 1 and establish whether this continued price reduction policy is the appropriate strategy for the future, even though it has produced a short-term financial loss. **(17 marks)**

7.4 Assess the proposed Strategy 2 under each of the following headings:

(a) Risks
(b) Marketing strategy **(12 marks)**

Total: 43 marks

Exhibit 1: Quarterly, summary management accounts

	3 months to	
	28 Feb 20X9	31 May 20X9
	£'000	£'000
Sales	10,000	10,350
Production costs		
Variable	5,000	5,750
Fixed	2,500	2,500
Distribution costs		
Variable	500	750
Fixed	250	250
Administration and other fixed operating costs	1,250	1,250
Operating profit/(loss)	500	(150)
Number of customers (ie retailers)	2,500	3,000

8   Evara Electrical Engineers Ltd

The date is June 20X9.

Evara Electrical Engineers Ltd (EEE) is a medium-sized private company which carries out electrical contract work, including wiring, electrical repairs, safety inspections and supplying and fitting electrical devices.

Company background

EEE was established a number of years ago in Manchester by Eric Evara, the managing director and sole shareholder. Initially, Eric ran the business from his home, carrying out electrical work alongside the three other electricians whom the company employed. Eric did all the administration tasks himself in the evenings, including invoicing, estimates and quotes, preparing wages, collecting of cash and writing up the accounts.

For a number of years Eric's sole role was to manage the business, no longer doing any electrical work himself. Twenty years ago he opened small business premises in Manchester for administration, and for storing materials. By the end of 20X8 EEE employed 25 electricians and two support staff.

Despite the growth, in early 20X9 EEE still had a basic organisational structure with Eric, as sole manager, taking all the key decisions, including negotiating prices with customers, allocating work to staff, overseeing work in progress, ordering materials and managing the office. Eric has external professional support from his accountants, legal advisers and occasionally from electrical engineering consultants where the jobs are particularly difficult technically.

Electricians are split into teams and there are five team leaders who are paid more than other employees. There are normally between two and seven electricians allocated to each job, depending on the size of the task. A team leader is in charge of each job on site, but their authority is informal, as employees tend to socialise together and regard each other as equals.

Eric exercises control informally. Team leaders telephone Eric about every two days to report the progress of work in general terms. Eric also visits each site personally, once a week, to review progress.

Eric keeps basic records of how much he spends on materials and labour for the business overall. He does not have any formal system of recording the material and labour costs incurred by each job. Through his day to day contact with operations Eric is, however, generally aware of whether costs differ significantly from his calculations made for the initial price estimate for each job.

Customers and pricing

EEE generates about £1 million in annual sales revenue. EEE's largest customer by far is Briggs Builders plc (BB), a UK listed company, which has factories in and around the Manchester area. BB has historically made up about half of EEE's annual sales revenue. Prices on the BB contract are set on a strict cost plus formula basis.

Other than BB, EEE's customers are smaller businesses (such as builders and property developers), almost entirely located within 35 miles of Manchester. Some of these customers offer regular work to EEE, whilst others are one-off jobs, frequently acquired through local reputation. Eric once described his pricing policy for these smaller customers as follows:

'I price jobs for smaller customers according to what I think they are willing to pay. I always negotiate directly with the budget holder who will effectively be the decision maker. Also, the price quote initially agreed is subject to 'variations', which means I can charge extra if there are unforeseen problems in the building structure, or additional faults are discovered when hidden wiring is exposed or the customers change their minds. I always find some of these variations so I can add on 10% to the price even if the problem is fairly trivial. The customers normally don't understand electrics so it is hard for them to dispute any variation. Also, if there is a problem in price variation negotiations, I give the budget holder tickets to sports events or concerts. That normally makes them more co-operative.'

A major expansion

In May 20X9 BB was acquired by Sharrow & Sline plc (SS), a major listed company with sites located throughout Europe. Eric was concerned at this time that EEE would lose the BB contract following the acquisition and began to make tentative plans to downsize his business. To Eric's surprise, however, he was offered a one-year contract to be the preferred supplier of electrical contracting services to the entire SS group, including BB, commencing on 1 January 20Y0. Under this contract, about 10% of EEE's jobs for SS would be in continental Europe, with the remainder spread throughout the UK.

The conditions offered to EEE on the SS group contract for 20Y0 were as follows:

- The pricing formula is the same as that used previously on the BB contract.

- The contract is estimated to be worth £4 million for the first year, but it may be more or less than that depending on requirements.

- Assurances are needed by SS that EEE can cope with the volume of work required.

- If EEE refuses the contract it will be offered elsewhere, including the work for BB.

- Renewal of the contract for 20Y1, and beyond, will depend on performance in the first year. To judge this, SS requires detailed data reports for each job including labour hours analysis, materials used and technical updates of the work completed.

- Details of EEE's project management procedures are to be presented to SS prior to commencement of the contract.

- EEE must act in accordance with SS's strict ethical code. This will also impact on EEE's behaviour towards its other customers.

New equipment and procedures would be required to fulfil the contract. As a consequence, EEE would be unlikely to make a significant profit in the first year. In addition, some of the operational work would be complex and outside the experience of Eric and his current employees.

Eric is keen to take on the new contract, but he has two major concerns about it:

(1) The only way he can see to staff the new contract is either to recruit 100 new electricians by January 20Y0 or to outsource the new work by sub-contracting it to other electrical firms.

(2) Irrespective of whether outsourcing is used or not, Eric knows that EEE would need a new organisational structure and new information systems to enable him to manage the individual jobs and the business overall. Eric also realises he would no longer be able to carry out all management functions and all quality control procedures himself. He appreciates that he would need better information systems to generate the data reports required by SS to judge performance and to decide whether the contract should be renewed.

Requirements

8.1 Ignoring the potential new contract with SS, explain how far EEE's organisational structure and information systems are suitable for managing its current strategy and operations.   **(10 marks)**

8.2 Discuss the ethical issues that arise from EEE's current pricing policy for its smaller customers.

(6 marks)

8.3 As a business adviser, prepare a draft report for Eric giving advice relating to the proposed SS contract as follows:

(a) Describe, and justify, potential new organisational structures for EEE which would be suitable if the SS contract is undertaken. From these alternatives, make a recommendation of the most suitable structure for EEE.

(b) Explain the factors that Eric should consider in deciding between outsourcing and recruitment of more staff, in order to meet the needs of the SS contract.

(c) Briefly advise Eric, with reasons, whether he should accept the SS contract.   **(16 marks)**

Total: 32 marks

9   Rugeley Tableware plc

Rugeley Tableware plc (Rugeley) is a niche manufacturer of quality ceramic tableware, based in the UK.

Company history

Rugeley was founded over two hundred years ago by William Rugeley, a local businessman and entrepreneur. It specialises in the design and manufacture of exclusive ceramic tableware (sets of plates, bowls etc), which is sold direct to the hotel and restaurant industry and also to individual consumers. Rugeley's products are stocked by major retailers and can be purchased online via its website.

From the beginning, Rugeley created a reputation for manufacturing tableware of the highest quality which it originally sold to wealthy individuals. For more than two centuries, Rugeley tableware was used at dinner tables in sophisticated private houses and hotels and the brand name became associated with an elegant lifestyle. As a result of its innovative patterns and designs, Rugeley was recognised as a prestigious brand throughout Europe and the US and was sought after because of its quality and English heritage.

Rugeley enjoyed many years of profitability and was converted into a public limited company at the peak of its success, when it became listed on the London Stock Exchange. 40% of the equity share capital remains in the hands of the Rugeley family, 45% is held by institutional investors and the remainder is owned by individual investors.

Declining fortunes

Several years after it was listed, Rugeley's results began to deteriorate. In 20X0, Rugeley decided to outsource some of its manufacturing operations to Asia, in an attempt to reduce costs and to address competition from the following sources:

- Cheaper imports, which were almost entirely being produced in low labour cost countries.

- Large global retailers that had begun to introduce mass produced, own-label product ranges, designed to resemble high quality tableware.

- More diversified competitors in the tableware market that also offered glassware and table linen.

- Major international companies that were able to benefit from economies of scale by manufacturing a wider range of ceramics for use in the home (including bathroom sanitary ware, kitchen sinks, tiles and tableware).

These sources of competition have become more powerful since 20X0 and sales and profits have continued to decline, despite the outsourcing decision. The most recent results (for the year ended 30 June 20X9) show a fall in revenue of 15%, a fall in profit of 25% and negative operational cash flow. The business urgently needs to make changes if it is to avoid becoming loss making.

For nearly a year, institutional shareholders have been openly critical of the chairman and chief executive, Belinda Rugeley (a direct descendant of William). Belinda runs the company in an authoritarian manner. She has refused to appoint non-executive directors, on the basis that they would not be as committed to the company as its executive directors, whose remuneration is based on the financial performance of the business. Some institutional investors have suggested the company should consider seeking a buyer from among the major international manufacturers.

Future options

At a recent board meeting to discuss Rugeley's future strategic options, the following views were expressed:

Marketing director (Malcolm Enderby): 'For years we have set worldwide standards in tableware design and manufacturing, but people's attitudes to dining have changed. As formal dining has given way to more relaxed eating habits, so our traditional products have become unfashionable. As a result, our sales to individual customers are now concentrated on a very narrow market, consisting largely of customers over 40 years of age. What's more the recession is unlikely to help matters as it will inevitably depress sales of what is seen as a luxury item.

I think we have taken too narrow a view of Asia as the solution to our manufacturing. I believe we should also focus on Asia as a new sales market. There is an opportunity here to build a brand image of exclusive tableware, based on our English style and heritage.

We also need to target the new, younger generation who are unfamiliar with our products. The recession may work in our favour here, as more people choose to dine at home instead of eating out. We can exploit this by introducing a new range of everyday designer tableware. Melinda James, the famous chef, owns a well-respected design and marketing business and she has agreed to cooperate with us in a joint venture to launch such a product.'

Production director (Alex Rodin): 'I think the lack of sales is more about supply chain issues than anything else and these have impacted on our customer service capabilities. At the moment there is a mis-match between the high quality of our product and the level of service we are providing to customers. Although we carry very high levels of inventory, these are not always of the right product lines. Because of the lead times associated with overseas manufacturing, production and delivery times have increased and our level of overdue orders is unacceptably high.

The problem is exacerbated by the fact that all our key strategic and operational decision making is carried out by the board, so production is based on centrally produced sales forecasts and not driven by real customer demand. Our centralised management structure has given rise to inflexibility and slow response times. It has also stifled local sales initiatives and design innovations. I believe we need to address our supply chain issues and at the same time change our decision making structure so that more authority is delegated, and sales planning is undertaken by the local manager within each sales market.

A former colleague of mine now works at PCE plc, a company which manufactures portable consumer electronics such as digital radios, MP3 and DVD players. They have just completed a review of their own supply chain with amazing results, and they've published some of their data on this. I think we could learn something from what they have achieved.'

Chairman/chief executive (Belinda Rugeley): 'I really don't see how we can learn anything from PCE plc – they are in a completely different industry from us. Surely they don't know anything about the manufacture of ceramic tableware and any targets they set for their supply chain will not be a relevant benchmark for ours?'

Requirements

Acting as a consultant to the board of directors:

9.1 Prepare a SWOT analysis of Rugeley's current strategic position, and highlight the key issues facing the company. **(8 marks)**

9.2 Using Ansoff, analyse the proposals made by the marketing director. **(8 marks)**

9.3 Evaluate the production director's proposals to decentralise decision making. Explain the change management issues that Rugeley would need to address if it were to go ahead with the proposed new decision making structure. **(10 marks)**

9.4 Discuss the comments made by the production director and the chairman/chief executive in respect of PCE plc. **(7 marks)**

9.5 Explain the principles of good corporate governance which would be relevant and the ways in which non-executive directors would be of benefit to the running of Rugeley. **(7 marks)**

Total: 40 marks

10 Pitstop Ltd

Pitstop Ltd (Pitstop) operates a well-known chain of roadside restaurants in the UK.

Company information

Pitstop's target market is road users, in particular business travellers and families with children, who want to break up a long journey and stop for refreshments. Pitstop has 65 restaurants, which occupy prime sites along major roads.

The restaurants all have the same internal design, décor, menu and prices. They are open 07:00 to 19:00 for 360 days in each year, and each has the capacity to seat 50 customers.

All procurement is done centrally and Pitstop sets strict guidelines regarding staff levels and the purchasing and preparation of food. Each restaurant is set a target for cost of sales of 68% of revenue so that waste is kept to a minimum and food and labour costs are carefully controlled.

All other costs incurred by Pitstop are fixed. These include the salaries of the restaurant managers, rent, marketing, procurement administration and other central costs. For reporting purposes, these are totalled and then divided equally across the 65 restaurants in the chain.

Key factors that influence performance for an individual restaurant are customer numbers and average amount spent by each customer. Pitstop's restaurants are all leased. Results have suffered recently as rents have increased considerably, whilst at the same time customer numbers have fallen.

The market is highly competitive and there is a variety of other outlets which cater for a similar need to Pitstop: petrol station forecourt shops, roadside facilities operated by regional and national chains, fast food outlets, coffee chains and local family friendly bar/restaurants. In addition, the volume of customers is highly affected by roadworks, the weather and the time of year.

The current focus on healthy eating has given rise to criticism that Pitstop's traditional menu places too much emphasis on fried food with a high fat content. In addition there have been changes in driving habits. The advent of in-car entertainment systems has made it easier for families to occupy children on a long journey. Many drivers prefer to purchase a snack that can be eaten quickly rather than stop for the time required to order and consume a meal.

Strategic proposals

Pitstop's board of directors has been discussing two possible strategies to improve profitability:

Strategy 1: Widen the appeal of the restaurant

Pitstop would attempt to increase customer volumes by a third in all its restaurants by:

- Targeting local families who could be encouraged to make regular visits to Pitstop as a neighbourhood restaurant.

- Encouraging business executives to view the restaurant as a meeting point, by creating a special office area within each restaurant, with facilities for laptop computers and free internet access.

- Attracting more road users with the introduction of a new snack menu. This would provide an alternative for customers who are short of time and wish to resume their journeys as soon as possible.

The finance director is on long-term sick leave. In her absence, the sales director has produced a forecast of the likely impact of this strategy on an **average** Pitstop restaurant, which is set out in **Exhibit 1** along with actual results for an **average** restaurant in the year ended 31 July 20X9. On the basis of these figures he is keen to implement the strategy across all Pitstop restaurants.

Exhibit 1: Strategy 1 projections for an average Pitstop restaurant

Year ended 31 July	Actual Results 20X9 £	Forecast Strategy 1 20Y0 £
Revenue	486,000	648,000
Food costs	170,100	226,800
Labour costs	160,380	213,840
Cost of sales	330,480	440,640
Gross profit	155,520	207,360
Marketing	20,000	20,000
Rent	75,000	75,000
Other overheads	60,000	60,000
Profit before interest and tax	520	52,360
Average amount spent by each customer	£9.00	£9.00

Strategy 2: Reduce prices

This strategy would involve reducing prices by 15% to make Pitstop more competitive. Although gross profit margins would fall as a result, the sales director is confident that the increase in customers would more than compensate for this.

The operations director is concerned about the downside risk associated with this strategy. In particular he has pointed out that if the lower prices do not attract more customers, then the majority of Pitstop's restaurants will fail to break-even.

Risk assessment

To assist in assessing the risk of the two strategies, the operations director has provided some information about the variability of customer numbers, average spend and margins during the year ended 31 July 20X9. This is set out in **Exhibit 2**, together with his estimate of the impact that Strategy 2 would have on gross profit margins.

Exhibit 2: Variability of Pitstop customer numbers, average spend and margins

	Worst performing restaurant	Average restaurant	Best performing Restaurant
Year ended 31 July 20X9 (actual)			
No of customers per day	95	150	245
Average amount spent by each customer	£7.50	£9.00	£10.50
Actual gross profit margin	30%	32%	34%
Year ended 31 July 20Y0 (estimate)			
Estimated gross profit margin with Strategy 2	18%	20%	22%

Requirements

10.1 Using both Exhibits and the other information provided:

    (a)   Analyse Strategy 1 and evaluate its impact on an average restaurant.

    (b)   Assess the reasonableness of the sales director's forecast and assumptions as a basis for projecting the results for all Pitstop's restaurants.

    Show any additional calculations that are relevant.   **(12 marks)**

10.2 For Strategy 2:

    (a)   Prepare calculations which demonstrate the increase in customers per day that would be required to maintain existing gross profits for an average restaurant.

    (b)   Discuss the likely impact of the proposed price reduction on the profitability of the company as a whole, showing any additional calculations.   **(10 marks)**

10.3 Explain any other factors that Pitstop should consider when making a decision about how to improve the company's profitability.   **(5 marks)**

                                       Total: 27 marks

11   Somborne Zoological Park Ltd

Somborne Zoological Park Ltd (Somborne) is a charitable, not-for-profit company. It is engaged in animal conservation and research and operates a well-known zoo in the UK. (**Note.** Conservation is the securing of long-term populations of species in natural ecosystems and habitats wherever possible.) Somborne is home to more than 2,600 animals and attracts around two million visitors a year. In addition to income from visitors, the zoo receives financial support from corporate sponsors, grants for research, donations from benefactors and subscription income from its membership programme.

Governance and regulation

Somborne is managed by a board of trustees which has overall responsibility for the zoo's operations. Somborne is a member of the International Zoo Federation (IZF), a global industry body, which requires each member to achieve certain standards in conservation, education and animal care and to meet certain inspection criteria annually in order to maintain its licence to operate.

Staffing

Somborne has a staff of about 200 paid employees, and more than 1,500 volunteers. The zoo is led by a manager who is responsible for the maintenance and growth of the animal collection and who has overall responsibility for the staff. The day-to-day care of the animals is undertaken by zookeepers, supported by qualified vets. In addition Somborne employs a number of staff in catering and retail roles at the zoo's café and shop.

Aims and objectives

Somborne's mission is 'To focus the zoo's resources on animal conservation and to support this through sustainable commercial activities, including managing the zoo as a first class visitor attraction.'

Somborne's strategic goals are stated as follows:

- To maximise the impact of our conservation activities and to undertake research activities which make contributions to conservation programmes both in captivity and the wild

- To promote and support the zoo through marketing and the provision of learning opportunities for the public

- To identify and develop alternative income streams to reduce dependency on visitor income

In addition, as part of a desire to gain accreditation for sustainability and environmental management from the IZF, the board has recently identified a fourth goal:

- To follow ethical principles to guarantee the well-being of our animal collection and to manage the operations and development of the zoo to ensure long term sustainability

A new chairman has recently been appointed to assist the board in implementing this sustainability initiative and has approached you, as a member of the zoo's finance department, for help:

'I think I am clear about the vision for the zoo but there appears to be a lack of detail on how the zoo intends to implement that vision. Please could you explain to me the relevance of strategic planning for a not-for-profit organisation such as ours, and give me some specific examples of detailed operational objectives that would allow us to meet our first three strategic goals.

As you are well aware we only have a finite budget and so the other thing I am concerned about is how to allocate the resources that we do have, between the various goals and projects that we could undertake.

In order to gain accreditation from the IZF we need to carry out an environmental audit to establish some baseline performance measures in four areas: financial, environmental, human resources and social. These measures will be used for monitoring during the first year of implementation of the sustainability initiative and subsequently. I have attached an extract of the guidance issued by the IZF on sustainability and environmental management in the **Exhibit** below which should explain more.'

Exhibit: Extract from the IZF report on 'Achieving Sustainability'

Achieving sustainability can be defined as reaching a state where all operations of a zoological institution are neutral in the environment.

All IZF members are expected to work towards sustainability by reducing their environmental impact and to lead by example, using green practices and educating staff and visitors about sustainable lifestyles.

An environmental management system (EMS) can provide a structured approach to implementing an environmental programme.

An EMS is a set of processes and practices that enables an organisation to reduce its environmental impacts and increase its operating efficiency.

An environmental audit measures and assesses the environmental impacts that a zoo's activities have on its surroundings. It considers all stakeholders and also takes into consideration historical and potential future impacts. An environmental audit is a first step in a successful EMS.

'The board of trustees has spent some time defining what sustainability means for the zoo in the four areas identified by the IZF:

- **Financial** – Somborne's income needs to match the zoo's growing expenditure. We want to ensure the application of environmental and ethical standards to our purchasing, sponsorship and investment.

- **Environmental** – Somborne must conduct activities in a way which minimises any negative impact on the environment (water, waste, energy, transport). Many zoo animals spend considerable periods of time in water and all rely on a plentiful daily supply for health and survival. The zoo intends to implement measures to reduce, reuse and recycle water. Our special exhibits, such as the reptile house, use lots of energy, and in addition to the volume of waste generated by visitors, care of the animals generates considerable natural waste. We need to reduce the amount of energy used and increase efficiency. We want to encourage staff to adhere to environmentally friendly principles and promote environmentally friendly methods of transport for staff and visitors.

- **Human resources** – We are committed to the management and development of talent and the application of ethical employment practices.

- **Social** – We are committed to extending the concept of corporate social responsibility to the wider community. Somborne will only use suppliers and contractors that follow ethical principles. In addition we are keen to increase our participation in the local community, in particular with local schools, to help educate the future generation about the need for sustainable living.'

Requirements

Prepare a report, in response to the chairman's request for help, which covers the following:

11.1 (a)   Explain the benefits of strategic planning for the zoo.

(b)   Give two examples of specific objectives for each of the first three strategic goals identified in the scenario.   **(8 marks)**

11.2 Identify the issues that Somborne is likely to face in deciding how to allocate limited resources.   **(6 marks)**

11.3 (a)   Explain the likely costs and benefits for the zoo of implementing a sustainability initiative.
(b)   Assess the likely impact of such an initiative on the zoo's staff and one other key stakeholder.   **(9 marks)**

11.4 Explain how the zoo could use an information system to assess the success of its sustainability initiative and suggest some appropriate performance measures that could be used for each of the four areas identified by the IZF.   **(10 marks)**

Total: 33 marks

12   Green Cards Ltd

Green Cards Ltd (GC) is a specialist retailer of good quality greeting cards, operating through a chain of shops.

Industry background

Greeting cards are traditionally purchased by consumers and sent by post to celebrate special occasions such as birthdays, religious festivals, weddings, births, and other important personal events.

The greeting card market in the UK is substantial, with estimated retail sales of £1,500 million in 20X9. It is a mature market which has experienced slow, but steady, growth (**Exhibit 1**).

There are several different types of retailer of greeting cards. Specialist retailers, such as GC, are those companies which sell greeting cards as their only, or major, product. These retailers are dominated by the 'big five' companies with large chains of shops spread throughout the UK. Non-specialist retailers include department stores, supermarkets, stationery shops, charity shops and small general shops.

There is significant competition in the industry at all levels, with smaller retailers constantly leaving and joining the industry. The larger retailers tend to be mid-market, selling for an average of about £2.50 per card and paying suppliers about £1.50 per card. The smaller retailers try to compete on the quality of the cards and customer service. The highest quality hand-made cards with special design features are sold through small specialist shops. A recent entrant to the retail market, Cardworld Ltd, sells very low price cards, all at £1.00 each, while paying suppliers about £0.90 per card.

A recent alternative to a traditional greeting card is electronic cards (e-cards) sent via the internet. While there has been rapid growth in the use of e-cards, they have not, to date, significantly affected the traditional greeting card market.

Suppliers of cards

Greeting cards are supplied to retailers by card manufacturers, as even the largest retailers do not design and print their own greeting cards. The card manufacturing industry is concentrated, with 88% of the

UK market being controlled by the 19 largest companies. In developing the market, card manufacturers have shown innovation in designs and features and have invested heavily in highly specialised greeting card printing machines.

The card manufacturers sell their cards to retailers, but also sell directly to UK and international consumers through mail-order and the internet.

Company history

GC currently has over 40 shops located in large towns and cities in the UK. It sells good quality cards with up-market designs. GC has retail prices averaging about £4.00 per card and it pays suppliers an average of £3.00 per card. GC's sales have grown slowly, but steadily (**Exhibit 2**). The company chairman, Louise Green, explained the company's strategy:

'We cannot compete with the larger retailers on price or range as we do not have their scale. By far the largest retailer in the industry is Mood Cards plc (Mood Cards), (**Exhibit 3**). We therefore sell in a market niche of higher quality cards, although this niche is only around 10% of the total market, as most people do not want to pay any more than necessary. We do not, however, sell the most expensive hand-made cards, which retail at two or three times the price of our cards, as the market is very small. Also, we pride ourselves on customer service.

We import most of our cards from a large card manufacturer in the Netherlands, Haad Cards. We have formed a good relationship with Haad Cards and they don't sell to many other retailers in the UK, so our cards tend to be different from those of other retailers. However, prices from Haad Cards have risen over the past year or two.

We are constantly looking to expand. When we see an opportunity to open a new shop in a new town or city, we will take advantage, but it can take some time for it to become known in a new local market. We try not to have more than one of our shops in the same town or city.'

Environmentally friendly cards

'Last year we launched a range of cards to take advantage of consumer support for environmental issues. These 'environmentally friendly' cards are displayed on separate shelving units in each shop, occupying about 5% of floorspace. The cards are purchased from new suppliers at an average cost of £3.00, and they retail at an average price of £5.00. They are printed on a mixture of 10% recycled paper and 90% ordinary paper, and we have made sure they contain the label '*Made from Recycled Paper*'. For each card sold, we donate £0.01 to environmental charities supporting the sustainable planting of trees.

After a recent review it was decided we are not making enough profit on these cards, so we will withdraw from this market as soon as possible.'

Proposals for a new strategy

Louise and the board have become impatient with slow growth, despite the fact that profits are being made. Two alternative strategies have therefore been put forward.

Strategy 1

GC has been approached by a high quality cake and confectionery company, Cakes4Occasions Ltd (C4O), with a business proposal. C4O makes cakes and other decorated confectionery for particular occasions such as birthdays, weddings and birth celebrations. It makes the decoration specific to the customer (ie with the individual's name or a special message written onto the cake).

C4O has proposed that it takes 20% of the floorspace in all GC shops, in order to make its own sales. C4O's marketing director explained the proposal at a recent meeting between the two companies:

'Our proposal would give us space in key locations, and it would link our product to GC's cards which are also up-market and are bought for special occasions. This cross-branding would benefit both companies. We would be prepared either to pay GC a rental of £100 per square metre per annum, or to pay a fee of 10% of the revenue that we generate in GC shops. Initially a one year agreement would be appropriate.'

Strategy 2

GC's finance director has proposed an alternative strategy. He argued: 'If we can't increase sales, then we need to improve profit by cutting costs. Staffing is the largest cost, so I propose we reduce staff by the equivalent of one full-time employee in each GC shop. I think we will see the benefits in profits quickly.'

It is not possible to undertake both *Strategy 1* and *Strategy 2*.

Exhibit 1: UK greeting cards retail sales data

	20X9 estimated	20X8	20X7
Sales revenue (£m)	1,500.0	1,435.0	1,396.0

Exhibit 2: Data for GC

	20X9 estimated	20X8	20X7
Sales revenue (£m)	10.58	10.08	9.50
Operating profits (£m)	0.846	0.806	0.760
Number of shops	46	42	38
Total floorspace (000s sq metres)	6.9	6.3	5.7
Number of employees	460	420	380

Exhibit 3: Data for market leader – Mood Cards plc

	20X9 estimated	20X8	20X7
Sales revenue (£m)	460.0	418.0	380.0
Operating profits (£m)	46.0	37.6	30.4
Number of shops	920	930	940
Total floorspace (000s sq metres)	184	186	188
Number of employees	9,200	9,300	9,400

Requirements

12.1 Prepare analyses for the following sections of the Porter's Five Forces model for the greeting cards retail industry in the UK:

    (a)   Power of suppliers

    (b)   Threats from substitutes   **(7 marks)**

12.2 Using the Exhibits and other information provided for the years 20X7, 20X8 and 20X9:

    (a)   Prepare an analysis of GC's competitive position in the greeting cards market, and explain any threats to GC's competitive position.

    (b)   Evaluate the performance of GC and draw comparisons with Mood Cards plc's performance.

              (18 marks)

12.3 Discuss the ethical and business implications of GC's participation in, and withdrawal from, the environmentally friendly cards market.   **(6 marks)**

12.4 As an assistant to the finance director of GC, prepare briefing notes which:

    (a)   Evaluate each of the two proposed new strategies; and

    (b)   Give clear and reasoned advice as to which of the strategies GC should choose.

    Use relevant data and calculations to support your arguments where appropriate.   **(12 marks)**

Total: 43 marks

13   Efficiency Systems Ltd

Jon Toman and Mike Landowne resigned their lecturing posts in Computer Science at the University of Northern England in 20X7 in order to set up Efficiency Systems Ltd (ES), which develops and markets software for operational processes in businesses and public sector organisations.

Expanding the business

After an initial two year period establishing ES, it became apparent that more finance would be needed to expand. Great Western Bank (GWB) offered to consider making a loan, provided that ES produced an appropriate business plan.

Jon and Mike, the two directors, have drafted some sections of the business plan, but have approached their firm of business advisers for assistance in completing the plan in a form that can be presented to GWB. The directors also require advice on the likely risks arising from their strategy and operations that may concern GWB.

Exhibit

DRAFT BUSINESS PLAN – EFFICIENCY SYSTEMS LTD

Efficiency Systems Ltd

Contents

1. Introduction and management
2. Products and services
3. Fees
4. Marketing
5. Competition
6. Financing requirements
7. Revenue and cash flow
8. Mission statement **(to be completed)**
9. Critical success factors **(to be completed)**

1.   Introduction and management

ES was established in 20X7 by ourselves (Jon Toman aged 45 and Mike Landowne aged 62) in order to develop software to promote efficiency in clients' operational processes. We are the sole shareholders and directors and we do not currently have any employees.

2.   Products and services

ES's key product is a process scheduling software programme, Comax. This measures and monitors the efficiency of operational processes in a wide range of industries by recording and monitoring the time and resources spent on individual tasks. This data can be applied to optimise how labour and other resources are used in operational processes. Comax works as a standard programme, but it can also be adapted and customised to suit the needs of each client.

ES owns the intellectual property rights to its products and has recently rejected an offer of £500,000 from a large company for the rights to all its programmes currently in operation and under development.

Example – Case study

One existing client provides gas maintenance, repairs and fitting services to individuals and businesses. The use of our Comax software enabled:

- Visits to be scheduled more efficiently, thereby improving labour usage
- Inventories of parts held on vans to be managed more effectively to prevent return visits
- The client to monitor the output of its service engineers more effectively

We intend to develop ES by writing new programmes which will link to mobile phone technology. We call this 'Z-Info'. This will enable real-time monitoring of clients' operations and the immediate capture of information. Z-Info has not yet been fully completed, but initial testing is promising.

3.   Fees

Fees are generated from a number of sources:

(a)   Initial sale and installation of our software

(b)   Initial training of client's staff to use the software

(c)   Continuing advisory work on systems and operations to enhance cost reduction by using the software

As most of the fees are earned from initial installation and training undertaken in the first year with a new client, it is essential that more new clients are attracted in future. New finance for the development of the Z-Info system is therefore essential for the expansion of ES.

4. Marketing

Our existing client base comprises small companies. In order to obtain larger clients we need to win competitive tenders. Public sector organisations, service companies, and industrial maintenance and repair businesses are our key target markets. To win tenders we need to operate on a larger scale.

With the additional funds Mike will complete the development of Z-Info. A pilot version has been well received in a trial run at one client. However, it needs further refinement before it can be sold commercially. We will also employ two support staff.

5. Competition

The key competition comes from eight medium-sized firms (with over 10 employees) offering similar services to ours.

We expect between three and five credible tenders to be made for each contract we try to win. These will mainly be from among the medium-sized firms, but one or two will come from smaller companies such as ourselves.

We believe ES's competitive advantage comes from a product that is superior to that of most of our immediate competitors.

6. Financing requirements

We each initially invested £100,000 in the business through personal borrowing. ES currently has no debt as it previously had no historic record of trading.

ES needs to borrow £250,000 and we are prepared to use our homes, in which there is equity of £400,000, as security for the company loan.

7. Revenue and cash flow

	Revenue	Net operating cash flows	
20X7	£200,000	£50,000	
20X8	£320,000	£60,000	
20X9	£350,000	£60,000	(estimated)
20Y0	£550,000	£100,000	(forecast)
20Y1	£750,000	£200,000	(forecast)

Assumptions

- Directors' remuneration will continue at £40,000 per year each

- Sales of Comax and Z-Info for 20Y0 and 20Y1 are stated on the assumption that new finance will be available to finish the development of Z-Info and that one tender in three is won (which has been the average achieved to date)

Requirements

As a senior in the firm of business advisers acting for ES:

13.1 Prepare the following sections for inclusion in the business plan:

    (a)   Critical success factors

    (b)   Mission statement   **(8 marks)**

13.2 Critically assess each section of the directors' draft business plan (see Exhibit) to be presented to GWB to raise the required finance. Identify additional information that should be included.

    (15 marks)

13.3 Explain the key risks facing ES, assuming that the required finance is provided by the bank.

    (9 marks)

    Total: 32 marks

14 Total Equipment Hire Ltd

Total Equipment Hire Ltd (TEH) hires out plant and equipment to construction companies and small building firms. The company has a high level of debt.

Company background

TEH has three product lines:

Product line	Examples	Customer type and period of hire	% of TEH's revenue
Heavy equipment	Bulldozers, cranes, diggers, excavators and concrete pumping vehicles (includes trained operator)	Large construction companies for periods of over a month	70%
Small tools and equipment	Hand tools and small items of plant, such as generators and pumps	Small building firms for periods of less than two weeks	20%
Scaffolding	Scaffolding	Existing customers who will also hire large or small equipment at the same time as scaffolding	10%

Each product line is run as a separate division, although all equipment is stored and maintained at one site, so many of the costs are incurred jointly.

TEH's equipment is of good quality, reasonably new and well maintained. The company's support service is also good, with prompt and efficient delivery to the customer's site for all items. As a result, the business is perceived as being above average quality and hire charges therefore include a price premium over many rivals.

Total revenue was £240 million in the year ended 31 December 20X8, but is estimated to fall to around £180 million in the year ending 31 December 20X9. The reduction is reasonably evenly spread, in proportionate terms, across the three divisions and is due to both volume reductions and price discounts.

Impact of the recession

The building and construction industry has suffered in the recession. As a consequence, demand for equipment hire has reduced very significantly in 20X9 compared to 20X8. There has been a significant reduction in the number of days hiring, but also there is fierce competition in the industry resulting in downward pressure on hire charges.

The key industry benchmark is a utilisation rate of 90% (ie equipment is being hired out nine working days in every ten) but, up to the end of 20X8, TEH operated with a utilisation rate of around 80%. This lower utilisation rate was due to TEH holding a wide variety of equipment to satisfy customers' occasional needs for infrequently used equipment. Customers were therefore attracted to TEH for all their equipment needs as a comprehensive service was provided. In 20X9 TEH's utilisation rate has fallen to 70%, compared to an industry average of 78%.

TEH estimates that it will make a loss for the year ending 31 December 20X9. Operating cash flows have been negative and the company is unable to borrow further. As a result, there is doubt over whether the company will be able to make the half yearly interest payment of £15 million that is due on 1 January 20Y0. A board meeting has recently taken place.

The board meeting

Helen Chen, the **finance director**, opened the meeting: 'We need to generate cash quickly by selling some of our equipment. I know we will make a loss on sale, but I think we need to sell off about 20% of our equipment in order to generate cash of around £60 million. Where we have more than one item of the same type of equipment we could sell off one, so we maintain our product range. We also need to cut costs. We spend far too much on customer service and delivering equipment promptly. We need to reduce our labour and transport costs, even if the service to customers deteriorates.'

Paula Penny, a **non-executive director**, interrupted: 'I agree that cash needs to be generated from selling equipment, but we should be more focused on closing down one division: either small tools or scaffolding. The performance of these divisions needs to be measured to decide which one to close.'

Frank Fitt, the **operations director**, was furious with these suggestions: 'If we sell off that amount of equipment we will destroy our whole strategy, as we will lose customers who want a complete product range from one hirer. During the recession, we know we will also only raise cash for about half what the equipment is worth.'

The **managing director**, Jeff Jones, joined in: 'I prefer not to sell equipment. Instead, I have entered into some tentative negotiations with a multinational shipping and transport company, International Transport and Trading plc (ITT). A central African country is having a major dam constructed and it has an urgent, but temporary, need for heavy plant and machinery. ITT has suggested a joint venture whereby, under a three year contract, we would make available up to 40% of our heavy plant and machinery.

According to the proposed contract, this equipment needs to be available for immediate transport to Africa on request. ITT would transport the equipment to Africa and deal with the customers in return for 50% of the rental fee. ITT would collect the fees directly from the client and then pay TEH its share. It is estimated that the gross rental fees would be about 75% of the equivalent hires in the UK, but utilisation will be near 100% for requested items during their time in use on the project in Africa. ITT has offered, on signing the agreement, to make an upfront payment of £10 million to TEH in respect of our share of future hirings on the project, to help us with our short-term liquidity problem.'

Requirements

14.1 Explain the potential impact on TEH's strategy and operations which could arise from Helen Chen's proposals for divestment of equipment and cost reduction. **(8 marks)**

14.2 Discuss the issues to be considered in measuring the financial and non-financial performance of the small tools and scaffolding divisions in order to determine which division should be considered for closure, in accordance with Paula Penny's suggestion. **(8 marks)**

14.3 Evaluate the benefits and problems of Jeff Jones' proposed joint venture arrangement with ITT. Identify any matters that need to be clarified between TEH and ITT before a decision on whether to proceed with it can be made. **(9 marks)**

Total: 25 marks

15 Blazing Bicycles Ltd

You should assume that the date is March 2010.

Blazing Bicycles Ltd (BB) is an independent bicycle retailer which operates a chain of ten stores across the UK, selling high quality bicycles and bicycle accessories.

UK bicycle industry information

The number of bicycles sold in the UK since 1930 and key dates in the history of the UK bicycle industry are set out in the graph and table in **Exhibit 1**.

Exhibit 1

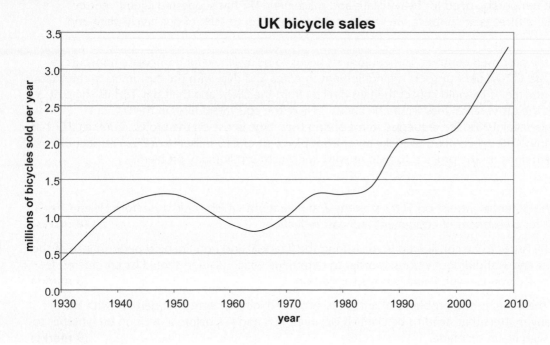

Key dates

1930s	Bicycles become popular as a form of transport
1950s	Motor cars become more affordable
Mid 1960s	Development of small-wheeled bicycles gives rise to the concept of leisure cycling
Early 1970s	Range of popular children's bicycles developed based on the small-wheeled design
	Popularity of motorcycle cross-country rallying leads to the creation of the bicycle motor cross (BMX) market – a range of small-wheeled 'off-road' bicycles specifically for children
Mid 1980s	The concept of off-road cycling is extended to adults with the development of small-wheeled mountain bikes for recreational cycling
Late 1990s	Technological advances including suspension bicycles and carbon fibre frames lead to radical changes in competitive cycling
Early 21st century	Concerns about health and the environment increase the popularity of cycling as a lifestyle activity and mode of transport for short journeys

History of the UK bicycle manufacturing industry

After the bicycle in its modern form was developed in the UK in the late 1800s, the UK became a major manufacturer of bicycles, using the metalwork and engineering expertise of its armaments and sewing machine industries to facilitate production. For the first half of the 20th century, the UK was the world leader in bicycle manufacturing, exporting bicycles to the USA and mainland Europe, and it remained a net exporter until the early 1980s.

By 1999 all the major bicycle manufacturers had ceased production in the UK. Although a number of UK-based small-scale bicycle manufacturers remain, UK-manufactured bicycles now only account for around 5% of UK bicycle sales. The majority of bicycles and parts are imported from China and Taiwan, where wages (which account for approximately 25% of production costs) are less than a third of those paid in the UK.

The UK bicycle retailing industry today

Bicycle retailing is a fragmented industry. There are over 2,000 independent bicycle retailers with a collective market share of approximately 45%. Some, like BB, are regional chains, but many are local owner-managed businesses operating from a single shop. Some cater for a wide range of cycling interests, while others specialise in a particular market segment eg top of the range bicycles for the competitive racing cyclist.

The UK's leading mass-market bicycle retailer, 'Benhonda', has approximately a 30% market share. The remainder of the industry consists of large sports retailers, supermarkets, toy shops, mail-order catalogues and online retailers which often offer a wide range of sporting and outdoor equipment.

Total UK bicycle retailing industry revenues amounted to approximately £510 million in 2009 and are forecast to reach £550 million in 2010. The breakdown of the average independent bicycle retailer's revenue is 47% bicycles, 36% parts and accessories and 17% bicycle repair services. The average retail price in 2009 of a bicycle was just over £150. Prices typically range from £45 for a basic child's bicycle to £2,000 for a high specification racing bicycle. Gross margins on bicycles average 37% of revenue, whereas margins on parts and servicing are generally higher at 48% of revenue. As a result of the recession, people are keeping their current bicycles for longer periods and so revenues from specialist workshop and repair services are increasing.

Market environment

The industry relies on discretionary spending and sales are affected by economic conditions and unusual weather.

Technological innovation has played a key part in the industry. In the 1950s most bicycles were made of low cost metals, had thick rubber tyres and a single gear. Since the mid 1980s new materials such as titanium and carbon fibre have become more common in bicycles and multiple-gear systems have become standard. There has also been increasing focus on aerodynamically efficient designs for racing and competition bicycles.

Concerns about environmental sustainability, escalating fuel prices and increased traffic congestion have led to the return of the bicycle as a mode of transport for short journeys, including use by commuters. Folding bicycles, which can be taken on public transport, and e-bicycles (a pedal bicycle with a small electric motor to aid with hills and speed) are becoming increasingly popular. E-bicycles are already in widespread use in countries such as China where there is a strong cycling culture. In addition to offering consumers a fast, environmentally-friendly mode of urban transport, they also have commercial applications (eg for postal deliveries).

The UK Government has introduced a number of cycling initiatives to address health problems related to inactivity and to tackle climate change. These include funding for cycle training in schools, and tax incentives for employees and employers under 'cycle to work' schemes. The UK bicycle industry has also benefited from public enthusiasm for cycling as a competitive sport, generated by the success of the British cycling team in the Beijing Olympics and the prospect of the 2012 Games in London.

Company information

In addition to selling high quality bicycles and accessories, BB provides limited repairs and servicing for customers who have purchased a bicycle from BB. Its ten out-of-town stores are held under operating leases. BB only employs staff with a keen interest in cycling and appropriate technical knowledge and expertise.

At a recent Board meeting the managing director expressed some concern about the external issues and risks facing the company:

'We have recently analysed the external environment and the nature of our industry, based on PESTEL and Porter's Five Forces. Using the results from this I have undertaken a risk analysis and identified the following four principal commercial risks that might prevent BB achieving its long term strategic objectives:

(1) Economic and industry conditions
(2) Competition
(3) Responsiveness to changing consumer preferences
(4) Reliance on foreign manufacturers

We have always operated in a difficult market but competition has intensified as a result of the recession. Although we have opened several new stores since 2007 our profits have fallen.'

Exhibit 2: BB financial performance in 2007 and 2009

Year ended 31 December	2007	2009
Number of stores	6	10
Total number of bicycles sold	9,200	11,000
	£'000	£'000
Sales:		
Bicycles	3,245	4,380
Accessories and servicing	2,198	2,798
Total sales	5,443	7,178
Gross profit:		
Bicycles	1,091	1,314
Accessories and servicing	938	1,268
Total gross profit	2,029	2,582
Administration and Distribution overheads	(928)	(1,493)
Profit before tax	1,101	1,089

Future direction of the business

In response to the managing director's concerns, the sales director outlined two possible strategies:

Strategy 1

'We could consider expanding the product range to offer sporting and outdoor equipment (for activities such as camping, hiking and surfing). This is consistent with what the larger retailers are doing and will reduce our reliance on the uncertain bicycle market.'

Strategy 2

'A significant proportion of our customers come to us to buy high specification bicycles, because of the knowledge and expertise of our staff. We could capitalise on this by setting up specialist bicycle workshops within each store. These will offer a range of services to new and existing customers, such as expert assembly, repairs and annual service plans. Our Manchester store has recently started doing this with excellent results.'

Requirements

15.1 Using the data in Exhibit 1 and the other information provided, discuss the extent to which the concept of the industry and product life cycle can be applied to the UK bicycle retailing industry and to sales of different types of bicycle. **(7 marks)**

15.2 Identify the factors that may have resulted in the UK's competitive advantage in bicycle manufacture for a significant period in the industry's history. Explain why this advantage now appears to have passed to countries such as China and Taiwan. Where appropriate, refer to relevant models of international trade. **(7 marks)**

15.3 Using the data in Exhibit 2 and the other information provided, analyse the performance of BB and its competitive position within the UK bicycle retailing industry. **(12 marks)**

15.4 Explain the relevant external factors that have led the managing director to identify the four commercial risks listed. **(8 marks)**

15.5 Discuss the merits of Strategy 1 and Strategy 2 as possible future directions for the business. **(8 marks)**

Total: 42 marks

16 Deeshire Council

For the purposes of local government, the UK is divided into different administrative regions. Deeshire is one such region, covering an area of 2500km^2 with a population of one million people. It is run by Deeshire Council (DC), an administrative body made up of elected, paid councillors who represent the views of the people within the region. DC receives funds from the UK central government, together with local taxes paid by the residents and businesses within Deeshire. This income is used to provide services for the community, and DC has to decide which services to provide and how much money to spend on them in areas such as education, health, housing, policing, transport, leisure and waste management.

Waste management

DC provides domestic waste collection and disposal services to its residents. The services are currently operated 'in-house' by DC's own employees. Each household is required to leave its waste at the boundary of the property for collection on the appointed collection day. There are two types of household waste: general refuse and recycling.

- General refuse is collected once per week and then disposed of by being buried in the ground ('landfill').

- Recycling is waste such as aluminium, glass, plastic and paper which can be re-used or re-processed into other materials. This is collected once every two weeks and taken to a disposal site for sorting, before being sold for re-use/re-processing.

Two million tonnes of household waste are collected annually by DC, of which up to 50% is suitable for recycling. The waste management costs that will be incurred by DC in the financial year ended 31 March 20Y0 are estimated to be £17.65 million and are detailed in **Exhibit 1**.

Exhibit 1: Estimate of waste management costs incurred by Deeshire Council
Year ending 31 March 20Y0

		£ million	£ million
General refuse			
Direct costs	1.5m tonnes @ £3 per tonne		4.50
Overhead costs			6.50
			11.00
Recycling			
Direct costs	0.5m tonnes @ £4 per tonne	2.00	
Overhead costs		3.20	
		5.20	
Less revenue generated from sale of recycling	0.5m tonnes @ £2.50 per tonne	(1.25)	
			3.95
Other central overheads			**2.70**
Total waste management costs			**17.65**

The UK central government has set DC a target for reducing waste, and for recycling as much as possible, so as to minimise the amount of general refuse going to landfill. Failure to meet the targets would involve DC incurring financial penalties in the form of a 'landfill tax'. DC is therefore considering two options to reduce costs and increase recycling rates (the options could be undertaken at the same time).

Option 1

Save £2.5 million annual overhead costs by reducing the collection of general refuse to once every two weeks and running a recycling campaign which will result in households converting a further 20% of their existing general refuse into recycling.

Option 2

Outsource the recycling element of DC's waste collection. The collection and disposal of general refuse would continue to be operated in-house. To comply with legislation, the contract has to be awarded by tender to an external contractor on the basis of the following three factors:

- The tender price submitted
- The contractor's capability to provide the recycling services required
- The financial strength of the contractor

DC will need to improve its existing information systems in order to manage the outsourcing contract and measure the performance and delivery standards of the external contractor. DC would therefore incur costs related to the management of the contract which have been estimated at £100,000 pa. As a result of the outsourcing decision, all the current costs specifically attributable to recycling would however be saved.

Tenders have been received from two applicants: Contractor A has submitted a tender price of £5 per tonne for the duration of the contract. Contractor B has quoted an overall total fixed tender price of £4 million pa. The successful contractor will be awarded a contract for the next four years.

The chief executive of Contractor A, who is also chairman of a prestigious golf club in the region, has approached a group of councillors, who are all members at the club. He has offered to fund life membership of the golf club for these councillors, if they ensure that his company obtains the contract.

You are employed by DC's strategic planning and policy group. The chairman of DC has asked you to prepare a briefing note which will be circulated to all councillors in advance of the next DC meeting, where the waste management strategy is to be discussed.

Requirements

Prepare the briefing note on waste management requested by the chairman of DC:

16.1 Using the data in Exhibit 1 and the other information provided, evaluate the financial impact of both options to be considered by DC and comment on the implications of your figures for DC's waste management strategy. **(13 marks)**

16.2 Explain the change management issues that need to be considered by DC under each option. In your answer you should refer to change management models where appropriate. **(10 marks)**

16.3 With respect to Option 2 only:

(a) Explain the principles of public sector governance that the councillors must apply when choosing between Contractor A and Contractor B. Recommend any appropriate action the councillors should take. **(6 marks)**

(b) Describe how DC could use an information system to monitor performance if an outsourced contractor is appointed. **(7 marks)**

Total: 36 marks

17   NP Ltd

NP Ltd (NP) is a small company which manufactures and sells steam cleaning machines in the UK only. These are used to clean surfaces and equipment in the healthcare and leisure industries. The use of steam reduces water and chemical usage and results in surfaces that are instantly clean and dry. NP is owned and managed by Nilesh Patel, a former research scientist with a keen interest in sustainability and the environment.

Applying the knowledge gained from operating the steam cleaning business, Nilesh has developed a new energy-efficient washing machine technology for laundering clothes and fabrics. This involves the use of special nylon beads to dissolve and absorb dirt and stains during the washing process. The beads reduce the amount of detergent required, and also reduce water consumption by 90% compared with conventional washing machines. As a result the clothes are almost dry at the end of the washing process and therefore considerable savings are made in terms of energy.

The technology has been fully tested in laboratory conditions and initial research suggests it would be appropriate for use in both the domestic and industrial laundry markets.

The domestic laundry market consists of consumers who purchase small washing machines for use in their own homes.

The industrial laundry market consists of commercial businesses which use large-scale industrial washing machines to provide washing services to:

- Companies – cleaning corporate clothing such as protective garments and uniforms, and linen for the hotel and leisure industry.

- Consumers – cleaning of specialist items of clothing, and household textiles such as duvets and curtains.

The majority of washing machines are manufactured by a few large international companies. Each company manufactures machines under a variety of different brand names for both the domestic and industrial laundry markets.

Nilesh has been granted worldwide patents for the new technology but recognises that, as a small company, NP may need additional help and expertise to exploit its full potential. He is currently considering three development strategies:

Option 1

CDT plc (CDT) is a company that specialises in helping organisations successfully develop new technological products. CDT would contribute finance and commercial support in exchange for a 50% equity stake in NP, with a view to growing the company as a manufacturer in order to obtain a listing on a stock exchange within five years. The commercial support would include creating a supply chain, developing a distribution network and identifying appropriate commercial partners.

Option 2

Eco Laundry (Eco) is a well-known, environmentally-friendly industrial laundry company that does not use chemical solvents. Eco owns a chain of industrial laundry businesses across the US, with an established customer base of both companies and consumers. Eco wants to create a strategic alliance with NP to promote the use of the new technology in its own business and also to sell it to other companies operating in the industrial laundry market in North America.

Option 3

NP would remain independent and set up a licensing arrangement whereby NP grants the right to use the technology to manufacturers of domestic and industrial washing machines.

Requirements

Prepare a report for Nilesh which:

17.1 Advises him on the issues to address when selecting the best market for the new technology, using the following headings:

    (a)   Market research
    (b)   Segmentation and targeting

    For this part only, ignore the three proposed development strategies.   **(10 marks)**

17.2 Discusses the desirability of pursuing a development strategy with a third party and advises him as to the relative merits of the three options being considered.   **(12 marks)**

                                                    Total: 22 marks

18   Executive Travel Ltd

Executive Travel Ltd (ET) operates a chain of 21 upmarket travel agent outlets which are located in major cities throughout the UK.

The travel industry

Tour operators traditionally sell trips (ie holidays and business trips) that include flights, accommodation and other services to consumers through travel agents which act as intermediaries. After offering a consumer advice and information from tour operators' databases, the travel agent makes a booking of a trip with the tour operator for the consumer using a sophisticated IT-based booking system. In return for these services, the travel agent receives a commission from the tour operator for each booking, based on a percentage of the value of the booking. For example, if a consumer pays £1,000 to a travel agent for a holiday, the commission earned by the travel agent may be £100 and then the net price paid over by the travel agent to the tour operator would be £900.

For a number of years travel agents have faced competition from internet bookings made on-line directly by consumers with the tour operators. Until 20X5, the tour operators' on-line price to consumers was the same as the consumer would have paid when booking via a travel agent, so in saving the travel agent's commission the tour operators made a higher profit. Since 20X5, however, tour operators have lowered on-line prices to consumers to around the net price paid by travel agents to the tour operators. As a consequence, there has been intense competition in the industry with many small travel agents ceasing to trade.

There are approximately 6,800 travel agent outlets in the UK. The 'big three' chains of travel agent outlets are part of vertically integrated companies which also comprise tour operators, airlines and hotels. They have about 1,750 travel agent outlets between them. The remainder are mainly small, independent chains.

Executive Travel Ltd

ET's business model is to sell upmarket leisure and business trips to long distance locations. These normally include business class or first class air tickets and luxury hotel accommodation. The trips are frequently designed by ET to meet the individual requirements of a consumer, rather than being a standardised package.

ET also attempts to make high margins from selling 'extras' such as car hire, travel insurance and limousine airport transfers.

ET has maintained a network of 21 travel agent outlets since 20X1. Of these, 20 are shops in city centres, but a key part of the ET business is called Outlet21. This is located in an office within a large investment bank, Garrett Inc (Garrett), in London. Outlet21 deals with all the business travel arrangements for Garrett's London-based staff. Garrett employees needing to make a business trip provide details to ET staff, who make all the arrangements and the booking. ET staff are authorised to make payments to tour operators from the bank's funds and then to record the costs against the appropriate cost codes in the bank's management accounting system. ET is paid fees by Garrett at the end of each month based on a percentage of the value of the trips arranged. Garrett's finance staff make very few checks on the costs incurred through ET and considerable discretion is given to ET employees over the cost and quality of the trips booked.

A crisis board meeting

The global economic downturn has caused a decline in ET's sales. As a consequence, a crisis board meeting was called. Jo Walker, the chief executive, explained the problem: 'In the recession, higher-priced upmarket travel has suffered even more than other sectors of this market. In order to compete and make sales therefore, since January 20X9 the managers of each ET outlet have been given the authority to reduce the price that the consumer pays. This is done by reducing our commission percentage by up to a half. Unfortunately, many managers seem to be discounting too often and our margins have suffered.'

The finance director, Carol Gull, who is a chartered accountant, added: 'I don't believe that discounting is the right pricing strategy for an upmarket travel agent. It sends out the wrong message to consumers. On the positive side, however, we have tried to keep sales volumes high by giving managers an incentive to increase the number of bookings being made: the number of bookings is now a key performance indicator, and part of the managers' remuneration is based on this figure.'

The marketing director, Henry Hall, was looking ahead. 'I think the way forward for increasing volumes is in entering into a contractual arrangement with an upmarket provider of travel or accommodation. I have had tentative negotiations with the Snooty Hotel Company (SHC). This company operates 25 luxury hotels, situated in high quality resorts around the world. Normally SHC would charge consumers £300 per room per night, but they are suffering low utilisation in the recession. To improve utilisation, SHC is willing to reduce its price to consumers. SHC has therefore offered to sell to our clients for £200 per room per night. We would need to guarantee to SHC that we would book a minimum of 1,600 room nights over the next year. Any shortfall would be payable by ET itself. Consumer bookings for SHC through ET were about 1,000 room nights last year, all at the full price of £300 per room per night. The commission rate for ET from SHC would remain at 10% of the room night price charged by SHC.'

At the board meeting the finance director provided data on the UK travel industry and on ET (**Exhibit**). It was agreed at the end of the meeting to conduct a thorough review of ET's business.

Exhibit

UK industry data

Years to 31 December	20X7	20X8	20X9
Revenue of tour operators (£m)	36,500	35,800	35,300
Commissions of travel agents from making bookings (£m)*	4,380	3,938	3,530
Number of bookings through travel agents (000's)	68,600	65,200	64,100

* Includes transfer prices of vertically integrated companies

Company data – ET

Years to 31 December	20X7	20X8	20X9
20 city centre outlets			
Revenue of tour operators (£m)	90	84	78
Commissions from making bookings (£m)	9	7.56	6.24
Number of bookings (000's)	30	27	24
Sundry commissions (car rental, travel insurance etc) (£m)	1	1.1	1.1
Outlet21			
Fees from Garrett (£m)	3	3	3

Ethical issue

One of the ET employees working at Outlet21 recently resigned and sent the following letter to Carol Gull, the finance director.

I want to draw your attention to a couple of matters that have concerned me whilst working in Outlet21. ET employees have considerable discretion over the quality of the hotels and flight tickets being booked. As a result, relatively junior Garrett employees are being given the best accommodation and travel by some ET employees who are then 'rewarded' with gifts from these bank employees – sometimes amounting to over £100 per gift.

Also, Garrett has a charitable trust for education in Africa to which the bank's clients, employees and suppliers voluntarily contribute. Senior bank employees sometimes book with ET to go to Africa to open new schools that have been purchased from the trust's funds, and so gain publicity for the bank. When they do so, they stay in the best hotels and travel first class. I think that if this had been bank business then it would be fine, but it is becoming a major cost for the charitable trust and it seems unnecessary and inappropriate. Sometimes the travel costs of the trips are even charged in full to the charitable trust, even though some commercial banking business also takes place.

Requirements

18.1 Using the Exhibit and other information provided, evaluate the performance of ET over the period 20X7 to 20X9. Make comparisons with the performance of the industry as a whole where appropriate. Indicate any additional key information that would be needed to make a fuller assessment of ET's performance in the period. **(16 marks)**

18.2 As part of ET's review of its business:

(a) Discuss the likely effects of the pricing policy of discounting by reducing commission percentages; and

(b) Assess the likely impact of the incentives for outlet managers being based on the key performance indicator of the number of bookings.

Ignore the contract with SHC. **(11 marks)**

18.3 Regarding the proposed contract with SHC:

(a) Assess the benefits and risks that need to be taken into account before deciding whether to enter into the contract; and

(b) Explain how risk can be managed if the contract is entered into. **(8 marks)**

18.4 Discuss the key ethical issues that arise from the letter sent to Carol Gull and explain what actions she should take. **(7 marks)**

Total: 42 marks

19 Hutton Haulage plc

The date is June 20Y0.

Hutton Haulage plc (HH) is a listed company which currently specialises in road haulage operations. It is one of the largest companies in the UK haulage industry.

Industry details

The road haulage industry offers a transport service by road for the goods of its customers and it accounts for 65% of all goods moved within the UK. The UK road haulage industry is in competition with transport by rail, water and air, while competition also arises from road haulage operators based in other EU countries, where diesel fuel for commercial vehicles is cheaper than in the UK. A relaxing of transport regulations by 20Y2 will allow EU haulage companies even greater access to UK markets in the coming years.

Barriers to entry in the industry are low but, during the recession, many haulage companies merged or ceased trading due to cash flow problems caused by narrow profit margins.

Company background

HH has a fleet of 1,500 trucks, most of which are less than five years old and are reasonably fuel-efficient. Twenty of the most recent trucks purchased have been fitted with 'green technology' engines and are significantly larger than the other trucks. This reduces the number of journeys, cuts total emissions and saves HH money over time, although the initial outlays are significant for this type of vehicle.

HH's major area of expansion in recent years has been to specialise in the road haulage of chilled and frozen food and drinks, which requires specialised containers. HH is one of the market leading road haulage companies for food and drinks manufacturers and for small to medium-sized retailers of these products but, to date, it has managed to secure only one specialist contract with a major supermarket. This is a five-year contract with Goonhill plc signed in November 20X6. This contract finishes next year.

About 75% of HH's journeys are within the UK but, in the last two years, HH has successfully expanded its trade to, and from, EU countries. A key location is Spain, from where fresh fruit and vegetables are imported for HH's UK customers in chilled conditions. About 50% of this trade with Spain is for Goonhill plc.

Part of HH's competitive advantage has been in controlling its costs. Its utilisation level is 85% (ie only 15% of the annual distance covered is with an empty load). This is achieved through detailed scheduling of journeys using IT systems which link resources with HH's wide network of customers. The utilisation rate is also facilitated by high annual volumes, which enable the goods of several customers to be transported in a truck at the same time (a shared load). In addition, HH's trucks enable drivers to sleep in their vehicles during rest breaks and at night. The truck and driver can therefore undertake journeys over several days serving a network of different locations for several customers, before returning to the home depot.

Current plans: Contract with Freshco

HH has been trying to finalise an outsourcing arrangement to supply transport services to Freshco, a large supermarket. Freshco has a good reputation for selling fresh food and it sources about 15% of this from Spain, with another 15% from other EU countries. The outsourcing arrangement would have no fixed term or any minimum guarantee of volume or value of services required. It would therefore be on a 'pay-as-you-go' basis. Freshco would however declare its intention to use HH as its preferred road haulage company for its distribution of fresh, chilled and frozen food and drinks from its suppliers to its central warehouses and to its 209 supermarkets located throughout the UK.

Freshco currently uses its own trucks to transport its fresh, chilled and frozen food and drinks, but it has been concerned that its supply chain operations have not been efficient with low utilisation rates and an aging fleet of vehicles. It is looking for service improvement and cost reduction. Freshco is therefore asking HH to show how it can improve Freshco's supply chain management compared to their existing, internally-resourced transportation policy.

In the negotiations with HH, Freshco has, in the last month, introduced new conditions. All Freshco's suppliers, including HH, are now required to present a plan showing how they will reduce their carbon emissions and enhance environmental sustainability in their activities to supply Freshco.

Current plans: Acquisition of RailTrans plc

RailTrans plc (RailTrans) operates rail transport facilities across Europe including the chilled transport of food and drink products. HH is considering whether to acquire RailTrans, as this would enable HH to offer more flexible transport methods to customers. Its trucks could collect or deliver goods at a rail terminus close to a major ferry port in the south of England, enabling efficient connections to many EU countries.

The fixed initial investment in RailTrans would be significant, but the variable cost of transporting goods on long journeys by rail across Europe would be up to 50% cheaper than by road, although this depends on a large volume of goods being transported on a regular basis. Food would be chilled more efficiently and trains are quicker than road transport. In addition the carbon emissions from trains are substantially lower than from trucks.

Requirements

19.1 Prepare a SWOT analysis for HH, explaining each of the points made. Highlight the key issues in a summary. **(10 marks)**

19.2 Prepare a memorandum for discussion by the HH board that explains:

    (a) How the outsourcing arrangement with HH can improve the efficiency of Freshco's supply chain; and

    (b) The actions that HH can take in order to enhance environmental sustainability in its activities for Freshco. **(12 marks)**

19.3 Explain the factors which should be considered in deciding whether to acquire RailTrans. **(9 marks)**

Total: 31 marks

20 Cutting Edge Ltd

The date is June 20Y0.

Cutting Edge Ltd (CE) is a private company that owns 50 hairdressing salons (ie outlets), located in six cities in the north of England. CE is owned by an upmarket hairdressing company, Cupitt Inc (Cupitt), which is based in New York.

Company history

CE was established by Stella Edge a number of years ago with a single salon. Stella was both entrepreneurial and a good hairdresser, expanding her business and winning national awards. Prices charged were about 30% higher than the average for hairdressing salons in similar locations. In 20X5, when CE had 75 salons, Stella retired and her son, Peter, took control of the business.

Peter was a good hairdresser, but he had poor management skills and the business therefore suffered. Peter sold 25 salons in the period 20X5-20X9 as they became unviable due to falling revenues.

New ownership

In March 20Y0, Peter sold CE to Cupitt. Within the UK, Cupitt had salons only in London at that time and it believed the acquisition of CE was a good entry into the non-London, UK market. Marketing surveys show that the Cupitt brand name is well-known and valued in the London area, mainly among higher socio-economic groups, but it is not well-known outside London. Cupitt's prices are about 20% higher than those of CE.

On acquisition, the Cupitt board set up a separate division (the new 'CE division') to manage and monitor the performance of the CE salons. Jane Jackson, a young manager in Cupitt's Paris office, was transferred to take charge of the CE division. The Cupitt board made it clear to her that they expected the performance of the CE division to improve substantially within three years. During the initial three years to March 20Y3, however, Jane would have no central funds to open new salons; any new openings would therefore need to be financed from the operating cash flows of the CE division.

After an initial review, Jane prepared a document summarising what she considered to be the key issues facing the business. These were as follows:

- The good reputation of the Cutting Edge brand had been damaged in the period 20X5-20X9 but, in the cities where CE had salons, it was still a well-recognised and valued brand.

- Staff turnover is high. Newly-appointed employees possess only basic hairdressing skills and are poorly paid.

- Salon managers are generally of low quality and are poorly paid. Prices are standardised, so managers have no control over the price list. They also have no discretion to make purchases of equipment. They can however recruit new employees within the overall salon budget.

Jane's two main strategic concerns are: first, to decide on the most appropriate divisional structure for developing the CE division; and second, how to monitor the performance of each salon in both financial and non-financial terms.

Jane is considering the following mutually exclusive options on how to structure the CE division:

Option 1

All salons to provide detailed weekly reports directly to Jane covering staffing, inventory requirements, sales and other operational matters. All detailed operational decisions for each salon would in future be taken by Jane, including staffing, services offered, purchasing and setting prices.

Option 2

Franchise the salons, whereby franchisees would control the prices and services offered in each salon.

Option 3

Give salon managers authority and control over all key operational decisions for their salon, including staffing, purchasing, pricing and the opportunity of widening the services offered to include beauty treatments. Jane would monitor each salon's performance using a balanced scorecard.

Requirements

20.1 Prepare notes for Jane which set out the advantages and the disadvantages of Option 1 and Option 2. **(15 marks)**

20.2 Assuming that Jane decides to follow Option 3:

(a) Prepare a balanced scorecard for the CE division describing goals and key performance indicators for each salon; and

(b) Discuss whether a balanced scorecard is likely to be the best method of monitoring the performance of each salon. **(12 marks)**

Total: 27 marks

21 Supaspeed Ltd

The date is September 20Y0.

Supaspeed Ltd (Supa) is a parcel delivery company which specialises in the home delivery of parcels to consumers on behalf of business clients in the Business-to-Consumer (B2C) market. Supa's main clients are mail order companies, traditional store-based retailers fulfilling consumer orders, internet retailers and businesses selling via online auction sites.

Parcel home delivery industry

The parcel home delivery market is highly competitive. There is a wide variety of choices open to clients, both in terms of the number of companies operating in the industry and the range of different services that each delivery company offers.

Within the UK, the parcel home delivery market is fragmented:

Parcels delivered to UK households (B2C market)	*Market share*
UK national postal service operator (overall market leader)	30%
Four international courier groups (the Big Four)	45%
Eight national companies (including Supa) and over 1,000 smaller businesses	25%

Outside the UK, in view of their global coverage, the Big Four dominate the market for parcels delivered from UK businesses to international consumers, with a combined market share of 70%.

Most parcel delivery companies offer a choice between speed and price, ranging from speed-sensitive urgent delivery (same-day or next-day), to price-sensitive non-urgent delivery within 2-3 working days. In the B2C market, the required speed of delivery is usually chosen by the end consumer when placing an order.

Some companies, like Supa, concentrate only on the B2C market. Others, including the Big Four, also operate in the Business-to-Business (B2B) and Consumer-to-Consumer (C2C) markets.

Industry developments

The demand for parcel home delivery services predominantly comes from retail businesses which need to distribute goods to a variety of consumers. Free trade and increasing globalisation have led to these businesses expanding into new international markets and this has increased demand for the worldwide transportation of goods. Economic growth in the Asian market has created a need for new distribution networks, and the trend towards outsourcing has led many businesses to turn to parcel delivery companies as part of their supply chain.

Before the internet changed the way that businesses operate, clients for the UK parcel home delivery market mainly consisted of UK mail order businesses which needed to send goods to consumers, with delivery taking up to two weeks. The home delivery sector has benefited from the continued growth in online shopping. However, this has also led to increased consumer expectations regarding the speed, security and tracking of delivery, and to reduced tolerance of delays.

Margins within the industry have come under pressure as a result of the recession and high fuel prices. Measures to tackle pollution and congestion have increased costs for road-based delivery services, and heightened security measures have increased the costs of air freight operations. This has led to the failure of a number of smaller operators and some consolidation, as other small operators have been acquired by the Big Four.

Supa's operations

Supa's distinctive purple delivery vans are based at 20 depots across the UK. The vans deliver parcels to consumers in their area in the morning and then make collections from business clients in the afternoon, although a minority of clients take parcels directly to the depot for onward delivery.

Once a parcel arrives at the depot it is sorted according to its address and area code and then transported to its final destination via land, air or sea depending on the speed of delivery requested by Supa's client or the consumer. To meet client requirements, Supa has developed a chain of overseas partners, giving it cost-effective access to a global network of distribution centres. These strategic alliances also provide Supa with links to international businesses wanting to deliver to consumers in the UK.

Parcel delivery is a cyclical business so Supa has a core of full-time employees, who all belong to a trade union, supplemented by part-time staff at peak periods. Employees are treated as a valuable resource and Supa invests heavily in training, so employees are familiar with the range of services Supa offers, understand how to use the technology and are able to communicate with clients and consumers. To promote Supa's corporate identity, all employees wear a purple uniform.

The condition of the contents of a parcel is affected by the quality of its packaging. To reduce the risk of damage, Supa encourages clients to make use of its own-brand, environmentally-friendly packaging materials (bags, boxes, tubes, tape etc). Supa was the first UK company to introduce a carbon-neutral delivery service, which is available at a premium price.

Change of strategy

Supa found it hard to compete effectively in the non-urgent market, dominated by the major international and national companies. In July 20X8 therefore it withdrew its non-urgent delivery service and focused entirely on urgent deliveries by offering a time-guaranteed next-day delivery service. Clients and consumers have a choice of specified two-hour time slots at different prices, the most expensive slot being the first delivery of the day (between 07:00 and 09:00). The latest delivery slot ends at 19:00.

In order to achieve this, Supa has invested heavily in information and communications technology to increase the efficiency of distribution. All parcels are labelled with a Supa delivery notice, and bar-coded with a unique parcel identification code (PIC). This facilitates the sorting and tracking process. All delivery vehicles are fitted with global positioning systems (GPS). Drivers have a notebook computer, with handheld scanner linked to a centralised database, which captures electronic information about each parcel, including the time of collection and delivery and the consumer's signature. Supa's ability to track electronically both drivers and parcels throughout the delivery process facilitates more efficient scheduling of collections and deliveries, and provides clients and consumers with accurate information about expected delivery times, reducing the need for costly redeliveries. Using the unique PIC, both clients and consumers can access information via Supa's website so they can trace a parcel, ascertain expected arrival time or verify proof of delivery. Supa also sends a text message or email reminding the consumer of the impending delivery and reconfirming the time.

Supa is now carrying out a post-investment audit in order to decide whether the strategy it has implemented in the two years since July 20X8 has been successful. Summary financial results for Supa and for the next-day delivery market leader in the year ended 30 June 20Y0, together with a budget, historical data and a Balanced Scorecard of performance measures, are set out in **Exhibits 1 and 2**.

Supa's operational director has suggested that further service improvements could be made by rationalising its depots and restructuring its distribution system. This would involve halving the number of depots and creating a new centralised sorting facility. The remaining depots would no longer undertake any sorting but would simply act as a local base for Supa's vehicles.

Exhibit 1: Summary financial results

Years to 30 June	Supa Old strategy Actual 20X8	Supa New strategy Budget 20Y0	Supa New strategy Actual 20Y0	Market leader Actual 20Y0
Revenue	£35m	£42.3m	£46m	£380m
Operating profit	£1.05m	£2.1m	£1.61m	£17m
Number of parcels handled	4.7m	4.7m	4.6m	42m
Number of UK depots	20	20	20	50

Exhibit 2: Balanced Scorecard for the time-guaranteed next-day B2C delivery market

Year ending 30 June 20Y0

Key performance indicator		Supa Budget 20Y0	Supa Actual 20Y0
Financial			
Revenue growth percentage }	to be calculated from	?	?
Operating margin percentage }	Exhibit 1	?	?
Customer			
% of deliveries made within allocated time slot		99%	97.5%
% packages lost or unable to be delivered		2.5%	3.5%
Internal business			
% of successful first attempt deliveries		70%	65%
Average number of trips per vehicle per day		4	4.5
Innovation and learning			
% staff achieving certification for training on new technology		80%	95%
Information systems availability – % downtime		2%	5%

Requirements

21.1 Explain how the parcel home delivery industry has evolved in the face of changing consumer demand and other key external factors. **(8 marks)**

21.2 Analyse Supa's value chain and describe clearly its key value drivers. A value chain diagram is not required. **(10 marks)**

21.3 Using both exhibits and the other information provided, assess whether implementation of the strategy to focus on time-guaranteed next-day B2C deliveries since July 20X8 has been a success.

You should:

(a) Prepare calculations for each financial indicator (budget and actual) that is indicated as being missing from Exhibit 2, together with other relevant financial performance measures.

(8 marks)

(b) Use your calculations in (a), and the Balanced Scorecard in Exhibit 2, to evaluate the impact of the new strategy, justifying any further information that you would require in order to reach a conclusion.

(10 marks)

21.4 In relation to the operational director's proposal, explain how the depot sorting staff, as key stakeholders, would be affected by and have the power to resist rationalisation of the depots.

(7 marks)

Total: 43 marks

22 e-Parts Ltd

e-Parts Ltd (EP) is an online retailer which sells spare parts and accessories for a variety of domestic appliances. EP was established two years ago by Kamal Sheikh, who identified a gap in the market after he struggled to find a reasonably priced replacement part for his oven. EP has two types of customer:

- Small specialists who repair and service domestic appliances for individuals and need to access parts quickly at low cost; and

- Individuals who need either parts such as door hinges and seals to carry out their own simple, non-electrical repairs, or accessories such as fridge shelves or dishwasher cutlery baskets.

EP has grown as people try to save money in the recession and seek to extend the life of their existing domestic appliances by servicing them rather than replacing them. It now has a database of over two million customers. 90% of orders are placed and paid for online, with the remaining 10% handled by a call centre, which also offers after-sales service and support for online customers. In its warehouse, EP stocks 100,000 different products covering the appliances of 250 different manufacturers. EP's inventory control system allows it to despatch most items on the day that the order is placed.

Competition

Domestic appliance manufacturers charge premium prices for spare parts and accessories, primarily to encourage customers to buy new appliances, but also because they do not find it cost-effective to supply parts and accessories directly to customers. Domestic appliance retailers only stock items for the most popular appliances. EP prices are significantly lower than those charged by the appliance manufacturers. As a result, its only real competition is from other similar online businesses.

Brand and marketing

Kamal has positioned EP as 'a service business which helps customers to repair and enhance appliances'. Via the EP website's advice page, customers can access articles and videos to guide them through the most common repair processes. EP also takes advertising revenue from repair businesses in exchange for listing their services on the website. EP relies heavily on customer feedback. As well as a 'product and service review' facility on the website, Kamal has recently created a social networking page where customers can take advantage of special promotions, exchange information and access free advice from experts.

Risk management and business continuity

At a recent management meeting, Kamal made the following comments:

'Keeping our website operational is key for our business. If the site is down we don't make any money. If new customers visit our site and the online shop is not functioning effectively, they don't come back again. The other key issue for us is our inventory control system which allows us to identify quickly whether an item is in stock and where it is located. So far we have handled everything ourselves, but as a result of our rapid growth I am thinking of outsourcing all our operational systems to a specialist information technology (IT) provider. I have also been told that we should have a formal risk management policy, including a business continuity plan, for the business as a whole, so that if a major incident occurs we can continue to function.'

Requirements

22.1 Explain the relevance of risk management to the business as a whole and identify the main factors that would be covered in EP's business continuity plan. **(6 marks)**

22.2 Identify the key risks arising for EP as a result of its reliance on IT (other than those relating to business continuity) and recommend how they can be managed. **(8 marks)**

22.3 Explain the factors to be considered by EP in deciding whether to use outsourcing as a method of implementing its IT strategy. **(7 marks)**

Total: 21 marks

23 Marcham plc

Marcham plc (Marcham) is a major supermarket chain with a loyal customer base and a 30% share of the UK supermarket sector.

MarchamBank

Marcham is proposing to take advantage of recent turmoil in the banking sector and public mistrust of some retail banks by launching its own banking services, under the name of MarchamBank. This will reduce the pressure felt by Marcham's traditional mature retail business as a result of lower consumer spending during the recession, and will take advantage of rising margins for financial products. MarchamBank will operate from 30 branches within the largest existing Marcham stores and will also provide online banking facilities. The strategy is to offer Marcham customers simplified financial products and the marketing literature will emphasise 'face-to-face, relationship-driven banking from a name that our customers can trust'. Initially MarchamBank will offer simple savings products, short term loans, and a credit card. Once these have all been launched successfully, it will offer current accounts and a mortgage broker service to source mortgages for customers. It does not intend to offer mortgages itself.

Unlike other competitors which have moved into selected personal finance products via joint ventures with major UK banks, Marcham is planning to control its own banking operations. It will hire its own financial services specialists to run its branches and staff its customer service call centre. In view of the collapse of several banks during the financial crisis, the UK government is keen to increase competition in the banking sector and Marcham has already been granted a banking licence. Establishment of the customer service call centre in Scotland (rather than Asia where most competitors base their support services) will allow Marcham to receive a £5 million grant from the UK government.

Customer loyalty card scheme and integrated information system

Marcham has over 20 million customers in the UK and manages its relationship with them via a customer loyalty card. The loyalty card allows customers to earn points in return for cash spent in Marcham stores. Points can be converted into vouchers that can be used to reduce the cost of future purchases. The loyalty card forms part of an integrated information and knowledge management system which allows Marcham to track the shopping habits of its customers.

The other key element of the integrated system is a sophisticated Electronic Point of Sale (EPOS) and inventory control system. As soon as a sales transaction is recorded, this system updates inventory records, provides valuable sales information regarding product demand and profitability, and facilitates automated purchasing from suppliers. This has enabled Marcham to reduce costs by increasing the frequency and accuracy of ordering, leading to lower levels of inventory and wastage.

The data collected from the various elements of the integrated system are logged in a centralised database with an advanced search engine. Marcham uses the resulting customer profiling information for a variety of purposes including pricing, decisions as to which product ranges to stock, research, marketing and customer service. One of the key benefits is improved customer segmentation, enabling Marcham to promote low price or high quality items as appropriate. The information is also sold to a number of the company's suppliers which use it to refine and develop their products.

Whilst most other supermarkets operate similar customer loyalty schemes, none is as far-reaching as Marcham's, which was the first of its kind. Marcham's research suggests that one in four UK adults belongs to its customer loyalty scheme. A key advantage for Marcham is that the scheme enables it to extend its share of customer spend by identifying other products that the customer is likely to be interested in, based on their profile and spending patterns.

Marcham plans for the loyalty card scheme to be a key driver of competitive advantage for its expansion into banking services, especially as none of the existing retail banks operates a loyalty card scheme. It will provide an immediate customer list for direct marketing purposes and the data may help to assess a customer's credit-worthiness.

Marcham intends to offer its customers a MarchamBank credit card to stand alongside the standard loyalty card scheme. This will further enhance its database by giving it access to information about non-Marcham purchases made by its customers.

Marcham criticised

The following is an extract from an article that appeared recently in a national newspaper:

'Supermarket giant Marcham has been criticised recently. Its customer loyalty card scheme has been labelled as a sophisticated spy system by some critics, allowing it to exploit customers by capturing information that they are not in a position to withhold and then using it to sell them things they don't need. As well, there is a risk that this private shopping information could fall into the wrong hands and might one day be used against people.

Marcham has also been accused of further tightening supplier payment terms to improve its own cashflow, despite continuing to make huge profits – indeed this may be where the money for its proposed expansion into banking services is coming from. Suppliers are, of course, prevented from complaining about low margins and onerous terms and conditions because of fears that they will lose Marcham's business.'

Requirements

23.1 In preparation for a meeting of Marcham's senior executives, the operations director has asked you to prepare a report which:

(a) Explains the potential benefits of an effective information system for a supermarket and discuss how Marcham has used its information systems to create competitive advantage in the supermarket industry. **(8 marks)**

(b) Assesses the suitability, feasibility and acceptability of Marcham's proposed expansion into the banking sector. **(12 marks)**

(c) Discusses the relative merits of Marcham's intention to expand into banking via organic growth rather than having an established bank as a business partner. **(8 marks)**

23.2 Discuss the ethical issues raised by the newspaper article in respect of Marcham's customer loyalty card and its treatment of suppliers. **(8 marks)**

Total: 36 marks

24 Quantum Agencies Ltd

The date is December 20Y0.

Quantum Agencies Ltd (QA) is a medium-sized estate agent, with branches located in a prosperous area of the south of England. The business focuses entirely on residential properties (ie individuals' homes). It has no dealings with commercial properties.

The UK industry

Estate agents can provide a number of services relating to properties for individuals. The most important for estate agents, in terms of revenue generation, arises from assisting private individual vendors (ie sellers) with the sale of their residential properties. The services provided in this context include agreeing an asking price with the vendor, advertising the property, taking potential purchasers to view the property and assisting with price negotiations between the vendor and purchaser. A commission charge is made for these services averaging between 1.0% and 1.5% of the final agreed selling price of the property. This is paid by the vendor to the estate agent on completion of the sale. There is no charge if a sale is not made. Estate agents also normally offer other property services such as property management, valuations, surveys, auctions and financial services.

Branches of estate agents, which are usually located on busy town or city centre streets, are effectively offices with large front windows used as advertising spaces for vendors' property details (eg photographs of the property). Staff in the offices aim to persuade vendors to sign contracts which commit the vendors to the agency for the sale of their properties. Staff then encourage potential purchasers to inspect and then buy the vendors' properties.

For 13 years up until 20X8 the estate agent industry experienced strong growth with increasing selling prices and high volumes of sales.

From 20X8, the economic downturn caused a reversal of fortunes in the UK industry, causing many estate agent branches to close in the period 20X8-20Y0. Key features of this decline were: falling selling prices (from a UK average of about £203,000 in 20X7 to about £162,000 in 20Y0); declining sales volumes; reduced availability of loans for property purchases; and increased competition among estate agents. The decline in volumes arose mainly from potential vendors being reluctant to sell at historically low prices, while potential purchasers were waiting for market prices to fall further.

In late 20Y0 there were some tentative signs of recovery, but property sales volumes continued to be well below their 20X7 level. Both vendors and purchasers remained cautious about undertaking a major financial transaction in an adverse economic climate.

Estate agents are facing increasing competition from individuals who advertise and sell their own properties directly through the internet. There is also low-price competition from internet-based estate agents. A further issue in the industry is recent legislation stating that vendors must provide a certificate showing the energy efficiency of their properties.

Predictions for population growth show that, over the next 20 years, there will be a significant increase in demand for residential properties and therefore a worsening of the UK's historical long-term shortage of housing. To address this issue the government has required some local authorities, particularly in areas where there is high demand such as the south of England, to construct many new homes, including ecology-friendly towns and low-cost social housing.

Company background

QA was formed a number of years ago by Neil Smith and Steven Richards, its only directors. It deals with residential property sales, but it also offers a range of other property services.

QA started with only one branch but grew over the years and now has 20 branches. The branches are all held under operating leases and hence there are few owned assets. Each branch is located in a town where there are normally two or three branches belonging to other estate agents. QA branches are all of similar size and are normally at least 15 miles from each other.

In 20X7 each QA branch had 7 staff with a further 20 staff at head office. Following the reduction in sales volumes, there are now only 6 staff at each branch and 15 at head office. Significant cost savings have also been made in branch rents since 20X7, as a number of operating leases have been renewed at lower cost.

QA operates in the comparatively upmarket sector of the industry, offering high quality customer service. Up to 20X7 it maintained a normal commission charge to the vendor of 1.5% of the selling price for each property sold but, in order to compete during the economic downturn, a policy of offering extensive discounts on commission to vendors was introduced in 20X8. By 20Y0, QA's profits had reduced significantly.

Steven and Neil decided to call a meeting in early December 20Y0 to plan a new strategy for 20Y1 and beyond.

The meeting

Each director proposed a different strategy. They agreed it would not be possible to implement both proposals.

Proposal 1

Neil opened the meeting: 'The recession has been longer and more severe than expected. We can no longer sustain our present network of branches and staff. I've been thinking we need to close at least five of our 20 branches.

However, recently, a friend of mine who owns a firm of solicitors, GTA, suggested to me that QA and GTA link up. In the five towns where GTA has branches, GTA's large front windows would be used to advertise our clients' properties. When a potential purchaser or vendor makes an enquiry at that branch, GTA's staff would take their details and communicate these to us. GTA would therefore be our first point of contact with vendors and purchasers. We would deal with the customer as previously, but by visiting their homes rather than having our own premises.

In return, where a QA property is sold following an introduction by one of GTA's branches, GTA would receive a half of one percent of the selling price as commission. QA would keep the remainder of the commission (eg 1.0%, if a full 1.5% is charged to the vendor). GTA may also benefit from selling legal services to the vendor or the purchaser. We could adopt this arrangement in the five towns where GTA operates. This would save about 75% of our branch costs in those towns, as there would be no need to rent premises, and staff costs would be significantly reduced.'

Proposal 2

Steven disagreed: 'I believe that the recession is ending and we need to start growing again.
Jim Terra, the owner of a rival firm of estate agents, Terra Ltd (Terra), told me recently that Terra has suffered in the recession as much as QA. He indicated that he would consider a merger of our two companies to form a new company, Terra & Quantum (TQ), with Jim having 50% of its ordinary share capital and each of us having 25%.

This seems like a generous offer to me, as Terra has 30 branches. There would be 10 towns where TQ would initially own two branches, but one branch could be closed in each of these towns to save costs. Jim has provided the following background details about Terra to help us evaluate a potential merger:

- Terra commenced trading over fifteen years ago and operates a chain of 30 branches. It only operates in the residential property market.

- Terra's business model is to attract as many vendors' properties as possible by offering a lower commission charge than most rivals. Terra normally charges 1.0%, but discounts may be given.

- Terra expanded rapidly with high volumes up to 20X7 but it has made losses every year since then. Branches are all held under operating leases, of varying duration, so there are few owned assets.'

Performance data

The following data shows estimated figures for the year ending 31 December 20Y0 for both QA and Terra, plus QA's figures for the year ended 31 December 20X7 (which was the peak of the housing market in terms of house prices and sales volumes).

	Quantum Agencies (QA)		Terra
	20X7	20Y0 estimated	20Y0 estimated
	£'000	£'000	£'000
Total value of properties sold	600,000	375,000	625,000
Commission from properties sold	9,000	4,500	6,000
Fees from other services	3,000	2,000	2,700
Branch costs	(8,500)	(5,000)	(7,200)
Head office costs	(1,500)	(1,400)	(2,000)
Pre tax profit/(loss)	2,000	100	(500)
	Units	Units	Units
Number of residential properties sold in the year	2,000	1,500	2,500
Average number of properties, advertised at any one time as available for sale	600	700	1,200
Number of branch employees	140	120	150
Number of branches	20	20	30

Requirements

24.1 Prepare a PESTEL analysis for the UK estate agent industry. **(11 marks)**

24.2 Using the data and other information available, analyse the performance of QA in 20Y0 compared with 20X7, explaining the key factors that have caused profit to decline. **(12 marks)**

24.3 Discuss the merits and problems of the strategic alliance with GTA in Proposal 1. **(7 marks)**

24.4 With reference to the merger in Proposal 2 and the analysis in requirement (b):

(a) Compare the performance of QA and Terra in 20Y0; and

(b) Explain the benefits and problems of the merger. Give advice on whether the merger should be undertaken by QA on the terms suggested by Jim. **(14 marks)**

Total: 44 marks

25   SkinDeepe plc

SkinDeepe plc (SD) manufactures and markets a range of skin creams and lotions.

Company background

SD's product range includes 33 different types of face creams, sun creams and body lotions.

About 75% of SD's products by volume are sold under SD's own brand, the 'Le Beauty' label. These are upmarket products selling at about double the average retail price for the industry. 'Le Beauty' products are sold through selected retailers across Europe in order to enhance the reputation of the brand. The other 25% of its products are sold to Tatton plc (Tatton) which owns a chain of exclusive department stores across Europe. These products are identical in substance to 'Le Beauty' products, but are packaged under the Tatton brand. The price paid by Tatton is about 20% lower than that paid by other customers due to the high volume purchased.

SD has two factories which produce and package its products. These are both located near Southampton, a major seaport in the UK. They are situated about 10 miles from each other. Factory A employs 150 staff and produces the creams and lotions in bulk form. They are then transported by road to Factory B where they are packaged by inserting the bulk products into a variety of attractive containers, suitable for retailing. These include sprays, tubes and tubs. Factory B employs 100 staff. SD's own fleet of trucks then distributes the packaged products to customers throughout Europe. Orders for Tatton go directly to its central storage facility.

A reduction in sales volumes and an increase in costs have caused pressure on profits and forced SD to reconsider its business model. The company recognises that a key asset is its brand and that its strength is in marketing and selling, rather than in production.

A cost reduction plan

Given the new challenges, in early December 20Y0 the board decided to implement the following plan in order to reduce costs:

(1) **Phase 1** – Immediately outsource production of the bulk cream and lotion products to a manufacturer in China, Huang Inc (Huang), to be delivered by ship to Factory B. Within one month, therefore, close Factory A.

(2) **Phase 2** – If Phase 1 is successful, in one year's time SD will close Factory B and Huang will then also package the products before transporting them to the UK by ship. On arrival in the UK, a distribution company, Fell plc (Fell), will collect the products from the ship, hold the inventory in a large warehouse, then deliver products directly to customers when requested to do so by SD.

SD will continue to be responsible for sales and marketing from its head office which is adjacent to Factory B, but in a separate building. About 30 of the Factory A and Factory B employees will be offered transfers, some to head office and some to China in quality assurance roles. These roles arise as quality assurance procedures are being put in place at Huang and in SD as part of SD's supply chain management procedures. All other employees will be made redundant.

SD's board is particularly concerned about how to implement and monitor the new strategy. The workforce at Factory B has tended to be loyal and most staff have been in employment with SD for many years. Factory A's workforce is mainly unskilled labour, on short-term contracts. Levels of job satisfaction in Factory A are low and there have been several strikes in the recent past.

Huang does not currently have the equipment to package the products during Phase 1, so this is purely a production phase. Also, even though operational due diligence procedures have been carried out to demonstrate that Huang can deliver on the contract, SD wants to implement the plan in two phases in order to obtain evidence about the level of service that Huang actually provides. A draft service level agreement with Huang is in place which emphasises quality management and quality assurance. This contains clearly defined measures for product quality and delivery times.

The plan is currently confidential but, as part of its implementation, the board has recently informed its biggest customer, Tatton, about it. A reply has just been received from Tatton as follows:

Requirements

25.1 With respect to the plan to source products from China, identify and justify the position of the following key stakeholder groups in Mendelow's power-interest matrix:

- Factory A employees
- Factory B employees
- Tatton   **(9 marks)**

25.2 Explain how barriers to change for Phase 1 may differ from those for Phase 2.   **(8 marks)**

25.3 Identify and explain the key performance indicators that SD could use to monitor the performance of Huang in Phase 1 of the plan, in order to decide whether to continue with Phase 2.   **(6 marks)**

25.4 As an employee, working for SD on its cost reduction project, draft a response to the two matters raised by Tatton.   **(10 marks)**

Total: 33 marks

26 Heaton Home

Heaton Home (HH) is a not-for-profit charity established forty years ago by Lady Alice Heaton when she gifted a large house to the charity. HH has a board of trustees responsible for its governance and strategy.

HH's history

The gift from Lady Heaton is a building of historical and architectural significance. The conditions attaching to the gift require the charity's board of trustees to use the house 'to provide reduced cost residential care home places for elderly people who have lived in the local town of Northport for ten years or more'. The trustees have always interpreted 'elderly' as meaning 'over 65 years old' when determining whether an individual is eligible for a place. The conditions of the gift by Lady Heaton also stated that the house itself should be 'maintained in good order'.

Lady Heaton also gave HH just enough money to establish the house as a residential care home, but not enough to cover annual running costs. There are no funds remaining from the original gift. Lady Heaton died a number of years ago.

Managers were appointed by the trustees and established three sources of funding to finance the running of the home:

- Fees from residents. These are currently £10,000 per year, per resident, which is much lower than the fees charged by other care homes in the region. However, fees were increased from £8,500 two years ago in order to meet the care home's rising costs.

- Contributions from local government have been agreed as a lump sum of £300,000 per year and an additional £5,000 per resident, per year. Local government has been willing to make a contribution since the alternative is for them to accommodate the elderly people in other care homes, which would cost local government substantially more. A condition of the contribution is the appointment of a trustee on the board who specifically represents local government.

- Charitable donations and bequests from the local community. These have been constant at around £250,000 per annum in recent years.

Experienced managers and care assistants are employed at a total cost of £800,000 per year. A quarter of the total labour hours required to run the home are provided by unpaid volunteers from the local community, where the home is well known and supported.

Some recent issues

The trustees have recently appointed a new manager to run the home. He identified a few problems in his initial review:

- The home has 50 places and historically these have been full, with a waiting list. Over the past two years, however, the number of occupied places has fallen to only 45 and there is no waiting list. Under the terms of HH's agreement with local government, £100,000 of the lump sum payment will be withdrawn if average occupancy in a year falls to 40 or below.

- There has been some deterioration in the state of the house which affects its appearance, but not the way it functions. The estimated cost of restoring the house is £300,000.

- The number of volunteer hours is falling by about 5% per year.

- Some residents will struggle to pay the full amount of their fees next year. Demand for places in the home has been sensitive to the increased price charged to the residents.

- The estimated full cost of running the home in 20Y0 is £1.25 million, which is almost entirely fixed costs and includes salaries. HH currently has cash accumulated from surpluses of previous years of only £100,000.

Meeting of the Board of Trustees

At a recent meeting, the trustees agreed that the current situation was financially unsustainable. There was also concern that the charity was failing to meet the needs of its residents, as evidenced both by the fall in demand, and by its failure to meet its obligation under the conditions attaching to Lady Heaton's gift, which required the house to be maintained. Legal advice suggests that the trustees are required to continue to comply with this building maintenance aspect of Lady Heaton's gift.

Hannah Khan, the local government trustee, put forward a series of proposals:

- To increase fees to residents by 20%

- In order to increase demand, to offer places to people living in a slightly wider geographical area around Northport, and to extend the eligible age range down to people who are at least 60 years old

- To reduce the staffing levels in order to save costs

Hannah argued that the conditions attaching to Lady Heaton's gift were not relevant to running the home in today's environment, but that any additional surplus arising from Hannah's proposals should be accumulated to restore the house.

Requirements

26.1 Prepare a mission statement for HH and briefly explain why a mission statement may be useful for HH.
(6 marks)

26.2 Based on the new manager's review, identify the key risks facing HH and briefly describe how these can be managed. Show any relevant supporting calculations.
(10 marks)

26.3 Evaluate the ethical implications of the proposals made by the local government trustee. (7 marks)

Total: 23 marks

27 Family Entertainment Company plc

The Family Entertainment Company plc (FEC) is a UK-based company which operates a chain of 20 family-oriented theme parks throughout Western Europe. Its mission is to provide 'a great all-round family entertainment experience'. Each FEC theme park consists of roller coasters and other thrill rides, live entertainment and themed exhibits (attractions linked to a specific concept such as outer space or sea-life). Each park also offers a variety of food outlets plus retail outlets that sell FEC branded merchandise. FEC's target market in each country is domestic customers and foreign tourists.

The theme park industry in Western Europe

In Western Europe the leisure and entertainment industry is mature. As well as an increasing number of theme parks, there is a wide range of alternative forms of entertainment available to tourists and domestic customers eg films, sports, zoos, and tourist and cultural attractions. Theme parks range from major complexes, operated worldwide by large multinational entertainment corporations, to regional chains such as FEC, to much smaller, simpler local parks. The multinational entertainment corporations gain marketing benefits from linking rides with film and television characters, and are also able to access the significant capital and technology required to develop the latest rides. Most multinational and regional chains add at least one new ride per year per park to attract visitors, and they spend on average 20% of annual revenue on building new rides and attractions.

Costs and revenues

Theme parks have relatively low variable costs and high fixed costs. They have low, mid and high seasons in terms of volumes of visitors. Seasonal attendance means that the effective cost per visitor is much lower in the high season. In addition, demand for rides fluctuates during the day, which can cause problems such as congestion and queuing at peak times.

Typically theme parks operate one of two pricing schemes:

Pay as you go – visitors pay a nominal price for entry to the park. Once inside the park, a separate price is payable for each ride or attraction, based on its popularity, with the most popular ones costing up to four times the price of the least popular.

Single admission price – visitors pay a single substantial admission price for which they receive unlimited use of nearly all attractions and rides. A small number of highly popular rides/attractions may not be included in the price or may incur a premium.

Competition is fierce. To improve profits in each period, parks need to attract more visitors, keep them in the park longer and increase the amount they spend. The key factors for a successful theme park are:

(1)   Convenience of location
(2)   Uniqueness/popularity of rides (performance and excitement)
(3)   Price
(4)   Availability and quality of wider amenities (food, merchandise etc)
(5)   Health and safety

The impact of the difficult economic climate on consumer spending has led to many theme parks suffering declining attendance and a fall in profitability. In view of increasing competition in the traditional markets of the USA and Western Europe, and the fact that land for expansion is expensive and restricted, a number of operators have started to look at other markets in Asia and South America. FEC has come under pressure recently from its shareholders, who are unhappy about falling earnings per share. To address this, FEC is now considering expanding into India.

Expansion into India

FEC's board believes that the Indian market is attractive for the following reasons:

- Strong economic growth

- Availability of large areas of dormant/unused land

- Government promotion of tourism and incentives for investment in the leisure industry

- Rising average household incomes and an increased willingness by the local population to spend resources on recreation and entertainment

There are over 100 theme parks in India, operated mostly by domestically-owned regional or local businesses, which tend to have a cultural or historical theme. These parks tend to be small, with fairly simple rides, partly because the owners lack the financial resources and technology to establish large parks with advanced, state-of-the art attractions.

FEC's theme park in India would be built on the outskirts of a major city (population of 14 million) that is recognised as one of the wealthiest in India; the residents are typically viewed as trendsetters in fashion and lifestyle. The city attracts many visitors and its tourist industry is very large.

FEC believes that the emphasis on families that is prevalent in Indian culture is a good fit with FEC's own values, and that there is an opportunity for an initial market entrant to establish a high degree of brand loyalty.

Financial projections for the Indian venture are to be produced on the basis of the assumptions set out in **Exhibit 1**.

Exhibit 1: Assumptions to be used for financial projections in respect of the Indian theme park

1. All costs and revenues will be incurred locally and will be denominated in US$

2. Figures are for revenues and expenses once the park is fully established

3. Total average revenue per visitor is made up of 50% admission price and 50% food and merchandise

4. The average admission price is $10 per visitor

5. Variable costs per visitor (excluding food and merchandise) are 20% of admission price. There is a 100% mark up on all food and merchandise

6. Estimated attendance figures:

	Attendance per month
High season (3 months)	90,000
Mid season (5 months)	75,000
Low season (4 months)	50,000

7. Annual fixed costs are $9,000,000

Health and safety

The theme park industry is in its development stage in India. Each theme park must undergo an annual inspection in order to retain a licence from local government in accordance with local certification standards. A national regulatory body for theme park health and safety has not yet been established so standards vary across the country.

FEC's operations director commented:

'Obviously the initial costs of creating and opening the new theme park will be huge, but once the park is open the annual overheads, including labour, will be much lower than in our European parks. This is important as the admission prices will need to be affordable to local customers. The industry is still at an early stage of development and regulation, and we can take advantage of this by reducing what we are normally forced to spend on park safety and ride maintenance. That should mean higher profits to keep the shareholders happy.'

Requirements

27.1 Prepare the following sections of the Porter's Five Forces model for the theme park industry in Western Europe:

- Threat of new entrants
- Competitive rivalry
- Substitutes

(8 marks)

27.2 Discuss the benefits and risks of FEC's proposed strategy to expand into India.   (7 marks)

panel manufacturers need proven technology and an established track record, because customers want confidence that the manufacturer will be in business for the duration of the panel warranty period.

Demand for solar energy

As the price of solar panels falls and that of traditional power sources increases, the global market for solar energy, which has grown rapidly since 20X5, is predicted to double again by 20Y4. However, demand for solar energy is unpredictable and varies considerably from country to country. Demand is driven by:

(1) Climate (the panels operate in daylight hours whatever the weather, however solar energy is most successful in areas of high sunshine)

(2) The price of electricity from traditional power sources

(3) Public awareness of and attitudes towards sustainability

(4) The state of the national economy

(5) Government policy/incentives for renewable energy

The political and economic framework

Government incentives offered to households and businesses to install solar energy systems vary from country to country but typically come in one of two forms:

- Investment incentives, where grants or loans are available to subsidise the initial cost of purchase and installation

- Varying levels of FITs, where the owner of the panels receives payment for all solar generated electricity that they feed back into the local network

In view of the long payback period for panels and to ensure stability of demand, government support schemes need to be available in the long term. As a result of its proven FIT scheme, finance opportunities, availability of skilled solar energy companies, and good public awareness, Germany has the highest proportion of solar power installations, followed by Italy, Japan and the USA. However each country's relative position is very dependent on its political and economic framework. For instance Spain, which had until recently been ahead of Germany, was forced to reduce solar energy subsidies in the face of its critical short-term budgeting and funding problems, resulting in an immediate and marked decline in demand.

SPV's competitive advantage

SPV uses special patented thin-film technology which is much lighter and cheaper to produce than the silicon used by other solar panel manufacturers, and which has a higher energy yield in the absence of sunshine. SPV owns factories around the world, including the USA, Germany and Malaysia, and derives economies of scale from its vertically-integrated manufacturing process which facilitates high-volume, low-cost production of efficient panels.

The uncertain industry environment and an increase in the number of Asian manufacturers offering quality products at low prices mean that, to maintain its competitive advantage, SPV needs a structure and culture which allows it to be forward-looking, innovative and quick to respond to changes in demand in different markets.

Recently, a number of environmentally-aware governments have set targets for their domestic utility companies requiring them to obtain up to 33% of energy from renewable sources over the next ten years. In view of this, SPV has approached UTILCO, a major utility company operating throughout the USA, to set up a joint venture where SPV's solar panels are attached to UTILCO's telephone and electricity poles. The solar energy will be captured and fed directly into the national electricity network.

Requirements

29.1 (a) Recommend and justify an organisational structure that is suitable for SPV given the nature of its environment. Refer to relevant models. **(5 marks)**

(b) Suggest operational strategies which SPV could adopt to encourage the culture necessary to maintain its competitive advantage. **(5 marks)**

29.2 Explain how the need for sustainability influences SPV's strategy, and assess the extent to which, as a result, SPV's success is driven by factors outside its control. **(8 marks)**

29.3 Discuss the relative merits of the proposed joint venture from the point of view of both UTILCO and SPV. **(6 marks)**

Total: 24 marks

30 Cauldron Cereals plc

Cauldron Cereals plc (CC) manufactures boxed breakfast cereals. It purchases grains such as wheat, corn and barley, processes them into breakfast cereals, packages the cereals in a range of box sizes and sells them to retailers which, in turn, sell to consumers.

Industry background

The boxed breakfast cereals industry in the UK is large and long established, with retail sales that make up about 2.3% of the UK grocery market. Despite being a mature industry, there was steady, long-term annual volume growth in UK retail sales of over 3% until the end of 20X8, since when retail sales revenues have been constant at around £1,200 million. The price to retailers and the final price to consumers of the average box of cereals have both been stable since 20X5 due to competitive factors in the industry and the economic recession.

One of the main drivers of growth in consumer demand up to and including 20X8 was a general trend among consumers towards healthy eating, in relation to which breakfast cereals have a positive image. This was exploited by manufacturers and retailers through new product development and marketing of innovative breakfast cereals designed to target healthy-eating consumers. More recently, however, the healthy-eating reputation of the industry has been tarnished by reports that, during the manufacturing process, high levels of sugar and salt are added to enhance taste. Manufacturers have been concerned about this publicity, but have had problems producing breakfast cereals of an equivalent taste with reduced sugar and salt content.

Competition in the industry is intense. Manufacturing output is dominated by the 'big three' (Astra Inc, Benn Inc and Ceel plc) which are all large international companies with manufacturing sites both in the UK and abroad. Jointly, they have dominated the UK industry for many years, defending their competitive positions with high marketing expenditure and regular launches of new products. The wide product range of the 'big three' includes the full spectrum of size, price and quality choices, including market niches such as healthy-eating and children's cereals. Many companies outside the 'big three' tend to focus on these market niches. Overall there is a wide diversity of companies in the industry (**Exhibit 1**). There are insignificant exports and imports of boxed breakfast cereals due to their bulk nature.

90% of sales by manufacturers of boxed breakfast cereals are made directly to supermarkets and other multi-outlet retailers, with the remainder to independent shops. The largest supermarket chains therefore have significant market power and use this to put pressure on all manufacturers to lower their prices. Many manufacturers, including some of the 'big three', supply 'own brand' products to supermarkets. These are products which are sold under the supermarket's brand label, so the consumer is unaware of which manufacturer made the product.

Company background

CC is a long-established manufacturer of boxed breakfast cereals focusing on the niche market of healthy eating. Within this niche it makes a range of products in terms of quality, price and size. It markets them to both adults and children. CC is small by comparison to the 'big three' but there are other companies in the industry of similar size, some of which have products in the same market niche (**Exhibit 1**).

CC sells directly to a wide range of retailers including the largest supermarket chains. CC products are currently only sold under the CC brand label.

CC historically used high quality grains in its breakfast cereals and the sugar and salt content was low at only 3% and 1% respectively, compared with 6% and 3% for many lower quality breakfast cereals. These figures have always been prominently disclosed on every box of CC cereal and are a key feature of advertising. Grains are bought on international commodities markets and represent nearly all of the variable cost of production. Current commodity prices are set daily by open market trading and tend to fluctuate significantly. Other variable costs of breakfast cereal manufacture, including sugar and salt ingredients, are negligible.

20X9 – A change in strategy

Despite the growth in sales in the UK breakfast cereal market as a whole up to 20X8, CC sales have not grown for some years and, at the beginning of 20X9, CC's chief executive was replaced.

The new chief executive, Eric Land, reviewed the company's strategy and decided that there was little CC could do to improve sales in the short term due to market competition and the economic recession. He therefore decided on the immediate tactic of cost cutting by reducing the quality of the grain purchased. Eric's instruction to production staff was: 'produce the same taste, at lower cost'. The cheaper grain was imported from Eastern Europe under a fixed-price, two-year contract signed in January 20X9. This fixed price contract proved surprisingly beneficial in saving further costs, as CC gained from lower grain prices in both 20X9 and 20Y0 when world grain commodity prices unexpectedly increased by 10% each year. Further increases in grain prices are now expected from 20Y1 onwards.

As a consequence of the cost-cutting policy, CC's profits increased in 20X9, despite there being some evidence that consumers were not as happy with the taste as they had been previously, resulting in a fall in sales volumes (**Exhibit 2**).

20Y0 – An ethical issue

Alarmed by the fall in sales volume, at the end of 20X9 Eric held an informal meeting with a small number of directors closest to him. They decided to increase the sugar and salt content of CC's products in order to improve taste and to compensate for the reduction in grain quality. The sugar and salt content was increased to 3.49% and 1.49% respectively from 1 January 20Y0. Eric explained at the meeting: 'We can legitimately continue to show sugar and salt content at 3% and 1% on our boxes, as these are now figures rounded to the nearest whole percentage point. I do not intend to disclose the fact that we have increased sugar and salt content, even to the other directors, as it may cause unnecessary problems.'

The change in sugar and salt content helped to improve the taste a little and, as a consequence, demand recovered slightly in 20Y0.

In March 20Y1 the finance director Jenny Jones, a chartered accountant, discovered the undisclosed increases in the sugar and salt content. She resigned immediately and then informed a number of newspapers. As a consequence of the bad publicity, weekly sales of CC products immediately fell to about 80% of their previous level. Eric was forced to resign. At the board meeting prior to his resignation he declared: 'How can you run a business when you can't trust your fellow directors to keep confidentiality as a basic principle of professional and ethical conduct? I improved the business and what she did was unprofessional and unethical. She has ruined this company.'

June 20Y1 – A new start

A new board was appointed and in May 20Y1, after reviewing the situation, they restored both the original grain quality and the previous sugar and salt content. Nevertheless, the reputation of CC had been damaged and sales were expected to remain at around 80% of their previous level for some time.

An offer has recently been received from a low-cost supermarket, FoodSave plc, to buy CC products at an average price of £2 per box. The cereals would be 'own branded' under the FoodSave name. Volumes would be a minimum of 400,000 boxes per year for two years.

Requirements

30.1 Using the data in Exhibit 1 and other information available, evaluate CC's long term competitive position in the UK boxed breakfast cereals manufacturing industry. For this purpose ignore the decisions made from 1 January 20X9. State any additional information that would be needed to make a more complete assessment of CC's competitive position. **(12 marks)**

30.2 Using the data in Exhibit 2 and other information provided:

(a) Describe and evaluate the financial and strategic performance of CC in the period 20X8-20Y0. In so doing, assess the impact on performance of the decisions to reduce costs and to change the quality of the grain content from 20X9; and

(b) Explain the risks facing CC in 20Y1 and beyond. **(16 marks)**

30.3 Explain the ethical issues arising from:

(a) The decision to increase the sugar and salt content; and
(b) Jenny's public disclosure of this decision. **(8 marks)**

30.4 Prepare a brief report which provides reasoned advice to the CC board on whether the new contract with FoodSave plc should be accepted. Include supporting calculations. **(8 marks)**

Total: 44 marks

Exhibit 1: UK boxed breakfast cereal industry – average annual revenue 20X8–Y0

Company	Average annual revenue from retailers in each year £m	Comment
Astra Inc	295	} The 'big three' have international operations and sell a wide range of boxed breakfast cereals.
Benn Inc	127	
Ceel plc	112	
Rival 1	65	Focuses on market niche of healthy cereals. Average wholesale selling price per box is £2.25.
Rival 2	40	Niche market of healthy cereals specifically for children. Average wholesale selling price per box is £3.
Rival 3	38	High quality producer using best grains. Sells a range of products but no particular emphasis on healthy cereals. Average wholesale selling price per box is £3.50.
CC	35	
Other smaller companies	268	There are about 125 other smaller companies in the UK manufacturing boxed breakfast cereals
Industry total	980	

Exhibit 2: Additional data

Financial data for CC

	20X8 £m	20X9 £m	20Y0 £m
Revenue	36	34	35
Fixed operating costs	(16)	(16)	(16)
Variable operating cost (grains)	(16)	(13)	(13.4)
Operating profit	4	5	5.6

Other data

	20X8	20X9	20Y0
Boxes sold by CC (millions)	12	11.33	11.67
Boxes sold by UK industry (millions)	490	490	490

31 Henford plc

Henford plc (Henford) is a conglomerate company with a diversified range of products.

Company history

Henford commenced trading a number of years ago as a manufacturer of traditional toys and games (eg board games, models, wooden toys and soft toys). The Henford brand is well respected and sells at a premium price, but operating cash flows are modest. Sales volumes have been falling for some years as the company has struggled for market share. There is severe competition from other toy companies, and particularly from companies which manufacture technology-based toys.

In 20X1, Henford appointed a new chief executive, Ian Palmer, who attempted to diversify while retaining the original toy business. His diversification policy was to make acquisitions, irrespective of the type of company or the industry in which the opportunity arose, using two criteria:

(1) The target company could be acquired at a price which represented good value; and
(2) Henford management could add value.

Since 20X1 Henford has acquired two other companies: Premium Paper Products Ltd (PPP) in 20X6 and Medicarex Ltd (Medicarex) in 20X9.

PPP was established in 20X1 and manufactures paper for all types of computer printer and copier. The paper is high quality and high price. The paper has been designed using significant research and development and has been shown to be one of the most efficient in the market in reducing blockages and solving other quality problems when printing. PPP has a very small market share compared to the market leader, but it has experienced rapid growth. Due to rapid expansion and new investment it has moderate profits, but a large negative cash flow.

Medicarex is a manufacturer of specialist containers for pharmaceuticals. In this niche sector Medicarex is a market leader, but growth rates for the company and the industry are low. Profit margins are reasonably high and, as the production technology is stable and long established, limited new investment is needed, so significant cash flows are being generated.

Each manufacturing site for toys, paper and pharmaceuticals is located in a different region of the UK. Henford's head office is located at the same site as toy production. Data is provided for each product (**Exhibit**).

Organisational structure

Until 20X1, Henford was managed by the Henford family with a fairly rigid, functional structure and a bureaucratic management style. Since 20X1, despite the two acquisitions expanding the size of Henford, the organisational structure had not been changed. However, Ian Palmer decided to modify the organisational structure with effect from 1 January 20Y1. As a consequence, the old and new structures were as follows.

Director	Old Structure (Pre-20Y1)	New Structure (20Y1 onwards)
Ian Palmer	Chief executive	Chief executive
Holly Huang	Finance director	Finance director
Simon Smart	Procurement director	Toys division director
Lisa Langford	Production director	Paper division director
Ali Akbar	Marketing director	Pharmaceuticals division director
Claire Cullen	Human resources director	Human resources director

All directors report to the chief executive under the old and new systems.

Under the old system each director had a small group of senior managers reporting to him or her.

Within the new structure, each of the three products forms a separate operating division under the leadership of a director who, as divisional head, is responsible for that division's profit. Each division carries out its own procurement, production and marketing, but finance and human resources remain as group-wide functions, each headed by a director as under the old structure.

The various senior managers in the old procurement, production and marketing functions have been allocated to the new divisions and each reports to the relevant divisional head.

Reaction to the change

Ian Palmer believes that the senior marketing managers have been very reluctant to accept the changes. He summarised the situation as he saw it at a board meeting:

'I made a decision to make changes in our organisational structure and I expect staff to implement that decision fully. It is clear that the senior marketing managers have been against these changes from the beginning, with a series of excuses as to why we should not carry out any proposed change every time we ask for consultation. Sales performance has fallen and this is not acceptable.'

Ali, the marketing director under the old structure, was much more sympathetic than Ian: 'The senior marketing managers and other marketing staff all used to be based at head office, but they are now spread across all three locations. We are all still in communication with each other, as we feel strongly that marketing should have remained as a centralised functional activity, like finance and human resources. Procurement and production staff were already spread across the three locations so they have not been affected much by the changes. Moreover, it has been reported to me that the other two new divisional heads do not understand the complexities of marketing and so can neither appreciate, nor control, the marketing staff's work. This is causing demotivation and a reluctance to perform to the best of their ability.'

Requirements

31.1 Using the data in the Exhibit and the other information provided, for each of Henford's three products (ie toys, paper, pharmaceuticals):

(a) Explain and justify its positioning within the Boston Consulting Group (BCG) matrix; and

(b) Based on your BCG analysis, explain where it is located within its product life cycle.

(13 marks)

31.2 In respect of Henford's organisational structure:

(a) Draw organisational charts for both Henford's old structure (ie prior to 20Y1) and its new structure; and

(b) Evaluate whether the change from the old functional structure to the new structure is likely to be beneficial for Henford. **(13 marks)**

31.3 As far as the information permits, explain the barriers to change that the senior marketing managers could potentially create. **(8 marks)**

Total: 34 marks

Exhibit: Product data

	Annual market growth rate	Sales £m	Largest competitor sales £m
Toys	zero	25	50
Paper	20%	5	50
Pharmaceuticals	3%	110	100

32 Felan Fashions plc

Felan Fashions plc (FF) is a designer, producer and retailer of ladies' fashion clothing. It has 27 retail outlets located in major cities throughout the UK, plus a central production site.

Current business model

FF has been very successful since being established by Tanya Felan over thirty years ago. Tanya had been a fashion designer working for a major fashion house when she decided to set up her own business.

Her business model was to base her latest designs on current trends set by the major international fashion houses, but to tailor FF products to UK market tastes and sell at prices well below those of the leading international fashion brands. These prices are still much higher than those of most good quality UK clothing retailers. FF's target market is young female professionals with high disposable incomes.

All the outlets are owned by FF and sell only FF products. FF clothes are made in a range of standard sizes at the central production site, but are fitted and adjusted to individual customer needs by FF's skilled staff at each retail outlet. The retail outlet staff also provide general advice and assistance for individual customers in making their fashion choices.

The business model has been successful and the FF brand has become well known in the UK, with 80% of young professional women recognising the FF brand name in market surveys. Specifically, the FF brand is perceived as desirable with an exclusive image, which is nevertheless affordable by young consumers on high incomes.

Future development

By 20Y1 Tanya believed that the UK market was saturated and therefore decided to expand by opening retail outlets in other parts of Europe. Only FF branded clothes would be sold.

An initial market survey showed that brand recognition among the target market in key European countries was only 20%, although it was 25% in France. As a result, Tanya recognised that marketing would be a key issue.

Tanya has identified two mutually exclusive strategies for European expansion as follows:

Strategy 1 – to open independent stores across four European countries (Germany, France, Italy and Spain) as opportunities arise for suitable prime locations in major cities in these countries.

Strategy 2 – to use floorspace within a chain of large, mid-market to upper-market French department stores, UneShop. This strategy would limit the expansion to France, but FF outlets could be opened immediately in all ten UneShop stores located in French cities. The available floorspace of each 'shop within a store' would be equivalent to one of FF's independent retail outlets.

Requirements

32.1 Explain the factors to be considered in developing a suitable marketing plan for FF's Strategy 1 using the marketing mix. **(12 marks)**

32.2 Compare and evaluate the two strategies for expansion and provide a reasoned recommendation as to which, if either, of the strategies should be adopted. **(10 marks)**

Total: 22 marks

33 KoganAir plc

KoganAir plc (KoganAir) is a listed, low-cost airline based in the UK. It flies only on 'short-haul' routes within Europe.

Industry background

The passenger airline industry consists of two sectors, scheduled and non-scheduled. The scheduled sector operates to a published timetable. It includes long-established airlines (eg British Airways, Emirates, Lufthansa) operating flights on both short-haul and intercontinental, 'long-haul' routes. It also includes low-cost airlines (eg easyJet, Ryanair) which operate flights almost exclusively in the short-haul sector. The non-scheduled sector comprises all other air transport which, in respect of passenger transport, consists mainly of charter flights operated exclusively by holiday companies to take their customers to a particular holiday destination.

Competition is particularly intense in the European airline industry as many low-cost airlines operate in this geographical region, competing with the established airlines of each country. Historically, the established airlines dominated the industry due to their size, enabling economies of scale. They were also often government-subsidised, national carriers with monopolies over certain routes (ie rights to operate flights between specified airports) and landing slots (ie rights for a given period, allocated to an airline by an **airport**, to schedule **landings** or **departures**).

However, international deregulation of airlines (sometimes referred to as the 'open skies' policy) has meant lower barriers to entry, which has led to many new entrants to the industry in the past two decades. Reduced government regulation over permitted routes has allowed market forces to increase access to landing slots and to determine mergers between airlines and pricing.

Despite deregulation, there is not yet full open access to routes and landing slots, as established airlines have retained some of their historical dominance at key airports. However, newer airlines entering the industry have cost advantages over traditional airlines, for example by setting up lower cost wage agreements.

Many of the new entrants have been low-cost airlines which have penetrated the scheduled market by attracting individual customers with low fares, popular routes, frequent flights and ease of booking on-line directly with the airline. In the past 15 years, many of these entrants have become market leaders in terms of short-haul passenger numbers.

The airline market has experienced long-term growth but has, more recently, suffered a decline in revenues and passenger numbers as a result of the global economic downturn. In addition, airline profits have been affected by high and volatile fuel prices, which comprise a high proportion of total costs. Other concerns facing the industry are: security issues, regulatory intervention, specific taxes on airlines, industrial action and ecological issues.

Company history

KoganAir was established a number of years ago and immediately acquired aircraft, along with the rights to landing slots and routes, from the liquidator of an insolvent airline. The fleet has since been expanded by both purchasing and leasing aircraft in approximately equal numbers.

As a low-cost airline, KoganAir quickly penetrated the scheduled market and has significantly increased its total number of passengers each year.

In order to offer low fares, KoganAir aims to operate at the lowest possible cost in its sector of the industry. It operates a 'no frills' service to passengers (eg no free food, drinks or films during flights) and it also constantly seeks to minimise the turnaround time spent by its aircraft at airports in order to maximise utilisation.

KoganAir has continued to expand but the November 20Y1 management accounts, released internally last week, make clear that profits for the year ending 31 December 20Y1 will be significantly lower than last year. This decrease has been expected and profit warnings were given to financial markets in October 20Y1. However, since then, analysts have made increasing demands for more details, including information about how much of the fall in profit is due to industry-wide factors, and how much due to company-specific factors. A meeting of executive management was called to evaluate the issue in more detail and to determine an appropriate strategy for moving forward.

Executive management meeting

The **chief executive** summarised the situation: 'In many ways we have been successful but, despite increasing revenues in 20Y1, we have suffered a significant decrease in profits and I do not believe we have adequately analysed the underlying reasons for this. Fuel costs increased, on average, by 17% per tonne in 20Y1 compared with 20Y0, driven by the world price of oil, but fuel costs are only one factor. I need an analysis of our basic financial and operating data (**Exhibit 1**) to explain in more detail why profits have fallen. I am also worried about the impact of further increases in global oil prices next year, as I fear these could cause our fuel costs to rise by as much as 30% per tonne. I have provided some key working assumptions for 20Y2 (**Exhibit 2**) to enable some scenario planning to be carried out. The aim is to better evaluate our risks and improve our forecasts for 20Y2.'

The **marketing director** had a different issue: 'I know costs are important, but we need to consider our long-term positioning in the market. We entered the market as a low-cost airline and, until recently, this approach has served us well, enabling us to penetrate the market and expand market share. Now, I think we need to reconsider our market positioning and pricing policies. Our margins are just too low to cover even modest cost increases. My proposal is to move to a mid-market position, sitting between the low-cost airlines and the higher priced, long-established airlines. My view is that we should increase passenger seat prices by, on average, 10% next year.'

Requirements

33.1 As an external adviser, prepare a report to the board which:

(a) Analyses the data in Exhibit 1 and the other information provided to explain, with supporting calculations, why the operating profit in 20Y0 is expected to turn into an operating loss in 20Y1, despite an increase in revenue generated; and **(15 marks)**

(b) Calculates the forecast operating profit for 20Y2 using the working assumptions in Exhibit 2. In addition, comment on the working assumptions and on the sensitivity of operating profit to fuel cost changes during 20Y2. (For this purpose ignore the suggestions of the marketing director.) **(9 marks)**

33.2 Explain the key risks for KoganAir that arise from factors within the economic, ecological and legal sections of the PESTEL framework. For each risk identified, explain how it might be managed by KoganAir. (For this purpose ignore the suggestions of the marketing director.) **(10 marks)**

33.3 Evaluate the suggestion of the marketing director, referring to Porter's generic strategies and any other appropriate strategic models. **(9 marks)**

Total: 43 marks

Exhibit 1: Financial and operating data

	Note	20Y0 Actual	20Y1* Estimated	20Y2** Forecast	% change 20Y0 to 20Y1
Total revenue (£m)	1	313	337		+7.7%
Fuel costs (£m)		(76)	(96)		+26.3%
Operating costs of aircraft fleet (£m)	2	(25)	(26)		+4.0%
Other costs (£m)		(211)	(227)		+7.6%
Operating profit/(loss) (£m)		1	(12)		
Available passenger seats (millions)	3	6.4	7.0	7.7	
Actual passenger seats sold (millions)	4	5.4	6.0	6.7	
Load factor %	5	84.4%	85.7%	87.0%	
Number of aircraft		49	50	53	
Routes operated		62	64	66	
Available seat kilometres (ASK) (millions)	6	7,271	7,868	8,500	

* The estimates for 20Y1 have a high degree of certainty as there are only a few weeks remaining in the financial year.

** Forecasts for 20Y2 use the working assumptions in **Exhibit 2**.

Notes

1   Seat prices increased on average by 2% in 20Y1 compared with 20Y0.

2   Comprises: (a) leasing costs and (b) depreciation of owned aircraft.

3   Available passenger seats are the total number of seats available for passengers to occupy on all flights in the year (across all routes and based on the total number of aircraft in operation).

4   Actual passenger seats sold are the total number of passenger journeys (ie seats occupied) actually flown in the year.

5   Number of actual passenger seats sold as a percentage of available passenger seats (ie (4) as a % of (3)).

6   Available seat kilometres (ASK) is the number of available passenger seats, multiplied by the average kilometres per flight.

Exhibit 2: Key working assumptions for 20Y2

In 20Y2, compared with 20Y1, the following are assumed:

- The cost of fuel per tonne will increase by 30%
- The average price per passenger seat will remain constant
- The amount of fuel used and revenue will vary according to ASK
- The operating costs of the aircraft fleet will remain constant
- Other costs will increase by 3%

34   Universal Office Supplies plc

Universal Office Supplies plc (UOS) manufactures office equipment for businesses and the public sector.

Products

UOS manufactures two product lines: communication systems hardware (including videoconferencing, audio conferencing and data sharing equipment) and office furniture (including desks, chairs and storage cabinets).

UOS began manufacturing office furniture twenty years ago as Office Supplies Ltd and added the communications systems hardware operation five years later on acquiring Universal Systems Ltd. After merging, the company became UOS and obtained a listing , setting up a single factory where each product line is manufactured in a separate section and operated independently. The product lines use very different methods of manufacturing. UOS has many clients who are customers for both product lines.

The communications systems hardware section aims to offer its customers the latest technology. Its products are differentiated from those of rivals by the nature and quality of the features provided. Jim Snape, head of communications systems manufacturing, is constantly changing the design and range of the products being offered in order to compete effectively in the market. New clients are frequently attracted to UOS by this product line, although existing clients are also lost to rivals on a regular basis. Prices are above the average for the sector.

The head of office furniture manufacturing is Pauline Parks. Office furniture is a mature industry so Pauline has tended to make few changes to manufacturing methods or to the nature of the final products. UOS produces mid-market office furniture and competes on price and service.

Current structure

UOS has three main operating divisions which are currently vertically integrated, being Procurement, Manufacturing and Marketing. There are also three support divisions: Research and Development (R&D), Finance and Human Resources.

By far the largest division is the Manufacturing Division, and the divisional head is Chen Li. This division has responsibility for manufacturing both product lines.

UOS attempts to maintain the autonomy of the operating divisions in its use of transfer pricing and by treating each operating division as a profit centre.

Inter-divisional transfer prices

The Procurement Division sources materials and parts according to the specifications provided by the Manufacturing Division. These materials and parts are sold by the Procurement Division to the Manufacturing Division at budgeted prices agreed between divisional heads at the beginning of the year. These prices include the budgeted direct cost of purchase, plus an allocation (based upon the value of the order) of the budgeted overheads of the Procurement Division. Any purchase discounts achieved by the Procurement Division therefore add to its divisional profit.

About 95% of the Manufacturing Division's output is sold to the Marketing Division at negotiated transfer prices which approximate to wholesale market prices. The remaining 5% of the output of the Manufacturing Division, consisting of both product lines, is sold directly to central government under a long-term contract. These items are not dealt with by the Marketing Division at all, but the prices in the government contract are used as a guide for the negotiated prices of all other transfers between the Manufacturing and Marketing Divisions.

The Marketing Division sells products to customers at the highest price it can obtain and also aims to sell, for both product lines, additional services such as installation and extended warranties. In recent years, however, the Marketing Division has struggled to break even.

The objectives of the R&D Division are product innovation and also cost reduction through improved efficiency. It is autonomous, initiating research projects that it believes will improve processes and products for communications systems hardware. Once a successful R&D project is completed, Jim Snape and Chen Li are informed and implementation of the development work is discussed. No charge is made by the R&D Division to the Manufacturing Division. No work is undertaken by the R&D Division in respect of the office furniture product line.

Proposed restructuring

The chief executive of UOS, Anna Tudor, wants to restructure the company after Chen Li retires next month. She proposes that, in future, divisionalisation should be on a product line basis, with two operational divisions – Communications and Furniture. Each division would have its own manufacturing, procurement and marketing sections.

For operational reasons the R&D Division would remain a separate cost centre and recharge its full costs, including overheads, to the Communications Division, which would initiate all R&D projects. The details, including costings, would be agreed between the two divisions before each R&D project commences.

The Human Resources and Finance Divisions would continue to operate as previously.

As part of the restructuring, Anna Tudor proposes changes in key positions which include the following:

	Current structure	Proposed structure
Chen Li	Head of Manufacturing Division	Retired
Andy Worrell	Head of Marketing Division	Head of Communications Division
Pauline Parks	Head of office furniture manufacturing	Head of Furniture Division
Jim Snape	Head of communications systems hardware manufacturing	Deputy head of Communications Division

Anna explained these changes to a fellow director. 'The communications systems hardware section has been underperforming and I largely blame Jim. He is a good engineer, but not a good manager. The focus has been too much on the technological features of the products and not enough on the needs of customers. I want to appoint Andy as head of the new Communications Division to address this problem. We need more of a market focus.'

Requirements

34.1 In respect of the R&D function:

    (a)   Explain how it can contribute to the business strategy of UOS; and   **(6 marks)**

    (b)   Compare and evaluate the current and the proposed structuring and recharging arrangements.   **(7 marks)**

34.2 Comment on the merits and problems of the company's current divisional structure in respect of the three operating divisions. Include an evaluation of performance measurement and transfer pricing arrangements.   **(12 marks)**

34.3 Evaluate the proposed restructuring of the three operating divisions. In so doing, suggest and justify the most appropriate method of divisional performance measurement under the proposed new structure.   **(8 marks)**

Total: 33 marks

35   Conchester Theatre

The date is December 20Y1.

The Conchester Theatre (CT) is a regional theatre, located 250 miles from London. It has a good artistic reputation and is operated on a not-for-profit basis.

History and background

CT was established over 60 years ago with a mission: 'To promote, in the local community around Conchester, traditional plays and musicals with high artistic merit. CT aims to break even financially'.

Plays are often the work of local playwrights, both current and those who lived in the region in previous centuries. Musicals are traditional and classical, as the theatre has avoided populist musicals in order to remain close to CT's mission. Each production of an individual play or musical normally has between one and seven performances.

Membership and demand

The theatre building is owned by the local government and leased to CT at a favourable rent of about half the full commercial rental. The theatre holds 800 people and is available for productions five days a week, 50 weeks a year, but it is not normally filled to capacity. It tries to stage many small productions (eg with local drama groups, colleges and schools) in order to keep the theatre in use even when utilisation is well below capacity.

The local population, living within 20 miles of the theatre, is approximately 200,000 people.

CT has 1,500 Members who each make an annual donation of £30. The membership is restricted to 1,500 and there is a long waiting list. The Members elect the board of Trustees which runs CT. If CT has any debts it cannot pay, the individual Trustees are potentially personally liable.

CT also has a mailing list of Friends of the Conchester Theatre (Friends) who receive information on the latest productions, but they do not need to make any donations. CT maintains a database of Friends with their details (address, age, profession, productions attended) so it can target mailings to those most likely to be interested in certain productions. There are about 4,000 people (including all Members) on this database.

Financing

The main source of revenue has always been sales of tickets, but ticket sales alone have never been sufficient to cover costs. Tickets all sell for £15 and there are currently no discounts available. Seats are sold to the public on a 'first come, first served' basis. However, Members are offered the opportunity to purchase up to four tickets for each production, one week before the general public. As a result, for popular performances, the Members sometimes take up the entire 800 seats available.

The other main source of revenue has been a government grant from the Arts Council. Following reductions in public spending by central government, in 20Y2 the grant will only be half its previous level, and will disappear altogether in 20Y3. A basic revenue summary is provided (**Exhibit**).

A dispute

The board of Trustees has met to discuss ways in which more revenue can be raised to compensate for the loss of the government grant.

The **chairman** started the meeting: 'We have had an offer of £125,000 in 20Y2 and £250,000 a year thereafter from a local businessman, Henry Strong. This would replace the government funding that we are losing. There are, however, some conditions attached, including that he sits on the board as a new Trustee. He would also have the right to choose ten productions each year and, as Mr Strong is a keen supporter of populist productions, we do not expect these to be the type of production we would normally put on. I do not like these conditions, but without this money we would start making large losses and we, as Trustees, could be personally liable. I think we should therefore accept Mr Strong's offer.'

The **treasurer** of CT objected strongly: 'Taking up the offer would be contrary to the historic culture of CT and the wishes of Members and other stakeholders. I do, however, recognise that we need to raise more revenue so I suggest we have more flexible pricing. We should stop charging £15 for every ticket and attempt to charge different prices, to different people, for different productions.'

Requirements

35.1 Discuss the ethical issues for CT's board of Trustees arising from the offer from Henry Strong.

(8 marks)

35.2 Explain each of the following:

    (a)   The purposes of market segmentation for CT;
    (b)   How the CT database may be used to segment the market; and
    (c)   How different prices may be set by CT in order to increase revenue.

(16 marks)

Total: 24 marks

Exhibit: Revenue summary

Year	Ticket sales £'000	Government grant £'000	Membership donations £'000
20X9	1,380	250	45
20Y0	1,440	250	45
20Y1*	1,500	250	45

* 20Y1 data has been reliably estimated given that the year is nearly complete.

It is estimated CT will break even in 20Y1, but it incurred small operating losses in 20Y0 and 20X9.

36 Bigville Council

Bigville Council (the Council) is the local government body responsible for providing community services to residents of Bigville, a large city in the UK. The Council is financed by central government, together with local taxes paid by residents and businesses in the area. Bigville is relatively strong economically. It has a respected university and is well-known as both a business and tourist destination. Around 500,000 people live and/or work in Bigville.

Demand for a community stadium

Bigville's professional rugby club leases its current sports stadium from the Council. As a result of recent success, the club is attracting large crowds to matches played at its stadium (home matches) and this stadium is at full capacity. Aware that Bigville's professional football club is also in need of a new stadium, the rugby club has asked the Council to consider the creation of a council-owned community stadium on a new site, with a shared pitch suitable for both rugby and football. It would also incorporate additional sports facilities which would be available for use by schools, colleges, clubs and other community groups throughout the year. On days when there are no home matches for either rugby or football teams the stadium could be used for a range of other commercial and social events (concerts, weddings, etc).

In the UK, football clubs compete in a series of hierarchical leagues, with the top clubs being promoted to the league above at the end of the playing season and the bottom clubs being relegated to the league below. The same system applies to rugby.

The attendance (number of people attending home matches at the club's stadium) and financial performance of any club is heavily dependent on its team's performance in the league. Bigville's two clubs currently play home matches on different days (football on Saturdays and rugby on Sundays) and their seasons overlap. The football season runs from August through to April, and the rugby season runs from February to September. Both clubs have a strong support base but have lower attendance than their respective league competitors due to restricted capacity. Neither stadium has the scope to be extended.

A new stadium would benefit the two clubs by allowing for increased attendance, which generates revenue from ticket sales, refreshments and merchandising. The improvement in facilities would increase the scope to raise some ticket prices by offering premium seating. For this reason, if the shared stadium goes ahead, the rugby and football clubs have pledged to make initial contributions of £1 million and £2 million respectively towards the capital cost.

Council's strategic priorities

The Council has recently stated publicly that its strategic priorities are as follows:

- To maintain and develop Bigville's successful economy and provide suitable employment opportunities for residents

- To ensure accessible opportunities for all to engage in culture, leisure and recreational activity

- To promote and provide support for local people to make healthy lifestyle choices

- To create, enhance and maintain cleaner, safer and more sustainable environments

The Council believes that a new community stadium would potentially assist in meeting some of these aims. It is therefore making a preliminary assessment of the business case for the community stadium. If this indicates viability, a more detailed feasibility study and financial analysis will be undertaken. The vision is to create a stadium with 6,000 seats, which both the football and rugby clubs will use for home matches and training.

The new stadium will incorporate a community sports centre with an athletics track and all-weather sports pitches. There is an option to enhance the stadium by adding a second level, which could be used commercially as a conference and events centre.

The Council has identified three criteria which it will use to assess the business case:

(1) Ability to raise finance for the initial capital investment
(2) Whether it is a commercially sustainable venture
(3) Alignment with the Council's overall strategic priorities

Council-owned land has already been identified as a suitable site for the stadium. This land is expected to meet the necessary planning criteria. The stadium would be partly sunk into the ground to limit noise problems, reduce the impact on the landscape and maximise environmental efficiency.

Capital costs and financial projections

The new stadium would be partly funded by the sale of the council-owned land on which the rugby club's current stadium stands. If sold to a developer for the construction of a retail site, this land would be expected to realise in the region of £6 million. Initial research suggests that some additional public sector funding would be available in the form of central government grants, provided certain criteria are fulfilled by the new stadium. These criteria include whether it can be demonstrated that the stadium actively increases community participation in sports, creates additional employment or contributes to the sustainability of the local environment. A sponsorship deal would be sought with a large credit card company, Finanex plc, whose headquarters are in Bigville and which is Bigville's largest private sector employer. The company has indicated that it would be prepared to pay an initial £1 million for the stadium to be named 'The Finanex Stadium', and then it would also contribute an amount annually for the right to display its company logos on the exterior and interior of the stadium.

The stadium is likely to cost a total of £10 million to construct. This comprises £6.75 million for the basic stadium and £3.25 million for the community sports facilities. An enhanced stadium, with an additional second level for conference and events facilities, would cost a further £1.1 million. Any shortfall in funding would need to come from the Council's cash reserves and/or debt finance. The Council's strategy department has researched similar community stadia funded by other councils and has produced some initial forecasts for the potential costs and revenue streams associated with the new stadium. These are set out in **Exhibits 1 and 2**.

Management and operation

If the new stadium goes ahead as planned, it will be owned by the Council and operated by a stadium management company (SMC) created as a joint venture between the Council and the two sports clubs. The Council will lease the stadium to SMC, which will then retain any profits or losses made from its operation. The Council, the football club and the rugby club will each have two directors on the board of SMC, although the Council will have a casting vote on certain specified issues. The Council is keen to ensure that it minimises its level of risk and, in particular, the financial liability to which it is exposed. It also wants to retain the ability to control the governance of SMC and the pricing, events scheduling and promotion of the stadium.

Exhibit 1: Forecast annual match revenues and costs for new stadium

	Number of home matches	Expected attendance per match	Total annual attendance	Total annual revenue	Total annual contribution	Traceable annual fixed operating costs	Forecast annual profit/ (loss)
	Note 1	Notes 2 and 3		Note 4			
Football	25	3,200	80,000	£800,000	£640,000	(£644,000)	(£4,000)
Rugby	15	3,000	45,000	£450,000	£270,000	(£214,000)	£56,000

Notes

1 Based on the average number of home matches played last season in each club's existing stadium. This can increase if a club is successful in various additional competitions which are run during the season.

2 Initial estimate of expected future attendance provided to the Council by each club, on the basis that it increases its capacity by moving to the new stadium and remains playing within its existing competitive league.

3 The average home match attendance at each club's current stadium is: football: 2,863; rugby: 2,234. Comparable data for similar clubs are as follows:

	Average attendance per match for typical club in:		
	League below	Existing league	League above
Football	1,800	3,050	5,000
Rugby	1,900	2,840	4,000

4 Based on expected average total spend per visitor on tickets, refreshments and merchandising.

Exhibit 2: Forecast annual non-match revenues and costs for new stadium

	Basic stadium £	Enhanced stadium with conference facilities £
Revenues		
Net income from community use of facilities	50,000	50,000
Stadium advertising/sponsorship from Finanex plc	200,000	250,000
Revenue from non-match day activities	187,000	537,000
Costs		
Stadium running costs, not directly traceable to rugby or football matches	(375,000)	(525,000)

Requirements

36.1 Discuss how the objectives of the key stakeholders (the Council, the rugby club and the football club) may conflict in relation to the shared stadium. You should ignore SMC as a separate entity for the purposes of this requirement. **(7 marks)**

36.2 (a) Using the data in Exhibit 1 relating to the new stadium, estimate the break-even attendance figures for each rugby and football match. **(4 marks)**

(b) Explain the implications of your calculations in (a) for the forecast match profits and discuss the potential variability in the annual attendance for each club, including the impact this is likely to have on the forecast in Exhibit 1. Show any supporting calculations. **(9 marks)**

36.3 Using the data in Exhibits 1 and 2 and the other information provided, prepare a report for the Council which evaluates the business case for the new stadium against the Council's three stated criteria, clearly identifying any further information required. **(14 marks)**

36.4 Assess the key risks for the Council in relation to the construction of the stadium and its operation by SMC. **(8 marks)**

Total: 42 marks

37 Beauty Soap Ltd

Beauty Soap Ltd (BS) is a large UK-based company which manufactures and sells personal care products (eg hand soap, deodorant, shampoo, face cream, toothpaste and other personal hygiene products) throughout Europe.

Company history

BS was established over one hundred years ago as a producer of soap. BS quickly established itself as a major player in the market because of the range of different product sizes and fragrances offered. Initially BS grew organically by investing in research and development to create a wider range of personal care products including shampoo and face cream. As the UK market became increasingly competitive, consolidation took place and the number of competitors reduced. BS however continued to expand through the acquisition of a UK company specialising in dental care products. It also acquired several manufacturers of personal care products in mainland Europe.

Strategic options

BS wants to reduce its dependence on the European market, as the market is mature and market prices are under pressure (see **Exhibit**).

Exhibit: European market for personal care products

	Revenue	
	20Y0 €m	20Y1 €m
Total European market	11,690	10,989
Market leader	1,489	1,297
BS	444	417

A number of competitors have targeted other international markets. BS is keen to expand into Latin America, as forecasts suggest there is considerable growth potential in some areas of the personal care products market, particularly in Brazil. The population of Brazil is culturally diverse. There are a number of affluent cities, but approximately one third of people live in rural areas, and there is significant poverty. BS is currently considering two alternative methods of development for expansion into Brazil:

(1) Acquire Gomera, a personal care products business based in Brazil. Gomera has an existing product range tailored to the needs of the local market and established supply chain and distribution networks. BS could either rebrand Gomera's products under the existing BS brand or keep Gomera's local brands and gradually introduce other brands from the BS range.

(2) Expand organically. Preliminary research has suggested that the market in Brazil would prefer smaller product sizes and lower prices than BS's traditional European product model, which the market perceives to be priced at a premium compared to local companies. BS plans to introduce new versions of products such as soap, shampoo and toothpaste in small packets containing enough product for a single use. BS already produces a range of similar single-use products for a major European hotel chain but does not currently sell these to individual consumers. The Brazilian government wants foreign-owned companies to demonstrate that they are creating value for the Brazilian economy. BS would therefore use a direct selling model with a workforce of local people, working from home and paid on a commission basis.

Competition

In Brazil the main competition in the personal care product market consists of:

- Two large multinational companies which have entered the market with their own global personal care brands

- Three domestic companies, one of which is Gomera, which produce a range of personal care products

The three domestic companies have established a strong presence in a variety of product segments and have the following advantages:

- An existing wide distribution network which extends to remote rural regions
- Low cost local manufacturing
- An established local supply chain network

They produce good quality products at competitive prices and make reasonable margins, although they lack the advertising budget and product innovation capacity of the multinational firms.

Educational marketing campaign

BS has recently announced plans to launch an education campaign, in conjunction with the governments in the countries in which it operates, to promote the regular washing of hands with BS soap to reduce infection and disease. The campaign will involve posters within schools and hospitals. If undertaken in Brazil there will be an advertising campaign featuring a well-known Brazilian footballer. BS's education campaign has been criticised by some as unethical marketing.

Requirements

37.1 (a) Using relevant strategic models, explain both the ways in which BS has previously chosen to expand its business and its future plans for Brazil. **(7 marks)**

    (b) Using the data in the Exhibit and the other information provided, evaluate the appropriateness of BS's plans to target markets outside Europe, given its current position. For the purposes of this requirement you should ignore the specific methods of expansion being considered. **(8 marks)**

37.2 Explain the choice that companies such as BS face between standardisation and adaptation of products in the context of the global market for personal care products. **(5 marks)**

37.3 Advise BS on the relative merits of the two options being considered for expansion into Brazil. **(8 marks)**

37.4 Discuss the ethical marketing issues raised by BS's proposed education campaign. **(5 marks)**

Total: 33 marks

38 Maureen's Motors

Maureen's Motors (MM), named after its female founder Maureen Docherty, sells motor insurance policies to car owners.

In the UK it is a legal requirement for drivers to have a minimum level of motor insurance cover. This provides compensation in respect of injury or damage to other people or their property resulting from an accident caused by the driver. The main driver of the car is usually the policy-holder, but the policy may also cover additional named drivers. Policy-holders can reduce their premium (the annual price of the policy) by agreeing to an excess (a fixed amount which, in the event of a claim under the policy, will not be paid out by the insurer).

Company background

A gap in the motor insurance market was identified by MM when industry research revealed that although there are many women drivers, a significant number were just covered as a named driver on their partner's car insurance policy rather than being the policy-holder.

MM therefore focuses on motor insurance for female policy-holders, by offering product and service benefits specifically tailored to women, which are not offered by standard car insurers.

MM provides additional cover for handbags and contents, pushchairs and child car seats; 24-hour accident and breakdown recovery (including a guarantee to be there within an hour of any call); a network of female-friendly car repairers; a helpline giving policy-holders advice on all vehicle-related matters; and, if a car is involved in an accident, MM provides a replacement child car seat even if the existing seat has not been damaged.

MM wanted to remove the image of 'insurance as a necessary evil' and to create a reassuring brand for 'real women with real lives'. Three famous actresses from a well-known TV comedy played the role of the '3 Maureens' in a long-running TV advertising campaign. Following this, MM was featured heavily in women's magazines. MM then ran a competition for existing and potential customers to star in a TV and poster advertising campaign. This campaign has significantly increased brand recognition, and using customers rather than celebrities has had the additional benefit of reducing marketing costs.

Pricing

The pricing of motor insurance premiums involves a risk assessment by the insurer of the likely risk of a claim being made and the amount that the insurer may have to pay out. The final price incorporates a number of factors, including:

- The insurance benefits offered
- The policy excess
- The type of vehicle, the expected annual mileage, and the location where the vehicle is normally kept
- The age and claims history of the policy-holder and any named drivers

The larger the pool of insured drivers, the more the risk is spread out for the insurer and the lower the premiums can be. MM offers discounts for customer loyalty and for referring a friend, to help retain customers and market share.

An EU Directive prohibits motor insurers from price discrimination between equivalent men and women. MM therefore offers its car insurance policies to male drivers at the same price as an equivalent female driver and men can also be named as drivers on a female partner's policy. However because of its brand image and the nature of its product offering, MM's current customer base of policy-holders is 90% female.

Insurance industry statistics show that women typically drive fewer miles than men, are responsible for fewer driving convictions and make significantly fewer claims. Where women do make claims, these are usually for less serious accidents and therefore smaller amounts. Statistically women are also less likely to switch insurer and this, coupled with their reduced risk profile, allows MM to make higher margins.

MM has recently attracted some adverse publicity in the national newspapers. It has been criticised for focussing too much attention on marketing to attract new customers rather than on delivering efficient claims handling and customer service to its existing ones.

Requirements

38.1 With reference to relevant models, discuss MM's generic strategy and market positioning.**(7 marks)**

38.2 Explain the key elements of the service marketing mix adopted by MM. **(12 marks)**

38.3 In light of the criticism received by MM, recommend, with reasons, three KPIs that MM can implement to help improve its claims handling and customer service. **(6 marks)**

Total: 25 marks

39 Grassgrind Garden Mowers plc

'I really do not believe that accepting this bid is in the best interests of our shareholders. The board needs to convince shareholders that they should reject the bid and support our strategy for growth.' The chief executive of Grassgrind Garden Mowers plc (GGM), Sundeep Shiller, was speaking at a board meeting last week.

GGM is a UK company that manufactures two types of upmarket, petrol-powered mower for use by UK households in cutting grass in their gardens. The meeting was held to discuss a take-over bid for GGM by Boston Batteries Inc (BB), a large US company.

You are a senior working for a firm of chartered accountants and business advisers,
Puller and Platt LLP (PP). Following the board meeting, Sundeep asked a partner in your firm, Jeff Nelson, to come to see him. You accompany Jeff.

The meeting

It was Sundeep who opened the meeting:

'In making the offer to GGM shareholders, BB has been critical of our strategy and our performance. The GGM board however believes that it has produced a reasonable performance recently and has a better strategy for future growth than BB.

The board needs PP to provide a report to shareholders which evaluates GGM's performance and compares the board's proposed strategy for growth with that of BB.

PP has not carried out any business advisory work for GGM in the past, so I have provided you with:

- Some background notes about GGM (**Exhibit 1**)
- A trade newspaper cutting about the mower industry (**Exhibit 2**)
- Details of the growth strategies proposed by both GGM and BB (**Exhibit 3**)
- Some financial, operating and market data about GGM (**Exhibit 4**)

'In looking at the data in **Exhibit 4**, I am concerned that we allocate fixed operating costs between our two types of mower on the basis of volumes sold. Is this distorting our assessment of profitability? I am wondering whether we should, instead, allocate such costs on the basis of the sales revenues generated by each type of mower, as this would provide a better measure of performance of each product line.'

An ethical issue

GGM recently received an email from Hetty Inc (Hetty), a company located in Eurasia, which is a developing nation. The following is an extract from that email:

'We would like to become your first export customer by placing a major order with GGM. However, in order to keep the price low, we would require a modification to your mowers, which is the removal of the safety guard. Unlike the UK, it is not a legal requirement in Eurasia, so it is not necessary for us to have this feature.'

Requirements

39.1 Using the data and other information provided, draft the report requested by Sundeep. In the report you should:

(a) Analyse the performance of GGM, and of each of its two products, in the financial years 20Y1 and 20Y2. **(15 marks)**

(b) Determine the current UK market share of GGM, highlighting any problems that arise in defining market share in order to produce a useful figure. **(5 marks)**

(c) Explain the competitive positioning of GGM in the UK mower market, and assess how this has changed between 20Y1 and 20Y2. **(7 marks)**

(d) Compare the growth strategy of the GGM board with that of BB. Make relevant calculations and refer to appropriate strategic models. **(12 marks)**

39.2 Explain the ethical issues that arise for GGM from Hetty's request to modify its mowers, and outline how GGM should respond. **(6 marks)**

Total: 45 marks

Exhibit 1: GGM company background

GGM was established a number of years ago and has always produced upmarket, petrol-powered mowers. Two types of mower are produced by GGM: (1) large mowers with a seat and a steering wheel for the user ('tractor mowers'); and (2) conventional mowers which the user steers by hand while walking. Tractor mowers are sold to high income households as they are only suitable for very large gardens. All tractor mowers are powered by petrol engines, while conventional mowers are powered in a variety of ways.

A feature of both types of GGM product is their high-quality steel cutting blades, which outperform most rivals. All of GGM's sales are in the UK.

GGM's customers are large do-it-yourself (DIY) stores, garden centres and other large retailers. As is normal in the industry, these retailers sell on to households at the price charged by GGM plus 25%.

While most companies in the mower industry also manufacture other types of powered garden tools and equipment, GGM has, to date, only produced mowers.

Exhibit 2: Extract from article in Mower Chronicle, 4th December 20Y2

Mowers – Battery power is cutting into the market

Sales of mowers to consumers in the UK amounted to £396 million in 20Y1 at retail prices, making up 45% of the overall gardening tools and equipment market.

The mower industry can be divided into sub-sectors in a variety of ways. These include by style of blade, by type (tractor or conventional) or according to how they are powered (petrol, electric, battery or hand-propelled).

Petrol-powered mowers have the largest market share by value as they are more expensive than electric mowers but, in terms of volumes, electric and hand-propelled mowers have a larger market share.

Conventional petrol-powered mowers have maintained approximately the same market share by value at about 35% of the UK mower market in the last five years, while tractor mowers make up about 9% of the UK mower market.

A recent development in the mower industry has been cordless mowers powered by batteries. Their market share by value reached 10% in 20Y1, from 5% in 20X7.

Exhibit 3: Proposed strategies for growth

GGM strategic plan

The GGM board proposes a new strategy, to diversify into a range of petrol-powered garden tools and equipment, including hedge trimmers, strimmers and chainsaws. The new range would use a smaller version of the petrol engine developed for the GGM mower. Customers (ie retailers) for the new products would be the same as for the mowers and the same GGM brand name would be used.

Budgets have been produced for the new range of petrol-powered garden tools and equipment, based on market research. The most realistic estimate indicates that 25,000 units will be sold each year, at an average price of £150 and with a 40% contribution margin on selling price. Additional annual fixed operating costs are expected to be £1.4 million. The market researchers have indicated that their estimate of sales volume could be up to 20% higher or 20% lower than their most realistic estimate, depending on market conditions.

BB strategic plan

BB is a US manufacturer of high performance lithium-ion batteries and has diversified in recent years by acquiring companies in industries producing industrial and domestic equipment which uses its batteries.

BB does not manufacture mowers, nor do any of its subsidiaries. As a result, its strategic plan is to acquire GGM and allow it to continue to produce petrol-powered mowers, and to commence producing mowers powered by lithium-ion batteries, using the same cutting blades as currently used by GGM. BB plans to encourage GGM to export battery-powered mowers to the US in future. BB has no plans for GGM to diversify away from mowers into other garden tools and equipment.

In the UK, battery-powered mowers would be sold to the same customers (ie retailers) as the existing products. The petrol-powered mowers would continue to be branded as GGM, but the battery-powered mowers would be branded under the BB name.

Budgets have been produced by BB that indicate 20,000 battery-powered mowers would be sold worldwide each year at an average price of £500 and with a 30% contribution margin on selling price. Additional annual fixed operating costs are expected to be £2 million, but could be as high as £3 million, or as low as £1 million.

Exhibit 4: GGM financial, operating and market data for years to 31 December

Profit per unit data	20Y1		Estimated 20Y2	
	Conventional mowers	Tractor mowers	Conventional mowers	Tractor mowers
	£	£	£	£
Price	400.0	2,000.0	400.0	1,800.0
Variable operating costs	240.0	1,000.0	240.0	1,000.0
Fixed operating costs*	112.5	112.5	120.0	120.0
Operating profit per unit sold	47.5	887.5	40.0	680.0

* Fixed operating costs are currently allocated to each mower based on GGM's total sales volume (see Sundeep's comments).

Operating and market data	20Y1		Estimated 20Y2	
	Conventional mowers	Tractor mowers	Conventional mowers	Tractor mowers
Volume sold by GGM (units)	8,100	2,700	7,380	2,820
UK market – volume sold (units)	1.5m	30,000	1.5m	30,600
UK market – sales value (at retail prices)	£360m	£36m	£368m	£36m

40   Care 4U Ltd

Care 4U Ltd (C4U) is a large private company which owns a chain of retail pharmacy outlets in the UK. These outlets supply consumers with prescription items (drugs and other products prescribed by health professionals for individual patients), general medicines and a range of other health and personal care products.

Industry background

Products and services

Retail pharmacies have two main sources of revenue:

(1)   About 80% from the provision of prescription items to patients by an appropriately qualified pharmacist

(2)   About 20% from retail sales by non-qualified staff of over-the-counter (OTC) general medicines and other products

In the UK, the key role of pharmacies is to provide patients with drugs and other items under prescriptions from their doctor or other health professional. Many prescriptions are wholly government-funded and provided free-of-charge to patients. Where the patient is required to pay a charge for a prescription item, this is a fixed amount which is the same irrespective of the purchase cost of the item. Most of a pharmacy's revenue therefore comes directly from the government which pays an amount for each prescription item supplied and makes an additional payment for the service the pharmacy provides to patients.

Many drugs can be obtained only on prescription from qualified pharmacists. However, many types of OTC general medicines, plus other health and personal care products, can be bought at their market price from non-qualified staff at pharmacies and other general retailers.

The retail pharmacy market

Total revenue for pharmacies has the potential to grow, as the volume of demand for prescription items is expected to increase. This is due to an ageing population and constant improvements in healthcare. However, reductions in government expenditure create doubt over the amount of future government funding that will be available for prescription items.

Despite increases in industry revenues, the number of retail pharmacy outlets has declined in recent years. This has been partly due to increased competition in the industry created by deregulation which has permitted price competition on OTC general medicines since 20X1. Since that time, supermarkets have introduced low-price, in-store pharmacies that are open, in some cases, 24 hours a day.

C4U company background

C4U was established over forty years ago. Since that time, commercial success through good centralised management has enabled expansion of the number of pharmacy outlets to 150 and significant growth in revenue per pharmacy.

All purchases are undertaken centrally at head office where key decisions are made. C4U's information technology system helps monitor and manage the performance of individual pharmacies. Typically, an average size C4U pharmacy, once established, would generate annual revenues of about £600,000 and an operating profit of 20% of sales revenue (this is before any central management charges, but after product purchases, salaries and overheads).

C4U has a reputation as a community pharmacy that offers services which are free to customers, including basic health tests (eg blood tests and health screening) and medical advice. The C4U brand has high and favourable consumer recognition throughout the UK.

At each C4U pharmacy there is a senior qualified pharmacist who, in addition to preparing prescription items, also runs the pharmacy's business activities, including being responsible for: ordering prescription drugs, OTC medicines and other products from head office; administration; hiring staff; and financial arrangements. Depending on the size of the pharmacy, there may be one or more other qualified pharmacists in addition to a senior qualified pharmacist.

A problem has arisen of high staff turnover among qualified pharmacists. Generous salaries are paid which have been successful in recruiting qualified pharmacists to C4U, but there have been problems in motivating and retaining them. In particular, many of C4U's pharmacists carry out the technical functions required of them, but have failed to manage professionally the business activities of the pharmacy by winning new customers, expanding sales and controlling costs. Other C4U pharmacists, having accumulated enough savings, have resigned from C4U to set up their own pharmacies on a self-employed basis.

C4U has borrowing facilities to obtain funding for its desired objective of further expansion, but the C4U board wants to ensure that available funds are used to best effect by opening as many new pharmacy outlets as possible.

C4U proposed expansion

The board has proposed two alternative strategies for expansion. Both strategies are designed to attract independent-minded, qualified pharmacists who wish to operate their own pharmacy, but who do not have enough funds to be self-employed by buying one outright. The two strategies are franchising and shared ownership:

Strategy 1 – Franchising

Under this proposal the number of C4U pharmacy outlets would be increased across the UK by offering qualified pharmacists franchise arrangements with the right to use the C4U brand name. Franchisees (ie the qualified pharmacists) could choose to benefit from some limited support and advice with respect to purchasing and administration, but could choose to reject this help.

C4U would purchase the property and basic fittings for each pharmacy outlet at an average cost of £200,000. The property would be acquired specifically for the purpose of opening a new pharmacy outlet. No existing pharmacy outlets would be franchised.

Each franchise agreement would last for five years and then would either be terminated (ie C4U would take full ownership of the property and control of the business) or, if both parties agreed, renegotiated on new terms. C4U would charge the franchisee an initial fixed fee of £25,000 and also an annual franchise fee of 5% of total annual revenue. Each franchisee would manage their own performance and would be entitled to all residual profit after franchise fees had been paid.

Franchisees would have strict responsibilities to abide by the terms of the franchise arrangement so C4U can protect its reputation. There would be no constraints on prices charged for non-prescription items, which can be determined by the franchisee.

Strategy 2 – Shared ownership

Under this proposal each new pharmacy outlet would be owned by a limited company, with ownership of the company shared equally between C4U and a qualified pharmacist. C4U would lend money to each new company to finance the remaining initial cash requirement of the pharmacy outlet. Typical funding for an average-sized pharmacy outlet would be as follows:

Share capital contributed by C4U	20%
Share capital contributed by pharmacist	20%
Loan from C4U to the company	60%

The average cost of opening a pharmacy outlet would be £200,000, so each qualified pharmacist would need to contribute £40,000 on average to acquire their share capital.

Each pharmacist would be paid a market salary by their company. C4U would receive a management fee from each company for providing intensive support, advice, administration and IT facilities at a market rate averaging £20,000 per annum. This support and monitoring would be a compulsory part of the agreement, so C4U can manage the performance of its investment. If the pharmacist wanted to sell his/her shares to C4U (or conversely to buy C4U's shares) at any stage in the future, this would be possible at a fair value, to be independently determined.

Requirements

40.1 Prepare a SWOT analysis for C4U. Each point should be clearly explained. Conclude by identifying the key issues and justify why they are significant. Ignore the strategies for expansion. **(12 marks)**

40.2 Explain and compare the two strategies for C4U's expansion under each of the following headings:

    (a)   Operating profit **for C4U** in respect of one outlet for one year (you should provide supporting calculations)

    (b)   Control and management

    (c)   Incentives for franchisees compared to shared owners   **(19 marks)**

                                                   Total: 31 marks

41 The Mealfest Corporation

The Mealfest Corporation (MC) owns a chain of over 100 mid-market restaurants, located in four countries across Europe: France, Germany, Switzerland and the UK. France and Germany have the euro as their currency.

Company structure and pricing

Until January 20Y2, each restaurant manager was responsible for performance and reported directly to the company's head office in Germany. Menu prices were fixed centrally in euro at 1 January each year and were uniform across all restaurants. The prices in euro were translated into Swiss francs (CHF) and sterling (£) using exchange rates prevailing at that date.

Head office specialists took responsibility for recruiting permanent staff for each restaurant. The same wage, which was reset and retranslated annually, was paid to all staff within each staff grade throughout the company.

On 1 January 20Y2 the company was restructured by having a separate division for each country. Each division has a divisional head. Restaurant managers now report their performance to their divisional heads, who then report total divisional performance to the company's head office. As with the previous structure, performance is evaluated by three measures: revenue, profit and return on assets.

From 1 January 20Y2 a new pricing policy was implemented. Menu prices are now set by divisional heads for their division each year, and can therefore vary between countries, but prices are required to be consistent within each country. Similarly, staff recruitment and remuneration are now decided at divisional level.

In both the pre and post-20Y2 structures, all meal ingredients are purchased centrally by MC from a French wholesaler. They are recharged to restaurants in euro at cost. Similarly, decisions on investment in new restaurants have always been centralised.

Monitoring the new structure and strategy

The MC board is having problems monitoring the success of the new structure and the new pricing strategy. It wishes to evaluate whether the method of assessing performance has improved following the restructuring.

The finance director summarised just one of the issues: 'It is very difficult to compare performance between countries due to exchange rate movements. Under the old pricing policy this meant that we set menu prices centrally in euro, then for the UK and Swiss operations we translated these to sterling and Swiss francs each year. Fluctuations over the year in exchange rates meant restaurant prices in the UK and Switzerland sometimes changed significantly when they were reset the following year. Under the new pricing system there is more pricing flexibility at national level, but we still need to make performance comparisons in euro as a common currency.

'I am not interested in hedging or in financial reporting issues, but I am concerned about the commercial impact of exchange rates on restaurants and customers, and their effect on measuring divisional financial performance.'

The chief executive responded: 'That is all very well in terms of financial performance, but I am interested in measuring all aspects of performance and in whether we now have the right structure and pricing strategy.'

Requirements

41.1 Compare MC's pre-20Y2 and post-20Y2:

    (a) Organisational structure and performance measurement; and
    (b) Pricing strategies.   **(14 marks)**

41.2 Explain how benchmarking may be used by MC to evaluate the performance of divisions and individual restaurants. **(10 marks)**

Total: 24 marks

42   Mayhews Ltd

Mayhews Ltd (Mayhews) is a family-owned business which runs three garages from freehold sites in prime locations in central England. Each garage operates a filling station, which sells fuel (petrol and diesel), and has a facility offering maintenance and repairs for motor vehicles.

Fuel retailing in the UK

Fuel retailing in the UK is a high volume, low margin business, characterised by strong competition. In the industry there are three types of filling station:

- Branded filling stations are either owned and managed by one of the major fuel wholesalers or operated on their behalf by licensees.

- Independent retailers, like Mayhews, are free to obtain fuel supplies from any wholesaler. Over 50% of all filling stations in the UK are independently owned.

- The big supermarket chains operate filling stations alongside their major stores. In recent years, whilst the number of branded filling stations and independent retailers has declined, the number of supermarket-owned sites has increased. This has coincided with the expansion of large out-of-town supermarkets with more people driving to do their shopping and buying fuel at the same time. As a result of their supply chain efficiencies and the large volumes of fuel that they sell, the supermarkets incur lower overheads per litre of fuel sold and are able to charge lower prices. In addition, many offer discounts on fuel based on the amount customers spend on goods in the main store. The average retail price charged by supermarkets in 20Y2 was 130.9 pence per litre compared to an overall UK average of 133.8 pence per litre.

Supply of fuel and pricing in the UK industry

The wholesale supply of fuel to retailers is dominated by a few large companies which produce and refine crude oil into a range of products including fuel. These wholesalers supply fuel to their own branded filling stations and to the supermarkets and independent retailers. 60% of the UK retail fuel price per litre consists of fuel tax and sales tax. On average 35% is paid to the wholesaler and the retailer earns 5% towards overheads and profit. Wholesale fuel prices in the last three years have been very volatile as the price of crude oil has varied significantly. Price volatility is a major problem for independent retailers. When market prices fall, independent retailers are often left with fuel supplies previously bought from the wholesaler at a high price. If they reduce the retail price then they may make a loss. If they keep retail prices high this is likely to have a negative effect on sales volumes. Conversely, when wholesale prices rise, the independent retailer may struggle to afford the increased cost of replenishing fuel supplies.

Demand for fuel in the UK market

Despite increased numbers of cars on the road, sales volumes of fuel are under pressure because of the improved efficiency of vehicle engines, increased fuel prices and the difficult economic climate. Government figures suggest congestion on motorways and major roads has been falling, indicating that people are undertaking fewer journeys by car.

Fierce competition between fuel retailers has led to a significant decline in the number of filling stations. There are now fewer than half the 18,000 filling stations that existed twenty years ago (**Exhibit 1**).

A fuel station's viability depends on two key factors: the gross margin per litre and the volume of fuel sold. Independent filling stations and those in less well-populated rural areas are at the greatest risk of losses due to declining sales volumes and below average margins. They also struggle to justify the additional capital expenditure required to comply with increasingly strict environmental and safety regulations. Many have tried to reduce their reliance on fuel revenue by creating alternative revenue streams such as on-site shops selling snacks, groceries and vehicle accessories. Mayhews does not currently operate a shop at any of its garages.

420 filling stations closed in the UK in 20Y2, of which two-thirds were independent. Some of these filling stations have been bought by property developers, although because of environmental regulations, sites have to be closed and the fuel tanks filled with concrete before being capable of alternative use.

Mayhews' business

The first Mayhews garage was set up a number of years ago by John Mayhew. The boom at this time in vehicle ownership and the later development of the UK motorway network led to a significant increase in demand for fuel and maintenance/repairs and Mayhews soon opened a further two garages. The business is now owned and managed by John's son Barry (aged 60), who is a well-known businessman in the region. After many successful years, Mayhews has been finding the filling stations market increasingly difficult and this is reflected in the company's recent results (**Exhibit 2**).

Although Mayhews has been experiencing a decline in fuel sales, the revenue and profit from maintenance and repairs have been increasing. This part of the business undertakes MOT testing (a compulsory annual test of safety for vehicles over three years old); replacement of parts due to wear and tear (brakes, tyres, wiper blades, lights etc); annual maintenance; and repairs.

Due to the economic climate, people have been slow to replace their old vehicles with new ones. Time pressure, lack of skills and the complexity of vehicles mean people no longer maintain their own vehicles, but they are reluctant to pay the high prices charged by the vehicle retailers for maintenance. Because of its longstanding presence in the region, and also as a result of Barry's contacts, each Mayhews garage has a loyal base of local customers. Mayhews also has contracts with a number of local companies for the maintenance of their corporate vehicles.

There are 32 million vehicles on the UK's roads and the maintenance and repairs market is fragmented. There are around 24,000 garage outlets in the UK offering motor vehicle repairs and maintenance. They are operated by retailers of vehicles, national and regional repairs and maintenance chains, fast-fit centres (specialising in tyres, exhausts and brakes) and many independents.

Strategic dilemma

Your firm acts as business advisers to Mayhews. At a recent meeting, Barry commented:

'We seem to be selling so little fuel these days I can't believe we are making much money from this side of the business. What do you think about us closing one or more of the filling stations and focussing on maintenance and repairs? This is a service-based market with many different providers where trust is really important to the customer. We already have a reputation for being honest and reliable and our brand is well-known locally.

We also have much lower overheads and labour costs than the main vehicle retailers. We can use this to differentiate ourselves by offering vehicle retailer quality service at affordable local garage prices.

Unfortunately, we simply don't have the appropriate technology to deal with the engine management systems in the more modern vehicles so currently we have to refer them to the vehicle retailer. We would need to invest in information technology by purchasing the relevant engine diagnostic equipment and a new computer system.

The new computer system would improve parts management and have marketing benefits. By maintaining their vehicles in good working condition our customers can improve fuel efficiency and drive safely. A key way we can help customers is to anticipate their needs for MOTs and maintenance and contact them in advance based on the age and mileage of their vehicle. The new system would provide us with an advanced data management system to do this, as well as allowing us to offer customers online booking for repairs and maintenance.'

Requirements

42.1 Prepare a Porter's Five Forces analysis of the UK fuel retailing industry which might be used to inform further discussions regarding the viability of Mayhews' filling station operations. **(9 marks)**

42.2 Using the data in the Exhibits, your answer to requirement (a), and the other information provided, evaluate the performance of Mayhews' overall business and compare the performance of the individual garages. Make and justify a preliminary conclusion as to whether Mayhews should consider closing one or more of its filling stations to focus on maintenance and repairs. **(17 marks)**

42.3 Discuss the advantages and disadvantages of making the investment in information technology referred to by Barry. **(6 marks)**

42.4 Explain how the use of critical success factors (CSFs) may assist Mayhews in establishing a strategic control system. Justify three CSFs for Mayhews' maintenance and repairs business and suggest one appropriate key performance indicator for each CSF identified. **(9 marks)**

Total: 41 marks

Exhibit 1: UK filling stations – market data 20Y2

	Branded filling stations	Independents	Supermarkets	Total
Number of sites	2,605	4,425	1,470	8,500
Millions of litres sold	10,520	7,425	14,950	32,895

Exhibit 2: Mayhews Ltd recent financial performance

	Breakdown of 20Y2			Total company	
	Garage A 20Y2 £'000	Garage B 20Y2 £'000	Garage C 20Y2 £'000	Mayhews Ltd 20Y2 £'000	Mayhews Ltd 20Y1 £'000
Sales:					
Fuel (Note 1)	878	738	776	2,392	2,686
Maintenance and repairs	688	454	755	1,897	1,604
Total sales	1,566	1,192	1,531	4,289	4,290
Gross profit:					
Fuel	103	76	91	270	304
Maintenance and repairs (Note 2)	355	218	415	988	836
Total gross profit	458	294	506	1,258	1,140
Operating costs (Note 3)	269	184	219	672	679
Profit	189	110	287	586	461
Litres of fuel sold (millions)	1.63	1.34	1.43	4.40	5.21

Notes

1 Fuel revenue is stated net of tax, ie, at 40% of the retail fuel price.

2 The gross profit on maintenance and repairs is based on the sales value of work done less the cost of parts and materials.

3 Operating costs include the wages and salaries of all garage staff. The operating costs for garage A also include £45,000 for Barry's salary.

43 Cabezada Ltd

Cabezada Ltd (Cabezada) is a relatively new company which uses steel shipping containers to create short-term living accommodation. The standard-sized containers can be transported anywhere by road, rail or sea, modified and then stacked to create the desired number of rooms.

The business is owned and managed by two directors: Sam Lowe, previously chief executive of a hotel group, and Anka Bien, formerly operations director of a large construction company.

Cabezada has two markets:

(1) Events clients, which require short-term accommodation for employees, media representatives, visitors and participants at a variety of sporting and leisure events.

(2) Contract clients, including the construction industry, the military and government, which typically require longer-term accommodation. Recent projects include key-worker accommodation and a temporary hospital.

Since starting the company, a number of projects have been completed very successfully for both markets. Cabezada's directors believe the business has significant global appeal and have started to draft a business plan which will be used to attract appropriate local partners to develop a worldwide business. The directors have already written some of the plan, which is included in the **Exhibit**, and have asked your firm of business advisers for help in developing it further.

Requirements

43.1 As a senior in the firm of business advisers, write the sections of the draft business plan indicated in the Exhibit, to cover:

(a) Strengths and realistic market opportunities (section 2.2.1)
(b) Weaknesses and threats (section 2.2.2)
(c) Benefits of partnership for both Cabezada and its local partners (section 3)

You should present your answer in an appropriate style and format, written in such a way as to help Cabezada to attract potential partners. **(16 marks)**

43.2 Recommend any further information that you believe should be included in the plan to enable potential partners to adequately assess Cabezada's partnership proposition. **(8 marks)**

43.3 Cabezada currently segments its market between events and contract clients. Explain the purpose and benefits of market segmentation and discuss other approaches to segmentation which Cabezada could adopt. **(8 marks)**

Total: 32 marks

Exhibit: Draft Business Plan provided by Cabezada's directors

DRAFT: Cabezada Local Partnership Programme 20Y3

1. Cabezada Local Partnership model

Cabezada uses steel shipping containers to create temporary living accommodation. Cabezada is regarded as a pioneer in the container accommodation industry and our brand name is well-recognised and trusted. The demand for cheap, flexible, temporary accommodation provided under a sustainable model is a global one. However we believe global business is best done using a local model and we are seeking the right local partners to help us target a wide range of potential markets.

Each local partner will set up a new company in their country or region called 'Cabezada (country/region name)'. Cabezada will have partial ownership of the company with a stake of 20%. The new company will pay a one-off franchise fee for exclusive rights to operate under the Cabezada brand in its defined area. There will be a monthly management charge for the use of all Cabezada information and infrastructure and a royalty fee on all container accommodation sold in the local market.

2. The Business

2.1. Our product concept

Shipping containers are highly durable and provide an ideal building module suitable for all climates and locations. Most new shipping containers are manufactured in China to international-standard sizes at a cost of approximately £4,000 each. Many countries import manufactured goods from Asia in shipping containers. Rather than pay to have these containers shipped back empty, it is often cheaper for Asian suppliers to buy new containers in Asia. As a result there is a plentiful supply of used shipping containers available globally, costing on average £1,000 per container.

Since the containers are designed to be easily transported by ship, road or rail, distribution costs are low, so accommodation can be provided in whatever location the client requires. Once adapted to make them suitable for living accommodation, the shipping containers can be quickly and easily combined in several storeys without requiring additional structural support.

The modular system offers flexibility of design and the standard of accommodation can range from very basic to luxurious. Depending on the client and location there is scope to create a building façade of brick, timber or marble. Cabezada's design system includes any necessary foundations, communal access arrangements, ventilation and connections to utilities.

For buildings up to five storeys high, container accommodation is significantly cheaper than the cost of erecting a brick-built structure, which takes much longer and requires larger, expensive foundations. Cabezada's whole product concept is more environmentally friendly, ideal for temporary use and consistent with the need for sustainability. Once a project is over, the containers can be refurbished and re-used. There is also a ready market for the sale of containers after use if Cabezada no longer requires them.

44 Chiba

Chiba is a Japanese company which manufactures a range of liquid foods including rice vinegar and soy sauce.

Different countries make vinegars from their indigenous crops, for example rice vinegar in Japan, oat vinegar in Korea, cider vinegar in the US, wine vinegar in Europe and malt vinegar in the UK. Rice vinegar has no fat or cholesterol and is very low in calories. It is also known for its anti-bacterial properties.

UK expansion strategy

Malegar, a division of a large UK listed food business, makes the UK's leading brand of malt vinegar. The division is currently for sale because Malegar's parent company (VM plc) has incurred significant borrowings and is now moving to a strategy of focusing on a few key profitable food brands.

Chiba wants to increase its market share in the UK and is considering setting up a subsidiary company, Chiba UK, to acquire Malegar, because of Malegar's strong UK heritage and identity. As well as targeting Malegar's traditional food market, Chiba is also keen to promote vinegar as a health product and as a cleaning product. However, Chiba's marketing director is concerned that VM plc would not be selling Malegar if it were a profitable business.

Contamination issue

The directors of Malegar are aware of a recent complaint from a major wholesaler concerning a contaminated batch of malt vinegar. The cause has not yet been confirmed and they are unsure whether the contamination arose in the glass bottles, which are purchased from an external supplier, or within the Malegar factory. Malegar takes health and safety and quality control very seriously, so the directors believe the fault is most likely to lie with the supplier. As Malegar was probably not responsible for the incident, the directors are planning to keep this issue confidential from all parties, including Chiba.

Human resource management

If Chiba's acquisition of Malegar goes ahead, all Malegar employees will transfer their contracts to Chiba UK following an appropriate consultation process. This may take up to twelve months.

Chiba's approach to human resource management is very different from Malegar's. Malegar has a hierarchical structure with a focus on short-term results, and with individual functional managers held accountable for the performance of their function. Employees within Malegar's factory have little involvement in the decision-making process and there is high staff turnover. In contrast, Chiba's approach emphasises job security for core employees, co-operation and mutual trust between employees and managers, collective responsibility and shared decision making. Chiba's directors are concerned about the change management issues that will arise from the integration of the Malegar employees into the Chiba culture.

Requirements

44.1 Explain the ethical issues that arise for Malegar's directors in relation to concealing the possible contamination. **(5 marks)**

44.2 In light of the comments by Chiba's marketing director, discuss the possible reasons for the divestment of Malegar by VM plc and the benefits to Chiba of growing by acquisition in the UK. **(8 marks)**

44.3 (a)   Contrast Chiba's and Malegar's differing approaches to human resource management. **(5 marks)**

(b)   Explain the change management issues that Chiba is likely to face when integrating the Malegar employees. Refer to relevant models where appropriate. **(9 marks)**

Total: 27 marks

46 Up 'n' Over plc

Up 'n' Over plc (UnO) manufactures garage doors for domestic properties. It sells entirely to retailers on a business-to-business basis.

Company history

UnO was established over twenty years ago and obtained a listing in 20X5. The directors own 20% of the ordinary share capital, with the other 80% being held by financial institutions.

From incorporation, UnO produced reasonable quality, basic garage doors at relatively low cost. It did not aim to be the cheapest, but it did aim to offer best value to customers, selling garage doors at prices towards the lower end of the market. UnO established a good reputation with end-consumers, who demand a reliable product at reasonable prices.

UnO sells to retailers located throughout the UK. They range from small shops, which buy from UnO only when they receive an order from a customer, up to very large retail chains, which have three-year purchase contracts with UnO. Large chains carry high inventories of UnO doors for immediate delivery to consumers.

A cost reduction policy

In December 20Y1 a new chief executive, Helen Earth, was appointed by UnO to increase profitability. After briefly reviewing the operations of the business, she decided on a cost reduction exercise, commencing in January 20Y2. This involved: reducing the quality of the materials used to make the garage doors; reducing staffing levels; replacing some staff at a lower skill level; freezing any unnecessary capital investment in machinery; and reducing maintenance. Strict performance management procedures were introduced to ensure that output volume was maintained, despite the changes.

The changes had a favourable effect on reported profit in the year ended 31 December 20Y2 (see **Exhibit 1**) but by June 20Y3 some problems were being reported. A board meeting was arranged.

Board meeting

Helen, the **chief executive**, explained the reasoning for her cost reduction plan. 'We have not yet developed a long-term strategy, but the cost reductions were immediately necessary just to make a profit.

'We've had some quality problems lately, but the cost of correcting these faults is small in comparison with the cost savings we have made. I realise that the durability of the current products is questionable. Problems will increase after about 18 months of usage of the garage doors, and there may be serious problems after three years of usage. I have made sure, however, that this is not going to be too costly to UnO, by reducing the guarantee period to customers from five years to two years. This means that by the time most doors start to develop serious faults after usage, they are out of guarantee and we have no obligation to repair them.

'As a result, I have prepared a schedule (see **Exhibit 1**) which shows that we expect to make a profit in the year to 31 December 20Y3, whereas we made a loss in 20Y1, and the share price is higher now than then. This demonstrates that the strategy is working. This is a competitive market and we need to compete on low prices, so we must keep our costs low.'

The **marketing director** disagreed: 'This business model is not sustainable. The number of complaints from our customers is growing and our reputation is declining. One of the large retailers has given us a final warning about quality standards and is threatening to stop buying our products when its long-term agreement period with UnO is completed. This cost reduction policy is just to improve short-term profits and share price. We should try to keep our customers happy in the longer term, so we must return to our previous policy of best value.'

The **chairman** joined the discussion: 'We need to balance the cost of rectifying faults with operating cost savings, but it's an increasingly competitive market. Personally, I doubt we can sustain our position as a manufacturer. One possibility is to close down our manufacturing facility and import garage doors from Thailand at a cost (including transport) that is just below our expected operating cost per door for 20Y3. In effect, we would become an importer and wholesaler of garage doors. To do this cost-effectively, we would need to order in large batches so we can fill a whole shipping container with each order, as there is a high fixed cost for transporting each container. I would like your views on whether we should consider this possibility further.'

Exhibit 1

Years to 31 December	20Y1	20Y2	20Y3 (expected)
Revenue	£32m	£32m	£30m
Selling price to retailer per door	£400	£400	£400
Fixed operating costs	£15m	£14m	£14m
Operating profit/(loss)	£(1m)	£3m	£2m
Number of doors repaired under guarantee	8	24	96
Price per share	£2.10 at	£4.50 at	£3.20 at
	31 Dec 20Y1	31 Dec 20Y2	31 May 20Y3

Requirements

46.1 On the basis of the information in the Exhibit, determine:

(a) The expected variable cost per garage door for 20Y3; and

(b) The break-even level of sales by volume for UnO in each of the years ended 31 December 20Y1 and 31 December 20Y2.

Briefly comment on the implications for operating risk of these calculations. **(9 marks)**

46.2 As a business adviser, prepare a report that evaluates the benefits and problems of each of the three strategies for UnO that were discussed at the board meeting:

(a) Return to the original strategy of producing in the UK at low cost and selling at best value, as suggested by the marketing director;

(b) Continue with the cost reduction programme introduced by the chief executive; or

(c) Cease manufacturing and import garage doors from Thailand, as suggested by the chairman.

In each case, include a brief assessment of the sustainability of each strategy. Provide a reasoned recommendation, justifying your preferred strategy. **(21 marks)**

Total: 30 marks

47 Moogle plc

You have recently joined Moogle plc (Moogle), one of the largest supermarket chains in the UK. You are the senior executive manager responsible for all Moogle's pet product sales in all its UK stores.

Initial briefing – chief operating officer

At an initial briefing, Moogle's chief operating officer, Fred Trueblood, outlined what he expected from you in your role:

'Moogle's pet products have underperformed compared with those of our rivals in recent years. I want you to make a difference. You will be responsible for procurement, pricing and profits in respect of all our pet product sales in the UK. This includes pet food and other pet-related accessories (eg toys, bowls, bedding).

I need you to think strategically and get ahead of market trends. Don't just copy what our competitors have already done, as your predecessor did. He also got too involved in what was happening at individual stores and did not see the bigger picture.

I have outlined a few details for you about the UK pet products retail industry (see **Exhibit 1**) and about Moogle (see **Exhibit 2**), as initial guidance.

I have also arranged for you to meet our head of IT, Walter Weasil. I want you to agree an information strategy, so you have the information that is necessary to guide the strategic and operational decisions you will need to take.'

Meeting with the head of IT

Walter Weasil opened the conversation:

'I need to know what key pieces of information you will need to guide your decision making and to help you monitor and control your area of responsibility. Your predecessor wanted every possible piece of information and just could not cope with it all. Try to be more selective and ask only for information that is appropriate to your function and level of management. Include any information you need to monitor any new strategies you may wish to adopt.

We can review matters later but, as a start, set out your regular monthly information needs by identifying three internal and three external pieces of information. In accordance with company policy, you must justify why you need each piece of information.'

Requirements

47.1 Prepare a PESTEL analysis for the UK pet products retail industry. **(11 marks)**

47.2 Respond to the head of IT's request by identifying **three** pieces of internal information and **three** pieces of external information that you will require each month in your role. Explain why you will need each piece of information. **(14 marks)**

Total: 25 marks

Exhibit 1: An overview of the UK pet products retail industry

The UK pet products retail industry grew steadily by around 3% per year until 20X8 when it reached total retail sales of £2,500 million. Since 20X8, UK pet products sales have grown more slowly at 1% per year due to the recession.

Pet food makes up about 75% of pet products sales. The remainder comprises: pet accessories (eg toys, bedding); veterinary services; and pet insurance. Pet insurance sales are growing rapidly, but insurance is highly regulated. Expenditure on products for dogs and cats makes up 93% of UK pet products sales. The highest growth in the pet food sector has been premium quality moist food, which has the highest price, largest margins and lowest consumer price resistance.

Animal welfare has become a key issue with new laws being passed requiring minimum standards of pet living accommodation, diet and medical care.

Pet owners now use social media network sites to share experiences and ideas and to recommend pet products to each other.

There has been a growing trend to tag dogs and cats electronically with microchips, so they can be recovered if they are lost.

On-line sales of pet products are increasingly common. There is also significant competition from pet superstores.

Exhibit 2: Moogle company background

Moogle is one of the largest supermarket chains in the UK, with stores throughout the world. Overall, Moogle positions itself as mid-market, but it has many low cost ranges and many premium product ranges.

Stores vary from large out-of-town superstores, to small in-town stores. All Moogle stores carry pet products. However, the proportion of total sales made up by pet product sales at each store varies significantly.

Moogle has a narrow product range for pets, focussing mainly on dogs and cats with a wide range of foods, plus a moderate range of accessories.

48   The Contract Cleaning Corporation Ltd

The Contract Cleaning Corporation Ltd (CCC) is a medium-sized company providing contract cleaning services to businesses in London.

The contract cleaning industry

The market for the contract cleaning industry arises from the outsourcing of cleaning activities by organisations which occupy offices, shops and factories. Contract cleaning market revenues in the UK amounted to £8,500 million in 20Y2.

Contract cleaners tend to be either small or medium-sized specialist cleaning companies or larger facilities management companies. The latter provide a wide range of services including, for example, contract cleaning, catering, building maintenance and security. A large facilities management company will often provide all these services to a client under a single contract.

Cleaning contracts tend to be awarded by clients for between one year and five years, with a break clause half way through in order to allow either party to terminate the agreement under specified conditions. At the end of the contract term there is usually a tender process, which may lead to a change in supplier. Alternatively, there may be a formal renegotiation between the current service provider and the client, resulting in a new price. The tendering process in the industry has become increasingly competitive, not just in terms of price, but also in terms of the quality and scope of the services provided.

The levels of staffing and the management of staff are key issues for cost control and operating efficiency. Small and medium-sized firms pay the statutory minimum wage, or just above this amount, to cleaners. Larger firms tend to pay more, as some of their cleaning processes require specialised skills. To check on the quality and security of work performed, there is a supervisor for each job, who is paid more than cleaners. Staff turnover is high for all companies in the industry.

The Contract Cleaning Corporation

CCC was established as a specialist cleaning company a number of years ago by two sisters, Gaynor and Lisa Harrison. Each owns 50% of the ordinary shares in CCC and they are also directors. Gaynor is primarily responsible for customer-facing activities. Lisa is responsible for internal activities, including staffing and day-to-day operations.

The business operates from leased office premises. There are few business assets, which comprise only vehicles, disposable cleaning equipment and office equipment. Operating staff (cleaners and supervisors) work 28 hours a week.

In April 20Y1, CCC's largest customer, Jarren plc (Jarren), announced that it would not be using CCC for its cleaning requirements after the current contract expired on 30 June 20Y2. In the year ended 30 September 20Y2, Jarren represented 10% of CCC's total annual revenue and 12% of its total annual operating profit.

Partly in response to the loss of Jarren as a customer, CCC engaged in a strategic review and decided to set up a new division to provide building maintenance services. This activity requires mainly part-time operating staff and they are managed separately from the Cleaning Division staff. The target market for the new Maintenance Division is existing contract cleaning clients who wish to widen the scope of services acquired from CCC, as part of a single facilities management contract. The new division commenced operations on 1 October 20Y2.

In November 20Y3, CCC prepared its management accounts for the year ended 30 September 20Y3 and this prompted concerns about performance. Gaynor and Lisa therefore appointed Sam Griffin, a newly-qualified ICAEW Chartered Accountant, as CCC's finance director and asked him to attend a board meeting to discuss performance.

The meeting

Lisa opened the meeting: 'Since we lost the Jarren contract I believe the business as a whole has gone into decline. We launched the Maintenance Division in October 20Y2, but it is taking time to become established. I would like Sam to review the performance of CCC and comment on our existing performance management system, which is a balanced scorecard that was introduced in 20Y1 by a university student on an internship with us. Frankly, we do not fully understand the balanced scorecard and we are unsure whether the key performance indicators (KPIs) we have adopted are appropriate. We have provided an outline of our current balanced scorecard and some operating and financial data (**Exhibits 1 and 2**).'

Gaynor joined the discussion: 'We have a potential new business opportunity. The CEO of a large facilities management company, Roizer plc (Roizer), approached me recently about a contract which might be mutually beneficial, even though they are a rival company. I have provided details (**Exhibit 3**).'

An ethical issue

As a consequence of decreasing revenues, Gaynor placed an advert in a London newspaper on 2 December 20Y3 which included the following:

The Contract Cleaning Corporation

The Contract Cleaning Corporation is the leading medium-sized cleaning company in London.

- All of our staff receive regular training
- We use environmentally-friendly cleaning materials
- Customer service is our main priority
- We also now offer maintenance services as a major part of our business

---

Sam discovers that:

- After initial induction training, staff training only takes place every three years
- CCC uses an equal mix of environmentally-friendly and standard chemical cleaning materials

Requirements

48.1 The directors have asked you, Sam Griffin, to complete the following tasks:

(a) Critically appraise the appropriateness of the KPIs in the balanced scorecard (Exhibit 1) that CCC has used in its performance management system. Explain how the performance management system can be improved, including suggestions for more suitable KPIs. You do not need to quantify the suggested KPIs. **(10 marks)**

(b) With reference to Exhibit 2 and the other information supplied, evaluate and explain the performance of CCC for the year ended 30 September 20Y3, compared with the year ended 30 September 20Y2. **(18 marks)**

(c) Using the data in Exhibit 3 and the other information provided, assess the benefits and risks which may arise from accepting the contract with Roizer. Provide supporting calculations, using the assumption that the Roizer contract would have the same contribution margin (ie contribution per £1 of sales) that the Cleaning Division had in the year ended 30 September 20Y3. **(9 marks)**

48.2 Discuss the ethical issues arising from the newspaper advert. **(5 marks)**

Total: 42 marks

Exhibit 1: CCC Balanced Scorecard KPIs

Key Performance Indicators currently used

Financial
  Revenue growth %
  Return on capital employed (ROCE)

Customer
  Total number of customers
  Number of customer complaints to the directors

Internal business
  Cost of cleaning products used
  Number of staff

Innovation and learning
  Hours of staff training carried out
  % of revenue from new clients

Exhibit 2: CCC operating and financial data

Income statements for the years ended 30 September

	Notes	20Y3 Cleaning Division £'000	20Y3 Maintenance Division £'000	20Y3 CCC Total £'000	20Y2 CCC Total £'000
Revenue		7,200	500	7,700	7,800
Direct labour costs		(4,048)	(324)	(4,372)	(4,128)
Other variable costs	1	(2,024)	(162)	(2,186)	(2,477)
Fixed operating costs	2	(950)	(50)	(1,000)	(1,000)
Operating profit/(loss)		178	(36)	142	195

Notes

1   Other variable costs comprise: transport (including vehicle depreciation), cleaning materials, disposable cleaning equipment.

2   Fixed operating costs comprise: administration salaries and other costs, training costs, directors' remuneration, office rent and other office costs including depreciation, insurance, accounting services.

Operating data – year ended 30 September

	20Y3 Cleaning Division	20Y3 Maintenance Division	20Y3 CCC Total	20Y2 CCC Total
Total number of clients during the year	80	5	85	77
Average number of operating staff (treated as direct labour)	440	30	470	430

Exhibit 3: Information for potential contract with Roizer – prepared by Gaynor

Roizer has recently won a facilities management contract with a large pharmaceutical company, GFP plc (GFP), for their London offices. The contract between Roizer and GFP is for four years from 31 January 20Y4, with a break clause after two years.

Roizer provides some cleaning services to existing customers, but cleaning is not a major aspect of their business and they will have trouble staffing this part of the contract at such short notice.

Roizer has therefore offered to sub-contract the GFP cleaning work to CCC on the following terms:

- CCC staff will perform all the cleaning tasks required under Roizer's contract with GFP in accordance with Roizer's service level agreement with GFP

- CCC will invoice Roizer for 60,000 chargeable employee hours per year, at £12 per hour

- CCC will provide all cleaning materials, disposable cleaning equipment, and transport, as for any other client

- The contract between Roizer and CCC would be annual, but renewable each year with the agreement of both parties.

49   The Foto Phrame Company

The date is December 20Y3.

The Foto Phrame Company (FPC) is a listed company manufacturing mid-market cameras from a single factory in Germany.

The camera industry

The first camera was produced over a hundred years ago and, since that time, new technology has enabled improved products to be launched with increasing frequency. Nearly all cameras now produced are digital cameras, which first appeared thirty years ago. However, technology advances quickly in the camera industry and each model of digital camera has a limited life cycle of five to eight years, before being replaced with an updated model. Within this life cycle, minor changes in technology mean that small variations in design, to improve a given model, are implemented each year.

Currently, there are broadly three types of camera: the compact camera (at the lower end of the market); the mirrorless camera (mid-market); the digital SLR (single lens reflex) camera (at the upper end of the market). Smart-phones are a major competitor for compact cameras, but are less of a threat to mirrorless and digital SLR cameras.

Research and development (R&D) is a key feature of product improvement and replacement. The industry is very competitive and owning intellectual property for the latest technology can be important in gaining competitive advantage. However, as technology changes rapidly, any such competitive advantage can be quickly eroded. Industry employees tend to be highly skilled.

The Foto Phrame Company

FPC products

FPC manufactures only mirrorless cameras. It has a highly skilled workforce and it spends a significant amount on R&D. FPC's markets are global. 40% of sales revenues are from European countries and 30% from the United States.

The lens is one of the highest cost components in a camera. FPC currently purchases all of its camera lenses from a German company, Zeegle, which has a factory located 40 kilometres from FPC's factory. Zeegle is in daily communication with FPC procurement staff regarding delivery quantities. However, there have been occasional delays in supply, so FPC holds the equivalent of 15 days of average usage of lenses in inventory. FPC believes that Zeegle's prices are higher than they should be. The Zeegle board has refused to lower the prices, but it has constantly sought to improve product quality and service delivery for FPC.

In June 20Y4 FPC intends to launch a replacement model for its best selling MirrorMinus3 (MM3) camera. This is the MirrorMinus4 (MM4), which has been redesigned to be smaller and lighter, with industry-leading technology. FPC undertakes a strategic review at the end of each model's life cycle. It is currently reviewing its procurement strategy and supply chain management policy as part of the strategic implementation of the new MM4.

Procurement and supply chain management

Two issues have arisen in terms of procurement and supply chain management:

Issue 1   FPC is unsure whether to procure its lenses for the MM4 from: (1) one supplier, Zeegle; or (2) a range of five suppliers, producing a single type of lens, but competing on price, product quality and service. One of the suppliers would be Zeegle, two other suppliers would be French, and two would be Japanese.

Issue 2   The MM4 has over 60 other separate components and FPC wishes to reduce costs. It wants to assess the benefits of undertaking a procurement review of all its direct suppliers ('tier 1' suppliers) in order to identify efficiencies. It is also considering managing further up the supply chain to ensure its suppliers' suppliers (ie 'tier 2' suppliers) are reliable and cost efficient. FPC is unsure whether to conduct its own review of operating procedures in tier 2 suppliers or to ask its tier 1 suppliers to carry out this task on its behalf.

Distribution

A further concern for the FPC board relates to distribution, particularly in the US which is a major and growing market for FPC. US sales have increased from 15% to 30% of FPC's total sales revenue in the last 10 years. Up to now, distribution for this market has occurred from Germany either to US wholesalers or directly to large US retail clients (eg large chains of specialist camera shops). No inventory is currently held by FPC in the US. However, demand in the US is variable and there have been an increasing number of complaints from US customers that lead times are too long and too uncertain.

The problems have been magnified by the fact that the version of the MM3 sold in the US differs in design from the MM3 sold to other global customers, due to the particular demands of US consumers. As a consequence, production runs for US design cameras at the factory in Germany only take place in the first week of each month. The company expects that variations in design for the US product will also be required for the new MM4.

FPC is considering developing its distribution facilities in the US by one of the following:

Distribution strategy 1:   Open a distribution centre in central US to hold significant inventory for distribution throughout the US using a third party courier.

Distribution strategy 2:   Set up a joint venture with a Japanese camera manufacturer to operate a distribution function in the US. The joint venture would acquire a distribution centre and vans to deliver the cameras of both companies to clients throughout the US.

Under both strategies, distribution would be both to wholesalers and directly to large retailers. However, a greater proportion of deliveries could be made directly to retailers, rather than through wholesalers, compared with existing distribution from Germany. Neither distribution strategy would involve FPC carrying out any further modification of cameras in the US.

Requirements

49.1 Explain the concept of the product life cycle and describe the factors which may affect the length of the product life cycle for FPC's cameras such as the MM3 and the MM4.   **(8 marks)**

49.2 Prepare a report for the board which explains the factors that FPC should consider in evaluating:

    (a)   The two procurement and supply chain management issues identified by FPC, providing reasoned advice; and   **(13 marks)**

    (b)   Each of the two US distribution strategies identified by FPC, providing reasoned advice.   **(14 marks)**

Total: 35 marks

50 FeedAfrica

FeedAfrica is a UK registered charity. It raises funds throughout the UK so it can support African communities faced with adverse conditions.

A summary of the issues

FeedAfrica has recently appointed Tom Reesing as its new chief executive because the trustees were unhappy with the charity's previous performance. The chair of the trustees summarised the situation in a conversation with Tom:

'We have been carrying out some really effective work in Africa, but we could do so much more. We are rejecting more and more requests for help, because we just do not have the financial or human resources to meet all the demands.

'The problems stem from a lack of public awareness of FeedAfrica's activities and a decline in funds raised in the UK. We need to market ourselves more intelligently to raise public awareness and increase our income. I have provided some background information and financial data (**Exhibit**) but, for me, FeedAfrica is about helping communities in Africa feed themselves sustainably. The charity can do this in three ways: by providing education on farming techniques; by supplying modern agricultural equipment; and by initiating projects to give long-term access to clean water. However, I do not believe we have got this message across to enough individual donors in the UK.'

The chief executive's initial review

Based on an initial review, Tom believes that, in order to increase donations from UK individuals, FeedAfrica needs to improve its market research and use this to target its promotional activities. Tom is very concerned that marketing expenditure has been wasted in the past, and that the costs incurred in raising funds have been too high in proportion to the funds generated.

Tom also believes that he could attract more donations from UK companies if he could better demonstrate that the charity's work in Africa is contributing to sustainable development there. However, to do this, FeedAfrica needs to provide appropriate evidence by measuring and monitoring its achievements.

Requirements

50.1 Explain the types of market research that FeedAfrica could carry out to help target its advertising and other promotional activities aimed at individual donors.   **(8 marks)**

50.2 Explain how market segmentation may be implemented by FeedAfrica to improve the effectiveness of its promotional activities towards individual donors.   **(7 marks)**

50.3 Explain how FeedAfrica can measure and monitor the impact it is having on sustainable development in Africa. **(8 marks)**

Total: 23 marks

Exhibit: FeedAfrica – background information and financial data

FeedAfrica was established thirty years ago in response to a long-term drought in central Africa which caused the failure of crops and led to the starvation of many people. Television coverage meant this hardship was well publicised and significant donations were received at this time by FeedAfrica from both individuals and companies in the UK.

The recession in the UK, and the absence of television coverage in recent years, have together meant that FeedAfrica's income has fallen. Draft financial statements for the year ended 30 November 20Y3 showed the following deficit:

	£'000
Donations from individuals:	
Cash and cheques	1,025
Planned giving (regular amounts by standing order)	1,345
Legacies and bequests	550
Donations from companies	840
Other income	260
Total funds generated	4,020
Costs of generating funds	(760)
Funds spent on charitable activities in Africa	(3,030)
Overheads	(540)
Deficit	(310)

Activities financed and organised by FeedAfrica have included:

- Drilling wells and accessing other water sources to enable irrigation of crops

- Educating farmers regarding fertilisation and crop rotation to improve crop yields

- Building roads for inward transportation of materials and workers to villages and for outward distribution of harvests to wider communities

- Encouraging the wealth generated by improved agriculture to be used in developing local communities

51 Emelius Ltd

Emelius Ltd (Emelius) offers document storage and management services in England. Its clients are organisations which typically process large volumes of paper and need to retain documents for a certain amount of time, for commercial or regulatory purposes. Clients include banks, professional services firms, local government organisations, utility companies and medical practices which find that managing their own documents requires significant amounts of time and storage space.

Document management companies benefit from economies of scale and can provide fast, cost-effective access to business-critical information. They use sophisticated systems to index information, protect documents from loss and alteration, and allow authorised access. Companies in the industry range from large global businesses, which offer comprehensive document storage and electronic data management, to smaller local or regional providers of paper-based storage facilities.

Company information

Emelius' current focus is the physical storage of paper documents. Documents requiring storage are collected from the client and taken to the nearest Emelius facility where they are bar-coded. This allows the documents to be catalogued and computer-indexed. Where relevant, a document is assigned an end-of-life destruction date, selected by the client, before being placed in long-term storage. When the agreed destruction date arrives, the document is shredded and the waste is recycled wherever possible.

Emelius' long-term storage system is suited to paper documents which clients are unlikely to need to access regularly. If access is required, the relevant documents can be retrieved from the storage facility and delivered to the client. Each Emelius storage facility is fitted with advanced fire detection systems and has comprehensive security with 24-hour off-site monitoring of the premises via surveillance cameras.

The document storage and management industry is quite capital intensive. In addition to premises and equipment, significant investment in IT systems is required. To reduce the amount of capital required, Emelius operates its business on a franchise model, with each franchisee granted an exclusive right to run the Emelius business in an agreed region of England. Strict franchise agreements allow Emelius to have tight control over the operations and quality of service provided, and to ensure Emelius' business model is applied consistently. Confidentiality of information and customer satisfaction are important and Emelius takes a strict approach to breaches of security and customer complaints.

Emelius has recently developed a new service, which franchisees will have the option to offer as an alternative to their customers. The new service is the digital data capture of paper documents that clients might need to access regularly. These are taken to the company's single central scanning house, where they are converted and saved in digital form. The original paper document is destroyed and the digital version is made available for clients to access using a web-enabled platform. A value chain analysis for Emelius' new digital data capture service is included in **Exhibit 1**.

Emelius Northern franchise

The Emelius Northern franchise (EN) was set up in 20Y2 by Lee Gryphon. The maximum storage capacity of its existing paper-based facility is 100 million sheets of paper. The business has been experiencing rapid growth (see **Exhibit 2**) and capacity could be increased to 150 million sheets by incurring additional fixed costs of £750,000 pa. EN does not currently offer the new digital data capture service.

Lee is in discussions with a large firm of solicitors, Swinburne LLP (Swinburne), about a potential new contract. Swinburne has five offices in the north of England and its paper document archive consists of 12 million sheets of paper. It wishes to outsource paper-based storage of all these documents to EN.

Swinburne has expressed an interest in using Emelius' new digital data capture service but Lee is unsure whether EN should start offering this service. Swinburne estimates that, once stored, 40% of its archive will need to be accessed regularly. The remainder needs storing for regulatory purposes but is unlikely to be accessed before end-of-life.

Requirements

51.1 Prepare a risk register setting out one significant risk facing Emelius' current paper-based document storage business, in each of the following four risk categories: strategic, operational, hazard and financial.

Use a table with four rows and three columns which explains, for each risk category:

- The nature of the one significant risk you have identified
- The possible impact of the risk and the likelihood of it occurring; and
- Appropriate risk management procedures **(12 marks)**

51.2 Explain four key drivers in the value chain for Emelius' new digital data capture service (Exhibit 1). **(12 marks)**

51.3 Using the data in Exhibit 2 and the other information provided in relation to the Emelius Northern (EN) franchise:

- Calculate the expected operating profit for 20Y4, without the Swinburne contract. Analyse the reasons for the improvement in performance of the EN franchise over the period 1 January 20Y2 to 31 December 20Y4.

- Quantify the impact on EN's 20Y4 expected operating profit of accepting the contract to manage Swinburne's document archive in paper format only.

- Explain your results and their implications for EN's decision about whether to introduce the digital data capture service. State any assumptions you have made. **(14 marks)**

51.4 Draft a letter on behalf of Lee Gryphon, the EN franchisee, to Swinburne, which covers:

- The benefits that digital data capture might offer Swinburne

- A justification of three performance measures that should be incorporated in the service level agreement for the contract between EN and Swinburne **(10 marks)**

Total: 48 marks

Exhibit 1: Value chain analysis for Emelius' new digital data capture service

	Inbound Logistics	Operations	Outbound Logistics	Marketing and Sales	Service
FI	10 regional franchises in England; head office provides support services (accounting, marketing, training) and centralised purchasing of all equipment and IT requirements; single centralised scanning house				
TD	Documents stored in standard image and text format to ensure maximum system compatibility	Powerful indexing system with multiple search function allows rapid document retrieval of main and any linked supporting documents			Multiple secure access controls to prevent and detect unauthorised creation, access, alteration or deletion of records
HRM	Relatively unskilled employees at scanning house, minimum wage, strict document processing targets			Existing franchisee responsible for deciding whether to offer new service in their region	Existing head office customer service team responsible for all customer support in relation to digital data service
P	Use of 24-hour national couriers to deliver paper documents from clients to central scanning house	Sole supplier agreement for all IT needs			
PA	High-speed scanners at single central facility, able to cope with multiple document formats and batch-process large volumes Once scanned, paper documents are destroyed	Key data captured and used to index documents Validation of accuracy of indexes Copies of digital documents stored across multiple servers	Web-enabled system allows multiple users to access the same files at the same time Paper copies of documents can be requested by authorised individuals	Distinctive Emelius branding on vans, staff uniforms, correspondence, website and social media	Certificate of destruction issued to client at end-of-life in accordance with regulatory requirements
	Inbound Logistics = Converting paper documents to electronic files by scanning	**Operations =** Indexing and storage of digital documents	**Outbound Logistics =** Providing clients with access to digital documents	**Marketing and Sales =** Informing customers and persuading them to buy	**Service =** Ongoing service support

MARGIN

KEY: **FI** = firm infrastructure; **TD** = technology development; **HRM** = human resource management; **P** = procurement; **PA** = primary activities

Exhibit 2: Emelius Northern (EN) franchise – operating performance summary

Year ended 31 December	Volume (sheets of paper)	Revenue	Variable costs	Fixed costs	Operating (loss)/profit
		£'000	£'000	£'000	£'000
20Y2 actual	50 million	1,800	675.0	1,500	(375.0)
20Y3 actual	75 million	2,700	937.5	1,650	112.5

20Y4 working assumptions (without Swinburne contract):

Maximum storage capacity = 100 million sheets of paper.
Anticipated volume = 90 million sheets of paper.
There will be no change in 20Y3 prices to customers.
Variable cost will be 1.15 pence per sheet.
Expected fixed cost = £1,755,000.

52   Boom plc

Boom plc (Boom) is a large, profitable mining company. It is engaged in extracting natural shale gas from underground rock formations at various sites around the world.

The hydraulic fracturing industry

Shale gas is projected to be one of the fastest-growing components of world energy consumption, with production expected to more than double between 2000 and 2020. A plentiful supply of shale gas is contained worldwide in underground rocks. It is much more abundant than conventional gas but cannot be reached by traditional vertical drilling. Instead a mixture of water, sand and chemicals is injected at high pressure, deep underground, to break up rocks and release the gas they hold. This process is known as hydraulic fracturing (fracking). The benefits claimed for shale gas include: reduced reliance on traditional fossil fuels, increased security of energy supply, reduced carbon emissions, and socio-economic development through jobs and tax revenues.

Project SA

Boom has recently discovered a new site in a remote but populated area of South America (Project SA). The local government is willing to grant Boom a lease to proceed with the fracking and the central government anticipates that there will be significant economic benefits from the production of shale gas, in terms of job creation, gross domestic product and tax revenues. Also, an abundant domestic supply of natural shale gas could be used to produce cleaner, cheaper electricity and fuel for the region.

However, there is opposition from environmental groups which claim that the local population has not been sufficiently informed about the long-term environmental issues associated with fracking. They claim that the development would place large demands on already restricted water resources and that Boom would compete with local farmers and residents for water. They also claim that fracking risks contaminating drinking water supplies. Industry experts disagree, pointing out that it is possible to make some use of saline (non-drinking) water and recycle the waste water from the fracking process.

Boom's mission

Boom's mission statement is 'to maximise the return on investment for our shareholders whilst striving to recognise our corporate responsibility to wider society.'

At a recent board meeting to discuss Project SA, Boom's finance director commented: 'Our responsibility as directors is to look after our shareholders. If we have to spend money keeping these environmentalists happy, at best we will reduce profits and at worst some of our projects will not be viable. I think the two parts of our mission statement contradict each other.'

One non-executive director (NED) took a different view. 'I recently attended a conference looking at the NED's role. They said that, as directors, we have a legal duty to promote the success of the company for the benefit of its members as a whole. This means having regard to the long-term consequences of any decision and the impact of the company's operations on the community and the environment as well as its employees, suppliers and customers. This leads to a sustainable business. Surely therefore we need to consider these environmentalists, if only from a risk management point of view.'

Requirements

52.1 Discuss the views of the two directors in relation to Boom's mission statement. In doing so, you should explain the directors' duties in respect of corporate governance and corporate responsibility.

(12 marks)

52.2 Discuss the commercial and ethical issues for Boom which are involved in the decision to extract shale gas in South America.

(10 marks)

Total: 22 marks

53 Tai Ltd and Jelk plc

Tai Ltd (Tai) is a Chinese company and Jelk plc (Jelk) is a UK company. They are currently considering a merger.

Tai Ltd – company information

Tai is well-established in China which is currently its only market. It manufactures and sells high-quality travelators (moving staircases and walkways) for use in shopping malls, offices, hotels, airports and railway stations.

Tai uses high quality materials and prides itself on its research and development team, which has created a range of technologically innovative products with outstanding energy efficiency. An integrated power control system means that Tai's travelators can run at full speed during peak times and automatically slow down or stop when there are no passengers. Safety is critical and the control system helps to minimise the risk of accidents as well as automatically shutting down power in the event of an emergency.

Tai has recently been asked to tender for the supply of 350 travelators for a railway expansion project in China. The contract will be awarded by the Chinese Ministry of Railways which requires the contractor to demonstrate its ability to cope with the scale and complexity of the project and to meet tight deadlines. Post-installation service and maintenance will also be key factors in awarding the contract.

Jelk plc – company information

Jelk is a UK listed company. It began as a manufacturer of elevators (mechanical platforms which move people or goods vertically between different levels of buildings). Jelk currently has contracts to supply and maintain elevators for a variety of major European clients in office and housing developments, hotels, railway stations and airports. Its products range from basic, cost-effective elevators for low-rise residential buildings to sophisticated multi-elevator systems for high-rise office buildings. Jelk has a reputation with its clients for excellent customer service and post-installation maintenance. Jelk makes extensive use of technology, including a state-of-the-art transport management and communication system which optimises travel within multi-elevator buildings, reducing energy use. This gives Jelk a competitive advantage. However the company recently lost a tender for a new project in Poland because the client wanted to install both travelators and elevators and decided to use a single supplier which, unlike Jelk, offered both services.

Jelk also designs, manufactures and installs stairlifts (motorised seats for transporting elderly or disabled people up and down stairs). Due to the decline in the European construction industry, Jelk has become increasingly reliant on its stairlift business. Each year, it sells thousands of stairlifts to individuals, of which 40% are exported from the UK, predominantly to Eurozone countries. Jelk is the acknowledged market leader in product safety, quality of service and innovative product design.

Jelk's headquarters, manufacturing and distribution operations are all based in the UK. It has an extensive network of installation and maintenance engineers located throughout Europe. Jelk does not currently operate in China.

Product life cycles

Travelators, elevators and stairlifts all go through similar stages in their life cycle:

- Installation of new equipment
- Modernisation and maintenance
- Replacement

However the useful lives differ: on average each travelator and elevator lasts 30 years, while each stairlift lasts only 15 years. The energy required to operate a travelator or elevator accounts for up to 80% of its environmental impact over its entire life cycle, so the primary objective when developing new models is to improve their energy efficiency.

Industry and market information: travelators and elevators

Collectively, the top four global manufacturers account for 65% of industry revenue. Demand for travelators and elevators is heavily linked to the construction sector, where macroeconomic conditions remain highly uncertain and market growth rates differ significantly between continents. The depressed construction sector in Europe has led to weak demand, increased competition and an increasingly price-sensitive market. Europe accounts for 48% of all travelators/elevators in operation, but only 23% of new installations.

In contrast, the construction sector continues to expand rapidly in South America and Asia. Due to high urbanisation rates, China represents the fastest growing travelator and elevator market, accounting for 30% of new installations. There is a developing awareness in China of the importance of quality and reliability, and increased demand for post-installation maintenance. There is also a need for basic, cost-effective elevators in the affordable-housing segment, since the Chinese government has announced plans to build 36 million mid-rise housing blocks for low-income families over the next five years.

Industry and market information: stairlifts

Apart from Jelk, the global stairlift industry largely comprises independent manufacturers which focus solely on stairlifts. Jelk is the global market leader, closely followed by two large competitors, both of which also originated in the UK. One of these competitors has recently been acquired by a major global company that provides a range of mobility products for the elderly and disabled.

Key drivers of industry demand are the age and health of the population, type of housing, disposable income and availability of government funding. Over 35% of worldwide sales currently take place in the UK, as government assists in paying for mobility aids for the elderly and disabled whereas, in most other countries, stairlifts are bought privately. Demand in China is growing rapidly because it has an ageing population with increasing levels of disposable income.

Proposed merger

'Despite our cultural differences, the proposed merger with Tai will bring tremendous benefits to both parties,' said Jelk's CEO. 'With Jelk's strong market share in the stairlift business, as well as Tai's well-established presence in China, the companies complement each other in achieving remarkable geographical market coverage and in offering a comprehensive product portfolio (see **Exhibits 1 and 2**). We are confident we can successfully manage the integration of the two entities.'

Requirements

Discuss whether the proposed merger should proceed, referring to relevant models where appropriate.

Use the following headings:

53.1 Product portfolio benefits	(10 marks)
53.2 Other key benefits	(7 marks)
53.3 Key strategic disadvantages and management issues	(9 marks)
53.4 Preliminary conclusions	(4 marks)

Total: 30 marks

Exhibit 1: Market data UK and China

UK market (figures stated in £ millions)

	Jelk sales	Largest competitor	UK market Annual growth rate
Elevators	£54m	£260m	–2%
Travelators	n/a	£182m	Nil
Stairlifts	£96m	£80m	8%

Chinese market (figures stated in US$ millions)

	Tai sales	Largest competitor	Chinese market Annual growth rate
Elevators	n/a	$4,550m	19%
Travelators	$19.6m	$342m	15%
Stairlifts	n/a	$12m	30%

Note. Assume an exchange rate of US$1 = £0.65

Exhibit 2: Analysis of sales revenue mix

	Jelk	Tai
Modernisation and maintenance	66%	12%
New installations	34%	88%

54 Albatross Golf Equipment plc

The date is June 20Y4.

Albatross Golf Equipment plc (AGE) is an unlisted company which manufactures golf clubs.

Market background

Golf clubs are used to play the sport of golf and are sold individually or in sets of clubs. They make up about 70% of the wider golf equipment market which also comprises golf clothing, bags, balls and other items related to playing golf.

Golf equipment is the largest single sector of the sports equipment market in the UK, mainly due to its high price compared to equipment for other sports. The UK golf equipment market amounted to £350 million in 20Y3, using manufacturers' selling prices. This represented a decrease of 16% since 20X8.

Distribution channels for manufacturers comprise general sports retailers and specialist golfing shops.

Company history

A number of years ago Ben Fogan opened AGE's factory in the UK to manufacture a range of high quality golf clubs. All raw materials have always been sourced locally in the UK. AGE has never made any other types of golf equipment.

When he started the business, Ben was a successful amateur golfer and a professional engineer. He made innovative adjustments to the standard design of golf clubs available at that time and patented his idea, under the LazySwing brand name. As a result, many golfers purchased the LazySwing branded clubs and reported improved scores when they played golf with them. Four years after opening the factory AGE's sales experienced a major boost when the winner of the Open Golf Championship, a globally recognised golf competition, used LazySwing golf clubs and this had a favourable reputational impact for the LazySwing brand.

AGE has, to date, sold only to specialist golfing shops, both in the UK and the rest of Europe. These shops are owned by a variety of companies and individuals, and Ben visited them personally on a regular basis to make sure that AGE products were being displayed and promoted, alongside rival brands, in an appropriate manner.

Ben continued to innovate with golf club design, but over time he could not match the rapid changes in technology achieved by larger competitors with significant research and development budgets. As a result, the LazySwing brand declined in reputation, with a decreasing customer base. Ben died in 20X4, by which time sales had fallen significantly from their peak in the early days. In October 20Y3, AGE was acquired by a private equity company, Fuller Finance plc (FF).

Lee Trebino was appointed by FF as the new chief executive of AGE. He immediately undertook a strategic review of AGE in order to explore opportunities for developing the company and returning it to growth. He asked Putt and Pitch LLP (PP), the firm of business advisers for which you work, to attend a meeting to plan the next steps following his review.

Possible strategies

Lee opened the meeting: 'When I took over as chief executive of AGE it was clear we needed to make changes to turn the company around. It was in decline and lacked a clear strategic direction. AGE has performed poorly in recent years (**Exhibit**).

'I would like PP to analyse why this is the case and to compare the performance of AGE with that of Galdo plc, the UK market leader in manufacturing golf clubs.

'The LazySwing brand still has a reasonably good reputation. However, it has now become a mid-range brand trying to compete in the high-end sector of the market. I believe it can no longer expect the required price premium or generate the required volume of sales in the high-end sector. I therefore propose a repositioning strategy for the existing LazySwing golf clubs, which is to move the LazySwing brand downmarket into the mid-range sector. We would continue to sell the existing clubs through specialist golfing shops, but at a reduced average selling price of £55 per golf club, to reflect the new mid-range market positioning.

'In addition to repositioning the existing clubs, I believe we can achieve real growth by importing some basic quality golf clubs from JiangGolf, a manufacturer in China. We expect these imported golf clubs to appeal to a wider market than our current range of clubs. We would need to guarantee to purchase a minimum of 100,000 clubs per year under a two-year agreement with JiangGolf. In return, JiangGolf has agreed it would supply AGE at an average price of £15 per golf club which, for the level of quality, is a lower price than any European supplier. I have two alternative strategies for the imported clubs:

Strategy 1: Sell the imported golf clubs under the LazySwing brand through the same specialist golfing shops as our existing LazySwing clubs, but price the imported clubs, on average, at £30 per club. They would therefore typically be the cheapest clubs available in these shops.

Strategy 2: Sell the imported golf clubs under a newly created brand name, 'Eagle', and distribute them through general sports retailers priced, on average, at £25 per club.'

Ethical issue

For the last few years, AGE has used a professional golfer, Gary Paler, to promote the LazySwing brand name. Gary signed a new four-year contract with AGE in 20Y2 to promote the LazySwing brand. He was chosen due to his success in golf competitions, but also because of his public image as a player with integrity. At a celebrity party in March 20Y4, Lee was told in confidence, by a professional golfer, that Gary regularly took performance-enhancing drugs. The possession and use of such drugs are banned in many countries.

Lee is aware that, if this information became public, it would significantly damage the LazySwing brand and severely harm Gary's career. Lee said nothing for a few months, but is now very concerned about the ethical implications of the following two options open to him: breach the confidence and disclose the information, which would damage all concerned, or stay quiet until the end of Gary's contract.

Requirements

54.1 Using the data in the Exhibit and the other information provided, analyse the performance of AGE:

    (a)   Over the period 20Y1-20Y3; and

    (b)   In comparison with the performance of Galdo, the UK market leader.

    Indicate briefly any further information that would be required to make a more complete analysis.

(18 marks)

54.2 As a business adviser working for PP, write a memorandum to the AGE board which evaluates the chief executive's strategies to: (1) reposition the existing clubs; and (2) import clubs. Use the following headings:

    •   Supply chain management

    •   Market positioning and branding   **(14 marks)**

54.3 Explain the ethical issues arising for Lee, and for AGE, in relation to Gary Paler. Set out and justify the actions that Lee should now take.   **(8 marks)**

Total: 40 marks

Exhibit: Financial, operating and market data

Financial data

	AGE			Galdo		
	20Y1 £'000	20Y2 £'000	20Y3 £'000	20Y1 £'000	20Y2 £'000	20Y3 £'000
Revenue						
UK sales	17,600	16,400	15,455	40,000	38,400	36,800
Export sales	4,400	3,600	2,945	60,000	57,600	55,200
Total	22,000	20,000	18,400	100,000	96,000	92,000
Manufacturing cost	17,600	16,400	15,456	70,000	67,200	64,400
Gross profit	4,400	3,600	2,944	30,000	28,800	27,600
Fixed operating cost	2,900	2,900	2,900	10,000	10,000	10,000
Operating profit	1,500	700	44	20,000	18,800	17,600

Operating data

	AGE			Galdo		
	20Y1	20Y2	20Y3	20Y1	20Y2	20Y3
Number of golf clubs sold (000s)	250	240	234	556	519	484

UK market data – golf equipment

	20Y1 £'000	20Y2 £'000	20Y3 £'000
UK market sales (at manufacturers' selling prices)	380,000	365,000	350,000

55 Best Fresh Bakeries Ltd

Best Fresh Bakeries Ltd (BFB) is a family-run company with five shops, each of which bakes and sells high quality, fresh produce including breads, pies, cakes and pastries.

Company background

BFB was founded by Henry Hardcastle thirty years ago when he opened one shop in a small town.

Over the following 15 years, Henry opened four further shops in the local area. All the food has always been freshly baked on the premises of each shop and BFB is well-known locally, with a loyal customer base. One of Henry's slogans is 'Baked and sold on the premises, on the same day.'

BFB is a key customer for some of its smaller local suppliers.

There has been no expansion in the number of shops since 20X1. However, in 20X4 Henry's two sons, Ralph and Nigel, joined the business. Henry gave each of them 10% of the ordinary share capital and retained the remaining 80%, with Henry taking the position of chief executive. Ralph and Nigel are the other two directors. Each director has one vote at board meetings. Brief biographies of the three directors are provided (**Exhibit**).

The net assets of BFB recognised in its financial statements are £3 million. Last year the board rejected an offer of £5 million from a large confectionery company for the entire ordinary share capital of BFB.

Henry intends to retire in 20Y9 and it is the intention that his two sons will then buy all his shares at their market value. Henry does not want to expand the business before then, but his sons are keen to grow the business as soon as possible. This caused conflict at a recent board meeting.

Board meeting – expansion strategy

Ralph opened the meeting: 'I think we should expand by centralising baking production at a single new centralised baking facility. We could then distribute the products each morning to our shops. This would give us greater capacity and enable us both to sell internally to our own shops and to make new sales to third parties. The new bakery would be set up as a separate division so we could monitor its performance after implementation. The five shops would together form the other division. I estimate my strategy would require initial capital of £2 million.'

Nigel joined the conversation: 'I agree with Ralph. We can expand the business this way, as larger scale production will deliver greater economies of scale, for instance by bulk buying raw materials and having larger production runs.'

Henry was not pleased with his sons: 'I will retire in five years at which time you can buy me out and do what you want with the business but, until then, I really do not want to invest more capital and incur the risk and effort involved in a major expansion. You both want to expand the business, but you have no money of your own to invest.'

Nigel rejoined the conversation: 'We believe the company can borrow £2 million to finance the new development, so we are not asking for any more personal investment from you. Ralph and I are serious about this; if necessary, we will vote together for the expansion plan at the next board meeting, where we will have a two to one voting majority.'

A governance issue

The day after the meeting Henry was still angry and discussed what had happened with a couple of good friends, Jon and Gemma, who are unconnected to BFB. Henry said: 'Ralph's suggestion might be the best strategy to expand the business, but I just do not want the extra strain from a personal point of view. It's my business and I don't want my sons to take control away from me at board meetings before I retire.'

Jon supported Henry: 'You're the chief executive and major shareholder, so why don't you appoint Gemma and me as non-executive directors? We will vote with you to make sure that you have a majority at board meetings.'

Requirements

55.1 Explain the risks that should be considered in evaluating the expansion strategy from the perspective of: (a) BFB; and (b) each of the three existing shareholder-directors. **(12 marks)**

55.2 Assuming the expansion strategy is implemented, briefly explain the factors that should be considered in determining transfer prices from the new centralised baking production facility to the five individual BFB shops, and recommend how the transfer prices should be set. **(9 marks)**

55.3 In light of Nigel's and Ralph's voting intentions, and Jon's suggestions, explain the governance issues for BFB. **(7 marks)**

Total: 28 marks

Exhibit: Biographies of the directors

Henry – aged 60: Henry owns his own house and has savings of about £200,000, but the proceeds from the sale of his shareholding in BFB will be his main source of retirement funding. Henry intends that his sons should buy all his shares at market value when he retires in about five years' time, even if they have to borrow from their banks to do so. Henry is risk averse.

Ralph – aged 35: Ralph is single, has no savings and rents, rather than owns, his house. He has an extravagant lifestyle, spending nearly all his income, but he has no debts. He believes in taking reasonably high risks.

Nigel – aged 30: Nigel is married with a family. He owns his house, but has a large mortgage. He has some limited savings. He is risk neutral, but ambitious.

56 ElectroInfo Ltd

ElectroInfo Ltd (EIL) operates in the electrical and IT services industry. The EIL board is currently reconsidering the company's pricing policy to customers.

Operations

EIL offers electrical and IT services to customers for their homes. These two types of service are offered independently and are provided by different EIL employees. The electrical services provided by EIL include traditional home electrical services, such as wiring and fuse box installation, and also broadband installation and maintenance. The IT services offer solutions to basic software problems experienced by customers on their home PCs, laptops and tablets.

EIL operates from 30 depots located on business parks in towns throughout the UK. The depots are located about 50 kilometres away from each other in places where there is less competition than in large cities and where local reputation can be established more easily. EIL employs qualified electricians and IT specialists. Typically there are three electricians and three IT specialists operating from each depot. Customers all live within 25 kilometres of a depot. The company aims to offer good quality customer service.

EIL has a centralised structure so prices and wages, plus most other aspects of operations, are determined centrally. Each depot head reports directly to EIL's board of directors.

Competition

EIL aims to have a market position between large service companies and small sole proprietor businesses which operate from proprietors' homes. The large service companies tend to carry out both commercial and consumer work, but charge higher prices at £38 per labour hour upwards. Sole proprietor businesses offer lower prices, charging £28 per labour hour or less, but they often lack the most up-to-date training.

Pricing

EIL charges all its services, to all its customers, at a single rate of £32 per chargeable hour. The average variable cost to the company for both IT and electrical services is £20 per chargeable hour.

To increase profits, some directors suggested raising EIL's price to all customers for both types of service, but the **finance director**, Denise Jones, was concerned about this. 'Some customers are willing to pay more, but many are on low incomes. They are resistant to price increases and many would move to lower priced competitors if we raised our price. Instead, I believe we should consider charging a different price for each of our two different services, IT and electrical, to all customers, even though it costs us the same to provide these services in terms of both wages and other costs.'

The **marketing director**, Amy Ashad, disagreed: 'We should be charging different prices to different customers, but pricing each of the two types of service the same.'

Market research

The board agreed to obtain more information about customers' attitudes to price through market research based on questionnaires and examination of actual behaviour in response to previous price changes. This research revealed the following information about the sensitivity of demand (chargeable hours per year) to selling price (£ per chargeable hour):

	£30	£32	£34	£36
Selling price per chargeable hour				
Demand (chargeable hours per year)	250,000	230,000	200,000	160,000

Further market analysis was completed, using two different approaches to segmenting the customer market for electrical and IT services, firstly by customer income, and secondly by service type.

Segmented by customer income

Selling price per chargeable hour	£30	£32	£34	£36
Demand (chargeable hours per year)				
Low income customers (Note)	85,000	70,000	45,000	20,000
Other customers	165,000	160,000	155,000	140,000

Note. Classified using the estimated value of the customer's house as a rough measure to indicate the level of the customer's income.

Segmented by service type

Selling price per chargeable hour	£30	£32	£34	£36
Demand (chargeable hours per year)				
IT services	125,000	120,000	110,000	100,000
Electrical services	125,000	110,000	90,000	60,000

The **chief executive** has now made a further suggestion: prices should be set locally by each depot head, rather than centrally for all the depots by the directors.

Requirements

56.1 Assume that the same price is charged for both electrical and IT services and that prices are set centrally:

   (a) From the four choices of price identified in the tables above, calculate the price per chargeable hour that EIL should charge in order to maximise total contribution under each of the following alternative assumptions:

        •   A single uniform price is charged to all customers (as per the current policy).

        •   One uniform price is charged to low income customers and a different uniform price is charged to all other customers.

   (b) Discuss the feasibility and benefits of Amy Ashad's suggestion of charging different prices to different customers based on income. Refer to your calculations in (a) above. **(12 marks)**

56.2 Evaluate Denise Jones' suggestion that a different price should be charged for the two different service types, IT and electrical. Provide supporting calculations. Assume the same single uniform price continues to be charged to both low income and all other customers, and that prices are set centrally. **(9 marks)**

56.3 Evaluate the chief executive's suggestion of depot heads setting prices locally and explain the issues which are likely to arise in implementing this policy. **(11 marks)**

Total: 32 marks

57   Forsi Ltd

Forsi Ltd (Forsi) provides forensic science services to private clients and UK public sector organisations, such as the police and HMRC.

Industry information

Forensic scientists examine materials and provide scientific evidence to assist in an investigation or court proceedings. As well as criminal cases, forensic science is used in private disputes concerning accidents, medical negligence, insurance claims and product liability.

Until 20X9, the government-owned Forensic Science Service (FSS) accounted for 60% of the total forensic science market in the UK and handled the majority of the public sector work. However, in 20Y0 a decision was taken to reduce the activities of FSS, leading to its complete closure in 20Y3. As a result there have been several new entrants to the market, which is now very competitive.

Forsi was founded in 20Y0 by four scientists who previously worked for FSS. Forsi and one other key competitor now dominate the UK market. Both offer a wide range of forensic science services to all types of client. A number of smaller providers have also emerged which typically specialise in one particular scientific field eg fire investigation, toxicology or genetics. Various UK police forces also have their own in-house forensic science laboratories but there is no national police policy, so many police forces outsource work to businesses such as Forsi.

Company information

From the outset, Forsi has operated with an informal structure, to minimise bureaucracy and focus on technical expertise and scientific analysis. The original founders spend little time on administration and management tasks, and instead concentrate on attracting clients and undertaking analytical work. Many support functions (including payroll, accounting and human resources) are outsourced.

As a result of the founders' reputations and technical expertise, and the range of forensic science services provided, Forsi has experienced steady growth. It now employs 40 scientists and five administrators. Work is organised on a project basis, with an appropriate project team created for each specific client request. On smaller projects, scientists may work alone. When they are not working on projects, Forsi's scientists are expected to undertake research to develop new scientific techniques or more efficient processes.

Although Forsi does undertake one-off projects for clients, most of its business is on a repeat basis, eg a succession of accident investigations for an insurance company. Obtaining such clients is key to revenue growth. Once Forsi has been confirmed as a client's approved supplier, client retention becomes important. Depending on the client and the nature of the work, some projects are negotiated at a fixed price and some are priced on a cost-plus basis. Increasingly clients prefer fixed-price projects so that they can avoid unexpected increases in costs. All dealings and discussions with clients are handled by the four founders.

As a result of the increased competition, Forsi's informal structure has started to present some difficulties and threatens to inhibit its growth. There has been a lack of collaboration between staff, with scientists preferring to work independently on each project, and Forsi has not maximised opportunities for shared learning.

Often, requirements change during the course of a project and delays have arisen whilst one of the founders renegotiates with the client, leading to client complaints. There are few in-house financial controls and although a budgeted cost is established for each project before work starts, this is often exceeded. As a result of these issues, Forsi's profits have fallen (**Exhibits 1 and 2**). It has started to lose some potential projects to competitors and has also had to accept lower margins on repeat business in order to retain clients.

A possible new owner

Recently, Forsi has been approached by an Australian multi-national, Aussi Ltd (Aussi), which undertakes work for global private and public sector clients. Aussi consists of several divisions, each offering a different scientific service (eg pharmaceutical research, forensic science, aerospace). All support services are provided by a centralised head office function.

Aussi's forensic science division is the market leader in Australia and Asia. In 20Y3 it spent £4.4 million on research and development and £9 million on marketing, and it generated sales revenue of £220.3 million (all figures translated from Australian dollars into £ sterling).

Aussi wants to acquire Forsi to further its expansion in Europe. However, it does not want to destroy Forsi's research-centred culture as it acknowledges that Forsi's success to date has been driven by the founders' knowledge and contacts, and by the skill of the scientists it employs. If the founders agree to sell their shares, Aussi will either allow Forsi to operate autonomously as a separate subsidiary company or integrate it within Aussi's forensic science division.

Whichever structure is chosen, Forsi will be required by Aussi to achieve a target return on capital employed (ROCE) of 15%. It will also have to comply with Aussi's formal project screening process whereby:

- All new projects are required to meet an expected minimum 20% gross margin
- The final agreed project price has to be signed off by Aussi's central finance department

In 20Y3, Aussi's forensic science division generated a gross margin of 25% and ROCE of 18% on net assets of £183.5 million. **Exhibit 2** sets out additional operating data for Aussi.

Requirements

57.1 Using the data in the Exhibits and the other information provided, analyse the performance of Forsi, contrasting it with Aussi's where appropriate. Suggest other non-financial information that may be useful in ascertaining the causes of the deterioration in Forsi's performance. **(16 marks)**

57.2 Discuss the appropriateness of Forsi's existing structure, referring to relevant models. **(7 marks)**

57.3 Assuming Forsi's founders do **not** agree to be taken over by Aussi, explain why knowledge management is important to Forsi and recommend the steps that Forsi could take to implement a knowledge management strategy. **(8 marks)**

57.4 Assuming Forsi's founders **do** agree to be taken over by Aussi:

(a) Discuss whether Forsi should be operated as a subsidiary of Aussi or as part of Aussi's forensic science division; and

(b) Recommend how Aussi should manage the change when the takeover is announced.

(14 marks)

Total: 45 marks

Exhibit 1: Financial data for Forsi for the years ended 31 December

	20Y2 £'000	20Y3 £'000
Sales revenue	5,400	5,088
Direct costs	(4,175)	(4,165)
Gross profit	1,225	923
Research & development	(254)	(260)
Marketing	(108)	(90)
Other operating expenses	(268)	(270)
Operating profit	595	303
Net asset value	4,020	3,910

Exhibit 2: Operating data for Forsi and Aussi

	Forsi 20Y2	Forsi 20Y3	Aussi forensic science division 20Y3
Number of employees	45	45	2,000
Number of projects undertaken in year	108	106	2,448
% of projects completed on time	83%	76%	89%
% of projects completed within budgeted cost	72%	65%	92%
Sales value of projects awarded, but not yet undertaken, at year end	£1,350,000	£855,000	£65,080,000

58 ToyL Ltd

ToyL Ltd (ToyL) is a start-up business. It intends to provide educational toys for children, which will be sold to individual customers and educational establishments.

ToyL has been founded by a husband and wife team, Pavel and Rosemary Bochev. They have prepared the first draft of a business plan to attract additional funding from private investors (**Exhibit**).

You are a consultant in a firm of business advisers that is assisting ToyL. Your manager has undertaken an initial review of the draft business plan and has some concerns about its structure and content. Rosemary and Pavel have never prepared a business plan before and lack financial expertise. Your manager is also concerned that they may have been over-enthusiastic in their desire to present the business in the best possible light to attract potential investors.

Requirements

58.1 Write a report for Pavel and Rosemary which critically assesses the content of the draft business plan and makes recommendations as to how the document may be improved. As part of your appraisal indicate the nature of any missing information and any additional sections of the plan that would be relevant to a prospective investor. **(15 marks)**

58.2 Explain the benefits of outsourcing as a production model for ToyL. **(6 marks)**

58.3 Assume that ToyL successfully raises the necessary finance. Explain how the information requirements of Pavel and Rosemary as managers will be different from the information requirements of the additional private investors, once the business is operational. **(9 marks)**

Total: 30 marks

Exhibit

DRAFT BUSINESS PLAN: ToyL Ltd
Contents
1   Executive summary 2   Introduction and management team 3   Products 4   Marketing 5   Competition 6   Strategy and operations

1.   Executive summary

Will be completed after the remainder of the business plan is finalised.

2.   Introduction and management team

ToyL Ltd (ToyL) will sell educational toys for young children. It is owned and managed by Pavel, an information technology (IT) specialist and his wife, Rosemary, an educational consultant.

Pavel will be in charge of operations, including the one-off manufacture of product prototypes. He has a computer engineering degree. Pavel started his career in the product development department of a large IT company, before moving to a consumer electronics company, where he was responsible for developing hand-held games.

Rosemary will be responsible for marketing and sales. She studied for a Master of Education degree and then spent several years developing educational tools for teachers of pre-school children.

Together Rosemary and Pavel's backgrounds have helped them design products that combine opportunities for learning with the fun aspects of a game.

3.   Products

ToyL has developed three distinct educational toys for young children, aged three to five years. These toys use interactive technology to teach numeracy and literacy.

- NumberToy: emits lights and sounds when the child touches a stylus on the appropriate number. In addition to teaching number skills, it also helps with hand-eye co-ordination.

- AlphabetToy: similar to NumberToy, but it teaches the child the alphabet and appears to improve their attention span.

- PhonicToy: an interactive toy that looks similar to a miniature laptop. It contains speech recognition software which allows the child to have a spoken conversation with a cartoon character. The character teaches word pronunciation and reads stories aloud. This is the most expensive product and is designed to help the child read and develop a vocabulary.

Although the toys are currently prototypes, they are functionally complete and ready for manufacture. The prototypes have been tested widely and were well received. Part of the testing has included Rosemary and Pavel observing a variety of children as they interact with the toys.

All products will be designed and initially manufactured in-house. However once a toy design has been tested and approved for sale, its on-going production will be outsourced to suppliers either in the UK or Eastern Europe. ToyL's product range is expected to grow over time as ideas for new toys are generated.

4.   Marketing

ToyL has identified two target market segments:

- Individuals, such as parents or grandparents, who will purchase the product for a particular child. We think this market segment currently has about 3.3 million prospective customers and is growing at around 8% pa. Typically these customers are well-educated and have higher disposable incomes. They are keen for the children to develop and believe they are getting value-for-money if the toys have educational as well as entertainment value.

- Educational organisations, such as pre-schools, day care centres and nurseries, which will buy products to use within their institutional environment. Typically they care for children in groups of between 7 and 25 in number. We believe that this market segment contains about 0.7 million prospective customers and is growing annually at around 10%.

ToyL has decided to sell direct to both groups. Its key marketing tool will be its website. Its marketing strategy will recognise the fact that there are two distinct groups that must be attracted.

5. Competition

The UK toy industry is a fragmented market, with many different toy manufacturers. Within the toy industry there is a niche of educational toy manufacturers which is dominated by two global market leaders (Knowall and Brightkidz). These companies sell toys under a range of different brand names to cover several price points. There are also several smaller, regional manufacturers of educational toys.

In addition, educational toy providers compete with the wide range of electronic products produced by the large game manufacturers.

We believe ToyL's competitive advantage comes from products that are superior to those already available in the marketplace. This quality will allow ToyL to achieve market penetration. ToyL will use its educational and engineering expertise to produce toys that are fun to use and which at the same time teach important skills for children. By recognising and exploiting its core competencies, ToyL will quickly gain market share as well as develop a reputation for making effective educational toys.

6. Strategy and operations

The company is in its first year. It has incurred set-up costs of around £24,000 but has not yet produced a finished product or made any sales. ToyL hopes to generate sufficient revenues to break-even by the end of year one and then expects strong sales growth for several years. Rosemary and Pavel anticipate sales of £367,000 in year two and £475,000 in year three.

Pavel and Rosemary have invested capital of £60,000 in the business (through personal borrowing) but to develop more products ToyL is seeking additional equity capital of £40,000 from one, or more, private investors.

ToyL has identified three critical success factors (CSFs) that will be instrumental in the sustainability of its business:

- The ability to develop creative, educational, engaging toys

- The need to listen to customers and create a feedback mechanism for new product development and existing product improvement

- The implementation of strict financial controls

59 Water On Tap

'Water On Tap' (Ontap) is a small social enterprise operating in central London. A social enterprise is a business which meets social and environmental aims by trading in a profitable and sustainable way.

Ontap's specific aim is 'to provide a cheaper and more sustainable alternative to bottled water.' Its founder, Nala Delmar, a keen athlete, founded Ontap because she was frustrated by the large amount of money she was spending on bottled drinking water.

Ontap's operations need to be financially viable because it relies on its business activities, not donations, for funding. 70% of Ontap's profits are donated to fund clean water projects in India. Remaining funds are reinvested in the business or used to raise awareness of the damaging effects of bottled water on the environment.

Bottled water industry in the UK

The retail market for bottled water in the UK is worth approximately £1.6 billion, by annual sales revenue. Industry statistics show that the average consumer drinks 33 litres of purchased bottled water per annum.

Despite legislation that requires any establishment serving alcohol to have free tap water available, it has become the social norm to purchase bottled water in such establishments. This has reduced the acceptability of asking for free tap water in restaurants, cafes and bars. It has also created a huge increase in plastic bottle waste. An estimated 18 billion plastic bottles are consumed annually in the UK, of which 75% are not recycled and therefore end up in landfill. The packaging and transportation involved means that bottled water also has a much higher carbon footprint per litre than tap water.

In 20Y2 several UK supermarkets were criticised for selling a product that should have been free, when it became apparent that some of their own-brand bottled water was simply filtered, purified tap water. Some multi-national bottled water companies have also attracted adverse publicity for spending huge sums on advertising in an attempt to make their brand fashionable and appear to offer variety for what is essentially an homogenous product.

About Ontap

The Ontap concept involves a re-fillable water bottle made from recycled aluminium foil, which carries the Ontap logo. Once purchased from Ontap, at a cost of £8, the bottle can be taken to a range of participating cafes and shops (currently only in central London) and re-filled with tap water. These businesses provide their re-filling services for Ontap's customers free of charge, in the hope they will purchase additional products. The Ontap website and free mobile app provide a list of refill sites, all of which prominently display the Ontap logo.

Plans for expansion

In London, Ontap has been a success and proved popular with athletes, commuters and students plus the participating cafes and shops. Ontap has received lots of social media coverage and the brand is currently very fashionable. Nala is keen to expand her original concept.

She is considering two possible options for expansion:

(1) A corporate sales scheme. Nala would like to persuade companies to buy water bottles to replace the plastic cups typically found beside water coolers in most offices. She has read a recent survey reporting that, on average in such offices, each employee throws away four plastic cups a day. Instead, the company would bulk purchase Ontap bottles for their employees, which would then be co-branded with the company's own name.

(2) Geographical expansion. This would necessitate finding cafes and shops outside the central London area which would be willing to be Ontap partners.

Requirements

59.1 Discuss the extent to which Ontap is a sustainable enterprise. **(7 marks)**

59.2 Compare and contrast the ethics of the marketing activities of Ontap with its competitors in the bottled water industry. **(8 marks)**

59.3 Discuss the problems Ontap will face in any expansion of the business and evaluate the two proposed options. **(10 marks)**

Total: 25 marks

60   Confo plc

Confo plc (Confo) is a listed company, operating in the packaged confectionery products (boxes of sweets) industry.

Confo was established a number of years ago, manufacturing boxes of sweets in its factory and selling them in its own shops throughout the UK. Since this time , some of the 240 shops have been operated under exclusive franchise arrangements, while the remainder are still owned by Confo. All products sold at Confo shops (both owned and franchised) are produced in Confo's factory. The company was structured as two separate divisions, Manufacturing and Retail, until 30 September 20Y3 (**Exhibit 1**).

Recovery plan

After a difficult period of trading, a new board was appointed in December 20Y2 and, following a detailed review, it implemented a radical three-year recovery plan from 1 October 20Y3. The recovery plan included: the closure of 70 owned shops; the opening of 30 franchised shops; and the creation of two new sales channels, commercial sales (to UK supermarkets) and export sales (to overseas retailers). As a result, Confo now has two additional divisions, Commercial and Export, and a revised system for pricing transfers (**Exhibit 2**).

Following preparation of the management accounts and operating data for the year ended 30 September 20Y4 (**Exhibit 3**), a board meeting was called to review progress in implementing the three-year recovery plan, and to consider whether any changes to the plan are needed.

Board meeting

The chief executive complained: 'This year's results are disastrous. This was supposed to be a recovery plan, but performance seems to have got worse, not better. Profit has fallen compared with last year.'

The marketing director disagreed: 'I believe that we have great potential for future growth from the commercial and export sales that we started this year. However, we need to give them time to get established and show their potential. You cannot judge performance on one year's figures.'

An ethical issue

From 1 October 20Y3, the sales manager of Confo's Commercial Division, Kirsty Keller, met regularly with John Drake, the procurement manager of a large customer, Lenton Supermarket (Lenton). In November 20Y3, John asked if he could have two small boxes of sweets for his family for Christmas. This type of small gift to customers' staff is common in the sweets industry. In December 20Y3, Kirsty delivered some Confo sweets, with a total value of £10, to John's home as a gift to promote good relations between Confo and Lenton. She informed Confo's commercial director about what she had done and he was happy with this action.

From January 20Y4, John made further requests for gifts of sweets, gradually increasing in both value and frequency. In order to keep a good business relationship with John, Kirsty continued to provide these gifts, but she stopped disclosing them to the commercial director in March 20Y4 when the value of the gifts reached £30 per week. In July 20Y4, when John started asking for gifts valued at £100 per week, Kirsty refused.

In September 20Y4, Lenton stopped purchasing from Confo. Kirsty never made any personal gain from the gifts and there is no documentary evidence relating to them.

Requirements

60.1 Compare and evaluate Confo's pricing of transfers before and after the changes made by implementing the recovery plan on 1 October 20Y3. Suggest and justify alternative methods of pricing transfers that Confo could have adopted on 1 October 20Y3. **(9 marks)**

60.2 Analyse and evaluate the performance of the Manufacturing Division and the Retail Division in the year ended 30 September 20Y4 compared with the year ended 30 September 20Y3. Highlight any problems in comparing the data and set out any additional information that would assist your analysis. **(15 marks)**

60.3 As part of the appraisal of the first year of the recovery plan, write a report which:

(a) Reviews the strategies adopted by the Export Division and the Commercial Division, and evaluates their performance. Include any relevant strategic models in your appraisal.

(b) Evaluates the success of the recovery plan for Confo to date.

(15 marks)

60.4 Explain the ethical issues for Kirsty, and for Confo, arising from the matters occurring with Lenton and John Drake. Set out, and justify, the actions that Kirsty and Confo should now take. **(7 marks)**

Total: 46 marks

Exhibit 1: Company structure and pricing of transfers – pre 30 September 20Y3

Up to 30 September 20Y3, both Confo divisions, Manufacturing and Retail, were profit centres. The factory's output was transferred by the Manufacturing Division to all Confo shops (owned and franchised) at the same price, full cost plus 20%. In addition to the Retail Division's profits from the owned shops, Confo also earned a total of £1.2 million annually from the fixed fees it charged to franchisees for use of the Confo brand name and for operational and management support.

Consumers are charged the same list prices at all Confo shops. Franchisees are also required to charge these list prices in order not to undercut the prices charged by owned shops, and to avoid cheapening the Confo brand.

The setting of the same prices for transfers from the factory to both owned and franchised shops caused some internal debate. The Retail Division management claimed that prices for transfers to owned shops were too high and should be lower than the prices charged to franchisees. They also believed that the annual fixed fees paid to Confo by franchisees were too low. Confo products are unique and valid comparison with the prices charged by rival manufacturers and retailers cannot be made easily.

Exhibit 2: Company structure and pricing of transfers – post 1 October 20Y3

Since the commencement of the recovery plan on 1 October 20Y3, Confo has operated with four divisions: Manufacturing, Retail, Commercial and Export.

Changes in the Manufacturing Division

From 1 October 20Y3, the Manufacturing Division became a cost centre. It transfers all its output at full cost to the Retail Division, to franchisees, and to the new Commercial and Export Divisions. The reduction in the price of transfers was, in part, intended to increase the volume of sweets purchased by existing franchisees and to encourage more franchises to be taken up. To offset the lost revenue, Confo increased the fixed fee charged to each franchisee. These fixed fees now total £2.5 million.

Changes in the Retail Division

Confo continues to make UK retail sales via owned and franchised shops. The Retail Division still comprises owned shops and remains a profit centre. The review by the new board identified that many owned shops in the retail network were under-performing. On 1 October 20Y3, as part of the recovery plan, 70 poorly performing owned shops were closed. Of these closed shops, 30 were immediately reopened under the management of new franchisees.

The new Commercial and Export Divisions

The Commercial and Export Divisions were opened on 1 October 20Y3 as separate profit centres.

The Commercial Division makes sales to UK supermarkets. The products are all made in Confo's factory, but are packaged by Confo in the client's brand and wrapping (ie 'own labelled') in order to minimise the loss of sales at Confo shops, and to make price comparisons by consumers more difficult. Prices charged by the Commercial Division are negotiated separately with each client. The supermarkets sell the products at retail prices that are lower than the list prices in Confo's owned and franchised shops.

The Export Division sells only Confo branded products, in bulk, to overseas retailers. It has taken some time to establish relationships with new clients and develop brand awareness, but sales have started to grow.

Exhibit 3: Management accounts and operating data

Confo: Management accounts for the year ended 30 September 20Y3

	Manufacturing £'000	Retail £'000	Total £'000
Transfers to franchised shops by Manufacturing Division	8,100	-	8,100
External sales	-	24,000	24,000
Divisional transfers	18,000	(18,000)	-
Variable costs	(13,050)	(2,400)	(15,450)
Fixed costs	(8,700)	(4,000)	(12,700)
Divisional profit	4,350	(400)	3,950
Fixed franchise fees			1,200
Operating profit			5,150

Confo: Management accounts for the year ended 30 September 20Y4

	Manufacturing £'000	Retail £'000	Commercial £'000	Export £'000	Total £'000
Transfers to franchised shops by Manufacturing Division	7,500	-	-	-	7,500
External sales	-	14,400	4,320	1,760	20,480
Divisional transfers	13,000	(9,000)	(3,000)	(1,000)	-
Variable costs	(12,300)	(1,080)	(720)	(320)	(14,420)
Fixed costs	(8,200)	(3,000)	(300)	(240)	(11,740)
Divisional profit	0	1,320	300	200	1,820
Fixed franchise fees					2,500
Operating profit					4,320

Confo: Operating data for the years ended 30 September

	20Y3	20Y4
Number of boxes of sweets sold externally:		
Retail Division (owned shops) (000s)	12,000	7,200
Franchised shops (000s)	5,400	6,000
Commercial Division (000s)	-	2,400
Export Division (000s)	-	800
Total products sold externally	17,400	16,400
Number of Confo shops:		
Owned shops	150	80
Franchised shops	90	120

61 Radar Traditional Radios Ltd

The date is December 20Y4.

Radar Traditional Radios Ltd (RTR) is a family-owned company which manufactures high quality portable radios at a factory in the UK. The particular styling of the radios, which appeals to UK market tastes, means sales are made in the UK only.

Radio broadcasting

In the UK, radio stations broadcast radio programmes via two main platforms:

- Analogue, using traditional analogue frequencies (AM/FM)

- Digital, using newer digital audio broadcasting (DAB)

Digital broadcasting was publicly launched in the UK twenty years ago. The broadcasting industry is encouraging digital radio broadcasting as it offers a wider choice of radio stations than analogue, is easier to use, and is resistant to localised signal interference.

However, on the negative side, the overall audio quality on digital is poorer than analogue, and digital reception is restricted in certain areas of the UK, so a lower percentage of the population can receive digital, compared with analogue. Digital reception was available to 80% of the UK population in 20X4 and to 90% by 20Y4. Analogue reception is available to 99% of the UK population.

Radio listening

In 20Y3, 35% of radio listening hours in the UK were on digital, 60% on analogue and 5% on other platforms.

Radio programmes that are broadcast on the analogue platform can be listened to only on analogue radios. Digital radio broadcasts can however be listened to on a variety of devices. The devices used to listen to digital audio broadcasts in the UK in 20X9 and 20Y3 were as follows:

Radio listening to digital broadcasts by device

	20X9 %	20Y3 %
Digital television	25	27
Digital radios	23	25
Internet	15	22
Smartphones	10	20
Other devices	27	6

In 20X9, there was significant optimism about the future of digital radio broadcasting. The UK government predicted that it would switch off the analogue platform in the UK by 20Y5. As a result, in 20Y1 a major UK electrical retailer announced that it would shortly stop selling analogue radios. In spite of this early optimism, however, growth in sales of digital radios has been much lower than anticipated. Digital radios are currently owned by a little less than half of UK households.

The government is now expected to require the switch-off of analogue radio frequencies in the UK by 20Y9, at the very earliest. Some industry analysts believe that digital may take many years to overtake analogue due to the modest levels of ownership of digital radios.

Radio manufacture

The manufacture of radios is a global industry with some multinational companies producing radios as part of a wide range of consumer electrical products. There are however many small national companies, like RTR, specialising in radio manufacture only for their home markets. Some companies have stopped making analogue radios. Most companies in the industry, however, currently manufacture both analogue and digital radios, though some have plans to greatly reduce, and then cease, the production of analogue radios, as analogue is being switched off in an increasing number of countries.

The price of radios to consumers in the UK varies widely. Analogue radios are significantly cheaper than digital radios, retailing from around £25. The cheaper digital radios retail at £35, and mid-market digital radios are typically £50 to £100, while top-of-the-range models are considerably more expensive.

With advances in technology, some radio manufacturers are adding additional features to digital radios including, for example, internet access. They have also added 'Bluetooth' technology, which allows the user to stream music wirelessly through a digital radio from other devices such as MP3 players and smartphones.

Company information - RTR

RTR manufactures both digital and analogue radios. Its radios contain up-to-date technology and are known for their quality, but they deliberately feature old-fashioned styling. This gives RTR a niche market, but there is continued pressure in the industry to keep the technology up-to-date to compete, not just with other radios, but also with the other devices, such as smartphones, which can receive digital broadcasts.

RTR radios are only distributed through upmarket stores in the UK, and are at the top end of the market. RTR's analogue radios sell for an average of £150 and their digital radios average £200. Over the past few years, RTR's annual sales volumes have remained constant at 100,000 radios, as follows:

RTR sales (units)	20X9	20Y3
Analogue radios	65,000	60,000
Digital radios	35,000	40,000

RTR has always had a policy of investing in research and development (R&D) to ensure its radios are innovative in function, as well as being distinctive in style. Recently it has added Bluetooth to one model in its digital range, but further investment is needed to introduce Bluetooth across the digital range and develop additional technology features.

It has become difficult for RTR to compete with larger manufacturers given rapidly advancing technology, both in radio broadcasting and in listening devices. RTR needs to decide whether to cease R&D and marketing expenditure on analogue radios, effectively phasing out their production over the next two to three years, so that all the R&D and marketing budgets can be focussed on digital radios. A board meeting was arranged to discuss these issues.

Board meeting

The R&D director was pessimistic: 'We are a small company in a big industry. We need to focus our R&D expenditure on digital products or the budget will just be spread too thin.'

The marketing director disagreed: 'We cannot abandon analogue, which is still our largest market. I agree we need to focus our resources. However, I would try to focus marketing expenditure at our target consumer groups for both analogue and digital radios, not just concentrate on one type of product. I agree the digital radio market is more challenging, so I have provided some data (**Exhibit**) to help us decide on a marketing strategy for digital radios.'

Requirements

61.1 Using Porter's Five Forces Model, explain the impact on competitiveness in the radio manufacturing industry, for the UK market, of the following TWO forces only:

- Substitutes
- Competitive rivalry amongst existing firms **(10 marks)**

61.2 Explain how market segmentation can be used by RTR to identify target groups of consumers for its digital radios, and discuss how each of the components in the marketing mix (4Ps) can be used by RTR to promote its digital radio product range to these groups. **(12 marks)**

61.3 Discuss and evaluate the factors to be considered by the RTR board in determining whether, and if so when, it should decide to abandon the manufacture of analogue radios to focus resources on developing and selling only digital radios. **(9 marks)**

Total: 31 marks

Exhibit – Analysis of UK consumers for digital radios

	UK industry average	RTR radios
Age of consumer	45	55
Average annual income	£23,000	£37,000
Gender	60% male	45% male

62 The Norgate Bank plc

The Norgate Bank plc (NB) is a bank whose customers are small businesses and individuals living in either the UK or France. It has no physical branches for customers to visit. Internet banking is therefore important to NB, but also its telephone call centres are key to communication and to building customer relationships.

Until last year, NB had only one telephone call centre, which was near London and served all its existing customers. Call operators included fluent French speakers to serve French customers. In December 20Y3, a major new investment was made in a new call centre in Vietnam, where some of the local population speak French. At that time, Ron Terry was appointed as the director in charge of all call centre operations.

Under the new arrangement, the UK call centre serves only UK customers. French customers are served by the call centre in Vietnam, where call operators are from the local, French-speaking population. Property costs and staff costs are much lower in Vietnam than in London. At both call centres there are two groups of call operators: one for business customers and one for individual customers.

Ron wants to conduct a post-implementation review of both call centres to ensure that physical and human resources are being used efficiently. Over the past year, Ron has used three Key Performance Indictors (KPIs) to measure call centre performance (**Exhibit**). These are:

- Average time taken to answer a customer call
- Average length of a customer call
- Scores from customer satisfaction surveys for handling calls (where: 1 = poor; 5 = excellent)

Ron is concerned about the validity of these KPIs, and he is unsure whether they are the most appropriate means of measuring performance. He is also unsure how they might be utilised to improve the efficiency of the call centres.

Wendy West, a senior manager reporting to Ron, used to work at a call centre in a large insurance company. She believes that NB's KPIs are poor by comparison to those of her previous employer.

Requirements

62.1 Evaluate the validity of the three KPIs used for measuring the performance of NB's call centres and suggest alternative measures. **(12 marks)**

62.2 Explain the benefits and problems of NB using benchmarking to evaluate performance, and to improve efficiency, in its call centres. Refer to different types of benchmark and use the data in the Exhibit where relevant. **(11 marks)**

Total: 23 marks

Exhibit – data for the year ended 30 November 20Y4

	UK call centre (UK customers)		Vietnam call centre (French customers)	
	Business	Individuals	Business	Individuals
Number of calls in the year (000s)	120	1,200	90	600
Number of call operators	20	100	12	30
Time to answer a call (minutes)	2	2	1	1.2
Length of call (minutes)	10	4	8	3
Average customer satisfaction score	3.9	4.1	3.1	3.3

63 Rocket Co

The date is March 20Y5.

Rocket Co (Rocket) is an accountancy practice with four partners. It operates from a single office in a European country that is not part of the EU and whose currency is the franc.

Information about Rocket

Rocket employs 17 professional staff, both qualified and part-qualified accountants, and five support staff. It specialises in accounting and tax advisory work in the sports and leisure sector. Rocket's clients are typically wealthy self-employed sportsmen and sportswomen. It competes with a number of big regional and national accountancy practices which service sports and leisure clients as part of a more general client portfolio.

Rocket has experienced impressive growth rates but the partners are concerned that growth appears to be slowing. An extract from Rocket's balanced scorecard for the years ended 31 December 20Y3 and 20Y4 is provided in the **Exhibit**, showing both financial and non-financial information. The partners' financial returns in 20Y4 were affected by a number of factors, including a fall in billable hours, a rent review and increased professional indemnity insurance (PII) premiums. Most significantly, Rocket had to pay higher salaries to its employees. Professional staff working on sports and leisure clients normally command a premium of around 10% on market salaries. During the recent economic recession, Rocket had been paying its 17 professional staff just below the market rates for general accountancy staff. This was accepted by staff while they had few other employment options available, however the market is now improving and external job opportunities are growing. As a result, during 20Y4, Rocket was forced to give professional staff a substantial pay rise.

Change in strategy: creation of a multi-disciplinary practice

A new regulatory framework for the legal services market was recently introduced in Rocket's country, to increase competition and encourage efficiency. This removed the previous restrictions on lawyers forming partnerships with other professions and created a new type of professional services firm, known as a multi-disciplinary practice (MDP). An MDP is a professional firm consisting of professionally qualified lawyers and accountants working together in client-facing roles. To operate as an MDP, a licence is required from the newly-created regulatory authority which is responsible for monitoring quality and compliance.

In February 20Y5, Rocket's four partners decided to take steps to become an MDP. Clients in the sports and leisure sector often need more than one professional service to deal with matters such as contract negotiations, sponsorship deals and personal injury claims. Rocket's intention is to capitalise on this by offering legal, tax and accounting advice to its existing clients. This should also allow it to attract new clients. Typically both legal and accounting firms face high fixed costs for salaries, premises and PII. The synergies involved in becoming an MDP will allow Rocket to provide a greater volume of client services more efficiently and cost-effectively, thereby increasing both revenue and margins.

Rocket estimates it initially needs six fully-qualified lawyers, with a view to increasing this to a team of ten once demand is established. Two possible ways of resourcing the change to an MDP are being considered:

(1) Recruit qualified lawyers on an individual basis

(2) Acquire a specialist team of qualified lawyers from a law firm to which Rocket has previously referred work

Announcement of the change in strategy

On 1 March 20Y5, Rocket issued the following email to its professional staff and support staff, in order to announce the firm's change of strategy and to set out the partners' expectations. There had been no prior consultation with the recipients of the email and it has caused considerable anxiety among all staff.

CONFIDENTIAL EMAIL

To: allstaff@Rocket.com
From: Rocket partners
Date: 1 March 20Y5

Re: New business structure and strategy

The partners have decided to take advantage of recent changes in legislation so, with effect from 1 June 20Y5, Rocket will become a multi-disciplinary practice (MDP) offering both legal and accounting/tax services. As you are aware, our high-profile sporting clients frequently also need legal services and this change in strategy will allow us to attract a greater share of their expenditure on professional advice, and to improve our competitive position. We are in the process of recruiting the necessary qualified lawyers.

We will be spending heavily on marketing the new services and to fund this over the next month we will be examining the potential for cost savings and efficiencies across the firm. This may have some impact on our staffing and management structure.

We estimate that 75% of a fully-qualified staff member's total workload is dependent on having completed their professional qualification. The remaining workload could be carried out by a combination of part-qualified professional staff and support staff. Therefore, we require all fully-qualified staff to identify immediately which parts of their work they can begin to pass on to other staff. This will result in financial benefits to clients as we can reduce certain fees, and it will allow our fully-qualified staff to focus on more value-added advisory work, which will enhance revenues.

From 1 June 20Y5, each client will be serviced by a multi-disciplinary account management team headed up by a partner, with at least one qualified lawyer and one fully-qualified accountant. There will be a single central support team providing administrative assistance to both legal and accounting/tax professional staff, so that clients receive a co-ordinated service. We need to improve the productivity of our support function with a view to maintaining a ratio of one member of support staff for every six professional staff (including partners).We expect all staff to be as co-operative as possible and ask you to do everything you can to make our new legal colleagues welcome. Please give them open access to your clients and all relevant client information.

Ethical issue

Alina Jay, an ICAEW Chartered Accountant with Rocket, has recently been involved in preparing a statement of personal assets and liabilities for a long-standing client of the firm, who is currently seeking loan finance. The final statement which was submitted to the client's bank was very different from the initial draft which Alina prepared and submitted to her manager at Rocket. She suspects that the Rocket manager, who is a personal friend of the client, may have agreed to a misstatement of the client's personal affairs. Alina is unsure whether she should report the client and/or the manager to her superiors, and is concerned about the impact on her job and career if she were to do so.

Requirements

63.1 Using the balanced scorecard in the Exhibit and the other information available, analyse and evaluate the performance of Rocket between 20Y3 and 20Y4. **(18 marks)**

63.2 Analyse the impact of the following factors that may influence Rocket's ability to create a multi-disciplinary practice:

- Human resource capabilities
- Legal and regulatory issues
- Competitors and market structure. **(10 marks)**

63.3 In relation to the email announcing Rocket's proposed change in strategy, discuss the extent to which Rocket's approach meets best practice in change management. Refer to an appropriate change model such as Gemini 4Rs. **(10 marks)**

63.4 Discuss the ethical issues associated with Alina's concerns and advise her on appropriate actions to take. **(8 marks)**

Total: 46 marks

Exhibit: Extract from Balanced Scorecard for Rocket

	Year ended 31 December	
	20Y4	*20Y3*
Financial		
Note: all monetary amounts are expressed in francs (F)		
Total fee income (F'000)	7,091	6,653
Growth in fee income	+6.6%	+9.2%
Mix of fee income - Accounting:Tax	47:53	45:55
Average fee charged per billable hour (F):		
Accounting services	335	300
Taxation services	415	360
Fee income per partner (F'000)	1,773	1,663
Net profit as a % of fee income	20.8%	23.1%
Clients		
Market share (sports and leisure sector)	12%	14%
% of satisfied clients (based on annual survey)	75%	85%
Innovation and learning		
Average training hours per qualified employee	14	14
Total staff turnover	23.5%	17.6%
Internal business processes		
Error rates (% of client assignments undertaken where mistakes by rocket employees are detected)	10%	8%
Utilisation rate (% of total professional staff hours spent on chargeable client work)	70.5%	66.5%
Staff ratio:		
Number of support staff: number of professional staff and partners	5:21	5:21

64 The Scottish Woodlands Commission

The Scottish Woodlands Commission (SWC) is a government department. It is responsible for all state-owned forests in Scotland.

SWC's mission and activities

SWC's mission is to 'manage, protect and expand the public woodlands in Scotland and to increase their value to society and the environment'. It is authorised to carry out woodland management, nature conservation and the provision of facilities for public recreation.

Woodland management requires a long-term planning process, typically involving a timescale of more than 20 years. Activities include:

- Maintenance of existing trees and removal of deadwood

- Felling of trees and extraction of timber

- Planting of new trees

- Identification and management of threats to woodland (eg, fire, pests, disease, impact of wildlife, soil erosion)

In addition to woodland management, SWC's secondary aims are:

- to protect and maintain habitats for wildlife and to manage wildlife populations

- to provide the general public with widespread access to the natural woodland environment and to promote the woodlands as a location for sports and leisure activities

SWC is governed by a board of trustees whose role is to make strategic decisions, monitor performance and liaise with stakeholders including the general public and other government departments. SWC is allocated a share of central government funds annually, but it is prohibited from borrowing money in its own right. Money is spent on replanting, making grants to private organisations and individuals engaged in woodland creation and improvement, providing education, and research. SWC is able to generate some revenue from the harvesting and sale of timber for use in house-building, paper, fencing and bio-fuels.

Holiday village

SWC has been approached by CabinCo Ltd (CabinCo), a private company, which operates a number of up-market, self-catering holiday villages in England and Wales. CabinCo has a database of around 400,000 customers. Its mission is 'to be one of the UK's leading providers of luxury short-breaks in natural surroundings'. CabinCo has been highly successful because of the high occupancy rates it achieves in its holiday villages. It wants to take advantage of the rapid growth in the short-break market (holidays of 3-5 days) and the increased demand for 'sustainable tourism' to create a new, high-quality holiday village in Campbell Forest, one of SWC's woodlands in Scotland. Customers will be able to rent a luxury self-catering log cabin and participate in a variety of activities in woodland surroundings. Due to Campbell Forest's location, on the edge of a lake surrounded by mountains, it is envisaged that there will be demand all year round and cabins will be available 365 days a year.

Structure of venture

A limited liability public/private partnership will be set up specifically for the new venture. The LLP will have two members: CabinCo and SWC. CabinCo will provide capital in the form of £2 million cash for building the cabins and developing the site, and will provide holiday management experience.

SWC will make its capital contribution by making available Campbell Forest (current market value £2 million) for use in the venture. It will also provide expertise in woodland management and woodland activities. The LLP will be operated as a commercial venture, with the members sharing profits and losses equally. The new venture will be known as Woodsaway LLP (Woodsaway). CabinCo and SWC will each be entitled to appoint three representatives on Woodsaway's senior management committee.

Campbell Forest will continue to be owned by SWC, which will grant a long lease to Woodsaway in exchange for an annual rent of £30,000. Woodsaway will have day-to-day management responsibility for operating the holiday village and the surrounding woodland. The village will consist of 100 high-quality two bedroom log cabins, built to a unique, eco-friendly design. Construction of the village will take approximately 12 months at an expected cost of £2 million, to be funded by CabinCo's contribution to the LLP.

The government has granted preliminary approval for creation of the public/private partnership, as it believes this is the most appropriate format for the management of risk and the exploitation of benefits from the village. The financial projections for Woodsaway make it clear that cabin occupancy levels will be critical to the venture breaking even:

Cabin occupancy	40%	65%	90%
	£'000	£'000	£'000
Cabin revenue	1,752	2,847	3,942
Variable costs	(526)	(854)	(1,183)
Contribution	1,226	1,993	2,759
Fixed costs	(1,502)	(1,727)	(1,985)
Rent to SWC	(30)	(30)	(30)
Operating (loss)/profit	(306)	236	744

If the initial venture proves successful then the concept may be expanded to other SWC woodland locations and Woodsaway will be given first right of access for the development of any new holiday villages in these locations.

Governance

At a meeting of SWC's trustees, one trustee expressed concern: 'Given SWC is a public sector body and we have a responsibility as trustees to deliver public benefit, by demonstrating selflessness and objectivity among other things, won't our involvement in Woodsaway give rise to possible corporate governance issues?'

Another trustee disagreed: 'Surely corporate governance isn't relevant. As the term *corporate* suggests, it is a matter for companies and their directors only, not a public sector body like SWC'.

Requirements

You are a strategic business adviser engaged by the government. Write a report for SWC's trustees, evaluating the proposed venture using the following headings:

64.1 Strategic fit	**(9 marks)**
64.2 Financial benefits	**(10 marks)**
64.3 Risks	**(7 marks)**
64.4 Governance issues.	**(8 marks)**

Total: 34 marks

65 WeDive Ltd

WeDive Ltd (WeDive) is a company which produces and sells high-performance drysuits for divers. It was set up some years ago, by a group of friends, after they experienced severe discomfort whilst scuba diving in cold waters because of leaks in their hired drysuits, which are supposed to work by keeping water out. The friends sourced a single supplier that was able to provide a special thermal fabric and designed a very tight-fitting durable suit with a unique neck seal, to offer maximum protection.

WeDive's drysuits are very expensive (up to £2,000 each) and are typically bought by professional divers (police, armed forces, oil companies, rescue organisations and salvage businesses). To achieve optimum fit the company produces a wide range of different sizes for both men and women. Each drysuit has a three year warranty and any repairs are undertaken at WeDive's production facility, located in the UK.

WeDive has grown successfully. It now has a number of major contracts with professional divers, but also distributes its drysuits to diving retailers for recreational users who want a high quality product. Total sales last year were approximately £13 million, comprising 65% professional divers and 35% recreational users. All sales were in the UK.

Drysuit production is very labour intensive. The market for recreational drysuits is dominated by several large manufacturers in China and South East Asia which benefit from economies of scale, although there are a significant number of smaller producers, like WeDive, which sell in niche markets.

WeDive's directors are keen to expand the business and are considering the following two mutually exclusive strategies:

Option 1: Expand the range of products for the UK market

WeDive would source supplies of lifestyle clothing (t-shirts, jackets and accessories) and sell them under its own brand. The products would be aimed at consumers in the UK market and distributed and sold through existing channels (diving retailers). This option would require marketing but, because of limited funds, WeDive primarily intends to use social media.

Option 2: Produce drysuits for export markets

Entering export markets would involve finding and partnering with new distributors, which WeDive hopes would promote the product on its behalf. A key aspect of WeDive's high-performance drysuit is the fit, so the product may need some redesigning or additional tailoring depending on the height and weight of the local population in each export market.

If Option 2 is pursued, a possible key market is New Zealand. If WeDive enters this market, there is a 90% chance that New Zealand market conditions will be favourable and it will generate a profit of £300,000. However, if market conditions are unfavourable, a loss of £100,000 is expected. Alternatively WeDive could delay its decision until it has undertaken market research, at a cost of £15,000, which would accurately predict the expected market conditions in New Zealand.

Requirements

65.1 So far as the information permits, evaluate the two strategic options being considered by WeDive's directors. Refer to models where appropriate. Ignore the specific information about the New Zealand market for this requirement. **(14 marks)**

65.2 Using a decision tree, calculate whether it would be worth WeDive paying for market research on the New Zealand market. Discuss your findings. **(6 marks)**

Total: 20 marks

66 Reyel plc

Reyel plc (Reyel) is an international company which owns and operates mid-market hotels.

On 31 March 20Y4 a new division, 'The Extended Stay Hotel Division' (the ESH Division), was set up so Reyel could enter the extended stay hotel market.

The extended stay hotel market

Hotels in this market target customers who wish to stay in a hotel for at least eight consecutive nights. Whilst customers can stay for as little as one night, the high prices charged for short stays discourage this.

The extended stay hotel market has two segments, business and private:

- Customers in the business segment include: project managers; professionals working on assignments; staff on short-term secondments; and contract workers.

- Customers in the private segment include individuals who are in the process of relocation, while looking for more permanent accommodation, or who have had to evacuate their houses due, for example, to floods or fire.

The business segment typically represents a higher proportion of total revenue than is the case for traditional hotels.

In order to meet the needs of the extended stay market, the guestrooms are larger than in traditional hotels and include living space with a kitchen as well as a bedroom. When averaged across the duration of the stay, the price per night is typically cheaper than traditional hotels, but the costs incurred are lower as the number of room change-overs (ie when one guest leaves and another arrives) is greatly reduced, and guestrooms are cleaned weekly on average, rather than daily. Occupancy is also typically higher than for traditional hotels.

The extended stay hotel market is well developed in the US, but it does not represent a significant proportion of the European hotel market, although it is growing.

The ESH Division

The ESH Division's business model is designed to: appeal to a different type of customer than Reyel's traditional hotels; exploit cost advantages; and strengthen the wider company brand in the business market segment.

The Clarre

In order to test the business model, the ESH Division commenced trading on 1 April 20Y4 with one hotel, called The Clarre, which is located in London. It has large guestrooms, each including a living area and a kitchen, but it does not have a restaurant or bar as there are many in the local area which guests can use. The hotel offers good quality rooms, but provides a limited range of services to guests. Each guestroom is identical.

The performance of The Clarre has been closely monitored and assessed each quarter. Sales appear to have been seasonal, with the quarters ending 30 September and 31 December being the periods of highest demand. Within each quarter, there is variation in demand where occupancy in some weeks is 100% (ie all guestrooms are full) and customers have to be turned away. There are fewer fluctuations in demand between days of the week than is the case with traditional hotels due to the longer duration of each guest's stay.

Kevin Kloster, the manager of The Clarre, has expressed concern over managing capacity and pricing:

- Managing capacity is a short-term concern involving coping with weekly and monthly fluctuations in demand. It is also a long-term concern in terms of being able to meet trends in demand over time.

- Pricing is complex with different standard prices at different times of the year. There is also a range of discounts available on the standard prices according to type of customer (business or private), length of stay and frequency of visits. Kevin also has discretion to offer a discount to achieve a booking when negotiating with customers.

The Zoy – a comparison

Performance measures monitored by the Reyel board include internal benchmarking in comparing The Clarre with a traditional hotel, called The Zoy, which is also owned by Reyel and is located nearby in the same area of London. The Zoy is a long-established traditional hotel, in a building the same size as The Clarre, but it has a restaurant and a bar which generate additional revenue. The Zoy's guestrooms are much smaller than The Clarre's, but there are more of them. Guestrooms are cleaned daily at The Zoy, but usually only weekly at The Clarre.

Quarterly financial and operating data is provided for The Clarre. Annual data is provided for The Zoy (**Exhibit**).

Concerns of The Zoy's manager

At a Reyel internal meeting, the manager of The Zoy expressed some concerns: 'Reyel should not be entering the extended stay hotel market. Our business is in traditional hotels and there will be customer confusion. Also, the cheaper prices for extended stays will damage the Reyel brand name. In the year ended 31 March 20Y5, revenues from The Zoy were 10% lower than the previous year and I think this is due to the opening of The Clarre in the same area of London, less than two kilometres away. I also believe Kevin Kloster is undercutting us on price and we just cannot compete as we need to offer a much wider range of services, which increases our costs.

'When we look at the performance of The Clarre we should look from a company-wide perspective and consider lost sales for other group hotels, not just the sales The Clarre is recording.'

An ethical problem

Most business customers in the extended stay hotel market are individuals who choose which hotel to stay in, then recharge the cost to their employers. To induce some of The Clarre's regular business customers to agree to pay a premium over the standard price for a guestroom, at their employer's expense, Kevin has been giving these individuals Reyel discount vouchers for private holidays with their families at Reyel hotels.

Requirements

66.1 Using the data in the Exhibit and the other information provided:

    (a) Analyse the performance of The Clarre for each of the four quarters to 31 March 20Y5. Briefly identify additional information that would help provide a more comprehensive assessment of performance.

    (b) Compare the performance of The Clarre and The Zoy for the year ended 31 March 20Y5.

                                                          (18 marks)

66.2 Explain, for the year ending 31 March 20Y6, the factors that the manager of The Clarre should consider in respect of:

    • Capacity management; and
    • Pricing.   **(10 marks)**

66.3 Explain how the Reyel management could estimate the loss in revenue of The Zoy for the year ended 31 March 20Y5 arising from the opening of The Clarre. **(7 marks)**

66.4 Discuss the ethical issues arising from the inducements given to individual business customers and advise on the actions that Reyel should take. **(7 marks)**

                                                                Total: 42 marks

Exhibit – Financial and operating data

Management accounts for the year ended 31 March 20Y5

	The Clarre					The Zoy
	Q1 £'000	Q2 £'000	Q3 £'000	Q4 £'000	Year ending 31 March 20Y5 £'000	Year ending 31 March 20Y5 £'000
Guestroom revenues	1,058	1,279	1,280	1,028	4,645	6,264
Other revenues	-	-	-	-	-	1,200
Operating costs	(864)	(920)	(920)	(857)	(3,561)	(6,106)
Operating profit	194	359	360	171	1,084	1,358

Operating data for the year ended 31 March 20Y5

	The Clarre					The Zoy
	Q1	Q2	Q3	Q4	Year ending 31 March 20Y5	Year ending 31 March 20Y5
Occupancy	72%	80%	78%	70%	75%	58%
Average guestroom price per night	£68.0	£74.0	£76.0	£68.0	£71.7	£100
Average length of stay (nights)	14	15	18	13	15	3

Notes

1   Both The Clarre and The Zoy are open for 90 days each quarter.

2   The Clarre has 240 guestrooms and The Zoy has 300 guestrooms.

3   Occupancy refers to the average number of nights that guestrooms are occupied as a percentage of the total available guestrooms.

4   'Other revenues' comprise restaurant and bar sales.

5   Quarterly accounting periods are as follows:

- **Q1** is the quarter ended 30 June 20Y4
- **Q2** is the quarter ended 30 September 20Y4
- **Q3** is the quarter ended 31 December 20Y4
- **Q4** is the quarter ended 31 March 20Y5

67   Home of Leather plc

The date is June 20Y5.

Home of Leather plc (HoL) is a company which manufactures good quality leather furniture. The company is located in the small town of Puddington in the South of England, where its site is comprised of a factory, distribution centre and office.

Company background

HoL was established many years ago and has been important to the Puddington economy throughout its existence. Most of the employees, who are mainly skilled workers, live in or around Puddington. Many of the suppliers, including suppliers of leather, are also from the local area. HoL is Puddington's largest employer.

Over the past 15 years, the reputation of HoL's products has grown. Its furniture is now sold throughout Europe, although 70% of sales are still in the UK market.

However, revenue growth has slowed in recent years. There has been increasing competition in the UK and European markets from overseas suppliers producing good quality leather furniture. These suppliers incur lower property and labour costs than HoL, and can therefore charge lower prices. The HoL board fears that sales could start to decline unless costs can be reduced to enable more competitive pricing.

A particular concern is that half of the UK sales come from a single customer, Grint plc (Grint), under a long-term contract. The contract is due for renewal on 31 December 20Y6 and the Grint board has already stated that the contract will be put out to tender. Grint's expectation is that prices will need to be reduced from their current average of £400 per unit to, at most, £360 per unit.

Strategic choices

The HoL board has decided that a fundamental change needs to be made in the next six months in order for HoL to continue to compete in the market. It has not yet made any announcement to the employees (including managers), but three alternative strategies have been proposed to reduce costs.

The board has set a target annual profit of £7.2 million, to be achieved irrespective of which strategy is selected.

Strategy 1 – Relocate within the UK

Close the whole Puddington site and relocate all operations to a larger site in the UK about 150 kilometres away. Most, but not all, employees would be offered continuing employment at the new site, but only about 40% of existing employees are expected to agree to relocate and carry on working for HoL at the new site. The new factory would have more automated production processes than the old factory and many of the working practices of skilled employees would need to change, along with the managerial reporting structure. The employees who do not relocate would be made redundant. HoL would continue to use most, but not all, of its existing suppliers.

Strategy 2 – Relocate manufacturing overseas

Close the factory in Puddington and relocate manufacturing to a larger factory in a lower cost, developing nation in South America. This would involve making 96% of existing employees redundant. The remaining 4% would continue to be employed in the existing distribution centre in Puddington, with senior managers operating from the Puddington office.

Strategy 3 – Cease manufacturing and import

Close the factory in Puddington and import furniture from overseas suppliers, thereby making HoL a wholesaler. Most employees would be made redundant. Only 4% of existing employees would be retained, operating from the Puddington distribution centre and Puddington office, as in Strategy 2.

Pricing

The quality of the output under Strategy 1 will be higher than under the other two strategies. As a result, the selling price for Strategy 2 and Strategy 3 will be about 90% of the selling price for Strategy 1. However, the sales volumes will be the same under all three strategies.

Estimated data is provided for costs and revenues for each of the three strategies (**Exhibit**).

Requirements

The board of HoL has asked you, as a business advisor, to prepare a report for it as follows:

67.1 Calculate each of the following, using the information in the Exhibit, for **each** of the three proposed strategies:

    (a)   The break-even selling price
    (b)   The volume of sales which would achieve an annual profit of £7.2 million   **(9 marks)**

67.2 Evaluate **each** of the three proposed strategies. Refer to your calculations in (a) above and make any further appropriate calculations. Ignore change management issues.   **(10 marks)**

67.3 For Strategy 1 **only**, explain power-interest using Mendelow's matrix for each of the following stakeholders:

    •   Existing employees
    •   Grint   **(7 marks)**

67.4 Identify and compare the change management issues for Strategy 1 and Strategy 2.   **(8 marks)**

                                          Total: 34 marks

Exhibit – Estimated data on costs and revenues

	Strategy 1	Strategy 2	Strategy 3
Expected sales volume	120,000 units	120,000 units	120,000 units
Average price per unit	£360	£324	£324
Average variable cost per unit	£200	£160	£280
Annual fixed costs	£14.4 million	£10.8 million	£1.8 million

68   Zuccini plc

The date is June 20Y5.

Zuccini plc (Zuccini) is a listed company manufacturing motorbikes, which it sells mainly in European Union (EU) countries.

The motorbike industry

Motorbike technology is constantly changing. As a result, research and development (R&D) is a key feature of product improvement and replacement. The industry is very competitive and implementing the latest technology can be important in gaining competitive advantage. However, as technology changes rapidly, any such advantage is difficult to sustain.

There were 1.2 million new motorbikes sold in the EU last year. Many of the most popular motorbikes sold in the EU are manufactured in Japan by multinational companies, which also make cars and other automotive products. There are also several smaller niche motorbike manufacturers located throughout Europe, such as Zuccini.

Company background

Zuccini is a relatively small company in the global motorbike industry. Currently it has an annual sales volume of 4,800 motorbikes. It has an R&D centre in Italy and two factories, one in Italy and one in the UK. The head office is in the UK.

The existing models

Zuccini currently manufactures two models of motorbike: the Typhoon4, a mid-market to upmarket motorbike; and the StormRaider, an upmarket motorbike.

The StormRaider is manufactured at the UK factory and was launched in 20Y3. Its launch was successful and monthly sales are continuing to increase. It is estimated to have a product life cycle of six years before it needs replacing in 20Y9.

The Typhoon4 is made at the factory in Italy. It is reaching the end of its product life cycle and sales have been gradually falling in recent months. The Zuccini board has not yet decided whether to:

(1)   Replace the Typhoon4 with a completely new model, the Typhoon5; or

(2)   Modify the Typhoon4 to produce a slightly updated version, the Typhoon4A, then replace the Typhoon4A with the Typhoon 5 two years later (ie in 20Y7 if the Typhoon4 were to be modified as the Typhoon4A immediately).

New capital investment will be needed for either alternative. The Typhoon5 would be a much more significant change than the Typhoon4A, although either of these alternatives could be implemented without much delay, once a decision is made. The board has not yet decided how long to carry on manufacturing the Typhoon4, but the timing of any change is under active consideration.

A new model under development
Another model of motorbike, 'the Hurricane', is currently in its R&D phase, but technical difficulties have caused delays and some uncertainties. It could be brought to market in June 20Y6 as a basic product selling at £6,000 or, with a further two years' development, it could be brought to market in June 20Y8 as a mid-market product selling at £9,000. The life cycle would be seven years from launch for the basic version of the product, as it is less susceptible to new technology developments and would sell on the basis of price rather than features. The life cycle would be six years from launch for the mid-market version. No estimate of production costs or volumes for either of these alternatives can yet be made.

Liquidity issues

Liquidity has started to become a concern for Zuccini. There is no immediate crisis, but cash flow projections indicate that further financing will be needed by 20Y7, unless sales improve.

Requirements

68.1 Referring to appropriate models, provide reasoned advice to the Zuccini board to help it decide:

- When production of the Typhoon4 should be ended; and

- Whether to replace the Typhoon4 with the new Typhoon5, or to modify it, initially, as the Typhoon4A. **(12 marks)**

68.2 Explain the strategic, operational and financial factors which would determine whether the Hurricane should be launched:

- In June 20Y6 as a basic product; or
- In June 20Y8 as a mid-market product. **(12 marks)**

Total: 24 marks

69   Kentish Fruit Farms

Kentish Fruit Farms (KFF) is a UK organic fruit farm that is owned and run by the Fielding family. KFF grows apples and produces apple juice, both of which it sells at local markets and to retailers.

UK organic farming and food industry

Organic food must be produced using environmentally-friendly farming methods, so no genetically modified (GM) crops, growth enhancers, or artificial pesticides and fertilisers may be used. Any farmer claiming to be organic must be certified by a government-approved body, such as the UK Soil Association. Food producers must also comply with Food Standards Agency regulations regarding the production, packaging and labelling of food.

Regulatory bodies can impose sanctions for breaching regulations. They can:

- Forbid the use of misleading labels and product descriptions
- Issue fines for inappropriate production
- Close down operations
- Seek punishment of those responsible for wrongful operations

Consumers increasingly want food that is healthy and is sourced both ethically and locally. Consequently, although initially perceived as a luxury niche product, organic food is now seen as a lifestyle choice by those consumers who regard non-organic products as more harmful to health and the environment. Major supermarkets have started to stock more organic and locally grown food.

A key issue for all farmers is the weather, which significantly affects the volume (yield) and quality of a crop and hence the market price. Organic farmers are unable to use artificial fertilisers or pesticides, so have developed alternative high-tech farming methods to improve profitability and cash flow. Weather information systems help plan planting, harvesting and irrigation. Climate-controlled growing tunnels and stores provide a pest-free environment with temperature, light and humidity control. These methods increase yields, extend the possible growing season and allow crops to be stored for longer before usage or sale, with no loss of flavour or quality.

KFF operations

KFF's profitability depends on crop yields and fruit quality, and its ability to use or sell all of the apple harvest. It is also affected by the overall level of supply in the market in any given year. KFF has a weather information system and uses climate-controlled technology.

The best of KFF's apples, which conform to retailers' specifications in relation to size, shape and quality, are sold to retailers as fresh fruit. Apples that do not meet retailers' specifications are either sold at local markets or used to produce KFF own-brand organic pressed apple juice in one-litre bottles. The juice is sold at local markets and has proved very popular so it is now also being stocked by retailers.

KFF's harvest normally begins in early summer and ends in late autumn. The production of juice follows on from the harvest cycle and, because of KFF's ability to store fruit, continues after the harvest has ended. KFF has a permanent labour force for its growing, production and bottling operations and additional seasonal workers are employed for harvesting and packing the fruit.

KFF uses its own vans to transport goods to the local markets. Distribution of products to the retailers, most of which are within 80 kilometres of the farm, is outsourced.

New strategies affecting the 20Y4 results

Demand for KFF's apples and juices in year ended 31 December 20Y3 exceeded KFF's production capacity. In 20Y4, capacity increased as a result of implementing the following strategies:

Strategy 1: KFF had acquired 15 hectares of land from a neighbouring farmer in 20Y0. The land was then intensively planted with apple trees of a modern variety which were expected to produce yields 30% higher than existing varieties. The first apple crop from these new trees was harvested in 20Y4. KFF's existing trees continued to give the same yield as in 20Y3, at the same cost per hectare.

Strategy 2: In 20Y4 KFF started to buy apples from other local farmers to use in its organic juices.

KFF's board set medium-term business objectives at the start of 20Y4. These were to:

- Achieve average annual revenue growth of 15%
- Increase gross profit margin to 45%

Financial and operating data for 20Y3 and 20Y4 is available **(Exhibits 1 and 2)**. The current management information system does not separately analyse cost of sales between the fresh fruit and juice operations.

Supply chain problem

In August 20Y5, a batch of KFF's organic apple juice was tested by the Food Standards Agency and found to contain artificial pesticides. The juice was made in a large production run using fruit from one of KFF's new suppliers. 20% of this production run has already been distributed to a major retailer which has just started to sell KFF organic juice. KFF is considering whether to issue a public recall of these bottles.

KFF's marketing manager, Joe Fielding, thinks this could be disastrous for KFF's reputation locally and has suggested that they do nothing in relation to the bottles that have already been distributed, but re-label and sell the remainder as non-organic. 'The thing that most concerns me,' said Joe, 'is why we didn't identify this as a problem earlier?'

Requirements

69.1 Identify and analyse the **three** key factors from the PESTEL model which are most relevant to the UK organic fruit industry. **(9 marks)**

69.2 Using the data in the Exhibits and the other information provided, evaluate the impact that KFF's two new strategies had on its performance in 20Y4. Identify any specific information that you require to explain more fully the effect of each strategy. **(18 marks)**

69.3 Discuss the ethical issues for KFF arising from the supply chain problem, and advise KFF on appropriate actions. **(8 marks)**

69.4 Explain how control procedures could be used by KFF to identify and prevent quality problems with suppliers. You should give specific examples of information that could be used to measure and monitor supplier performance. **(8 marks)**

Total: 43 marks

Exhibit 1: Financial data for KFF

Extract from income statement for the years ended 31 December

	20Y3 £'000	20Y4 £'000	% change
Revenue			
Fresh fruit	576	889	54.3
Juice	336	525	56.3
Total revenue	912	1,414	55.0
Cost of sales	(540)	(812)	50.4
Gross profit	372	602	61.8
Other operating costs	(259)	(456)	76.1
Operating profit	113	146	29.2
Interest paid	(53)	(74)	39.6
Profit before tax	60	72	20.0

Exhibit 2: Operating data for the years ended 31 December

	20Y3	20Y4
Hectares of KFF trees yielding fruit	40	55
Tonnes of KFF apples sold as fresh fruit	288	468
Tonnes of KFF apples used for juice production	192	252
Total tonnes of KFF apples harvested	480	720
Tonnes of apples purchased from local farmers for juice	-	48
Number of one-litre bottles of juice produced and sold	96,000	150,000

70 Premier Paper Products plc

The date is September 20Y5.

Premier Paper Products plc (PPP) prints banknotes and identity documents for a variety of central banks and governments. It operates three divisions: Banknotes, Cash Processing and Identity Systems.

Company background

PPP started over one hundred years ago with a contract to produce paper banknotes for its own country. Its reputation for high quality, elegant designs and innovative security features has made it a market leader - PPP now prints paper banknotes for over 100 countries, mainly in Europe and Asia.

To capitalise on its customer base, 60 years ago PPP started to produce banknote counting and sorting machines and banknote inspection equipment to assist banks in processing cash and detecting forgeries. It then applied its expertise in designing and printing security paper for government identity schemes. In 20X0 PPP won its first contract to print passports and driving licences, for its own government. PPP has continued to invest in the development of sophisticated security solutions. It produces passports and identity cards for 65 countries, including machine-readable e-passports with biometric data incorporated on an electronic chip.

Banknote production

A country's currency is issued by its central bank. The world's largest central banks produce all of their country's banknotes using their own state-owned printing works. However many smaller central banks outsource production to large paper and printing companies which benefit from economies of scale. As a result, PPP and its competitors print 20% of all banknotes worldwide. Since security is a major issue, banknote-printing companies must be certified and the ordering and distribution process is tightly controlled. Normally central banks outsource banknote printing to a single supplier, under a long-term contract, renewable every ten years.

Smaller countries outsource banknote printing for economic and technical reasons. Machines required to print modern currency are expensive and are designed to produce large volumes of notes which may significantly exceed a smaller country's requirement.

Some state-owned printing works attempt to achieve critical mass by producing notes for other countries. Rapid changes in technology make it difficult for a small state-owned printing works to keep up with constantly evolving anti-counterfeiting features.

New technology means that several central banks recently decided to change from using paper banknotes to plastic (polymer) notes. Polymer notes are lighter, cleaner and have more embedded security features to protect against counterfeiting. They are also more environmentally sustainable as on average each polymer note has a life of seven years compared to three years for a paper note.

Future strategic direction: Banknote division

Although PPP remains committed to the production of paper notes, its board is unsure whether the demand for polymer notes merits investing in the new technology.

The private banknote printing sector is dominated by PPP and two other companies, one of which, Uniquel, produces polymer notes. Uniquel's share of the banknote market has increased as 25 countries have recently moved from paper to polymer notes, because costs to the central bank are reduced over the life of the banknote despite high initial costs.

Several of PPP's central bank contracts for paper notes are due to come to an end in 20Y6 and some of the banks concerned are likely to adopt polymer notes. Producing and printing polymer notes would require a more highly skilled workforce and different machinery. To achieve critical mass for both existing and new machinery, PPP would need to find new customers for paper notes whilst persuading some existing customers to switch to polymer.

Extract from Banking trade journal article:

Is there a future for cash?

Society is increasingly moving away from cash to card-based and smartphone/contactless payments systems. Last year only 4.5% of the UK's money existed in the form of physical cash and the average value of a cash transaction was £9.50.

Will polymer bank notes help stop this move to a cashless society?

Polymer notes are waterproof, cleaner, more durable and more environmentally friendly than paper money and this will help them compete with plastic payment cards. Unlike credit cards and contactless payment systems, notes are not subject to identity theft.

In the UK cash is still important for person-to-person transactions and elsewhere around the world, cash prevails. In many emerging economies over 70% of all consumer transactions still take place in cash. Between 20Y5 and 20Y7 banknote volumes are expected to grow in some parts of Africa by up to 50%.

Requirements

70.1 Using relevant strategic models analyse the ways that PPP has expanded its business and identify the critical success factors (CSFs) which have facilitated this growth. **(10 marks)**

70.2 Prepare a risk register, setting out what you consider to be **three** significant business risks facing PPP's Banknote division.

You should present your answer in a three-column format, explaining, for each risk:

- The nature of the risk
- The possible impact of the risk and the likelihood of it occurring
- Risk management strategies **(9 marks)**

70.3 You are the manager of the PPP Banknote division. Prepare a memorandum for the board which explains the issues that should be considered in deciding whether to invest in polymer banknotes technology. **(11 marks)**

Total: 30 marks

71 Taxi Tracker

Taxi Tracker (TT) is a company which is trying to change the taxi market in a major capital city. The market currently consists of council-regulated city taxis (Citicabs) and private-hire vehicles (PHV).

Citicabs operate from taxi ranks and are also able to pick up passengers in the street. The city council controls the number of Citicab licences available and regulates fares. Critics argue that this increases waiting times and imposes high fares on customers. The council also issues licences to drivers of individual private-hire vehicles. PHVs cannot use the taxi ranks or pick up passengers in the street. They must be pre-booked but can charge whatever they like in fares. Some PHV drivers work for themselves, others register with private-hire companies which operate a centralised booking service and take a percentage of each fare charged in exchange for putting the driver in contact with passengers.

TT's business model

TT began operations in 20Y2 when it launched a 'driver for hire' application (app) for smartphones. The customer downloads the TT app for free and registers their personal details and payment card information. They can then see which PHVs are near their location, receive estimates of price and journey time, tap on the desired PHV to book, and track its arrival on their phone. TT fares are calculated according to distance and time, with the customer's phone acting as a meter. At the end of the journey the customer's registered payment card is automatically debited. TT promises to 'have a car with you within five minutes'. It seeks customer feedback on every journey and drivers are required to achieve a minimum average score of 4 out of 5.

TT does not own vehicles or employ drivers. Instead it acts as an intermediary between PHV drivers and customers. Drivers with an existing PHV licence can apply to TT, which carries out a criminal record check, and verifies licence and insurance details. Drivers who pass TT's screening process are then issued with a TT smartphone which allows them to be registered and tracked on the TT system. TT passes 80% of the fare it charges to the driver, retaining 20% as commission to cover costs and margin. TT's main operating costs are technology and marketing.

Since its launch, TT has faced intense opposition from Citicab drivers, who have argued to the city's transport regulators that TT essentially operates an unlicensed city taxi service. To the consumer, TT's service was initially cheaper than a Citicab, but more expensive than a conventional PHV. Due to the ease of booking, cashless payment, and improved customer service compared to both Citicabs and existing PHV, the number of journeys booked through TT grew rapidly.

Dynamic demand-based pricing

As a result of its initial success, in 20Y4 TT switched to a dynamic demand-based pricing model. When demand is high in relation to the number of cars available, the fare goes up in an attempt to balance supply and demand. The higher price encourages more PHV drivers to make themselves available, helping to avoid unfulfilled customer requests. For example, when it is raining, and during peak hours, the average fare typically increases by 50%. There have been some angry responses on social media suggesting this is unfair to TT's customers.

Proposed short-term fare reduction

Recently TT has been made aware of rumours that a rival firm is planning to launch its own taxi booking app in the city. TT is keen to protect its 'first to market' position. In order to generate brand loyalty from existing customers and attract new ones before the rival's launch, TT is considering cutting its fares by 25% for a limited period of four weeks. However it needs to retain the loyalty of its PHV drivers so wants to make sure it minimises the impact on them.

Requirements

71.1 Explain the concept of cost drivers and value drivers and briefly explain **three** key drivers in TT's value chain. **(8 marks)**

71.2 Discuss the benefits of TT's dynamic demand-based pricing model and comment on whether it is unfair to TT's customers. **(8 marks)**

71.3 You have been asked to evaluate for TT the impact of its proposed short-term 25% fare reduction. Assume that currently 130,000 journeys a week are booked through the TT app, at an average fare of £10 per journey.

(a) Calculate the impact on TT's profit for a four-week period if:

- Demand is unaffected by the fare cut, and TT retains 20% commission

- Demand increases by 15% and TT commits to maintaining PHV driver revenue at its current level

(b) Assuming that TT retains 20% commission, calculate the increase in demand that would maintain revenue for both TT and the PHV drivers at the same level as before the fare reduction.

(c) Evaluate the proposed fare reduction strategy in light of your results in both (a) and (b).

(11 marks)

Total: 27 marks

Answer Bank

Guidance on mark plans

Introduction

This guidance has been put together by the examining team. It is possible, over time, as a result of candidates' performance in the real exams, that there may be further developments in the way in which mark plans are constructed. A document such as this can only ever provide broad guidance. The examining team set mark plans for each question on an individual basis, taking account of the overall structure of the question, the scenario, and the complexity of the analysis and argument required.

Marking documents

Business Strategy has one of the highest skills content of all the Professional Stage papers as it leads on to the Technical Integration and Case Study papers. This is reflected in the marking process where the available marks for each requirement are divided into two pools: Knowledge marks (K) and Skills marks (S), with more marks awarded for skills than knowledge.

For any particular exam paper there are three separate marking documents:

- A detailed mark plan for the paper (a full answer, containing all the likely points that candidates may make, as published for students)

- A marking grid which breaks the paper down into the K and S mark pools available for each requirement

- A separate marking guidance document issued to markers, giving an overview of the typical K and S points for each requirement, to be used in conjunction with the detailed mark plan

The marking grid and marking guidance for the December 2014 paper are included in Chapter 1 of the Study Manual.

Knowledge and skills marks

Broadly speaking, the K marks are for demonstration of appropriate and accurate knowledge and understanding from the learning materials, explicit or implied (eg where the answer is developed using recognised models, tools and frameworks, not just common sense).

The S marks are for:

- Assimilating and using information
- Structuring problems and solutions
- Applying judgement
- Conclusions and recommendations
- Communication

For example, if the requirement was to 'analyse the competitive forces within an industry' then K marks would be available for selecting the right model and knowing the meaning of the key headings, in this case that 'competitive forces' suggests Porter's Five Forces model should be applied.

S marks would be gained for example by:

- Applying a model to the context in the question, eg identifying relevant information from the scenario

- Analysing the information, eg identifying causal factors that explain changes in data

- Reasoning and judgement, eg providing reasoned advice relating to the specific terms of the scenario

The marking information set out below is that used to mark the questions

Allocation of marks

Typically it is not possible to allocate a half/one mark per point as it is in the more numerical papers. This type of approach would encourage a scatter-gun approach and reward answers making a long list of minor points, even where they fail to identify and explain the key issues.

Marks are therefore awarded in small pools which attempt to give an assessment of a candidate's performance for each sub-set of a requirement. Markers are encouraged to use discretion and to award partial marks where a point was either not explained fully or made by implications.

It is often the case that the more succinct answers are better, since it is the quality rather than the number of points which attracts marks in Business Strategy.

As a general rule, the mark plan is constructed according to the following principles:

- **Numerical elements**

  Where the requirement includes a specific calculation, the total marks available will be broken down into a series of computations for the components of the calculation. Marks will be awarded for workings and not just for the correct final figure. Additional marks will be available for stating assumptions.

- **Data interpretation/analysis**

  Specific marks for any necessary calculations/numerical analysis will be awarded as for numerical elements above. Also, however, appropriate calculations will need to be identified by the candidate and marks will be awarded for addressing the key issues.

  A greater proportion of the total marks available will be awarded for the following skills:

  - Interpretation of data
  - Considering cause and effect relationships
  - Identifying implications of the analysis
  - And for linking the data analysis to the wider strategy or issue in the scenario

  In these respects 'making the numbers talk' will be a key feature.

  Additional marks will be awarded for highlighting additional information required and/or the limitations of the analysis undertaken, even if not specifically asked for (although this may form part of the requirement).

- **Use of specific theories/models**

  Requirements will generally be open ended and candidates may be expected to identify the appropriate model to use in a particular situation. For example, a requirement to analyse the ways in which the business has grown might be answered by considering Ansoff and Lynch.

  Where a requirement calls for the application of a particular theory or model, there will be a limited number of knowledge marks for identifying the correct model and explaining its use. A greater proportion of the total marks will be awarded for the skills shown in applying the model to the scenario and discussing its limitations in the particular context.

- **Written elements**

  Each component of the requirement will be assigned a 'pool' of marks. An element of the marks in the pool will be available for demonstrating the correct knowledge but the majority will then be awarded to a candidate based on the degree of application, analysis and judgement demonstrated by the answer. Thus it is possible to identify the characteristics of various possible answers, together with their mark scoring potential:

  (a) Generic comments from the learning materials, which are not expressed in the context of the scenario. Answer includes lists of unprioritised, undeveloped and/or irrelevant points. Points listed but not explained.

  This constitutes a poor answer, scoring less than half the marks available in the pool and hence a 'fail' on the particular section of the requirement.

(b) A number of generic comments but with some attempt to apply knowledge to the scenario in the question and to link points together in the form of key issues.

An adequate attempt, scoring a little over half the marks available in the pool normally generating sufficient marks to attain a marginal pass.

(c) Succinct points, made in the context of the question with little irrelevant comment. Some insights demonstrated. Logical argument backed up by analysis of the data/scenario. Demonstrates judgement by providing clear recommendations or advice where required by the question.

A high scoring answer which would be awarded the majority of marks available in the pool (in some cases the maximum) and achieve a clear pass.

Presentation marks and workings

Generally, where specifically requested in the requirement, one knowledge mark would be awarded for presentation of a report/memo/briefing notes in an appropriate format.

Headroom

As can be seen from the sample paper and previous real exam papers, all written questions contain a degree of 'headroom' (ie potentially there are more marks available than the maximum for the requirement), as a range of different answers are possible. For example, the requirement totals, say, 20 marks, but the mark plan contains a total of, say, 25 marks. This means that a candidate could, in fact, score 100% without producing an ideal answer.

The published answers are detailed mark **plans** and are designed to encompass many possible valid comments that a marker may see. As a result they are often more detailed than even a strong candidate would give in his or her answer.

Mark plans in the learning materials

The summary mark plans in the learning materials have been reviewed by the examining team.

However, tutors should bear in mind that the mark plans in the learning materials have not undergone the full development process as those for the real exams where mark plans are tested over a large sample of candidates' answers.

Nonetheless, the above guidance can be illustrated by looking at the past real exam papers included in the question bank.

The mark scheme provided with each solution indicates relative emphasis of the sub-areas of the question.

Note. The marks awarded in the real paper may exceed these where the candidate's answers merit this.

1 DA plc (March 2008)

		Knowledge	Skill	Marks
1.1	Factors creating competitive advantage	2	5	6
1.2	Analysis of strategic development	4	8	10
1.3	PESTEL analysis	2	7	8
1.4	Marketing strategy	2	7	8
1.5	Strategic and operational risks	2	7	8
		12	34	40

1.1 Factors creating competitive advantage

Competitive advantage is anything that gives one organisation an edge over its rivals. Critical success factors (CSFs) are the areas where an organisation must excel if it is to achieve sustainable competitive advantage. DA's critical success factors concern not only the resources of the business but how these can be used to advantage in the competitive environment in which it operates.

Here a key strategic resource is the possession of a licence to operate as a CRA. Complying with the terms of this licence is fundamental to DA's ability to continue in operation. Possession of the licence acts as a barrier to entry and while it does not give DA an advantage over CC Inc, it does protect its market share from new entrants.

DA may gain competitive advantage over CC Inc by virtue of being the only UK-based CRA.

According to the resource-based view of strategy, firms develop competencies and then exploit them. Sustainable competitive advantage is obtained by the exploitation of unique resources. Thus a firm should focus only on products where it has a sustainable competitive advantage and focus on core competences which competitors do not possess or would find it difficult to copy.

A threshold competence for CRAs is compliance with the relevant UK legislation, eg consumers have specific rights in relation to the information CRAs hold about them. Complying with this and other relevant legislation is crucial to DA's business, as it is to the business of competitors. Going beyond mere compliance, eg by extending its free advisory and education services may give DA a competitive advantage over CC Inc.

The key factors that appear to have given rise to DA's competitive advantage would include:

(1) First to market – DA began business a number of years ago and as one of the first to market, and a primary player, it has created a strong reputation and market dominance as a result of this.

(2) Scale – With 58% of the market there are scale economies in search costs and IT costs which would give DA an advantage over its main competitor and any potential entrants.

(3) Information and knowledge systems – DA's core competences are its ability to compile and manage vast quantities of information, giving it 'the most comprehensive credit database in the UK'. It also maintains a large database for the automotive industry.

For competitive advantage DA must have superior skills in Database management:

- Continuous access to a wide variety of information sources to ensure that the consumer profile or vehicle history is complete and accurate

- The ability to integrate vast quantities of information and organise it in a user friendly form

- Maintenance of up-to-date information

(4) Product development skills/Innovation – DA have a core competence in helping businesses reduce risk. Processes for new product development have enabled DA to expand the products and services it offers and the markets it serves, eg the development of the analytical decision business. By making this proprietary software, DA is able to protect their competitive position and prevent copying.

(5) Relationship management skills – DA's experience in personal selling has attracted business customers in the first instance. These customers have been retained through relationship management and by developing additional products to meet their risk management needs. As a result there is significant brand loyalty.

(6) Technical resources – DA's IT systems will be important in delivering an efficient service to customers, where customers will particularly value:

- Speed of processing
- Flexibility of delivery (online, phone etc)
- Confidentiality

(7) Organisation structure – DA has divisionalised by product or brand. This should facilitate communication and decision-making, at the level of the brand and allow a fast response to a rapidly changing market.

As a listed company DA will also have good access to finance.

1.2 Analysis of strategic development

The Ansoff model is a two-by-two matrix of Products (new and existing) and Markets (new and existing).

By relating product opportunities to markets, this mix identifies four broad alternative strategies open to DA.

Market penetration

This involves selling more of existing products to existing markets. This increases the organisation's market share. DA is the largest credit reference agency in the UK market and in this field the company has only one major competitor, CC Inc. As a result each company can only increase market share at the expense of the other, unless they can each persuade businesses to carry out searches with both organisations. To some extent DA's position is protected by the fact that organisations wishing to compile credit information need a licence. As DA is clearly the market leader it could be argued that they have been very successful in achieving market penetration. This has been based on their ability to create and retain successful client relationships and their core skills of database compilation and management.

Product development

This means developing new products for existing markets. As a credit reference business, DA initially focused on financial services businesses as its potential customers. It was then able to expand by developing the technology around its existing product. Knowledge of the specific needs of this market in terms of speed of decision making, reduction of risk etc enabled DA to build and develop a wider range of products relevant to its customers, eg the decision analysis software that E introduced was based on the premise that businesses would value analytical rather than just factual information.

Market development

This strategy takes existing products and finds new markets for them. Having recognised a core competence in database management, DA used this strategy to offer information products to the automotive industry. This market is similar to the financial services market, in that customers value information that assists in reducing the risk associated with decisions.

Diversification

This involves moving away from core activities and developing new products for new markets. Diversification stands apart from the other strategies. It involves the greatest risk of all strategies. It requires new skills, new techniques and different ways of operating.

Having focused on the business-to-business market, DA plans to diversify into the business-to-consumer market with its new product Checksta. While the broad product area is still credit information there are overtones of diversification because it is for individual consumers. This decision recognises that many consumers want to be more in control of their credit status, to be able to monitor their credit report at any time and to protect themselves against identity fraud.

Note. Although the company perception is that Checksta represents a new market, It could be argued that this is product development rather than diversification, since DA already offers the statutory credit report to the consumer market.

Lynch Expansion method matrix

The Lynch model is another two-by-two matrix of company growth (organic growth and external development) and geographical location (home (domestic) and international). Under this model, all of DA's growth appears to have been carried out organically and products/markets have been developed domestically rather than internationally.

DA has been able to grow organically as a result of having been an initial player in the market, allowing it to develop critical mass.

Overseas expansion

It is likely that a large number of existing customers, who value the DA brand, are global businesses. In the same way that CC Inc has expanded into the UK, DA could exploit this brand loyalty and apply its information management skills to Europe or the USA. If it wishes to target overseas markets in the future, then growth by acquisition might be considered as a faster way of getting access to the necessary licences and databases.

1.3 PESTEL analysis

Political

- Only companies that are licensed CRAs can provide credit reference services and access to consumer credit files. DA and CC Inc are the two largest CRAs. Lending organisations and retailers offering trade credit have a choice of organisation with which to do a credit search, and consumers may not know which business their prospective lender will use, thus consumers are likely to want to access their file with each organisation.

- Changes in regulation may restrict DA's freedom of operations, eg regarding pricing or ability to advertise.

- Government may choose to discourage credit, reducing the need for credit checks and hence DA's product.

Economic

- A consumer's willingness to take on credit depends on his or her confidence in their ability to repay the money. This confidence comes in part from job stability and faith in the economy. The relatively low and stable interest rates and stable employment have made consumers more willing to take on credit. While currently favourable, future changes, eg in interest rates, may reverse this trend.

- Consumer spending is often used as an indicator of how well the economy is doing. Credit is a key factor in fuelling an economic boom. Any boom in consumer spending will mean that there is an increase in the number of credit checks lenders make through DA.

- The rejection of credit applications, especially if it is unexpected, may be an opportunity for DA as it is likely to cause individuals to want to access their credit report.

Social

- Changing attitudes to money and credit have meant it is no longer traditional to save up for things. More and more people use credit as a way of buying things they do not have the money for.

- People can apply for credit from almost anywhere: over the Internet, by telephone, in a shop or supermarket, or in response to direct marketing campaigns.

- Consumers are much less loyal to one bank or finance provider and are more likely to shop around and approach several lenders to find the best deal. The above factors mean that individuals are more likely to shop around for credit and lenders have to carry out more credit checks. A desire to obtain credit on the best terms is likely to increase consumers' awareness of their credit history and increase demand for the credit scoring service provided in conjunction with Checksta.

Technological

- The credit industry has made huge technological advances. Financial products and services can now be bought online and e-commerce is now an important part of the global economy.

- The boom in e-commerce will continue to necessitate more frequent and rapid credit checks by businesses and increase the number of consumers who are likely to want real time online access to their credit history.

- DA has already upgraded its IT systems in response to changing technology but will need to ensure that these are kept up to date and that the necessary security systems are in place.

- The increase in identity crime represents a major opportunity for Checksta as individuals become increasingly aware of the possibilities of fraudulent access to their information and identities and will be keen to protect themselves against this.

Environmental

- Not really of major significance, though there could be a reduction in credit if society moves towards consuming less and conserving energy and resources.

- Environmental concerns, such as the desire to go 'paperless' may boost demand for an online product.

Legal

- UK legislation exists which governs how organisations can collect, use and share personal information and giving consumers specific rights in relation to the information CRAs hold about them. Continuing to comply with this and other relevant legislation is crucial to DA's business. DA needs to ensure that its plans for Checksta do not contravene this legislation or the terms of its licence.

- The consumer education programme that DA had to implement as a result of the tightening legislation has given it an opportunity to increase the awareness of its brand name among consumers and also consumer organisations.

In conclusion the environmental analysis would suggest that there is considerable scope for a product such as Checksta and that its planned introduction is well timed.

1.4 Marketing strategy

In the first instance DA should ensure that it has undertaken the appropriate market research. Market research is the systematic gathering, recording and analysing of information about problems relating to marketing of goods and services. Market research will therefore involve gathering information about the 7Ps of marketing (see below).

Target market

To the extent that it has identified customer needs and developed a product accordingly, DA would appear to have undertaken some preliminary market research and used this to identify the segments containing those potential customers that it wants to target.

In DA's case it wants to target a specific type of customer: personal rather than business, with certain behaviour preferences: users of credit and also of the Internet. As a result it will need to take account of people's ages, their gender and socioeconomic grouping in deciding on an appropriate marketing mix.

Checksta is a new UK brand. It is important to develop an image that would be appropriate for the product that is being offered. Having a profile of the most likely customer will help DA to develop a promotional campaign that positions the product in the minds of its potential customers.

Marketing mix

Next, DA needs to develop its marketing strategy using the marketing mix, which is traditionally done using the 4Ps.

Product

Checksta is based on a product that existed already – the consumer credit report. The product has been developed by allowing real time online access and augmented via support for ID fraud.

In this case, the service needs to be considered in terms of the attributes that are likely to generate demand (eg 24-hour availability; convenience of online access; security of information; ability to predict lender's scoring).

Checksta's unique selling points (USPs) are that it allows consumers to see their credit reports online and automatically alerts them to important changes to the information held about them. This helps consumers understand what makes them creditworthy and can help them to manage their credit commitments. If there is a problem, consumers get free phone advice from credit reference specialists.

Price

The price that potential customers are willing to pay could clearly be a specific objective of any market research exercise.

DA needs to consider whether there are any regulations governing the pricing of their service. Presumably the starting point for price is the price of the statutory report = £2.

It then needs to assess the value of real time access to the customer and the value of the other services on offer.

One possibility is to price elements of the package separately eg a basic price for online access, and then extra charges for the additional service elements such as the alert service, credit score and so on.

Some form of monthly membership scheme, with an initial free trial period would encourage new users to consider take up of the service. If they do not think the service is for them, members would then have to remember to cancel their membership, say at the end of the 30-day free trial.

DA could consider price skimming for early adopters or alternatively discounts for those who are quick to sign up, so as to build market share quickly.

Place

Checksta developed because of the growth in e-commerce communications technology. Its 'place' or channel by which it reaches its users is the electronic medium of the Internet – Checksta is an e-commerce product, available online for consumers.

Some of the support services are offered online but also via different channels – the alert service is offered via email or text (mobile phone) and the free phone help-line can presumably be accessed via landline or mobile. Thus in addition to Internet users, DA is also targeting those with mobile phones.

Promotion

As a new venture, the initial impact of advertising and other promotion on price and demand should be considered.

Until recently, DA has worked mainly in the business-to-business (b2b) market. Its expertise is based on personal selling and relationship building. To succeed in the business to consumer (b2c) market, DA will have to use a different promotional mix and needs to develop a range of different promotional strategies.

As a result of the tightening of credit legislation DA has already implemented a consumer education programme and been working with consumer groups. When DA launches its Checksta product in the UK, it should build on this existing awareness of its brand by ensuring that all free advice guides, consumer education programmes and conferences it attends also promote Checksta.

It could produce literature both online and as a paper product informing people of the dangers of identity fraud and explain how a monitoring service like Checksta could help protect them from the effects of this crime.

DA should consider using a public relations agency to help advertise the new online credit report with press releases and a television advertising campaign.

Advertising could be placed in the money/financial review sections of the press and appropriate financial/credit/consumer advice magazines.

DA could sponsor exhibitions such as the Ideal Home Show and events such as Credit Awareness Week 20X7, which its target customers may attend.

As the product is an online one and DA are targeting internet users, web-based advertising would also be appropriate. DA need to ensure there are links to its website from the various money supermarket and personal finance websites. Research should be done to ensure that DA and the Checksta brand appear when a potential customer uses a search engine.

DA could exploit links with other areas of its business, eg advertise the Checksta service to those customers seeking finance for vehicle purchases. Direct mail those people who have previously applied for a statutory credit report and include a leaflet about Checksta with each statutory report.

Note. As DA is a service company, the marketing mix could be extended to consideration of 7 Ps.

People

This refers to anyone that is to have regular interaction with the customer. In this case a lot of the service will be provided automatically and a substantial amount of any interaction will be electronic by text or email. Customers may make personal contact if they use the free advice phone line.

DA needs to ensure that the nature of any communication gives a good impression of the company, that staff have appropriate training on the new product and the flexibility to provide a good service and that staff manning the helpline are informative and suitably concerned and reassuring.

Processes

Accuracy of information, secure access and confidentiality will be key to determining how effective the service is. DA needs to implement standard operational procedures and ensure that staff apply these consistently.

The ease of application for membership and navigation through the website will be important.

There will need to be security systems in place to verify the identity of members both online and by phone.

DA needs to ensure that the IT systems operate efficiently and that there are no significant delays in the provision of the real time information or periods when the website is down.

Physical evidence

This is the evidence that the service has been performed. It may include electronic confirmation of membership, the online report, any alerts. DA could issue a credit card sized Checksta membership card, with membership number and key contact numbers/website addresses.

1.5 IT/IS risks

Strategic Risks	Risk Management
DA will lose competitive advantage if it fails to utilise IT/IS as effectively as CC Inc, particularly given its renewed focus on the UK market.	DA needs to keep up to date with new technology, continuously upgrade systems and ensure continuous advancements in the products/services offered.
	It should undertake regular benchmarking against competitors such as CC Inc.

Strategic Risks	Risk Management
Since all of DA's information management and in particular the Checksta product depends on IT/IS, a breakdown in its operations threatens the business. This could arise from systems failure or natural threats such as fire, flood, electrical storms.	DA should ensure that if major failures or disasters occur, the business will not be completely unable to function. It should implement protection measures to ensure continuity of operations and to minimise the risk of systems failures, eg back-up servers in alternative locations and regular back-ups of data.
The cost of updating and maintaining IT/IS and implementing the necessary security controls and risk management systems may reduce the operating margins that DA has enjoyed to date (currently around 25% on average). This is particularly true if, as a result of CC Inc offering a low cost web-based solution, DA has to reduce the price of its services.	The costs of the necessary systems controls and security measures need to be considered in the light of the benefits that these will bring.
Market dominance may result in DA being criticised for anti-competitive practices or investigated by the Competition Commission.	Care should be taken to ensure DA does not abuse its position and actively lay itself open to criticism.

Operational Risks	Risk Management
Loss of information as a result of corruption of the system by viruses or human error.	Particularly important is protection from viruses and the need for regular back-ups. DA needs to protect data and systems from unauthorised modification, eg via passwords and levels of access/modification authority.
Theft of information or deliberate misuse of data by hackers/employees.	DA must recruit trustworthy employees, and ensure detection and reporting of security-related incidents, eg unauthorised activity. Training is particularly important, with the aim that users are aware of information security threats and concerns and are equipped to comply with the security policy.
Penalties or intervention as a result of non compliance with regulations such as the *Data Protection Act* which could be imposed by courts if data is wrongly used or control procedures are not in place.	DA must put controls in place to ensure it monitors compliance with any relevant legal requirements such as the *Data Protection Act*.

Examiner's comments:

The scenario in this question considers a credit reference agency, DA, which is the UK market leader. DA provides information to financial services organisations and commercial businesses which want to check the credit rating of potential customers. It has developed its business by extending its database management skills to apply to other industries (eg vehicle history for automotive industry) and also by developing analytical software to help clients making lending decisions. DA is now considering a new online credit report service, Checksta, for individuals who are concerned about their credit ratings and also about the possibility of identity fraud.

At 40 marks, this was the longest question on the paper, although the requirements were broken down to help candidates in developing answer headings and assessing mark allocation. This seems to have been of benefit, as question 1 was well attempted, with the highest average score, although some candidates wrote too much, which was then reflected in their scores for questions 2 and 3.

Requirement 1.1 asked candidates to explain the factors that may have contributed to DA's competitive advantage. This was reasonably well answered by most candidates, who were able to extract key information from the scenario to evidence their comments (first to market, scale economies, core competences in database management, information technology and customer relationship management). Only the stronger candidates made reference to the need to outperform the competition, in this case CC Inc. Better candidates also discussed the possession of a licence to operate as a CRA as a barrier to entry for new competitors.

Requirement 1.2 requested an analysis of the ways in which DA had chosen to expand its business, using relevant strategic models. Answers to this part of the question were variable. A number of candidates simply repeated the information in the question about the development of DA's different divisions without examining it in the context of a strategic model. Those candidates who did apply a model, usually chose to use Ansoff's product market matrix, which was the obvious choice given the structuring of the information in the scenario. Weaker candidates simply described where each of the divisions would fall in the matrix, eg identifying the move into vehicle history as a new market for an existing product. Better candidates provided some analysis of the reasons for the choice of strategy and questioned whether the new product, Checksta, was indeed diversification as identified by DA. Although there was also scope to look at the method of growth adopted, only a few candidates identified that DA has chosen to grow organically, and only one candidate mentioned Lynch's expansion matrix in this context.

Requirement 1.3 asked candidates to prepare a PESTEL analysis on the credit reference industry. These points were largely contained in the narrative and as a result most answers were reasonable, however the weaker candidates simply repeated the facts from the scenario without considering the implications for DA's new product, which had been specifically requested.

Requirement 1.4 asked candidates to advise on an appropriate marketing strategy for the new product. This part of the question was the least well attempted, with candidates often restricting their comments to possible promotional strategies. Better marks were obtained by those who used the traditional 4Ps of the marketing mix to structure their answers. Since this was a service organisation there was scope to apply 7Ps although none of the candidates did so.

Requirement 1.5 required candidates to identify the strategic and operational risks associated with DA's use of information technology and to outline measures to deal with such risks. This requirement was well answered with candidates demonstrating a good awareness of the issues. Those who adopted a tabular approach, linking the risk management measures to each specific risk identified, tended to score very well.

2 Kraftvagen Gmbh (March 2008)

Marking guide

	Knowledge	Skill	Marks
2.1 Analysis of product and market positioning	2	4	
Other information	2	4	
			10
2.2 Emerging markets	2	5	7
2.3 Report	3	9	11
	9	22	28

2.1 Sales and market analysis

Note. The answer that follows covers the range of points that might have been made by candidates and is significantly longer than would be expected for the marks available.

Analysis of KV sales by market/production location

Market	Sales %	Production %	Sourcing by KV %
USA	17.3	14.2	82 local
Europe	41.5	35.1	85 local
Japan	33.8	19.5	58 local
Other	7.4	31.2	76 sold outside
Total	100.0	100.0	

Analysis of market share in core markets

	USA	Europe	Japan
Total luxury vehicle sales	2,320	2,220	1,560
Market share			
KV	12%	30%	35% (ML)
Lima	32% (ML)	14%	10%
Durant	5%	14%	28%
Conrad	17%	32% (ML)	15%
Relative share of KV compared to mkt leader	0.37	0.94	1.0
Average annual market growth			
20X2-20X7 actual	0%	–4.6%	+5.5%
20X7-20Y2 forecast	–2.5%	–6.2%	+3.2%
BCG analysis	Dog	Cash cow	Possible Star

Analysis of sales and market position

The market analysis highlights the dependence of KV sales on the European and Japanese markets. Over 75% of its sales come from these two markets, although it is not clear whether these contribute in the same ratio to the operating profit.

KV is the market leader in the Japanese market and very close to the market leader in Europe. It would be useful to know how long it has held this position and whether, in the case of Europe it was previously the market leader.

Europe – KV is one of two key players in the market but as with the USA the market is in decline, indeed the annual decline is forecast at 6.2% for each of the next five years. The decline is very significant and may give rise to damaging overcapacity. Protecting and gaining market share should be the strategy.

Japan – KV is the market leader with 35% of market and its nearest rival is Durant. Durant is maybe not a true luxury carmaker but has gained that perception in the Japanese market; this could be the result of clever promotional activities and may be giving them a high margin. KV could counter-attack by emphasising its true quality. Market research needs to be undertaken to find out why Durant is succeeding in this way.

USA – KV is well behind the market leader in volume of sales, in a market that is forecast to decline. There may be potential to take market share to achieve growth. The market share of the top three is less than half the total market indicating the presence of section of smaller players who could be attacked but some are possible niche players which may give them competitive advantages. Lima, the market leader, has greater diversity in its product range that may give it advantages over KV.

KV's current share of 12% of the US market, while low in relation to its share in Europe and Japan, may represent an increase on previous years.

Other markets – In India last year KV sold 300 cars, which is a market share of 2.5% (300/12000). The growth projections show that opportunities are available here despite decline in other markets. Were KV to set up the new factory, producing and selling 8,000 cars then they would have a market share of 28.6% in 20Y2 (8,000/28,000) or 14.3% in 20Y7 (8,000/56,000).

We do not know why the US and European markets are in decline, this may indicate switching from luxury vehicles to sports or smaller vehicles or maybe due to customers attempting to reduce their carbon footprints. Economic factors including taxation could also be causing a downsizing. It is unlikely to be due to population changes or socio-cultural reasons.

It would be interesting to undertake comparative analysis of the three main markets to explain why Japan is bucking the trend in luxury vehicles.

Location of production

The spread of production would tend to imply that KV continue to manufacture significant volumes from its original base in Europe (35.1%) and have then located production facilities in other markets outside Europe, USA and Japan (31.2%) – perhaps in order to take advantage of lower labour costs and scale economies.

To assess the benefits of this strategy it would be useful to have information about relative production costs and capacity for each location. The forecast decline in USA and Europe is likely to bring increased competition and pressure on margins and there may be scope for KV to reduce costs by closing factories and consolidating operations in areas where production costs are cheapest (subject to the increasing distribution costs that this may give rise to).

Stage of industry/product life cycle.

The available information suggests that the market for luxury cars could be assessed as follows in terms of the product/industry life cycle:

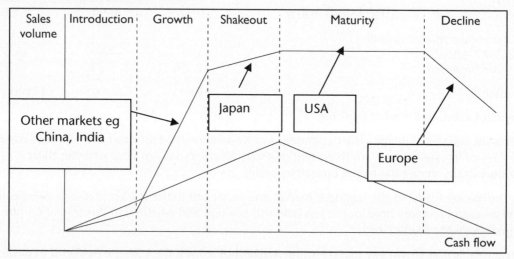

KV would appear to have markets at each stage of the life cycle, which should help smooth cashflows and create a balanced portfolio.

The major reliance on Europe may be of concern because industry information suggests a shrinking market for luxury cars. KV may be able to identify certain elements of this market that will continue to grow however and target these, eg the super luxury market where demand is probably relatively inelastic, alternatively it may be true that within Europe, demand varies by country and some countries are still exhibiting market growth.

The declines in sales of luxury cars are dramatic given that replacement cycles normally keep sales buoyant when taken across several years.

BCG analysis

Although traditionally used to assess product portfolios, A BCG analysis could also be undertaken of KV markets. Again on this basis there seems to be a reasonable spread:

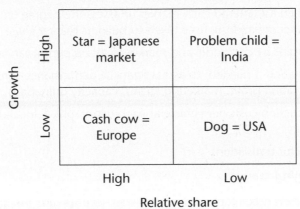

Other information that would be helpful:

External information

- A thorough analysis of the whole market and by vehicle type is required.

- The data we have may also need to be checked to ensure that the definition of luxury is being consistently applied.

- Details of the size of the passenger car vehicle market in total and the projected growth or otherwise, to ascertain whether the trend in luxury car sales is different from the underlying trend. This would help KV assess whether they should consider additional models/ranges of cars if the future for luxury cars is declining.

- Details of any individual trends within the luxury car market eg it may be that demand for cars at the lower end of the premium market is reducing as consumers are hit by higher taxes, environmental penalties etc but that at the highest level demand remains consistent.

- Information regarding the market leader in Europe, their range of vehicles and position in other markets. Also any plans they have to enter the Indian market (or whether they are there already).

- More detailed historic data on market size, growth and share to better identify the stage in the product life cycle.

- More competitive information for benchmarking costs and profitability, also to better understand KV's source of competitive advantage.

- We do not know the pricing, promotion and placing strategies of the key players nor do we know how their sales have been changing in recent years. It would be very useful to have information about the product life cycles of key models including refreshment and re-launching information. While it is likely that manufacturers use single global designs with local variants, an analysis of models with data on extent of design and component sharing would be useful. It would also be important to receive future model plans and examine trends in prototypes.

- Customer survey data is regularly collected for the motor industry and may help to explain competitive positions.

Internal information:

- A breakdown of the 'other market' sales for KV and industry information on market shares, growth and so on.

- An analysis of production across the 'other markets' – in particular number and location of factories, and capacity.

- Information regarding the range of luxury vehicles and a sales analysis by brand to assess stars and underperformers.

- Sales prices and margins by car model and market to assess performance.

- Historic analysis, by market, of sales, production and market share to better assess KV's business unit portfolio and understand the trends in its performance.

- Information as to when KV entered each market to assess the degree to which it has benefited from first mover advantage and the time taken to build its market share.

- Sales prices and margins by car model and market to assess performance.

- More internal information is needed to assess financial performance (gross margins, operating costs, operating profit, marketing spend, capacity utilisation).

- Information on production costs per vehicle at each geographical location in order to determine profitability.

- Exchange rates used for translation.

2.2 Reasons to target emerging markets:

- Reduces dependence on other core markets and therefore spreads risk, particularly given forecast decline in demand in USA and Europe.

- KV will face increased competition in its mature markets eg US/UK – it may face less rivalry in developing markets such as India initially and therefore enjoy better margins.

- Increased restrictions on carbon emissions/ fuel etc are changing tastes in mature markets like Europe. The governments of developing countries are probably not yet imposing environmental restrictions.

- UK and US tax systems now penalising luxury cars, so targeting other markets extends the possible life of this product.

- Stage of product life cycle is likely to be different in India and similar markets, eg China where the market for luxury cars is only just emerging. This offers the opportunity for increased profits and cashflow over a significant period.

- Western products and brands becoming very attractive in Indian market so this represents a good opportunity to increase sales volumes.

- Government spending on infrastructure will facilitate more luxury vehicles.

- Economic growth is likely to boost demand for vehicles in general and industry forecast suggests promising growth in luxury market.

- Production arguments for locating production in low cost countries and ensuring volumes are sufficient for economies of scale. May also reduce transportation costs to other countries outside core markets.

- Lack of export restrictions may mean cheaper to service KV's other markets from India.

- May be financial arguments for setting up:

  - Grants and incentives from Indian government
  - Lucrative emerging market
  - Possible tax benefits
  - Lowering of trade barriers

- Widen brand and enhance reputation/image as a truly global company.

- Level out possible seasonal fluctuations in turnover and cashflow.

- May be an opportunity to dispose of excess production and ensure factories in other countries are operating at capacity.

- Competitors are also doing this and KV needs to be either lead the way or follow.

Risks and issues to consider:

- **Risk profile**

  On the one hand, expansion into a developing market represents an opportunity to reduce reliance on other markets and spread risk. On the other it involves considerable extra risk, particularly as the market is an emerging one and is likely to change rapidly in ways that may be difficult to forecast.

- As with any overseas venture, KV will face political risk, dealing with a new country and an unknown government. Any political instability could adversely affect KV, as could changes in government attitudes to foreign ownership/investment, changes in legislation etc designed to discourage international trade or protect home producers.

- Economic and transaction risk will affect the exchange rate, the underlying cost of materials and labour, the value of profits extracted and so on.

  Exchange control regulations could be applied which might affect the remittance of funds.

- Government spending on infrastructure may not happen/may be delayed and as a result demand for luxury vehicles may not grow as expected.

- Economic growth may not continue as expected reducing the number of entrepreneurs and professionals attracted to India and hence the demand for luxury cars.

- The move to impose quotas/taxes on imports could affect KV's flexibility and prevent it continuing to export to India (see above on economic and transaction risks).

- Competition: As the market is predicted to grow there is a high threat of other potential entrants who may establish a reputation faster. Competitors, such as Durant, whose mid-range car is considered to be a luxury vehicle in India, may be able to make better returns from a cost-leadership perspective. KV may also face competition from local manufacturers.

- Is the financial return acceptable? Need to produce forecast profits and cashflow, and to consider the opportunity cost of investment, ie what else could have been done with the funds?

- Does KV have the necessary resources and management skills to exploit the opportunity – cash for investment, ability to recruit local workforce, people with experience of doing business in the Indian market? Again, experiences in other markets would suggest that it is able to manage this.

- KV will need to invest time and money understanding customer needs and preferences in the new market. It also needs to consider the extent to which production and marketing needs to be adapted for success in the Indian market.

- Are there any specific regulations that must be complied with or any hidden costs, eg restrictions on the acceptable mix of workforce, hours or days of operation?

  KV may run the risk of legal penalties of it fails to comply with the law or bad publicity if it is seen to apply less strict standards than it does in other countries.

2.3 **To:** Walter Bergen
  From: A N Consultant
  Date: XX March 20X8
  Subject: Developing the Indian market

This report sets out:

(a) Factors to consider in selecting the most appropriate option for implementation
(b) Ways to minimise the downside risks associated with each option

(a) **Options for implementation in India**

In choosing a method of development, there are two considerations for KV:

(1) To what extent the product, in this case the luxury car model, can be standardised across national boundaries or whether it needs to be adapted to local market conditions. It would appear that the basic manufacture of vehicles is likely to be quite standardised but that tailoring to the local market may be required in terms of branding, marketing and possibly additional features eg superior suspension.

(2) The extent to which the organisation's activities can be centralised or concentrated in a few limited locations as opposed to being widely distributed internationally. Concentration of production in countries with low cost labour would allow KV to take advantage of economies of scale but might increase the costs of distribution and potentially affect the quality of the vehicles produced.

Option 1

- Lower risk as no additional capital investment is required.

- It may be more cost effective to utilise spare capacity available at existing production plants – economies of scale are likely to be greater if KV concentrates production in a few core plants, rather then fragmenting it across all the different countries to which it is selling.

- India's reputation for restrictive labour laws may deter KV from setting up production locally.

- The trial run means KV may already have tried and tested distribution channels available for export.

- People are attracted by the Western brand name and brand image, so there may be no need to have a local brand image as a selling proposition.

- Would guarantee the existing quality – this is important given the luxury nature of the cars.

- Avoids any restrictions on KV's ability to extract profits from its Indian investment.

However:

- Possible supply chain delays if the product is not manufactured locally, although people are more likely to be prepared to wait for luxury car models, so any minor delays in the supply chain would not be a problem.

- Trade agreements may affect the freedom of movement and costs of imports/exports.

- Tariffs/quotas likely to be imposed by the Indian government on the import of finished goods, making the option to export finished vehicles to India more costly.

- Exchange rate movements may affect the costs and hence profitability/competitiveness if the product is not made locally.

- Lima and Durant are investing in plants in India. Their greater commitment to local expansion could enable them to establish a reputation and build market share faster than KV. In addition KV may face competition from local based auto manufacturers.

Option 2

- Will avoid any issues with restrictions on finished goods imports, although not on raw materials/components.

- Local government incentives/grants on offer may reduce costs of capital investment.

- Retains the quality of the existing components and yet gives a degree of local image. KV is seen to be promoting wealth for the local economy.

- May give KV the chance to test the market potential if it can build an assembly plant with the flexibility to expand production capacity or switch to assembly of a smaller luxury vehicle for example if Indian tastes prove to be different.

- A local presence may deter competition setting up facilities and help gain KV market share.

- This strategy is in line with the actions of Lima (KV's key competitor in the USA).

However:

- Would require significant capital investment and lead to an increase in operating gearing, although less than Option 3.

- Does not maximise access to low cost labour as a significant amount of costs will be incurred elsewhere in manufacturing the kits.

- Capacity is limited to 3,400 cars (two shifts at 1,700), whereas demand in five years is forecast to be 28,000. Unless there is scope to increase capacity beyond the doubling of shifts, this significantly limits KV's ability to fulfil an increase in demand and would require it to export production to India from other countries.

- Suitable premises will need to be located and staff recruited and trained.

Option 3

- Gives more scope to meet growing demand, although production is still limited to 8,000 cars, so if demand increase significantly then some top up of capacity by exporting to India will still be required.

- Full production in India may give KV access to low cost labour, raw materials, property, equipment and even capital.

- Any spare capacity in initial years could be exported to other markets but this will depend on trade agreements, tariffs/quotas and distribution costs.

- Speed of response to changes in demand is likely to be faster if production is based locally.

- KV may experience better hedging of foreign exchange risk through the matching of all revenues and costs in the same currency.

- Being seen to support local economy and the rapidly developing countries, may enhance/promote KV's image globally and avoids any import restrictions.

- Allows tailoring of the vehicle to the local market needs eg enhanced suspension to deal with lower quality roads.

- This is the strategy being pursued by Durant, KV's closest competitor in Japan.

However:

- Will benefit from lower labour and other costs but production numbers may still be too small to generate economies of scale.

- It will take time to establish a full production operation – premises will need to be located, machinery sourced, staff and management will need to be recruited and trained.

- There may not be a local supply chain eg available component manufacturers to support manufacture in India.

- If demand does not materialise then this strategy leads to highest exit costs: redundancies, penalty clauses on leases, reputational damage.

- Higher risk due to increased operating gearing from the additional capital investment.

- There may be quality implications of manufacturing the vehicles in India. KV's brand image and reputation would easily be damaged.

(b) **Ways to minimise downside risk**

Risk reduction can be achieved through the following:

- KV has already reduced some of the risk they face by conducting trial sales. It could also undertake more market research to obtain a more accurate forecast of the likely levels of demand.

- Risk would be reduced by adopting a 'wait and see' strategy and letting others such as Durant and Lima be first in the market. This will reduce the potential downside risk but also lose the returns associated with first mover advantage.

- Production strategies: The issues concerning production options have been discussed above. KV's management must strike a balance between contracting out production to local sources (thus losing control) and producing directly (which increases the investment and hence increases the potential loss). Alternatively to minimise losses, it may be better to locate key parts of the production process or the distribution channels abroad.

- Insurance: If KV decides to export, trading risks may be reduced with the help of banks, insurance companies, credit reference agencies and government agencies, which provide protection against various threats including nationalisation, currency conversion problems, war and revolution.

- KV may transfer risks contractually, eg obliging distributors to pay for any losses.

- Political risk may also be addressed by negotiations with Indian government to obtain a concession agreement. This would cover matters such as the transfer of capital, remittances and products, access to local finance, government intervention and taxation, and transfer pricing.

- Risk can also be reduced by cultivating relationships with legislators and influential individuals.

- Any foreign exchange risk could be addressed through hedging.

- If KV decides to produce in India, it should create a cost structure where costs are mainly variable, thus reducing operating gearing eg via use of outsourcing. It should also consider the use of Flexible Manufacturing systems to facilitate ability to switch production to other vehicles in response to demand changes.

- Risk of poor quality assembly or production can be minimised by implementing rigorous recruitment and training processes and maybe employing expatriate managers.

- KV may consider the use of strategic partners to share risk and give it the benefit of knowledge of local legislation, practice and cultural tastes.

- Possible methods include joint ventures or ceding control to local investors and obtaining profits by a management contract.

- If KV are producing and selling in India then this moderates exchange risk as revenues and costs are both incurred in rupees.

- Internal control procedures may be designed to minimise the risks from legal action, for example human resource policies, health and safety polices.

- Also KV can reduce risk to reputation through social and commercial good citizenship, complying with best practice and being responsive to ethical concerns.

The range of options facing KV is typical of an organisation looking to expand overseas.

Often risk of such expansion is reduced by achieved it in stages ie:

(1) Initially the market is targeted as an export market, possibly through an intermediary such as a sales agent.

(2) Some sort of base is established in the target market eg a distribution outlet or sales office.

(3) Full scale production is undertaken in the overseas market once demand is established.

This is typically the pattern that has been followed by the Japanese and European motor manufacturers.

Examiner's comments:

This scenario considers a German-based car manufacturer, KV, with a strong market position for luxury vehicles in USA, Europe and Japan. The chief executive has identified that the core markets are experiencing a decline and is looking to expand sales to India, to take advantage of growth opportunities there. Possible methods of expansion being considered range from export to setting up a full production plant.

Despite disappointing attempts at the data analysis element in part 2.1, candidates generally scored well on the rest of the requirements and as a result overall performance on this question was reasonable.

Requirement 2.1 asked candidates to evaluate the relative product and market positioning of KV and identify further information that might help assess its competitive position and performance. Most candidates produced calculations showing the sales mix across the various markets and KV's market share in each. Fewer candidates considered the sourcing of production and some misinterpreted this data, ignoring the fact that the question clearly states the production is valued at selling price and using it, incorrectly, to calculate a profit margin for each market. Having done some numerical analysis, many candidates then simply went on to describe their figures, producing little by way of interpretation or explanation. More analysis and reasoning, for example, might have elicited comments as to why the majority of KV's production is sourced from Europe (due to KV's origins in Germany) and other developing markets (perhaps to take advantage of cheaper labour). Better candidates used the market growth and share information to position KV's markets using the BCG analysis and to discuss the future implications for KV of having almost 60% of its sales in declining markets. Only one or two candidates discussed the likely position of each market within the industry life cycle.

A small number of candidates failed to do any numerical analysis and instead chose to apply a Porter's Five Forces analysis, scoring limited marks as a result.

The 'further information' element of the requirement was answered reasonably well and candidates appeared to be well prepared for this part of the requirement.

Requirement 2.2 requested candidates to explain the possible reasons for targeting emerging markets and the risks and issues to be taken into account.

This requirement was well answered, with candidates making good use of the information in the scenario to explain the reasons why India, in particular, might be attractive and the possible risks involved. Stronger candidates used their analysis from 2.1 to point out that emerging markets are likely to be at a different point in the industry life cycle and as such represent an opportunity for KV to reduce reliance on the more mature markets like Europe and USA which are forecast to decline.

Requirement 2.3 asked candidates to prepare a report advising on the factors to consider in the choice of expansion method and the ways that downside risks could be minimised. Again this was well attempted by the majority of candidates, who made sensible comments about the need to consider relative costs of production and distribution, possible barriers to imports, the need for a local image, balancing capacity and future demand, and the actions of competitors.

Candidates seemed well prepared to comment on risk management, with most making the obvious points about hedging foreign exchange risk and sharing risk though some form of JV arrangement.

3 Campaign for Trading Equitably (March 2008)

Marking guide

		Knowledge	Skill	Marks
3.1	Obectives	2	2	4
3.2	Mission statement	2	4	5
3.3	Stakeholders	1	6	6
3.4	Governance issues	1	5	5
3.5	Key performance indicators	3	6	
	Nature and sources of data	1	3	
				12
		10	26	32

3.1 NFP vs profit-focused organisation

As a charity, CTE can be considered a not-for-profit organisation (NFP).

The primary goal of a typical profit-focused trading organisation will be the wealth maximisation of its stakeholders.

The goals/objectives of CTE will not be based on profit achievement but rather on achieving a particular response from a much wider range of stakeholders, including:

- Founder members and others with an interest in equitable trade, donors and volunteers, beneficiaries such as targeted producers and workers, consumers, licensee companies and corporate sponsors.

When CTE sets objectives it must balance the interests and concerns of these audiences, which will often conflict. This may result in a range of objectives, rather than a single over-riding one.

In order to allow for this balance to be achieved, NFPs will typically feature much wider participation in the objective setting process. Indeed, it may be a legal condition in their constitution and essential to maintaining their legal status.

CTE's objectives are likely to be more intangible and less financially measurable than those of a trading organisation. Thus primary goals may include meeting the founder members' needs, contributing to the well-being of workers and producers, generating the support of consumers and pressing for political and social change.

Secondary goals will include the economic goal of remaining solvent and, ideally perhaps generating a financial surplus to invest in promotional activities or to give to specific projects to benefit those disadvantaged by trade.

To the extent that CTE, will seek to maximise the benefit derived from limited resources eg funds, they might be similar to a profit-focused trading organisation.

However CTE's objectives are likely to involve a much greater degree of corporate social responsibility than a profit-orientated organisation.

CTE's objectives are also likely to be more heavily influenced by external stakeholders such as the government than in a typical trading organisation.

3.2 CTE's mission statement

CTE's mission statement might be expected to describe its basic role in society and contain a statement of its overall objectives. In addition to its area of operations, the mission might provide a statement of the culture, its reasons for existence, its aims and the stakeholders served.

The *Ashridge College* model identifies four features of a successful mission:

(1) **Purpose**: Why does the organisation exist? Who does it exist for?

(2) **Strategy**: The competitive position and distinctive competence of the organisation.

(3) **Policies and standards of behaviour**: The policies and behavioural patterns underpinning its work.

(4) **Values**: What the organisation believes in which is replicated in employees' personal values.

These can be used to assess CTE's mission statement:

Purpose

CTE's mission statement has addressed this feature. It identifies its purpose as 'to promote the relief of poverty and suffering'. The choice of words is quite emotive. There is a lack of clarity concerning the definition of 'poverty and suffering' and in addition it is unclear whose poverty and suffering CTE is concerned with. The second part of the mission would suggest that this relates to the poverty and suffering experienced by the local producers, farmers and presumably their workers.

CTE has defined its area of operation as 'arising in connection with the conduct of trade in any part of the world.' This creates a very wide and as such, it might be argued, unachievable remit.

The mission goes on to acknowledge one group of stakeholders – the disadvantaged producers and workers – but does not explicitly consider the objectives of other groups, including for example employees, licensee companies, donors and sponsors. As the only group mentioned, there is an implication that the need of the producers and farmers take priority over all others.

Strategy

CTE has outlined its strategy for promoting relief: 'This will be achieved by providing assistance to disadvantaged producers and workers' and provided some opportunity for measuring the success of the strategy by stating its desire 'to help improve their social and economic position'.

Again there is no explanation of what constitutes 'disadvantaged' and if performance were to be assessed, CTE would need to consider how social and economic position might be measured.

The charity does not have direct competitors for its core activity, so in some ways its competitive stance is of less relevance, however it will be competing for people's time and funds.

One of the distinctive features of the charity is its use of the CTE logo as a consumer guarantee and some reference to this might reinforce the charity's unique position.

Policies and values

While CTE's mission addresses its purpose and strategy, it makes no real reference to policies, standards of behaviour and values.

The function of a mission statement is to:

- Communicate the nature of the organisation to its stakeholders

- Help instil core values in the organisation

- Provide a basis for control and evaluation of an organisation ie managerial and operational goals can be set on the basis of them and performance can then be reviewed

In its current form, CTE's mission statement is likely to achieve the first of these only.

At present it appears that the mission statement is largely a public relations exercise. The general nature of it would make it hard to tie down specific strategic implications or to develop meaningful strategic objectives. It is not clear to what extent the mission statement has been taken into account by those responsible for formulating or implementing the charity's strategy.

Suggested improvements

To make CTE's mission statement more effective it should:

- Incorporate references to a wider range of stakeholders and their goals

- Include the core values of the organisation eg transparency

- Refer to the unique nature of the CTE logo

- Be more specific about the area of operations so that the remit is not impossibly wide eg refer to target countries or specific types of farmer/producer

- Define the terms 'poverty', 'suffering' and 'disadvantaged'

- Refer to the charity's policies and standards of behaviour

3.3 **Stakeholder analysis**

Note. The answer provided covers the range of possible stakeholders that might have been identified, although candidates were only expected to focus on a few key ones in their answers.

Stakeholders: groups or persons with an interest in what the organisation does, what resources the organisation may have and what is to be achieved. They are affected by, and feel they have a right to benefit from, or be pleased by, what the organisation does.

All stakeholders will have an element of power in their dealings with an organisation to a greater or lesser extent and this will affect the way that CTE chooses to deal with that particular stakeholder or stakeholder group.

Stakeholder	Interests	Power and Influence
Founder members/ patrons	Achievement of aims/ greater good Political power Image of charity in the media/wider environment	Significant. May depend on the size of their annual contributions and the status/reputation of the organisation they belong to. They may well have power as a result of their areas of expertise and network of contacts.
Charity employees	Job satisfaction, security, pay, experience	Power is primarily resource based – they will provide services and time often for relatively low reward. The board will have a greater degree of influence over the day-to-day running and direction of CTE.

Stakeholder	Interests	Power and Influence
Government funding agencies	Value for money Promote the good name of the UK or EU	Depending on the proportion of funding they provide their power could be quite considerable. May have to balance the interests of the charity with the interests of large retailers, producers etc. Will have network power to influence other governments and funding agencies to assist CTE.
Donors	Proper use of funds, recognition or confidentiality as appropriate, satisfaction of having done the right thing	Power is not just about the size of any donation but also based on an individual's ability to raise the profile of CTE eg if a well known celebrity.
Corporate sponsors	Improved image, brand awareness, transparent and cost effective operations, reputational capital by association	Power depends on the value of sponsorship and possibly also on the value to CTE of any expertise that they can provide.
Farmers/ producers	Adequate and sustainable income, long-term contracts, ensure premium gets to farmers	Power virtually non existent unless they have unique products to offer.
Licensee companies	Produce commercial products, increase sales, reasonable margins, enhanced image	Given that the charity's success relies on persuading companies to take out licences, they may have some collective power to influence CTE as a group.

CTE's primary stakeholders can be analysed by considering Mendelow's power-interest matrix as follows:

Stakeholder	Interests	Power and Influence
Retailers	Wider range of products, increased sales/market share by being seen to adopt ethical stance	Again may have some power due to the relative size of the organisations and CTE's need for them to stock the products.
Consumers	Feel virtuous, increased range of products available, reasonable prices	Little power as individuals.
Consumer groups and others, eg World Trade organisation	Lobby govt/organisations to promote and stock goods Interested in the performance/success of the organisation	May have network power to influence other bodies to assist CTE with funding or expertise.
Supporters/ volunteers	Proper use of funds, ethical activities, governance, wide range of merchandise available, organise events	Little power as individuals.
Press/media	Coverage of topical and emotive issues may increase circulation	Need to be kept on side as they have the power to increase publicity or damage the reputation of CTE.

3.4 Governance issues

The following are the main issues that Ellen should be concerned with in respect of the governance of CTE:

Accountability and openness

This is fundamental to the corporate governance of the charity, with regard to both the proper stewardship of public and donated funds and the increasing demand for stakeholders to be involved in decision-making.

The trustees of CTE should be as open as possible about the decisions and actions that they take. They should give reasons for their decisions and restrict information only when the wider public interest clearly demands.

The Board of CTE must be prepared to submit to an appropriate level of scrutiny. This will lessen the risk of being accused of acting improperly.

Stakeholders

Since CTE has a wide number of stakeholders, issues of accountability are not clear-cut and conflicts can arise, eg the charity trustees have a legal duty to act in the interests of their beneficiaries, but this may not always coincide with the priorities of the founder members or the wishes of corporate sponsors.

Such conflict is illustrated by the founders' concerns regarding the marketing expenditure. On the one hand this may be seen to raise CTE's profile with consumers and retailers and increase the effectiveness of CTE as an organisation. On the other, since any direct link between marketing spend and effectiveness is hard to prove, it could be argued that this money would be better going directly to alleviate the poverty of the farmers or improve the conditions of their workers.

The board must have a clear policy statement about the amount of investment in and the purpose of the CTE logo.

Actions of the board

Board members must take decisions in line with the objectives of the charity and in the interests of its beneficiaries (the disadvantaged producers and workers). They should not do so to gain financial or other material benefits for themselves, their family or their friends. Nor should they place themselves under any financial or other obligation to outside individuals or organisations that might influence them in the performance of their duties.

The board have a duty to declare any private interests relating to their duties and to take steps to resolve any conflicts of interest.

Ellen has expressed concern regarding the acceptance of donations and sponsorship from certain multinationals. In considering such sponsorship CTE needs to take into account the likely benefits of increasing the funding available, the interests of its beneficiaries and the impact that this will have on the charity's image.

The trustees should draw up transparent and public guidelines about the source of grants and sponsorship.

The board would be advised to satisfy themselves as to the current trading practices and ethics of the prospective sponsors. They should provide as much information as possible about the reasons for accepting such money and ensure that they have complied with the principles set out above regarding transparency, honesty and self-interest.

Monitoring performance

The board needs to implement an effective system of performance measurement as this demonstrates to external stakeholders that the charity's mandates and objectives are being met.

3.5 Assessing performance

When assessing CTE's performance, three important issues must be taken into account. These are:

- There is no profit motive objective so many of the traditional financial performance indicators cannot be applied eg the ROCE.

- No particular stakeholder group dominates, unlike say the shareholders of a limited company.

- It may be difficult to find other, similar organisations that can be used as benchmarks for assessing the performance of CTE.

Despite these difficulties it is important that CTE maintains control by setting performance standards and implementing a system of monitoring, feedback and reporting on performance.

In order to assess whether CTE is achieving its objectives, key performance indicators need to be established, and actual performance measured and monitored for each of those indicators.

CTE will need to establish targets, thereby enabling measurement of the extent to which objectives have been achieved. A significant number of these are likely to be of a non-financial nature and as a result the balanced scorecard approach to performance measurement is likely to be particularly relevant.

The BSC approach looks at four perspectives in order to provide operational control so that the organisation's mission and objectives can be met. These perspectives are financial, customer, internal, and learning and growth. They are balanced in the sense that managers are required to think in terms of all four perspectives to prevent improvements being made in one area at the expense of another.

Financial perspective

In profit-making organisations this would be expressed in terms of shareholder value and return; however the financial perspective is still relevant to a non-profit organisation such as CTE.

Here the financial perspective will be in terms of economy and efficiency: allowing the available resources to be put to best use to add value to society, providing value for money for the sponsors and fund providers.

Appropriate KPIs include:

- Average donations
- Sales of CTE merchandise
- Licence fees received
- Level of marketing spend
- Costs of producing/sourcing merchandise
- Costs involved in setting up and monitoring licence agreements

Customer perspective

A not-for-profit organisation such as CTE needs to know what its users and beneficiaries feel about its services. CTE aims to ensure that the licensee businesses offer farmers and producers a guaranteed income and to make money available for community projects.

Appropriate KPIs include:

- Actual income received by farmers/producers compared to guaranteed income promised
- Increase in average wages received by workers/wages received in comparison to other workers
- Amount contributed by CTE to producers/workers as a proportion of total funding received
- Increase in number of beneficiaries and/or number of regions/areas covered by CTE aid
- Amount spent by CTE/licensee companies on community projects

Internal business process perspective

This perspective asks the question what processes must CTE excel at to achieve our financial and customer objectives and it aims to improve internal processes and decision making.

CTE must assess how it goes about delivering its services and what impact this has on its effectiveness.

Appropriate KPIs include:

- Number of new licences

- Percentage of revenue spent on admin

- Percentage of revenue that is spent on the publicised cause (eg rather than on advertising or administration)

- Speed of processing of licence applications

Learning and growth perspective

This considers CTE's capacity to maintain and grow its position through the acquisition of new skills and the development of new products or services.

CTE will benefit from learning from the past (both successes and failures), to enable processes to improve over time leading to improved user satisfaction.

Ellen has identified a need to raise the profile of the charity and so might look at innovative ways to raise awareness, attract new funding, or bring in new products to the CTE logo.

Appropriate KPIs include:

- Number of new products carrying the CTE mark
- Increase in range of products available
- Amount of training undertaken by staff
- New fundraising initiatives undertaken

The introduction of a new performance measurement system may create fear and uncertainty among staff since it raises their visibility and accountability. It will be important to implement an appropriate programme of consultation, communication and training.

Information requirements

The following information may be useful in assessing CTE's performance:

Strategic information: Derived from both internal and external sources and summarised at a high level

- Activities of other charities engaged in similar activities
- Government (and in some cases overseas government) policy on trade
- Public and retailer attitudes to equitable trade

Tactical information: Primarily generated internally (but may have a limited external component). Prepared on a regular basis to help monitor and control performance

- Percent of revenue spent on admin
- Average donations
- 'Customer' satisfaction statistics
- Statistics regarding awareness of CTE brand/mark

Operational information: Derived from internal sources. Prepared on a very frequent basis to help track the organisation's specific and day-to-day operational activities

- Households collected from/approached
- Banking documentation
- Number of new licences
- Licence fees received
- Sales of CTE merchandise

Examiner's comments:

This scenario is a charitable company engaged in promoting the relief of poverty through the conduct of fair trade. Its primary activities are the certification of products, via a fair trade logo and the granting of licences to companies wishing to operate under this logo. The newly appointed director, who has no experience of the charitable sector, wants to raise awareness of activities and extend the range of certified products on offer. She has asked for help in measuring performance but also needs to address concerns raised by the founder members about spending money on promotional activities and accepting donations from large multinationals who have previously adopted unfair trade practices.

Many attempts at this question were marginal. Some scripts were very weak due to poor performance on the requirements concerning mission and objectives, a failure to answer part 3.4 on governance and possible overall time pressure at the end of the exam.

Requirement 3.1 requested candidates to discuss the extent to which the objectives of the charity will differ from those of a typical profit-focused organisation. Answers to this requirement were disappointing. Weaker answers simply stated that the objective of a trading organisation is to maximise shareholder wealth whereas a charity aims to provide aid for its beneficiaries. Better answers related their points to the scenario, identifying the need to balance the interests of a much wider range of stakeholders and commenting that as a result objectives might be less easily measured. The best scripts identified similarities to the extent that both organisations would be aiming to maximise returns from limited resources and went on to say that increasingly there is a need for even profit-focused organisations to consider corporate social responsibility and its wider group of stakeholders.

Requirement 3.2 asked candidates to critically evaluate the content of CTE's mission statement and to suggest improvements. Most candidates explained that a mission statement should identify the general purpose of an organisation and that CTE's mission statement did indeed do this. Better candidates commented on the use of unspecific terms such as 'poverty and suffering' and pointed out that CTE's mission is very far reaching in terms of remit and as such potentially unachievable. Some candidates failed to make recommendations for improvements, despite this being specifically requested. A number attempted to apply the 'SMART' principles but in doing so, seemed a little confused by the distinction between a mission statement and the objectives of an organisation.

Requirement 3.3 asked candidates to identify the key stakeholders of CTE and explain their interests and likely influence. Candidates were clearly well prepared for this part of the question, with most demonstrating a good knowledge of Mendelow's matrix and an ability to apply it to the scenario in question.

Requirement 3.4 requested candidates to advise Ellen on the specific governance issues arising as a result of the concerns raised by the founder members. Many candidates did not attempt this requirement at all and those that did often discussed whether the concerns of the founders were valid, without advising Ellen on the implications for governance. Better scripts addressed the need for the board to apply principles such as transparency, ethical behaviour and accountability to the stakeholders.

Requirement 3.5 asked candidates to explain how Ellen might measure the performance of CTE. In addition to suggesting appropriate key performance indicators, candidates were also required to describe the information that would assist in the measurement process.

Many candidates did not attempt the first element of the requirement at all and those that did tended to make a brief comment on the need for both financial and non-financial measurement. Only the better candidates identified that a balanced scorecard approach would be appropriate in these circumstances and explained the benefits that this would bring. The section on performance measures was normally well answered and it was pleasing that these were on the whole tailored to the scenario. Most candidates were able to give some examples of useful information and some discussed benchmarking as a means of comparing CTE's relative performance in the charitable sector.

4 Embury Ltd (September 2008)

Marking guide

		Knowledge	Skill	Marks
4.1	PESTEL	2	8	8
4.2	(a) Capacity planning/procurement	3	4	
	(b) Outsourcing benefits and problems/risks	2	5	
				12
4.3	Ethical procurement	2	4	5
4.4	Change management problems	3	4	
	How to address	2	4	
				11
4.5	Pros and cons of product development	2	6	6
		16	35	42

4.1 PESTEL analysis

Political

- Current and future restrictions imposed by governments and/or the water companies on the use of water eg for garden purposes may limit demand for garden equipment

- Legislation or changing attitudes of overseas governments may affect the availability of low cost labour in other countries

- Any future restrictions placed on imports by the UK government or exports by overseas governments would affect costs and possible competition

Economic

- Changes in interest rates and the state of the economy will affect disposable incomes and hence demand for gardening products which are discretionary purchases

- Rising charges for water services will reduce the amount that individuals are prepared to spend on non-essential water such as for gardening purposes

- Changing exchange rates may affect the cost of manufacture and hence margins on the outsourced products

- Recession in the housing market may affect the number of households and the size of gardens. An increase in the proportion of people choosing to rent for example is likely to mean less interest in gardening

- Availability of low cost resources in other economies means increased pressure on margins for UK manufacturers

Social

Demand for gardening equipment is derived from the demand for gardens and gardening:

- Increasingly busy lifestyles may reduce people's desire to have a garden and hence decrease the need for gardening equipment

- Modern housing developments with small gardens decrease the need for gardening and equipment

- Alternatively increasing concerns about the quality of the environment may stimulate demand for an outdoor lifestyle and hence garden products. If market research is to be believed, a desire for a better quality of life may increase demand for natural surroundings and gardening as a form of leisure

- An increasingly ageing population may mean there are more retired people with time on their hands for leisure and gardening

- Peer pressure may mean that consumers do not want to be seen watering their gardens or washing their cars. Conversely this may boost demand for water conservation measures and other environmentally friendly products

Technological

- Technological developments may mean cheaper products become available to Embury or its competitors

- Alternatively modern technology may allow the production of more efficient watering equipment to bypass restrictions

- As developers are forced to become more ecological, all new houses may be built with underground rainwater tanks and garden irrigation systems, avoiding the need for gardening equipment or offering companies like Embury an opportunity to sell its new product range to developers

Environmental

- Climate changes and the weather are uncontrollable factors which may increase or decrease the demand for gardening equipment

- Increased environmental concerns may cause households to reduce the non-essential consumption of water for leisure purposes thus reducing the demand for hosepipes and sprinkler systems

- An increased desire to be sustainable may cause households to switch to alternative approaches to irrigate their gardens or alternatively to plant different types of trees and shrubs which do not need so much watering

- May be an increase in environmental groups lobbying for sustainability, which widens the stakeholder groups that need to be considered

Legal

- Legislation regarding the environment, the use of water etc may affect production processes or demand. It might also influence the types of product Embury is able to offer

- Embury will need to comply with minimum wage legislation and other Health and Safety issues

- Embury will also need to ensure it complies with any legislation regarding factory closures and redundancies which could increase costs

- The water industry is regulated by law in the prices it can change (by OFWAT) and thus changes in regulatory policy may affect water prices as well as the pricing policy of the water companies. This will affect the amount of the charge, but also the form of the charge (eg compulsory water metering)

- Penalties for breaching water use regulations might be both public and quite severe

Summary

Demand for garden equipment is significantly affected by factors outside the control of the industry, such as the weather. This is exacerbated by the increasing cost of water, the drive for water conservation and the restrictions on water use imposed by governments. Certain demographic factors are favourable but a key threat for UK-based manufacturers such as Embury is the increasing competition in the industry (as evidenced by GZ's entry to the UK market) and the pressure on margins as a result of the availability of other lower cost products.

4.2 (a) **Capacity planning and procurement**

Capacity planning

Capacity planning involves consideration of Embury's capability to supply both existing and future demand but with an understanding of the costs of providing spare capacity as a buffer for uncertainty and a buffer for seasonality.

Capacity planning also links to supply chain management since supplier capabilities and reliability will affect Embury's own capability.

- **Variations in demand**

  The key issue for Embury is the fact that demand will vary considerably with the time of year and also the weather conditions.

  Embury has always faced the fluctuations of seasonality for watering products leading to spare capacity or tight periods. However while Embury is likely to be able to predict that demand for its products is higher in the spring and summer than autumn and winter, within these periods demand is subject to unexpected climate changes or problems created by restrictions placed on water use. Hence Embury faces issues of overstocking and stock-outs which are largely caused by factors outside its control.

  Longer term trends are also affecting demand:

  – The new generation of gardeners and the generally predicted shift to increased demand for gardening and leisure products

  – The nature of products in the mix may change as water saving products are demanded more in the longer term and at peak times due to drought and government restrictions on water use

- **Balancing capacity and demand**

  The major retailers will expect Embury to respond flexibly and quickly to changes in demand.

  There is a significant problem with capacity utilisation. Unit costs are likely to be high as facilities and staff will be underutilised in off-peak periods. Hence the proposals to reduce the number of factories and staffing levels would appear to make sense.

  The MD has identified the need to move to more flexible manufacturing. Embury must try to anticipate variations in demand and alter its capacity accordingly, eg by having minimum numbers of full time staff and taking on part time staff or working overtime in peak demand periods.

  Variations in equipment levels might also be necessary, perhaps by means of short-term rental arrangements.

  Embury needs information and data to support forecasting and modelling of the future and possibly IT models to assist in analysis. Models may need to link to integrated ERP and supply chain management systems with data sharing backwards and forwards in the supply chain. Inventory control systems may be required to control buffering costs.

  Embury may have opportunities to expand market share through marketing and will need to build these potential increases in demand into its planning and procurement models.

  Embury may be able to smooth production and pass some of the risks of weather on to the retailers, for example by negotiating fixed early season orders at off-peak prices.

Procurement

Embury needs to decide on a strategy for sourcing materials and or products.

From a business perspective Embury will need greater access to supplies to lower risk of procurement shortages.

Also Embury as raw material prices increase, Embury needs to be able to compete with companies who are able to produce lower cost products.

Procurement issues would include whether to buy in raw materials and components, part assembled products or to sub contract the whole manufacturing process for certain products (see discussion below on outsourcing).

Additionally Embury needs to decide whether to choose one or more different suppliers.

The advantage to Embury of creating a long term, single-source strategic relationship with a supplier is that it facilitates economies of scale and can increase competitive advantage by affording cooperation and flexibility. However, Embury would need to choose the supplier carefully as reliance on a single company exposes Embury to possible disruptions in supply.

(b) **Benefits of outsourcing**

- Faced with increasing raw material costs and low cost products from competitors, outsourcing production of certain products may enable Embury to reduce costs because the external supplier can source raw materials cheaper overseas, gain access to lower costs of labour or take advantage of economies of scale.

- E may also gain access to cheaper products due to exchange rate advantages.

- This may improve competitive advantage and hence improve sales and performance. The MD's comments imply that competitors have benefited from this and it is particularly important given the entry to the UK market of GZ, together with the existing presence of competitively priced own-brand products.

- Given the variability of demand and the seasonality of the product, Embury may want to reduce operating gearing by making its cost base more variable.

- Risk may be managed better by outsourcing, eg may pass risks on to the supplier such as overproduction in the face of a sudden drop in demand but this will depend on the flexibility built into the outsourcing contract in terms of a minimum level of demand.

- There may also be scope to shift legal liability to the supplier and levy charges for breakdowns in performance or delays in delivery that will mitigate losses.

- Gain from outside expertise or competence – an external supplier may have better or different knowledge in relation to certain product lines eg the new water conservation range. This may improve Embury's ability to differentiate its product from competitors and/or lead to increased product innovation.

- Embury may shop around and choose to use different suppliers for different products according to their competences, flexibility, costs and so on.

- Embury can improve its competitive advantage by creating a network of long-term relationships with the suppliers in its value chain. Some of these benefits may be lost if E only outsources certain product ranges.

Problems and risks

- Choice of partner – Embury is exposed to risks if the supplier is unreliable/unstable or the product produced is poor quality.

- May be problems in controlling supply chain: there will be admin costs and time spent in co-ordination.

- May be harder to guarantee supply eg delays in delivery may arise if products are being imported from overseas locations.

- May be harder to control quality, particularly with a variety of suppliers. Embury will need to ensure that there is an appropriate contract and performance measures.

- There may be hidden costs eg impact of 'kick backs' required to do business in certain countries.

- Costs will also be affected by exchange rate fluctuations. A relatively weak pound would increase the costs for Embury, despite these being manufactured in low cost countries.

- There is a risk that Embury's learning and intellectual property is being transferred. The in-house operation may be a source of significant learning leading to product and process improvement. Embury may face direct competition from the supplier after any contract comes to an end.

- Closure costs may be prohibitive: redundancies, exit penalties etc and will lead to bad publicity. If the outsourcing agreement fails, Embury may find it hard to source alternative supplies but will no longer have the production facilities in house.

- Managing this change will require considerable time and effort on the part of management.

4.3 Ethical procurement

An ethical procurement policy is an attempt by Embury to fulfil its own Corporate Social Responsibility commitments by demanding similar commitments and standards of behaviour from suppliers.

As an ethical approach becomes increasingly popular with customers and investors, it may also contribute to Embury's longer term business success.

Embury may however be accused of being hypocritical if while demanding ethical behaviour from suppliers it attracts adverse publicity for the way its own employees are being treated as a result of the factory closures.

Embury is likely to expect all suppliers to comply with the policy and may choose not to do business with companies that are not prepared to comply or to take corrective action.

An ethical policy is likely to lead to:

- Reduced choice/range of suppliers
- Increased costs of the product
- Requirement to monitor compliance and costs incurred as a result
- Additional terms in outsourcing agreement

However it might also be used as a USP to differentiate Embury from competitors such as GZ.

When Embury is considering its choice of suppliers and the drawing up of contracts, ethical procurement would have an impact in the following areas:

(1) **Working in partnership with suppliers**

Embury's policy may cover the need for fair contracting terms and conditions with suppliers and transparency of negotiations.

This would include fair prices, adherence to reasonable payment terms and having a grievance procedure to deal with suppliers' grievances. It would also make clear timescales for contract re-tendering and award/non-renewal.

(2) **Human rights**

The human rights of workers within supplier firms must be protected so that:

- Employment is freely chosen and no child labour is used
- Working conditions are safe, hygienic and humane
- Working hours are not excessive and reasonable wages are paid
- No discrimination is practised

(3) **Health and safety**

There would be an expectation that proper health and safety standards should be maintained in operations that may affect employees and the general public.

(4) **Environmental protection**

Embury is likely to have objectives for sustainable development which would mean that suppliers are expected to comply with all relevant local and national environmental regulations and to work to minimise the harmful effects of their activities.

(5) **Fraud and corruption**

There will be zero tolerance of the offering of gifts and inducements by suppliers and also of conflicts of interest.

4.4 Change management

There are two separate change management issues:

(1) The leaked email
(2) The planned closures

(1) **Leaked email**

The leaked email may have put information into the public domain prematurely or even when it was never intended to be public information. There are risks of inaccuracy and of escalation of rumour.

The leaked email gives rise to issues for shareholders and wider stakeholders who may use information to advantage or react to information from their stakeholder view, commercially or emotionally. There are political implications and social issues.

The press describe the potential closures of two factories as 'shocking' and talk of 'lost' jobs in an emotive way. The implication is that there was no proper consultation and that maybe profits come before people. The news report also 'mocks' the reason as if it is all down to water shortages.

The MD of Embury has been quoted addressing only his shareholders and not all stakeholders. His response appears economically rational. He also uses the opportunity to mention outsourcing that has positive economic benefits to shareholders but potential social issues for other stakeholders. Longer-term job losses may be implied.

His final reported comments appear to say that job losses are just collateral damage in the pursuit of return and growth and management of risk the implication is that there is an opportunity as well as a threat.

Embury may need to consider some additional PR communications to reduce the negative social messages and internally will need to manage the rumour and people issues. There is potential for resistance to change and local protest from staff and the community. There is a risk of broader reputational damage.

(2) Planned closures

All changes tend to be resisted by employees. The nature of the changes such as Embury are proposing which involve downsizing and redundancy will be resisted even more strongly – particularly if, in the first instance, employees find out about the proposed changes as a result of the leaked article.

- **Cultural barriers**

    The new proposal puts forward fundamental changes that will affect the culture of the organisation. Power structures within E may be threatened by the redistribution of decision-making authority or resources, or the changing of lines of communication.

    This will in particular affect management and thus management may be reluctant to implement changes which will be against their own interests eg the managers of the two factories that are to be closed.

- **Stakeholder groups**

    Group inertia may block change where the changes are inconsistent with the norms of teams and departments, or where they threaten their interests.

    Examples from Embury might include:

    - Strikes and other forms of resistance to change implementation by Embury staff to be made redundant

    - UK raw material suppliers taking legal action for contract termination if the business is now to be switched to overseas suppliers

    - Shareholders selling shares as a result of the changes

- **Individuals**

    There are also barriers which affect individuals and result in them seeing the change as a threat to earnings and job security. This may affect not only the UK factories that are to be closed but also the employees in the remaining consolidated site where there are likely to be substantial changes in work practices and also redundancies of old skills in favour of new skills.

Addressing the issues and managing the change

Change management will involve two project levels a technical project and a people project, the two are interlinked:

Technical

- Shifting production and technology to one site
- Liquidation of old sites
- Redesign of processes for efficiency
- Redesign of supply chain processes
- Setting up of new departments for R&D

People

- Managing the rumour internally and externally
- Ensuring the need for change is understood
- Dealing with redundancy announcements, implementation and exit support
- Building new teams to implement the change
- Getting staff onside and positive for the change
- Getting staff ready for the additional work and pressure of change
- Building the new culture internally and across the supply chain
- Managing news to motivate
- Managing investor relations issues

A change agent should be appointed to oversee the change process. Ideally someone from outside who can clearly communicate the benefits of change and where possible involve the remaining staff in the process. This will help strengthen the forces for change.

Embury needs to identify key stakeholders and encourage them to support the change.

Communication will be an essential part of the process:

- Shareholders will be interested in the impact on share price and profitability and dividends. Embury will need to provide reassurance re the state of their investment and how strategy will benefit them/improve results.

- Key customers (retailers etc) will need reassurance about quality and reliability and availability of supply. They will also be interested in any impact on prices.

- Unions and staff must be consulted and the case for change to ensure the long term survival of the company made clear. Participation in the process may improve motivation. If staff are to be made redundant, they may be motivated by making negotiation of redundancy terms, references and assistance with alternative employment contingent on smooth transition.

- Embury will need to preserve PR by communicating information to the financial press and analysts about how and why has decision been made and how will it be implemented.

Once the changes have taken place Lewin would argue that it will be necessary to refreeze the new methods. This will involve ensuring that the remaining staff adapt to the new business model and are motivated to work within it.

Techniques such as introducing new reward systems and changing the way in which activities are carried out should help embed the model.

4.5 Product development

Advantages

- Embury would benefit from having a range of products to reduce dependence on any one product and ensure a balanced portfolio of products that smooths out cashflow. It appears to have devoted too little attention in the past to developing products that will be the future of the company.

- Introducing water conservation products widens the product base and reduces total reliance on products that require plentiful water supplies.

- Water conservation products would appear to be a growing market and Embury can establish an advantage if it can be first to the market with these types of product. Market research should be undertaken to assess demand.

- A different balance of products may lessen some of the supply chain pressures by spreading demand more evenly.

- The current proposal still links to existing area of expertise so within Embury's competence.

- Being seen to be environmentally friendly may enhance the company reputation and image and may help it be looked on more favourably by government/legislators and environmental groups.

- May help compete with GZ and protect market share in UK.

Disadvantages

- New products may be expensive to purchase or install and as a result demand may be limited.

- The products still rely on the availability of water which is subject to factors beyond Embury's control.

- Use of household waste may be unsanitary and lead to litigation claims and/or bad publicity.

- Given the size of GZ and its reputation for innovation, Embury's technology and products may be superceded.

- Current proposals represent only limited diversification of the product range. Thus there will only be a limited reduction in the impact of the weather on the seasonality of revenues and cashflow.

Conclusion

The development plans probably do not go far enough. Larger businesses all produce across the whole range of gardening equipment which is likely to reduce the risks of their portfolios and extend the season of demand for their products eg leaf blowers in autumn and sprinklers in summer.

Perhaps Embury needs to consider additional new products eg pond and water equipment or selling its products to markets where the seasons are opposite to those in the UK.

Examiner's comments:

The scenario is based on the UK's leading manufacturer of garden watering equipment which is facing unpredictable demand due to environmental issues. It is also confronted with increasing raw material costs and competition from a multi-national garden equipment company that is expanding into the UK. As a result it intends to widen its product range to reduce dependence on seasons. The company has recently suffered bad publicity when its previously unknown plans to reduce costs by closing two factories and outsourcing certain product manufacture to China were leaked to a local newspaper.

This question is the mini case and, at 42 marks, was the longest question on the paper, although the requirements were broken down to help candidates in developing answer headings and assessing mark allocation.

Overall good scores on 4.1, 4.2(b) and 4.4 made up for poorer scores in 4.2(a) and 4.3. Part 4.5 tended to be variable in quality.

Requirement 4.1 asked candidates to prepare a PESTEL analysis on the garden equipment industry. Most candidates found this requirement reasonably straightforward as the bulk of the points could be discerned from the text of the scenario. A number applied their analysis to the company rather than the garden equipment industry as a whole and weaker candidates restricted their marks by producing tables or lists of undeveloped points. Some candidates wrote far too much here for the marks available, leaving themselves short of time for later requirements. Only the best candidates indicated the relative importance of the various factors or attempted to summarise the overall implications of their analysis for the industry.

Requirement 4.2(a) asked candidates to describe the capacity planning and procurement issues currently facing the company and (b) to explain the benefits and risks involved in the outsourcing proposal. The subject of capacity planning and procurement is new to the learning materials and many candidates seemed to lack specific knowledge here. As a result many did little more than repeat the information from the question regarding the unpredictability of demand and the issue of stock-outs/overstocking; often failing to discuss procurement at all. Better candidates explained the implications for fixed cost recovery and the value chain, commented on the need for a more flexible manufacturing strategy (as highlighted by the managing director) and discussed the importance of reducing fixed costs and developing closer relations with suppliers.

Candidates were better prepared to discuss the pros and cons of outsourcing in 4.2(b). Most scored well here, although higher skills marks were earned by those who applied their points to the case eg pointing out that most of Embury's competitors were already adopting this strategy. Only the stronger candidates linked their discussion back to the issues in 4.2(a), explaining that outsourcing might help to reduce fixed costs and transfer some of the risks of variable demand to the supplier.

Requirement 4.3 involved ethics. Candidates were asked to explain how the company's proposed ethical procurement policy might affect any outsourcing agreement. Answers were quite poor on the whole. Most candidates appreciated that such a policy would probably increase the cost to the company and limit the available suppliers, but only the better ones went beyond this to explain fully what such a policy would cover (labour, environmental issues, raw materials) and how the agreement would be drafted (monitoring, sanctions, termination etc). A number were highly critical of the likely ethics of a Chinese manufacturer and the impact this might have on the company's reputation but seemed to ignore the fact that the recent press article cast a shadow on Embury's own ethical behaviour.

Requirement 4.4 asked candidates to explain the change management problems that are likely to occur as a result of the newspaper article and the planned factory closures and to discuss how these might be addressed. As usual the majority of candidates showed good knowledge in this area but often failed to earn the skills marks available for applying this to the scenario. Weaker candidates either made general points without reference to any theory or discussed barriers to change and possible change management approaches including Lewin's 'unfreeze/move/refreeze' model, in generic terms. Weaker answers tended to focus solely on the employee aspects of closure, rather than considering also the wider commercial issues and the other stakeholders. Many completely ignored the effect of the change being announced by the newspaper article.

Requirement 4.5 requested a discussion of the advantages and disadvantages of the plans for product development and was reasonably well attempted by the majority of candidates.

Skills marks were earned by those who linked their discussion back to the PESTEL analysis and the impending competition.

5 DT Ltd (September 2008)

Marking guide

		Knowledge	Skill	Marks
5.1	SWOT	1	8	8
5.2	Evaluation of expansion proposals			
	(a) Governance and control	1	3	
	(b) Risks	2	4	
	(c) Resource requirements	1	3	
				12
5.3	Business plan			
	(a) Business model	1	4	
	(b) Basis of competitive advantages	1	3	
	(c) Benefits for a franchisee	1	3	
				12
		8	28	32

5.1 SWOT ANALYSIS

Strengths

- DT has a successful business model that has delivered a profitable and rapidly expanding business in just a few years.

- David has been prepared to reinvest profits and not just run a 'lifestyle' business.

- David's technical expertise has allowed him to develop an innovative training product which appears to have attracted customers.

- Training requires less time, costs less and results in improved success rates – part of the core competence in attracting trainee drivers – which will give DT a competitive advantage.

- DT is able to compete with both types of business – self-employed driving instructors based on time and quality and large schools based on time and cost.

- Proprietary knowledge is protected by patent which restricts competitors copying the product.

- Well known brand name locally – the brand name seems to have become well known and is thus recognisable. This reinforces reputation and allows DT to capitalise on referrals.

- Extended life of product and wider potential market – ability to use the simulator for more experienced and commercial drivers widens DT's target market and hence increased sales opportunities. It also means that DT can continue to sell to existing customers once they have a licence.

- Ability to use simulator in winter months reduces seasonality of revenues and cashflow.

- May appeal to environmentalists due to reduced costs.

Weaknesses

- Reliance on David – much of the control and culture appears to depend on one person. David also is the real innovator with software. There is thus a risk if David leaves or is ill.

- There is also limited capacity for one person to control expansion as the business grows.

- Rapid growth may have put pressure on systems and led to overtrading.

- Profits and cashflow affected by seasonality (though this may have been minimised by the use of the simulator).

- Lack of further debt finance – expansion is constrained by lack of financial resources.

- David has a high level of personal debt which needs servicing – the high debt creates financial risk.

- Expansion has been limited to the known London geographical market, where the company has a reputation. Wider geographical expansion may be outside management's experience and the business may take time to develop a reputation and customer base outside London.

Opportunities

- Provincial expansion – there is an opportunity to expand in other cities/areas of the UK.

- Further organic growth eg raise share capital via friends and family.

- New investors such as IMS appear to be available to supply new resources for expansion.

- Brand name and proprietary software mean the business is capable of being franchised.

- Develop the commercial driver training element of the business eg through corporate contracts.

- Expand the concept of training for extreme conditions.

- Develop complementary products eg DVDs/CD Roms or simulator products for other industries.

Threats

- Contestable market – there are few barriers to entry and competition is intense. Eventually David's patent will expire and in the meantime rivals may develop other innovative training methods and compete away DT's profits. The patent will only protect the specific programme used rather than the idea of driving simulation as such.

- There is a threat to the personal control of David if more shareholders are needed – David may eventually lose control of the company under the strategy option above. Thus while the business may succeed, David's investment may not if this source of external finance is used.

- There is a need to change organisational structure as the business grows – this may affect the business model. If David's 'hands on' approach is making the business succeed this may not be available as the business expands and new management is brought in.

- Any bad publicity would damage reputation and lose clients and referrals.

- Inability to service high debt costs if business declines or over-expands.

- A fall in pass rates would affect demand.

- The product is IT-based and as such open to the inherent risks of system failure, malfunction, viruses etc.

- Takeover by a national chain (could be seen as an opportunity).

Key issues

David's technical expertise has allowed him to develop an innovative training product which has given DT a competitive advantage. However, the business is heavily reliant on David and has limited resources for expansion. In view of this and given the low barriers to entry and the intense competition in the industry, organic growth is likely to be difficult to achieve. DT's brand name and proprietary software make it attractive as a partner and thus offer a good opportunity to expand either through franchising or in partnership with another business such as IMS.

5.2 **Evaluation of expansion proposals**

Proposal 1 – Franchising

Under a franchise a firm grants other firms the right to use its brand, its product or its know-how. There is also likely to be some degree of central control and support. In return, the franchisee will normally provide a lump sum, share of earnings and specific payments.

In the current context, a franchise is likely to be on a geographical basis in order to segregate the markets of the individual franchisees.

(a) **Governance and control**

DT maintains some general contractual control over franchisee but loses some operational control.

If franchising is to be taken up by many small operators, then DT is not dominated by its business partner(s).

There is a need to monitor franchisees and there may be quality control issues. Franchisees must be chosen carefully and contracts need to be drawn up to ensure DT's reputation is protected.

(b) **Risk**

Reduced financial risk by having franchisees' own capital.

There are fewer risks from franchisee losses as cost of failure is shared with franchisee. This reduces the maximum potential loss from the failure of an outlet but also provides an increased incentive for the franchisee to succeed.

Poor quality franchisees may harm brand name eg lower quality instructors may have an impact on success rates.

May be more difficult to change the strategic direction of the business in the future if franchisees have a degree of autonomy in the running of their outlet.

There is a need to monitor the franchisees as they may have different objectives, approaches and abilities compared to DT. David may find he is overburdened as the number of franchises grows.

Franchisees gain access to intellectual property and may misuse or copy the software or break away and set up in competition.

May invite national competition.

Franchisees may not want to take up the opportunity – there needs to be some incentive to purchase a franchise and without successful establishment in the market outside London this may be unlikely.

(c) **Resources**

This method offers quicker business expansion than using DT's own financial resources as the franchisees offer a new source of capital.

David will be required to provide training in the use of the simulator. Franchisees may also expect support with marketing. DT may need to take on additional manpower to provide training and support and manage the franchisees.

Franchisees are likely to be individuals so unlike IMS will not be able to provide any large scale expansion or financial support.

The need to share profits with franchisee means fewer profits can be reinvested in the expansion of the business than if DT were to grow organically.

DT gains access to the local knowledge/reputation of the franchisee which may attract candidates, increase awareness of the brand and increase referral rates.

Proposal 2 – New share capital via IMS

IMS offers economies of scale in two respects: increased financial capital and access to IMS driving schools across Europe as a wider market.

(a) **Governance and control**

Initially David retains control of the business because of his majority stake, although IMS will have a significant stake and may interfere in the day to day running of the business.

Control of the business will remain centralised and David may have more influence over instructors than under a franchise arrangement.

After five years, David may lose control of the company if IMS takes up the option to increase its shareholding. He will become more dependent on IMS who may decide to change the control and reporting structure. David is likely to have reduced influence on the board of directors and this may lead to stalemate for important operating decisions.

(b) **Risk**

The brand name may be unknown outside London and thus needs to be established in each individual city. This may not be easy or quick.

IMS has no experience of the UK and there may not be the local knowledge and core competences within DT to operate successfully in provincial cities.

Expansion outside UK may not be as successful, or may be more uncertain. Competition for the simulator training product may already exist.

Simulator may need modification eg for right hand driving.

Rapid expansion may carry the risk of overtrading and loss of David's investment in the event of failure.

Requirement for dividend or exit route by IMS may limit future availability of funds.

The terms of which IMS can expand its shareholding from 33% to 50% need to be clear or there is a risk that resources input may not compensate for the loss of control by David.

IMS may not fulfil their promises in respect of resources or finance.

May reduce risks as effectively a venture which eliminates competition.

Additional equity capital will lower financial risk through reduced gearing (although this depends on the extent to which DT takes advantage of the loan finance offered by IMS).

The additional debt represents increased gearing risk.

(c) **Resources**

If significant new capital is provided by IMS then growth could be rapid in terms of the number of outlets.

The sites in provincial cities are likely to be lower cost than London thus enhancing profitability.

DT will be able to benefit from access to IMS expertise in the market place.

IMS will be able to provide DT with support for advertising, training etc, which is the inverse of the franchise situation.

Conclusion

Before deciding on which option to pursue David should carefully consider his and DT's objectives in expanding and his eventual plans for exit. Both options address the issue of limited resources and share the risk of expansion but also require David to share the control and the future profits of the business.

The deal with IMS gives DT access to a large pool of funds and expertise and is likely to offer more opportunity for significant growth; however David's control will be greatly diluted. Contractual protection may be needed if and when IMS gain a 50% shareholding.

Franchising offers a slower growth route, with DT providing the expertise, but David is much more likely to retain control of the direction of the business and may benefit from the local knowledge and reputation of franchisees. More detail is required regarding the terms of the franchise and the number of interested franchisees.

David's key skill is the development of the software, rather than the management of an expanding business. Thus developing the business under a license system may free him up to concentrate on further product innovations.

5.3 Extract from business plan to attract franchisee

(a) DT Limited: Business model

DT's mission is 'to provide high quality, convenient and comprehensive driver education courses at the lowest cost'. We operate five successful driving centres in and around the London area, which provide training for learner drivers, via a virtual reality driving simulator, similar to those used in airline pilot training. The simulator is used in addition to traditional road-based instruction and learning.

Three years ago, when the company was founded, David Thomas (the founder and sole shareholder) realised that there was an untapped opportunity in the driver education industry.

No company was providing what the customers truly demanded, high quality driver education at the lowest possible cost. Large companies were charging too much for their services and the local companies were not providing enough programmes and services or they were poor quality.

DT is at the cutting edge of driver training by instituting the use of computer simulators. The technological revolution in computers has enhanced our abilities to teach.

Simulator training widens the market opportunities as it can be offered to:

(1) Learner drivers
(2) Existing drivers wanting refresher courses or needing advanced driving skills
(3) Commercial drivers

The company will continue to seek new ways to provide a better and more convenient teaching environment through technology.

DT's steady growth in a mature market is a sign of the firm's viable business strategy and our success in the London area has proven that our product works. Now the company is ready to expand and is seeking like minded individuals who want to participate in our success.

Through franchising, DT aims to create a national network of driver instructor centres providing cheap, effective driver training at the forefront of technology.

In return for an initial capital investment, DT will provide franchisees with the necessary equipment, training and ongoing support to establish themselves as the premier instructor in their region. Franchisees will retain the profit from their business, after paying a percentage to DT to cover ongoing costs.

(b) DT's competitive advantage

The driver education industry is highly competitive. Each company within this field has high capital and running costs, low margins, and a high intensity of competition.

In addition buyer power is also very high. Buyers are willing to search for the most favourable combination of price and acceptable service. Also under the conventional model there is a lack of opportunity for repeat business.

DT's unique, patented driving simulator has allowed us to create a new low cost position while still being able to compete with the larger driving school companies on quality.

DT believes that the critical success factors for this industry are all met by our new and innovative training approach:

(1) Excellent reputation which will stimulate referrals
(2) Improved driver success rates which provides sustainable competitive advantage
(3) Minimises time commitment required from the learner
(4) Reduces cost of training for trainee
(5) Lowest possible cost base for instructor

(c) **Benefits to you as a franchisee**

(1) An innovative training product that is patent protected and a unique selling point compared to other instructors in your area

(2) The benefits of running your own business but with the initial training, advice and ongoing support to establish yourself as a driving instructor

(3) Risks of set up are shared with DT, as are some of the initial costs

(4) Lower running costs for your business – less vehicle wear and tear, lower repairs, reduced fuel costs

(5) A better return on your time since using the simulator four drivers can be trained at any one time 'off road'

(6) Increased market potential as you can extend your services to existing and commercial drivers and extend the revenue from learners by offering them advanced driving courses via the simulator

(7) You will benefit from national advertising and awareness of the DT brand

(8) Reduces the seasonality of your business as the simulator can be used to maintain driver training and hence income in the winter months and for non daylight hours

Examiner's comments:

This question involves a relatively new UK business providing training for learner car drivers, via a virtual reality driving simulator. The business is keen to expand but the owner is unsure whether to achieve this by offering franchise arrangements to would-be driving instructors or an equity stake to a European driving school wishing to expand into the UK.

Marks on this question were polarised. There were some very good attempts but it was also noticeable that candidates who had mismanaged their time allocation failed to score well on this question.

Requirement 5.1 requested candidates to prepare a SWOT analysis of the current strategic position of DT. This was reasonably well done although many candidates failed to indicate the major issues, despite a specific requirement to do so. Some weaker candidates mixed up the internal nature of strengths and weaknesses with the external nature of opportunities and threats, and candidates who used a grid presentation with undeveloped bullet points scored limited marks.

Requirement 5.2 asked candidates to evaluate the key factors to be considered with respect to the two proposals for expansion. Candidates did well here, with almost all clearly distinguishing the governance/control, risks and resource requirement issues of each of the two proposals. Better candidates linked their comments back to the key issues identified in 5.1 and skills marks were awarded to those who recognised that there were two parties involved in the expansion. Thus for example, while DT might need to provide resources for franchisees, it would also benefit from the sharing of risk and reduced exposure should the franchised business fail.

Requirement 5.3 asked candidates to produce three sections of a business plan to attract potential franchisees, covering DT's business model, the basis of DT's competitive advantage and the benefits for a franchisee.

Weaker candidates failed to appreciate that the business plan asked for in part 5.3 was specifically aimed at attracting potential franchisees, and so should be couched in appropriate terms, not in overly academic ones; also that a discussion of the 'cons' of DT's strategy would be inappropriate. Some struggled to distinguish adequately between DT's business model and its competitive advantage, repeating the same points under both headings and a significant minority limited their mark by concentrating on the benefits for DT rather than the franchisee.

6 CWI International Ltd (March 2009)

		Knowledge	Skill	Marks
6.1	Report format	1	–	
	Data analysis/explanation/financial and non-financial	2	9	
	Other information	2	4	
				14
6.2	Barriers and overcoming them	3	4	6
		8	17	20

General comments:

This was the data analysis question. CWI International Ltd (CWI) operates a chain of English language schools in a range of African, European and Asian countries. Each CWI school offers course for two types of qualification leading to an external exam: International Baccalaureate Diploma (IBD) and Test of English as a Foreign Language (TOEFL). These are aimed at 16-18 year old students and entrance is selective. CWI are in the process of applying for accreditation by the English Language Board (ELB) and as a result need to introduce a new performance measurement system (covering tutors, results, class sizes, materials and management), since the current approach is simply to monitor pass rates against world-wide averages. The chief executive believes this will also help identify underperforming schools and tutors and might be used to differentiate CWI when talking to prospective students. Candidates were provided with some financial and operating data for the company as a whole, together with recent statistics on pass rates for both qualifications.

Overall, candidates performed fairly well. Some candidates started off badly on this question by failing to produce it in the required report format.

To: Chief Executive of CWI Ltd
From: AN Consultant
Date: XX March 20X9
Subject: CWI – Performance measurement system

This report sets out the issues to consider in implementing the proposed performance measurement system in order to gain ELB accreditation.

6.1 (1) Performance analysis

> **Tutorial note:**
>
> Here are potentially a lot of different figures that could be calculated by candidates in answering this question, given the richness of the data provided. The skill here is analysing and discussing the key data and not crunching all available numbers. It is suggested that candidates include the key figures in an Appendix to the report.
>
> Here, in addition to the suggested appendix, which contains the analysis discussed in the report, a separate schedule of possible calculations has also been included at the end of the answer, for marking purposes.
>
> Where different approaches to calculations are possible, and acceptable, candidates are advised to show their workings or explain their method eg candidates adopted a number of different approaches in calculating gross profit and some chose to include grant income in calculating gross profit margin.

Key indicators of the financial and non-financial performance of CWI during 20X7 and 20X8 are set out in Appendix 1 to this report.

Commentary on performance

There has been a significant growth in fee income over the period (31%), which as course fees have remained constant, must relate to the increased volume of students (56% for IBD courses and 14% for TOEFL).

However as the revenue per school has only increased by 5% year on year, a substantial amount of the increase is presumably a result of the increase in the number of schools from 8 to 10. More information would be needed as to when these came on stream in 20X8 and how many courses each was offering.

The fact that revenue has increased because of expansion in the number of schools rather than improved efficiency is underlined by the fact that while sales have increased by 31%, expenditure has increased by 36%.

Allowing for the increase in the number of schools, it is clear that whilst IBD revenue has gone forward, TOEFL revenue has gone backwards. This is reflected in the sales mix, with IBD income increasing from 41% sales in 20X7 to 48% in 20X8.

IBD courses

The average figures per school suggest that the growth in IBD revenue appears to have come from CWI schools offering additional courses (an average of 3 per school in 20X8 compared to 20X7). However it is unlikely that all schools have increased the volume of IBD courses on offer.

Instead it is possible that CWI has acquired two additional schools during the year whose focus is IBD courses, although if there has been no organic growth within the existing 8 schools, then the additional schools would need to be very sizeable to account for the additional 14 IBD courses. The reality is likely to be somewhere in between.

Certainly the increase in revenue appears to have come at a price, as the average class size has dropped from 20 to just fewer than 17, leaving CWI with spare capacity, although this may be looked on favourably by the ELB.

Whilst the reduced class size might be expected to lead to improved pass rates, this has not happened. In fact the IBD pass rate has dropped and is now only 7% above the worldwide average (compared to 10% in 20X7). This could mean that CWI have had to accept less able students in order to fill places or that the new schools are not as successful as the existing ones. However as the IBD is a 2 year course it is likely to be the end of 20X9 before the true impact on results can be seen.

Overall the impact of the change in sales mix and the spare capacity created in the IBD classrooms is to reduce the gross profit margin from 60% to 56%. A breakdown of staff costs is required in order to assess the margins made on each type of course, as well as the breakdown of the financial results by school to assess the profitability of each school.

TOEFL courses

Although the average figures suggest that the existing schools have reduced the number of TOEFL courses they are offering, as mentioned above, more information is required about the number and breakdown of the courses offered by the two new schools to properly assess the position.

If the majority of courses offered by the new schools are IBD courses then the existing schools have managed to grow their TOEFL revenue organically.

These courses are likely to have been more profitable in 20X8 due to the increased class size (12.8 students compared to 12).

TOEFL pass rates have remained largely consistent across the two years and are considerably above the worldwide average. It is possible that IBD get the best quality students and the pass rates are therefore higher because of the ability of the students rather than the quality of the courses. Also the courses could be more intensive and costly than the opposition so the pass rates are higher as a result. (Other students could be self taught which lowers the general pass rate.)

Expenditure

Key resources within the school are staff costs and premises which accounted for 64% of fee income in 20X8 compared to 62% in 20X7. This increase is likely to be due to the additional staff and rooms associated with the increase in the number of courses.

Other expenses have remained largely consistent as a percentage of fee income, with the exception of marketing which has increased from 7 to 10% of revenue. This is likely to have been incurred to market the new schools and to generate demand for the additional IBD courses.

Net profit

Since the schools are largely a fixed cost business they will have high operating gearing and need to operate courses at full capacity to ensure a good overhead recovery rate. Thus despite the significant increase in revenue, the reduction in the gross profit margin and the increase in marketing expenses has led to a net profit margin of 7% compared to 12 % last year.

Without the grant income, CWI would have made a loss in 20X8 and more information is required as to the nature of the grants and the extent to which this is regular, recurring income.

(2) **Additional information and performance measures**

> ### Tutorial note:
>
> This answer is longer than a candidate would have been expected to produce but a variety of different points have been included below for marking purposes.

Detail on individual schools

The analysis above is based on data for an average school. In reality the 10 schools may be different sizes and offer a different mix of courses. Depending on the nature of the staff and/or the student catchment, some may have more success at one qualification than another.

In order to assess each individual school, a breakdown of revenue, costs, staff and pass rates by school is required.

Comparative information

In order to interpret performance, information is needed regarding budgets and targets, competitors and industry norms, so that CWI can benchmark performance not just between its schools but against others in the industry. This would help CWI assess which schools are performing well and which are not, both currently and with respect to changes over time.

The stated ELB criteria covers teachers, results, class sizes, materials, management, student welfare and premises. CWI need to obtain information regarding the targets which will be set by the ELB in each of the performance areas and specifically any restrictions that they are likely to place on class sizes which will affect CWI's flexibility and efficiency.

It is also important to distinguish the performance of the school from the performance of the manager. A badly performing school could be improved by changing the manager or it could be the inevitable consequence of its local market, additional competition or other non-controllable factors.

Internal benchmarks – comparisons of pass rates, resource utilisation, revenue growth and profit compared to the best performing school in CWI. The problem with this measure is that the performance of any school might be a function of its location, as well as its management, nevertheless, perhaps some lessons could be learned.

External/Competitive benchmarks – compares to the industry leader in the sector and the locality. Information might be hard to come by for competitive language schools, however, indicators are: fees charged, courses offered, pass rates.

In looking at performance, revenues are generated throughout the world. The ability to charge high fees in say Africa is different to a prosperous nation (eg Germany) and this will impact performance. Expenditure if incurred locally is also likely to be lower.

Exchange rate volatility is a further issue in measuring performance consistently.

Multiple performance measures

As the ELB will use a range of assessment measures, any system implemented by CWI should use as wide a range of measures as possible, both financial and non-financial.

One tool by which this can be achieved is the balanced scorecard which looks at the following perspectives:

- Financial
- Customer
- Innovation and learning
- Internal business
- Thus in addition to the analysis above, other useful information would include:

  - Financial – staff costs split by IBD/TOEFL to assess profitability by course

  - Customer – customer satisfaction surveys/student feedback forms regarding standards of tuition, facilities, pastoral support etc

  - Innovation and learning:

    (1) External recognition of student/tutor achievements
    (2) Qualifications held by staff
    (3) No of staff undertaking extra training/qualifications
    (4) No of candidates accepted for further education

  - Internal business:

    (1) Staff turnover
    (2) No of staff whose teaching is assessed as satisfactory and above
    (3) No of student drop outs
    (4) No of applicants vs no of places available
    (5) Value added by school ie actual pass rates vs predicted pass rates
    (6) Extracurricular activities offered
    (7) Details of the course materials used by CWI

Future performance

Other useful information would be budgets for the forthcoming periods and the assumptions on which the budgets are based.

Projections of eg student numbers, staff and premises costs, fee income, capital expenditure would be useful.

It would also be useful to know the basis on which grant income is awarded and the extent to which this is recurring income.

Market research could indicate whether the data that is available for past periods can be projected into the future with any reasonable degree of reliability.

Appendix 1: Analysis of financial and non-financial performance 20X7/X8

	20X8	20X7
Financial analysis		
Sales mix:		
IBD	48%	41%
TOEFL	52%	59%
Profitability:		
Gross profit margin (tuition fees – tutor costs)/tuition fees	56%	60%
Net profit margin (PBIT/total income)	7%	12%
Resources: expenditure as a % of total tuition fees		
Staff costs and premises	64%	62%
Marketing	10%	7%
Performance indicators		
Tuition revenue per school	£744k	£708k
IBD		
No of courses per school	3	2
Ave class size	16.7 students	20 students
Percentage points above worldwide average pass rate	7%	10%
TOEFL		
No of courses per school	24	28
Ave class size	12.8 students	12 students
Percentage points above worldwide average pass rate	15%	15%

	% Increase between 20X8/X7
IBD tuition fees	56.25
TOEFL tuition fees	14.29
Total fee income	31.36
Total expenses	36.04
Revenue per school	5.08

Examiner's comments:

Requirement 6.1 was the data analysis section of the paper which has been indicated as a regular feature of Business Strategy papers. It asked candidates to evaluate the financial and non-financial performance of CWI, based on the data and other information provided. They were also asked to identify and justify any additional information required to better assess the performance of the individual schools.

Most candidates coped reasonably with the analysis of performance and were engaged with the financial and non-financial data and understood the links. Most were also happy to try to explain why changes in performance had come about, not just describe what had come about, and appeared to have spent about the right amount of time calculating ratios. Some weaker candidates only provided qualitative analysis or only made a nominal quantitative attempt by just repeating data from the question. Where candidate did address the data, some set out their quantitative analysis at the beginning of their answer, then provided the discussion. Others interspersed calculations and comments throughout their answer. Either approach was acceptable, although better candidates normally tended to use the first of these methods.

It was somewhat disappointing that the majority of candidates failed to appreciate that the ELB was looking at particular indicators such as class sizes, and therefore the company may have been seeking to reduce class sizes in order to gain accreditation. However, in the course of their analyses a pleasing number of candidates did pick up on the importance of performance by school and by course, which informed their suggestions for other information that would be useful. Whilst clearly prepared for the requirement to specify additional information, weaker candidates lost marks by failing to justify their answers or by merely listing further information in the context of performance measurement in general rather than in respect of individual schools.

6.2 Barriers to change and approaches to overcome

Barriers to change

All changes tend to be resisted by employees. The nature of the changes such as CWI are proposing may be resisted strongly by staff or schools that feel they are underperforming – particularly if employees find out about the CEO's plans to use the new system to help identify and address this.

(1) **Cultural barriers**

Structural inertia: the existing system of performance measurement that is focused purely on exam results may act as a barrier to change to a new wider measurement process.

Power structures within CWI may be threatened if it becomes clear that a particular school or particular members of staff are more important or more successful than others. This will in particular affect management and thus management may be reluctant to implement changes which will be against their own interests.

Group inertia may block change where the changes are inconsistent with the norms of team working and departments, or where they threaten their interests. Thus schools may resist comparison with each other as they are not used to working within a competitive environment. CWI may also face resistance from unions which are common in the teaching profession.

(2) **Personnel barriers**

There are also barriers which affect individuals and result in them seeing the change as a threat eg to earnings and job security. Teaching staff may be worried by what they see as implied criticism of past performance. They may resist the new appraisal system as a result of their fear of the unknown or use selective information to justify their position. As they are not used to being appraised in this way, the new system is likely to make them feel uncomfortable.

(3) **Psychological contract**

Pressures will arise if the changes affect the current set of expectations between the employee and the employer. In this case the staff may perceive a change in the way in which they are being managed.

Approaches to overcome the barriers

Staff are likely to get used to the new performance measurement system if given sufficient time to do so.

Information about the proposals should be freely circulated and staff should be given an opportunity to talk about their concerns.

The change must be sold. Staff need to be convinced that accreditation by the ELB is a good thing and that the measurement system is a necessary step to achieve this. Rather than focussing on the more threatening angle of identifying the underperformers, the positive aspects of the change need to be encouraged eg the ability to differentiate the school using these measures, the ability to rewards schools and staff for good performance, CWI should provide learning/training opportunities for staff. They will need help to adapt and reassurance about the impact of the system on pay and job security.

Resentment and fear is likely to be lessened if staff feel that they have been involved throughout the change process.

The project manager will need to act as a change agent in order to drive the new system through.

The Lewin/Schein three stage (Iceberg) model could be used to summarise the necessary approach:

(1) Unfreeze existing staff behaviour by selling the reasons for change (eg the need for accreditation to attract more students)

(2) Move the attitude by communicating the new norms and encouraging staff to welcome and adopt the new measurement culture (through learning and participation)

(3) Refreeze the new behaviour eg by offering incentives/reward system to motivate staff to pursue the accreditation targets

Examiner's comments:

Requirement 6.2 asked candidates to explain the barriers that may be encountered in implementing the new performance measurement system and to indicate how these might be overcome. As usual, the majority of candidates showed good knowledge in this area, but often failed to earn the skills marks available for applying this to the scenario. Weaker candidates either made general points without reference to any theory or discussed barriers to change and possible change management approaches including Lewin's 'unfreeze/move/refreeze' model, in generic terms. Better candidates made reference to the nature of the staff and the context of accreditation. It was evident that quite a number of candidates simply equate 'change' with 'redundancies', an assumption that was not really supported by a scenario based on amending a performance measurement system.

7 Kemmex Ice Cream plc (June 2009)

Marking guide

		Knowledge	Skill	Marks
7.1	Barriers to entry	3	6	8
7.2	Market share evaluation and definition	2	5	6
7.3	(a) Data analysis and explanation	3	9	
	(b) Price reduction – Strategy 1	2	5	
				17
7.4	(a) Risks	3	4	
	(b) Marketing strategy	3	4	
				12
		16	33	43

General comments:

The scenario in this question looks at a listed company which manufactures ice cream in the 'economy' sector of the market. The company has attempted to expand recently by lowering its selling price in order to increase sales volumes. While sales revenues have increased, profits have fallen and there is a dispute between the finance director and the marketing director as to whether it is appropriate to continue with this strategy. An alternative strategy has been put forward by the marketing director which is to enter the premium branded sector of the market using a licensing agreement to utilise a brand name of a large confectionary manufacturer.

7.1 Economies of scale and capital investment

The lowest barriers to entry are in the 'economy' sector of the ice cream market which is characterised by smaller manufacturers. The smaller scale of production and lower quality levels mean that the production process is less capital intensive and thus the direct entry costs of capital investment are lowest in this sector. As a result, economies of scale would be less significant as a barrier to entry than in other sectors of the ice cream market.

Moreover, as this ice cream is not branded, then there is not the requirement for marketing expenditure which is necessary in other sectors to compete with larger producers.

In the premium branded sectors, economies of scale are more significant as large scale production is needed to cover significant capital investment and brand advertising. Smaller new entrants may therefore find it hard to compete. Existing small ice cream companies in the 'economy' sector could also find it difficult to enter the premium sector from their existing market position (see notes below concerning KIC's Strategy 2).

Product differentiation and switching costs

There is little branding in the economy sector of the market, thus there is little brand loyalty by consumers. This means that switching is possible by consumers so it is less difficult for a new entrant to enter the 'economy' market.

In the premium sectors there is more branding and thus loyalty may be significant, making switching more restricted and thus new products would take longer, and at greater cost, to become established.

It would appear there are near zero switching costs for a consumer to transfer from one brand to another so this is unlikely to be a barrier to entry.

Access to distribution channels

The requirement to deliver ice cream to retailers in chilled conditions adds greater costs. Larger incumbent operators are likely to have the advantage of economies of scope with a larger distribution chain.

Small new entrants can avoid the initial capital cost of delivery vehicles if they outsource deliveries, but this may increase operating costs and reduce flexibility of supply.

Distribution barriers can also include access to retailers.

Tutorial note:

A practice of restricting access to manufacturer-owned freezers located at retailers would have been a major barrier to entry. It is an advantage that this practice is now illegal but there remains the issue of attracting retailers, as customers, as well as appealing to consumers.

Cost advantages to incumbents irrespective of scale

These may include:

- Access to suppliers of ingredients on favourable or exclusive terms
- Knowledge and expertise on health and safety issues
- Knowledge and expertise on production processes
- Brand rights

These are all more likely to occur in the premium ranges where the skills and ingredients are less generic.

Response of incumbents

Large incumbent companies may defend their market positioning by aggressive marketing to counter new entrants. This might include targeted advertising in the product or geographical sector of the new entrant. Similarly, targeted price cuts or discounts may prevent new entrants gaining a foothold.

These are more likely to occur in the premium ranges where larger incumbents are more likely to defend specific brands where there is a similar new entrant launching a product in similar price-quality space, rather than for more generic ice creams.

Examiner's comments:

Candidates' answers were generally of a good standard. The two most common approaches were either (1) to structure answers according to the barriers existing in each market segment or (2) to consider each type of barrier to entry sequentially and explain how it affected the different market segments. Either approach was acceptable.

Better answers considered the relative strengths of the barriers to entry in the individual segments. Weaker candidates described the relevant barriers but did not explicitly state why they would deter entry.

7.2 Market share

If the UK ice cream market is £1,000 million and the quarter ending 31 May is typical for KIC then a full year's sales would amount to £41.4m (£10,350,000 x 4). This means the market share is 4.14% (£41.4m/£1,000m). Alternatively this would be 4% based on the quarter to 28 February 20X9 in applying the previous strategy.

This is fairly small, but the market can be redefined in terms of the take-home market as KIC only operates in this market. The size of this market is 72% of £1,000m which is £720m. This gives KIC a market share of the 'take-home' market of 5.75% (£41.4m/£720m), which is far from insignificant.

The market share could, however, be further refined to the take-home regular/economy sector. More information would be needed for this purpose.

The market share of KIC by comparison to smaller competitors is illustrated by the average size in the UK market. Total sales are £1,000 million and there are 200 manufacturers of varying sizes so the mean annual sales achieved per company in the industry in the UK is only £5m. By comparison KIC has sales of over £40m. Given that the industry is characterised by two large companies then the median size is likely to be much lower than the mean. Similarly, the average size of the manufacturers is lower in the economy sector. KIC is therefore quite large for this sector.

KIC is clearly at the low cost end of the market and with its narrow portfolio of products (currently) it is entirely dependent on this sector. Its size within this sector makes it a reasonable sized player in the market, particularly in its focussed geographical region.

The product is commodity type and largely undifferentiated so competition is in the form of distribution, service and price through cost leadership.

The above discussion excludes the European market, given the problems of transportation, although it could be argued that market share needs to consider the import/export market.

Examiner's comments:

This requirement was poorly attempted in general. Many candidates did not perform a calculation of market share but just discussed the different ways of segmenting the market in general terms. There was a lot of repetition of the facts in the question, often with little analysis. The stronger answers were those which attempted to compute market share under different market definitions and drilled down further by redefining size. Only the best answers assessed market share in relation to the likely share of most other competitors.

7.3 (a) Evaluate and explain performance

	3 months to 28 February 20X9 £'000	3 months to 31 May 20X9 £'000	% change
Sales	10,000	10,350	+3.5%
Production costs			
Variable	5,000	5,750	+15%
Fixed	2,500	2,500	–
Distribution costs			
Variable	500	750	+50%
Fixed	250	250	–
Administration and other fixed operating costs	1,250	1,250	–
Operating profit/(loss)	500	(150)	
Number of customers	2,500 outlets	3,000 outlets	+20%

Sales prices have been reduced by 10% thus, comparing the two quarters on a constant price basis, growth in sales volumes can be determined:

$$\frac{10,350}{10,000 \times 0.9} = 15\%$$

Alternatively:

$$\frac{10,350/0.9}{10,000} = 15\%$$

This increase in sales volumes is consistent with the objective of increasing market share.

Variable production costs have therefore changed in direct proportion to sales volumes.

Despite the sales volumes increasing by 15% and sales prices decreasing by only 10% this has had an adverse effect on profits. The reasons for the fall in profits are best analysed in the first instance prior to distribution costs.

The changes can then be analysed according to the impact on the existing customer base and the impact of the new customers.

In terms of the existing customers, the loss of contribution is just the loss of 10% of sales revenue (as 'sales volumes to existing customers have been consistent with those in the quarter to 28 February 20X9').

As a consequence, controlling for the price change and comparing sales to existing customers, the profit before distribution costs would be:

	3 months to 28 February 20X9 £'000	3 months to 31 May 20X9 £'000
Sales	10,000	9,000
Production costs		
Variable	5,000	5,000
Fixed	2,500	2,500
	2,500	1,500

There is therefore a loss of contribution of £1m of sales to existing customers as a consequence of the price reduction.

Sales to new customers are therefore the remaining sales. Thus the profit before distribution costs for new customers would be:

	3 months to 31 May 20X9 £'000
Sales	1,350
Production costs	
Variable	750
Incremental fixed costs	–
	600

Overall therefore the contribution prior to distribution costs has fallen by £400,000 from £2.5m to £2.1m (£600,000 + £1.5m). The extra contribution of £600,000 from sales to new customers, is insufficient to compensate for the lost revenue from existing customers due to reducing selling prices to them (£1m).

The increase in distribution costs of £250,000 reduces the contribution from new customers further to £350,000 (£600,000 – £250,000).

This means an overall reduction in profit of £650,000 (£400,000 + £250,000) which explains the reduction in operating profit from £500,000 to an operating loss of £150,000.

The fact that distribution costs have risen by 50% while sales volumes have risen by only 15% is a matter for concern. This may be due to the following:

- The new sales are to 'retailers well beyond the 100 mile limit that we used to have and this is where most of our new customers have arisen.' The distribution costs are therefore greater due to larger distances.

- The new customers cover a wider area so are likely to be more spread out giving diseconomies of scope.

- The new customers are smaller on average than existing customers. At the new prices average quarterly sales to existing customers are £3,600 (£9m/2,500). Average sales to new customers are £2,700 (£1.35m/500). If order costs are fixed per delivery, then smaller deliveries are (for the moment at least) being made to new customers so there is less profit per sale to cover delivery costs.

Overall, therefore, short term financial performance has been poor as a consequence of the price reduction. It may be, however, that the marketing director is correct is saying it is too early to judge, as there may be other effects not considered:

- Lagged effects – customers and consumers may take a while to react to the new prices (eg terminating existing contracts with other ice cream suppliers may take a while before they can buy more from KIC).

- Competitor reaction – if competitors do not copy the price reduction then sales volumes may increase substantially in future. If, however, competitors follow the price reduction, then the market sector may be locked into lower prices with lower profits in the industry sector.

(b) **Evaluate the price reduction strategy**

A reduction in price should generate more sales, but the extent to which it does so will depend on the elasticity of demand. Current evidence suggests that demand is elastic as sales volumes have increased by 15% in response to a 10% price reduction. However, while this indicates an improvement in revenue, it has already been demonstrated that profits may fall due to the increases in variable production costs and distribution costs.

The source of the increase in sales volumes is also important. Potentially it could increase the sales volumes to existing customers, but it could also generate new customers. To date, the new strategy only appears to have achieved the latter of these two goals. To the extent that early data is reliable, this would suggest that the policy of reducing all prices by 10% was inappropriate as the price reduction to existing customers yielded no benefits and was just a deadweight loss of £1m.

A policy of price discrimination on a geographical basis may therefore have been more appropriate. Assuming no leakage between the two markets, this would have generated an incremental contribution from new customers of £600,000 while maintaining the existing operating profit of £500,000. This would have given an overall operating profit for the quarter of £1.1m.

If this price discrimination is not possible, through market leakage or alienation of existing customers, then the new policy may be justified despite short term losses, as part of a strategy of price penetration. This is where price in a new market starts low in order to penetrate the customer base and gain market share (ie in new geographical markets for KIC). Having gained some customer loyalty, prices can then be gradually increased again. If market research deems this to be feasible, then the low initial price may be an appropriate sacrifice, notwithstanding the short-term reduction in profit.

If price discrimination and/or price penetration are not possible then the price reduction policy needs to be judged on its longer term financial merits of increasing sales volume at the new lower prices on a more permanent basis.

Taking Jane's assumption of an increase of 25% this would yield the following quarterly results in steady state (assuming all new growth is out of the 100 mile radius and thus distribution costs for new customers are similar to that occurred in the last quarter).

	WORKINGS	3 months to 31 May 20X9 £'000
Sales	10,350 × 1.25	12,938
Production costs		
Variable	5,750 × 1.25	7,188
Fixed		2,500
Distribution costs		
Variable	500 + 250 + (250 × [43.75 – 15]/15)*	1,229
Fixed		250
Administration and other fixed operating costs		1,250
Operating profit/(loss)		521

* Given a 10% price reduction, sales volumes have risen by 15% (10,350/9,000). However, at the margin, variable distribution costs have risen by 50% from £500,000 to £750,000. This is because the new customers are located further away from the factory than existing customers. If sales volumes increase by a further 25% then these are also likely to be to more distant customers. Assuming that the additional variable costs for the 25% increase will be similar to the 15% increase then the overall increase is 1.15 x 1.25 = 43.75%.

On this basis profit would increase from £500,000 to £521,000, but only if Jane's assumption of 25% growth is correct.

Examiner's comments:

This requirement was the data analysis section of the paper which has been indicated as a regular feature of Business Strategy papers. Part (a) asked candidates to assess and explain the performance of KIC in the most recent quarter using the available data. Part (b) asked candidates to evaluate the price reduction strategy (Strategy 1). In general, answers to this requirement were weak.

For part (a), typically the data analysis was poor – often only amounting to quantifying the movement year on year, with a commentary of what had happened, rather than an explanation of the causal factors giving rise to the changes in the figures (ie why it had happened). Many candidates did work out sales or contribution per customer, but it was disappointing how few worked out that the volume increase was 15% which was a fundamental part of the answer. As a result, many candidates incorrectly talked about variable production costs being out of control and rising disproportionately to sales. Many recognised the significant rise in distribution costs and provided reasonably good explanations for this in terms of the location of new customers. Better candidates linked evaluation to the stated objective to increase market share. Those who prepared a table of calculations at the beginning of their answers generally produced a more coherent analysis than those who made occasional, and sometimes random, calculations within their narrative. Some candidates seemed determined to produce a long list of additional info (possibly having clearly learnt this by rote!)

In part (b) there was not much numerical analysis, although a few candidates did talk about elasticity. Some candidates briefly mentioned price discrimination and market penetration. A significant minority evaluated Strategy 1 through the use of SFA (Suitability, Feasibility, Acceptability) analysis, but the discussion tended to be descriptive as opposed to analytical. Answers were awarded good marks where price elasticity of demand and break even analysis were explained.

7.4 This is a new product being sold in a new market, so it would be regarded as diversification in the Ansoff matrix. As it is in a related area of ice cream it would be regarded as related diversification.

(a) **Risks**

Break-even risks

If the price is set at the equivalent of competitors at around 50p then break-even is:

Contribution per unit is £0.50 – £0.20 – £0.05 = £0.25

Annual fixed costs are £3m + £1m = £4m

Thus sales of 16 million Chocnuts would be needed per year to break even.

This would generate annual sales of £8m (quarterly sales of £2m assuming no seasonality) just to break even.

This is an increase of 20% based on existing sales (at pre reduction prices).

There is clearly a significant risk that the break even level of sales will not be achieved and thus the new product will not make a profit.

Operating gearing

The level of fixed costs is high by comparison to the existing products. Indeed, although sales are only 20% of the existing sales (at the break-even point) the incremental fixed costs are equal to the existing level of fixed costs at £4million. In compensation, the contribution margin ratio is high for the new product at 50%. (25p contribution per 50p sale.)

As a consequence, if sales are around break-even level then operating gearing is very high, making changes in profit very sensitive to changes in sales.

Exit costs

There is a high level of initial investment, both in terms of manufacturing capability, but also in terms of an up-front royalty to the holder of the 'Chocnut' brand name rights. If the launch fails there may be high exit costs from the loss of the royalty payment and low realisable values for the machinery.

Royalty relationship

If the brand rights are short term or renewable on different terms then, if the product is a success, the owner of the brand, Yocolate, may increase the royalty to take up any excess profit.

New market

This is a new product being launched in a new market and there are therefore significant risks of product acceptance in the market and production learning for a new product.

Exchange rates

If the 'Chocnut' is to be sold in Europe then exchange rate variation provides an additional risk.

Reversal of price increase

It has been assumed that the reversal of the 10% price decrease will reassert the status quo before the change. However, the changes in price may have altered customer and consumer perceptions and there may be an unfavourable response to the restoration of the original prices applying prior to 1 March 20X9.

(b) **Marketing strategy**

Marketing strategy can be considered using the 4Ps model:

Price

The price of the product needs to be determined according to the estimated market willingness to pay and the prices of competitors for similar products. This clearly needs to be achieved through market research in order to establish the viability of the launch and this should be before any capital commitment is made.

A price penetration strategy may help establish an initial market, but may damage consumer perception about the quality of the product and therefore make it difficult to raise prices at a later date.

Product

Product marketing includes the nature of the actual product, but also the customer perception of the product that needs to be managed.

The product needs to be of high quality to achieve premium pricing. The low quality perception of the existing ice creams will need to be overcome.

The appearance of the product also needs to be appropriate in addressing consumer perceptions.

Branding is a key issue and the use of the Chocnut brand is key as it uses the instant recognition of a well know product (at a price). Using similar packaging, similar outlets and making the appearance of the product the same as the Chocnut chocolate bar will reinforce the branding image.

Brand recognition of the Chocnut brand in the rest of Europe will need to be tested by market research and the rights to use the brand outside the UK will need to be established in any contract.

Place

'Place' includes the whole issue of distribution. The existing distribution area of 100 miles appears inappropriate but this then raises similar issues of cost and economies of scope as those noted above with respect to Strategy 1.

The issue of distribution into Europe is more significant, not just in terms of cost, but for communications, currency and knowledge of markets. The extent to which a viable launch is dependent on significant European sales needs to be established and separate market research carried out.

Place refers not just to the geographical area, but also to the distribution channels used. The new product appears suitable both for the 'take home' market in the form of multipacks and for the 'impulse' purchase market.

There may be some overlap of distribution channels with existing products in the 'take home' market but this is only in a limited geographical area. The impulse market is likely to require a strategy to set up an entirely new customer base.

Sharing distribution channels with Yocolate may save costs and help access their customer base. The need for chilled distribution of ice creams may however prevent or restrict this.

Promotion

In order to support the brand, significant advertising is likely to be needed, or at least enough to match competitors. Joint advertising with Yocolate may be possible but this would assume they are willing to do this and there may be additional cost.

Promotion would need to be to both the customer (retailers) and the consumer to obtain both a push and a pull effect.

Larger customers would be a major advantage and may be the target of any promotion strategy. This might include supermarkets but also the use of intermediary wholesalers who may widen distribution through their own networks more efficiently than could be achieved by KIC directly.

Examiner's comments:

In part (a) the risks described tended to be very general, ranging from new markets, exchange rate risk and the possibility of new products. Answers were often brief, with no real development of points or application to the scenario. There were some good attempts and a reasonable number calculated break-even and discussed the implications of this for risk.

Part (b) was generally well done and most candidates used 4 Ps, or in some cases 7 Ps. Typically, the weaker candidates did not apply this analysis sufficiently to the scenario but on the whole, this section was answered well.

8 Evara Electrical Engineers Ltd (June 2009)

Marking guide

		Knowledge	Skill	Marks
8.1	Structure	3	3	
	Information systems	2	4	
				10
8.2	Ethics	3	4	6
8.3	Report	1		
	(a) New structure and recommendation	2	5	
	(b) Outsourcing v new staff	2	5	
	(c) Advice re contract	1	4	
				16
		14	25	32

General comments:

The scenario in this question involves an electrical contracting company with one large customer and a number of small commercial customers. It has a flexible pricing policy with respect to small customers which gives rise to some ethical issues. Following an acquisition of the largest customer there is the possibility of taking on the work for the entire new group under a proposed new contract, which will very significantly expand the scale of EEE's activities. A key question is whether the company can cope with the new level of activity and the most appropriate organisational structure to do so.

8.1 Organisational structure

EEE has an entrepreneurial structure where all the key decisions are centred around one person.

In terms of Mintzberg's organisational forms, Eric is at the strategic apex as a single owner-manager who exercises direct control over the operational core below him. Other functions are reduced to a minimum and are fulfilled by the two administrative employees and external professional assistance.

The organisational structure is very flat as there is only Eric and then the team leaders and general employees. There is no middle management layer and no internal technostructure. Co-ordination is achieved through direct supervision, so the structure is flexible and suitable for a dynamic environment.

The small size of the business and its geographical concentration means that it is feasible for Eric to devote adequate personal time to mange the jobs and staff personally without being unduly distracted from managerial tasks and managing the wider strategy of the business.

Eric's ability to control the operations of the business is enhanced by his technical knowledge of electrics. His control over purchases and pricing also means that significant direct control is exercised over key functions without delegation.

Information systems

Eric needs information for a number of purposes. These include:

Strategic planning: internal information includes knowledge of which are the most profitable elements of the business to develop in future (eg BB or other work) and external information about competitors and markets. Also information about future regulations that may constrain the business or provide new opportunities.

Tactical planning: Resource utilisation, staff planning; overall customer satisfaction; average recovery rates.

Operational issues: management of individual assignments; pricing and costing individual jobs; customer needs and feedback; resolving operational issues and customer needs.

A particular need may be to have information systems that are capable of producing data that can be evidenced in order to support the cost plus pricing nature of the contract with BB. Audit and verification by BB seems likely. Informal systems may be difficult to support the contract information needs for BB.

In terms of managing the business, the day to day involvement of Eric reduces the need for formal detailed information as he is likely to be aware of the labour time and materials being used on each job given his personal involvement. As the business expands, whether through one of the two suggested strategies, or otherwise, the level of detailed personal involvement becomes less and less thus more formal information systems are likely to be needed, irrespective of any contractual obligations for verifiable information to third parties.

Examiner's comments:

The identification of an entrepreneurial structure and the advantages and disadvantages associated with this was generally reasonably well done. Well prepared candidates discussed Eric's control and direct management style. Weaker candidates tended to describe the structure rather than evaluate whether it was suitable.

The information systems part was normally rather briefly answered, with some candidates omitting it all together. Candidates did note that systems were very simple and may cause problems for pricing and job cost identification.

8.2 Ethical issues exist at the level of the business and the individual. In the case of Eric however the interests of the business and the individual are closely aligned as he is the sole shareholder and managing director.

Ethics may also relate to the society and to corporate responsibility. In this case of pricing however the primary issue relates to Eric's dealing with one particular stakeholder group – the smaller customers.

EEE does not currently appear to have an ethical code thus the ethics of the company tend to be the personal ethics and morals of Eric – especially in relation to pricing, where Eric has sole responsibility.

In terms of ethical constraints Eric does not belong to a profession so there is no issue of abiding by a professional ethical code. Clearly, his dealings with customers must be legal and thus comply with the law relating to fraud and misrepresentation.

The policy of pricing on a 'willingness to pay' basis is legitimate and does not appear to be in breach of any major ethical principles, even though some customers are paying more than others for the same work. This is a common business practice of price discrimination, and is normally ethical as the customer is not forced to accept the contract and could obtain alternative quotes from other electrical firms.

The key issue is that of variations in price once the contract has commenced and it is then more difficult to go to an alternative contractor.

The ethical issues that arise are:

(1) **Honesty** – there appears to be an attempt to exaggerate faults and charge a substantial premium of 10% for a minor change to the agreed work by falsely claiming it to be major.

(2) **Transparency** – there is a lack of transparency as the customers do not have the technical knowledge to determine the extent of the variations to ascertain a fair price. EEE appears to be exploiting the lack of transparency to further its own ends.

(3) **Equity** – there is a lack of fairness in the pricing of variations compared to the main agreed work by EEE exploiting its superior technical knowledge.

Aside from the procedures of pricing variations, there is the ethical dilemma of making gifts to the budget holder. Depending on the value of the gifts, there is the potential for deception and fraud in this case. There is a potential conflict of interest as budget holder may gain personally from the gifts and, as a consequence, authorise payment of funds by his/her employer to EEE. The key ethical issues here are:

(1) The size of the gifts and whether they are sufficient to strongly influence a decision

(2) Whether the gifts are conditional upon favours being received by EEE or whether they are just given in the hope of influencing the budget holders' behaviour

(3) Whether there is transparency and the budget holders' line managers are aware of the gifts

Overall, the key ethical issue is whether the price variations are carried out openly and honestly in accordance with normal business practice. In this respect the customers have a responsibility to protect themselves (eg by limiting price variations in the contract or by obtaining third party verification of major variations). It is not an ethical obligation by Eric or EEE to do this on the customers' behalf.

Note. This may have been different if the customer had been an individual consumer who is more vulnerable.

A further ethical issue arises in respect of the SS contract. If it is signed, there is an obligation for EEE to comply with the ethical code of SS for all customers. If the pricing of variations falls outside this code then it may be misleading not only to the smaller customers, but also to SS, in dishonestly claiming compliance with its ethical code when it does not do so. If discovered, this may also have commercial consequences for EEE.

Most answers to this requirement were rather disappointing. Many did not distinguish the three different issues – pricing policy, variations and gifts. Most commented about the tickets as gifts being a bribe but many seemed to think it was unethical, rather than normal business practice, to charge different customers different prices. Better candidates mentioned price discrimination and linked the ethical issues to the new contract demands.

Many candidates failed to state explicitly the ethical issues involved eg honesty or conflict of interest. Instead, they merely described the actions that had occurred and asserted they were unethical, as if it were self evident. Some candidates appeared to believe that the ICAEW code applied to electricians and were all for contacting the ICAEW to report Eric's behaviour!

8.3 (a) **Organisational structure**

With the SS contract there would be a number of fundamental changes in the nature of the business which would require reassessment of the organisational structure. These include:

- The scale of the business would increase by 350% from revenue of £1 million to £4.5 million
- The business would be geographically dispersed, not just throughout the UK, but throughout Europe
- The complexity of the operational tasks is likely to increase requiring new skills
- Possible management of outsourcing

Personal management by Eric therefore seems unfeasible with the new contract as he is unlikely to have the time or expertise to manage operations personally, as he has done in the past. Therefore the entrepreneurial structure would probably be inappropriate for the new needs with the SS contract.

Features needed in the new structure are likely to be:

- More non operational managers in the business, perhaps as an additional layer within the organisational structure
- Greater technical expertise
- Flexibility as the SS contract may be temporary
- More formal reporting and control lines
- More support and administration staff

This is likely to lead to a taller organisational structure than EEE has at present with a narrower span of control for Eric.

Options for organisational structure include:

- *Customer or market segment divisionalisation*

  This would have a separate division responsible for each type of customer. This may however only require two divisions: SS group and other smaller customers. Key advantages are that it:

  - Focuses on customer need and customer service
  - May enable profit centre responsibility

  A key disadvantage is that the division responsible for SS is 8/9ths of the entire company and thus the divisional manager would have many of the same control problems as already cited for an entrepreneurial structure. To manage this he or she may need sub divisions (eg for the UK and Europe; or for different aspects of the work).

  Even with divisionalisation there may need to be some functional responsibility eg for finance, administration, human resources, purchasing).

- *Geographical divisionalisation*

  This could be similar to the above but based on geographical areas. Such as each region within the UK and one for continental Europe.

  A key advantage is that it could focus on local resources (eg staff located in an area) a key disadvantage is that it may lack a customer focus and require some centralisation (eg a company-wide safety inspection for SS).

- *Functional structure*

  This would divide the company according to work specialism, with departments defined according to functions. For example: operations; finance; purchasing; human resources; outsourcing management.

  Problems for EEE would include:

  – A lack of customer focus
  – Does not reflect business processes of individual assignments
  – More difficult to attribute profits and losses

General issues

(1) Within any of these structures, the apex would be likely to require a board of directors rather than just Eric as an individual. The board is likely to need a range of skills (finance, technical, HRM) as well as responsibilities (eg divisional managers in a divisionalised structure). The apex would then be given a greater capacity for strategic planning and operational control.

(2) While there is a need to manage the increased size of the business there is a danger that the SS contract may be lost after a year and EEE revert to a smaller organisation with a revenue of only £0.5 million from smaller customers (as work for BB would also be lost under the new regime). If this is the case, then an entrepreneurial structure may again become appropriate. Any new structure should therefore be flexible and capable, as far as possible, of reversal. The probability of losing the contract needs to be assessed as early as possible.

(3) A different type of management structure may be needed according to whether the additional capacity is acquired through outsourcing or with new staff (see below).

(b) **Outsourcing or new staff**

A significant increase in the size of the business means that new capacity is essential. Key issues in acquiring the new capacity are:

(1) The scale of the increase relative to the existing size of the business is immense (350%) therefore the new work will dominate the existing work. There may be problems in hiring sufficient employees with the right skills, in the right locations in should a short period given the scale of the labour increase.

(2) There is a need, not just for more staff, but for greater skills, including some which the existing staff do not possess. Outsourcing may provide more immediate, more flexible and more reliable access to these skills than attempting to employ individuals. This is particularly the case if these skills are only needed occasionally.

(3) While greater human resources is a key need, there is also a requirement for additional support services for these people. If new electricians are employed then there is likely to be the need also to acquire the additional support services to manage these employees and the operations that they will carry out. With outsourcing some of the support services may come with the additional human resources (eg equipment, training, technical support). If new electricians are employed then there is likely to be the need also to acquire the additional support services to manage these employees and the operations that they will carry out.

(4) There is a risk that the new contract with SS will not be renewed after a year or, if it is, then it may not be renewed at some stage in the near future if there are annual contract reviews. Given that this contract will make up 89% of the revenue of EEE, then there will need to be major downsizing if the contract is lost. These exit costs are likely to be

significant if 100 new employees are hired in terms of redundancy costs and disposal of support assets. Outsourcing is likely to be more flexible in this respect if the duration of the outsourcing contracts match those of EEE's contract with SS.

(5) Cost is likely to be a major factor. Outsourcing is likely to be much more expensive than employing individuals as the outsourcing companies will charge a significant premium over the wage costs of their employees.

(6) Both outsourcing and employment of additional staff raise quality problems of different kinds. Outsourcing would require contractual control over quality with penalties for any shortfall. Nevertheless, while some control over technical quality can be exercised, the control over service delivery and customer satisfaction can be more difficult.

Similarly, however, staff recruitment and training to obtain so many new, good quality employees in such a short period may be difficult.

(7) The cost plus pricing formula with SS needs to be considered for the impact on the contract price of (a) outsourcing (where most of the costs are direct) compared to (b) internal hiring of more staff (where support costs may be largely overheads).

It should not be assumed that any costs incurred can be recovered in full from SS with a profit mark up. Nor should it be assumed that the price to SS under the formula will be the same irrespective of whether outsourcing takes place.

Summary

The key issues appear to be:

- Immediacy of the requirement, being in only six months' time
- Cost
- Flexibility as the need may be temporary
- Impact on contract price

A possible decision may include:

(1) Employ staff on temporary contracts where possible (although this may influence the quality of the staff that can be acquired).

(2) Obtain a mix of new staff and outsourcing, where outsourcing provides the flexible top slice and the technical skills, with temporary employees providing the core.

(c) **Decision to accept the contract**

The status quo of having the small customers plus BB does not appear to be an option that is on offer. Therefore some significant change is required.

The choices are:

- Significant downsizing to have only smaller customers with a revenue of £0.5 million (ie half the previous size)

- Scaling up to £4.5 million revenue by accepting the SS contract but taking on the risk annually of losing the contract

One view may be that the SS contract would make more profit in one year than downsizing would make in many years thus accepting the contract would be advantageous even if it is only temporary. This, however, ignores the initial investment in assets and new procedures to engage in the contract and the exit costs to be incurred if, and when, the SS contract were to be terminated.

The key issue therefore is to determine the likelihood of renewal. This depends partly on EEE's strategic capability of delivering on the contract and the intentions of SS. Given that at least some of the new contract appears to be beyond the current core competences of EEE, then significant risks are apparent and there is significant reliance on the ability of EEE to engage successfully in change management and on the ability to acquire new key skills and resources in the next six months.

Answers to this requirement were good overall. For part (a), there were some rather generic answers. Most candidates concluded in favour of restructuring on a divisional or functional basis. There was also some support for matrix structures and Handy's shamrock. The inappropriateness of continuing with the entrepreneurial structure and the point of Eric being unable to maintain direct control over activities was well recognised.

In part (b), knowledge of outsourcing was good. A pleasing number identified key points including the volume of employees, skills required, contract renewal issues, control of staff, standard of work and availability/influence over staff. A number of candidates seemed to think Eric would outsource the whole contract to one company which is unlikely to be the case and only better candidates realised a mix of employees and subcontractors could be an option. The impact of the decision on the cost plus contract pricing formula was considered by some better candidates.

In part (c), some did a full SFA (Suitability, Feasibility, Acceptability) analysis despite the 'briefly advise' requirement. Better candidates discussed the need for change management and talked about Eric's future objectives. Few made the point that the status quo was not an option and that refusal of the contract would mean the loss of a major customer. Only a minority of answers were linked to, and flowed from, the points made in other parts of the question.

9 Rugeley Tableware plc (September 2009)

Marking guide

		Knowledge	Skill	Marks
9.1	SWOT	1	9	8
9.2	Ansoff	3	6	8
9.3	Decentralisation	3	3	
	Change management issues	3	3	
				10
9.4	Benchmarking	3	5	7
9.5	Corporate governance and NEDs	4	4	7
		17	30	40

General comments:

The scenario in this question looks at a listed company which is a niche manufacturer of quality ceramic tableware, based in UK. The company has attempted to address competition from cheaper imports by outsourcing some of its manufacturing operations to Asia, however this has not halted the decline in sales and profitability. The institutional shareholders have been openly critical of Belinda Rugeley (the Chairman and Chief executive) who runs the company in an authoritarian manner and has refused to appoint non-executive directors. The board is considering the future strategic options. The marketing director has suggested a strategy of both market and product development to attract a wider range of consumers. The production director on the other hand believes the lack of sales is a result of supply chain issues and the centralised management structure. He has identified a consumer electronics company that could be used to benchmark the supply chain and has also suggested changing the decision making structure of the company.

9.1 (1) Swot analysis

Strengths

- Long established business with a previously good record of growth and profitability
- Prestigious brand image and reputation and client base includes top hotels and restaurants
- High quality exclusive luxury product (may be recession proof as truly wealthy unaffected by credit crunch)
- Reputation for innovation (although not clear if this is still true today)
- Move to outsourcing is evidence that management are prepared to change
- Listed company therefore should have access to finance

Weaknesses

- Falling profits and negative operational cashflow are a cause for concern
- Unfashionable product, hence limited market with focus on older generation which restricts sales
- Poor customer service and high level of overdue orders may lose business
- High inventories lead to increased costs including obsolescence
- Long lead times due to overseas manufacturing will lead to dissatisfied customers
- Inflexibility and slow response times due to centralised structure and Belinda's authoritarian approach may mean alternative strategies are not fully considered
- More expensive than alternative products offered by cheap imports and retailers own brands
- Lack economies of scale of global ceramics manufacturers and presumably also can't match their marketing budget
- Not diversified so no spread of risk
- Lack of compliance with principles of good corporate governance
- Institutional shareholders have been openly critical of Belinda Rugeley which will undermine confidence in the company and its management

Opportunities

- New product ranges eg designer everyday tableware
- New markets eg Asia, younger generation
- Expand into related products eg glassware, crystal, gifts
- Get taken over by one of global manufacturers
- Take over a competitor
- Re-engineer supply chain
- Change the structure of the company and the decision making

Threats

- Changing dining trends mean product has reached end of life cycle
- Credit crunch means further sales decline is likely
- High levels of competition from cheap imports, large global retailers and more diversified competitors may further reduce market share

- Liquidation as a result of poor cash position

- Dissatisfaction of institutional shareholders may cause them to force change

(2) Key issues

The key issues are:

- The declining financial position raises questions over the long term viability of the business

- The long term change in dining habits which has significantly impacted on R's sales and means that its core product appears to be at the end of its life cycle, as a result R urgently needs to pursue other opportunities for growth

- Poor customer service which is inconsistent with premium product

- The centralised authoritarian structure and the dissatisfaction of the institutional shareholders which needs to be addressed as a matter of priority

Examiner's comments:

In requirement 9.1 candidates were asked to prepare a SWOT analysis of Rugeley's current strategic position, highlighting key issues. Most candidates scored well here and it was pleasing to note an increase in the number of candidates providing explanations as to why a particular point was a strength or weakness etc. Some weaker candidates produced an imbalanced SWOT with a long list of strengths, when the weaknesses and threats were of far more concern in this scenario. A surprising number also made little effort to highlight the key issues, despite the specific requirement to do so. Those candidates that chose to include a summary at the end highlighting the need for Rugeley urgently to address the issues of declining demand, increased competition and negative cashflow, tended to score very well.

9.2 Strategic options proposed by marketing director

The following matrix, developed by Ansoff, can be used to analyse the possible growth strategies available to Rugeley.

	Existing product	New product
Existing market	Internal efficiency and market penetration	Product development
New market	Market development	Diversification

(1) Internal efficiency and market penetration involve attempts to reduce cost or further penetrate existing markets by taking market share from the competition. The outsourcing of some manufacturing in 20X0 was presumably an attempt at increasing internal efficiency in order to match competitors through low cost manufacturing, but this does not appear to have generated additional sales. Thus to achieve market penetration, it may be better, as the marketing director suggests, to focus on differentiating itself from its competitors on a quality basis.

A marketing campaign aimed at emphasising the traditional English heritage might achieve this, although the problems identified by the SWOT analysis (and the marketing director) suggest that this approach may not be viable given the change in dining habits, the narrow customer base and the credit crunch. Indeed given that Rugeley are operating in a niche market, their market share/level of penetration may already be high and there may be little scope to increase this, unless they can persuade customers to buy multiple dinner services for different occasions or increase penetration of sales to hotels and restaurants eg through links with Melinda James.

Hence increased sales growth is likely to necessitate other strategies.

(2) Product development involves selling new products to existing customers and normally requires research and development expenditure.

The introduction of the Melinda James everyday designer tableware range could be said to represent product development, although it is also possible to view this as simply an extension of the existing product range.

The fact that R intends to introduce this by way of a joint venture would be deemed 'External domestic development' according to Lynch's expansion matrix. This shares some of the risk and may allow R to save on marketing as it will enjoy additional publicity from the association with Melinda.

Alternatively, as this product is not going to be targeted at existing customers, who are in the older age range and may not associate with the celebrity chef, it could be argued that it is a means of market development (see below).

Other possible product development opportunities include: increased R&D to make innovations in patterns and designs; own brand ranges for large retail chains; giftware, glassware and other associated items for dining.

(3) Market development involves selling existing products to new customers and involves investment in marketing.

In this case the marketing director is proposing two elements of market development:

Domestic expansion in terms of targeting a new market segment of younger customers (discussed above).

Overseas expansion in the context of exporting to the Asian market. According to Lynch this could be achieved organically or through some form of JV/licensing agreement. The fact that the marketing director is keen to emphasise the English heritage may mean that use of a 'local' partner is inappropriate.

R could also consider overseas development of other markets eg India.

(4) Diversification involves making new products for new markets. It can be vertical (backward or forward in the firm's existing production chain), horizontal (acquisition of competitors) or conglomerate (a move into a totally different area). R does not appear to be considering diversification at this point in time.

Possible diversification opportunities include wider ceramics manufacture for bathrooms and kitchens. As they have no experience of this, it would be sensible to use 'external development' methods eg JV/acquisition

Note. It is possible to argue that the JV with Melissa James (everyday tableware for the younger market) is related diversification (new product and new market).

Examiner's comments:

In requirement 9.2 candidates were asked to use Ansoff to analyse the marketing director's proposals. Candidates tended to score well here. Not all candidates depicted the Ansoff matrix and provided an explanation of the framework but most were able to explain where the marketing director's strategies would be positioned on the grid. Better candidates went on to discuss the appropriateness of each growth strategy in light of their SWOT analysis and the risks involved, pointing out that the risk of introducing a new designer range of everyday tableware might be reduced via the joint venture with a celebrity chef.

9.3 Decentralisation and change management issues

Decentralisation proposals

Currently it appears that Belinda Rugeley has adopted a very authoritarian, centralised management structure, with all key decisions being taken at Board level. The structure of the business does not appear to have changed despite growth.

The production director suggests that this has stifled innovation, and led to inflexibility and slow response times. He also implies that the sales forecasts produced centrally may have been inaccurate causing problems of overstocking and at the same time outstanding orders.

There are four bases for benchmarking:

- Internal – comparisons within the business over time, or between business units
- Competitive – comparisons with other firms in the same industry/sector
- Best in class/Activity – best practice in a completely different industry
- Generic – against a conceptually similar process

Internal and competitive benchmarking would involve making comparisons within R's own industry. To an extent R has done this in the past, as competitive benchmarking led it to outsource some of its manufacturing in 20X0.

When a company or its whole industry is performing badly or losing out to other industries, there is a case for the wider perspective offered by 'best in class' and generic benchmarking. This would involve identifying suitable benchmarking partners.

The production director is thus correct that there may be lessons to learn from PCE's experience in re-engineering their supply chain and this would be in the context of activity/best in class benchmarking.

Whilst the industry is different, they both sell consumer products and the concepts of lead times, responsiveness, overdue orders and inventories would still apply. Also PCE may well have experience of outsourcing production to Asia.

The chairman's concerns that PCE operate in a different industry might in fact be an advantage rather than a constraint, as it could encourage R to think more widely and be more innovative in its approach, rather than being limited by the way things are normally done within the industry. This might lead to an approach which is different from competitors and hence generates competitive advantage (something that the outsourcing in 20X0 appears to have failed to do).

One approach does not preclude the other, so R could identify the competitor with the best supply chain in the ceramics industry at the same time, although it may be harder to get the necessary information. PCE may be more inclined to share information as it will not feel the need to be protective of trade secrets and some data has already been published.

The Chairman is correct that PCE's targets may not be appropriate for R, but benchmarking is more than just collecting data or setting targets. R needs to identify the drivers of good performance. So comparisons with PCE might indicate the areas of the supply chain that R needs to focus on and may give R an insight into the problems that were experienced by PCE in managing the changes. This may help R obtain better results or facilitate the implementation of the change.

In addition to improving the efficiency of operations, benchmarking may also enable R to identify scope for improving its management structure and decision making processes eg the need to decentralise the system of sales planning and decision making.

A possible downside of benchmarking is that managers may feel their role is reduced to copying others and thus any benchmarking programme would need careful management.

Conclusion: R urgently needs to establish or regain its competitive advantage and benchmarking the supply chain against PCE may help it do so. It might also consider other forms of benchmarking and perhaps undertake a value chain analysis.

Examiner's comments:

In requirement 9.4 candidates had to discuss the differing views expressed in the scenario about the relevance of using a company (PCE) in a different industry to benchmark Rugeley's supply chain. Answers were varied. Some candidates failed to spot that this requirement was about benchmarking and limited their marks by discussing the potential comparison only in general terms. Better answers explained the different types of benchmarking available to Rugeley and went on to consider whether PCE plc was an appropriate choice for benchmarking. Many also provided consideration of supply chain issues. Candidates who discussed the use of value chain analysis as a means of identifying improvements to the supply chain and increasing competitive advantage were awarded credit.

9.5 Corporate governance and NEDs

Corporate governance involves the set of rules which governs the structure and determines the objectives of a company and regulates the relationship between a company's management, its Board of directors and its shareholders. It is not about the day-to-day management of operations or the formulation of business strategy.

Key aspects of good corporate governance involve the transparency of corporate structure and operations; the accountability of managers and boards to shareholders; and corporate responsibility towards employees, creditors, suppliers and the local community.

The UK Corporate Governance Code 2014 issued by the FRC sets out best practice which R currently does not comply with:

- There should be a separate chairman and chief executive, whereas Belinda currently does both roles

- The Board should consist of sufficient non-executive directors to prevent domination by the executive directors

- Non-executive directors (NEDs) should establish a remuneration committee to decide on directors' remuneration and an audit committee to work with the external auditors. As there are no NEDs it is assumed that R does not have either of these currently

The Code is only a legal requirement for premium listed companies so non-compliance by R in some ways is not an issue, as there is a 'comply or disclose' policy. Thus as a condition of its continued listing R is simply required by the Stock Exchange to disclose the areas where it has not followed the Code. However a bigger issue may be that the institutional shareholders are becoming increasingly unhappy with the situation.

Belinda would be advised to appoint NEDs and form a remuneration committee as this would protect her and the other executive directors from the criticism/accusation that the company is being run for their personal benefit.

NEDs would provide a better balance of power on the Board and may encourage Belinda to delegate some of the decision making to others.

NEDs could also help improve the efficiency and effectiveness of the remuneration system and act as a buffer between the Board and the auditors.

The benefit to Belinda of the NEDs is that they would be seen by the institutional investors and other shareholders as independent, which would improve the perception of the company.

In addition they may bring skills and experience that improves the quality of decision making which could lead to better performance. NEDs would also be able to help R appoint new directors should the need arise.

Overall the appointment of NEDs may increase institutional shareholder confidence in the running of the company, and if they are reassured by the move they are less likely to demand that the company seeks a buyer.

Examiner's comments:

Requirement 9.5 asked candidates to explain the principles of good corporate governance and the ways that non-executive directors (NEDs) might be of benefit to the running of the business. A disappointing number of candidates failed to explain the concept of corporate governance and restricted their answer to a discussion of NEDs. Better candidates considered corporate governance in the broader context of agency theory, talked about the applicability of the Code and the need for a separate Chairman and CEO, discussed the issue of directors' remuneration being linked to performance and highlighted the need for better governance given the concerns of the institutional shareholders.

10 Pitstop Ltd (September 2009)

		Knowledge	Skill	Marks
10.1 (a)	Strategy 1 analysis	2	6	
(b)	Assumptions/overall	2	6	
				12
10.2 (a)	Strategy 2 calculations	1	4	
(b)	Impact of Strategy 2	2	5	
				10
10.3	Future profitability	1	5	5
		8	26	27

General comments:

Pitstop Ltd is a chain of 65 roadside restaurants, operating in an increasingly competitive market. The company has a good track record but increased site rental costs have led to a recent decline in financial performance. Two alternatives are being considered to improve profitability: Strategy 1 – widen the appeal of the restaurant in order to increase customer volumes by one third; Strategy 2 – reduce prices by 15% to become more competitive. As the finance director is on long term sick leave, the sales director has prepared forecasts of the likely impact of the two strategies. The operations director is particularly concerned about the downside risk associated with Strategy 2. Candidates were provided with two exhibits: the actual and forecast results for an average restaurant (Exhibit 1), together with some data on margins and average customer spend for the best and worst performing restaurants in the chain (Exhibit 2).

This, the data analysis question, was by far the least well attempted question on the paper and many attempts were marginal. Few candidates made use of the additional data in Exhibit 2 regarding the best, worst and average restaurants – those who did tended to score highly.

The question required candidates to analyse forecasts for two new strategies in relation to the current actual performance. Both forecast and actual data was provided in order to test candidates' ability to apply basic data analysis skills to data in a variety of forms but weaker candidates seemed unable to show flexibility in analysing forecast data. It appears from tutor feedback received, that some candidates may have been led by tutors to assume that there is a 'normal' data analysis question involving the analysis of only historic business performance. The learning materials are clear that this area is not limited in this way: 'the key requirement in the BS exam is to be able to interpret financial and other data provided in the exam and relate it to the business strategy'. In addition 'the ability to analyse the impact of a new project or strategy' is listed in the material as one possible area that might be examined, which includes the ability to analyse the reasonableness of forecasts.

10.1 (a) Evaluation of forecast for Strategy 1

Appendix 1:

	Actual 20X9	Forecast 20Y0
Food as % of turnover	35%	35%
Labour % of turnover	33%	33%
Gross profit margin	32%	32%
Net profit margin	0.1%	8.1%
No of customers pa (Revenue/Ave spend)	54,000	72,000
No of customers per day (based on 360 days pa)	150	200
Turnaround of tables (daily customers/50)	3	4
Gross profit per customer (gross profit/no of customers)	£2.88	£2.88

	% Increase 20X9-20Y0
Revenue	33.3%
Gross profit	33.3%
Overheads	Nil
Net profit	9,969%
Customers per day	33.3%
Ave spend per customer	Nil

Commentary: Impact on current position of an average restaurant

Currently the 'average restaurant' is making a contribution of £155,520 but only just breaking even (net profit of £520) after its allocated share of the rent, marketing and other overheads. This appears to be consistent with the suggestion that results have suffered as a result of significant rent increases.

Overall the new strategy would therefore appear to significantly improve the situation, with the 33% increase in customers generating a £51,840 increase in gross profit and hence PBIT.

Assuming there is no change in fixed costs, and that gross margins remain at 32%, any increase in customer volumes will increase capacity utilisation and hence lead to extra profit.

On the face of it, the sales director's forecasts suggest the proposal is a good one, however this depends on whether the sales director's forecast of both volumes and cost behaviour is realistic, and whether the increased customer numbers can be achieved across the chain in the manner suggested. Given the FD's absence, it is possible that the sales director lacks the necessary experience to produce accurate forecasts and this is examined below.

(b) **Reasonableness of forecast and assumptions for predicting company-wide results**

Customer numbers

The sales director has assumed that widening the target market will increase the number of customers by 50 per day or 33.3% overall. The implication is that these will come from the new target market.

This target seems quite ambitious and equates on average to an extra sitting a day, as the turnaround of tables increase from three to four times. Whether the planned increase is achievable will depend to an extent on the location of the restaurant and the competition in the surrounding area.

In reality the increase is unlikely to be spread evenly across the week – business customers are more likely to use the restaurant Monday-Friday, whereas local families may be more inclined to visit at weekends. The restaurant may encounter problems if, for example, the additional custom is all generated at lunch time, when the tables may already be full.

Also in view of the strong competition, if Pitstop continued with its existing strategy customer numbers may decline between 20X9 and 20Y0, requiring even more customers to be generated from the new target market.

It would be helpful to break the forecast down, to more clearly identify the forecast revenue and customer numbers under both the existing and new strategies.

Average spend and margins

The forecast is based on average spend remaining constant at £9 per customer and gross margins continuing at 32% or £2.88 per customer. Thus the 33.3% increase in customers leads directly to a 33.3% increase in overall gross profit. The forecast does not appear to take account of the fact that the new target customers may have a different spending pattern. Business customers who use the restaurants for meetings are likely to occupy a table for longer but may spend less if they only purchase several cups of coffee.

The introduction of a new snack menu may attract increased volumes of travellers but is likely to lead to a reduction in the average spend. This type of food may require little preparation however, so it is possible that margins will increase on these menu items as there is less labour cost involved if the product is offered on a self service basis.

Average spend is thus likely to vary by type of customer and time of day and margins will vary by menu dish, thus more information would be required to make a more accurate prediction.

Overheads

The sales director has assumed that allocated overheads will remain constant. In reality overheads are likely to increase for the following reasons:

- Pitstop will need to raise awareness of its new strategy and menu. This will necessitate promotion to business customers and local families, and printing of new menus. Widening the target market will therefore involve increased marketing costs unless Pitstop believes that it can attract sufficient coverage via articles in local newspapers and word-of-mouth.

- Pitstop will incur capital costs to fit out part of the restaurant as an office area and ongoing IT costs to support and maintain this strategy.

- Certain costs may be subject to annual price increases eg rent and utilities.

Extrapolation of results company-wide

As the gross profit margin is broadly the same across all Pitstop restaurants and all other costs incurred by the business are split equally across the 65 restaurants, the only variables are customer numbers and average spend.

In order to properly predict the results for the chain as a whole, the customer numbers and average spend for each individual restaurant would be required and these could be amalgamated to create a group forecast.

In the absence of such information, the sales director's forecast for the average Pitstop restaurant could be extrapolated.

With the average restaurant only just breaking even after allocated overheads, the company's PBIT for year ended July 20X9 could be estimated at £33,800 (65 × £520) which is unlikely to be a sufficient return for investors after interest and tax payments.

Leaving aside the inaccuracies noted above, then the overall forecast group PBIT for year ended July 20Y0 under Strategy 1 would be estimated at £3,403,400 (65 × £52,360) – a substantial improvement.

Range of possible results

To get a better idea of the variation in performance, the range of individual restaurant results could be considered:

Actual 20X9

Gross profit:

Worst: 95 customers × 360 days × £7.50 × 0.32 = £82,080

Best: 245 customers × 360 days × £10.50 × 0.32 = £296,352

After deducting overheads at £155,000 this means PBIT in 20X9 ranged from a loss of £72,920 in the worst restaurant to a profit of £141,352 in the best.

Forecast 20Y0

Assuming the worst and best restaurants were also forecast to increase their customer numbers by 33.3%, 20Y0 forecast profits under Strategy 1 would range from:

Gross profit:

Worst: £82,080 × 4/3 = £109,440

Best: £296,352 × 4/3 = £395,136

PBIT

Worst: £109,440 – £155,000 = Loss £45,560 (a reduction in the loss of £27,360)

Best: £395,136 – £155,000 = £240,136 (an increase of £98,784)

Thus the new strategy would increase profits in the average and best restaurants but would still result in Pitstop's worst restaurants being loss-making after the allocation of overheads.

The competition is likely to vary from one restaurant to another and this will affect the results and whether the planned 33% increase in customer numbers will be achievable uniformly across all Pitstop restaurants.

Also some restaurant locations may be more suitable for business/family trade than others. It may not be appropriate to convert all restaurants for business use for example.

Conclusion:

Strategy 1 may be feasible but requires more market research and competitor analysis. Pitstop could attempt to assess the impact of this strategy by running it as a trial in certain restaurants before phasing it in across the whole chain.

Examiner's comments:

Requirement 10.1(a) asked candidates to analyse Strategy 1 and evaluate its impact on an average restaurant. Requirement 10.1(b) then asked candidates to assess the reasonableness of the sales director's forecast and assumptions as a basis for predicting the results for all the restaurants in the chain. Well-made points in 10.1(b) generally made up for poor analysis in 10.1(a).

In 10.1(a) weak candidates tended to avoid numerical analysis of the exhibits and concentrate on the suitability, feasibility and acceptability of Strategy 1, without reference to the sales director's forecasts, thereby failing to answer part of the requirement 'to assess its impact on an average restaurant'. Better candidates pointed out that the average restaurant was currently only just breaking even and therefore, on the face of it, the sales director's forecast indicated that the strategy would improve financial performance considerably. Given that fixed costs were forecast to stay the same, the strategy to increase customer volumes by one third whilst maintaining average spend and gross margins would, if it were achievable, increase capacity utilisation – and the additional volume would lead directly to additional profit. The better scripts identified that the crux of the matter was therefore whether the sales director's forecast of both volumes and cost behaviour was realistic, and whether the increased customer numbers could be achieved across the chain in the manner suggested.

In 10.1(b) most candidates provided a comprehensive discussion concerning the limitations of the sales director's assumptions regarding overheads, customer numbers and spend, and margins, although surprisingly few pointed out that, in the FD's absence, the sales director may lack the necessary experience to produce accurate forecasts. Disappointingly few candidates picked up on the other aspect of the discussion which was whether the situation could be considered on an average restaurant basis at all, given the wide variation of customer numbers and average spend between the worst and best performing restaurants.

10.2 (a) **Strategy 2**

Customers required to maintain 20X9 PBIT

Calculation of new contribution per customer

	Average restaurant £
Current average spend	9.00
New average spend (85% × current spend)	7.65
New contribution (20% × new spend)	1.53

Customers required to maintain profits:

	Average restaurant
Total 20X9 Contribution	£155,520
New Contribution per customer	£1.53
Customers required per annum	101,647
Hence customers required per day	282
Increase in customers per day (282-150)	132

Alternative approach to calculations:

Contribution per customer

Gross profit per customer at existing prices 10.1(a)	£2.88
Reduction in gross profit due to price decrease	15% × £9.00 = £1.35
New contribution per customer	£2.88 – £1.35 = £1.53

No of customers required:

Lost contribution = lost revenue from price reduction = 150 × 360 × £9.00 × 15% = £72,900

Thus increase in customers required = £72,900/£1.53 = 47,647 pa or 132 per day

(b) **Likely impact of Strategy 2**

Impact on average restaurant

Unless there are potential savings in staff and food costs, the 15% reduction in price causes the gross profit margin to fall from 32% to 20% for an average restaurant. The calculations show that to compensate for this, the average restaurant would need to attract 282 customers per day. This is more than the best performing restaurant currently attracts and for an average restaurant represents an additional 132 customers per day (an increase of 88%).

This looks unobtainable and even if it were successful in doing this, the average restaurant would only be operating just above breakeven. In reality such additional volumes may also necessitate an increase in marketing expenditure or other fixed costs which would further reduce profitability.

Thus the sales director's confidence would appear to be misplaced unless demand is very price elastic.

Impact on the company as a whole

In 20X9, using the existing pricing strategy, after allocating fixed costs, the worst restaurant made a loss of £72,920, the average restaurant was just breaking even, and the best restaurant made a profit of £141,352.

The operations director is worried about the downside risk of the price reduction strategy.

In the worst case scenario, if the price reduction failed to attract any additional customers, the calculations in Appendix 2 show that the worst and average restaurants would become loss making (£115,773) and (£72,380) respectively and the best restaurant would only make a small profit of £18,489. Thus the likely effect on the company as a whole is a significant deterioration in profitability, which would render it loss making.

Impact on breakeven point

An alternative way to assess the risk of the strategy is to consider the impact of the 15% price reduction on the breakeven point:

Compared to the actual number of customers in 20X9, with the 15% price reduction the worst performing restaurant would need to generate an extra 280 customers a day just to break even – almost three times its existing customers and more than the number of customers of the best performing restaurant in 20X9!

The average performing restaurant would require 131 customers and the best performing restaurant would have a margin of safety of 26 customers.

Conclusion

The price reduction of 15% proposed in Strategy 2 would not appear to be viable and without significant increase in numbers or major cost reductions is likely to increase the chain's losses. Rather than reducing all prices by 15%, Pitstop could consider implementing price discrimination strategies eg offering senior citizen or early bird discounts to smooth out the peaks and troughs of trade.

Appendix 2 of possible calculations:

	Worst	Ave	Best
New contribution per customer	£	£	£
Current Ave spend	7.50	9.00	10.50
New ave spend (85%)	6.375	7.65	8.925
New contribution (new spend × 18/20/22%)	1.147	1.53	1.963

Impact on profits of the price reduction if there were to be no increase in customer numbers:

	Worst	Ave	Best
Existing customers per day	95	150	245
New contribution per customer	£1.147	£1.53	£1.963
Annual Gross profit	£39,227	£82,620	£173,137
PBIT (after £155,000 overheads)	(£115,773)	(£72,380)	£18,137
Existing 20X9 PBIT	(£72,920)	£520	£141,352
Reduction in profitability	(£42,853)	(£71,860)	(£123,215)

Impact of price reduction on breakeven point

	Worst	Ave	Best
Overheads	£155,000	£155,000	£155,000
New contribution per customer	£1.147	£1.53	£1.963
Break even no. customers	135,135	101,308	78,961
Breakeven customers per day	375	281	219
Actual customers per day 20X9	95	150	245
Increase in customers required to break even	280	131	(26)

Examiner's comments:

Requirement 10.2(a) asked candidates to prepare calculations showing the additional number of customers per day that would be required to maintain the gross profit of an average restaurant if prices were reduced by 15% in accordance with Strategy 2. Overall this was poorly attempted and it was disappointing to see many candidates failing here, despite the simple nature of the calculation (a variant of break-even). The most common error was to calculate the number of customers required per day in an average restaurant to maintain revenue rather than gross profit. Those that correctly performed the calculation in terms of profit often assumed that, despite the 15% price reduction, the GP margin would be maintained at 32%, when the scenario clearly stated that margins would fall and indeed, the new estimated margin of 20% was provided in the Exhibit.

In requirement 10.2(b) candidates were then required to discuss the likely impact of Strategy 2 on the profitability of the company as a whole and to provide any supporting calculations. Most fared a little better here, with many performing calculations of the impact on profit if the price reduction failed to generate an increase in customer volumes, although only the better candidates referred back to their calculations in 10.2(a). Better candidates pointed out that the sales director's assertion that any increase in revenue would more than compensate for the reduction in price depended on the price elasticity of demand. There was some confusion on the part of weaker candidates regarding elasticity however, with many stating that as the price reduction had led to increased volumes, then demand must be elastic (therefore failing to recognise that this is the case for all downward sloping demand curves and that elasticity requires the increase in volume to be more than proportionate to the reduction in price). Only the best answers included comments about the need to consider the impact of this strategy on the other restaurants in the chain and the possibility of applying price discrimination rather than a universal price cut.

10.3 Additional considerations for future strategy

Note. This answer includes a complete range of points for marking purposes and is far more than would be expected in the time available.

In order to decide on the future direction of the business Pitstop needs:

(1) To more accurately evaluate the proposed strategies

(2) To assess the current position of each individual restaurant in order to identify the underperforming restaurants

(1) To assess the proposed strategies

Budgets – Predictions of customer numbers, average spend and overheads for 20Y0 if Pitstop continued with the existing strategy would be useful as a baseline to assess the impact of the new proposals.

Capital expenditure – More information is required regarding the cost of fitting out the restaurants as a business centre.

Competitor analysis – This needs to be done on an overall company and individual restaurant basis to establish the appropriate target market and strategy for each restaurant.

Market research – Pitstop needs to carry out some market research:

- Regarding the target market (local families, business users) and the new snack menu to accurately predict increased customer numbers and average spend for Strategy 1.

- To assess the likely impact of reducing prices and the price elasticity of demand for Strategy 2. Each Pitstop restaurant should also compare their prices to those of the local competition.

(2) To assess underperforming restaurants

Detail on individual restaurants

Pitstop's reporting system assumes constant gross profit margins and an equal allocation of overheads. In reality not all restaurants will successfully keep to the target for food and labour costs. Also the actual rents are likely to vary depending on the restaurant location eg those near London or on prime routes are likely to pay more rent than those in more rural areas. By allocating overheads evenly Pitstop is likely to be overstating the profit in some restaurants and understating others.

In order to assess each individual restaurant, a breakdown of revenue, costs and staffing levels is required. Pitstop also needs to make an attempt to split overheads between those that are traceable per restaurant eg rent, utilities and other premises costs, and those that are central costs eg marketing and management that need to be reallocated.

Seasonality

Trade is likely to be seasonal and the clientele is likely to vary at different times eg:

Time of year – the summer may be busier because of tourists

Time of week – more trade at weekends from families

Time of day – more business trade in the earlier part of the day

More information is required about the utilisation of the tables in order to assess when a restaurant needs to generate additional trade eg is the restaurant usually full on weekday lunchtimes but empty between 9.30am and 11.30am? This would help identify the type of clientele to be targeted.

Popularity and profitability of menu items

Some meals will be more popular than others and the profitability of the various menu items will differ. This information would help assess which menu items should be offered.

Comparative information

In order to interpret performance, information is needed regarding budgets and targets, competitors and industry norms, so that Pitstop can benchmark performance not just between its restaurants but against others in the industry. This would help Pitstop assess which restaurants are performing well and which are not, both currently and with respect to changes over time.

It is also important to distinguish the performance of the restaurant from the performance of the manager. A badly performing restaurant could be improved by changing the manager or it could be the inevitable consequence of its local market, additional competition or other non-controllable factors.

Multiple performance measures

Pitstop might consider using a wider set of assessment measures to identify the drivers of an individual restaurant's success or failure, including non-financial areas such as level of customer complaints, waiting times, staff turnover. One tool by which this can be achieved is the balanced scorecard.

Conclusion

Pitstop may be unable to return to profitability unless it has sufficient information to identify and either turn around or close underperforming restaurants.

Strategy 1 may be feasible but requires more market research and competitor analysis. The price reduction of 15% proposed in Strategy 2 would not appear to be viable and without significant increase in numbers or major cost reductions is likely to increase the chain's losses.

Other possible strategies to consider include:

- Offer takeaway or drive through service
- Get taken over by another chain
- Sell franchise to one of the fast food chains

Examiner's comments:

Requirement 10.3 asked candidates to explain any other factors that the company should consider before making a decision about how to improve the company's profitability. A wide range of points could be made here (identifying the worst restaurants with a view to closure, considering the impact of the competition, undertaking market research to provide better information for decision making etc). Most candidates made sufficient sensible comments to make up at least in part for weaknesses elsewhere in the question.

11 Somborne Zoological Park Ltd (September 2009)

Marking guide

	Knowledge	Skill	Marks
11.1 Report format	1		
(a) Strategic planning benefits	1.5	2	
(b) Objectives (2 per goal)	1	4.5	
			8
11.2 Allocating limited resources	2	5	6
11.3 (a) Costs and benefits of sustainability initiative	2	4	
(b) Impact of staff/key stakeholders	1	3	
			9
11.4 Information system	3	3	
Performance measures	2	4	
			10
	13.5	25.5	33

Report

To: Chairman of Somborne Zoo
From: A.N.Other
Date: September 20X9
Re: Proposed Sustainability Initiative

11.1 (a) **Strategic planning – benefits**

Strategic planning involves setting goals and then designing strategies to meet them.

Purpose and benefits of planning:

- To ensure Somborne meets the needs of its diverse stakeholders. A strategic plan will help communicate the purpose and values of the zoo to staff, visitors and sponsors, and help identify the priorities for the zoo

- Attract and maintain funding and public support, avoiding over-reliance on any particular source of income. The availability of a plan may help sell the zoo to the public and sponsors in particular

- Ensure optimum use of resources which, as with most NFP organisations, are likely to be limited

- Ensure day-to-day operations are consistent with the long term goals of the zoo. As part of its strategic planning process Somborne has already identified four strategic goals. The strategic plan needs to set out in more detail how each of these goals will be pursued and will consider areas such as financial strategy and the raising of funds, marketing, visitor services, the organisation and scale of the site and exhibits, development of the animal collection, intentions for breeding, forming strategic partnerships for conservation and research

- Guide the development and evolution of the zoo – coordinate the growth and ensure coherency of the site plan and exhibits. May help increase chances of gaining IZF accreditation

- Relate the zoo to its external environment

- Improve performance of zoo and its chances of survival

- Help to identify and manage risks

(b) **Objectives**

Whilst the zoo's goals may be stated quite generally, the specific objectives need to be SMART (specific, measurable, achievable, relevant and with a timescale attached):

Goal: To maximise the impact of conservation and research activities

- Ensure at least five research papers are published during the year
- Secure x number of new animals from threatened species within five years
- Gain recognition from conservation bodies for activities eg be cited for or win awards, press coverage/media accolades within one year
- Ensure x animals born per year under the zoo's breeding programme

Goal: To promote the zoo and provide learning opportunities

- Increase the number of return visitors to 20% of total over three years
- Increase admissions revenue by 15% per year
- Complete the development of the panda exhibit by July 20Y0
- Introduce a quarterly 'Friends of Somborne' newsletter in 20Y0
- Upgrade the zoo's café and restaurant facilities by May 20Y0
- Appoint a schools coordinator by Dec 20X9 and visit five schools a month to promote the zoo's school programme
- Ensure the zoo is featured in local press and current affairs programmes at least every month

Goal: To develop alternative income streams

- Have approached 20 potential corporate/sponsors by Dec 20X9
- Attract five new benefactors in 20Y0
- Increase the annual membership of the 'Friends of Somborne' by 15% by summer 20Y0
- Promote the zoo as a venue for corporate events and hospitality such that this forms 10% of the income in 20Y0
- Increase the sales of zoo merchandise by x%

Examiner's comments:

Requirement 11.1(a) asked candidates to explain the benefits of strategic planning for the zoo and (b) to provide examples of some objectives for the strategic goals identified in the scenario. Candidates were well-prepared for this requirement and tended to score highly, particularly in 11.1(b), where a significant majority recognised the need for SMART objectives. Some candidates provided a generic list of the features and benefits of strategic planning, but better ones related their discussion to the case, focusing on the inherent conflicts in strategic planning for the zoo due to scarce resources and diverse stakeholder needs – issues that were highlighted in the later requirements.

11.2 Allocation of resources

In common with other not for profit (NFP) organisations, Somborne is likely to face the following issues in making decisions:

- Multiple objectives (driven by diverse stakeholder needs)
- Conflicts between stakeholders
- Need to take a long-term view of the impact of short-term decisions
- Not always easy to measure results or to quantify the impact of decisions
- Requirement for greater awareness of corporate responsibility and sustainability issues
- Financial and other resource constraints
- Operations in the public eye

In view of its limited resources, Somborne therefore needs to prioritise its goals, audiences, and activities.

In order to make a decision on how best to use resources and what projects the zoo can afford to carry out each year, Somborne first needs to identify the resources available, not just in terms of finances but also staffing and space. Potential projects will be constrained by any physical limitations of the actual site. Increasing Somborne's use of volunteers will help increase the resources available.

In making a choice as to which exhibits and programmes to allocate funds and space to, Somborne must strike a balance between the needs of the animals, visitors and staff.

Somborne's licence may require resources to be dedicated in certain areas and the desire for accreditation will affect the zoo's priorities. There may also be conditions attached to certain donations which restrict what the funds can be used for.

The mission statement acknowledges the dual role of the zoo as a visitor attraction and as an organisation engaged in animal conservation.

Thus it may appear that there is competition for resources between Somborne's revenue-producing activities and its conservation desires and needs eg the zoo may face a choice between dedicating more money for conservation and spending this on visitor facilities.

An improved entrance or a new exhibit may bring extra visitors and increase the number of returning visitors. This in turn may generate more funds for conservation and research activities.

Conversely good conservation or recognition of successful research may enhance the zoo's budget by attracting funding. This would then allow development of the zoo's visitor attractions.

Thus the two roles are not necessarily in conflict.

Having decided to spend money on either conservation/research or its commercial activities, Somborne still faces competing choices.

Resources for research are finite and must be carefully targeted. In choosing between potential research or conservation projects, priority must be given to research that has clear implications for saving species, populations and habitats.

If Somborne decides to spend money on new visitor features, then it will need to consider how best to spend this. Thus it may need to consider choice of location within the zoo, order of construction of exhibits, amount of space to be allocated to visitors/staff/animals.

There is also a distinction between short and long term goals. Somborne needs to focus on the ultimate goal of conservation, but also on meeting the immediate day-to-day needs of the living creatures for which it is responsible. Thus in allocating funds it needs to consider how to provide the best possible conditions for the animals in its care and whether funds will be available in future years for projects to continue.

One of the problems facing Somborne is how to measure the return on its investment. It is likely that the spending on projects within the zoo, rather than conservation research, will have a more direct impact which is easier to quantify – eg if a new gorilla exhibit is created, Somborne can measure the impact in terms of number of visitors, press coverage, increased admissions revenue, adoption of the animals etc.

It may take much longer to assess the impact of conservation and research activities and this is also likely to be affected by wider and possible uncontrollable influences eg climate change, natural disasters eg fire and floods, other parties engaged in similar research.

Examiner's comments:

Requirement 11.2 asked candidates to identify the issues the zoo is likely to face in deciding how to allocate resources. Answers here were polarised. Most candidates identified the issue of limited resources in the context of funding and the need to choose between conflicting objectives, sometimes referring back to the wide range of goals identified in 11.1. Better candidates recognised the dual role of the zoo – as an organisation dedicated to conservation and as a visitor attraction – and the trade-off between allocating resources to animal welfare and research and spending on marketing and promotion to attract more visitors to the zoo. They also noted that the zoo's licence and its sponsors may impose certain constraints and that resources were not limited to cash but extended to labour, both paid staff and volunteers.

11.3 (a) Sustainability

Costs and benefits of sustainability

Sustainability involves using natural resources in a way that does not lead to their decline. In the context of the zoo, sustainability has been identified as having an impact not just on the environment but also in other areas: financial, human resources and social.

Costs of implementing a sustainability programme

In the short term this may lead to:

- Increased costs eg using greener energy sources, buying fair trade products, paying higher wages to workers
- The environmental audit will take time and money, as may the accreditation process
- Increased admin time in screening suppliers and contractors, and reduced number of parties available
- Possible reduced income eg no donations from non-ethical sponsors
- Additional management considerations eg regarding the ethical HR policies

Benefits:

- Sustainable activities will help to improve the environment and will fulfil the zoo's moral obligation to be involved in such practices
- Accreditation by IZF for its sustainable activities may enhance the reputation of the zoo particularly if, as a result, it qualifies for official awards and recognitions
- If Somborne stresses sustainable activities as a basis for promotion and marketing it may become a more attractive option to visitors, donors, investors, and strategic partners and thus increase net income. Accreditation may help attract ethical investors
- Green practices adopted by the zoo may lead to cost savings through eg reduced costs of utilities such as water and energy
- This strategy will improve employees' awareness of environmental issues and responsibilities, enhance employee morale and help to ensure that Somborne is seen as a desirable employer
- Somborne will stand as a model for sustainable practices, encouraging others, especially in the same community, and setting an example for 'greener' governance
- The sustainability initiative will improve their image as champions for environmental responsibility, enhance compliance with environmental principles and, even better, help to inform and shape future legislation

(b)   **Impact on staff and one other key stakeholder**

Stakeholder group	Area of interest	Impact
Staff	Financial	Will want the zoo to operate as a going concern to safeguard jobs
	Environment	Can enhance sustainability through own personal convictions eg view on environment. May contribute to change and innovations or may resist change due to extra workload
	HR	Will be interested in development opportunities, HR practices, health and safety
	Social	May feel rewarded through participation in educating the local schools and community
Suppliers/contractors and other business partners	Financial	Will be concerned about the potential impact on their contracts and working practices which could lead to additional costs
	Social	May be concerned about the cost implications eg if required to use recyclable packaging
		May welcome ethical procurement if it increases their chances of winning work or the price that they will receive

Candidates may have instead analysed any of the following which were deemed to be key stakeholders:

Visitors	Environment Social	May have a genuine concern about the welfare of the animals, the environment and the sustainability of the zoo's performance
Investors/sponsors/ donors	Financial	May contribute if they believe that the zoo's activities and its financial position is sustainable
		May want to ensure funds given are allocated for specific causes
Local community	Social	Will expect the zoo to provide socio-economic development through jobs, links with the schools, cooperation with local business

Examiner's comments:

Requirement 11.3(a) asked candidates to explain the likely costs and benefits of implementing a sustainability initiative and (b) to assess the likely impact of such an initiative on the staff and one other key stakeholder. Overall this was reasonably well done, although weaker candidates interpreted sustainability quite narrowly in terms of being 'environmentally friendly', failing to use the information provided in the scenario which extended this concept to ethical purchasing, sponsorship, and HR policies; staff development; and visitor education.

Stronger candidates referred to time lags and the potential in some cases for tangible benefits in the future arising from costs incurred today.

There were a number of other key stakeholders that could have been identified in (b), including visitors, suppliers and sponsors. Better answers discussed the positive and negative impact that the initiative would have on the staff and one other group. Some candidates wasted time by discussing more than one stakeholder or alternatively failing to pick one that was 'key' – those candidates who talked about the impact on the animals or animal rights activists fell within this category!

11.4 Use of information to assess sustainability initiative

Somborne needs to implement a system which provides the appropriate type and amount of information for managers to implement and control the sustainability initiative and assess its success.

The current information management system may need to be enhanced to allow collection of new types of data, eg may need to first measure energy usage before can implement policies and procedures to reduce it.

In addition certain specific information may be required by IZF to demonstrate achievement levels and in order for Somborne to acquire accreditation. Thus S needs to establish any specific performance criteria that will be used by IZF in order to decide what indicators need to be measured and monitored in each of the four areas identified.

Some of the information that needs to be gathered may be qualitative as well as quantitative, eg impact on visitors' willingness to adopt a sustainable lifestyle will be hard to measure and may be based on responses to surveys/conversations etc.

Somborne may make use of exception reporting eg to highlight problem areas where energy or water usage has overrun, breaches of relevant guidelines.

One purpose of an information system is knowledge management so that best practice with regard to sustainability can be shared. Staff may need training to formally record data/information necessary if such records have not been kept in the past.

Once the environmental audit has been conducted Somborne will have information about the current level of achievement in various areas. Baseline performance can be defined and targets set for future achievement.

On an ongoing basis performance can then be measured against these targets/budgets and deviations from the plan can be investigated. S may benchmark performance targets against other zoos (IZF may be able to provide appropriate information).

The zoo will need to undertake staff training, communicate the new system and establish procedures for cost control.

Baseline performance measures:

Overall impact

- Increase in positive zoo/conservation news stories or features
- Increase in partnerships with other conservation bodies

Financial

- % of revenue from zoo based activities

- Retail revenue per visitor

- Increase in number of visitors per month.

- Funds received from research and development activities

- Donations received

- Responses to pledges and petitions

- Increased zoo membership numbers and increased sponsorship schemes, especially those prompted by support for conservation/sustainability

- Deficit/surplus of income over expenditure

- No. of suppliers/contractors subject to screening

- No. of suppliers meeting sustainable criteria

- % procurement from fair trade countries/suppliers

Environmental

- Volumes of waste disposed of vs recycled
- Monthly levels of energy consumption
- Monthly water usage
- Volume of recycled water
- Methods of visitor travel to and around zoo
- No. of fair trade and organic products in the shop and cafe
- No. of new environmentally friendly initiatives implemented
- CO_2 and other emissions
- % of energy from alternative sources

Human resources

- Staff and volunteer injury rate
- Hours and expenditure on sustainability training
- Number of certificates awarded to staff and others trained at the zoo
- Percentage of staff receiving recognition from professional organisations
- Percentage of staff who have completed their professional development plan each year
- Percentage of staff walking/cycling or using car share schemes to get to work

Social

- Number of training programmes offered by zoo staff covering topics related to sustainability

- Number of presentations and publications that connect and inform the general public and the professional community about sustainability

- Attendance figures at specific education projects

- Assessments of the educational effectiveness of different exhibits via surveys and questionnaires, observations of visitor behaviour, conversations

- Number of research programs, citations, no. of papers published

- Number of news stories that cover sustainability initiatives at the zoo

- Records of media coverage, and teacher feedback on formal programmes

- Records of sales of products in the zoo that have been associated with particular messages or campaigns

Examiner's comments:

In requirement 11.4 candidates were requested to explain how the zoo could use an information system to measure the success of its sustainability initiative and to suggest some appropriate performance measures that could be used. Candidates were obviously comfortable suggesting performance measures under the headings of finance, environment, HR and social, although to score well these needed to be related to the specific sustainability goals identified by the zoo. Most were less well-prepared to discuss information systems, a topic which came into the syllabus for the new Business Strategy paper and which has not yet been examined in any depth. A small minority made some good points about the need to design a system around the reporting requirements of the industry body (the IZF), the use of exception reporting to identify areas of underperformance and the benefits of introducing a knowledge management system to share information and experience.

12 Green Cards Ltd (December 2009)

		Knowledge	Skill	Marks
12.1 (a)	Power of suppliers	1	4	
(b)	Threats from substitutes	1	3	
				7
12.2 (a)	Competitive position/threats	3	7	
(b)	Performance and comparison	2	9	
				18
12.3	Withdrawal – ethical and business	2	5	6
12.4	Briefing note format	1	–	
(a)	Evaluation of strategy 1	1	4	
	Evaluation of strategy 2	1	4	
(b)	Advice	1	2	
				12
		13	38	43

General comments:

The company in this scenario owns a chain of shops retailing greeting cards. Green Cards Ltd is positioned towards the quality end of the market, but it is small by comparison to the market leaders. The company recently introduced a range of environmentally friedly cards but it is now seeking to withdraw from this market. Two strategies have been proposed to improve performance. Strategy 1 is to allow a confectionary company some floorspace where the fee is to be based either on the square meters occupied or on a share of revenue generated. Strategy 2 proposes to cut costs by reducing staffing.

12.1 (a) Power of suppliers

The key suppliers to the retail greeting card industry are card publishers (ie manufacturers).

The fact that the card manufacturing industry is concentrated, with 88% of the UK market being controlled by the largest 19 publishers, means that on average the producers are of significant size by comparison to all but the largest retailers. This may indicate that they have some power over smaller retailers to negotiate high prices and extract profits from the retail card industry.

There are however other factors which would affect the power of the publishers.

- There is a sufficient number of UK suppliers at 19 for there to be competition

- The card publishing industry is international so this generates further competition from overseas and weakens the power of UK suppliers over UK retailers

- The publishers may be reliant on the greeting card industry if they specialise in this type of printing and thus their power is reduced as they have nowhere else to sell their output other than to greeting card retailer

- The suppliers' product is a major cost for retailers (GC has a margin of 25% and even Mood only a margin of 40%). There will therefore be greater resistance to price increases

- There is low (but some) differentiation between suppliers' products, so switching is fairly easy for retailers, thereby lowering the power of suppliers

- In a recession there may be surplus production capacity for producers thereby increasing the power of retailers

Producers may be able to sell directly to consumers (mail order; internet) which would increase the suppliers' power by cutting out the retailers as intermediaries if the gap between wholesale and retail prices becomes too large.

Other suppliers to the retail card industry should also be considered – for example, lessors of high street retail properties. In a recession their power may be significantly reduced as many properties become vacant and retailers have more choice at the end of contractual rental periods.

(b) **Substitutes**

The most obvious substitute for the traditional greeting card is the e-card which may be sent more cheaply and can have additional features (eg sound, personalised photos). This will limit the prices that consumers are willing to pay for traditional cards but may also increase the demands made from the format of traditional cards. It would be easy for consumers to switch to the e-card.

The fact that producers may be able to sell directly to consumers could also be seen as a substitute for the service that greeting card retailers offer.

Other forms of communication on a special occasion may substitute for greeting cards if prices rise too much (eg text messages, emails, telephone calls, letters, delivered presents such as cakes/flowers/wine etc).

One of the major threats to the card industry is that it is a non essential purchase which may be forgone in a recession or as a response to using paper which is an environmentally unfriendly activity. In this case some consumers may cease purchasing cards and substitute this with not buying any form of greeting or communication.

Examiner's comments:

Requirement 12.1 asked candidates to provide an analysis the industry using two of Porter's Five Forces: the power of suppliers and threats from substitutes.

Nearly all candidates were able to discuss the power of suppliers. However a large majority only discussed the card manufacturers and failed to mention any of the other suppliers to the business. As required, answers were generally industry focussed, with only weaker candidates discussing company specific issues. Candidates were reasonably good at using the information in the scenario to explain the card manufacturers' position and mentioned issues such as switching cost, and differentiation. Few candidates picked up on the threat from overseas suppliers. Stronger candidates included a conclusion on the power of suppliers.

With regards to substitutes, a majority of candidates only mentioned e-cards as a possible substitute. Hardly any candidates picked up on the issue raised in the question about the manufacturers supplying directly to the public. Stronger candidates thought more broadly and mentioned text messages and social networking sites as substitutes. Stronger candidates included a conclusion.

12.2 (a) **Competitive position**

GC is a small participant within the greeting card retail industry. It cannot therefore compete on cost with larger companies such the 'big five' and with Mood in particular. This is due to the fact that larger companies have economies of scale. These may include:

- Large orders with publishers giving discounts
- Ability to have power over suppliers (per Porter's Five Force Model) to negotiate superior terms of trade. This includes not just suppliers of cards but other major costs such as rental agreements with leaseholders
- Greater customer awareness
- Larger shops with a wider range of cards to attract customers
- Better financing terms
- Fixed administration costs on a larger scale spread over more units of output

GC does not attempt to compete on the basis of cost. Instead it differentiates the products it sells by selling good quality cards and providing a high level of service. Given that the quality card market is 10% of the total market, it could be described as competition in a niche market, although this description might be more appropriately applied to retailers selling hand-made cards.

Within this market, GC is growing its market share. However this increase is very minor and is only being achieved through more investment in more outlets rather than through generic growth (see below).

Even though GC's market share is growing slowly, the market itself is growing by 4.5% in 20X8 and 2.8% in 20X7. This may, at first sight, be indicative of a reduction in competition in the industry. However it is clear that there are few barriers to entry as set up costs are low, and this is evidenced by 'small retailers constantly leaving and joining the industry'. As a consequence, if the market continues to grow, then this may draw in new entrants and increase competition. Conversely however there appear to be few barriers to exit so if the recession becomes more severe then retailers exiting the industry may reduce the impact on remaining participants.

One caveat is that the growth in the overall market may not be reflected in a growth in the 'quality' market. It would only be growth in this sector that would benefit GC and here there are fewest barriers to entry, so there may be little benefit as new entrants are drawn in. However, it is at the higher end of the market that the effects of the recession are most acutely felt, and this will serve to deter potential new entrants.

More generally, a product can be positioned in a number of ways eg via a price or emphasis on a particular characteristic or set of characteristics. In other words, positioning means giving a product or service a place relative to its competitors on factors such as quality, price, image, providing status, etc. The price-quality trade-off is therefore just one aspect of market positioning.

The overall market could be seen in the diagram below.

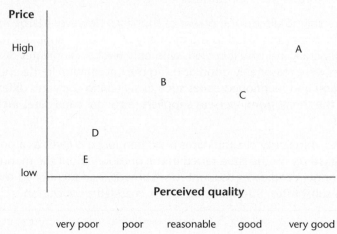

In the diagram:

C represents GC where price and quality are maintained at a high level

D represents Mood and other big retailers where price and quality are mid market ranges

B could represent Strategy 2 (see below) if service was cut and price increased

E represents Cardworld Ltd

A represents the specialist retailers with hand-made cards charging high prices

Within this mapping, one might regard any of the positions on the price-quality trade off as acceptable, other than **B** (which is dominated by GC's position C which offers better quality at a lower price). However:

- Quality is a question of perception where it is not always readily observable by the customer.

- The relative price difference between companies is more observable than quality.

- Short term and long term price/quality effects may be different as reputation may ultimately be affected.

One further issue is the profit margin achieved by GC which is only 25% compared to 40% for Mood. This is despite being a differentiator where one would normally expect greater profit margins. In terms of competition by price if there were to be a price war then there is limited scope for GC as once other operating costs are deducted the operating margins are much lower.

Threats to GC's competitive position

- If the recession deepens then there may be more pressure on the 'quality' market as consumers may substitute cheaper cards for quality cards.

- If the larger participants in the industry are suffering reductions in sales then they may attempt to become more broad-based by selling across the range of quality rather than focussing on up-market and mid-market sales.

- There is the threat of substitutes with competition from internet and mail order sales and from e-cards. This may increase in future even though e-cards in particular have not yet had much impact.

- Exchange rates variations with the £/euro may make supplies more expensive and GC only has one significant supplier, which is in the eurozone. Increases in costs may not be able to be passed on in full. Other retailers appear to be mainly UK-supplied, so they will not experience similar problems to the same extent.

(b) **GC's performance**

Superficially, GC has experienced growth in sales and operating profits of around 5% in 20X9 and 6% in 20X8. However this growth can be attributed largely to expansion in the number of outlets. The increase in profit is not therefore, of itself, evidence of improved performance. The business was expanding over this period and an element of the increase in profitability was due to larger scale activity rather than increased efficiency or improved market conditions.

Indeed, the data analysis shows that over the period 20X7 to 20X9 there was a reduction in performance after allowing for scale differences in terms of the increase in the number of new outlets. Specifically, the above table shows that the revenue per shop fell by around £10,000 per annum in each year, which is about a 4% pa reduction. Similarly, operating profits per shop fell by around 4.7% in 20X9 and 3.6% in 20X8.

This is also reflected in floorspace, as the data shows, the average floorspace per shop is unchanged following the opening of new outlets. So, controlling for shop size, the average revenue and operating profits per sq metre will parallel the figures per shop.

Overall therefore, while there has been some growth in sales and profits this cannot, with any certainty, be attributed to improved performance. The major contributory factors in improving sales/profits appear to be a larger scale of activity from an increased number of shops. This would be reflected in a greater investment (even if the shops are leased) and thus a greater overall expected return.

The increased in market wide sales may have also benefited GC.

It should however be recognised that, while the performance of the company may not have improved, the results have been achieved with the onset of the recession. The performance of management may therefore have been reasonable. Nevertheless, market growth would indicate that the recession has not, as yet, affected the overall UK industry significantly.

Comparison with Mood Cards

Caution needs to be exercised in comparing the performance of GC and Mood Cards as:

- The scale of activities is so significantly different that the nature of the operations and financing is unlikely to be comparable

- Whilst the two companies operate in the same industry, they address different sectors of the market and thus their fortunes may have been affected differently by different factors

Notwithstanding these reservations about making comparisons, it is clear from the data that Mood is performing rather better than GC. This is clearly true in absolute terms but also, adjusting for scale in terms of outlets, Mood appears to significantly outperform GC.

The comparison of revenue/profit per outlet is not valid as Mood has a larger average floorspace for each of its outlets. The data for sales per sq metre of floorspace is a more valid comparison and this shows Mood generating revenues of £2,500 per sq metre (£460m/184k sq metres) compared to £1,533 per sq metre (£10.58m/6,900 sq metres) for GC (which is 63% greater).

Examining the change in performance of the two companies over the period 20X7-20X9 it appears that while GC is expanding the number of shops, Mood is contracting its shops. Despite this, Mood it still expanding sales by over 10% and operating profits by 22.3% and 23.7% in 20X8 and 20X9 respectively.

When adjusting for scale, in terms of the number of shops, Mood is increasing operating profits by 25.0% (£40,430/£32,340) and 23.7% (£50,000/£40,430) in 20X8 and 20X9 respectively. This is far greater than GC.

One comparison with Mood is using the BCG matrix which looks at the relative market share (market strength) compared to the market leader or major competitor (Mood) and the overall market growth rate (market attractiveness).

Relative Market share

	High	Low
HIGH	STAR	QUESTION MARK
LOW	CASH COW	GC x DOG

Market growth (label at left, rows HIGH / LOW)

Examiner's comments:

Requirement 12.2 was the data analysis section of the paper which has been indicated as a regular feature of Business Strategy papers. Part (a) asked candidates to analyse GC's competitive position and explain any threats to that position. Part (b) asked candidates to evaluate the performance of GC and draw comparisons with the market leader.

Most candidates used the data available to help them in their discussion of competitive position and performance. Stronger candidates set out the information coherently in a table format and included data relative to the size of the business (eg revenue or operating profit compared to floorspace/shops/employees). However, only a minority fully explained cause and effect relationships based on this relative data analysis.

Most candidates identified Green Card's position in the overall market, a number using the BCG matrix to assist them in their discussion. Stronger candidates went on to discuss Green Card's position in the niche market. A fair number used a SWOT analysis to discuss Green Card's position. Most candidates gave suitable specific threats for Green Cards. Candidates who had planned their answer well, could analyse the performance of Green Cards and compare it to Mood. Again, those who had considered size relationships were able to give stronger explanations.

Weaker candidates demonstrated a lack of planning in their answer and used the data randomly on an ad hoc basis in the main body of their writing, with a surprising number of candidates failing to relate the data to floorspace/shops/employees. Some weaker candidates also failed to distinguish clearly between parts (a) and (b) of the requirement and produced a merged answer. Also, some very weak candidates produced a largely, or entirely, descriptive answer with little, or no, use of the data.

Comparing the staffing of GC to Mood then:

	20X9 estimated
Employees per shop	
GC	10
Mood	10
Sq m of floorspace per employee	
GC (6900/460)	15 sq m
Mood (184000/9200)	20 sq m
Revenue per employee	
GC (£10.58m/460)	£23,000
Mood (£460m/9,200	£50,000

While GC's staffing per shop is the same as Mood, this is not comparable as Mood's shops are one third larger. Once this is considered, then GC appears to have more staff per 1,000sq m of floorspace, ie they have only 15 sq m each to cover rather than 20 sq m as for Mood.

Mood staff also generate more sales per employee.

The key question however is about the marginal impact to GC of reducing staff as it has a higher quality ethos than Mood.

Also the comparison may not be valid, as some staff may not be employed in the shops but in head office. Due to economies of scale Mood may have proportionately fewer than GC.

(b) **Recommendation**

Overall a review of staff is needed before any decision is taken but if there is evidence of overstaffing this is likely to be the better option as it retains the core competences of GC and does not concede operating capacity to an unknown partner for uncertain benefits.

Examiner's comments:

Requirement 12.4 asked for an evaluation of the two proposed strategies with clear and reasoned advice. A majority presented their answer in briefing note format.

Strategy 1 was generally well attempted with candidates discussing how it could affect the reputation (positively or negatively) and that there could be an opportunity for cross branding. Only strong candidates utilised the data provided in the scenario to discuss the fee and compared the two fee-based options. Those that did this scored highly on this requirement.

For scenario 2 most candidates discussed quality and reputational issues, however, again only strong candidates utilised the data provided in the scenario. Many answers tended to focus on the effects of redundancies on staff morale and the costs of redundancy. Better answers concentrated on the lack of fit with the service-related strategic position of the firm, but very few made the link back to any per-employee analysis produced in requirement 12.2.

The majority of candidates gave a recommendation, but in many cases the reasoning was thin, or was just an assertion of the best course of action.

13 Efficiency Systems Ltd (December 2009)

		Knowledge	Skill	Marks
13.1 (a)	Critical success factors	2	3	
(b)	Mission statement	1	3	
				8
13.2	Business plan assessment/additional information	4	12	15
13.3	Key risks	3	7	9
		10	25	32

General comments:

The scenario in this question involves a small, recently formed enterprise with two entrepreneurial owner/directors. The company develops and markets software to improve the operational processes of organisations. The directors are seeking additional finance and they require assistance in drawing up a business plan to present to the bank is support of a loan application. An assessment of the key risks facing the business, assuming that the loan is granted, is also required.

13.1 (a) Critical success factors

For ES the critical success factors in seeking to expand the business may include:

- Successful development of the Z-Info system in a reasonable period of time at reasonable cost

- Z-Info and existing Comax software must be constantly developed so they continue to outperform similar products from closest rivals in terms of delivering cost savings to clients

- The service delivery and support must outperform rivals in combination with software

- Winning an adequate number of tenders to secure new larger customers at a reasonable tender price that generates adequate profit

- Securing adequate finance to develop the Z-Info and employ the new staff required to install and operate the system for clients

- Appointing and retaining key staff to deliver the core competences of the business

- Retain sufficient agility compared to competitors, in a fast moving industry in terms of products and skills of staff

(b) Mission statement

To develop and supply our software products and to provide supporting services in order to deliver significant cost savings to our customers. This will be achieved by developing staff's skills and other resources to compete with the market leaders in our sector of the industry.

Examiner's comments:

Requirement 13.1 asked candidates to prepare sections for the business plan on critical success factors and a mission statement.

The majority of candidates provided reasonable critical success factors that specifically related to the scenario. Good answers addressed the requirement fully and wrote the CSFs as though they syere part of the business plan. The critical success factors were sometimes insufficiently linked to customer needs.

Mission statements were generally of good quality, although some candidates spent too long explaining what a mission statement was without actually providing one. Mission statements varied from short succinct statements to longer and more comprehensive sets of goals.

13.2 Introduction and background

Management

There is insufficient detail about managerial skills and background. The respective roles of the two directors need to be explained in more detail.

More information may be required to assure the bank on the following matters:

- Dependence of ES on the two directors for skills and finance

- Lack of skills and experience outside IT for the two directors (eg management or finance experience)

- The age of Mike is a concern as he is 62 and nearing retirement, in particular because he is developing the new software and customising the existing Comax software. His knowledge, as program writer, would be difficult to replace

Products and services

More detail is needed on the nature of Comax, the existing software. For example:

- How software works in relation to clients' systems

- The amount of work needed to turn the standard Comax program into one customised for a client's needs

- More evidence than one case study of how existing clients have been helped by existing software (evidence of satisfaction, such as repeat business)

In respect of Z-Info, much more information and evidence of its current and future operational capability is needed. Specifically:

- Detailed specification of the software, what it is intended to achieve and how it differs from existing software in the industry

- Comparisons to other commercial software available (industry standard)

- Evidence of field tests

- Trial runs with clients' systems

- Project plan for Z-Info development and time-line for completion

Fees

A more detailed description of each of the activities is needed including how much revenue each has generated in the two years of business.

A list of clients is also needed, perhaps with revenues generated for each and contracts in place with each.

Marketing

A much more detailed marketing plan is needed which specifies the nature and size of the market that the business is in. Detail is needed about target companies and the process about how the right to tender will be awarded.

More detail on pricing is needed. How are prices set generally and particularly the strategy for tender pricing? Winning a tender needs to be distinguished from making a profit on a contract. Cost analyses are therefore also needed.

The aim of achieving a high success rate needs to be supported by marketing evidence. Also evidence is needed from any past tender experience.

A policy on relationship marketing for existing customers is needed.

Competitors

More details of competitors will be needed, eg:

- The names of the entities that are likely to be in the tender process with you
- The nature of their products
- An outline of their programs for developing new products, to the extent this may be known
- A summary of the customer base of main rivals
- Evidence to support claim that Comax is a 'superior' product

Financing requirements

A detailed financial history is needed including financial statements and cash flows for the years of operation.

The assumptions underlying the forecasts need to be spelt out and justified. Full forecast financial statements are needed, including cash flows, for perhaps three years ahead.

Show separately the impact of:

- Existing contracts (highly certain)
- Probable contracts (eg under final negotiation or repeat business with existing customers)
- More speculative future contracts that may be won with new customers

A success rate of 'one in three' on new contracts is very high if the number of tendering companies is large. This needs to be justified but is likely to be viewed as unduly optimistic. Some sensitivity analysis is needed to explore risks and the consequences of over-optimism.

A more detailed explanation of what borrowed funds will be used for is also necessary.

Given the level of profit being earned, the directors' remuneration totalling £80,000 seems high for a growing business as it is taking much-needed cash out of the business.

Additional information

Also needed in the business plan are:

- Detailed business strategy
- Executive summary
- Supporting documentation

The supporting documentation in appendices may include:

- Tax returns of ES since incorporation
- Statement of personal wealth of Jon and Mike (eg independent valuations of directors' houses)
- Copies of Jon and Mike's personal tax returns
- Copies of any key contracts
- CVs of Jon and Mike
- The bid documentation from the company offering £500,000 to acquire ES

Summary

As it stands, there is little in the business plan to support a loan of the size being requested. Specifically:

- The profit projections appear uncertain as they depend on a new product not yet fully developed

- The projections appear optimistic as they depend on a one in three success rate for tenders when there are three to five tenders expected for each contract

- The key corporate asset is the software which is poor security on a loan

- The cash flows appear to be weak even with optimistic sales predictions

A major positive point, however, is that the bank may still lend based on the fact that the directors' houses provide sufficient security to cover the loans requested, provided that the valuations are credible given reductions in house prices in the recession.

Examiner's comments:

Requirement 13.2 asked candidates to critically assess each section of the draft business plan and identify any additional information. This requirement produced mixed responses. The majority of candidates presented their answer with structured headings as per the question. A minority of candidates did not take this approach, which often resulted in disjointed and weaker answers. Stronger candidates thought about the user's needs and focussed on information that the bank would want to know. In asking for additional information some answers were too vague just noting 'more detail' was needed while others seemed unrealistic in asking for almost every possible piece of information. The best answers addressed all sections and indicated, selectively, the need for key additional information, both in the body of the answer and in a section at the end.

13.3 Risks:

- Failure of the business may lead to loss of directors' homes

- Failure of Z-Info to outperform competitors would mean there is no competitive advantage and winning new substantial business would be unlikely. (Given it is in development stage its feasibility may even be in doubt)

- Reliance on few products (existing software) means there is no diversification of risk if one product fails

- Reliance on two key personnel. Risks of them leaving, retiring, having conflicts, illnesses may put the entire future of the business into doubt

- High fixed costs in developing Z-Info mean high operating gearing and volatility of profits

- High debt finance means high financial gearing and volatility of profits with interest needing to be paid. Jon and Mike initially invested a total of £200,000 in equity. The current borrowing request at £250,000 is greater than this amount. Even if there are some retained earnings, financial gearing is around 50%

- Intellectual property rights over software may be questioned if it was developed while working at University of Northern England

- The industry is rapidly changing and any competitive advantage that does exist can be eroded away quickly

As the business grows, there needs to be reliance on new staff rather than the owners themselves carrying out all the work. Staff selection and retention is a key risk in this respect.

Examiner's comments:

Requirement 13.3 asks candidates to explain the key risks assuming that the bank loan was to be made available. This requirement also produced a mixed response.

Good answers gave detailed specific risks relating to the scenario. Weaker candidates took a text book approach and presented risks that any business could face without relating them to the circumstances facing the company in the specific scenario. Sometimes this approach appeared to arise from the use of a form of the PESTEL framework to analyse risks, and thereby tended to provide rather generic analysis which was insufficiently focused on the firm. This highlights the more general problem of over-reliance on frameworks in an inflexible manner, often resulting in very generic discussion.

14 Total Equipment Hire Ltd (December 2009)

	Knowledge	Skill	Marks
14.1 Divestment and cost reduction	2	7	8
14.2 Closure, measuring performance	3	6	8
14.3 Joint venture	3	7	9
	8	20	25

General comments:

The company in this scenario hires out plant and equipment to other businesses in the building and construction industries. It has three divisions: heavy equipment, small equipment and scaffolding. Due to the recession the building industry has suffered significantly and TEH has similarly suffered a significant reduction in trade. As a consequence, there is doubt over the company's liquidity and going concern as it may be unable to make a forthcoming interest payment. In order to improve liquidity a number of proposals have been put forward; first, to sell off about 20% of equipment and to reduce labour and other costs; second, to close a division; and third, to enter into a joint venture to hire equipment at deeply discounted price to an overseas development project.

14.1 Divestment

The divestment of equipment would release £60 million cash. However operating capability would be downsized significantly by 20%. If the operations director is correct in stating this cash is only half what the equipment is worth, then this would mean that to restore operating capability in future would be possible only at significant cost. There is therefore a significant risk that, in order to attain short term liquidity in this way, the company will be smaller for some time to come.

This may have effects on costs and efficiency as economies of scale (eg better utilisation of support activities over more output, spreading of fixed costs, ability to satisfy large orders) and economies of scope (eg simultaneous deliveries to common sites or common regions) would be reduced.

Although the suggestion is that disposals will only be made where there are multiple items held, there is still likely to be an impact on the marketing strategy of having available for customers a wide variety of equipment at all times. If utilisation rates are (even in a recession) 70%, then a reduction of 20% in equipment would put average utilisation at around 87.5% (70/80). Minimal daily or weekly usage variability – and variability of usage between different items of equipment – would mean customers could not be supplied reliably with the items they wish. This is likely to have an impact on TEH's 'quality' market positioning.

As the economy recovers and underlying utilisation rates improve, this problem is likely to become more pronounced.

The reductions are likely to affect each division differently. For instance in the heavy equipment division the cost of losing a sale from hiring will include the loss of hiring out operators who may need to be made redundant.

The amount of cash raised from the sale is much greater than the half yearly interest payments. This may be a financing issue to give more liquidity than immediately necessary. Also however it may give more strategic flexibility to discount prices or invest in some new, but different, items more suitable to demand during a recession.

Cost reduction

The cost reduction exercise may have strategic consequences as TEH has positioned itself as a provider of a differentiated product (per Porter's generic strategy). If costs are cut, and as a consequence the service quality is reduced, then the marketing message may be confused with that of cost leadership. This may result in long term damage to the brand.

Other criticisms of this approach would be that it may increase cash over time, rather than immediately, as with the sale of equipment. It may also be that, in net terms, it is not cash generating if customers are put off by the change in service levels. This would mean that the changes could be revenue reducing which may offset any cost savings.

The case in favour of cost reductions is that if equipment is scaled down by 20%, then support costs to maintain, deliver and operate equipment could also be reduced (eg administration and maintenance costs and heavy equipment operators). In this respect, the two aspects of the finance director's strategy may be seen as consistent.

It would also appear that hire charges have been reduced. Utilisation has fallen by 12.5% (from 80% to 70%) while revenue has fallen by 25% (from £60m to £45m). This would imply that prices have fallen by 14.3% . [Where i = price change then $(1 - i) = 0.75/0.875)$]

This may mean that this is a strategy to become a low cost provider and cost reductions are consistent with this pricing policy. However, this would be a hasty conclusion as the key issue is relative prices compared to competitors. If all sectors of the market are reducing prices in the recession then the relative position of TEH as a quality provider may be maintained in terms of its relative pricing strategy. Service reductions would not therefore necessarily be consistent with price reductions.

Examiner's comments:

Requirement 14.1 asked candidates to explain the impact of the proposed strategy to divest equipment and reduce costs.

Most candidates made a reasonable attempt, but a significant minority did not refer directly to the fundamental cash flow problems facing the firm.

Stronger candidates answered both parts of the question and included headings for divestment and cost reduction. Nearly all candidates mentioned the effects the strategies would have on quality and reputation and most mentioned that this was moving away from their core strategy. Some noted the need for a major cultural change in the organisation if the cost reduction strategy is pursued, questioning whether or not this was feasible. Most focussed upon the downside of the suggestions with little focus in the fact that it would actually solve the immediate problem of paying the interest and the threat this was posing to going concern.

Very few candidates used the data given in the scenario to calculate revised utilisation rates, or that hire prices have fallen. Weaker candidates largely ignored the cost reduction element of the requirement and focused mainly, or solely, on divestment issues.

14.2 Financial performance

The financial performance of the divisions is likely to be difficult to determine as, although they are controlled separately, they are not operationally independent. In particular:

Interdependence of revenues – customers come to TEH for a comprehensive range of products which can be delivered simultaneously. Thus, for instance, scaffolding is requested alongside other items of equipment and delivered together. The closure of (say) scaffolding might therefore have an adverse impact on the revenues of small tools. The converse would also be true if the small tools division was closed.

The extent of this interdependence of revenues needs to be determined.

As the heavy equipment division and the small tools division have few, if any, common customers there is likely to be less interdependence of revenues in this case.

Interdependence of costs – there are likely to be a number of costs incurred jointly between the divisions which may have been allocated. Also, there may be some scale economies for storage and maintenance of equipment and administration, so closure of one division would impact on the costs of the other divisions. As already noted, there are likely to be efficiencies of delivery costs in terms of economies of scope.

The impact of closing a division might be slightly different than 'across the board' cost savings as suggested by the finance director. Specifically, if the cost drivers relate to a product line the costs may be saved but, more likely, the cost drivers are likely to relate to functions which cut across the three product divisions. In this case, performance is difficult to identify as the costs are common and the cost savings from closure may be limited due to these interdependencies.

Non-financial performance

Given the recession and the significant impact on the building industry, poor financial performance may be viewed as inevitable in the short term. If the divisions, however, are still satisfying customers and outperforming competitors then the company may be well positioned to improve performance with the recovery. Some divisions may, in this respect, be better than others and this may form the basis of any performance assessment and closure decision rather than financial data. Possible approaches include:

Benchmarking – This may be internal, where the divisions are benchmarked against each other but this is not likely to be helpful in determining closure where there are many common functions between the divisions (eg delivery).

Competitive benchmarking may be more helpful in assessing performance against competitors (eg delivery times, range of products, prices).

Activity benchmarking (generic) could be fairly close to existing activity and look at say specialist scaffolding firms. More generally, for the function of delivery it could be compared against couriers and specialist logistics companies.

KPIs – These could be developed from benchmarking or internal measures but may include customer satisfaction, delays in availability of request products, delivery time once product is available, collection times, product failures/breakdowns per 100 hires.

The Balanced Scorecard could form a framework for these KPIs but would need to be focused on the closure decision, rather than measuring performance generally.

Examiner's comments:

Requirement 14.2 asked candidates to explain the issues to be considered in measuring financial and non financial performance in order to determine which division should be closed.

Again, the biggest criticism is that the immediacy of the liquidity issue was ignored and most candidates failed to talk about this being a longer term solution. Most candidates split their answer between financial and non-financial issues. Joint costs were mentioned by most, but only stronger candidates discussed the interdependence of revenues and costs.

Many candidates discussed performance generally without relating it to the immediate purpose of deciding which division to close. Many of the candidates taking this approach used the Balanced Scorecard framework rather too inflexibly and thereby tended to miss many of the key issues concerning closure. This again highlights the problem of the inflexible use of frameworks and their application in an uncritical manner.

14.3 Benefits

- Cash is raised without selling off the assets

- The assets will be available to restore growth to the business when the recession is ended

- While the prices are discounted below UK levels, some revenue would be generated from underutilised equipment

- The joint venture structure would share the risks of the project without needing to establish any permanent relationship with the other party

- The JV would allow incentives for both parties to exploit the rewards, while contributing their (very different) core competences. A mere transport contract may just provide a fixed reward for ITT and not the incentive for it to seek further opportunities for the mutual benefit of both parties

Problems

There will be a significant reduction in the availability of equipment in the UK if there is a commitment to it being used overseas on the new project. In this respect many of the problems noted above for the finance director's strategy of 20% divestment would be repeated here. There are however some key differences:

- 40% of the heavy equipment could be unavailable and, as this makes up 70% of total equipment held for hire, this would be a reduction of 28% in operating capability compared to 20% with the FD's proposal

- The focus of the reductions is even more significant in the heavy equipment division and these customers may be disproportionately affected

- The upfront cash amount is lower than with the FD's proposal and does not cover the interest payment. Thus, the immediate liquidity issues may not be resolved by this venture as they were by the FD's proposal

- The JV agreement requires equipment to be made immediately available if requested. This means that they may need to be withheld from longer term hire in the UK. This could create a situation where equipment is not rented out in the UK at relatively high rates, but is only being reserved for use overseas so is not actually earning any fees

- The JV arrangement is for three years so it may extend into the recovery period after the recession when utilisation rates increase and there may be a much greater opportunity cost in lost UK revenues

- The joint venture structure may give rise to conflict as it relates to the conduct of an entire project rather than just a contract for specified transport services. There is therefore a need for independent assurance over the parties (eg over fees collection and sharing)

Issues for clarification include:

- There may be a risk of damage or loss of equipment in transport or overseas. It is not clear who bears this risk (eg who stores the equipment while it is not being used overseas)

- The heavy equipment requires a skilled operator in the UK and who incurs the cost of providing this needs to be established

- As ITT is dealing directly with the client, any additional benefits arising from the contract may accrue to ITT rather than jointly with TEH

- The hire days need to be defined, as days in transit will not attract revenue but will be days out of use for TEH

- The fee split seems unreasonable given that ITT are merely transporting the goods and supplying the client contact. In effect, if ITT is getting half and the fee is 75% of the UK fee then this is only 37.5% of the UK fee coming to TEH. The basis of the split needs to be justified and may be renegotiated

- Is there exclusivity or could ITT also be using rivals and leaving TEH products largely unutilised but held in reserve in case they are requested

- There may be reputational damage if ITT does not provide a good quality of service – although the impact in the UK may be restricted given the location and specialised nature of the contract. The need for a service level agreement needs clarification

Examiner's comments:

Requirement 14.3 asked candidates to evaluate the benefits and problems of the proposed joint venture and to identify any matters to be clarified. This part of the question resulted in the weakest answers.

The majority of candidates discussed generic issues relating to joint ventures. Only stronger candidates related their answer to the specific points in the question. Most seemed to think that the joint venture was a good idea – better candidates discussed the shortfall of £5 million for the required interest payment, and the fact that the contract may not be a good deal after assessing the costs and benefits involved. Again, only the better answers attempted any data analysis or recognised the change in the situation likely to be faced by the company as the economy emerges out of recession, together with the implications for the other proposed strategies.

15 Blazing Bicycles Ltd (March 2010)

Marking guide

		Knowledge	Skill	Marks
15.1	Industry and product lifecycle	3	5	7
15.2	International competitive advantage	3	5	7
15.3	Calculations	-	8	
	Evaluation of performance and competitive position	2	6	
				12
15.4	External risk factors	3	6	8
15.5	Evaluate Strategies 1 and 2	2	7	8
		13	37	42

General comments:

The scenario in this question involves an independent bicycle retailer which operates a chain of ten shops across the UK, selling high quality bicycles and bike accessories. Information was given in the question about the development of the UK bicycle retailing and manufacturing industry since the 1930s, together with detail regarding the nature of the competition and relevant environmental and market factors. The company's recent financial results (which were provided) are giving some cause for concern, with profits falling despite a number of new stores being opened. Candidates were also supplied with a risk analysis prepared by the Managing Director which listed the key commercial risks currently facing the company. Two alternative strategies are being considered to address these issues: expand the product range to offer other sporting and outdoor equipment or set up specialist in-store bicycle workshops to offer repairs and servicing.

This question was the mini case, incorporating some data analysis and, at 42 marks, was the longest question on the paper. The requirements were broken down to help candidates in developing answer headings and assessing mark allocation. Overall candidates performed reasonably well on this question, showing good knowledge of the models tested and on the whole demonstrating improved data analysis skills.

15.1 Industry and product life cycle analysis

The concept of life cycle analysis is used to describe the phases of development that an industry or product goes through.

The key stages of the life cycle are:

*   **Introduction** – a newly invented product or service is made available for purchase and organisations attempt to develop buyer interest.

*   **Growth** – a period of rapid expansion of demand or activity as the industry finds a market and competitors are attracted by its potential.

*   **Maturity** – a relatively stable period of time where there is little change in sales volumes year to year but competition between firms intensifies as growth slows down.

- **Decline** – a falling off in activity levels as firms leave the industry and the industry ceases to exist or is absorbed into some other industry.

Some industry life cycles are identical in pattern and timing to that of their product (eg the steel industry). Others have longer life cycles than the particular products, eg the music industry which has endured from sheet music till MP3 and downloads, merely releasing (and re-releasing) its music as new products as the format changes. This appears to have been the case with the bicycle retailing industry which has seen a variety of products come and go within the industry life cycle.

Thus the cycle has been influenced by two factors:

(1) Changes in the usage to which bikes are put (transport, leisure etc). Such changes lengthen the industry life cycle but may not necessarily involve a new or separate product.

(2) Changes in the types of bike (products).

The industry appears to have followed a traditional pattern of introduction, growth, maturity and decline from 1800 through to the mid 1960s, when the product was essentially a bicycle as a means of transport.

Thus it took a while for sales to develop after the introduction of the bicycle in its modern form in the late 1800s. Then from 1930 onwards the industry experienced a period of growth and expansion as bicycles became a popular form of transport. After a short period of stability, the industry can be seen to enter decline in the 1950s with the advent of more affordable motor car transport, lasting to the mid 1960s.

From the mid 1960s the industry appears to enter a different phase, with the bicycle becoming a leisure rather than transportation product.

In terms of the product life cycle it is common within an industry for products to overlap. As one product declines, another is in maturity and another is growing (either because of changes in consumer demand or technological change). This can be seen in the bicycle industry from the mid 1960s onwards where the product life cycles of individual products such as small wheel bikes or mountain bikes have overlapped at different times. It could however be argued that these are design modifications to the same basic product, rather than different products themselves.

The overall trend from the mid 60s to 2010 is one of growth (sales of 0.75m increasing to around 3.25m per the graph), punctuated by periods of rapid expansion then slow-down as a variety of products have come and gone. Hence the small wheeled bicycle and children's version accounted for much of the growth in the late 60s and 70s, then there was a period of relative stability until the industry developed the mountain bike in the mid 80s, leading to another rapid expansion.

The apparent slowing down in the 90s is likely to have led to intensified competition but changing attitudes to health and the environment have seen the bicycle reinvented as a mode of transport again, leading to another period of growth in the 2000s.

Hence the concepts of both product and industry life cycle do appear to apply in the bicycle industry, which has managed to extend the life of its product by continual innovation and to revitalise its product by responding to changes in the external environment (such as technological developments) and consumer preferences.

Examiner's comments:

In requirement 15.1 candidates were asked to consider the extent to which the concept of the industry and product lifecycle could be applied to the bicycle retailing industry and to sales of different types of bicycles. Most candidates scored well here, demonstrating appropriate knowledge when describing the lifecycle in its different stages, often with an accompanying diagram. It was pleasing that the majority were able to apply this knowledge well to the scenario. Most candidates distinguished between the industry and product lifecycles, pointing out that the lifecycle of an individual type of bike, eg BMX was typically much shorter than that of the industry and that continued product innovation had allowed the industry lifecycle to be extended. Weaker candidates wrote about the lifecycle in overall terms or incorporated lengthy comments about the impact of the various stages of the lifecycle for a manufacturer, which did not answer the question.

Tutorial note:

Candidates were not necessarily expected to use two models but both are produced here for marking purposes.

The International Trade Life Cycle suggests that many products pass through a cycle during which high income, mass-consumption countries are initially exporters but subsequently lose their export markets and ultimately become importers of the product from lower-cost economies. This is consistent with the information in the scenario where the UK moved from a net exporter to a net importer of bikes.

From the perspective of the initiator high income country, the pattern of development is as follows:

- **Phase 1. The product is developed in the high income country** – here the UK which was the source of innovation for the modern version of the bicycle. There are two main reasons for this.

    - High income countries provide the greatest demand potential.

    - It is expedient to locate production close to the market during the early period so that the firm can react quickly in modifying the product according to customer preferences.

- **Phase 2. Overseas production starts**. Firms in the innovator's export markets (such as mainland Europe) start to produce the product domestically. Thus, for example, the European market is then shared by the innovative UK firms as well as local manufacturers. This has the effect of reducing the level of exports.

- **Phase 3. Overseas producers compete in export markets**. The costs of the other producers begin to fall as they gain economies of scale and experience. They may also enjoy lower costs of labour and materials than the UK firms (this is particularly true of China and Taiwan). These firms now start to compete with the UK producers in third-party export markets such as, say, the USA.

- **Phase 4. Overseas producers compete in the firm's domestic market**. The new firms become so competitive, due to their lower production costs (the scenario refers to wages in China and Taiwan being less than a third of UK costs), that they start to compete with the UK firms in the UK domestic market. In the bicycle market this eventually led to all major bike manufacturers ceasing production in the UK by 1999 and the majority of bikes and parts being imported from China and Taiwan.

Porter's diamond also provides a framework for assessing the relationship between location and competitive advantage and could be used to explain the UK's historic dominance of bicycle manufacturing:

Factor conditions – the resource inputs needed by the business. Since the UK was instrumental in the development of bicycles a workforce will have developed with the necessary knowledge and skills to design and manufacture bikes.

Home market demand conditions – these shape a firm's priorities and the way it responds to buyer needs. Thus UK manufacturers were successful in places such as USA and mainland Europe which are generally similar to the UK market.

Supporting local industries – manufacturers of gears, brake cables, frames and tyres will have grown up around UK bike manufacturers. Thus the metalwork and engineering expertise of the sewing and armaments industries helped the UK become a world leader in cycle manufacture.

Firm strategy, structure and rivalry – emergence of firms with strong competitive characteristics which are then able to dominate worldwide markets. Since the UK was credited with developing the modern bicycle it had a strong presence in the industry until the later part of the 20th century.

Using this framework the competitive advantage may have passed to China and Taiwan for the following reasons:

- Factor conditions – the availability of a large pool of low cost labour means bikes can be manufactured at a much lower cost

- Home market demand – a large population with a very strong cycling culture

- Supporting local industries – major steel industry and a reputation for expertise in electronics and technology will have supported the development of new carbon fibre frames etc

- Firm strategy, structure and rivalry – the UK has witnessed the decline of its manufacturing base and as it has moved towards service businesses, China and Taiwan have increasingly benefited from the outsourcing of manufacture

Examiner's comments:

In requirement 15.2 candidates were asked to use models of international trade to explain why the UK had a historic competitive advantage in bicycle manufacture and why this had now passed to countries such as Taiwan and China. The majority of candidates tackled this using Porter's Diamond. Less frequently applied, though also relevant, was the concept of the International trade lifecycle. Most answers explained the UK's historic advantage in terms of its role in developing the modern bicycle, the knowledge and resources available from the sewing machine and armaments industries, and the sophistication of demand. They also identified the key point from the scenario that as a result of low labour costs this advantage had now passed to China and Taiwan. Better candidates developed their answers further, referring to the change in focus in the UK from manufacturing to service industries such that now only 5% of bicycles are manufactured in the UK, China's increasing experience of outsourced manufacturing and technological innovation and its strong cycling culture.

15.3 Refer to appendix for supporting calculations

(1) **Competitive position**

Market positioning

The information suggests that in 2009 BB had around 1.4% of the UK bicycle retail market (7.178/ 510).

It is clearly a small player relative to Benhonda (30% share) and the other large retailers which between them account for 25% of the market. However it is probably reasonably large in terms of the independent cycle retailers which between the 2,000 of them hold 45% (or an average share of just 0.0225%). This is further borne out by the fact that BB has 10 shops whereas a large number of the independent retailers are local owner managed businesses with a single shop.

Each BB outlet has a market share of 0.14% (1.4%/10). An average BB outlet is therefore over 6 times (0.14/0.0225) larger than the average independent outlet.

Competitive stance

Although BB stocks a range of bicycles, it focuses on the sale of high quality bikes and employs staff with specialist knowledge and expertise. This (and its premium pricing discussed below) suggests that it is a differentiator according to Porter's generic strategies.

Pricing

BB's average price is significantly higher (£398 in 2009) than the retail industry average of £150+. This could mean that BB charges more for similar models than competitors but is more likely to be a result of the types of bike sold by BB, which focuses on the higher specification models and may exclude children's bicycles.

The overall market could be seen in the diagram below:

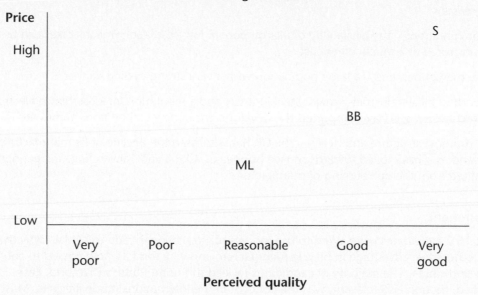

In the diagram:

BB represents BB where price and quality are maintained at a high level

ML represents Benhonda and other big retailers where price and quality are mid market ranges

S represents specialist retailers selling high performance competition bikes

(2) **Performance**

The key issue here is that although the additional four stores appear to have led to an increase in sales revenue of 32%, this is not sufficient to cover the 61% increase in admin and distribution costs and as a result, overall profit before tax has fallen from £1.1m to £1.089m despite the increase in sales revenue.

Sales volumes

The MD suggests that BB has recently been affected by increased competition as a result of the recession. Although the number of bikes sold has increased from 9,200 in 2007 to 11,000, four additional stores have been opened in this period. Thus the number of bikes sold per store has fallen from an average of 1533 in 2007 to 1100 in 2009.

More information is required to assess the cause of this, as some of the stores may only just have opened or may be smaller than the original six stores. Alternatively the drop in sales could be due to consumers trading down or delaying the purchase of new bikes as a result of the recession.

The average price per bike has increased by £45 from £353 to £398. Since this is an average price for all ranges, BB might have changed the mix of bikes sold. Alternatively if this is due to BB raising prices, it could have resulted in a decrease in volume.

Sales mix and margins

The proportion of bicycle sales has remained largely consistent at 60-61% of total revenues. This is significantly higher than the average retailer, where bikes amount to just under 47%, but again could be accounted for by the fact that BB sells items of higher individual value.

BB's margin on bicycle sales is lower than the industry average of 37% and disappointingly has dropped from 34 to 30%. This is perhaps surprising given BB's focus on higher quality bikes, as it might expect to make better margins, but the decrease could be due to increased import prices as a result of changing exchange rates.

The higher margin sales of accessories and servicing account for only 39% of BBs sales in 2009, compared to 53% for the average retailer. This suggests that there is scope for BB to improve overall margins by increasing this side of the business, as proposed by the sales director under Strategy 2.

Profitability

As discussed above, overall profits have fallen, as have profits per store (£109k 2009 compared to £183k 2007).

The increase in admin and distribution overheads is not unreasonable given the additional operating leases for the four new stores, so the key to understanding BB's profitability lies with its sales figures.

Allowing for certain one-off set up costs and assuming the new stores take a while to achieve the same level of sales as existing ones, BB's future performance may improve. Alternatively BB may have opened stores too close together which are competing for sales, or in poor locations.

Further information

As the figures are summarised for the business as a whole, more detail is needed on a shop by shop basis to identify those shops that are doing particularly well or underperforming.

A breakdown of prices and sales volumes by type of bicycle, for BB and the average retailer, would allow for a better analysis.

Appendix of calculations:

Tutorial note:

Candidates were not expected to produce the full range of calculations which are included here for marking purposes.

	2007	2009	Mkt average 2009
Sales mix			
Bikes %	60	61	47
Access. and servicing %	40	39	53
Margins			
Bikes %	34	30	37
Access and servicing %	42	45	48
Total GP margin	37.3	36.0	
Total PBT margin	20.2	15.2	
Store performance			
Sales/store £'000s	907	718	
GP/store £'000s	338	258	
PBT/store £'000s	183	109	
Analysis per bike			
Average price per bike	£353	£398	£150
Bikes sold per store	1533	1100	
GP per bike	£119	£119	£55.50
Market share			
BB market share		1.4%	Market leader = 30%
Share per outlet		0.14%	
Share relative to market leader (1.4/30)		4.67%	
Ave independent share 45/2000			0.0225%

Examiner's comments:

Requirement 15.3 was the first of two requirements in this paper that required some data analysis, which has been indicated as a regular feature of Business Strategy papers. Candidates seemed well prepared for the requirement in this question which asked them to evaluate the company's performance and competitive position based on historic results. Most, but not all, candidates used the data available to help them in their discussion.

Stronger candidates set out the information coherently in a table format, included data for both position and performance, and made calculations of revenue and profit on a per shop or per bicycle basis. However, only a minority fully explained cause and effect relationships based on this relative data analysis and made full use of the industry information that had been provided for benchmarking purposes. A number concentrated on revenue growth, without identifying the key point that whilst revenue had increased, probably as a result of opening four new stores, overall profits had fallen.

In terms of competitive position, most candidates identified BB's competitive strategy in terms of Porter's differentiation and a significant number produced a price/quality diagram to show BB's relative positioning. Typically BB's market share was calculated in relation to the overall market. Stronger candidates related this to the share of the market leader, Benhonda, and the average share of an independent retailer and went on to discuss BB's position within its niche market.

Candidates who had planned their answer well analysed both performance and competitive position. Those who had produced analysis on a per bike or per shop basis were able to give stronger discussions. Weaker candidates demonstrated a lack of planning in their answer and used the data randomly within the main body of their writing. Some very weak candidates produced a largely, or entirely, descriptive answer with little, or no, use of the data, or limited their data analysis to a long list of the % movements from 2007 to 2009. A number of weaker candidates only showed numerical analysis relating to performance and omitted completely any numerical analysis of the competitive position.

15.4 External sources of risk

Tutorial note:

Models such as PESTEL or Five Forces might have been used to help generate ideas here but whatever approach is adopted, it is important to consider the implications of such industry factors for BB and explain why they might be considered to be sources of risk.

Economic and industry conditions:

Political – changes of attitude by the government or differing levels of support may affect demand for bikes. The attitude of the current government appears favourable for the industry but spending priorities may change as a result of the recession or a new government. This will have an impact on the industry as a whole but may affect some product ranges more than others. The government may be more likely to subsidise basic ranges rather than the higher quality bikes offered by BB.

Economic – the economy has a major influence on levels of spending. Recession may have both positive and negative effects. The downside risk is that consumers could cut back on spending, or trade down to lower quality bikes which may adversely affect BB as they appear to be operating at the higher end of the market. Alternatively people may keep bikes longer, thus delaying spending on new bikes but increasing the likelihood of sales of parts and servicing. BB's sales and profits may be at risk unless it caters for this additional demand, as suggested by Strategy 2.

In an attempt to save money eg on fuel people may use bikes in preference to cars for short journeys and commuting. As far as BB is concerned the risk is that this may change the mix of products being demanded.

Technology – BB may experience price deflation caused by technology development or radical developments could render existing stock obsolete. This is particularly likely to affect the high end of the market and the competition bikes.

Competition

The industry is highly competitive and has become more so as a result of the recession. BB faces competition from a variety of small independent UK retailers, as well as international companies and internet-based operators. Failure to compete with competitors on areas including price, product range, quality and service could have an adverse effect on BB's financial results. The market share calculations in 15.3 suggest that BB is small compared to Benhonda and other big retailers. There is a risk that if they choose to offer similar ranges to BB, it will be unable to compete on price.

Responsiveness to changing market preferences

The history of the bike market demonstrates that over time consumer tastes have changed rapidly. There are also a wide variety of substitutes both for bicycles as a form of transport and also as a form of entertainment eg interactive games consoles. If BB fails to offer products that reflect the changes in demand, there is a risk that its sales will decline. In addition it may be left with high levels of unsold stock.

Reliance on foreign manufacturers

A significant amount of parts and bikes are imported. This gives rise to risks associated with international trade including exposure to different economic conditions, regulatory requirements, trade restrictions and changing foreign government policies.

Transportation problems may affect BB's ability to meet customer demand, which is a problem given low customer switching costs.

Given the majority of bikes are imported, the weak sterling exchange rate may have a significant impact on the costs of the business and hence erode margins.

15.5 Evaluation of Strategy 1 and 2

Strategy 1: Expansion of product range

This represents a new product for BB and may attract a different type of customer or alternatively may offer BB the chance to increase the amount spent by existing customers, since bike enthusiasts may also need sporting and outdoor equipment.

This may increase sales per shop provided that BB has unutilised floorspace in its stores.

Development of the product range will reduce the company's reliance on the difficult bicycle industry and hence reduce risk.

However BB lacks experience in this area and there is a high level of existing competition from companies which are much larger. As a smaller player BB would find it hard to get economies of scale and may lack purchasing power with new suppliers.

This strategy does not focus on BB's core competences, as staff are cycling experts and may lack knowledge in other areas.

Strategy 2: Integrated workshops

Servicing and parts is the higher margin business so this strategy should improve results and may increase customer retention as BB can try and tie in customers with after sales plans.

The specialist workshops build on existing expertise and provide BB with an added differentiation factor. Given its knowledgeable staff, BB may be able to achieve this with relatively low investment.

This strategy is also consistent with environmental conditions where consumers are retaining bikes for longer and therefore spending more on repairs and servicing. The fact that BB has already trialled this in the Manchester store reduces the risk of failure and suggests it may be successful.

This strategy does not however reduce reliance on the bicycle industry although it helps diversify within it, and avoids competition with larger retailers.

Other options

Strategy 2 is the most obvious one for BB to pursue in the first instance. The strategies are not necessarily mutually exclusive however and BB might consider testing Strategy 1 in certain stores, as it has done with the workshop in Manchester.

BB should also consider whether it is losing out on sales by internet/mail order.

Performance may be improved by identifying which shops are performing well and why, as it may be worth closing some down. Similarly some product ranges may be better than others and it may be worth specialising in certain bike ranges only.

Examiner's comments:

In requirement 15.5 candidates had to discuss the merits of the two options set out in the scenario. This was typically well done. The better candidates related their points back to the risks identified in 15.4 and attempted to reach a conclusion as to which strategy was more viable, in some cases recommending other options to be considered.

16 Deeshire Council (March 2010)

| Marking guide |

	Knowledge	Skill	Marks
16.1 Briefing note	1	-	
Calculations	-	11	
Implications for strategy	-	5	
			13
16.2 Change management issues for each	4	7	10
16.3 (a) Principles and action	3	4	6
(b) IS to monitor performance	2	7	7
	10	34	36

General comments:

This question asked candidates to play the role of an employee working in the strategic planning and policy department of a local council. Domestic waste collection and disposal services are currently operated 'in-house' by the council. Estimates of the council's waste management costs for the latest financial year were provided. Under pressure from the government to reduce landfill and increase recycling rates, the council is considering two proposals to reduce costs and avoid the government's landfill tax penalties:

Option 1: Reduce the number of general refuse collections from weekly to fortnightly in the hope of improving recycling rates

Option 2: Outsource the recycling element of the waste collection. The council have received two tenders for the four year contract: Contractor A based on a variable price per tonne and Contractor B which is a fixed annual sum. Councillors face and ethical dilemma since the chief executive of Contractor A has offered to fund life membership of the local golf club if they support his tender.

This question, which also incorporated some data analysis, was the least well attempted on the paper with reasonable performances on part 16.2 often failing to make up for poor attempts at either 16.1 or 16.3. A disappointing minority did not produce their answer in the style of a briefing note.

16.1 Evaluate financial implications of options

Briefing Notes

To:	Deeshire Councillors
From:	Strategic planning and policy group
Date:	March 20Y0
Re:	Waste management strategy

The attached notes set out the financial implications of the proposals under consideration and other issues that Councillors need to consider in deciding on an appropriate waste management strategy.

Option 1: reduce collections and promote recycling

General refuse becomes $0.8 \times 1.5m = 1.2m$ tonnes and hence recycling = 0.8m (0.5 + 0.3 converted from refuse).

Note. This is within the limit for recyclable waste of 1m tonnes

Financial implications

(1) **Incremental approach:**

The primary saving is the £2.5m reduction in fixed costs as a result of the once per fortnight general refuse collection.

In addition the Council saves £1.50/tonne by getting households to convert general refuse to recycling (VC of general refuse collection are £3/tonne, recycling costs a net £1.50 per tonne – £4 less £2.50 revenue generated), so the saving is $£1.50 \times 0.3m$ tonnes = £0.45m.

Thus the total saving is £2.95m.

The maximum amount of current waste that can be recycled is $0.5 \times 2m = 1m$ tonnes, so the total potential saving if recycling rates increase from 09/10 levels would be an additional 0.5m recycling at £1.50 = £0.75m.

(2) **Alternative approach: Calculation of total cost**

		£million
General refuse		
Variable costs	1.2m tonnes @ £3/tonne	3.6
Fixed costs	6.5-2.5 saving	4.0
		7.6
Recycling		
Variable costs	0.8m tonnes @ £4/tonne	3.2
Fixed costs		3.2
Less		6.4
Revenue generated from sale of		
recycled waste	0.8m tonnes @ £2.50/tonne	(2.0)
		4.4
Other overheads		2.7
Total waste management costs		14.7

Since existing costs are £17.65m, option 1 would save the Council £2.95m per annum once established. The increase in recycling rates may also help the Council avoid the government's proposed landfill tax.

Further information required:

- Can further general refuse fixed costs be saved if more waste is recycled?

- Alternatively will the FC of recycling increase as limits of existing capacity are reached?

- What are other overheads and how will these be affected?

- Are any inflationary price increases expected or changes in rates at which recycling can be sold?

- Projections for number of households and levels of waste over next four years?

- Any additional fixed costs as a result of campaign to promote recycling?

Option 2: Outsource recycling

Financial implications

(1) **Incremental approach:**

	Contractor A £m	Contractor B £m
In house costs saved	3.95	3.95
Contract management costs	(0.1)	(0.1)
Contract price	(2.5)	(4.0)
Net saving/(cost)	1.35	(0.15)

(2) **Alternative approach: Calculation of total cost**

	£million
Existing general refuse costs	11.0
Contract management	0.1
Other overheads	2.7
Total waste management costs excluding contract price	13.8

Total cost with contractor A = 13.8 + (0.5 × £5) = £16.3m

Total cost with contractor B = 13.8 + 4 = £17.8m

Comments

Contractor A is cheaper assuming the current level of recycling is maintained, but overall Option 2 is more expensive than Option 1.

However the options are not necessarily mutually exclusive, so the Council could outsource recycling and switch general refuse collection to once per fortnight, to increase recycling rates.

If Option 2 is combined with Option 1, total cost becomes:

	£million
Option 1 general refuse costs	7.6
Option 2 outsourced costs for 0.8m tonnes	4.0
Contract management	0.1
Other overheads	2.7
Total waste management costs	14.4

Overall it appears that this is the best decision from a financial point of view.

Choice of contractor

Contractor A: has tendered a price of £5 per tonne, hence total cost of contract increases as quantity of recycling increases. Thus it is in the contractor's interest to promote increased recycling (which benefits the Council as far as the government targets are concerned but costs it more).

Contractor B: fixed price of £4m, hence cost per tonne for the Council is reduced as amount of recycling increases. There is less incentive for the contractor to promote recycling but it will be in the Council's interests to do so as it reduces cost and helps meet government targets.

Contractor A is significantly cheaper at the current levels of recycling. If the Council can increase recycling as planned to 0.8m tonnes, then both contractors are the same price. B becomes cheaper if either the number of households or the levels of recycling increase substantially.

There are however ethical issues surrounding the golf membership offered by Contractor A – see later notes 16.3.

Summary of total annual costs for various options:

Option	Quantity recycled	Total cost £		Saving £m
Current	0.5m	17.65m		
1 only	0.8m	14.7m		2.95
2 only	0.5m	A: 16.3m	B: 17.8m	A:1.35
1+2	0.8m	A: 14.4m	B: 14.4m	3.25
Max recycle	1m	A: 14.8m	B: 13.8m	B: 3.85

Other issues:

The quantity of recycling achieved by the external contractor will impact on the costs of general refuse collection for the Council. This would affect the decision if it is felt that one contractor is likely to achieve different recycling rates than another.

It is possible that other overheads may be reduced if all recycling is outsourced.

Contractors will pursue a profit maximisation objective which may cause them to ignore or reduce unprofitable activities eg waste collection in rural areas, reduction of number of collections.

As the Council remains responsible for the services, poor performance on the part of the contractor will reflect badly on the Council. It may also result in risks to health and the environment and give rise to claims for damages.

Redundancies of in-house workers may cause dissatisfaction and damage the Council's reputation. The Council may need to consider the degree of unionisation (see notes on change management).

Outsourcing may not improve recycling rates as a private contractor may be less likely to be joined up with other Council activities in this area.

It will be hard to go back to in-house provision if the decision proves to be the wrong one.

Examiner's comments:

Requirement 16.1 asked candidates to evaluate the impact of the two proposals in financial terms and to comment on the implications for the council's waste management strategy. This was one of the least well attempted requirements on the paper and many attempts were marginal.

Most candidates were able to produce sensible calculations for options 1 and 2, either by recalculating the total costs for each option, or by calculating the cost savings on an incremental basis. Either approach was acceptable, although the incremental approach would have been faster. Common errors included: calculating the additional amount to be recycled as 20% of the current recycling, instead of 20% of the current volume of general refuse; ignoring the additional £100,000 monitoring costs for outsourcing; treating the contractors' bids as revenue for the council, rather than costs.

Comments on the implications were less insightful and often amounted to a statement of the overall cost saving for each option. Only the better candidates discussed the accuracy of the estimates and questioned whether the residents would be satisfied with fortnightly collections or whether the promotional campaign would achieve the necessary increase the recycling. The stronger candidates also realised that given the government's desire to increase recycling rates and avoid landfill taxes, the volumes of recycling were likely to increase in future. As a result, the fixed price offered by Contractor B might become a more attractive option during the four years of the contract. Any attempt at sensitivity analysis here to identify the volume of recycling at which the council would be indifferent between the two contractors was awarded credit.

Disappointingly few candidates picked up on the fact that, as the two options were not mutually exclusive, combining the proposal for fortnightly collections with the outsourcing of recycling would potentially lead to the biggest savings. There were sufficient marks available for candidates to pass the requirement without addressing this higher skills issue, but those who recognised the possibility and produced calculations to prove it, scored very highly.

The weakest candidates tended to avoid numerical analysis almost entirely and instead discussed the impact of the proposals in more general terms, selecting one or two figures from the question to back up their comments. This approach typically failed to generate sufficient marks.

16.2 Change management issues

The following issues are relevant when changing the way in which waste management is operated:

(1) Pace, manner and scope of change
(2) Barriers to change
(3) Ways to implement and manage the change process

(1) **Pace, manner and scope of change**

The change may be incremental (building on existing methods) or transformational (a new model of waste management) and may take place gradually or require a rapid one-off change. Option 1 is more likely to involve incremental change whereas Option 2 is more transformational.

Here outsourcing is new in the context of waste management but the Council may already have experience of managing outsourced contractors in other areas of service provision. The government is putting pressure on Councils to improve recycling rates and some funding may be dependent on reaching appropriate targets, so the changes will probably need to be introduced relatively quickly. The switch to outsourcing is likely to be done in one go rather than being gradually phased in.

(2) **Barriers to change**

A very important aspect of successfully implementing the changes required will be identifying all the factors that could hinder change and then reduce them. At the same time it is important to identify those factors that will promote change and strengthen them.

The capacity to undertake change must be considered in terms of the resources the Council have available and whether there are any cost or time constraints which could prohibit change.

The barriers to change need to be considered by looking at the stakeholders who will be affected by it – specifically here the Council employees who currently operate the waste collection services and the residents who are used to a certain level of service. Their readiness to change or their resistance to it will have a significant impact on the success of the new recycling strategy. Other important stakeholders might include the local media who have the power to support and promote the Council or alternatively damage its reputation.

Given the size of the county there will be a wide variety of communities and issues will differ from one to the other.

For Option 1, the greatest barriers to change are likely to come from the residents who will be used to a weekly collection and will have ingrained habits concerning the disposal of waste which are difficult to change and may prevent recycling targets being achieved.

For Option 2, the barriers to change are likely to be highest among the Council workers, who may well be unionised. These will be split into two groups – those who are to be made redundant, who will no longer be involved, and their colleagues in general refuse who will continue with the current ways of doing things but may feel their job security is threatened (either because of a reduction in number of collections and less volumes of waste or perhaps because ultimately the Council may decide to outsource all aspects of waste collection).

(3) **Implementing the change**

The way in which the changes are introduced will be very important in them being implemented successfully.

Resistance needs to be acknowledged and discussed and can be lessened by involving both the employees and residents in the planning and implementation. The change needs to be sold to all those involved and communication will be key to this.

Within the Council work force employees must be helped to change their attitudes and behaviours.

Lewin/Schein's 3-step iceberg model of change would prescribe the following approach:

- Unfreezing standard operating procedures (identifying the restraining forces and overcoming them)

- Changing to new patterns of behaviour (carrying out the change and switching to the outsourced contractor) and

- Refreezing to ensure lasting effects ie reinforcing the new system and behaviour

The **Gemini 4Rs** framework could also be used here:

Reframe – create the will and desire to change (the Council may focus on the need for a sustainable environment and the benefits to the environment and future generations of reducing landfill).

Restructure – redesign the structure and culture to facilitate the new approach. This may involve holding meetings with residents, setting up appropriate targets and measures and creating a culture of teamwork between the contractor and the Council's own staff to promote recycling.

Revitalise – ensure an appropriate fit with the environment eg issue promotional literature regarding the Council's plan.

Renewal – ensure the change is supported on an ongoing basis and that individuals involved have the necessary skills eg education of residents as to what is recyclable, reward systems for contractor's achievement of new recycling targets.

Examiner's comments:

Candidates were clearly more comfortable with requirement 16.2 which asked them to explain the change management issues that might need to be considered by the council under each option, referring to change management models where appropriate.

Most candidates showed good knowledge of change management (types of change, barriers to change and Lewin's 'unfreeze/move/refreeze' model) although relatively few mentioned Gemini's 4R approach. Weaker candidates failed to earn the skills marks available for applying this knowledge to the scenario, simply providing a text book list of generic points. Better candidates identified the fact that the nature of the change, the size of the barriers and the stakeholders affected was different for each option, with the greatest resistance likely to come from households in option 1 and employees to be made redundant in option 2. A minority of candidates limited their marks by writing about change management in general, rather than for each option separately, and/or by only discussing 'employees' in each case, which tended to result in some repetition of points.

16.3 (a) Principles of public sector governance

Corporate governance in the context of Deeshire County Council will be concerned with the way in which the Council manages and applies public funds in providing services to the community and its relationship with its various stakeholders. It incorporates the Council's responsibilities and mandate, its decision making processes, and accountability.

The Nolan Committee set out seven Principles of Public Life which apply to public sector governance: selflessness, integrity, objectivity, accountability, openness, honesty, leadership.

- **Selflessness**: Holders of public office should take decisions solely in terms of the public interest. They should not do so to gain financial or other material benefits for themselves, their family or their friends.

- **Integrity**: Holders of public office should not place themselves under any financial or other obligation to outside individuals or organisations that might influence them in the performance of their duties.

- **Objectivity**: In carrying out public business, including making public appointments, awarding contracts or recommending individuals for rewards and benefits, holders of public office should make choices on merit.

- **Accountability**: Holders of public office are accountable for their decisions and actions to the public and must submit themselves to whatever scrutiny is appropriate to their office.

- **Openness**: Holders of public office should be as open as possible about the decisions and actions that they take. They should give reasons for their decisions and restrict information only when the wider public interest clearly demands.

- **Honesty**: Holders of public office have a duty to declare any private interests relating to their public duties and to take steps to resolve any conflicts arising in a way that protects the public interest.

- **Leadership**: Holders of public office should promote and support these principles by leadership and example.

The offer of lifetime golf membership would appear to directly conflict with the principles of **selflessness** and **integrity** and threatens the **objectivity** of the relevant Councillors.

To comply with the **honesty** principle, Councillors would need to declare the offer that has been made and it is likely that the appropriate response would be to withdraw from the decision-making process.

Were the Councillors to be involved in awarding the contract it is possible that the media and the electing public might question the reasons for their decision on the basis of personal interest. The Council needs to be seen to apply the decision criteria fairly and not leave itself open to appeal by unsuccessful contractors.

In making a decision, the remaining members of the Council must review each case against the criteria set down by local government and award the contract on merit ie based on:

- Contract price
- Capability of contractor to provide services
- Financial strength

As members of the Council will be accountable for the decision they need to consider whether they have sufficient experience to select and manage the best contractor. If not they may need to engage external advice or support.

They also need to consider whether the process has attracted sufficient suitable responses. It is possible that the Council may feel none of the applicants is suitable.

The Council may struggle to elicit sufficient information from their own in-house contractors in order to specify the performance terms of the contract as they may fear for jobs.

Aside from the Nolan principles, there are general ethical issues involved here (where ethics are defined as the moral principles governing or influencing conduct).

The Institute of Business Ethics suggests that 3 questions be applied in deciding whether a situation raises ethical issues:

(1) Transparency – do I mind others knowing what I have decided? It is likely that the Councillors involved would not wish the information regarding golf membership to come to light as it suggests a conflict of interest.

(2) Effect – whom does my decision affect or hurt? In this case it might be the unsuccessful contractors, or the local community if it transpires that the best contractor has not been appointed.

(3) Fairness – would my decision be considered fair by those affected? The public and media are likely to question Councillors' motives in awarding the contract.

There are also ethical issues surrounding the behaviour of the waste management contractor's chief executive which would give the Council general cause for concern about the organisation's corporate responsibility. Even if this organisation were to meet the various decision making criteria, it may be inappropriate for the Council to engage this contractor because it is not the type of company that the Council wants to be involved with.

Examiner's comments:

Requirement 16.3 which covered public sector governance, ethics and information systems, was poorly attempted by many. In part (a) candidate were asked to explain the principles of public sector governance that the councillors must apply when choosing between Contractors A and B and to recommend any appropriate action that the councillors should take. Few candidates seemed to be familiar with the Nolan seven principles of public sector governance set out in the learning materials. Despite this, candidates who applied their corporate governance and ethics knowledge to the public sector were able to gain marks. Sensible comments regarding the non-profit making nature of the council, its need to consider wider stakeholders and the requirement for transparency, honesty and accountability in decision making were sufficient to score a pass. Weaker candidates referred to Deeshire as if it were a company rather than a council and some completely failed to discuss the ethical issue involved with the lifetime golf membership being offered by Contractor A. Those that did tended to state that the golf membership offer was essentially a bribe which should be rejected. Better candidates identified that given this threat to objectivity, the councillors concerned should declare it and remove themselves from the decision making process. They also pointed out that the behaviour of Contractor A called into question its suitability to work with the council.

(b) **Information system to monitor performance**

An information system can be used for monitoring and control purposes, to check adherence of the contractor to the service level agreement, but also for decision-making in respect of contract renewal and future waste management strategy.

The Council can collect data in order to measure actual results in relation to the promised standards set out in the contractor's service level agreement and in relation to any specific targets the Council are required to meet eg by the government.

Data might be collected in different ways, eg using electronic chips in bins to measure volume and type of waste being disposed of/recycled, or via contractor reports and customer satisfaction surveys.

Exception reporting may help to highlight areas of concern in terms of cost overruns, resource utilisation, customer dissatisfaction, or failure to meet recycling targets.

- Compliance with legislation/environmental standards
- Quality control procedures
- HR policies and employment issues (diversity, training etc)
- Effectiveness of contractors' own monitoring and reporting systems

Measures of delivery standards would include:

- Number of collections weekly
- Number of collections made on time
- Number of vehicle breakdowns
- Number of complaints received from residents
- Rates of recycling
- Number of litigation cases/damages claims
- Employment record
- Compliance with legislation and other environmental standards

Financial stability will affect ability to resource the contract now and in future. This can be evidenced by recent accounts, bank references and credit ratings, all of which should be monitored closely.

Comparatives

The Council will need benchmarks to assess performance. In addition to specific comparatives eg Council targets and standards agreed in the contractor's SLA, the Council may be able to compare itself to other Councils which have achieved high rates of recycling.

As a minimum the Council will need to monitor performance in the following areas, against the three decision making criteria:

- Contract price (ie costs incurred)
- Capability of contractor to provide services
- Financial strength

Price

The actual costs incurred may not reflect the original price tendered, either because the contractors lack the detailed information to provide a realistic price or as a result of later variations in service requirements.

In establishing whether the outsourcing decision has been a success, any price must be compared to the cost of in-house service provision but calculations of cost savings should factor in any exit costs for the current arrangement eg redundancies.

Measures: Annual spend vs budget, Cost overruns.

Provision of services

The Council will need to consider:

- Standards of service delivery
- Contractors' capacity to continue to resource contract and flexibility to cope with increased volumes in future (information about vehicle fleet, staffing levels, working partnerships, disposal facilities)

Examiner's comments:

Requirement 16.3(b) asked candidates to describe how the council could use an information system to monitor the performance if an outsourced contractor is appointed. Most were less well-prepared for this topic, which came into the syllabus for the new Business Strategy paper and which has not yet been examined in any depth. Many answers were limited to a brief discussion of the use of systems to monitor costs and service levels, with one or two basic performance measures suggested. A small minority made some good points about the use of IS to check adherence to targets specified by the council or the government; assess resident satisfaction, monitor recycling trends; benchmark the contractor and council's performance and make decisions regarding contract renewal. Stronger answers made imaginative suggestions about methods of data collection (eg electronic chips in wheelie bins), identified a range of relevant KPIs that could be used (sometimes involving a balanced scorecard) and discussed the use of exception reporting to identify specific areas of underperformance.

	Knowledge	Skill	Marks
Report format	1	–	
17.1 (a) Market research	2	4	
(b) Segmentation and targeting	2	4	
			10
17.2 Joint development/CDT/Eco/Licensing relative merits	5	9	12
	10	17	22

General comments:

This question involves a small manufacturing company which currently operates in the steam cleaning industry. It is owned by a former research scientist, Nilesh Patel, who has recently been granted worldwide patent for a new energy-efficient washing machine technology which uses nylon beads to reduce the energy and detergent required and significantly lowers water consumption. The company faces a choice of whether to develop the technology for the domestic or commercial laundry markets and also how to structure the business to exploit the new technology. Options under consideration are a company offering venture capital style funding and support, a strategic alliance with an environmentally friendly dry cleaning company that has a chain of businesses across the US or a licensing agreement(s) with manufacturers of domestic and industrial washing machines.

There were some very good attempts at this question and a number of candidates chose to attempt this question first on the paper. A disappointing minority did not produce their answer in the report format requested.

17.1 (a) Market research

Report

To: Nilesh Patel
From: A.N.Other
Date: March 20Y0
Re: Exploiting proposed new washing machine technology

This report sets out the issues to be considered when selecting a market for the new technology and the relative merits of the joint development strategies under consideration.

(a) **Selecting the best market**

Market research can help in identifying the potential size of specific markets and provide information about customer characteristics, needs and wants, attitude to price and quality, and competitors' products. Market research may also help in defining appropriate elements of the marketing mix (product, price, place, promotion).

Desk research would involve gathering and analysing existing (secondary) data to ascertain which customers might be interested in the new washing machine technology. This is usually cheaper as the data is already published eg by governments, trade journals and commercial companies but as the technology is new it may not provide all the information required.

External databases may help identify customers in prospective markets eg the major manufacturers of industrial and domestic washing machines, and any competitors with similar products or similar technologies. It might also provide factual information about the economy, legal and political considerations, environmental protection standards etc.

Desk research may be a useful initial step in identifying certain markets as unattractive or lacking in profit potential. It may also assist in setting prices eg by ascertaining how much people could save on overheads by using the new technology.

More detailed information can be obtained by **field research** which involves the collection of new data from respondents. This might be in the form of surveys, interviews, focus groups and discussion with company heads.

Field research can be used here to determine which markets are likely to have the highest demand and also what price different users are prepared to pay for the new technology:

- Who is the target market and who is the decision maker in the purchasing process?

- What product features must the product incorporate?

- What benefits will the product provide?

- How will consumers react to the product?

- How will the product be produced most cost effectively?

- Will the product be profitable when manufactured and delivered to the customer at the target price?

In selecting the best market relevant factors will include:

- Where the most profits can be made
- The sustainability of these profits into the future
- How barriers to entry can be preserved or raised to discourage competition

Market research may also help NP in identifying other applications of the technology beyond those already decided.

Having undertaken the necessary research, NP must:

- Estimate likely selling price based upon competition and customer feedback
- Estimate sales volume based upon size of market
- Estimate costs to produce, profitability and breakeven point

(b) **Segmentation and targeting**

Market segmentation is the practice of identifying homogeneous sub-groups within a market, which can then be marketed to in different ways. Here NP can segment the market for the new washing machine technology based on the type of customer, their needs and also possibly their geographic location.

It would be normal practice to divide consumer and industrial markets – the two distinct markets available to Nilesh – particularly since these will have very different buying characteristics and product requirements.

	Consumer (Domestic)	Industrial
Buying frequency	Rare (low volume, high value)	Often
Reliability	Recommended	Essential
Size of machine	Small	Large
Load	Light	Heavy
Economy	Relatively important	Very important

Within the market for consumer durables (low volume, high value purchases) NP's new technology is likely to be attractive to innovators who typically are the first to try various new products (relatively young, intelligent, socially and geographically mobile and of a high socio-economic group).

A key characteristic for NP to focus on is the growing eco-awareness of consumers. NP would be best identifying those markets which are most environmentally aware – this may be a particular group of consumers or a particular geographic location.

Issues to consider in deciding on whether to target consumer or industrial markets:

Targeting involves selecting the best market segments. This will depend on:

- The sales potential (market size and growth forecasts)

- The ability to manufacture and distribute the product according to customer requirements

- The likelihood of the segment providing a stable income stream

- The profits available given the capital investment required

- How defendable the market is from competition eg the barriers to entry in the form of the patent may prevent competitors developing similar products initially

NP may decide to concentrate on a single market segment eg domestic washing machines, or adopt a multi-segment strategy, offering smaller machines for the domestic market and much larger machines for industrial purposes. Given the size of the existing company and the limited resources available to NP, it is likely that if it grows organically, a single market segment would be advisable (see part b below).

NP could adopt a price skimming strategy, targeting those who are keen to be early adopters of the new technology, then lowering the price later to develop the market further.

Test marketing might involve a trial run of all elements of the marketing mix in a sample market segment that is small, self-contained, representative and with adequate promotional facilities.

Examiner's comments:

Requirement 17.1 asked candidates to advise Nilesh on the issues to address when selecting the best market for the technology, considering (a) market research and (b) segmentation and targeting. As usual, candidates were well-rehearsed in the marketing knowledge required and in most cases applied this to the scenario. As well as giving examples of both types of research, better candidates pointed out that desk research might be less relevant for a situation involving new technology but also that the cost of field research might be an issue for Nilesh. Most answers identified the need to segment the market between domestic and industrial buyers and good answers went on to explain the differences that were likely to arise between the two markets. Only the strongest candidates pointed out that given the size of the company, it may not have the resources available to target all segments successfully, hence the need to consider some form of joint development strategy.

17.2 Joint development strategies

NP is facing two issues:

(1) Can NP successfully commercialise the new technology?

The patent and the initial testing suggest that the new technology has a number of possible successful applications.

(2) Would it be better doing so independently or in co-operation with a larger partner?

Desirability of a joint development strategy

The need for a joint development strategy stems from the inability of NP to exploit the full potential of the new technology using existing resources or those that could easily be acquired, and NP's lack of experience in the laundry market. Development in association with a third party would provide access to their core competences – here NP requires the other party to be able to engage in large scale production and to have access to a wide distribution market.

Another important issue is that the new product is subject to a high degree of risk and the impact on the existing business needs to be considered.

The key advantages of combining with a third party are as follows:

- Growth can be achieved more quickly and efficiently as expertise can be shared eg third party may have experience of overseas operations.

- A partner may provide access to countries or companies that it would otherwise be impossible for NP to access (eg America).

- Will increase access to resources and/or capital for growth, both of which are likely to be limited but critical at the start-up stage.

- Third party may bring purchasing power and economies of scale which are unlikely to be available to NP due to its limited size.

- Risks are shared and it reduced the risk of failure due to Nilesh Patel's inexperience and possible inability to control growth.

- May provide access to existing supply and distribution chains, on an international scale.

- May allow NP more time to ensure that the existing business does not suffer because with organic growth all the focus may have to be on the new technology.

Third party may add value to the brand if it is an established brand name

However:

- NP will suffer a loss of control

- If the venture is successful NP will make less profits since these have to be shared

- May lose rights to intellectual property which in this case is of fundamental importance

- Change may happen too fast (inefficiencies, inability to control, lack of appropriate systems). Organic growth may be easier to control

- Association with the wrong third party may devalue the brand

Relative merits of the joint development strategies under consideration

Option 1: Offer from CDT

Benefits:

- Established business with experience of converting ideas into commercially viable businesses
- Provide financial investment for promotion and marketing
- Greater network of contacts and bargaining power
- Help in choosing outsourcing partners for production and distribution
- Prestige and rewards from flotation which offers NP an exit route

Drawbacks:

- Loss of controlling equity stake and introduces another key stakeholder as a 50% shareholder. Also CDT will help 'identify appropriate commercial partners' which may further dilute control.

- CDT likely to be major player and therefore dictate to NP; it may interfere in the day-to-day running of the existing business.

- Differing objectives and priorities may be a source of potential conflict. CDT may be looking for a fast return on their investment, rather than being interested in NP in the long term.

- Differences in culture.

- May be problems after exit when NP is on his own.

NP needs to ascertain the exact nature and form of the financial and commercial support and clarify certain issues eg how the patent rights will be affected, the impact on the existing business, and whether CDT will expect to be involved/share returns from this business too.

Option 2: Strategic alliance with EcoLaundry

Nature and terms of the alliance need to be negotiated and this will depend on the relative strengths of the two parties – EcoLaundry is likely to be the stronger party in this respect with more commercial experience so NP, as the smaller partner needing access to economies of scale and a wide distribution network, may be disadvantaged.

Benefits include:

- Faster growth than would be possible organically.

- Access to capital provided by Eco and to marketing expertise.

- Synergy from the fact that the Eco brand name is well-known and linked to environmentally friendly laundry.

- Will give access to wider geographical markets internationally. Eco has a chain of businesses across the US with an established customer base of both companies and consumers.

Disadvantages:

- Unclear who will be responsible for manufacture
- Gives away a share of the benefits of the innovative technology
- Likely to lead to some loss of control since Eco wish to sell the technology to other companies
- Disputes may arise over the rights and obligations of the parties involved
- Access to know-how is given away
- Exchange risk affecting the remittance of NP's share of profits from the US

Option 3: Licensing

NP can license to one or two large companies or many smaller companies. The form of licence would need to take into account the geographic spread or could be on a product basis eg the right to manufacture domestic machines rather than industrial ones.

There needs to be some incentive for the companies involved to purchase the licence.

The technology is patented so competitors will therefore be restricted in their ability to copy, but prospective licensees may need some more evidence of commercial viability beyond initial testing of technical functionality.

Advantages of licensing

- Will offer faster expansion than using own resources
- Affords opportunity for much greater worldwide coverage
- Reduce risks for NP
- May enhance recognition of NP brand name and stimulate sales of dry-steam cleaners
- Depending on strength and life of patent, it may guarantee revenues for a significant time

However:

- Growth is likely to be slower than the other options as NP will need to convince others about the potential of the new technology

- Involves sharing profits and know-how with larger companies which may exploit this when licence period ends

- Multi-nationals with economies of scale and distribution networks are likely to have much greater bargaining power than NP so may drive down terms

Conclusion

If NP wants to retain control of the business and his intellectual property, then he could segment the market and exploit his patents on a worldwide basis by implementing Option 3. The options are not necessarily mutually exclusive so one possibility might be to undertake the strategic alliance in respect of the American industrial laundry market and then use licensing as a strategy for the domestic market and for countries other than USA.

Examiner's comments:

Requirement 17.2 asked candidates to discuss the desirability of pursuing a joint development strategy and the relative merits of the three options being considered. This was a relatively straightforward requirement and most candidates demonstrated good understanding of the differences between the options. Once again the distinction between a strong and weak answer tended to depend on the candidates' ability to apply this knowledge to the scenario, thereby prioritising the points of relevance to Nilesh which centred around control, retention of intellectual property, risk and resources. Weaker candidates tended to ignore the requirement to consider the desirability of a joint development strategy and simply assess the three options, sometimes only listing the advantages of each option, without considering any downside. The strongest scripts identified that as a small company, NP was likely to need help to exploit the full potential of the technology and having considered the relative merits of the options, made a recommendation as to the best course of action.

18   Executive Travel Ltd (June 2010)

	Knowledge	Skill	Marks
18.1 Evaluation of performance of ET	–	18	16
18.2 (a) Likely effects of pricing policy	3	4	
(b) Likely impact of incentives	1	5	
			11
18.3 (a) Benefits and risks	1	4	
(b) How the risk can be managed	1	4	
			8
18.4 Ethical issues and action that should be taken	3	5	7
	9	40	42

General comments:

The company in this scenario (ET) owns a chain of 21 upmarket travel agent outlets. The company has been significantly affected by economic downturn and, as a response, it has introduced more flexible pricing methods, with greater discretion given to branch managers to offer discounts. Also, performance incentives have been given to branch managers based on sales volumes achieved. Data was provided on the performance of both the company and the industry. The company has recently had a crisis board meeting to review the price discounting policy and consider a contract with a hotel company for a guaranteed minimum number of booking next year. Ethical issues have arisen at the company's Outlet21, which is based in an investment bank. These issues arise from a letter sent to the chartered accountant FD from an ex-employee, concerning gifts received by ET staff in return for upgraded bookings, and the charging of business expenses against a charitable trust which is supported by the bank.

18.1

	20X7	20X8	20X9
Industry (per question)			
Value of trips	36,500,000	35,800,000	35,300,000
Commissions	4,380,000	3,938,000	3,530,000
Trips	68,600	65,200	64,100
Company (per question)			
Value of trips	90,000	84,000	78,000
Commissions	9,000	7,560	6,240
Trips	30	27	24
Sundry Commissions	8,000	9,000	10,000
	20X7	20X8	20X9

Analysis

Industry

Value per trip (£)	£532	£549	£551
% Commission/value	12%	11%	10%
Commission per trip	£63.85	£60.40	£55.07
Growth in value of trips		(1.9)%	(1.4)%
Growth in commissions		(10)%	(10.4)%
Growth in number of trips		(5.0)%	(1.7)%
Company			
Market share (value)%	0.25%	0.23%	0.22%
Market share (comm)%	0.21%	0.19%	0.18%
Commission per trip (£)	£300	£280	£260
Value per trip (£)	£3,000	£3,111	£3,250
% comm/value	10%	9%	8%
Growth in value of trips		(6.6)%	(7.1)%
Growth in commissions		(16.0)%	(17.5)%
Growth in number of trips		(10)%	(11.1)%

ET Performance

ET is trading in difficult market conditions, hence the decline in performance must be judged against this background. In common with many industries, companies operating in upmarket sectors are suffering more than those in mid-market and downmarket sectors as people 'trade down' in the recession.

The market demand for the services of travel agents is a derived demand from the market demand for holidays/tours. Performance can therefore be explained, in part, by the changes in market demand for holidays/tours.

The industry data provided indicates that there was a modest decline of 1% to 2% in the value of trips in both 20X8 and 20X9. Unusually for industry data there is also a measure of volume in the travel industry in terms of the number of trips. This shows a more severe decline of 5% in 20X8, although the 20X9 fall of 1.7% is broadly in line with the fall in value. The discrepancy between the fall in value and volume in 20X8 is explained by the increase in the value per trip from £532 to £549 (3.2%).

By contrast, the data for ET indicates that there was a more substantial decline of 6.6% in 20X8 and 7.1% in the value of trips in 20X8 and 20X9 respectively. This may indicate that ET has performed poorly in attracting new customers compared to the industry average or it may indicate that the upmarket sector is performing poorly as a whole by comparison to the industry. A more valid comparison might be how well ET is performing relative to upmarket competitors (ie in the same sector of the travel market).

For any given level of demand for holidays, travel agents face competition, not only from each other, but also from direct on-line bookings between the consumer and the tour operator. In a recession, when market conditions are difficult, the level of competition is likely to be more severe and this may take the form of price competition, putting pressure on travel agents' commission levels.

In terms of the industry, % commissions have fallen from 12% to 11% then to 10% over the period 20X7-20X9. This means there have been reductions of around 10% in each year in commission, which amplifies the fall in volumes of trade already considered.

The percentage commissions (ie commissions to trip value) of ET were lower than the industry average at the start of the period and they have maintained this gap, falling broadly in line, from 10% down to 8% over the same period. The lower level of the commissions to value % is likely to be due to the fact that the value per trip for ET is far greater than the industry average. Thus, for instance, the average value per trip in 20X7 was £3,000 for ET compared to the industry average of £532 (ie 5.6 times greater). The commission per trip booked is therefore far larger for ET than the industry average, despite the lower commission to value %.

Nevertheless, the significant fall in volumes, combined with the reduction in % commission rates, has caused a very severe reduction in the overall absolute value of commission income for ET. Overall commissions from holiday sales have fallen from £9 million in 20X7 to £6.24 million in 20X9 – a 30.7% reduction in primary income in two years.

Two areas where there is a better performance are 'Outlet21' and sundry commissions.

Outlet21 has a flat level of performance of £3 million each year. This means it has not suffered from the recession. More detail is need on commission rates and volumes, but if these have changed the changes have compensated each other. Whilst performance in these conditions can therefore be regarded as good, and has a stabilising effect on overall revenue, there is a risk that such a high proportion of income now comes from one source (at £3 million it is almost half of the core commissions on holidays of £6.24 million generated by the other 20 outlets).

Sundry commissions have performed very well with a 10% increase in 20X8 to £1.1 million and maintaining revenues at this higher level in 20X9. The performance has been all the more creditable as it has been achieved against a reducing volume of trips on the core business. Thus, for instance, in 20X8 the number of trips fell by 10% and sundry commissions rose by 10%, so the sundry commissions per trip increased by 22%.

Overall the table below shows that revenue has fallen by 10.3% in 20X8 and 11.3% in 20X9. The sundry commissions and Outlet21 have moderated the reduction in core commissions but dependency on these areas in future is uncertain as they depend on the core business to generated customers for sundry commissions and to enhance reputation.

	20X7 £'000	20X8 £'000	20X9 £'000
Commissions	9,000	7,560	6,240
Outlet21	3,000	3,000	3,000
Sundry	1,000	1,100	1,100
Total	13,000	11,660	10,340
% change		–10.3%	–11.30%

Thus the poor performance in terms of revenues may be due to market conditions, in whole or in part, but in assessing the performance of the business, as opposed to the performance of the managers of the business, there has been a very severe reduction in trade and a poor performance.

Additional key information

- Details of performance of rival companies in the same sector as a benchmark

- Breakdown of performance for each branch

- Detailed analysis of costs. Given that all the 20 outlets have high fixed costs and are maintained in operation, then the impact of a downturn on profit is likely to be much more severe than that on revenue as operating gearing is high

- Breakdown between sectors (eg business and leisure)

- Industry projections

Examiner's comments:

The performance on the data analysis section showed general improvement from previous sittings and this was reflected in a majority of candidates' answers to this question. Nevertheless, there continues to be some variability in the quality of answers. The better candidates were able to calculate meaningful ratios which focussed on both the company and industry changes with appropriate evaluation of performance in explaining the data and identifying causal relationships, both for ET and for the industry. Better candidates also tended to set out a structured table of calculations at the beginning of their answer, then provided a narrative commentary which evaluated this data.

Weaker candidates tended to provide random calculations intermingled within a general narrative. Weaker answers also tended to focus merely on the company with little or no coverage of the industry, despite this specifically being required in the question. More generally, weaker answers tended to describe what has happened to various ratios (eg increased or decreased) rather than attempting to address how it has happened (eg analysing the data in more detail) or why it has happened (eg identifying underlying factors discussed in the scenario which may have caused the changes in the ratios/data). Weaker answers were also very repetitive and more often than not attributed all aspects of the declining performance to the worldwide economic recession. Some weaker answers also omitted any mention of Outlet21.

The additional key information from the weaker students was the usual list of cash flows, balance sheets and management accounts. However, the highest scoring answers produced excellent lists of additional information, including other companies specialising in luxury holidays, costs, performance on a branch by branch basis and sector information.

18.2 (a) Discounting pricing policy

ET is an upmarket provider and therefore prices of travel are high. While, in most industries, upmarket sectors tend to be less price sensitive and more quality sensitive than downmarket sectors there is significant competition in travel. For simple products such as a first class flight or a specific hotel the product is homogeneous between providers and price comparisons can easily be made. These conditions may therefore force discounting in order to match competitors.

More generally, however, where there is a bespoke package of travel arrangements the price is less comparable and the level of service may be more important.

A key point also is that the travel agent is only able to discount its commission, which has only a marginal impact on the overall cost of the holiday cost. Thus, if commission is £100 and this is 10% of the holiday value then a 50% reduction in this commission to £50 is only a 5% reduction in the overall cost of the trip to the customer.

It should also be noted that price is a signal of quality. If, as the FD suggests, discounting indicates a perceived cheapening off the service provided then this may have a long-term reputational effect.

Overall, the elasticity of demand is key, in that if discounting increases the volume of sales significantly then it may be advantageous.

The policy of discretionary discounting does seem more appropriate than a general overall discount. This is because it enables price discrimination on a customer by customer basis as the manager can make an assessment of the price resistance of each individual. If however the discounting becomes more or less automatic by the manager, or expected by the customer, then the policy moves de facto from discretionary to general discounting.

In terms of the evidence available, it should be noted that, despite discounting, the number of trips has continued to fall. Clearly, without discounting it the number of trips may have fallen more sharply but the success of the policy may nevertheless be questioned.

(b) Managerial incentive policy

The policy of rewarding managers on the basis of volumes sold and, at the same time, giving them the discretion to discount may cause a conflict of the managers' personal interests with ETs underlying objectives. The incentive for managers could be to discount to maximise sales volumes rather than to maximise commissions from revenues or profits.

Some sales that could be made at full price may be needlessly discounted by managers who are over-anxious to make the sale even if it reduces ET's revenue unnecessarily.

The policy also ignores costs. Although variable costs tend to be low, the manager may incur search costs for holidays (staff time, international telephone calls etc) which are out of line with the value of the commissions generated.

Managers would also have the incentive to promote small trips rather than the high value large trips if they are rewarded on a volume count as these incur less staff time and generate the same bonus. This may lead to key, high value customers not receiving the level of service that they require and the high commissions that they pay would warrant.

Examining the evidence however the value per trip has risen from £3,000 in 20X7 to £3,250 in 20X9, so there is no evidence to support the notion that incentives have caused lower value trips to be sold. Further scrutiny is needed but one possible explanation is that very high value holidays are more resistant to the recession.

Examiner's comments:

Most answers in (a) focussed on the impact on the image of ET and recognised that customer perception could be adversely affected. Better candidates discussed the price elasticity of demand and were able to link their answers to the data. This was very encouraging and demonstrated good knowledge and application of skills. Price discrimination between individuals, given the management discretion, was surprisingly not discussed by many candidates. A minority pointed out that despite the drop in commission per trip for ET, demand had decreased rather than increased.

In (b) answers to this section were generally good and recognised the motivational issues involved and that there could be a potential conflict of interest for managers. Given that managers are rewarded on volume rather than value, answers focussed on managers' tactics to sell lower cost holidays which were heavily discounted. Some answers went one step further and suggested alternative policies for management incentives such as value of booking and performance of their particular branch. Few answers referred back to the data to evaluate whether there was any evidence to support a falling value of per trip arising from these incentives.

18.3 (a) **Benefits**

- The proposed arrangement with Snooty Hotels offers accommodation that is appropriate to the customer base (as it has been used previously) but this year is offered at a significant discount

- There is a cross branding facility whereby the luxury brand of Snooty Hotels is linked with that of ET as an upmarket provider of leisure services

Risks

- The key risk is that the price reduction will not be sufficient to increase demand from last year's level of 1,000 room nights to 1,600 room nights. As a consequence, ET will need to pay for the shortfall.

- At 1,600 room days at £200 the total cost is £320,000. At last year's rate it would be 1,000 room days at £300 per day which is £300,000. This may imply a maximum probable exposure of £20,000. However, with declining sales volumes, it would be wrong to assume that last year's sales volumes could be sustained. The risk exposure could therefore be far greater than £20,000.

(b) **Managing the risks**

SHC operates in a number of cities and resorts. If ET has in the past recommended alternative accommodation in these locations then it may be advisable to push customers towards SHC instead. This would ensure that the minimum target was achieved, and thus no penalties would arise.

More generally, given the potential exposure to low demand, ET could attempt to persuade customers to take trips to these locations instead of other locations.

If closer to the departure date there were excess rooms with SHC then they could be sold off down to cost price of £200. Indeed, ultimately even a price below £200 at the last few days would yield some contribution rather than ET pay the full guaranteed price.

Examiner's comments:

In part (a), the benefits and risks section, coverage was good on the whole. The main points discussed centred on the compatibility of SHC and ET with the luxury holiday label being retained. The main risks noted were that ET may fail to let out all 1,600 rooms and that SNC's reputation was not well known to ET, in turn potentially having an impact on the overall business. Better candidates used numerical data to illustrate the relatively small increase in annual commission and the extent of the risks.

In part (b), on managing risks, performance was generally poor with many candidates struggling to come up with reasonable approaches to mitigate risk. Answers were typically too general and often asserted that ET could transfer or reduce the risk but did not elaborate further on how this might be achieved. Some of the methods suggested for risk mitigation, for example taking out insurance, were unreasonable and showed a lack of commercial reality. A number of candidates produced generic descriptions of different approaches to risk management, and thereby scored some knowledge marks, but low marks in terms of skills.

18.4 The issue of ET staff receiving rewards from the bank's staff represents a potential conflict of interest between promoting ET's goals, promoting the bank's goals and promoting the staff's own personal goals. The disbursement of the bank's resources in order to gain personal benefits may also be fraudulent. However given that discretion and judgement are involved this may be difficult to demonstrate. A policy of transparency of gifts received or a prohibition of any significant gifts may prevent such behaviour, or at least make it more apparent.

The issue of senior bank staff travelling at the charity's expense would depend on the agreement with the charity, the charities internal rules and disclosure of administration costs compared to donations would be appropriate. If such expenditure was contrary to the charity's basic trust terms then this may be not only an ethical breach but a fraudulent act which would make any excess cost repayable.

If the charity is being charged with travel costs which should properly be due to the commercial activities of the bank then this may be fraudulent and may amount to money laundering.

As Carol is a chartered accountant then she is bound by the ICAEW ethical code for accountants in business. This could require the disclosure of fraudulent activity, notwithstanding the general duty of confidentiality. There may also be a duty not to act for the bank although as Carol does not work for a firm of chartered accountants this would not be a duty on the other directors. Carol may therefore need to resign her position where there is fraud and the fellow directors continue to act for the bank.

Examiner's comments:

This requirement was not well answered. Many candidates addressed the issues in terms of a lack of controls by the company to limit these actions, rather than the ethical implications that were asked for in the question. Similarly, some candidates pointed out the commercial consequences of the actions, rather than their ethical implications. A number of candidates failed to acknowledge the fact that Carol was a Chartered Accountant and was therefore bound by the ICAEW code of ethics. More generally, candidates failed to apply their knowledge of ethics to the situation provided. Most candidates did address the two ethical issues individually, drawing separate conclusions, although did not always go on to suggest actions, even though this was a specific part of the requirement.

19 Hutton Haulage plc (June 2010)

		Knowledge	Skill	Marks
19.1	SWOT analysis	2	8	10
19.2 (a)	How outsourcing can improve supply chain efficiency	3	5	
(b)	Actions to enhance environmental sustainability	2	4	
				12
19.3	Factors to be considered – acquisition	3	7	9
		10	24	31

General comments:

The scenario in this question relates to a listed road haulage company specialising in the transport of chilled and frozen food and drinks. The company operates mainly in the UK, but increasingly in Europe. It is considering two developments of the business. The first development is to accept an outsourcing contract from a supermarket, Freshco, to supply all its transport needs. The second potential development is the acquisition of a European rail transport facilities company, RailTrans in order to provide multi-modal transport to customers.

This was the best attempted question on the paper and overall the performance of most candidates was good.

19.1 SWOT analysis

Strengths

- High efficiency leading to low cost service provision due to volumes, IT system, shared loads, and drivers sleeping in cabins
- A large customer in Goonhill giving volume and reputation
- Wide general customer base
- Strong core assets in modern trucks
- Specialisation in chilled food (market leader)
- Operating in an essential industry

Weaknesses

- Solely in road transport and therefore undiversified
- Comparative disadvantage compared to EU haulage companies on diesel costs
- Road congestion compared to rail and water transport
- Low profit margins in the industry

Opportunities

- Acquisitions to increase size and maintain economies of scale and economies of scope
- Diversification opportunity into rail with RailTrans
- Freshco agreement is near finalisation

Threats

- Potential loss of Goonhill as a large customer with the existing five year contract finishing next year
- Failure to enter into agreement with Freshco by not satisfying new conditions

- Volatility in diesel fuel costs reflecting oil price volatility and fuel tax changes

- Further economic downturn would be reflected in a decline in industry volumes and increased competition

- Increased EU regulations opening up UK market to European competition

- Increased general pressure on carbon emissions and specific pressure from Freshco

- Competition from water, rail and air transport may increase if road transport becomes slower (eg congestion) or more expensive (road pricing or taxes)

- Low barriers to entry may increase competition when recession ends

- Even if Freshco agreement is signed it may withdraw or reduce volumes as it is a 'pay as you' go basis

- Exchange rate volatility with euro changing competitive position with EU haulage companies

Summary – key points

The key points would seem to be:

- The high utilisation and operating efficiency giving a competitive advantage in terms of low cost and quality service

- Potential loss of Goonhill on contract renewal

- Diversification opportunity into rail with RailTrans

Examiner's comments:

The SWOT analysis was well done in general. Candidates did struggle to state weaknesses other than the fact that there was only one large major contract. Some candidates thought that weaknesses were the same as threats and vice versa, when weaknesses identified should be internal to the company and threats should be external factors. Most, but not all, addressed the requirement to provide a summary, although in the case of the weakest candidates this tended to be a generic comment about building on strengths to counter threats.

19.2

From:	A. Candidate
To:	HH Board
Date:	14 June 20Y0
Subject:	Outsourcing and sustainability

(a) **Outsourcing and efficiency improvements for Freshco**

HH needs to provide a more efficient transport service for Freshco, than the company is currently providing internally. It also needs to charge a price which is lower than the costs currently being incurred by Freshco, but still makes a profit for HH.

HH is a long established road haulage company with a core competence in the industry. Freshco is a supermarket and does not necessarily have the core competences in road distribution. These core competences do not just arise in the road transport industry generally, but in the specific function that is the subject of current negotiations between HH and Freshco – the transport of chilled and frozen food in the supermarket industry. This has arisen most obviously with the Goonhill contract over a four year period but also this is an area 'where HH is a market leader'.

In addition to greater experience in the industry compared to Freshco, HH also has advantages of scale and scope. HH serves a range of customers and therefore deals with large volumes giving economies of scale with fuller loads, fewer empty loads, more networked journeys, fewer simple return journeys, and a larger fleet of trucks giving flexibility of size, availability and specification.

Economies of scope are achieved through servicing several customers simultaneously in a given area (eg shared load).

Other issues include:

- The high specification modern fleet will give a more reliable delivery (eg fewer breakdowns, less service time and repair time off the road)

- The IT system can enable monitoring of trucks, but may also facilitate data transfer from Freshco to HH on a real time basis

- More frequent deliveries may be possible as the fleet is more heavily utilised and can operate viably by dual loading which is often not possible with a single customer internal provider

- Multimodal travel from Europe may soon be possible with the acquisition of RailTrans. This gives a faster, more rapid and more reliable supply chain over distance

- The 'pay as you go' system enables Freshco to use HH's services without a long term binding commitment. Service improvement therefore needs to be demonstrated quickly to retain the contract even in the short term

Overall the efficiencies and cost savings can enable a better service to be delivered at lower cost but clearly much will depend on how Freshco determines its costs internally (eg Full cost with allocation of overheads? Are the old trucks fully depreciated?). A focus on service improvement rather than cost reduction may therefore be appropriate.

(b) **Environmental sustainability**

Environmental sustainability relates to environmental policies that meet the needs of the present without compromising the ability of future generations to meet their own needs. In so doing it considers the inter-relationship between the environment, society and business.

The proposed acquisition of RailTrans is a transparent and clear signal of carbon reductions. Rail transport has much lower carbon emissions than trucks and the acquisition would signal a major commitment towards rail and away from road only transport.

Moreover, if the volumes increase with the Freshco contract, then the train becomes an even lower producer of carbon emissions, for instance on the Spain route where containers may be shared with Goonhill.

Other possible environmental sustainability contributions from carbon savings:

- Increase the proportion of modern fuel efficient vehicles by a replacement programme for old vehicles

- Use of larger vehicles with full loads as volumes increase

- Use of cleaner, high grade diesel fuel even where this is more expensive

- Improve utilisation to decrease the number of 'empty load' journeys which waste fuel without benefit (more IT, more common loads, greater flexibility in drivers' contracts)

- Better refrigeration to reduce emissions from this source

- Compliance with EU regulations in advance of implementation

Examiner's comments:

In (a) most candidates performed well. There were good discussions centred around the fact that there were differences in HH's and Freshco's core competences, the provision of up to date vehicles and alternative transport routes and the opportunity to diversify into other areas. Candidates identified the main issues and made reference to cost savings because of the ability of drivers to sleep in their vehicles, new routes and modes of transport which would open, plus access to more sophisticated IT systems which would in turn, lead to efficiencies.

Application skills on this requirement were generally good, and high skills marks were accordingly awarded.

In (b) environmental sustainability was not answered as well as expected. This was surprising as it is very topical. Many candidates tended to cite 'trucks fitted with green technology' but did not elaborate further nor give any other points. Many also failed to answer this in the context of the Freshco contract. This was quite disappointing.

Only a minority attempted to provide some generic definition of environmental sustainability, and those who did tended to provide only weak definitions. Only a significant minority mentioned the contribution of RailTrans.

19.3 Potential acquisition of RailTrans

Benefits

The acquisition of RailTrans is a major diversification away from road transport and therefore reduces dependence, to an extent, on the road transport industry. Thus, fuel cost increases, more adverse regulation, road congestion, road pricing may all put pressure on the viability of the road haulage industry. In this case, access to rail transport may give some alternative if only at the margin.

The access to rail transport gives HH the chance to offer multimodal transport which may combine the benefits of multiple methods in a single journey eg long distances or large loads by train (eg from Spain to the UK), then shorter distances to multiple destinations (onward transport within the UK).

Observable and clear carbon reductions to meet Freshco's requirements and more generally.

Compete more effectively with EU road haulage.

Reduced variable costs.

Potential to use rail for two major customers, Goonhill and Freshco, if these contracts are retained and entered into respectively. Common usage on the Spain route will give scale benefits.

Expansion into Europe to give greater European presence. May be benefits for integrated rail and road transport for acquiring new customers in Europe.

Problems

High initial cost which:

- Increases operating gearing with high fixed costs

- Damages liquidity if it is a cash acquisition which may be a particular issue in a recession

- Increases sun costs if venture fails (eg lose Goonhill contract and/or Freshco contract not entered into)

HH has no core competence in rail transport.

Integration costs may be high with two separate sectors.

Synergies may be low given different sector unless a degree of co-ordination and integration can be achieved through multi-modal transport. What HH can add to RailTrans's existing business may need to be significant to make the acquisition viable.

Rail transport may be leased rather than acquiring an entire company to enter this sector of the market.

Overall much will depend on the acquisition price as to whether this would be viable.

Examiner's comments:

This section was generally well answered with candidates noting the obvious benefits and risks, with some application to the scenario. The better candidates presented their answers in terms of acceptability, feasibility and suitability or (less frequently) Porter's attractiveness framework. This enabled them to produce more structured answers. Weaker candidates produced largely generic lists, with minimal application, and which could been applied to almost any acquisition.

	Knowledge	Skill	Marks
20.1 Advantages/Disadvantages of Options 1 and 2	6	10	15
20.2 (a) Prepare balanced scorecard	3	6	
(b) Discuss whether balanced scorecard is the best method of monitoring performance	2	3	
			12
	11	19	27

General comments:

This scenario relates to a chain of hairdressing salons, CE, which has recently been acquired by an international company, Cupitt, which also operates in the hairdressing industry. CE had been poorly managed in the few years prior to the acquisition. Cupitt has maintained CE as a separate division after acquisition and appointed one of its managers, Jane, to turn the division around. One of the key issues for CE is divisional structure and control. Jane has identified three options: (1) centralise control with Jane taking all the key decisions, (2) franchise the salons and (3) give salon managers significant autonomy over operational decision making and monitor performance through the use of a balanced scorecard.

Overall the performance on this question was very variable, with too many poor answers.

20.1 Option 1 – Direct control by Jane

This would mean a wide span of control for Jane with significant centralisation.

The current organisational structure of CE was entrepreneurial with key decisions being taken by the main shareholder. Jane has replaced that role as CE is now a division within Cupitt.

This proposal is very centralised, with Jane taking most of the key decisions, not just at divisional level but for the key operations at the level on the individual salon (pricing, staffing, inventories of products).

The managers therefore have little strategic or even operational autonomy in the day to day affairs of the salon. All these will be imposed by Jane with little responsibility for managers.

The **advantages** of central control for CE include the following:

- If managers are of poor quality (as suggested by Jane's initial review) then they may not be capable of making good decisions if they had autonomy. While good local managers may add benefits with knowledge of local conditions, poor local managers may be worse than good a central manager.

- The close geographical proximity of the salons in Northern England enables close personal control by Jane (eg frequent personal visits).

- There is effective communication and monitoring of the salons using the new IT system so Jane can readily monitor performance at each salon.

- Co-ordinated decisions can take place so a coherent brand image is presented.

- The decentralisation of key strategic decisions would be important where rapid responses are required in a changing and dynamic environment. However, hairdressing is a reasonably stable environment which is suitable to slower, more considered centralised decision making.

- CE is a small division where the span of control is wide, but reasonable, so Jane is not overburdened in making centralised decisions and can have reasonable knowledge of each salon.

- The more diverse the organisation, the greater the need for lower down decision making and specific expertise. In the case of CE however there is a large degree of homogeneity between salons so centralised control of decisions may be more appropriate.

The **disadvantages** of central control for CE include the following:

- Individual managers cannot be held directly accountable for the profitability of individual salons. They may be able to improve the service and motivate more customers to visit the salon but this is limited if there are poor quality staff who are not properly trained or if prices are too high.

- Salon managers may become demotivated with their lack of control an inability to influence performance. This may increase if they are to be held responsible for performance.

- Highly centralised structures tend to stifle innovative strategic solutions and result in less flexibility to react to changing marketplaces or requests of individual customers.

Option 2 – Franchise

Under a franchise a firm grants other firms the right to use its brand, its product or its know-how. There is likely to be central control and support, advertising of the brand. In return, the franchisee will provide a lump sum, share of earnings and specific payments.

In the current context, a franchise could be on a geographical basis (eg one for each city) in order to segregate the markets of the franchisees. Alternatively each salon could be franchised out individually.

The **advantages** of franchising CE include:

- Attract better new managers than CE's current managers

- If CE's current managers took over a franchise they would take on the risk

- Enables new salons to be opened to expand the CE business, so there would be quicker business expansion than using Cupitt's own financial resources alone

- Reduced risk by having franchisees' own capital

- Generates incentives with franchisees' keeping residual rewards and using local knowledge

- Maintains some control over salons

- If franchising is temporary then CE could retake control of the business after salon's have been improved

- Ultimately could abandon the CE brand to the franchisees and expand using the Cupitt brand

The **drawbacks** of franchising CE include:

- The need to share profits with franchisees

- The need to monitor franchisees

- Poor franchisees may harm CE brand name but given problems with previous this risk is small and brand may actually be improved by enthusiastic franchisees

- There needs to be some incentive to purchase a franchise and with the poor performance recently under Peter this may be difficult

- Risks of operational and contractual disputes with franchisees

- Increased monitoring costs which may vary depending on the perceived risk of the franchisee

Examiner's comments:

Candidates identified the main points on both centralised and franchised structures. Good answers included the fact that a centralised structure would be demotivating for managers of salons, there would be overall goal congruence and control but it would limit management being able to have independence, which could in turn stifle ideas and adaptation to the local conditions facing each salon. In addition candidates identified that Jane was not experienced in this sector and was also a very young manager with no knowledge of how the salons were run in practice, and with a very wide span of control.

The points on franchises which were commonly made centred on the loss of control for Jane, problems with branding, maintaining standards across salons, risks to reputation and lack of consistency of products.

20.2 (a) Financial perspective

Goals	KPIs
Profitability	Operating profit per salon
	Profit from each activity (hairdressing, beauty treatments, sun tanning)
	Gross margin %
	Net margin %
Revenue	Revenue growth
	Revenue from each activity
	Annual revenue per customer
Shareholder value	Return of capital employed
	Projected profit growth
Liquidity	Operating cash flows
	Projected cash balances

Customer perspective

Goals	KPIs
Overall Customer satisfaction	Scores on customer surveys (satisfaction)
Customer acquisition	% of sales from new customers
	New customers taking up offers
	Growth in customer numbers
Reliability of service	% of customers commenced on time
	% of customers completed on time
Customer dissatisfaction	Number of written complaints per salon
Market share	Revenue as % of sector revenue
Competitive Price	Comparison to competitors
	Price based complaints
	Response of customers to price changes

Internal perspective

Goals	KPIs
Quality of service	Number of repeat bookings
Quality of assets	Average age of facilities
Utilisation	Appointments made/total available appointments
Quality of staff	Hairdresser training expenditure
	Qualifications achieved

Innovation and learning perspective

Goals	KPIs
New hairstyles and treatments	% of revenue from new styles
	% of profit from new styles
Employee satisfaction	Staff turnover
	Staff complaints
Technology capability	Customer complaints concerning IT booking
	Use of new equipment
Widening of services	% of profit from new services
	% of revenue from new services
	Growth in revenue from new services
	Growth in profit from new services

(b) **Balanced Scorecard**

The BSC approach seeks to develop a range of measures that are linked to strategic objectives and the operations to achieve those objectives. As such, it has the following advantages:

- It emphasizes long term strategic business development rather than just short term financial achievement (eg customer satisfaction this year may determine profits in future years)

- Financial measures alone may ignore strategic goals

- A range of financial and non financial objectives are addressed which balance strategic and operational goals

- Short-term financial measures only offer a single perspective on performance

- Short-term financial measures can be subject to distortion

Overall a BSC approach enables Jane to measure whether key strategic goals are being achieved.

A disadvantage is that BSC may have too many goals which may conflict or lack prioritisation and this may confuse managers.

Alternative measures could include: financial measures only and benchmarking.

If the performance of managers, as opposed to the performance of the salons themselves is to be measured using a balanced scorecard then it is important that managers have control over the factors affecting the KPIs. This appears to be the case under the new suggested organisational structure where managers have significant autonomy.

Examiner's comments:

In section (a), candidates' performance was surprisingly disappointing. Even in terms of the knowledge of the format and structure of the BSC, many candidates where unable to demonstrate these basics and hence lost many of the knowledge marks. There was even confusion as to the nature of basic goals and KPIs. Some answers were little more than a general narrative, while others grouped a series of goals together, then grouped a series of

KPIs, without ever relating individual goals to individual KPIs. The KPIs were often very general and sometimes not relevant to this particular business. However, some answers were excellent and showed skills by applying the BSC very specifically to the scenario and using KPIs such as profit from different treatments within the salons, number of repeat customers, number of additional products (such as shampoos etc) bought by customers, number of complaints, staff retention and ability to attract experienced stylists. This type of answer was however all too infrequently produced by candidates.

In (b) better answers evaluated the BSC both generically and in terms of its applicability to CE. A minority ignored the BSC almost entirely and devoted most of the answer to a discussion of benchmarking as being more appropriate.

21   Supaspeed Ltd (Septemeber 2010)

Marking guide

	Knowledge	Skill	Marks
21.1 Industry evolution	2	7	8
21.2 Value chain/key drivers	4	7	10
21.3 (a) Calculations	–	9	8
(b) Evaluation of new strategy, including other info	–	11	10
21.4 Stakeholders	2	6	7
	8	40	43

General comments:

The company in this scenario (Supa) specialises in the home delivery of parcels for the Business-to-Consumer market. The market is highly competitive, with a wide variety of choice in terms of different companies and different delivery services. The industry has been significantly affected by free trade and globalisation, technological advances and the development of the internet/online shopping. This has led to a wider customer base, changed the nature of delivery services and increased customer expectations. Having found it hard to compete with the major players, Supa decided to exit the non-urgent delivery market and invest heavily in technology in order to offer a time-guaranteed next-day delivery service. It is now carrying out a post investment audit to decide whether the strategy, implemented at 20X8, has been successful. The operations director has suggested Supa could improve results further by closing half of its depots and creating a new centralised sorting facility.

Overall candidates performed well on this question.

21.1 Evolution of parcel home delivery industry

Tutorial note:

Models such as PESTEL or Five Forces may have been used to generate ideas. Use of the industry life cycle model to explain the development of the industry was also acceptable.

Evolution of parcel home delivery industry

Development of global distribution networks

Reduced protectionism and increased global trade have widened cross-border trade and increased the trend for businesses to outsource. Business customers need to send parcels to customers in many different countries. This requires parcel companies to have a global distribution network and has led to consolidation within the industry as the leading companies grow by acquisition. It has also led to increased co-operation as a business model, with smaller companies creating global networks through the use of strategic alliances or partnerships.

The economic development of countries such as China and India also provides new customers from different cultures who may need dealing with in different ways from the traditional domestic customers. Using local partners helps to address this.

Finally the development of partnerships as a business model is facilitated by the ease of communication and technology which allows the sharing of data/information between business partners.

Range of services offered

Historically the industry offered a standard delivery service for mail-order businesses. A wide range of services has now been introduced to address the changing expectations of customers:

- Development of express service due to customers' reduced tolerance of delays (want speed of delivery to match speed of ordering on the internet)

- Significant reduction in time for non-urgent deliveries (2-3 working days compared to the previous 14 days for mail order customers)

- Introduction of specified time/date deliveries – facilitated by technology which allows better logistical planning

- Automated tracking service for customers to address their need for visibility

- Premium priced environmentally friendly (carbon neutral) services

Customer base

A big increase in internet trade has widened the target market for delivery companies and reduced their reliance on mail order customers. Also new market segments have developed due to the use of online marketplaces such as eBay and this may lead to an increasingly significant C2C market.

Delivery methods

Increased focus on the environment has led to a change in packaging materials offered to ensure they are recyclable, and the development of carbon neutral delivery services.

There has been a reduced focus on air transportation methods due to rising costs and security concerns. Higher fuel prices have increased costs and put pressure on margins.

Pricing and competition

The internet has made pricing structures more transparent.

The industry has become increasingly competitive with companies constantly differentiating themselves by offering different service features.

Impact of technology

The internet and IT have already been mentioned as having had a major impact on the industry in a number of areas:

- Increased demand as the use of e-commerce provides a wider geographic market and new customers

- Greater ability of customers to compare prices and services between competitors and increased expectations concerning speed of delivery

- Use of IT to improve logistical planning and efficiency of distribution, and also to increase levels of customer service through delivery reminders and tracking

Examiner's comments:

Requirement 21.1 asked candidates to explain how the parcel home delivery industry has evolved in the face of changing consumer demand and other key external factors. Answers were of a good standard, with most candidates extracting the key information from the scenario. High marks were awarded to those who structured their answers so as to distinguish between consumer and external factors, and who demonstrated clearly the impact of those factors on the industry. A number of candidates applied strategic models such as PESTEL and/or Industry life cycle to help them develop a balanced answer.

21.2 VCA

Value chain

A value chain is the sequence of business activities by which value is added to the products or services produced by a company. Primary activities create value and are directly concerned with providing the product/service. Support activities do not create value in themselves, but enable the primary activities to take place with maximum efficiency.

VCA recognises that it is the way that a company's resources are organised that ensures that its products or services are valued by its customers. Thus it is the relationship or linkages between the company's resources, activities and processes that are important and which create a profit margin – the margin being the excess that the customer is prepared to pay for the service over the cost of providing it. Competitive advantage is sustained by linkages in the chain and the wider value system that extends to a company's various business partners. VCA can also be used to identify activities in the chain which are not adding value.

Supa's value chain consists of the following:

Primary activities:

Inbound logistics – collecting the parcel from the customer (or receiving it at the depot)
Operations – sorting, storage and transportation scheduling

Outbound logistics – delivering the parcel to the end customer

Marketing and sales – advertising and promotion

Service – handling of redeliveries, lost or damaged parcels, complaints

Support activities

Infrastructure (the way the company is organised, its management structure etc)
Technology
HR
Procurement

Competitive advantage for a parcel delivery company centres on providing an excellent service, which involves two key aspects: the physical collection and delivery of a parcel and the management and utilisation of the information relating to that delivery.

In terms of Porter's generic strategy, Supa is a focussed differentiator and the key value drivers within Supa's value chain include:

Use of technology to

- Increase cost efficiency of collection and distribution through better logistical planning due to real time information provided by GPS system, notebook computers etc

- Increase likelihood of first time delivery (use of chosen time slots and delivery reminders means customers are more likely to be in), reducing costly redeliveries and the risk of lost parcels

- Provide better customer service due to enhanced visibility/automated tracking facility

- Share information with JV partners in the distribution network thus generating a more seamless service

Customer service

- Ability to specify timed delivery slots
- Automated tracking facility
- Text/email messaging services
- First to introduce carbon neutral delivery option

HR

- People treated as a valuable resource not a commodity

- Strong customer service ethos

- Investment in training and development, particularly with reference to using the technology and customer service

- Corporate uniform generates strong cultural identity

Marketing

Distinctive company branded purple uniform, vans and packaging

Extended value system

Use of strategic partners which provides global coverage and better understanding of local customers' needs. Again this is facilitated by technology and sharing of information

Examiner's comments:

Requirement 21.2 asked candidates to analyse Supa's value chain and describe clearly its key value drivers. Most candidates demonstrated a good understanding of the components of the value chain and were able to explain them in the context of Supa's parcel delivery. A disappointing number failed to highlight the key value drivers and, when they did so, often focussed simply on trivial issues such as the use of purple vans and uniforms. The best candidates identified that Supa was a focussed differentiator and that, as such, its use of technology to improve speed of delivery and customer service was key to its competitive advantage. Despite an instruction to the contrary in the question, a minority of candidates produced a value chain diagram.

21.3 Evaluation of performance

(a) **Exhibit 2 missing figures:**

Revenue growth:

Note. To assist with interpretation the figure for 20X8-20Y0 could be annualised.

Budget 20X8-20Y0 = 42.3-35/35 = 20.86%, annualised = 10.43% (simple) or 9.94% (compound)

Actual 20X8-20Y0 = 46-35/35 = 31.43%, annualised = 15.71% (simple) or 14.64% (compound)

Operating profit margin:

Budget 20Y0 = 2.1/42.3 = 4.96%

Actual 20Y0 = 1.6 1/46 = 3.5%

Appendix of financial performance indicator

	Supa Budget 20Y0	Supa Actual 20Y0	Supa Actual 20X8	Mkt leader 20Y0
BSC missing financial measures				
Annualised revenue growth	10.43%	15.71%	n/a	n/a
Operating margin	4.96%	3.5%	3.00%	4.47%
Parcel stats				
Average revenue per parcel	£9.00	£10.00	£7.45	£9.05
Operating profit per parcel	£0.45	£0.35	£0.22	£0.40
Operating costs (£m)	40.20	44.39	33.95	363.00
Operating costs per parcel	£8.55	£9.65	£7.22	£8.64
Depot stats				
Parcels handled per depot (m)	0.235	0.230	0.235	0.840
Average revenue per depot (£m)	2.12	2.30	1.75	7.60
Operating cost per depot (£m)	2.01	2.2195	1.6975	7.26

(b) All calculations are provided in the supporting appendix.

In assessing whether the implementation of the new strategy has been a success we can consider:

- Whether actual performance has improved since 20X8 (actual 20X8 to 20Y0)

- Whether the performance achieved is as good as Supa intended (actual 20Y0 compared to budget 20Y0) and compares favourably with that of the market leader

- The non-financial perspective provided by the other BSC indicators

Intended impact of strategy

A review of the budget suggests that in the first two years of the new strategy Supa intended to maintain the volume of parcels handled at 4.7m but increase revenue and profit, by more than doubling the operating margin per parcel from 22 pence to 45 pence. Further analysis indicates that this was to be achieved by increasing the average revenue per parcel from £7.45 to £9.00. This can be explained by Supa's decision to pull out of non-urgent deliveries market (the most price sensitive market) and focus on overnight deliveries with a specified time slot, which are likely to command a price premium. Supa has had to invest heavily in technology to offer this service and is likely to have had to increase the frequency of deliveries given the number of time slots it is now offering. This is reflected by the budgeted 18% increase in operating costs from £33.95m to £40.2m.

20Y0 Actual performance (new strategy) in relation to Actual 20X8 (old strategy)

The change in strategy appears to have resulted in revenue increased by over 31% from £35m to £46m (or 15.7% per annum). This has been achieved by a marginal reduction in the volume of parcels handled (4.6m compared to 4.7m) and a significant increase since 20X8 in the actual average revenue per parcel from £7.45 to £10, reflecting the change in strategy towards the higher value deliveries.

Operating costs per parcel have increased significantly from £7.22 to £9.65. This is likely to be due to the increased frequency of customer deliveries and the additional costs incurred for the new technology required in order to offer guaranteed time slots, provide delivery reminders and track parcels.

The increase in the prices charged to the client more than outweighs the increased cost however, so operating profit has increased from £0.22 to £0.35 per parcel, resulting in an increased operating margin (3.5% compared to 3% in 20X8).

20Y0 Actual performance in relation to budget

20Y0 revenue is 8.7% more than budgeted despite the volume of parcels being slightly down at 4.6m compared to the budget of 4.7m. The fact that the average revenue at £10 per parcel is higher than the budget of £9 may reflect a difference in the product mix compared to that forecast eg relatively more deliveries than expected being undertaken during the most expensive 7am-9am slot. Alternatively Supa may have been forced to increase prices in an attempt to cover the increase in operating costs and this could have reduced demand.

Overall operating costs are 10% higher than budgeted and, at £9.65, significantly more expensive per parcel than the budget of £8.55. Since a high proportion of Supa's costs are fixed, an increase in the volume of parcels handled would reduce the average cost per parcel. If total costs were to remain at the 20Y0 level of £44.5m, Supa would need to handle 5.2m parcels in order to achieve the target cost of £8.55. Alternatively it needs to reduce its operating costs and this may be what has motivated the operations director's suggestions regarding the rationalisation of depots.

Comparison with market leader

It is hard to compare Supa directly to the market leader (ML). Supa's market share is only 21% of theirs. The ML has 30 more depots and the appendix shows that these are significantly larger, handling an average 840,000 parcels per depot (Supa 230,000), generating 3.3 times the amount of revenue (£7.6m compared to Supa's £2.3m) and incurring average operating costs of £7.2m (Supa £2.2m).

In terms of market positioning, Supa's target implies they intended to price themselves just below the market leader at £9, although in practice they have achieved average revenue of £10 per parcel. This may be because of a change in pricing strategy or alternatively because Supa has different types of customer or product mix.

The ML is likely to have greater international coverage than Supa and so it may be more relevant to compare Supa's performance with the ML results for the UK deliveries, if they were available.

Balanced scorecard indicators

The balanced scorecard indicators may be viewed as a vertical hierarchy, with the quality of the processes (as measured by innovation and learning) leading to increased business efficiency (internal business) and hence customer satisfaction. Conversely the failure of internal processes may explain inefficient operations or lower customer satisfaction.

Looking at the innovation and learning perspective, Supa has successfully implemented employee training with respect to the new IT systems which reinforces its commitment to HR as a valuable resource. It is however falling short of its target in respect of IT downtime.

The new service with specified time slots relies on technology, hence delivery problems may have arisen as a result of the system being unavailable (eg an inability to text or email the parcel recipient to remind them about the delivery), resulting in a failed first attempt. As we can see from the internal perspective, Supa has only managed to achieve a first attempt delivery rate of 65% against a target of 70%. The other internal measure is the number of trips made per vehicle. Utilisation rates will be a key factor in driving operational efficiency and lack of system availability may have caused scheduling problems and hence delivery failures.

This could explain why both the customer perspective measures are less than the target, and also explain why costs per parcel are relatively higher. Failed attempts at delivery potentially increase the chance of the parcel going missing or having to be returned to the sender as undelivered. They also lead to Supa incurring additional administration and transport costs associated with the redelivery, for which there will be no additional revenue. Certain customers may have built targets into their service level agreements allowing them to claim discounts or refunds if Supa fails to meet these targets, making failed deliveries even more costly as a result of a negative impact on revenue as well as increasing cost.

Quality and standard of budget/targets

When considering performance it may be that the 'budget' rather than the 'actual' is at fault. It is possible that the targets set were too ambitious, given the changes in system and strategy, and failed to take into account teething problems/learning curve issues. Alternatively the targets may have been deliberately ambitious in order to motivate staff to aim for the top and management may be very pleased with the results.

What is not clear is how Supa has performed in comparison with previous years or competitors, and more information is required to do this (see below).

Further information required

Breakdown of results

- Detailed breakdown of operating costs to assess areas of over-/under-spend and scope for rationalisation

- Analysis of revenue, costs and profit for 20X8 by type of service would allow us to see how Supa's performance has improved in the speed sensitive delivery market

- Analysis by depot – to assess performance of individual depots/managers

- Analysis of pricing structure and revenue by time slot (pre 9 am or weekends are priced more highly than afternoon deliveries)

- Results for 20X9 in order to consider year on year performance. 20X9 was the transition year

- Monthly management accounts to assess any seasonality impact

- 20X8 and 20X9 balanced scorecard measures for next day deliveries to assess whether the service has improved as a result of introduction of the new technology

Comparatives

- Details of the industry average prices for the different services on offer

- Benchmarks for the other indicators in the BSC to assess how Supa is performing in relation to the best overnight parcel delivery company (competitor benchmark) and also any other market leaders in distribution or companies renowned for their fleet management/distribution capabilities

- Could also do internal benchmarking by comparing individual depots with Supa's best depot. This might help the operations director decide which depots to consider for rationalisation

Objectives/budgets/targets

- In order to assess performance fully, details of the aims and specific objectives for the change in strategy would be helpful (eg increase market share by x%, retain more customers)

- Part of a post-investment audit would include assessing the quality and accuracy of the forecasts and budgets. In order to do this more information would be required about assumptions made

- Details of management expectations regarding the appropriate level of achievement of the target would also be useful

Preliminary conclusion

On the face of the initial analysis, the strategy appears to have been a success, having grown both revenue and profit, but there is more scope for Supa to increase its operational efficiency. Comparisons with the market leader would suggest that one way of achieving this is to reduce the number of depots but increase the size of each.

Examiner's comments:

Requirement 21.3 was the data analysis requirement and dealt with whether the implementation of the new strategy had been a success. Candidates were provided with actual company results for 20X8 and 20Y0, a budget for 20Y0 and relevant data for the market leader. They were then asked (a) to prepare two specific calculations (revenue growth and operating margin) together with other relevant financial performance indicators; and (b) to use their calculations in (a) and the balanced scorecard indicators provided in the scenario to evaluate the impact of the new strategy. An indication of useful additional information was also required.

Almost all candidates were able to calculate the two specific performance indicators requested, although very few recognised that to aid interpretation it might be sensible to annualise the figures for revenue growth. There was some variability in candidates' ability to calculate other meaningful ratios, and those that were weak in this area then struggled to provide a meaningful interpretation of financial performance in (b), as they had little on which to base their discussion.

The better candidates were able to identify the need for calculations on a per parcel basis such as average revenue/operating profit/cost per parcel, and also to provide comparisons between Supa's 20Y0 actual results and the figures for 20Y0 budget, 20X8 and the market leader.

Weaker candidates tended to focus only on revenue calculation, or only considered the comparison between 20Y0 actual and budget, producing relatively few calculations for the 8 marks available. Those candidates who focused on calculations per depot appeared to have given little thought to the figures that would be relevant in determining Supa's performance, since the number of depots had remained static throughout the period.

In part (b) most candidates produced a reasonable evaluation of the financial impact of the strategy and the non-financial performance measures provided, and a larger proportion of candidates seemed well-prepared for the balanced scorecard than at the previous sitting. Some weaker candidates did however ignore the balanced scorecard measures. Better candidates linked their discussion, using the increased system downtime to explain the failure to meet certain delivery targets and then suggesting that this might explain the increased operating costs. Stronger candidates also questioned the accuracy of the initial budget, and/or identified that it was still very early to judge the success or otherwise of the strategy.

As in the past, weaker answers tended to describe what had happened to various figures (eg increased or decreased) rather than attempting to address how it had happened (eg analysing the data in more detail) or why it had happened (eg identifying underlying factors discussed in the scenario which may have caused the changes). The additional useful key information from the poorer students was also the usual generic list of cash flows, balance sheets, management accounts and competitor information.

21.4 Depot closure

Power/interest matrix

The impact of the proposed depot rationalisation on the employees can be assessed by the Mendelow power-interest matrix.

The interest of the employees will certainly be high. The extent of their power may be less so.

Interest

Interest will be high due to:

- Concerns about job security and possible loss of jobs

- Impact of any proposed relocation for example to the new central sorting hub

- Inability to find replacement work locally due to economic slowdown and general level of unemployment

However if the redundancy payments offered are sufficiently high, some employees may favour voluntary redundancy to continued employment and thus have a positive interest in closure of the depot (eg if they were going to leave anyway or were close to retirement).

Power

The power of employees to stop or moderate any decision is limited. As individuals the employees have low power, however their collective power will partly depend on the extent to which the workforce is unionised. It will also depend on the level of support for the depot staff from the rest of Supa's workforce. If the entire UK workforce is united, then significant costs can arise from disruption. Once the decision is announced and implemented however, then the remaining employees who are to retain their jobs have a much lower negative interest in the decision.

Where depot employees may have some power is in resisting the change and therefore increasing the costs involved. In this respect the threat of action may make the perceived exit costs higher, particularly when the costs of damaging the brand are taken into account. Employees may expect to have more power/influence as Supa has historically treated them as a valuable resource and they are a key factor in providing good customer service.

Examiner's comments:

Requirement 21.4 asked candidates to explain how the depot sorting staff, as key stakeholders, would be affected by and have the power to resist the operational director's proposal to rationalise the depots. A significant number of candidates used Mendelow's matrix, and may considered staff on both an individual and a group (unionised) basis. Stronger candidates identified both positive and negative consequences of the rationalisation proposals and the fact that staff resistance might disrupt the process or increase the company's costs, but would be unlikely to prevent closure.

22 e-Parts Ltd (September 2010)

Marking guide

	Knowledge	Skill	Marks
22.1 Relevance of risk management/contents of BCP	3	4	6
22.2 Key IT risks and management	4	5	8
22.3 Outsourcing to implement IT strategy	3	5	7
	10	14	21

General comments:

The scenario in this question relates to an online retailer which sells parts and accessories for domestic appliances. 90% of orders are made online, and the owner has identified the dependence of the business on the inventory control system and the importance of keeping its website operational. The business has grown significantly during the recession and is now considering outsourcing all its operational systems to a specialist IT provider. The owner has also been made aware that the company needs a formal risk management policy and a business continuity plan.

Answers to this question varied in standard and although the overall performance was quite good, there were some very poor answers.

22.1 **Risk management and business continuity planning**

Risk management is the process of identifying and assessing the risks facing EP's business and the development, implementation and monitoring of a strategy to respond to those risks, in order to reduce threats to acceptable levels.

When running a business, risk is unavoidable and will include financial, strategic, operational and hazard risks arising from both internal and external sources. Risk management is a corporate governance issue as there is the danger that directors of companies might take decisions intended to increase profits without giving due regard to the risks. They may also continue to operate without regard to the changing risk profile of their organisation.

The point of risk management is that risks can be mitigated if management have plans to deal with problems if they occur. Risk management should be carried out by all businesses and involve all levels of staff and management. The aim is to prioritise the risks according to the ones that threaten the business most and then to take action to reduce or otherwise address the risk.

In addition to the general risks faced by all businesses, as a retailer EP faces additional risks because it carries large volumes of stock and also because business is largely done online (see 22.2). A key issue for an online business is that technical failure has a significant and immediate impact. Problems with the ecommerce site are immediately visible and it is easy for customers to switch to a competitor if the website is unavailable. Thus it is important for EP to take action to prevent/reduce losses due to excessive risk exposure that may include theft, fraud and data insecurity.

Kamal must ensure that all staff are trained and fully aware of ecommerce security issues and fraud risk.

Whether EP thrives or fails will partly be dependent on how as a business it manages risk and exploits opportunities. The aim is to reduce the probability and/or consequence of failure but retain as far as possible the benefits of success. Thus effective risk management is integral to EP's competitive advantage and will help ensure EP's survival in the longer term.

Business continuity planning is the process through which a business details how and when it will recover and restore operations interrupted by the occurrence of a massive (but rare) risk event eg natural disaster such as a warehouse flood or fire or a major breach of security causing the website to be down for an extended period.

Where risk management is largely pre-emptive, BCP is designed to deal with the consequences of a major realised risk. The difference is also linked to the extent of the impact – for instance the difference between website disruption due to a temporary loss of internet connection and a denial of service attack that places the business's existence in jeopardy.

A BCP is concerned with crisis management and disaster recovery. It must specify the actions to be taken in order to recover from any unexpected disruptive event. Factors that should be considered by a BCP include:

- Securing interim management and staff
- Inventory replacement
- Restoration of data and other IT systems
- Securing interim premises
- Management of the PR issues

Methods of recovery might include:

- Carrying out activities manually until IT services are resumed (eg via the call centre)

- Moving staff at an affected building to another location

- Agreeing with another business to use each other's premises in the event of a disaster

- Arranging to use IT services and accommodation provided by a specialist third-party standby site

All members of ES staff should be aware of the importance of business continuity planning, training should be given and the plan tested regularly.

Examiner's comments:

Requirement 22.1 asked candidates to explain the relevance of risk management to the business as a whole and to identify the main factors that would be covered in a business continuity plan. Overall answers were of a poor standard with many candidates failing this requirement because they were uncertain about the nature and content of a business continuity plan, despite the clear hint given in the scenario about ensuring the business could continue to function in the event of a major incident. Explanations of risk management tended to be extremely generic and only the best candidates pointed out that risk management was critical given the risks faced by EP as a result of its inventory levels and the e-commerce nature of the business. Weaker candidates often mentioned Turnbull, which demonstrated a lack of understanding of its application.

22.2 Risks of ecommerce and how to manage them

EP must take steps to minimise the risk of systems failure, protect the integrity of its systems, safeguard information and ensure the continuity of its operations.

Risks may be transferred, avoided, reduced or accepted.

Specific risks arising for EP and recommendations for risk management:

- Inaccessible website/Website too slow/payment system for ecommerce website goes down. This is critical given that 90% sales are online and is likely to result in frustrated customers and lost sales as they can easily switch to another online competitor.

  Risk can be reduced by ensuring appropriate systems development and maintenance takes place and by having back-up servers. EP could also reduce the risk by providing other channels to market and ensuring that customers are directed to alternatives such as the call centre in the event of system delays or failures.

  EP could transfer the risk by outsourcing the provision of the website to a specialist provider (see 22.3).

- Identity theft/credit card fraud arising due to online payments – this would damage EP's reputation and may result in lost customers.

  EP should ensure it reduces the risk by having access controls, appropriate payment verification software, firewalls and secure communication.

- Loss of critical data, particularly given there are 2m customers on the database and 100,000 different products to control. Failure of stock control system may cause inaccurate information to be provided regarding stock levels or wrong products to be despatched. Failure to comply with the Data Protection Act could also result in penalties/litigation.

  EP should reduce the risk of inadequate or inaccurate information by performing regular physical stocktakes and reconciling these to computerised records.

  EP must ensure the stock system and customer database are kept up-to date, backed up regularly and hard copies kept off site. It must have systems in place to monitor compliance with data protection regulations and ensure all data held is secure (eg via encryption).

  Reduce the risk by ensuring all feedback is screened regularly and ensuring appropriate security features are in place to control access and content.

- IT system becomes out-of-date or is less capable than that of online competitors.

  Systems need to be upgraded regularly to ensure they are capable of providing the necessary capacity, particularly given the growth EP has experienced.

Where risks cannot be reduced or eliminated it may be possible for EP to transfer them via:

- Insurance (however this may be costly and it may be problematic to quantify the extent of business loss from a security incident)

- Contracting out the management of ecommerce to a third party who can host the system. The loss may still occur and impact on the business, but the service level agreement can stipulate penalties

Other more generic IT risks include:

- Virus attacks and/or hackers exploiting vulnerabilities in the system (steal data, damage system or corrupt information)

- Website defacement (impact on reputation/brand image)

- Denial of service

- Infrastructure failure eg loss of internet connection

- Software/hardware systems malfunction

- Loss of key IT personnel eg website designer/IT manager

- Risk to corporate information/intellectual property

- Human error

- Deliberate sabotage

- Fraud

- Natural threats (fire, flood, electrical storm)

More generally EP can reduce vulnerability and increase its level of confidence in its technical environment by:

- Installing firewalls, using strong authentication processes and secure communication

- Implementing policies to manage activities eg internet and email usage

- Setting standards for firewalls, servers and procurement of PCs

- Establishing a high level of Information security and access controls, and measuring to detect unauthorised access

- Ensuring there are regular back-ups

- Undertaking appropriate systems development and maintenance

- Ensuring physical and environment security

- Complying with relevant legislation

Examiner's comments:

Requirement 22.2 asked candidates to identify the key risks arising for EP as a result of its reliance on IT and to recommend how they could be managed. Answers were quite variable. Good answers concentrated on relevant IT risks for EP, including the possible failure of the website, loss of customer database information, identify theft and the possibility of damaging reviews on social networking sites. The best candidates tended to set out their answers in the form of a table, clearly identifying, for each risk identified, the way that it could be managed. A significant number of answers discussed IT risks and the TARA model for risk management in very generic terms. The weakest candidates failed to concentrate on IT risks, mentioning any types of risk they could think of.

22.3 Considerations in outsourcing the provision of the website and inventory control system

EP is considering outsourcing all its systems relating to the website and inventory control.

Factors to consider include the following:

- EP has experienced substantial growth and its current systems may no longer be able to cope with the increasing volume of transactions. Outsourcing may reduce the chance of system breakdown and give EP access to back-up servers and systems.

- Outsourcing would provide access to specialist IT knowledge and allow Kamal to concentrate on the strategy of the company.

- As specialists, with the potential for economies of scale, an outsourcer may be able to provide better, more efficient systems for EP at a lower cost. They are also more likely to be able to keep the systems up-to-date and develop new applications which may help EP maintain its competitive advantage.

- By outsourcing, EP can transfer the risk of systems failure to the IT provider and may have recourse to compensation in the event of financial loss.

However:

- EP has a database of 2m customers. Outsourcing would require it to share confidential information with the IT provider, who may also work with competitors.

- Any problems experienced when transferring the systems over may disrupt EP's business and cause it to lose sales/customers.

- Once EP has decided to outsource it may find it difficult to switch suppliers and is unlikely to be able to revert to in-house provision as it will no longer have its own web designers/IT experts.

Other factors to consider:

- Fees charged by contractor
- Costs currently incurred in own service provision
- Potential redundancies of staff no longer required
- Time and cost involved in agreeing and monitoring service level agreement
- Attitude of influential stakeholders
- Previous incidence and consequence of system breakdown

Conclusion: If EP does decide to outsource it will need to choose a partner carefully, and assess their financial stability and track record of delivering suitable services elsewhere.

It must then agree a series of performance targets and penalties in the event of the contractor's failure to deliver.

Examiner's comments:

In requirement 22.3 candidates were asked to explain the factors that should be considered by EP in deciding whether to use outsourcing as a method of implementing its IT strategy. Candidates were clearly well rehearsed for this requirement in terms of knowledge but many weaker candidates failed to obtain the available skills marks. This was due to the fact that they produced largely generic lists of pros and cons, with minimal application of EP and its IT strategy, which could have been applied to almost any outsourcing scenario. Better answers focussed specifically on the factors that would influence the choice between in-house and outsourced IT provision and the impact on risks for EP.

---

23 Marcham plc (September 2010)

Marking guide

	Knowledge	Skill	Marks
23.1 Report format			
(a) Info system benefits/competitive advantage	3	6	8
(b) SFA of expansion into the banking sector	3	10	12
(c) Organic growth v joint development	3	6	8
23.2 Ethical issues	3	6	8
	12	28	36

General comments:

This scenario relates to a major supermarket chain which is proposing to take advantage f the recent turmoil in the banking sector by launching its own banking services (rather than as a joint venture with another bank). Marcham has a 30% share of the supermarket sector and was the first supermarket to introduce a loyalty card. Along with an EPOS and inventory control system the loyalty card forms part of an integrated information and knowledge management system and is to be a key driver of competitive advantage for the expansion into banking. Candidates were provided with an extract from a national newspaper which has recently criticised Marcham for using its loyalty card to spy on customers and for abusing its suppliers.

Overall the performance on this question was quite good, although weaker candidates struggled with the requirement on ethics.

23.1 Report

To: Operations Director
From: AN Other
Date: September 20Y0
Re: Information systems and proposed expansion into banking

(a) **Benefits of and use of information system for competitive advantage**

- Increased revenue (from customers and also from sale of data to suppliers)

- Reduced costs (better stock control)

- Increased customer service and hence improved customer retention – effectively the loyalty card acts as a barrier to exit for the customer

- Improved decision making (forecasting, scenario planning, market analysis)

- Existing database for direct marketing

- Targeted discount coupons as a form of price discrimination

- EPOS system facilitates better stock control, allowing for a Just-in-Time approach which reduces costs and wastage

Marcham's competitive advantage (CA)

In the supermarket industry, most players have EPOS systems and loyalty card schemes. In order for CA to arise, Marcham not only needs to be better at capturing information than competitors but also better at using it.

The loyalty scheme is a form of relationship marketing whereby Marcham is trying to build a long-term relationship with the customer. Marcham's CA arises because in terms of capturing the information:

- It was the first of its kind to introduce the scheme and therefore captured (and retained) an initial loyal customer base, obtaining first-mover advantage

- Its dominance within the market (60% of the UK population shop at a Marcham store at least once a month and one in four adults in the UK belong to its customer loyalty scheme) means it has a more extensive database than any other competitor (data about more customers and also collected for longer)

In terms of its ability to use the information:

- It has reduced costs by increasing the frequency and accuracy of ordering, leading to lower levels of inventory and wastage

- It has more effective marketing which facilitates market segmentation and targeting, so low price goods can be promoted to certain customers and high quality ones to others

- It has better price discrimination and hence increased margins

- It can to trade up sales by targeting promotions

- The percentage of customer spend can be extended by identifying products customers are likely to buy but may currently be buying elsewhere

- It has higher margins – it is cheaper to keep existing customers and to sell more to them than it is to attract new ones

- It is likely to result in a higher success rate for new product lines as it has already identified what customers want

- It shares this with suppliers, generating revenue from the sale of the database, promoting better captive relationships with the supplier and improving the matching of products with demand

Within the financial services sector none of the competitors has loyalty cards so Marcham will have first mover advantage if it uses the loyalty card within the banking sector.

Examiner's comments:

Requirement 23.1 asked candidates to write a report which (a) explains the potential benefits of an effective information system for a supermarket and discusses how Marcham has used its information systems to create competitive advantage in the supermarket industry (b) assesses the suitability, feasibility and acceptability of Marcham's proposed expansion into the banking sector and (c) discusses the relative merits of Marcham's intention to expand into banking via organic growth rather than having an established bank as a business partner.

A minority of candidates did not use the report heading which was disappointing.

In 23.1(a) most candidates were able to discuss the benefits of an information system in a retail environment citing better inventory control and improved supply chain management to help minimise costs and prevent wastage. In addition, if buying habits of customers could be tracked then market segmentation, targeted marketing and price discrimination could be undertaken.

The better candidates considered the benefits for the industry and then the reasons for Marcham's competitive advantage separately. Weaker candidates tended to simply discuss information systems in the context of Marcham but in doing so did not explain clearly the reasons for the firm's potentially sustainable competitive advantage. Thus they failed to recognise that most supermarkets have EPOS systems and many have loyalty cards, and that the benefits for Marcham arise because of it being the first to introduce a loyalty card, its dominance in the market and its integration with suppliers – all of which allow it to capture more data and be better at using it than competitors.

(b) **Suitability, feasibility, acceptability**

Suitability (strategic logic and fit)

There is a precedent as Marcham would not be the first major retailer to get involved in financial services (Tesco, Sainsbury, M&S) although it would be the first to set up a full banking service.

Strong brand name – timing is good given some people's loss of faith in the banking sector and perceived lack of transparency surrounding banks' behaviour. The issue is whether Marcham will be seen by consumers as a credible provider of banking services, although the fact that they have been granted a licence suggests the FSA believe they are.

Both banks and supermarkets are about serving personal customers and Marcham already possesses core competence in customer service and responsiveness.

There is also a strong link between retail spending and the need for credit.

Both banks and supermarkets require a presence on the high street and Marcham can use existing infrastructure.

The loyalty card scheme offers exposure to a large number of customers and the opportunity to increase share of customers' spend.

However:

- Are financial services a core competence for retailers?

- It is a very competitive market

- Relatively Marcham will be a very small player faced with large competition

- Core competences in procurement and logistics would be less relevant in banking than if it expanded into other retail areas

- There are onerous compliance requirements related to data protection, identity confirmation, regulatory compliance and money laundering of which Marcham has limited experience

- Many customers now use online banking so Marchambank's presence in stores may not be that attractive to them

Feasibility (can the strategy be implemented?)

This looks at whether Marcham have the necessary resources.

Marcham has already been granted a licence which demonstrates government support.

Branches will be located in existing stores which reduces the overhead costs associated with the operation.

Cash appears to be available although there is an opportunity cost if it is not invested in other new stores.

The loyalty card provides instant access to a database for direct marketing and profiling information which will allow Marcham to tailor products to different groups of customer.

Marcham already has systems in place to collate data about customers and process applications, so credit assessment would simply be a bolt-on.

Marcham would need to hire new staff and management with appropriate financial services knowledge – there is likely to be a big training requirement.

The pricing of financial services and processes are much more complex than individual retail transactions eg selling a loaf of bread.

The banking sector will entail onerous compliance requirements related to data protection, identity confirmation and money laundering.

Financial services are long term in nature so Marcham will need to commit resources for a significant period. It will take time to recoup initial set-up costs and for the venture to become profitable.

Acceptability (to stakeholders)

This considers the likely benefits to stakeholders (returns) and the likelihood of failure and its associated consequences (risk).

Returns

More information is required to assess the proposed financial impact of the strategy. Here we are told that it will offer access to higher margins at a time when the retail business is under pressure, so it may result in increased profitability for shareholders. The core retail business is mature and growing slowly so this offers an opportunity for continued growth.

The government grant reduces the cost of setting up the call centre.

Customers may perceive the strategy as enhancing the service on offer which may help retain/attract new customers for the retail business.

Given the government's stated aim to increase competition they may well look favourably on the venture by Marcham.

It may provide additional career opportunities for some employees.

Risk

The biggest risk is that management have no experience/expertise in financial services products, which are complex.

From a risk point of view, adding financial services spreads the risk profile of Marcham's business. However according to Ansoff this strategy would be classed as unrelated diversification and as a result is a high risk approach to increasing profits. Given recent events, banking is no longer the safe and secure business that it was once deemed to be. Institutional shareholders will already have well diversified portfolios and it could be argued that if shareholders wanted ownership of a bank then they could just buy shares in one themselves.

Shareholders may be concerned that management will be distracted from the core business.

There is a big reputational risk for the existing business if Marcham gets it wrong and it would need to ring fence this area of the business as a separate company.

Marcham may lose customers from the retail business if it rejects applications for loans or credit cards.

Conclusion:

The fact that a number of other supermarkets have launched financial services products suggests that the strategy is viable, although further consideration needs to be given to the best method of implementing the strategy.

Examiner's comments:

Answers to 23.1(b) were generally of a good standard, with many candidates scoring well on the skills marks. The strong candidates clearly knew the difference between 'suitability, feasibility and acceptability', describing how these would be judged more generally, before assessing each in relation to Marcham's expansion into banking. Weaker candidates tended to blur the distinction between the three areas.

The best answers were extremely well-balanced and contrasted the positives (Marcham's brand name, loyal customer base and loyalty card, the grant of £5m, the FSA licence) with the negatives (no experience, increased regulatory requirements, high competition and the fact that space would be taken up in supermarket branches by the banking section which could impact on Marcham's core business.

Some candidates did appear to struggle with the 'acceptability' part of the question and there was a distinct lack of recognition that whiles the proposal had to be acceptable to a variety of stakeholders (investors, customers, government) the impact on risk and return for shareholders was likely to be of critical importance.

(c) **Organic growth versus joint venture**

Arguments against organic growth (in favour of joint venture)

Gaining competences via organic growth takes time. Marcham does not have any expertise in financial services so will need to buy it in. A partnership with an existing bank would ensure rapid access to the relevant expertise.

There are significant regulation and compliance issues in the banking sector, including barriers to entry such as the licence. Although Marcham has already been granted a licence it will lack expertise and systems to ensure compliance in areas such as money laundering legislation.

The FSA may be more favourable in the long term towards a venture that has already demonstrated financial expertise and compliance.

Most other retailers have chosen to move into financial services through partnership with banks, thus combining banking expertise with the retailer's brand strength and reputation.

Risk is shared.

Arguments in favour of organic growth (against joint venture)

Organic growth gives Marcham full control over the venture and avoids the need to share profits.

Having to buy-in operational expertise from a bank may restrict the scope for Marcham to do banking in a different way, which is a key driver for its strategy.

An alliance with a bank would not address the issue of the public's mistrust of the banking sector. Marcham's loyalty card provides access to existing customer base.

The government grant may not be available if Marcham expands with a partner.

The available choice of partner would be limited as there would be relatively few options available to choose from in terms of a bank with a reputation still intact.

It avoids placing reliance on the future reputation of the chosen partner.

Organic growth avoids any potential clash of strategy or disagreement - banking partners may be reluctant to sanction new financial services products that are critical of their own service provision or that overtly compete.

It saves the time and cost of negotiating terms of a JV agreement, profit share, exit options etc.

Conclusion:

Other supermarkets have chosen to enter financial services with banking partners for a reason and Marcham needs to consider carefully the risks involved in pursuing this strategy alone.

Examiner's comments:

In part 23.1(c), candidates were well prepared to discuss the merits of organic growth vs joint venture in terms of cost/time/risk. However a disappointing number of answers tended to repeat the learning materials and were not in the context of the scenario. Those candidates who scored higher marks highlighted relevant factors such as the regulation required by the FSA, Marcham's lack of expertise, its information systems and loyalty card and customers' generally poor perception of existing banks.

23.2 Ethics

Tutorial note:

This answer includes more points than is necessary for the marks available but a full range of points has been provided for marking purposes.

Loyalty card:

The issue concerning the loyalty card is really one of ethical marketing and relates to the collection, use and sale of the data gathered in this way. Is Marcham behaving in a fair and transparent manner and what is the likely effect on its customers?

It is partly a question of boundaries – how much data is it reasonable to collect, what is acceptable use and is it legitimate to sell the data on?

Collection of data

The ethical argument is that collection of the data is an invasion of privacy and that it could be abused if it falls into the wrong hands.

Effectively consumers who join the loyalty scheme trade information for product savings. Customers have a choice as to whether to shop at Marcham and whether to join the loyalty card scheme. The fact that one in four adults belong implies they do not have a problem, or perceive that the benefits are sufficient to compensate for the lack of privacy.

The Data Protection Act (DPA) strictly regulates the confidentiality, storage and use of personal information and Marcham is likely to have sophisticated security and access systems to ensure it does not fall into the wrong hands.

Marcham will also have a stated policy explaining what data is collected and how it is used/shared with preferred partners (transparency) plus an option for consumers to tick a box if they don't want their data shared.

Critics might argue that consumers know what data they have given when they apply to take out a card but lack awareness of how much data is subsequently captured and how it is used. The key ethical issue here is therefore transparency and whether informed and willing consent has been given by consumers to Marcham to utilise data in an agreed manner in return for the benefits of the scheme.

Use of data

Issues concern motives and transparency.

The debate about marketing centres on whether it is about meeting people's needs and expectations or selling people things they don't need.

It could be argued that Marcham uses the loyalty card to better identify the specific needs of different groups of customers and so wastes fewer resources because marketing is targeted. As a result it becomes more efficient at stocking shelves with products consumers want, and can therefore pass the savings on in lower prices, although some argue that this is at the expense of higher prices paid by non-loyalty card holders (lack of fairness/negative effect on some).

Marcham could use data captured to promote healthy food and provide improved education re healthy diets, hence offering a benefit to society.

Profiling could however also be used negatively to exclude undesirable customers (eg recent case of the customer wearing pyjamas whilst shopping at Tesco) or to concentrate on a wealthier class of customers, and this would be regarded as unethical.

Sale of data

The potential issue regarding the sale to third parties (suppliers, direct mail companies, telemarketers) is that Marcham has less control over it and has also made money from it.

DPA means it is illegal for companies to sell on people's details without their consent or for uses other than those they were originally told about. Thus Marcham will give consumers an option on the loyalty card application form to tick a box if they don't want their data shared. This is standard practice engaged in by most retailers.

It is not in Marcham's interests to breach DPA as it will face consequences in terms of damaged reputation and lost customers.

Conclusion

Ultimately Marcham is no different than a whole host of other retailers also operating loyalty card schemes and consumers have the choice of whether to belong to the scheme or not. They can also shop elsewhere if they don't like it.

Treatment of suppliers

Business ethics covers the way a firm as a whole behaves and thus any victimisation of suppliers by Marcham would contravene this. Corporate responsibility would also suggest that Marcham owes a responsibility to society and its wider stakeholders and that a balance needs to be struck between making profits for the shareholders and treating suppliers fairly.

Marcham is being blamed, like a number of other supermarkets and large retailers in the press recently, for exacerbating the poverty of farmers and other weak suppliers.

The issue centres on whether Marcham is merely implementing good supply chain management or is guilty of unethical treatment due to exploitation.

Marcham's ability to dictate terms and conditions to suppliers is evidence of its bargaining power as a customer (Porter) – the bigger the company the greater its likely power to push prices down and demand better payment terms. Lower prices achieved from suppliers may benefit consumers if they are passed on. Thus terms and prices may differ between suppliers depending on their relative bargaining power in relation to Marcham.

The policy of extending payment terms is good cash flow management and could be argued to be in the interests of shareholders.

Even if it adopted standard payment terms, Marcham would be a relatively cash rich business - cash sales mean it has few receivables and JIT policies keep inventories relatively low, leading to an effective cash operating cycle.

The argument against extending payment terms is that Marcham's monopoly position in the market allows them to exploit suppliers by driving prices down, which can force smaller suppliers out of business. Marcham's terms could be compared to the industry average and to other organisations of its size to assess whether they are reasonable. Marcham might be said to be being unfair if it significantly differentiates terms between large and small suppliers, thus abusing its position of power, or if it is not adhering to Industry codes of practice.

However it is unlikely to be in Marcham's interest to drive suppliers out of business as it would then be faced with disruptions in supply or emergency supplies at premium prices. As a major player in the market and a successful plc, Marcham will not want to risk damaging its reputation. Outwardly at least Marcham it is likely to argue that that it supports local businesses and works in partnership with suppliers, adopts ethical procurement policies with transparent payment terms and conditions agreed in advance, and has grievance procedures available to unhappy suppliers.

A lack of personal ethics might lead individual managers to abuse their position or make threats to suppliers and Marcham must ensure it creates an ethical culture and has procedures in place to deal with such inappropriate behaviour.

Note that the OFT has the power to act if it believes that a firm in a dominant position within an industry is abusing its monopoly power.

Finally it is worth pointing out that the newspaper article may be guilty of sensationalism and some of the criticisms may be unfounded.

Examiner's comments:

Requirement 23.2 asked candidates to discuss the ethical issues raised by the newspaper article in respect of Marcham's customer loyalty card and its treatment of suppliers. This requirement was often not well answered. Weaker candidates failed to apply their knowledge of ethics (in terms of transparency, fairness and corporate responsibility) to the situation provided and a significant number addressed the issues in terms of the commercial consequences of these actions and/or how to manage bad publicity, rather than the ethical implications.

Many answers were extremely one-sided. Weaker candidates adopted the approach that Marcham was acting extremely unethically, was breaching the Data Protection Act in using customer data for other purposes and was intimidating suppliers with its behaviour. Whilst there was merit in some of these propositions, better candidates contrasted this with the fact that customers do have some choice in providing their data and can choose whether they wish their information to be shared with third parties. In addition, Marcham does have significant bargaining power and influence and, whilst there is an obligation for Marcham to act responsibly, what it was doing with suppliers was not illegal and not uncommon within the industry.

The strongest candidates questioned the reliability of the newspaper report.

24 Quantum Agencies Ltd (December 2010)

Marking guide

	Knowledge	Skill	Marks
24.1 PESTEL	4	8	11
24.2 Evaluate performance of QA compared to 20X7	–	14	12
24.3 Merits and problems of strategic alliance (Proposal 1 GTA)	2	5	7
24.4 Proposal 2 (Terra)			
(a) Performance comparison	2	5	
(b) Benefits and problems	3	4	
			14
	11	36	44

General comments:

This scenario related to a medium-sized, upmarket estate agency, QA with 20 branches. After a number of years of growth in the industry, the recession in the property market has made trading conditions for estate agents difficult. The performance of QA has deteriorated and the two owner-directors are considering two proposals to improve matters. Proposal 1 is to close some branches and enter into a joint venture with a local firm of solicitors, GTA. Proposal 2 is to merge with a rival firm of estate agents, Terra, then rationalise the branch network. Performance data was provided for QA is respect of 20X7 and 20Y0 and also for Terra in respect of 20Y0.

24.1 PESTEL

Political

Political influences relate to the extent to which it is government policy to support the housing market (social housing, owner occupied housing, increased 'new builds') for example in the form of local and national governments' incentives (taxes, grants) and reductions in regulations which are a deterrent to house purchase.

Also, however, given the dependence of the housing market on the prosperity of individuals, the success of a government's economic policies is likely to impact on the housing making.

Economic

The factors affecting the estate agent industry are very closely linked to prosperity and activity in the residential housing market.

One of the major factors that has influenced the industry was the recession, as estate agent sales are strongly dependent on house sales, which in turn are closely correlated with economic prosperity.

The housing market has suffered severely in the recession as disposable incomes have fallen and economic confidence to make major financial commitments has been reduced (eg through redundancies, pay freezes, and general economic uncertainty).

Adverse credit market conditions have meant obtaining mortgage credit is more difficult, although lower interest rates have reduced the cost of credit with some low borrowing rates in evidence.

Social

The increasing population and the change in demographics have expanded the long run potential growth of the housing market. Social trends can also affect the types of houses (eg single dweller or large houses) and the balance between purchased and rented accommodation.

Technological

Increased usage of the internet, and other electronic means of communication, is a threat as a substitute sales channel for direct transactions between buyer and seller without the need for an intermediary estate agent.

Also however internet technology is an opportunity to advertise the stock of each estate agent more effectively to a wider audience.

Ecological/environmental

The requirement for increased energy efficient homes can be both a capital cost to new buyers but also a potential cost saving in energy bills. This may change both the quantity and types of housing sold, but also require estate agents to become more knowledgeable about energy issues.

The continued regulation for an energy efficiency certificate makes buyers and sellers conscious of the environmental factors in addition to energy costs.

Legal

Legal issues can be both a benefit and a cost to the industry. Legislation may directly affect the practices of estate agents, but also impact upon the housing market.

The energy efficiency certificates have been a cost to sellers and thus may have deterred them from putting their houses on the market. However the certificates may have encouraged buyers by reducing uncertainty.

Examiner's comments:

This requirement was generally well answered, with most candidates covering all six elements of the PESTEL framework and generally including appropriate factors under each heading. However, some candidates did not relate their comments specifically to the estate agency industry and discussed only the property market. Some discussions were very well developed, with candidates identifying the issues in the question and being able to explain their impact. Some answers missed out the ecological and environmental impacts completely, even though the new energy efficient certification procedures were mentioned in the question. Poorer answers did not cover all six elements individually, sometimes combining political and legal and/or including wrong content under certain headings. Poorer answers were also characterised by a lack of detail, with only one or two brief points under each heading.

24.2 Data analysis

	Quantum		Terra		Industry
	20X7	20Y0	20Y0	20X7	20Y0
Average value per property (000s)	300	250	250	203	162
% fees earned	75	69.2	69		
% fees from other services	25	30.8	31.0		
% profit/sales	16.7	1.5	−5.7		
Branch costs (000s)	8,500	5,000	7,200		
Total costs (000s)	10,000	6,400	9,200		

QA change data

% change in fees	(45.8)
% change in profits	(95)
% change in sales transactions	(25)
% change in branch costs	(41)
% change in total costs	(36)

Data per branch

Fees from sales (000s)	450	225	200
Other fees (000s)	150	100	90
Total fees (000s)	600	325	290
Costs (000s)	425	250	240
Profit per branch (000s)	175	75	50
Number of sales made	100	75	83.3
Number of employees	7	6	5
Number of properties on books	30	35	40

Data per sale made

Total fee per sale (000s)	6	4.3	3.48
Sales fee per sale (000s)	4.5	3	2.4
Branch cost per sale (000s)	4.25	3.33	2.88

Other data

Sales made: average prop held	3.33	2.14	2.08		
Sales revenue per employee (000s)	85.7	54.17	58		
Sales made per employee (no. of properties)	14.3	12.5	16.67		
House price per sale (000s)	300	250	250	203	162
% commission on sales	1.5%	1.2%	0.96%		

> ### Tutorial note:
>
> The detail of the data analysis is more than would be expected from any one candidate but reflects the range of data that may be used by candidates generally.

There is clearly a very substantial deterioration in Quantum's overall company performance between 20X7 and 20Y0.

The fall in fees of almost 46% was a very significant reduction in the level of trade. Due to the fixed nature of many costs, the total cost fell by only 36% resulting in a fall in profit before tax of 95%. In comparing the performance at branch level with the overall picture for the company there is little additional information provided as the branch network was maintained at 20 branches and thus it is a linear picture of the overall situation.

A factor in the reduction in performance is the fall in the number of properties sold of 25% from 2,000 to 1,500. However, this reduction needs to be compared to the fall in the volume of transactions in the UK industry generally, in order to isolate industry effects.

In terms of obtaining houses under contract (ie on its books) QA has done well as the average number of houses available for sale has increased by 12.5% from 600 to 700. However, in terms of the company's ability to sell these houses, performance has been poor as properties sold have declined by 25% from 2,000 to 1,500. This implies that in 20X7 it took on average about 110 days to sell each house ([600/2,000] × 365 days). However in 20Y0 it took about 170 days ([700/1,500] × 365 days).

Also the fall in the volume of sales is less than the fall in fees generated so there has been pressure on pricing as well as on volumes.

The key assessment in measuring performance and assessing its causes is therefore to measure the extent to which the decline in the performance in QA can be explained by the decline in the industry performance, which is uncontrollable, and how much it may be due company specific factors.

There is clearly an industry effect on QA in terms of the general fall in sales volumes, but there has also been an industry effect in falling house prices. For QA the average property sold has fallen by 16.7% from £300,000 to £250,000. Whereas, for the industry, the average property sold has fallen by 20.2% from £203,000 to £162,000. This may reflect the local housing market for QA or may be a failure to continue to attract higher value house sales.

While QA has, along with the rest of the industry, suffered a decline in sales volumes, it appears to have done so despite reducing its effective commission charges below 1.5%. In 20X7 its average commission was 1.5% implying there were no discounts. In 20Y0 however the average commission was 1.2% (a 20% reduction) as a consequence of the discounting policy.

The adverse impact in the fees reduction % is magnified by the fall in the average property price such that the fall in commission per sale made fell by one third from £4,500 in 20X7 to £3,000 in 20Y0.

Fees from other services remain around the same proportion of total fees in 20X7 compared to 20Y0. This appears to have suffered in the same way as may be expected if the property sales are falling which is likely to be the revenue driver for other sales.

Examiner's comments:

This requirement was well answered on the whole, showing continued improvement in candidates' ability to deal with data analysis. Most answers included sufficient quantitative analysis of the data to assist in making some relevant comments on the decline in performance. The best responses focused on the relationship between sales volume decline, decreases in house prices and the decrease in the percentage commission earned. Poorer answers tended to ignore cause and effect relationships in that they provided a commentary on what had happened to key figures, but failed to provide further computations (such as ratios) to break down how it had happened or to provide any detailed explanation of why it had happened.

24.3 Merits and problems of a merger with GTA – Proposal 1

The strategic alliance with GTA offers the opportunity to save most of the costs of maintaining five branches while attempting to link the QA brand with that of GTA.

The disadvantages are that one third of the commission would be lost and the volume of trade may be lower if vendors are not able to visit the estate agent's premises and receive the level of service which was previously provided.

In pure financial terms, assuming a best case scenario that no customers are lost under the new arrangement, if the new arrangement would 'save about 75% of our branch costs' then the saving per branch would be £187,500 (£250,000 × 75%). The loss of fees would be £108,333 (£325,000 × 33.33%) assuming the agreement applies to all fees.

An alternative calculation would be to assume they only give away the commission and that as the average commission for 20Y0 is 1.2% they are giving away 0.5 and keeping 0.7:

The loss then becomes 0.5/1.2 × £225,000 = £93,750

However there is also a significant risk that there will be a loss in trade volume arising from QA not maintaining its own premises. Market research would need to be carried out to assess the magnitude of this potential loss.

The fee sharing agreement allows a half percent to GTA, but if there is a discount to the customer this would appear to be out of QA's 1% in full, thereby representing a disproportionate reduction in fee.

A source of revenue may be that GTA should pay to QA a percentage of the legal fees it earns from QA clients.

Other issues to consider are:

- The need to build a working relationship with a different, but complementary, type of business

- An alliance can be reversed beyond a contractually agreed period if the market recovers, unlike a merger

- There are likely to be exit costs (eg redundancies, lease termination costs) but also some minor exit benefits from the sale of surplus assets arsing from branch closures (Note. As the properties are leased they will not be surplus assets)

Examiner's comments:

Most answers provided a general qualitative evaluation of the merits and disadvantages of the proposed strategic alliance, often relating discussion to generic features of such alliances. Only a minority of candidates addressed, in any detail, the specific terms of the arrangement in the scenario by attempting financial calculations of savings and fee loss arising from the alliance and indicating the disproportionate drop in commission for QA arising from the fee sharing proposal.

24.4 (a) Comparison of the performance of QA and Terra

Key differences between QA and Terra which make performance comparisons more difficult are: the larger branch network of Terra; and its different business model of low price, low cost service provision.

In terms of size it therefore appears more valid, initially at least, to compare performance at the branch level in order to compare like with like.

Both companies operate in a similar geographical market, but also appear to operate in the same sector of that market as they both have an average property sales price of £250,000.

In financial terms the fees per branch are greater for QA at £325,000 compared to £290,000 for Terra. Terra has some cost advantage with cost per branch of £240,000 compared to QA's £250,000. Nevertheless, the profit per branch of £75,000 for QA is greater than the £50,000 per branch for Terra.

In operational terms, Terra appears to be more successful in attracting new properties onto its books with 1,200 in all (40 per branch) compared to only 700 for QA (35 per branch). This may be a reflection of the lower effective commission rate of 0.96% for Terra compared to 1.2% for QA.

In 20Y0 Terra also made more sales per branch at 83.3 compared to QA at 75. However this is only 11% more sales per branch compared to 71.4% more properties on the books available to sell. As a consequence, Terra appears to sell a lower proportion of the properties on its books than QA. However the figure of average properties on the books may be misleading as it depends on the time taken to sell and the realism of the prices being asked by vendors.

The proportion of fees from other services is around the same for each company and thus does not appear to impact on an assessment of relative performance in any significant way.

In overall financial terms, the branches of QA generate a profit of £1.5m (£75,000 × 20) which, after head office costs of £1.4m, reduces overall profit to £100,000.

The branches of Terra also generate a profit of £1.5m (£50,000 × 30) but, after higher head office costs of £2m, there is a loss of £500,000.

It is clear therefore that in pure financial terms QA has overall outperformed Terra, but nevertheless there are serious questions about the performance of both companies.

(b) Benefits and problems of a merger with Terra. Advice on merger

Both QA and Terra operate in the same industry and therefore share many of the same core competences.

The business models are however significantly different. QA purports to operate in the upper end of the market, in terms of service provided, while Terra is a low cost provider. If a merger takes place there is therefore the potential for brand confusion with customers as to the positioning of the new company. A clear strategy will be needed for the new firm in terms of pricing and quality of the provision.

There are some synergies that would be gained from a merger. Potentially the closure of one head office would save significant costs as many activities would be duplicated. Similarly, in the towns where there are two branches, one may be closed to save costs. However, it does not follow from this that all the sales will be transferred from the previous businesses to the new branch. Each of QA's branches 'is located in towns where there are normally two or three branches of other estate agents'. Where one branch is closed some potential customers may be attracted to the rival estate agents.

Also, although the branches are held under operating leases, these may be of significant duration and there may be exit costs in terminating the lease either by a period of vacant possession or in terms of a sub lease on adverse terms.

In terms of a best case scenario, one head office could serve the new company at the existing cost of Terra's head office of £2m. If all customers are retained in the ten towns where one branch is closed then there could be a saving of £2.4 million (£240,000 × 10 taking the lower average branch cost of Terra).

The best case scenario would then be the existing contributions from branches:

QA	£1.5
Terra	£1.5
Branch cost savings	£2.4m
Head office costs	(£2.0m)
Profit before tax	£3.4m

In terms of cost savings this is optimistic, but nevertheless even with more modest savings there is potential for the merged entity to make significant profit. Economies of scale in a number of functions are likely to exist, but not to the extent that the head office or a branch could be closed with costs maintained at the previous level of only one entity.

While Terra is a larger estate agent chain than QA this appears to yield little benefit as it is loss making. Also, while it is larger, there do not appear to be significant assets in either company as branches are held under operating leases. Indeed, if branches held under operating leases were originally entered into at the peak of the market, the company may be bound into excessive and onerous rental contracts representing an effective liability rather than an asset.

If the general UK industry is about to recover, then there is more potential for revenue generation and further increased profit, but positioning within a merged entity may not be ideal, particularly given the different business models.

Governance is a key issue as the shareholders would be split 50:50 and this may make decision making difficult where the coalition is split evenly in this way. Overall the most important issue is integrating the two companies' strategies where market positioning and business models are so different. This will be important in establishing the new brand.

Advice

Overall, in concept, an alliance or a merger may yield benefits given the reduced volume of activity in the recession. In each case however the terms of the agreement and the proposed partners may be worth further consideration and negotiation. As it stands neither proposal seems particularly favourable either in the current downturn or in terms of strategic positioning for a recovery.

Examiner's comments:

In (a) answers were variable in quality, with only a minority providing calculations on a per branch basis. Poorer answers thereby displayed confusion over the relative performance of QA and Terra, with the poorest minority suggesting that Terra's performance was better overall. Even better efforts sometimes fell into the same trap, to a degree, but then qualified their answers in light of the fact that Terra is forecasting losses. It was apparent that, whilst candidates are comfortable producing basic data analysis calculations, answers often lack more detailed quantitative and qualitative analysis to explain underlying causes of differences.

In (b), answers tended to polarise, with weaker attempts referring only to generic benefits of mergers, while better attempts focused on the terms of the specific proposal in the question. The majority provided direct advice as to whether or not the merger should go ahead in their conclusions, but this advice frequently took the form of a one-line assertion rather than a reasoned position on the issue.

25 SkinDeepe plc (December 2010)

Marking guide

	Knowledge	Skill	Marks
25.1 Mendelow	2	8	9
25.2 Barriers to change	2	6	8
25.3 KPI	2	4	6
25.4 Response to Tatton	3	8	10
	9	26	33

General comments:

The scenario in this question relates to a company which manufactures and markets skin creams and lotions. 75% of sales are under the SD brand but the remaining 25% are to a single large retailer customer, Tatton, using its own brand. Difficult trading conditions have caused the company to implement a cost reduction plan. This involves, in Phase 1, closing one UK factory and outsourcing production to a Chinese company, Huang, with immediate effect. If this is successful then in one year's time Phase 2 will be implemented which involves closing the other UK factory and also outsourcing packaging and distribution to Huang. After being informed of these proposals, Tatton has written to SkinDeepe expressing concerns about quality assurance and the reliability of delivery times.

Candidates were required to:

- Identify and justify the positions of key stakeholders in the Mendelow power-interest matrix, in respect of the proposed changes

- Explain how barriers to change may differ between Phase 1 and Phase 2

- Identify and explain key performance indicators to monitor the performance of the outsourcing company, Huang, in Phase 1

- Provide a response to the letter from Tatton raising concerns

25.1 Factory A employees

Power – Low

Interest – High negative

Factory A employees have high negative interest as they are under immediate threat of losing their jobs.

The power of Factory A employees to stop or moderate any closure decision is limited. If the entire UK workforce is united, then significant costs to SD can arise from disruption. Given however that sales and marketing jobs are not under threat then there may be limited co-operation in industrial action from these employees – unless they perceive themselves to be under threat from unannounced changes.

Once Phase 1 is implemented, Factory B employees are likely to be affected, but have a year to find alternative work, so they may not support Factory A employees in resisting closure during Phase 1.

Given that Factory A workers have short term contracts they have little contractual protection or other powers to resist change.

Perversely, if the redundancy payments are sufficiently high, some employees may favour redundancy to continued employment and thus have a positive interest in the plan (eg if they were going to leave anyway).

Factory B employees

Power – Moderate

Interest – High negative

Factory B employees have high negative interest in Phase 2 of the plan as they are under threat of losing their jobs when it is implemented in one year.

They are also likely to have a high negative interest in Phase 1 as this may be perceived as being a very probable stepping stone to Phase 2.

The power of Factory B employees to stop or moderate any closure decision is very limited, but is probably slightly greater than Factory A employees. Once Phase 1 is implemented SD still needs Factory B employees for a year until Huang is in a position to carry out packaging. This gives them slightly more power but ultimately there may be little to be achieved.

The individuals making up the 30 employees transferred to head office will be less resistant to the change once it has been announced who they are.

Tatton

Power – High

Interest – Moderate

Given that 25% of SD's sales in volume terms are with Tatton they have considerable power over SD and are likely to be in a position to influence the decision to source production in China. The cost savings from transferring production are unlikely to compensate for losing 25% of sales. As their letter specifies, they will, as a minimum, need assurances, if products are to be manufactured overseas, as to quality and delivery schedules.

Tatton is only moderately interested in the production transfer as skincare products manufacture is a competitive market, with a range of alternative suppliers being available if Tatton fails to deliver. Nevertheless, SD is currently Tatton's preferred supplier for presumably good reasons, so there may be a moderate wish to continue the relationship, despite the concerns expressed in their letter.

The uncertainty over quality and supply may mean that they have a negative moderate interest in the proposal. However, Tatton may also be positively interested in the decision, if part of the cost savings made by SD are to be passed on to Tatton.

Examiner's comments:

This requirement was well answered on the whole. Most displayed a good understanding of Mendelow's framework. The application part of the question was quite variable with candidates producing a range of positionings within the matrix for each stakeholder's power and interest. This variability in the conclusions drawn by candidates is acceptable if it is supported by appropriate reasoning.

25.2 The closure of a factory is an extreme form of change where the barriers that can be put in place by individuals and groups are limited.

A key difference between Phase 1 and Phase 2 is timing. Irrespective of differences in the nature and culture of Factory A and Factory B, Phase 2 comes one year later so there is greater opportunity for employees in Factory B to resist change over time.

Aside from timing, a series of cultural barriers may exist to resist change. There are to be fundamental changes in the structure of SD as it moves from a manufacturer of its products alongside marketing, to become a leaner marketing organisation that outsources most other key functions, including production and distribution.

This threatens power structures by the redistribution of decision-making authority and resources, and the changing of lines of communication. This will impact on the roles of employees in head office as well as in the factories (though perhaps not so fundamentally). Phase 1 is likely to give people an insight into the changes and determine whether they are favourably or adversely affected. Phase 2 is more likely to extend the established trend of structural change so there may be less fear of the unknown.

Group inertia may block change where the changes are inconsistent with the norms or where they threaten stakeholder interests. In this respect Factory B appears a more organised and cohesive group to resist change and is closer to the norms of head office (if only in geographical proximity and length of service).

Examples of group resistance include:

- Strikes and other forms of resistance to change implementation by staff.
- Suppliers taking legal action for contract termination.
- Gathering the support of other groups to resist change.

There are also personal barriers which affect individuals and result in them seeing the change as a threat. This may affect not only the factory that is closed but also the employees in head office where there are likely to be substantial changes in work practices and also redundancies of old skills in favour of new skills.

Phase 2 will demonstrate a significant period of uncertainty for many individuals (eg if they will be part of the group offered alternative positions in head office or in China) hence there is more scope for individual resistance and disruption. Phase 1 is much quicker and hence the period of uncertainty and opportunity for resistance is less.

Examiner's comments:

Answers to this part varied in standard significantly. There were mainly two approaches. One was purely knowledge based and explained, in general terms, the various barriers to change such as group inertia, cultural barriers and structural barriers, defining what each meant. The second approach was very scenario focussed and discussed barriers such as skills of the workforce, the impact of moving production to China and the problems with the distribution network. The best responses related the scenario discussion to generic barriers, drawing comparisons between the phases as well as recognising the importance of the sequencing of events and timing.

25.3 Quality of product

Maintenance of quality is a key factor in making the outsourcing successful. Any cost advantage gained would be quickly eroded if reduced quality leads to reduced sales. It is therefore important to provide metrics to measure various aspects of quality.

- Number of defective batches delivered (measures the proportion of batches of unacceptable quality)
- Consumer satisfaction surveys with the smell, texture and effectiveness of products (measures the extent to which consumers are happy with average quality, perhaps by comparison to the results of any previous surveys that are available from when products were made in the UK)

- Satisfaction reports from Tatton (feedback from the major customer which may survey its own consumers, or sales levels)

- SD quality management procedures satisfaction levels compared to previous in-house production (looking at internal measures of quality control within the factory)

Distribution

- Number of late deliveries (pre ordered) (measure fact, length and reason for delays)

- Ability to respond to short term orders (assess the minimum lead times. This may vary by product but also by volume – eg small volumes could be flown from China if this was key to a customer's relationship such as Tatton)

- Number of goods damaged or perishing in transit (measure amount, cost and reason for damage)

Price

- Correct invoicing (number of errors discovered)
- Conformity with contracted prices (measure variances)

Examiner's comments:

This part was surprisingly poorly answered, overall, particularly given the broad clues provided in the question in the memo from Tatton regarding costs, quality and reliability of delivery. A significant minority did not provide specific measures and merely talked around the subject. Also, those who attempted to produce a Balanced Scorecard often missed some key measures.

25.4 To: Tatton plc
From: Skin Deepe plc
Date: 13 December 20Y0
Subject: Outsourcing plans

Product quality assurance

Quality assurance procedures are being put in place to ensure there is no loss in product quality from the outsourcing arrangement. Specifically:

- Care and due diligence has been undertaken in selecting Huang as a quality provider of our manufacturing needs.

- A service level agreement provides benefits and costs to Huang from the quality of the product delivered which will lead to strong incentives.

- SD staff in the UK and China will be appointed to new quality management positions to monitor the quality of Huang's processes and output.

- Our approach is one of quality assurance which focuses on the way a product or service in produced. Procedures and standards are devised with the aim of ensuring defects are eliminated (or at least minimised) during the production process, rather than detected and corrected afterwards.

- Once the goods arrive in the UK there will be additional quality checks made by newly appointed employees.

Distribution

It is recognised that there will be a delay in transporting manufactured goods from China to the UK such that short term orders cannot be directly supplied from China within a reasonable period.

We have 33 product lines and it is our intention to hold all 33 lines packaged with the Tatton branding in the UK sufficient to satisfy a wide range of variable quantity demands by Tatton.

To this end, from next year we are outsourcing our distribution systems and inventory holdings to a reputable distribution company in the UK, Fell plc. They will hold and deliver inventories on SD's instructions at short notice to meet your needs.

Statement of relationship

Overall our view is that our relationship with Huang is one of strategic procurement and is therefore the development of a true partnership between SD and a supplier of strategic value. The arrangement is intended to be long-term, single-source in nature and addresses products, materials, development, capacity and delivery.

This recognises that the need for, and benefits of, establishing close links with companies in the supply chain. This has led to our view of an 'integrated supply chain' with Huang.

I hope this reassures you that we will continue to deliver the highest quality of product and level of service.

Examiner's comments:

The communication style adopted by candidates was generally good, adopting the format and approach of a letter to a major customer. However, answers were often brief and sometimes did little more than mention that a service level agreement was in place and that existing staff would move. There was frequently no explanation provided of assurance of quality or due diligence.

26 Heaton Home (December 2010)

Marking guide

	Knowledge	Skill	Marks
26.1 Mission statement and benefifs of a mission statement	2	4	6
26.2 Risks and managing risks	4	6	10
26.3 Ethical issues	3	4	7
	9	14	23

General comments:

This scenario relates to a not-for-profit charity (HH) which operates a residential care home for elderly people who have lived locally. The house was gifted by a rich individual, with the gift be subject to conditions for resident care and eligibility, and for maintenance of the property. The home is run by trustees, but is partially funded by local government. The number of residents has dropped recently which is placing the viability of the home in question. Possible withdrawal of local government funds as a consequence of decreased resident numbers is a major issue. There are also problems of deterioration of the property. A new manager has been appointed and reviewed the position of HH. The local government trustee has also proposed: an increase in fees; wider geographical eligibility; and reduced staffing to save costs.

Candidates were required to:

* Prepare a mission statement for HH and explain why this might be useful
* Identify the home's key risks and describe how these might be managed
* Discuss the ethical issues of the proposals of the local government trustee

26.1 (1) 'To offer high quality, affordable, residential nursing care in a safe and caring environment to elderly residents of the town Northport.

The board and its managers will work together with staff, volunteers, local government and the local community to deliver this service and to provide finance to reduce the cost for residents.'

(2) A mission statement is a useful formal document for incorporating the objectives and values of an organisation and to communicate these to internal and external stakeholders.

They can include: purpose, strategy, policies and values

For a not-for-profit organisation, such as HH, where there is no clear profit motive, the mission statement can provide clarity as to the objectives of the organisation for key stakeholders and how these may be achieved.

Examiner's comments:

This requirement was generally well answered. The majority, but not all, provided an attempt at a mission statement and were able to give appropriate reasons as to why one would prove useful for HH. Poorer efforts produced mission statements which were either too brief, being little more than advertising slogans, or far too long. Better answers referred to the need for the inclusion of purpose, strategy, policies and values, particularly in the context of a not-for-profit organisation, often with conflicting stakeholder interests. Weaker answers provided only a general justification for a mission statement without referring to the nature and circumstances of HH.

26.2 Key risks

The fall in demand for places in the home represents a key loss of income to HH both from the residents themselves and the per capita fee paid by local government.

The table below indicates that a surplus of £50,000 is made at current fees levels when all the places are full. However, at the current level of occupancy of 45, a deficit of £25,000 per annum is being made. It is not immediately clear whether this deficit on an accruals basis is equivalent to the cash deficit but, if so, the cash reserves of £100,000 would only last four years.

More significantly, if occupancy declines further to 40 residents, then the local authority will withdraw one third of its lump sum funding. In these circumstances HH would not be viable.

Management of risk

The reasons for the fall in demand need to be established. A key feature could be the increase in price two years ago. While this was intended to raise more funds, it may not have done so if the price change was the sole cause of the reduction from 50 to 45.

Under this assumption, the gain in revenue was £67,500 (45 × £1,500) from the residents who stayed and paid the additional fee. The loss in revenue was also £67,500 (5 × (£5,000 + £8,500)). Given that the costs are 'are almost entirely fixed costs' there was therefore no net revenue gain.

In managing this risk, the sensitivity of the residents to price needs to be explored to aim, as far as possible, to the fill the 50 beds while earning some fee from the marginal residents (eg waiving of some fees for needy local residents).

Alternative, non-price, explanations for the reduced number of residents also need to be explored (eg reductions in service levels through fewer volunteers, decaying of the fabric of the building, competition, local reputation).

At the margin of 40 residents the risk is significant of losing £100,000 of local authority funding. At the margin this could be controlled by (in the extreme) giving away a few free places to lift the average above 40.

The clause in the gift limiting the home for the benefit of 'elderly people who have lived in the local town for ten years or more' could be explored with the trustees. The definitions of 'elderly' and 'local town' could be explored to see if the potential resident base could be widened. (See 26.3 below.)

The building

A condition of the original gift was that the mansion should be 'maintained in good order'. There is a risk that the 'deterioration in the fabric of the building affecting its appearance' may be in breach of this element of the gift conditions and there may be consequences for HH for its rights over the continued use of the building.

Management of risk

The terms of the gift need to be clarified to see if there is a definition of 'maintained in good order'. Discussions could be held with the trustees to establish their view and the likely course of action they would take.

The necessary repairs to meet the conditions of the gift should be fully costed and perhaps a special appeal for donations could be launched that had a focus of maintaining the building.

Volunteers

The reduction in the number of volunteers is not only a financial risk in needing partially to replace them with paid employees, but also a risk in terms of the quality of the service provided. It may also be a reflection of the esteem with which the home is held in the local community. If the support of the community is reducing this may have a significant impact on the home's role, charitable contributions and wider support.

Management of risk

- Exit interviews could be held to explore the reasons why people have ceased to volunteer or reduced their hours
- The role volunteers play and how they are treated by paid employees could be explored
- A recruitment drive in the local town and local schools could be carried out to raise awareness of the voluntary scheme and promote the home

Current Full capacity 40 residents

	Current	Full capacity	40 residents
Residents (45 × £10,000)	450,000	500,000	400,000
Local authority (45 × £5,000)	225,000	250,000	200,000
Local authority	300,000	300,000	200,000
Donations	250,000	250,000	250,000
Costs	(1,250,000)	(1,250,000)	(1,250,000)
Surplus/(deficit)	(25,000)	50,000	(200,000)

Examiner's comments:

Answers varied in quality. Better candidates identified most of the key risks and attempted to provide guidance as to how they should be managed. Others often only listed the risks without any attempt at consideration of their management. Answers which provided numerical analysis and/or considered price elasticity of demand were in a minority. Only a minority made reference to generic risk management techniques, often using TARA, but often not applying this very well to the scenario.

26.3 The ethical issue of raising the price to residents is that some may not be able to afford the increase and therefore may need to leave the home. Also many potential residents may not be able to take up a place in future. This may be in conflict with the charitable aims of HH providing 'reduced cost' places for the elderly in the area.

There may be an additional ethical issue in terms of the conflict of the objectives of the terms of the gift between maintaining the building and providing care to elderly residents. If the proposed scheme is an appropriate means of funding the repairs then ethically it may discharge the duty of the directors to fulfil this element of the terms of the gift.

The additional funding may also be ethically defensible if it is a means of sustaining the financial viability of HH and ensuring that it can continue to operate as a going concern and fulfil its intended charitable purposes.

Given the evidence of price elasticity (see 26.2 above) raising prices may not secure the additional revenues desired if occupancy levels fall. The local government director has suggested expanding the age range and the geographical area where HH can target residents. The ethical question here is whether this is in accordance with the terms of the gift by Lady Heaton by which managers are bound in using the property.

If the definitions of age and geography are unclear in the terms of the gift then the ethical issue is whether the directors can act against what are perhaps the implied wishes of the founder in order to promote their strategy, even if there is no legal constraint in doing so.

27 Family Entertainment Company plc (March 2011)

Marking guide

	Knowledge	Skill	Marks
27.1 Five forces	3	6	8
27.2 Benefits and risks	2	6	7
27.3 Data analysis	–	17	15
27.4 Market segmentation and pricing	3	6	8
27.5 Ethical issues	3	4	7
	11	39	45

General comments:

The company in this scenario (FEC) is a UK-based company which operates a chain of family-oriented theme parks throughout Western Europe. As its existing market is mature and profitability is under pressure, it is considering expansion by opening up a new theme park in India and is in the process of assessing the potential benefits and risks of this strategy; approaches to marketing and pricing; and issues concerning health and safety. The operations director has suggested that one benefit of the Indian park would be lower annual running costs, especially for labour, and that in addition, because of limited regulation, FEC can reduce its normal expenditure on park safety and ride maintenance.

This question was the mini case, incorporating some data analysis and, at 45 marks, was the longest question on the paper. The requirements were broken down to help candidates in developing answer headings and assessing mark allocation. This was the best attempted of all three questions, with the majority of candidates performing well, showing good knowledge of the models tested and with many demonstrating good data analysis skills. Disappointingly the requirement on ethics (27.5) was poorly done by a significant minority.

27.1 Porter's Five Forces is a model that considers the level of competition in an industry. In addition to the three forces below, there are two others, bargaining power of customers and suppliers.

Threat of entry

The barriers to entry to the theme park industry in Western Europe are high due to high capital cost for rides and also the expense of the site. In addition the potential sites for park development are limited due to scarce supply of land. Finally the maturity of the market, the major brand names and domination by existing multi-national entertainment corporations such as Disney would act as a barrier. The economic climate may also act as a barrier currently since consumers are inclined to spend less and have more constraints on their disposable income. Overall the threat of new entrants in Western Europe is probably low.

Competitive rivalry

Global competition is great in the industry. There are major international players and national/local smaller scale parks. The mature market in Western Europe means competition is intense, companies have to spend money to maintain state of the art rides, sites are difficult to come by (other than through acquisition) and only the most powerful players will survive. The economic climate means companies must fight even harder as consumers spend less money. Many of the multinationals are better placed to withstand competition as they gain marketing benefits from linking rides to TV/film characters, have access to wider resources and are more diversified – offering a wide range of entertainment (TV, films, retail outlets, parks). As a result of all these factors competitive rivalry is intense.

Threat of substitutes

There is a wide variety of other tourist attractions, cultural and entertainment offerings, all competing for a share of household leisure spend, thus the threat of substitutes offering an alternative 'day out' is quite high. Some of these alternatives are less affected by poor weather and the impact of the recession may be to encourage some people to switch to cheaper alternatives for a day out.

However there is an element of thrill/risk associated with theme parks which may mean these other leisure pursuits are not perfect substitutes.

Conclusion

The forces examined suggest that the theme park industry in Western Europe is fiercely competitive and that there is pressure on its long-run profit potential.

Examiner's comments:

Requirement 27.1 asked candidates to prepare three sections of a Porters Five Forces analysis for the theme park industry in Western Europe – threat of entry, competitive rivalry and substitutes.

Answers were of a good standard, with most candidates extracting the key information from the scenario and using it to assess the strength of each particular force; the majority concluding that the threat of entry was relatively low but competition was fierce and there were many substitutes for a 'day out'. High marks were awarded to those who, in addition, summarised the overall impact of the three forces on the potential for long term sustainable profits in the theme park industry in Western Europe. Some weaker candidates confused competitive rivalry and substitutes and a very small minority answered the wrong question by applying the analysis to the theme park industry in India. It was noticeable that some weaker candidates wrote far more than was necessary for the 8 marks available, causing themselves unnecessary time pressure on other parts of the paper (normally question 3).

27.2 Proposed expansion strategy

Benefits of expansion:

- Mature market in UK/US so opportunity to expand into market at different stage in product life cycle
- Lack of further development opportunities in existing markets due to scarcity and cost of land means FEC needs new markets such as India
- Availability of land in India reduces barriers to FEC's entry
- Indian government policy appears favourable and there may be incentives to invest
- Increasing economic growth and wealth of local population provides a ready market
- No existing international competition – existing parks are small and often simple, so FEC would be a dominant player and have competitive advantage, particularly as a first mover
- FEC's values fit with the family culture in India
- Better spread of risk as diversified business worldwide so not just exposed to macroeconomic factors in Europe. Also the business is seasonal but the seasonality in India may differ from that in Europe, creating better smoothing of cashflows
- May improve earnings/profits to keep shareholders happy

Risks of overseas expansion

- Significant investment required in infrastructure

- Opportunity costs of funds required to invest overseas

- European/US theme park model is untested in India. FEC may need to adapt product model culturally to ensure local success (global v local) but may lack knowledge to do this. Existing parks are quite different and appear to have a local cultural/historical theme. Appropriate food, beverage and merchandise may be quite different from European parks

- FEC may lack experience/knowledge of how to do business outside Europe and there may be hidden costs of which it is currently unaware

- Impact on profitability of factors/risks outside FEC's control – foreign exchange, government policy

- The government may remove its support and/or the licence to operate if it believes FEC are compromising on health and safety

- Indian climate is very different from Europe. There is a possibility of natural disasters – floods, monsoons – so FEC may not be able to operate all year round

- High exit barriers

- Threat of expropriation of assets – may mitigate via possible JV/government equity stake and also by demonstrating local wealth generation via employment etc

- Sensitivity of tourist industry to strikes/war/exchange rates/terrorism

- Other multinationals may not have entered the market either because they believe it is not viable or because the risks are too high

- Lucrative emerging market may attract other major players increasing competition in the longer term

- If the Indian venture fails this may have a damaging effect on FEC's reputation and European parks

Conclusion

The industry in Western Europe is highly competitive and FEC is under pressure from its shareholders to address falling EPS. The fact that a number of other operators are expanding in Asia and South America suggests expansion outside its traditional markets may be a suitable strategy. It needs to consider the financial projections to determine whether the Indian venture is likely to generate sufficient returns to compensate for the additional risks and uncertainty involved.

Examiner's comments:

Requirement 27.2 asked candidates to discuss the benefits and risks of the proposed expansion. Again answers were of a good standard with most candidates extracting information from the scenario and explaining the implications for FEC in the context of benefits and risks. Better candidates used their knowledge of overseas expansion to generate additional points and concluded that, subject to appropriate financial returns, the strategy seemed a sensible one, given the challenges faced in Western Europe and the shareholders' concerns about falling EPS. Weaker candidates merely regurgitated points from the scenario or discussed generic risks, such as cultural and foreign exchange risk, without applying them to the specifics of the scenario.

27.3 (a) Profit forecast

Attendance	Number of months	Visitors	Total attendance
High Season	3	90,000	270,000
Mid Season	5	75,000	375,000
Low Season	4	50,000	200,000
Visitor numbers pa			845,000

Revenue	$
Admission 845,000 @ $10	8,450,000
Food and merchandise @ $10	8,450,000
Total revenue	16,900,000

Variable costs	
Admission 8.45m @ $2	1,690,000
Food and merchandise (8.45m × 0.5)	4,225,000
Total variable costs	5,915,000

Contribution	
Admission (8.45m × 0.8)	6,760,000
Food and merchandise (8.45m × 0.5)	4,225,000
Total contribution (16,900 – 5,915)	10,985,000
Less	
Fixed costs	(9,000,000)
Net profit	1,985,000

(b) Break-even calculations

Annual fixed costs	$9,000,000
Total revenue per visitor (10/0.5)	$20
Contribution per visitor (0.8 × 10) + (0.5 × 10)	$13
Break-even visitors (9m/13)	692,308 visitors

(c) Sensitivity

To fixed costs

Annual fixed costs	$9,000,000
Current estimated net profit	$1,985,000
Fixed costs can increase by 1.985m/9m	22.06%

To admission price

Admission revenue	$8,450,000
Current estimated net profit	$1,985,000
Admission revenue (and hence price) can drop by 1.985m/8.45m	23.5%

Notes

1   Assumes each visitor continues to spend $10 a head on merchandise and food/beverage.

2   The attendance fee is calculated on an average basis. In reality FEC may not charge the same fee at all times of the year or to all visitors.

(d) Commentary and further information

Commentary on figures

On the basis of the estimates the park looks set to make healthy profits, with an average contribution margin of 65% and a net profit of £1.985m once the park is up and running, which represents an 11.7% margin. However it will take a while for the park to be established, considerable investment is required and there may be losses in the first months/year(s) of operation.

In terms of sensitivity to the estimates: The breakeven attendance figure is 692,308 so the estimated attendance of 854,000 gives a margin of safety of 18% (845,000 – 692,308/845,000).

Fixed costs can increase by 22% before the Indian venture becomes loss-making, which would seem to be a reasonable margin of safety. This does however assume that the other estimates for attendance, admission and other revenue and margins are achieved.

Similarly the admission price could fall by 23.5% assuming that other revenues for food and merchandise and other costs remained constant.

Note. Figures given assume that once the park is up and running attendance will be static. As the market is new, the annual attendance is likely to grow whilst the park is being established. It would be more accurate to prepare forecasts of demand year by year.

FEC also need to prepare projections for capital expenditure and set-up costs. Typically given the size of investment FEC would probably use a 10-15 year time period to evaluate the theme park and a cash flow forecast will also be required.

Information to assess accuracy of assumptions

Need to compare results to the performance of FEC's existing parks.

Need to know whether the assumptions are based on European parks or have been tailored to the Indian market – the entrance fee at $10 would probably suggest the latter as even though it is an average, it looks low. However the Indian market may spend a different proportion on food and merchandise than Western Europeans for example.

Fixed costs are high and profits depend on admission numbers and revenues. The key to accurate assessment of prospects is the ability to predict demand. Need results of any market research undertaken to ascertain where estimates have come from for the seasons and the attendance – are these figures based on competitors in India or FEC's experience in Europe? How likely is the attendance to drop below the break-even figure of 692,308?

Park may not be able to be open for 12 months of the year – many parks find it is not viable to open for the low season as operational costs may outweigh the revenues in this period. The seasonality is also likely to be different from Western Europe.

Admission price is an average and in fact may vary depending on age and nature of visitor and time of visit. The amount spent on food/beverages and merchandise per head is also likely to vary. Could benchmark these figures against the prices charged by existing Indian parks.

No detail is given about what is included in fixed costs – is it just the cost of running the park or does it also include depreciation on equipment, interest charges on finance?

Need to also consider:

- Tax
- Exchange rate differences
- Any compliance fees

Examiner's comments:

Requirement 27.3 was the data analysis requirement. Candidates were provided with assumptions regarding estimated attendance figures, admission price, other revenues, and costs in order to produce some financial projections for the Indian park. This requirement was broken down into four clear parts covering: (a) calculation of the park's estimated annual profit (b) break-even analysis in terms of attendance figures (c) sensitivity to fixed costs and admission price and (d) a commentary on the significance of the calculations together with any additional information required. The calculations were designed to highlight that, with high fixed costs and seasonal attendance, profits would be highly dependent on estimated attendance numbers and revenue per visitor.

This requirement tested candidates' ability to apply basic data analysis skills in the context of forecast data. Answers to the calculation elements of this requirement ((a) – (c)) were quite polarised, with a significant number of candidates scoring full marks, but a small minority failing to make all but the briefest attempt.

The performance on the data analysis section of the paper has shown general improvement over recent sittings, although it appears that some candidates were unable to apply their skills in this context, having perhaps been led to expect that data analysis equates to the analysis of historic business performance which, the learning materials are clear, is only one possible area that might be examined.

Almost all candidates attempted the calculation of projected profit, the most common errors arising in the calculation of revenue and costs for food and merchandise. Where candidates made an error with the cost structures or profit figure at this point, they were awarded full credit for using their figures in the subsequent calculations and commentary. There was some variability in candidates' ability to calculate the break-even attendance figure, the most common errors being to base the calculation on revenue rather than contribution, or to ignore the contribution from food and merchandise.

A number of candidates correctly calculated the sensitivity of the profits to estimated fixed costs but were unable to assess the sensitivity of the proposed admission price.

Marks were awarded to those sensible candidates who, despite being unsure of the exact calculation, adopted a 'what if approach' by calculating how much profit would vary for a given change in the relevant estimate.

Even if they had found elements of the calculations demanding, most candidates produced a reasonable commentary on their figures, with many pointing out that the profit projections were highly dependent on the assumptions made and on exchange rates. The strongest candidates also pointed out that, as the figures related to revenues and expenses once the park was fully established, it would take some time to reach this point and that the initial capital expenditure to acquire land and build rides would be considerable.

The additional useful key information from the poorer students was the usual generic list, including requests for breakdowns of cost, cash flows and competitor information. However, the highest scoring answers produced excellent lists of additional information, typically including the need to understand whether the assumptions had been based on a typical European park or tailored to the Indian market, the benefits of market research to confirm seasonality and attendance figures, benchmarking of the admission price and other data against existing Indian parks, and the need to produce forecasts for the set-up period.

27.4 Market segmentation and pricing

Market segmentation is the division of the market into homogenous groups of potential customers. In FEC's case this is likely to be:

- Local residents
- Tourists (domestic and foreign)

FEC may then also choose to sub-divide these groups by income level or age.

The benefit of market segmentation is that FEC can adjust components of the marketing mix to improve returns from each group according to spending potential, location, needs and tastes.

Foreign tourists to India – can capitalise on existing brand, will have sophisticated expectations of rides, attractions, food and merchandise based on prior theme park experiences.

Domestic tourists and local residents – may need or expect a product experience which is more tailored to local culture. Alternatively the attraction of FEC's park may be its Westernised nature.

Tourists are probably prepared to pay more than residents but will offer less opportunity for repeat business and the tourist business is likely to be more seasonal.

Pricing

In the theme park industry there are two approaches to pricing – pay as you go tickets may work better for one group than another.

(1) Pay as you go

This involves visitors paying a small fee on entry to the park then, once inside the park, a separate amount for each ride/attraction. The cost of each ride/attraction is based on its popularity, with the most popular costing up to four times the price of the least popular.

Advantages

- May be more attractive to less wealthy customers as they only pay for what they experience

- Can vary prices etc to cater for changing demand

- More scope for price discrimination

Disadvantages

- People are more conscious of what they are spending so they may limit it
- Need more staff to sell tickets/take money round the park
- Visitors may spend less on food/beverage and merchandise

(2) Single price

This involves visitors paying a single large admission fee for which they receive unlimited use of attractions and rides. Some specific high value attractions may not be included in the price or may incur a premium.

- Easier for customers to budget
- Don't need as many staff at park to take ticket money
- But customers have to pay for rides and attractions they don't want to experience

Price discrimination means setting different prices for a similar product in different markets. The reasoning behind this is that a universal price may be lower than some people eg foreign tourists would be prepared to pay (losing revenue) and higher than others (local residents) can afford (losing volumes). Thus the best strategy is to charge each group the maximum they are prepared to pay. Successful price discrimination relies on segmentation and differing price elasticities of demand.

FEC could operate differential pricing by:

Market segment – eg loyalty schemes for locals who are regular visitors or who purchase annual passes Timing eg peak/off peak – seasonality around festivals/ tourist periods; weekdays vs weekends.

Dynamic pricing – according to levels of demand compared to normal patterns.

Captive product pricing eg for food, beverage and merchandise once in the park.

Other options: loyalty cards, discounts for groups or families, seasonal pricing of admission fee.

Recommend: Suggest a multi-tiered pricing structure to take account of ride popularity, attract customers for repeat visits and increase business during quieter periods.

Tutorial note:

Consideration of the 3 Cs would also be an acceptable approach for discussing pricing.

Examiner's comments:

Requirement 27.4 asked candidates to explain how FEC might segment the market as part of its approach to marketing and also to discuss appropriate pricing strategies.

Most candidates discussed segmentation in terms of domestic residents and tourists and better candidates went on to identify opportunities for breaking these markets down further eg by income or age. Candidates seemed well prepared to talk about pricing and many referred to the benefits of adopting price discrimination to maximise revenues. The highest marks were scored by those candidates who linked their discussions on price to the market segments they had identified.

27.5 Ethics and stakeholder conflict

Ethical issues

Ethics are the moral principles governing or influencing conduct which is deemed acceptable in the society or context in question. Ethics exist at three levels: personal, business and corporate.

- **Personal ethical behaviour** eg the suggestions of the operations director to keep maintenance costs low because the market is not yet developed perhaps calls into question his personal ethics.

- **Business ethics** – the way FEC as a firm behaves. FEC's management needs to consider the ethical implications of its proposed strategies before implementing them. Customers and employees have a right to expect certain standards of ethical behaviour. As a business FEC has an obligation to maintain proper health and safety standards and it is unlikely to be acceptable to take advantage of lower standards or lack of procedures in one country compared to another.

- **Corporate responsibility** is the belief that the firm owes a responsibility to society and its wider stakeholders, not just its shareholders. This links to the discussion of stakeholder conflict below.

In deciding whether the operations director's suggestion raises ethical issues, FEC could adopt the Institute of Business Ethics tests:

- **Transparency** – would FEC mind others knowing that it had decided to reduce maintenance expenditure?

This may depend on whether health and safety is compromised because of the planned level of expenditure. FEC may be planning to spend what they believe is necessary to maintain good health and safety, albeit that this is lower than the levels enforced on them in Europe. If however the motivation was because the current lack of safety standards allowed them to get away with it, then it is likely that FEC would not want the reason for this to come to light.

- **Effect** – Who does the decision affect/hurt?

From a health and safety angle, lack of maintenance may increase the risk of workplace injury to employees and also customer injury in the event of a ride breakdown or accident.

An accident would also have financial consequences for FEC – increased costs of insurance, compensation payments, legal costs – as well as reputational consequences: lost customers, loss of employees, possible loss of licence, knock on effect on image and attendance at European parks.

- **Fairness** – would the decision be considered fair by those affected?

This partly depends on whether the actual level of expenditure is seen as a justifiable business decision, which might take into account cost/benefit analysis, risk assessment and the normal level of expenditure in European parks.

Stakeholder conflict

Stakeholders are groups of people who are interested in what FEC does. In the case of FEC's approach to health and safety this would include internal stakeholders (employees, management), connected stakeholders (shareholders, customers) and external stakeholders (government/regulatory bodies).

Here the issue of maintenance costs highlights the potential for conflict within and between various stakeholder groups:

Shareholders want profitability – indeed the Indian venture is partly to address their concerns about falling EPS – so some may prefer FEC to only spend what is absolutely necessary on maintenance.

The theme park employees, customers and local government may value safety more highly however.

Whilst only local regulation exists at present, the national regulator may publish standards that are more onerous if it feels that FEC is not taking its responsibility for employee and customer safety seriously. Also any safety incident may lead to the withdrawal of government support/licence.

Which stakeholders' interests determine FEC's actions will depend to an extent on their relative power. Clearly FEC's primary focus is to maximise shareholder wealth. However in the context of a new park, customers are very important to success and may choose to go elsewhere if they think their safety is being compromised. Also shareholders may acknowledge that higher levels of expenditure on health and safety in the short term will establish FEC's reputation and ensure government and public support, giving FEC a competitive advantage and higher profits in the long term.

Examiner's comments:

Requirement 27.5 asked candidates to discuss the ethical issues raised by the operations director's comments on health and safety and the potential for stakeholder conflict that might be present. As has been the case with most previous papers, the ethics requirement was often not well answered. Some candidates failed to discuss the ethical issues and simply restricted their answers to stakeholder analysis. Weaker candidates who did cover both areas often failed to demonstrate any knowledge of ethics (in terms of transparency, fairness and corporate responsibility) and addressed the issue in terms of the commercial consequences of cutting back on health and safety and the likely effects in terms of bad publicity and litigation, rather than the ethical implications.

Whilst there was merit in some of these comments, better candidates pointed out the fact that the operations director might be operating legally, within the scope of the existing Indian regulations, but went on to discuss the impact of the proposed strategy in terms of transparency, effect and fairness and whether FEC might be better served by applying a higher standard of corporate responsibility. They then went on to consider the likely interest and influence of various stakeholder groups, including visitors, employees and the Indian government and regulatory authorities.

Many weaker answers were extremely one-sided with a number of candidates implying that all shareholders would be happy to make profits at the expense of the safety of visitors and employees. The strongest candidates concluded that there may not in fact be conflict as shareholders might recognise that setting high standards of health and safety would establish FEC's reputation, capture market share, and ensure government support, leading to long term sustainable profits for the shareholders.

28 MPW Ltd (March 2011)

Marking guide

	Knowledge	Skill	Marks
28.1 Evaluate comments (inc. report)	4	10	13
28.2 Supply chain and performance	4	7	10
28.3 CSFs and KPIs	3	6	8
	11	23	31

28.1 To: The Board of MPW
From: A N Other
Date: March 20Y1
Re: Growth strategy

The purpose of this report is to consider whether MPW's growth strategy has been successful and to make recommendations for improvements in the supply chain, performance measurement and incentive schemes.

Directors' comments

The wholesale phone business is very competitive with narrow margins. In order to be successful MPW needs to operate with high sales volumes, hence the growth strategy would appear in the first instance to be sensible, as is the focus on improved customer service to penetrate the market. Also the board's attempt to gain commitment to the strategy and motivate employees via incentive schemes appears to have led to happy staff and the company has recognised the need to monitor strategy by using KPIs.

In the context of these KPIs, the managing director is right that the strategy has been successful, however achievement of these KPIs has not led to an increase in overall profitability since, according to the MD, net profit has in fact fallen, and MPW needs to understand the reasons for this.

Sales Director's comments

The sales director believes the purchasing strategy is at fault.

MPW's new strategy involves guaranteed next day delivery which will necessitate large amounts of inventory, but if this inventory is not sold quickly it risks becoming obsolete which will reduce profitability.

The fact that the purchasing manager's bonus is based on manufacturer discounts seems to have encouraged the buying of handsets that do not appear to have matched demand – a point raised by the sales director. This is partly due to the fact that the manager may have bought excessive quantities in order to achieve a bulk-buy discount but it is also likely that manufacturers are offering the best discounts on older handset models or models that they know are soon to be upgraded.

It is in the purchasing manager's interests to maximise their bonus by buying the cheapest inventory in large quantities which demonstrates a lack of goal congruence. This has the following impact:

(1) Bulk buying may have generated discounts but will involve increased inventory holding costs (cost of capital tied up, insurance, warehousing) and have a negative effect on profitability and cash flow.

(2) If the discounted handsets can be sold at normal prices then the discount obtained will improve the gross margin. However the fact that over 40% of MPW's inventory is over two months old means that the firm will suffer reduced margins on these models, if indeed it is able to sell them at all. Thus, as highlighted by the MD, it is likely that MPW are making money on some handsets and not others.

The sales team, whose bonus is based on % gross margin, will ensure they only sell items with positive margins (as the sales director comments) and will have little incentive to push sales of these older models if they will at best just recover cost. The longer the inventory is held, the more it is likely to become unsaleable and the write-off of such inventory, particularly if it has been bought in large quantities, will significantly reduce future gross profits.

(3) Inventory that the sales director believes the company could sell (newer, more popular models) is probably not being purchased, since manufacturers are unlikely to be willing to offer discounts on such items. Given the competitive nature of the market and the fact that there are low switching costs for buyers, it is likely that MPW will lose customers to competitors if it consistently fails to meet demand for such items.

Also the more popular items may earn lower margins, but if retailers prefer a one-stop shop, the newer models may act in the same way as a 'loss leader', forming part of a larger order for a range of different, more profitable handsets.

Purchasing director's comments

The purchasing director believes the issue is with the sales strategy. According to the purchasing director the existing customer base has changed its purchasing strategy to take advantage of next day delivery and this has had a damaging effect.

By focussing its attention on gross margin the business is not taking all costs associated with selling the product into account, particularly the costs of processing and distributing orders.

If we consider the financial results for sales to existing customers, MPW may be making the same level of revenue and gross profit as before but, unless it has passed on the extra charges to its customers, MPW will almost certainly have seen a reduction in net profit due to the costs involved in handling more frequent, smaller volume orders and in distributing to retailers daily. This is not just a short term issue and, in answer to the MD's question, MPW may well be losing money on customers placing small orders, if the costs of ordering and distribution outweigh the gross profit per order.

As a result of the sales growth and the sourcing of new retailers, the volume of orders will have increased but the increase in custom may not have been sufficient to offset the increased administration and delivery costs.

Finance Director

Although the targets MPW set are both financial (sales growth and gross margin) and non-financial (% deliveries on-time), they are not looking at the whole picture, which is what the new FD is concerned about.

Ultimately for long term financial success, as well as sales and gross margin, overall profitability is important and the KPIs do not currently take this into account. They also do not consider MPW's internal processes or the company's innovation and learning capabilities. Use of a wider set of measures may have helped the board understand sooner that the strategy was not as successful as first hoped and the reasons behind this (see 28.3 for more details).

A large proportion of MPW's costs are likely to be fixed overheads and these will have increased with the new warehouse facility. As the new strategy has only recently been implemented, it is possible that it will take time to achieve the increase in volumes necessary to cover the additional fixed costs, so the lack of profitability may be a short term issue.

The new FD has also raised the issue of incentives. Incentives are a good way to gain commitment to a strategy and motivate staff but, as discussed above, the current incentives may be causing a lack of goal congruence. For example, if the incentive scheme for the sales team is based on % gross profit then they may go for high price and low volume which could be entirely contrary to the growth strategy.

Conclusion

In the context of the existing KPIs, the strategy has been successful, however the growth in sales and the improved customer service levels have been at the expense of overall profitability. MPW needs to ensure it sets targets that are consistent with the overall objectives of the business and which promote long-term as well as short-term interests.

Examiner's comments:

Requirement 28.1 asked candidates to evaluate the comments made by the directors to explain the unexpected decline in net profit. A minority of candidates started off badly by failing to produce their answers in the required report format.

Strong candidates produced a structured analysis of each director's comments, addressing the key issues, namely: poor inventory control, failure to predict and meet demand, failure to take account of increased selling and administration costs, inappropriate performance incentives causing a lack of goal congruence and the use of a narrow range of performance measures. Thus the strategy has delivered growth in revenue and better service levels for customers but has significantly increased costs for MPW in terms of inventory holding, selling, distribution and bonuses. Weaker candidates reiterated the comments made by the directors in the scenario but failed to link them back to the managing director's question or to use their knowledge of performance management issues to make any insightful comments as to why the situation might have arisen eg the purchasing manager's bonus is based on discounts negotiated from suppliers, so the high inventory holding of older model (potentially obsolete) handsets is likely to have come about because these would be the ones on which suppliers were prepared to give the biggest discounts.

28.2 Recommended improvements to supply chain

Supply chain management (SCM) is the management of all supply activities from the suppliers (in this case the phone manufacturers) through to the customers (the phone retailers).

Key aspects of SCM are:

- Responsiveness – ability to supply customers quickly with the goods they want
- Reliability – ability to meet agreed service standards
- Relationships – better integration between MPW and its suppliers

MPW may want to address the following issues in order to improve its supply chain efficiency and performance:

Co-ordinate purchasing with demand

- MPW need to move to a demand pull rather than cost push system

- Use forecasting for handsets with predictable demand in order to reduce inventories of these items

- Identify which phones are most popular and in short supply and focus efforts accordingly

- Ensure communication and co-ordination of effort between sales and purchasing departments, so they don't buy inventory at a special price unless MPW believes it can market and sell it

- Ascertain minimum order volumes required to make next day delivery viable or pass on increased costs to customers

- Adopt different pricing strategies for fast and slow moving items

Reduce inventory levels

- Co-ordinate pricing and inventory – use promotional pricing, discounts etc to manage fluctuations in demand and to reduce excessive inventory holdings/sell off aged inventory

- Levels of inventory required will depend on lead times for receiving orders from manufacturers and the predictability of demand. There may be scope for JIT system to reduce inventory so that MPW only order from manufacturers in response to retailer demand

Reduce costs

- Use value chain analysis to ascertain cost and value drivers. Profitability can then be improved by focussing on these. Here a key cost driver appears to be the number of orders placed, so MPW should investigate ways of reducing the costs of order processing eg implement an e-procurement system to automate order processing and reduce costs through online ordering, payment and invoicing eg impose a minimum order size/value on customers to ensure that gross profit from the order is sufficient to cover costs of processing and distribution

- Another factor that has increased costs is the new warehouse. If inventory levels are reduced and purchasing is more in line with demand, MPW may find that they do not need so much space. If exit costs in the form of lease penalties and redundancies are high then one possibility may be to sub-let space

Increased use of technology

- Increased use of technology for forecasts and then to track actual demand, orders placed, inventories etc

- Possible use of Enterprise Resource planning (ERP) software to manage the key aspects of the supply chain: product planning, purchasing, inventory control, order tracking

- Consider linking computer systems with those of phone manufacturers/retailers to reduce paperwork and administration

Customer relationship management

- Use of relationship marketing to build longer term relationships with retailers, thereby increasing loyalty, minimising chance of losing customers if MPW does not have inventory, sharing information with customers concerning expected demand

- Emphasis on improving profitability through customer retention as well as new customer attraction

- Identify the best and most profitable customers eg reduce number of customers served and concentrate on those customers placing larger volume orders with high margin products

Examiner's comments:

Requirement 28.2 asked candidates to advise on the steps that MPW could take to improve the efficiency of its entire supply chain and hence its performance.

This requirement was often badly done. Only the strongest candidates demonstrated a clear understanding of the fact that the supply chain covers all the activities from acquiring inventory from suppliers through to delivery of the product to the customers. Few discussed supply chain management in terms of responsiveness, reliability and relationships. Many candidates confused supply chain management with value chain analysis and whilst the latter was worthy of consideration, it was not the sole focus of the requirement. Candidates who used their analysis in 28.1 to make sensible suggestions about coordinating purchasing and demand, reducing inventory levels, controlling costs (eg by setting minimum order sizes for next day delivery), and using information systems to improve inventory control and assess customer profitability scored well.

28.3 Performance measurement and incentives/CSFs and Revised KPIs

Critical success factors (CSFs) are the areas that are vital if MPW is to achieve competitive advantage. These should guide KPIs, the setting of targets for incentive schemes and the reporting of information for control and decision making.

CSFs are likely to include:

- Ability to meet customer demand (availability of wide range of handsets)

- Ability to offer high level of customer service (guaranteed next day delivery)

- Good relationships with retailers to retain customers and encourage repeat purchase

- Good inventory control to encourage fast turnaround and minimise inventory obsolescence/write offs

- Efficiency and cost of order processing

Improvements to performance measurement

MPW is currently looking at performance from two angles: financial and customer. It needs to use additional measures in these two areas but also to widen its system of performance measurement.

A balanced scorecard approach may be useful to MPW, since in addition to KPIs covering the financial and customer perspective, this would have highlighted the need to consider internal business processes and decision making, and innovation and learning.

MPW may also improve its approach to performance measurement by benchmarking performance with competitors/other wholesalers.

Incentives

Changes in the incentive scheme would encourage staff to take decisions which are in line with the overall company objectives and hence improve performance.

MPW needs to make the sales team aware of the overall costs of meeting orders so it is important that any bonus offered takes into account net margin per order, not just gross margin.

In awarding the purchasing manager a bonus, MPW needs to incentivise the manager to purchase the right inventory at as good a price as possible – currently the only factor being considered is price. Thus the purchasing manager needs to be encouraged to consider MPW's ability to sell the items purchased and the incentive could perhaps be based on gross margin per order. In this way the purchasing manager will only get a bonus if the sale is made and will get a bigger bonus if they have negotiated a good supplier discount as the margin earned will be higher. Any bonus could be restricted by taking into account aged inventory levels, inventory write offs etc.

To ensure co-ordination of the purchasing and sales team's efforts, an element of everyone's incentive should be based on the overall results of the business.

Additional measures

> **Tutorial note:**
>
> Only four are required and a prioritised list addressing CSFs raised above will score more highly than a generic list.

Four additional measures that could MPW usefully use to widen its KPIs are:

(1) Overall profitability: operating and net profit margins. MPW should also report profitability per order and per product.

(2) Since the MD is concerned that MPW may be losing money on some customers it should consider customer profitability – both gross and net of selling and distribution costs, number of orders per customer and average order value.

(3) The purchasing director has highlighted the importance of considering the efficiency and cost of order processing. MPW could do this using a measure such as average processing cost per order.

(4) Inventory management is also critical and appropriate management information here would include an aged inventory analysis. MPW could measure inventory write-offs/write-downs as a percentage of inventory held.

> **Tutorial note:**
>
> Alternative approach for marking purposes.

As an alternative, candidates may adopt a balanced scorecard approach when discussing how MPW could improve its performance measurement, which is set out below:

Financial perspective

MPW is already measuring sales growth and gross margin but has failed to consider overall profitability.

Additional measures should include looking at:

- Cost control eg overheads as a percentage of revenue

- Overall profitability: operating and net profit margins and also profitability per order, per customer and per product

- Market share

- Revenue mix

- Cash flow

Customer perspective

MPW are currently measuring satisfaction based on on-time delivery. It would also be useful to monitor satisfaction in terms of number of products demanded that are out of inventory.

In addition to satisfaction, MPW should also measure customer profitability, both gross and net of selling and distribution costs, number of orders per customer and average order value.

Since it typically costs more to attract new customers than to keep existing ones it could also measure customer loyalty in the form of retention rates and assess whether it is a preferred supplier based on its share of the key retailers' spend.

Internal business processes and decision making

The purchasing director has highlighted the importance of considering the efficiency and cost of order processing, using measures such as average processing cost per order, time taken to process each order.

Inventory management is also critical and appropriate management information here would include:

- Product profitability analysis
- Sales vs inventory reports
- Weekly inventory holding
- Aged inventory analysis – eg % inventory held over two months
- Inventory write-offs as a percentage of inventory held
- Exception reporting of aged inventory and small order values

Innovation and learning

This looks at whether MPW can continue to improve and create value. For example they may consider the number of new products added to the range as this might encourage them to include more captive products such as mobile phone accessories.

They could assess employee satisfaction, particularly given the potential changes that may take place in the incentive schemes. They could also assess productivity of employees in terms of sales and order processing.

Examiner's comments:

In requirement 28.3 candidates were asked to identify MPW's critical success factors and discuss how it can improve its performance measurement. The issue here was that the company needed to widen its KPIs, linked also to changing the incentive targets. Most candidates were able to suggest appropriate critical success factors for MPW although these were sometimes too narrow, focussing exclusively on customer needs and failing to take account of the internal need for operational efficiency and better inventory control as identified in the earlier requirements. The best candidates went on to link their suggested performance measures to the CSFs they had already identified. A minority did not provide four specific measures (as per the requirement) and some confused KPIs with goals. Candidates who used the Balanced Scorecard as a framework to identify a key performance measure for each of the four areas (financial, customer, internal and innovation) tended to produce wider answers and score more highly than those who gave a range of measures for the customer perspective. A number of candidates restricted their marks by suggesting KPIs that the company was already using.

29 SPV plc (March 2011)

		Knowledge	Skill	Marks
29.1 (a)	Structure	2	3	5
(b)	Operational culture	2	3	5
29.2	Sustainability	3	6	8
29.3	Joint venture	2	4	6
		9	16	24

General comments:

The scenario concerns a manufacturer of solar energy panels, which uses a unique patented thin-film technology. Demand for solar energy is unpredictable and dependent on a variety of external factors, including government incentives for renewable energy (detailed background information was provided in the scenario for those candidates who were unfamiliar with the technology and the nature of the industry). SPV is considering how to maintain its competitive advantage in the face on an uncertain industry environment and increasing competition from Asia. One strategic option is a joint venture with a major utility company in the USA.

Overall the performance on this question was very variable with too many poor answers. The weaker candidates performed poorly on the skills-bases elements of this question (requirements 29.1(b) and 29.2). Although there was no general evidence of time pressure (all but one of the candidates attempted every question), some weaker candidates who spent far too long on the Q1 mini case made a very truncated attempt at Q3. As a result there were a number of very low marks for this question which is reflected in the question average.

29.1 Structure and culture for success

(a) Structure

Organisational structure defines how the various functions in an organisation are arranged. A successful strategy requires effective organisation of people and decision making.

The contingency approach takes the view that there is no one best structure and emphasises the need for flexibility. The most appropriate structure depends on the stage of development of the organisation and the nature of its competitive environment.

SPV needs a structure which is quick to change but which can cope with the levels of growth anticipated.

Entrepreneurial structures can be flexible and quick to change but would not be suitable here as SPV is likely to be already too large and such structures tend to limit expansion capability.

Highly centralised structures or bureaucratic structures tend to stifle innovation and the rigidity makes them unsuitable for the unpredictable environment of the solar power industry.

SPV needs to be able to respond to rapidly changing demand from country to country and technological developments on the part of Asian competitors. In a complex, dynamic environment such as that faced by SPV, Mintzberg recommends an adhocracy/innovative configuration which is essentially a matrix structure. In this type of business the operating core who work directly on the product are the key building block of the organisation, and work autonomously. Whatever co-ordination is necessary is achieved by mutual adjustment which involves interaction and informal communication.

The matrix can be a mixture of functional, product and territorial organisation and is most suitable for complex/hi-tech industries. Such a structure offers great flexibility and is ideal where, as in the case of SPV, there are many geographic areas with distinct needs but the firm needs to exploit economies of scale to keep production costs low. The use of multi-skilled teams where employees are trained to undertake a variety of tasks would further enhance flexibility.

Burns and Stalker identified two extremes of structure – mechanistic or organic. Organic structures are flexible and adaptive and suitable for fast-changing environments and would therefore be appropriate for SPV.

(b) **Culture**

A successful company is often one that is outward looking, and has accepted the reality of constant change and the necessity to review its product-market policy continuously. It places emphasis on vigorous initiative, always looking to the future towards new markets, innovative products, better designs, new processes, improved quality and increased productivity.

SPV has developed and patented thin-film technology but needs to continue to innovate if it is to maintain competitive advantage. It can help foster a culture of innovation by:

- Recruiting and retaining the best talent – innovative organisations tend to attract and retain higher quality staff, who want to gain experience with the market leader and want the opportunity to contribute to the development of a forward-looking organisation.

- Getting the best from its employees. Cross-disciplinary teams allow employees to be more involved in the development of new products or processes, to move around and experiment with fresh ideas. Training and development will also be key.

- Creating a culture that promotes and rewards creativity and inventiveness and supports individual and team abilities. This is evidenced by the adoption of the employee suggestion to offer leasing to customers.

- Implementing a management style and structure designed for innovation: praising new ideas, encouraging staff to explore off-beat possibilities, and giving them a high degree of autonomy.

- Being aware of and making use of common information/resources available to industry. Certain managers can be made responsible for obtaining information about innovative ideas from outside and disseminating it throughout the organisation.

- Spending on R&D and market research and risking capital on new ideas.

- Using multiple sources of innovation – R&D, employees, customers, suppliers, partners, outsourcing and joint ventures, working with government or other public sector initiatives.

- Going beyond product innovation to consider how they can innovate their processes, their structure, their business model and even their market.

Examiner's comments:

Part (b) was less well done, with too many failing this part of the requirement. Weaker candidates overlooked the requirement to focus on operational strategies and instead discussed Porter's generic strategies of cost leadership and differentiation or focussed on high level strategic options. Better candidates identified that innovation and flexibility were critical success factors and discussed ways that SPV could promote this internally eg recruiting and retaining talent, empowering employees with a high degree of autonomy, promoting/incentivising creativity and innovation, collaborating on research and development.

29.2 Sustainability and control

Sustainability and SPV's strategy

Sustainability is about maintaining the world's resources rather than depleting or destroying them. The Bruntland report defined sustainability as 'the ability to meet the needs of the present without compromising the ability of future generations to meet their own needs.'

Sustainability is not limited to the environment and encompasses social, environmental and economic issues.

Protecting the environment and preserving its resources are at the core of SPV's activities. It is engaged in the provision of sustainable energy where the source of the energy is sustainable and there is little disruption to the environment. Such energy will help promote worldwide sustainability by reducing dependence on fossil fuels and mitigating the effect of greenhouse gases. Thus sustainability is integral to SPV. The world's increasing consciousness of the need for sustainability offers SPV a wide range of opportunities but also presents it with considerable risk.

There is a clear need for SPV to be a sustainable enterprise (a company that generates continuously increasing stakeholder value through the application of sustainable practices). The payback period for its panels can be up to 10 years and customers want confidence that the panel manufacturer will stay in business for the duration of the panel warranty period.

Ability to control success

SPV's established reputation and track record help to reduce the risks it faces, as it will be seen as a stable business partner, which is critical given the long term nature of the product. As the market expands, SPV may therefore be more attractive as a partner for utility companies who are typically risk averse.

SPV has used patents to protect its proprietary technology which will reduce the risk of copycat products for a period of time until newer, cheaper products are developed. We discussed in 29.1 how SPV can help ensure success through careful design of its structure and culture and this could facilitate ongoing innovation to stay ahead of the market.

In addition to SPV's use of cheaper thin-film rather than the more expensive silicon, its vertically integrated process and economies of scale mean that it can provide relatively affordable panels. Compared to traditional silicon, the panels also have a high energy yield in the absence of sunshine, making them more suitable for a wider range of climates and countries. Thus if demand exists, SPV is likely to capture market share, at least in the short term.

However demand for SPV's product is heavily dependent on the level of industry demand, which is itself dependent on the political framework and also the economic climate, both of which are outside SPV's control. Thus SPV may choose to invest in certain countries, only to find that a change in government or financial position render the market unattractive. This is evidenced by the case of Spain reducing green energy subsidies due to budget constraints.

In the absence of government subsidies, sustainability may become less popular when levels of disposable income fall and consumers and businesses are either unprepared to pay the price premium to be green or alternatively cannot wait so long for the payback.

To an extent SPV can mitigate against this risk through careful choice of markets, operating in a range of different locations, and cultivating appropriate networks and relationships for lobbying purposes but ultimately if alternative cheaper forms of renewable energy are developed/become widely available or governments worldwide stop supporting sustainable energy initiatives then SPV's long term success is largely outside its control.

Tutorial note:

Candidates may also approach the discussion of controllability by using the 5 factors listed in the scenario as drivers of demand as a structure for their answer (climate/price of electricity/public awareness/economy/government).

Examiner's comments:

Requirement 29.2 asked candidates to explain how the need for sustainability influences SPV's strategy and assess the extent to which its success is driven by factors outside its control. Weaker candidates struggled with the first part of this and had little to say other than quoting the Bruntland Report definition of sustainability and discussing fossil fuels. Better answers appreciated that sustainability is wider than just the use of green technology, picking up on the points raised in the scenario about the need for SPV to be a sustainable business given the long payback period for its panels and the fact that customers want confidence that SPV will be in business for the duration of the panel warranty period.

Many candidates extracted the information from the scenario about the drivers of demand for panels (climate, price of traditional power sources, state of economy, government attitudes and public attitudes) and noted that in the main these were uncontrollable by SPV. The stronger candidates went on to produce a more balanced answer by discussing the fact that SPV has already managed to create a market leader position through its use of unique patented technology and that by having an appropriate structure and culture and strengthening its position, eg with the proposed joint venture, it will be able to create sustainable competitive advantage. Thus when the demand drivers are favourable it will be able to profit more than most.

There is a high emphasis on skills in the Business Strategy paper because it is a fundamental part of the preparation for Advanced stage. Thus in certain parts of the paper candidates are expected to be able to apply their knowledge and exercise judgement. Where a requirement is more skills-based, as this one was, those candidates who recognise that a lot of the necessary information is provided in the scenario and have the confidence to use their knowledge of the learning materials in that context can score well even if they struggle to use their skills fully. Candidates who fail to produce an answer to a requirement because, to quote the tutor commentaries it is 'not widely practised' or 'a regular requirement', cannot be awarded credit for a blank page.

29.3 Joint venture with UTILCO

A joint venture is a contractual arrangement whereby two or more parties undertake an economic activity which is subject to joint control. Here SPV's solar panels will be attached to UTILCO's existing telephone and electricity poles throughout the USA.

Attractiveness to UTILCO

- Need to comply with government policy and the 33% target for renewable energy, so is going to be forced to increase renewable energy

- Does not have the technology itself and is unlikely to have the expertise to develop it in-house

- SPV is a well-established, market-leading company with tried and tested technology therefore likely to be a preferred partner

- Longstanding track-record and financial stability of SPV will reduce risk

Attractiveness to SPV

- Utilco have access to a very large distribution network and an extensive customer base

- Will be able to take advantage of the growth opportunities arising from the government policy, without having to find all the finance/bear all the costs

- May be further scope to collaborate eg on the development of major solar power plants

- Likely to have access to resources and capital which are critical to the development of the solar powered industry and may help facilitate further technological development

- Will help raise awareness and demand for solar power which may further stimulate demand for panels by households and businesses

Conclusion

The joint venture looks to be beneficial for both parties and, subject to the ability to agree appropriate terms and conditions, should be pursued.

In requirement 29.3 candidates were asked to discuss the merits of the proposed joint venture and appeared well-prepared to do this, with many showing an improved ability to apply their knowledge in the context of the scenario rather than providing a generic list of points. A minority however ignored the requirement to consider this from the point of view of both UTILCO and SPV.

30 Cauldron Cereals plc (June 2011)

Marking guide

	Knowledge	Skill	Marks
30.1 Analysis of competitive position	3	10	12
30.2 (a) Analysis of performance	–	10	
(b) Risks	3	4	
			16
30.3 Ethics	3	5	8
30.4 FoodSave contract	2	6	8
	11	35	44

General comments:

This is the mini case and data analysis question. The scenario relates to a manufacturer of healthy eating breakfast cereals, Cauldron Cereals (CC). CC is at the higher end of the quality spectrum, but it has performed poorly in recent years. In 20X8, a new CEO was appointed and, in an attempt to improve profits, he cut costs by lowering grain quality. At the same time, he entered into a two-year contract with a supplier to fix the price of grain. Demand fell so the CEO, with the agreement of only a few directors, increased the salt and sugar content, without internal or external disclosure, in order to improve taste. Profits at first increased, but then discovery of the undisclosed change in salt and sugar cased a fall in sales and the removal of the CEO. An ethical issue is that the finance director discovered the undisclosed change, resigned and disclosed this to the newspapers. A new board is considering a contract to sell to a supermarket under its own label at a lower price, while the core product reputation has time to recover.

30.1 Average revenues using Exhibit 1:

CC average sales	£35.0m
Industry average	£7.4m (£980m/132)
Big three average	£178m ((295 + 127 + 112)/3)
Average of non-big 7	£2.144m (£268/125)

CC's market share (by value ie sales revenue) 3.57%(£35m/£980m)

CC's sales are only 11.9% of Astra's sales and only 19.7% of the average of the big three companies. Despite this, CC is one of the larger companies in the UK industry with revenue 16.3 times the average of the smaller companies outside the 'big seven'.

In order to assess the competitive position of CC it may however be more appropriate to view it as competing in a niche market with the general industry. Its niche appears to be defined by both the type of cereal (healthy) and by the quality-price relationship. In this latter context it can be seen from the other information available that the average price per box is £3 for CC ($35m/11.67m) and £2 for the industry average (£980m/490m). The contention is therefore that in selling £2 boxes of cereals there is a rather different market segment than for £3 boxes of cereals and thus they are not, in normal circumstances, in direct competition. (Care must be taken in using this data as the average size of a cereal box is assumed to be constant for companies in the industry. The assumption will be made that boxes are approximately the same size but more information would be required to verify this.)

This is not to argue however that there is no competitive effect outside the market niche. In recession, cheaper cereals may be a substitute for expensive cereals as people trade down. Similarly, there may be a competitive effect from outside the breakfast cereals industry from substitutes (eg other type of health food for (say) lunch, or other types of breakfast eg croissant).

However, taking a primary view of competitive position as within the market niche then the main competitors appear to be:

- 'The wide product range of the 'big three' includes the full spectrum of price and quality choices, as well as market niches such as healthy-eating and children's cereals.' This means that at least a segment of the big three are in direct competition with CC. More information is needed about the extent of the activities of the big three in the healthy eating sector and the manner of pricing within that sector. Nevertheless, the advertising budgets and economies of scale and scope are likely to mean that big three brands are major and direct competitors with CC products, significantly affecting the company's competitive position.

  Rival 1 is a direct competitor of CC in terms of producing primarily healthy cereals. Its sales are almost double those of CC in value terms, and more than double in volume terms so it would benefit from greater economies of scale.

  However, in terms of price and quality it does not appear to be in direct competition with CC as it has an average price of £2.25 compared to £3 for CC. There is therefore likely to be some limited impact in terms of competitive position and this is likely to be greater in a recession where substitution of Rival 1's lower price products, but still within the 'healthy' sector, may be common.

- Rival 2 is closer to CC in terms of size and average price than Rival 1, but it seems only to compete in a niche within a niche, as it specialises in children's healthy cereals. It therefore appears to be a prime and significant competitor to CC within this sub-sector. The impact on the overall competitive position of CC would depend on the proportion of sales falling within the children's healthy food sector. More information is needed on the sales mix of CC in respect of adult cereals and children's cereals to evaluate the competitive risk from Rival 2.

- Despite being a similar size to CC, Rival 3 does not appear to be a primary rival in the context of healthy breakfast cereals. It does however compete with CC in the quality market with an average price of £3.50 compared to £3 for CC. The difference in price however may be regarded as fairly significant and therefore is probably the least direct competitor for CC of the three similar-sized rivals.

- Other smaller companies are not likely to be major competitors individually but, collectively, groups of smaller companies may have competitive impact on CC. The smaller companies may, if successful, grow sufficiently in the longer term to be more substantial competitors to CC and similar companies in the industry.

Using Porter's Five Forces model, CC's competitive position can be seen as not only being affected by competition within the industry, but also by relationships with suppliers and customers. The relative power of larger buyers (such as supermarkets and other large multi outlet retailers) over CC is likely to be substantial as most sales by CC are to these groups. If there is pressure on prices from powerful buyers this affects CC's profitability and price competitiveness compared to large competitors who may have more bargaining power with buyers such as large supermarkets. If the 'big three' are better able to resist price pressure from supermarkets then this would strengthen their competitive position compared to CC.

As a general indication of buyer power in the industry, the profit margin of retailers is given by comparing total retail sales of £1,200 million to wholesale sales of £980 million. This is a healthy margin for retailers of over 18% on a basic food product. In 20X8, before the changes by the new CEO, CC only had a profit margin of 11.1%. This may be an indication of CC's lack of competitiveness in the market, but other explanations such as cost inefficiencies may also be contributory.

A similar argument could be made with respect to power over suppliers but international grain markets are likely to be robust even for the big three to obtain and advantage.

Competitive threats from overseas manufacturers are significantly reduced 'due to the low-cost, high bulk-volume of breakfast cereals, which make transport costs high.' This may limit new entrants which would need a UK manufacturing base to compete effectively, rather than just export into the UK.

In terms of changes in competitive position, it would appear that the market share of CC is worsening. Long term industry sales have increased by 3% whilst CC has not shared in this growth.

Tutorial note:

Candidates may also use a BCG matrix approach using the data that CC's sales are only 11.9% of the market leader, Astra, and there is currently zero market growth.

Examiner's comments:

Requirement 30.1 asked candidates to use the industry data provided and other information to evaluate CC's long term competitive position. Any additional information needed was also requested. Answers to this part varied in standard.

There were few calculations produced, other than the 3.57% market share, which most candidates correctly determined. The most common model used was Porter's Five Forces and salient points were normally made using this framework. The better answers focussed on CC's immediate competitive position in comparison to its rivals and also in relation to the 'big three'. Good discussion was seen in terms of CC's position in the niche market and as a differentiator. Some candidates, however, chose to do a SWOT analysis for this part of the question, which did not tend to bring out the key points. It was surprising to note that most candidates produced no calculations on CC sales, compared to the industry average or the average of the big three. Some candidates produced price/quality trade-off diagrams to depict the relative strategies of CC and its close rivals.

The request for further information led to a standard shopping list in many cases. It was quite apparent that candidates approached this element of the question very generically and did not really think about what further information would be useful. For example, there were some requests for information which has already been given in the question itself.

30.2

	20X8	20X9	20Y0	
Revenue	£36m	£34m	£35m	Per question
Grain cost	£16m	£13m	£13.4m	Per question
Operating profit	£4m	£5m	£5.6m	Per question
Volume	12m	11.33m	11.67m	Per question
Price	£3	£3	£3	
Grain cost per cereal box sold	£1.33	£1.15	£1.15	
% change in revenue	–	(5.5)	2.9	
% change in volume	–	(5.6)	3.0	
% change in total grain cost	–	(18.75)	3.0	
% change in grain cost per box	–	(13.5)	Nil	
% change in operating profit	–	25	12	

(a) **Performance**

Financial performance

In pure financial terms, the operating profit has increased substantially by 25% and 12% in 20X9 and 20Y0 respectively.

Looking at factors which may have given rise to this improvement, it does not appear to be the selling price as this has remained constant. Similarly, fixed operating costs have remained constant. Neither does it appear to have been sales volumes, which have decreased and therefore have had the opposite effect in reducing overall sales revenue and profit.

The key causal factor driving the increase in operating profit therefore appears to be the reduced cost of grain. There are three interrelated factors in respect of the change in grain cost which need to be understood to evaluate their impact on financial performance. These are changes in total grain cost due to:

- Lower unit costs due to lower quality
- Lower total volumes of usage
- Contract pricing effects

Unit costs and volumes

20X9

Ignoring the contract pricing effects for the moment, in 20X9 the overall grain cost has fallen by 18.75%, but the cost per box sold has only fallen by 13.5% this is due to the fall in volumes of 5.6%. At a constant volume of 12 million boxes then the profit at the new grain prices for 20X9 would have been £6.2m (£36m – £16m – (£1.15 × 12m). To the extent that the deterioration of grain quality has impacted demand, then this is a harmful effect as, at constant quality, profit would be £6.2m. Thus the unfavourable profit impact of the quality deterioration (assuming all the volume change is attributable to this) is £1.2m. However, this is outweighed by the cost saving resulting in an overall increase in operating profit in 20X9 of £1m.

20Y0

In 20Y0 there has been no change in selling prices, fixed operating costs or grain prices per box. The increase in operating profit of £0.6 million is therefore attributable to the increase in sales volumes. This can be demonstrated by the change in total contribution of £1m – (£1.15 × 0.34m) (subject to rounding).

This financial gain appear to be attributable to the increase in salt and sugar content which 'helped to improve the taste a little and, as a consequence, demand recovered slightly in 20Y0'. To the extent that this is true there has been a short term narrow financial benefit to the decision to include more salt and sugar content, but ideally we need to estimate what would have happened in 20Y0 in the absence of this action rather than assume that the 20X9 performance would automatically have been repeated.

Fixed price contract

The final element of financial performance has been the fixed price contract. This has enabled the acquisition of grain at artificially low prices compared to its fair value on world commodity markets. Performance can therefore be analysed between (1) operating activities and (2) financial contracts.

In terms of assessing sustainable business operating performance, the financial contract performance can be separated out (as it is unlikely to be sustainable that the commodity market can be predicted in the long term). This can be achieved by charging the fair value of grain, which 'unexpectedly increased by 10% each year', rather than the artificially low cost attained in the contract.

In this case grain prices would be:

20X9	1.1 × £13m	=	£14.3m
20Y0	1.1 × 1.1 × £13m	=	£15.7m

Profit would then be as follows:

Financial data for CC

	20X8 £m	20X9 £m	20Y0 £m
Revenue	36	34	35
Fixed operating costs	(16)	(16)	(16)
Variable operating cost (grain)	(16)	(14.3)	(15.7)
Operating profit	4	3.7	3.3

Reviewing the revised figures shows that profit has now fallen and the company's performance has deteriorated. This is not to suggest however that the management has, of necessity performed badly as profit would have fallen anyway under the old strategy of high quality grain due to the global grain price increases (see below).

The value of the contract over two years has been the difference in profit of £3.6 (5 + 5.6 – 3.7 – 3.3).

Strategic performance

Overall there has been an improved financial performance in the short term.

This is largely due to a fortuitous raw material hedging contract that has generated significant profit.

If the existing strategy has been maintained with the grain price increases as follows:

| 20X9 | $1.1 \times £16m$ | = | £17.6m |
| 20Y0 | $1.1 \times 1.1 \times £16m$ | = | £19.36m |

then the following would have arisen assuming no other changes in volumes:

| | Financial data for CC | | |
| | 20X8 | 20X9 | 20Y0 |
	£m	£m	£m
Revenue	36	36	36
Fixed operating costs	(16)	(16)	(16)
Variable operating cost (grain)	(16)	(17.6)	(19.36)
Operating profit	4	2.4	0.64

These profits are lower than those that would have been achieved above of £3.7m and £3.3m under the new strategy in the absence of hedging. This could superficially lead to the conclusion that the change in strategy was advantageous.

A key problem is that the policy is unsustainable as once the salt and sugar changes became transparent to the consumer a new level of demand based on fuller information was established which is only at 80% of the previous level, at which point the company makes a loss (see 30.4 below).

Thus the strategic cost of a short-term financial gain has been:

- Loss of reputation
- Damage to the healthy eating brand characteristic
- Reduced sales and profit in the longer term

This impacts on CC's market positioning and its future long-term viability.

(b) **Risks**

A key risk facing CC has been its long-term decline compared to the industry average.

Note. '… long-term annual volume growth in UK retail sales of over 3% until the end of 20X8… Despite the growth in sales in the UK breakfast cereal market as a whole up to 20X8, CC sales have not grown for some years.'

Therefore, despite the risks in the new strategy adopted from 20X9 there were also risks in doing nothing and continuing with the old strategy.

Aside from any particular business strategy adopted, the volatility of grain prices is a key risk. The magnitude of the changes is illustrated by the calculations above indicating the impact on profit that would have occurred had the hedging contract not been in place.

This risk has been effectively managed by CC in the period 20X8-20Y0 through the fixed price contract. However, to the extent that long-term grain prices have remained high, then CC became exposed to the higher prices and future volatility when the contract expired at the end of 20Y0. The contract was only therefore a temporary means of risk management.

The risks from the market appear to be relatively stable as it is a long established company in a mature industry where prices and volumes appear to be stable and, despite the maturity, there appears to be longer term growth in sales outside the recession period. This is not therefore a highly contested market.

Moreover, the size of the market leaders and their advertising spend tends to create barriers to new entrants which restricts future competition, albeit that the big three are better able to do this rather than CC.

A key short-term risk is the recession where high quality producers are at particular risk of falling sales through consumers trading down.

Change in consumer tastes, particularly with respect to healthy eating, is another key risk. In the case of CC it is also a potential benefit although a reduction in health consciousness in the population may have a dramatic effect on sales as it directly impacts the core values of CC's marketing.

In addition to the above market and industry risk there are also a number of risks that apply specifically to CC as a consequence of their recent decisions. These include:

- Reputational risk. The reputation risk of the company has been damaged by the public disclosure of salt and sugar content and grain quality. Future decision making needs to consider the possibility of further reputational damage.

- Alongside harm to the company's reputation, there is likely to be impairment of the overall brand and the brand names of individual cereals. This mainly relates to the quality of the product which, to the extent it may vary in future, represents an additional risk to which consumers are likely to be sensitised. Consumer goodwill is therefore likely to be fragile.

Examiner's comments:

Requirement 30.2 requested candidates to: (a) analyse the financial and strategic performance of CC using the data provided; and (b) explain the risks facing CC in 20Y1 and beyond.

Candidates produced a range of calculations in answering part (a). The recurring calculations were operating profit margin, % change in revenue and % change in costs of grain. The better answers recognised that although there was an improved profit in the short term, this was not sustainable in the longer term as, strategically, the reputation of the business had been damaged by the change in grain quality and increase in salt and sugar content. The weaker answers merely focussed on trying to explain the reasons for the increased short term profit without acknowledging that financial performance will deteriorate as the full impact of the change in strategy was felt. A minority considered the 'same taste at lower cost' tactic as a conscious change of strategy towards cost leadership in the niche although, at the same time, not reflecting on the fact that the price had not been lowered. Only a minority recognised the favourable, and fortuitous, impact on profit of the long term contract fixing grain prices. Even fewer attempted to extract the impact of the grain contract quantitatively, in order to assess the underlying operational performance in financial terms.

Part (b) on risk was generally done quite well, with most candidates discussing the reputational risk to CC, the damage to the brand and the loss of consumer goodwill. The higher scoring answers highlighted various types of risk bringing in wider economic impacts and discussing recession.

30.3 (a) The key ethical issues in this case are transparency and honesty. Despite the increase in salt and sugar content, the action of adding more of these ingredients to improve flavour in not, in itself, illegal or unethical as levels remain well below the industry average and are not therefore a material or unacceptable risk to health in the view of the consumers who continue knowingly to purchase these products.

The issue of transparency is both internal to CC and external to customers.

Internally, this is a question of corporate governance. An important decision has been made, not by the board in a formal meeting, but by a subset in an informal meeting where the decision was deliberately not communicated. This was a breech of good faith and an improper process of decision making. Its legality may be called into question.

Externally, the communication of 1% and 3% rather than 1.49% and 3.49% could be regarded as a lack of transparency and deliberately misleading the customers. The ethical implications would depend largely on the industry norms as to the level of accuracy with which these ingredients are disclosed. The magnitude of the changes is however significant, being a 49% increase in salt and a 16.3% increase in sugar. A phrase such as 'to the nearest whole percentage' may have gone some way towards a defensible ethical position but transparency in line with rival companies and consumers' expectations would have been a preferable position.

(b) The ethical issues with respect to Jenny are confidentiality and whistleblowing. In terms of confidentiality, there is a presumption that private information acquired from within a company by employees and officers should not be outwardly disclosed to the public without authorisation. This presumption can however be overturned, and whistleblowing can be ethically justified where there has been an illegal act committed.

As it stands, it is unclear whether the CEO has deliberately attempted to deceive the public or has acted within acceptable norms of accuracy of disclosed data. To the extent that he may have acted illegally then the breach of confidentiality by whistleblowing can be justified on ethical grounds within the ICAEW Code of Ethics. Authoritative guidance should have been obtained by Jenny however prior to public disclosure.

Examiner's comments:

Requirement 30.3 asked candidates to explain the ethical issues arising from: (a) the CEO's decision to increase salt and sugar content without disclosure, either internally or externally; and (b) the FD's decision to resign and publicly disclose the decision.

Weaker answers tended to adopt extreme ethical positions, for example by regarding the increase of the salt and sugar content as illegal so on this basis the FD had acted in the public interest and her actions were correct in amounting to whistleblowing. The better scoring answers adopted a more balanced approach and identified the key ethical issues using ethical language. In terms of the FD's actions, better candidates identified that Jenny could have potentially breached confidentiality and should have sought further advice before making a disclosure to the press.

30.4 To: Cauldron Cereals plc Board
From: An Accountant
Date: 13 June 20Y1
Subject: FoodSave Contract

The contract with FoodSave is fixed price. A significant risk therefore arises to CC from volatility in grain prices over the two year contractual period which has a minimum quantity clause as costs may increase significantly without any corresponding ability to increase selling prices to FoodSave.

In simple financial terms the new contract creates a positive contribution per year as follows:

First year		
Sales	(400,000 × £2)	£800,000
Grain costs	(£1.77 × 400,000)	£708,000 (see Note)
Contribution		£92,000
Second year		
Sales	(400,000 × £2)	£800,000
Grain costs	(£1.95 × 400,000)	£780,000 (see Note)
Contribution		£20,000

Note. The original grain quality has been restored. In 20X8 the cost of grain per box is £1.33; by 20Y0 this has increased by 10% per year and so is £1.61 per box. The contract is being considered in July 20Y1 and we know: 'Further increases in grain prices are now expected from 20Y1 onwards'.

As a working assumption it has been assumed that grain prices will increase by a further 10% in the first year of the contract which would be £1.77 per box.

In the second year of the contract if (say) grain increases by a further 10% then the price of grain per box is £1.95.

There may be further benefits:

- There is significant slack capacity as sales are only 80% of their previous levels so this keeps staff and other resources employed while the company tries to recover its reputation and volumes

- The 400,000 volume is a minimum and sales to FoodSave may be much higher

- Other supermarkets may offer similar contracts if CC can show it can satisfy FoodSave's needs

- The reputational damage of the old board may be limited by the vote of confidence by FoodSave

Disadvantages may be:

- If it becomes known by consumers that the FoodSave cereal is the same, in substance, as the CC cereal they are likely to buy the FoodSave version for £2 rather than the CC version for £3

- There may be further reputational damage as a quality provider if it becomes known that CC is supplying a low cost supermarket

- The contract is small relative to the size of CC so the balance between reputational damage and financial benefit leans towards rejecting the contract

- There is a risk that volatility in grain prices outside the assumed 10% may create a negative contribution, particularly in year 2 where the margin in thin. If this is the case, CC's cereals may be the lowest cost that FoodSave can obtain and it may demand large quantities from CC thereby magnifying the negative contribution

Examiner's comments:

Requirement 30.4 asked candidates to produce a report which provides advice on whether to accept the FoodSave supermarket contract, including supporting calculations.

Many candidates produced few, if any, calculations, despite the specific request in the question to do so. A significant number of candidates appeared to assume that the additional cereals could be sold without any additional costs being incurred such that the full £800,000 revenue was added to profit each year. Amongst those who did address costs, there was frequently a misconception that grain prices would remain stable. Few addressed risks in any detail.

31 Henford plc (June 2011)

Marking guide

		Knowledge	Skill	Marks
31.1 (a)	BCG	2	4	
(b)	Life cycle	2	6	
				13
31.2 (a)	Organisational charts	2	4	
(b)	Function structure to new structure	2	6	
				13
31.3	Barriers to change	3	6	8
		11	26	34

31.1 (a) The relative shares of the three products compared to the major competitor are:

Toys   5.0
Paper   0.10
Pharmaceuticals 1.10

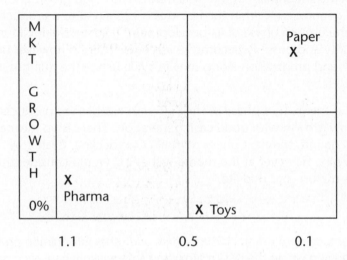

MARKET SHARE (compared to market leader)

Toys

The traditional toys section is trading in a zero growth market. Its sales are also only half that of the largest competitor so market share is relatively low. Operating cash flows are modest.

Toys may have been a cash cow in the past but as a result of increasing competition from IT-based toy manufacturers it has suffered new entrants in a competitive market.

As a consequence, the BCG matrix is likely to view toys as a 'dog' product with limited potential for growth and development.

Paper

Henford's paper products section has high growth but the market share is small relative to the main competitor, being only 10% of its size by sales.

The paper products could therefore be regarded as a question mark (or problem child). This means that there may be a case for additional capital expenditure to expand the product in order to gain critical mass.

With a portfolio of products as a conglomerate, the cash cows could help finance the question marks to stimulate early growth.

Pharmaceuticals

Henford's pharmaceuticals section is a market leader with a high market share. There is low growth at 3% as this is a mature market so new entrants are less likely. There is a limited need for new investment in production assets as expansion is low and there is little need to defend market position from new entrants. As a consequence there is high positive cash generation.

As a consequence, Pharmaceuticals could be viewed as a cash cow within the BCG matrix.

(b) **Product life cycle (PLC)**

The product life cycle can be adapted to use the same market growth, market share and cash generation classification as the BCG matrix. The PLC however tries to explain these factors as sequential over the life of the product.

Traditional toys

This product is between the maturity and decline phases of the life cycle. This is characterised by low market share and zero growth, with modest cash flows. Within the PLC this places it between a dog (as in the BCG matrix) and a dodo. The key issue however is not the exact position in the PLC but the direction of movement. This is a product which is past its peak and is now struggling to compete, with poor cash generation.

The next phase would be to cease production at the end of its PLC as cash flows may move to be negative.

Paper

Paper is classified as a question mark in the BCG matrix with high growth, low market share and poor cash generation. Within the PLC this is explained as a product still trying to establish itself in the growth phase of its development. If successful it can move to the next section of maturity and possibly become a cash cow. There is however uncertainty over its development and progression along the life cycle hence the title question mark.

Pharmaceuticals

Pharmaceuticals are in the mature phase of the PLC with established products having high market share, low growth with good cash generation. There is no inevitability that mature products will go into the next phase of the PLC of decline. Cash cows are often sustained for many years. However at the moment the PLC would consider the cash cow in the BCG matrix as mature and mid life.

Examiner's comments:

Requirement 31.1 asked candidates to use the industry data and other information provided to: (a) explain and justify its positioning within the BCG matrix; and (b) explain where each product is located within the product life cycle model.

In part (a) most candidates performed relatively well and sound knowledge of the BCG matrix was demonstrated in qualitative terms. However, while a majority of candidates correctly positioned each product in the correct quadrant, the numerical data relating to market growth and market share percentages were not discussed in much detail or used to position products within a quadrant.

In part (b), the majority of candidates were able to discuss the phases of the product life cycle in general terms and accurately link each product to the correct phase. However parts (a) and (b) of the question were often answered in isolation and many candidates failed to make linkages between the product life cycle and the BCG matrix. High marks were awarded where the linkage and understanding of the interaction between BCG and the product life cycle were demonstrated.

31.2 (a)

Old structure: functional

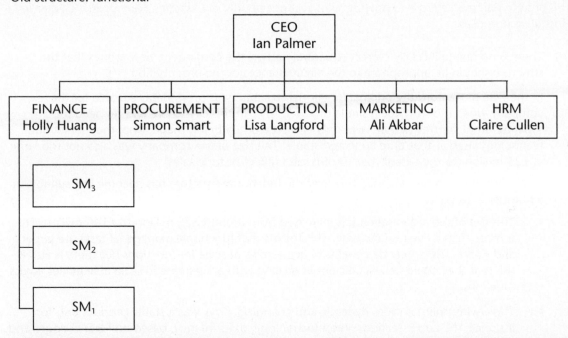

Tutorial note:

The senior managers of only one division have been included for illustrative purposes.

New structure: Product divisionalisation with some centralised functions

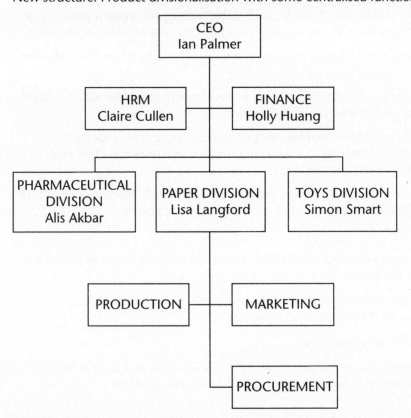

Tutorial note:

Different versions of this diagram were acceptable provided the reporting lines and the distinction between the operating divisions and the centralised functions were clear.

(b) There is no one universally correct structure. Rather, the contingent view argues that the structure should be appropriate to the circumstances of the organisation.

In the case of Henford the original functional structure was presumably suitable for the company when it only made a single product, toys. In this case there was no need for separate profit centres as there was only one type of toy being made. Also, the market and technology used at that time appeared stable. The size of the company was also not too large at £25 million (to the extent that current sales reflect historic sales).

As the organisation has changed however the functional structure has become less suitable in a number of respects.

- The size of the organisation has increased from around £25 million to £140 million. This is more than a five-fold increase. This means that functional managerial tasks are larger and wider. There may be benefits of economies of scale for functions but there is also a risk that they could be less efficient in dealing with an increase in scale of activities across functions.

- The environment is more dynamic and changing. Toys was a stable product but, for instance, the paper section is high technology, in its infancy, based on R&D changes and expanding. Functional structures tend to be bureaucratic and may not cope will with changes particularly in co-ordinating changes for a product across functions and may therefore hamper creativity and future change.

- There is now greater diversity in the range of products, as Henford is a conglomerate. Functional structures are not normally best suited to dealing with this diversity as the nature of the function could vary. Thus production technology for paper is different to that for toys and uniting them in one function may have few shared skills and benefits.

The new structure is a movement towards divisionalisation but it retains a functional element in finance and HRM.

The structure is one of product divisionalisation but, as the factories are in separate locations, it can also be regarded as geographical divisionalisation.

The new structure enables a divisional manager to take holistic responsibility for the performance of a product by coordinating a range of functions and resources. This enables profit centre responsibility to be implemented.

The fact that Henford is a conglomerate makes the product lines largely independent of each other and therefore segregated management of each product is facilitated.

Advantages for Henford are:

- Managers are held accountable for profitability so the objectives of the reporting unit parallel those of the company

- Functional product specialisation can be developed within divisions, eg marketing pharmaceuticals may be different to marketing toys

- Coordination of functions is facilitated

- The focus of managerial goals is outputs in terms of performance and achievements (profits), rather than inputs in terms of carrying out functional activities

Disadvantages for Henford are:

- The divisional managers may not have the competencies and skills to run a division as their experience and background is in managing a specialised function.

- There may be some duplication of effort and tasks within functions.

Examiner's comments:

Requirement 31.2 addressed changes to the organisational structure of Henford. It required candidates to: (a) draw organisational charts for the new and old structures; and (b) evaluate the changes.

In part (a) most candidates produced reasonable diagrams. There were some omissions in relation to the new structure, mainly around the lower level senior managers within each function/division. A minority of candidates incorrectly considered the new structure to be a matrix structure as opposed to divisional.

In part (b) the discussions on the new structure compared to the old structure were very general but the key principles of autonomy and lack of specialist knowledge were reflected in most answers and candidates appeared to be very comfortable with this element of the question.

31.3 Marketing managers appear to dislike the change, which for them is transformational since all their reporting lines and even their location have changed.

They 'are still in communication' so clearly identify themselves with the culture of their previous group as a function rather than their new group as a division. The marketing managers appear to have their own culture based on the old function of marketing which may have been built up over many years.

Cultural barriers include:

Group inertia: Barriers to change may take the form of cultural barriers to change based on group resistance despite their recent geographical separation. The changes make the group dispersed and perhaps their professional skills less understood. Performing less well may be a means of emphasising their role especially when this appears to be a coordinated effort to make the case.

Structural inertia: this is the cumulative effect of the systems and processes. These include promotion and reward systems. These can act as a barrier to change in resisting the new systems by lack of cooperation and the seeking of further changes through board representation with Alan.

In addition to the group of marketing managers resisting change, individuals who are affected by the change may have individual resistance. This may arise because marketing managers have moved geographically (if not working in the Toys division) or there may be a change in role position or rewards.

Barriers to change may be deliberate attempts to resist change but may also be genuine difficulties in coping with the new system or dealing with different people with dissimilar backgrounds.

Individual barriers may include:

* Working less efficiently when reporting to a non-marketing line manager who may not fully understand a marketing role and cannot therefore easily observe or monitor marketing staff

* Failing to interact appropriately with non-marketing staff

* Leaving the organisation (eg to seek a job locally without moving house)

* Lacking appropriate skills in a multi-discipline environment

* Declining morale and motivation

Examiner's comments:

In requirement 31.3 candidates were asked to consider the barriers to change that the senior marketing managers could potentially create.

Many answers were very generic in describing barriers to change from the learning materials with limited application to the scenario. At the opposite extreme, some candidates commented on the specific changes made by just adopting common sense and without relating the suggestions to relevant models. Those candidates adopting a more balanced approach performed well, although some answers drifted from discussion of the marketing managers to the more general impact on all marketing personnel or all staff.

32 Felan Fashions plc (June 2011)

Marking guide

	Knowledge	Skill	Marks
32.1 Marketing Mix	4	10	12
32.2 Compare two strategies	2	10	10
	6	20	22

General comments:

The scenario in this question concerns a company which designs, produces and retails upmarket ladies' fashion clothing. Felan has a wide coverage of stores in the UK and is seeking to expand into Europe. It is considering two alternative strategies. The first strategy option is to open independent stores across Germany, France, Spain and Italy. The second strategy option is to expand only into France using an agreement to take floor space within a chain of French department stores.

32.1 The marketing mix is the set of controllable marketing variables that a firms blends to produce the response it wants in a target market.

Product

In the marketing mix, 'product' refers to the qualities of the product as perceived by potential customers. This relates to the product's benefits to the consumer and its suitability for its stated purpose including aesthetic factors, durability, brand and associated services.

What is particularly important is not how well these factors are satisfied as such, but how they are perceived in comparison with the key competitors in the market niche selected. The low market recognition for FF of 20% represents a problem in this respect as presumably domestic brands in target countries have higher recognition than FF.

With respect to the product itself, FF has expertise in manufacture, retailing and service delivery in the UK that has proved to be successful. A key question is whether this can be replicated in European countries which may have different tastes, even where there is recognition of the FF brand. Whilst the business model was 'to base her latest designs on current trends set by the major international fashion houses', Tanya attempted to 'tailor FF products to UK market tastes' and may not have the core competences to adapt fully to European tastes which themselves may vary across the target range of countries.

The FF brand name is part of customer product perception. Although it is not widely recognised, a key issue is what it is recognised for. If it develops a good reputation and recognition widens, then the perceived value of the product may increase in customers' perceptions.

The test of success of the product will be in consumers' reaction to the product and this could be revealed in market research, market testing or initial market entry.

Place (distribution)

The use of FF's own shops under Strategy 1 controls the quality of the immediate environment within which FF's clothes are sold. This environment can then be made consistent with the marketing image and the supporting personal service can also be provided.

Unfortunately, FF may not benefit from economies of scope if it uses stores spread across western Europe and it may be unable to take advantage of common distribution channels with its products assuming they continue to be made in the UK. The high value and low volume/weight is likely to reduce this problem as clothes can be sent by courier if needed urgently.

Price

The pricing policy needs to be appropriate to the wider marketing strategy. A low price may penetrate the market and achieve recognition more quickly, but it also sends a signal about the quality of the product. Once established as below the designer range in market positioning, it could be difficult to improve its image and increase the price later.

- Costs

  There may be greater costs of operation and distribution in Europe than in the UK and the influence of costs on price needs to be considered alongside marketing issues. In the long term, price should be expected to cover average costs. However this in turn may depend on the volumes sold in Europe and the economies of scale achieved.

- Customers

  Customer tolerance of prices may vary from country to country for the target group according to how important clothing expenditure is in an individual's budget. Market research will be needed to assess price resistance in this sector of the market. A key issue in this respect is price elasticity.

- Competitors

  The prices charged by competitors may be different than UK competitors as cost structures may vary, as may the intensity of competition. Also there may be some variation, as the £:Euro exchange rate may alter, possibly significantly.

Promotion

Promotion is about communication – informing consumers about the product and enhancing their perception of the product in a manner that persuades them to buy it. The means and method of promotion needs to be appropriate to the product and its positioning. The cost of promotion also needs to be considered in relation to the benefits.

In terms of promoting to consumers, there is a range of methods including: advertising; sponsorship, offers, discounts. Not all these are likely to be appropriate in an upmarket context.

Advertising is likely to be the most important means of sales promotion for FF. If the brand is to be up-market then this needs a significant marketing effort to promote this image compared to maintaining the brand image in the UK. If a new local European market is to be accessed, a greater initial marketing effort will be required, perhaps reflected by the use of outside marketing specialists with local knowledge and a significantly larger marketing budget.

Whilst it normally takes significantly more resources to establish a brand image in a new market, there may be enduring benefits once brand reputation and recognition are established.

Market research may reveal a particular market segment where FF clothes most appeal in terms of their attributes, image and appearance. This may mean that more effective advertising could take place as efforts could then be targeted using a segmentation strategy. Each target country may be different to the UK and to each other.

The 7Ps

The 4Ps model can be expanded into the 7Ps model and this is particularly relevant in the marketing of services. While FF sells goods, a high level of FF customer service is important and may be as much of a key feature in marketing FF in Europe as the clothes themselves.

People

Recruiting appropriate staff in Europe would be a key feature of the service element of the marketing plan. The people working for an organisation which has an interface with customers often say more about that company than the product being sold. In the case of FF, this may include the ability to sell clothes as well as knowledge of local fashions and tastes in advising customers. It may also include skills of altering and fitting the clothes. Assessing the nature and extent of staff recruitment and training will be an important feature of the marketing plan.

Physical

Physical refers to items that give physical substance surrounding the delivery of a service, such as logos, staff uniforms, carrier bags and packaging, and store layout/design. FF's clothes are upmarket and the physical evidence of the quality of the stores in which they are sold is an important part of the image and context within which the clothes are sold. The marketing plan therefore needs to consider the size of the stores and decor etc.

Processes

The ways in which the clothes are sold and customer service is delivered have an impact on the way in which FF customers perceive the organisation. As part of a customer service, efficient administrative processes underpin a high quality of provision. For instance if a customer cannot obtain the size or colour of clothes they want then they may go elsewhere. Efficient processes for FF would include: maintain an appropriate level and type of inventories; ordering services for customers where an item is not held in inventory; and an efficient fitting service.

Examiner's comments:

Requirement 32.1 asked candidates to set out the factors to be considered in a marketing plan for Strategy 1 using the marketing mix.

Most candidates produced answers which used the 4Ps marketing mix model. Although points made specifically in relation to Felan were brief, some good application skills were demonstrated. A minority extended the analysis to 7Ps or, at least, considered 'people' as an extra factor in addition to the 4Ps. Most candidates were able to state the main points in relation to the fact that FF is an unknown brand outside the UK, moving abroad meant migrating into a different market with different consumers and that distributing the unknown product abroad may be difficult. Some excellent answers were produced which focussed on different fashion tastes, other established brands in the market and the fact that the alternative strategies would have an impact on how and where the product was to be distributed. The higher scoring answers focussed on consumers, competition and push/pull pricing. Some poorer answers were also produced in this part which did not even discuss the 4Ps.

32.2 General issues of overseas expansion for both strategies

Lynch's Expansion Method Matrix identifies the proposed strategy as 'international development'. The two options of acquisition and direct investment are identify in Lynche's Expansion Method Matrix as 'Organic Growth' (or internal development) in an international market.

Core competencies

The core competencies that have allowed FF to prosper in the UK may not exist in an overseas country. Specifically, core competencies may relate to design and production.

Within this framework, Kay's sources of core competencies are:

Architecture

- Internal architecture – is the relationship with employees. These are likely to be entirely or largely new employees where a new relationship needs to be established.

- External architecture – this includes relationships with external stakeholders such as suppliers and customers. There is likely to be a need to establish some new local suppliers as entire supply from the UK is unlikely to be feasible.

- Network architecture – collaboration between businesses and local networks needs to be established from scratch.

Reputation

It is likely that FF will need to establish a new reputation locally. This may prevent it from initially charging a price premium as in the UK.

Innovative ability

Innovation in design is likely to be able to be 'transported' from the UK to the overseas markets but it is an industry where tastes vary across countries and thus is unlikely to give the same competitive advantage.

Risks

The risks are substantial from the overseas venture and include:

- Foreign currency translation, as revenues would occur in euros. This is however partially naturally hedged by the fact that costs are also partly being occurred in the same currency.

- Lack of knowledge of overseas markets.

- High level of sunk costs in entering the new market with associated high exit costs if the venture fails and there is a need to withdraw from the market.

- This is a strategy of market development within the Ansoff Matrix. In order to penetrate this new market it is necessary to have core competencies that at least match established local competitors. This is uncertain given the established positions of local competitors.

- The fact that the expansion will reduce dependence on the UK market and the UK economy may reduce risks but only if the other countries are not correlated with the UK in terms of its economic cycle.

Comparison

Issues in favour of Strategy 1

- There are fewer limitations on the scope of development compared to Strategy 2 as there are only 10 UneShop stores. Strategy 1 has no such limits.

- With Strategy 1, FF can develop its own independent market positioning, whereas with Strategy 2 it is questionable whether UneShop has a reputation consistent with FF as it is mid to upper market.

- High street space is likely to be at ground level and prime locations. UneShop floor space may be less prime space (perhaps a corner of the top floor).

- There may be greater operational independence with Strategy 1 than with Strategy 2 in operating with UneShop eg regarding opening times, presentation, staff and other shared facilities.

- Greater scope to choose prime locations in major European cities rather than be restricted to only 10 French cities.

Issues in favour of Strategy 2

- Greater initial impact as 10 stores can open immediately whereas under Strategy 1 it may take time to find and develop 10 new sites

- There is cross branding between UneShop and FF so greater initial market recognition is achieved

- There is more immediate footfall from existing UneShop customers who would visit FF

- Rentals may be lower than high street space depending on the location

- Economies of scope as geographically is more condensed from operating in France alone

- May be able to use UneShop distribution channels and joint marketing

- Greater initial market recognition in France at 25% with Strategy 2 compared to 20% elsewhere in Europe with Strategy 1

- Less range of culture and tastes by focusing in one country

Recommendation

The recommended course of action will depend largely on the terms of agreement with UneShop (eg the cost of renting the floor space, restrictive conditions etc). Assuming, however, that there is no significant difference in rental cost or other conditions between the two strategies, then Strategy 2 appears to offer much better long term scope for expansion and gives more control and autonomy.

The above recommendation is of course provisional and will depend on market research demonstrating evidence of viability of the project. It may be that the evidence demonstrates the opposite, in which case neither strategy should be accepted.

Examiner's comments:

Requirement 32.2 asked candidates to compare and evaluate the two alternative strategies and to provide appropriate advice. Answers to this part focussed on organic growth compared to a joint venture. Many answers lacked detail and focussed on: Felan's lack of knowledge of overseas markets, exposure to foreign currency risk, the fact that fixed costs would likely remain constant and that there would be an established customer base with Strategy 2. Although it was apparent that candidates had understood the key advantages and disadvantages, it would have been encouraging to see development of these points and an assessment of the impact of the strategies on business, customers, strategy and performance of FF.

Weaker candidates tended to list advantages and disadvantages of each of the two strategies as two separate propositions, while stronger ones compared and contrasted them. The majority provided recommendations, with most opting for Strategy 2. Some suggested that use could be made of an emergent strategy approach, starting with Strategy 2 and then possibly moving on to wider expansion.

33 KoganAir plc (December 2011)

Marking guide

		Knowledge	Skill	Marks
33.1 (a)	Analyse operating profit	1	16	15
(b)	Forecast profit and working assumptions	2	8	9
33.2 (a)	Risks/PESTEL	1	4	
(b)	Risk management	2	4	
				10
33.3	Marketing director and Porter	3	7	9
		9	39	43

General comments:

This is the mini case and the data analysis question. The scenario relates to the airline industry. The company in the scenario, KoganAir, is a low-cost airline operating routes within Europe. The company has expanded the number of routes this year and increased revenue. Despite this, profits have fallen and losses are expected in the current year. Data is provided to show changes in key financial and operating elements of the business. KoganAir is evaluating the impact of future fuel cost increases. It is also examining a strategy of repositioning itself in the market between the low cost airlines and the national airlines by increasing prices and service quality.

33.1 (a)

	20Y0	20Y1	% change
Basic analysis of operational data given in question			
Available passenger seats (millions)	6.4	7.0	+9.4
Actual passenger seats	5.4	6.0	+11.1
Load factor %	84.4	85.7	+1.5
Number of aircraft	49	50	+2.0
Routes operated	62	64	+3.2
ASK (millions)	7,271	7,868	+8.2
Revenue analysis			
Revenue	313	337	+7.7
Revenue per passenger	£57.96	£56.17	(3.1)
Revenue per available seat	£48.91	£48.14	(1.6)
Revenue per aircraft	£6.39m	£6.74m	+5.5
Revenue per route	£5.05m	£5.27m	+4.4
Revenue at 20Y1 prices (ie 2% inflator on 20Y0 revenue)	£319.26m	£337m	+5.6
Cost analysis			
Operating costs per aircraft	£0.51m	£0.52m	+2.0
Total cost per passenger	£57.8	£58.2	+0.7
Fuel cost at 20Y1 prices (ie 17% inflator on 20Y0 fuel cost)	£88.92m	£96.0m	+8.0
Fuel cost per 1 million ASK	£10,452	£12,201	+16.7
Fuel as a % of total cost	24.4%	27.5%	
Operational analysis			
ASK per aircraft	148.4m	157.4m	+6.1
ASK per route	117.3	122.9	+4.8
Load factor	84.4	85.7	+1.5
Average flight length (ASK/available passenger seats flown)	1,136	1,124	(1.1)

Revenue

Overall the data shows an operating profit of £1m in 20Y0 being turned into an expected operating loss of £12m in 20Y1. This is not due to a reduction in the level of revenue or number of passengers, both of which have increased.

Revenue has increased fairly significantly by 7.7%. Part of this increase is due to an average increase in prices of 2%. The real terms increase is shown in the above table as 5.6%. This could be explained by (1) an increase in the volume of sales (2) a change in the mix of sales or (3) changes in exchange rate where tickets are sold in a foreign currency.

The number of passengers and ASK have increased by 11.1% and 8.2% respectively so this suggests that the sales mix has changed with a greater number of lower value journeys and/or there have been unfavourable currency movements with the £ strengthening relatively against other European countries where tickets are sold overseas.

These factors (mix and currency) are demonstrated in a fall in revenue per passenger of 3.1% despite the overall increase in prices and volumes. It may be that the new routes introduced are shorter, lower value routes (the average flight length has fallen by 1%, for instance) or just an overall shift away from higher price flights.

Fuel costs

Fuel costs have risen substantially in 20Y1 compared to 20Y0, by 26.3%. This is significantly in excess of the revenue increase and increases in other costs and is therefore a major reason for the decrease in operating earnings.

The increase can be divided into a price increase and a volume increase. Prices increased by 17% according to the chief executive. ASK increased by 8.2% (the determinant of volume of fuel used according to the CEO's working assumptions). This gives an imputed change in total fuel spend of 26.6% (1.17 × 1.082). The actual increase in fuel spend is 26.3%. The difference in actual and imputed fuel spend could be due to fuel efficiencies arising perhaps from the increased load factor. (The relationship with ASK is only approximate according to the working assumptions.)

Overall, fuel makes up a significant proportion of total costs and this has increased from 24.4% in 20Y0 to 27.5% in 20Y1. The increase in fuel price is therefore significant in affecting profit in terms of its importance in the cost structure and the % increase.

In absolute terms, fuel spend increased by £20m which is greater than the change in operating profit of £13m.

Other costs

Other costs changed broadly in line with the change in revenue. They reflected capacity increases (aircraft and routes) but also inflationary increases.

Operating efficiency

Operating efficiency in terms of asset utilisation appeared to have improved in 20Y1 compared to 20Y0.

The ASK per aircraft increased by 6.1% which may reflect better utilisation (quicker turnaround or more demand). It might have reflected longer flights but the data does not support this as the above table shows that the average flight length has fallen by 1.1%.

Similarly, the load factor increased from 84.4% to 85.2% showing that the proportion of occupied seats was greater in 20Y1 than in 20Y0. This is important as it generates revenue at the margin, but the marginal cost of an additional passenger on an existing flight is likely to be minimal.

Examiner's comments:

Requirement 33.1(a) was fairly well answered on the whole, however the main drawback for the majority of candidates was an inability to distinguish correctly between volume and price effects on the growth of revenue and fuel costs between 20Y0 and 20Y1. Many did not recognise any volume effect at all. Thus, when attempting to explain the difference between KoganAir's increase in fuel costs of 26% and that of the industry as a whole (17%), many incorrectly explained this as being due to, for example, inefficient operations, old planes etc. The poorest answers made little if any attempt at explaining changes, merely describing what percentage changes occurred, without suggesting how, why or when these may have arisen. Many weaker answers did no calculations of their own and merely repeated calculations which had been given in the question, such as the 7.7% revenue increase, without adding any analysis or explanation. The rise in fuel costs tended to be the major factor which candidates picked up and discussed in detail – bringing in global oil prices generally. The best answers understood the volume change effect, and the possible impact of changes in the sales mix. Additionally, only a very few candidates explicitly referred to the importance of load factor improvements, given that the marginal cost of an extra passenger is virtually zero.

(b)

	20Y1 Estimated	20Y2 Forecast	Comment
Total revenue (£m)	337	364.1	Prices are constant so revenue varies in accordance with ASK £337m × (8,500/7,868)
Fuel costs (£m)	(96)	(134.8)	£96m × (8,500/7,868) × 1.3 Increase related to the price per tonne increase of 30% and the increase in ASK

	20Y1 Estimated	20Y2 Forecast	Comment
Operating costs of aircraft (£m)	(26)	(26)	Assumed constant despite three new aircraft. This may imply that larger aircraft have been replaced by a larger number of smaller aircraft or other cost efficiencies made (eg leasing contracts renewed on better terms given recession in industry)
Other operating costs (£m)	(227)	(233.8)	Increase only 3% – more info needed on these assumptions
Operating (loss) (£m)	**(12)**	**(30.5)**	

With a 30% price rise assumed, the total increase in fuel costs in 20Y2 would be 40.4% (in 20Y1 there was a 26.3% increase). In absolute terms this is £38.4m which is larger than the increase in the forecast operating loss of £18.5m. The fuel price increases are therefore driving the increase in operating losses.

This analysis of fuel spend however needs to be considered both in terms of increased usage of fuel (assumed to vary according to ASK) and increases in the price of fuel per tonne.

If fuel prices per tonne were constant in 20Y2 compared with 20Y1 then total fuel spend would rise to £103.7m (£96m × (8,500/7,868)) ie an increase of £7.7m (£103.7m – £96m).

In terms of basic sensitivity analysis therefore it would take a total fuel spend of £116.3m to achieve the same overall operating loss of £12m as in 20Y1. The maximum fuel price increase would be 12.2% (£116.3m/£103.7m) to maintain the operating loss at its current level.

To achieve break even overall, fuel spend would need to be £104.3m (£134.8m – £30.5m). This would require an increase in price per tonne of fuel of only 0.58% (£104.3m/£103.7m).

These calculations of course depend on the validity of the working assumptions but a limitation of sensitivity analysis is that it only considers one factor at a time while holding all other factors constant.

Working assumptions

Fuel prices – the assumption of a 30% increase is a possibility and may be a worse case scenario for scenario planning purposes, but it is unlikely to be the most probable scenario as oil is a traded commodity and is likely to be priced efficiently. If a 30% increase next year is the most likely estimate then this would lead to speculation, thereby immediately forcing up current fuel prices.

Average price per passenger – in a recession, constant prices appear reasonable as a prudent assumption. It may however be the case that prices need to fall if competitors reduce prices.

Fuel and revenue vary according to ASK – fuel varying according to ASK seems a reasonable assumption if there are no major changes in the fleet of aircraft such as size of aircraft or fuel efficiency. Revenue varying according to ASK may not be a reasonable assumption as the price of a flight is unlikely to vary in direct proportion to distance travelled (ie twice the price for twice the distance). However, if the portfolio of routes remains similar in 20Y2 then ASK appears a reasonable short term measure of activity against which to evaluate revenue changes.

Operating costs will remain constant – this assumption seems unlikely as three new aircraft are to be acquired in 20Y2 which will increase leasing costs and/or depreciation.

Other costs will increase by 3% – this assumption seems a reasonable approximation of inflation (eg of wages) given that the recession creates downward pressure on wages and other costs. However, this assumes that 'other costs' are fixed, whereas there is likely to be a variable cost element which will increase with the predicted increase in activity for 20Y2 (eg ASK is estimated to increase by 8% in 20Y2).

Examiner's comments:

Answers to requirement 33.1(b) tended to be highly variable in quality, with some scoring virtually full marks while others struggled to achieve a pass mark for the question. The key discriminating factors were whether or not candidates could provide correct calculations for the 20Y2 forecast, and make a reasonable attempt to calculate and explain the sensitivity of operating profit to changes in the cost of fuel.

The most common errors in the calculations for 20Y2 were to arrive at a revenue figure of £376m, rather than £364m, and a fuel cost figure of £125m rather than £134.8m. The £125m ignores the volume effect ie simply increasing £96m by 30%. The revenue figure of £376m uses forecast passenger seats sold as the driver rather than basing the projection on ASK (as stipulated in the key working assumptions of the question itself) which reflects the length of journeys in addition to just the number of journeys.

Sensitivity analysis was ignored by many candidates and also tended to vary in quality amongst those who did attempt it. Poorer efforts merely provided some form of calculation, often just fuel costs as a percentage of profit or revenue, with little attempt at interpretation. Most candidates did recognise profits to be sensitive to fuel price changes. The comments on the working assumptions were quite weak with many candidates focussing their answers purely on the fuel price rise, without taking into consideration the impact of other costs on overall profit.

33.2 PESTEL

Risk and impact	Risk Management
ECONOMIC	
Fuel costs Sudden sustained and significant changes in fuel prices would unexpectedly increase costs	Buy fuel on forward market (hedge) Fuel is a common cost in the industry and so may be covered by common price rises Scenario analysis and planning Contingent fuel surcharges on tickets (ie charge passengers extra if fuel prices increase, even on tickets already sold)
Currency movements Changes in exchange rates which reduce the sterling value of revenues (eg ticket sold overseas) or increases the sterling value of costs (oil is priced in US$)	International diversification Hedging
Recession Lower passenger demand and more price resistance leading to lower revenues	Sensitive and flexible prices Flexible operations (eg short term leases on aircraft)
Industrial action Loss of flights leading to uncertainty and lower reputation. Increased wage costs	Human resources policy Regular employee engagement Appropriate wages for the industry
ECOLOGICAL	
Environmental issues Impact on consumer perception and reputation. Increased environmental compliance costs Pollution from aircraft	Sustainability policy Environmental public relations policy Use of modern fuel efficient aircraft Recyclable materials

Risk and impact	Risk Management
LEGAL	
Security (illegal acts)	
Terrorist incident or accident leading to loss of reputation and direct financial cost	Checking of baggage Liaison with authorities and airports Regular maintenance checks Passenger safety procedures
Regulatory intervention	
Increase of costs or reduced flexibility due to new laws affecting the industry or one jurisdiction	Lobbying of governments International diversification
Taxation	
Increases in general tax, fuel tax or industry specific tax (could also be classified under economic)	Monitoring of budgetary proposals Lobbying

Note. Many of the risks are industry wide (eg fuel prices) thus while they may have an impact on the competitiveness of the industry, they will have a limited effect on the competitiveness of individual companies within the industry as the effects would be common to most airlines.

Examiner's comments:

Requirement 33.2 requested candidates to explain the key risks for KoganAir that arise from factors within the economic, ecological and legal sections of the PESTEL framework and to explain how these risks might be managed.

This requirement was generally well answered, with the majority of candidates displaying a good understanding of the PESTEL framework and correctly categorising risks between Economic, Ecological and Legal. Most candidates considered how the firm could manage risks but the risk management techniques were not always linked to the specific risk to which they related. Many better candidates used a columnar format to link risks to the relevant risk management technique, but other methods of providing this linkage were also acceptable.

Some of the risk management techniques were very general and not really appropriate to the risk identified. For example, for Ecological issues, most candidates identified that there were pollution issues with the use of aircraft. However, instead of using their knowledge on sustainability or CSR and applying it to the airline industry, some candidates chose to offer development by KoganAir of alternative means of transport, such as diversifying into coach and sea travel, which was entirely unrealistic for an airline operator.

Also, despite being specifically instructed in the question to deal only with Economic, Ecological and Legal matters, some candidates wasted time outlining the political, social and technological risks, which were not required and received no additional marks.

33.3 Porter argued that competitive pressures are such that only two competitive strategies will deliver competitive advantage (ie superior ROI).

- **Low cost**: a firm following this strategy will withstand the shrinking margins better and so, as rivals fall away, may be left as a major player with enhanced power against the power of suppliers and buyers.

- **Differentiation**: a firm presenting itself as a superior provider may escape price pressure by avoiding straight-forward price comparisons with rivals.

Porter's generic strategies can be represented as follows:

Porter's generic strategies

	LOW COST	DIFFERENTIATION
BROAD	COST LEADERSHIP	DIFFERENTIATION
NARROW	COST LEADERSHIP FOCUS	DIFFERENTIATION FOCUS

(left axis label: COMPETITIVE SCOPE)

Cost leadership

As a low cost airline KoganAir is attempting to adopt a (focused) cost leadership strategy whereby it is seeking to achieve the position of lowest-cost airline in its sector of the industry (ie European short haul). By operating at the lowest cost, KoganAir has been able to compete on price with every other airline in its sector of the industry, and still earn profits.

Key factors in cost leadership may include

(a) Economies of scale as operations increase (aircraft/routes).
(b) Use the latest technology to reduce costs and/or enhance productivity (eg online booking).
(c) High utilisation of aircraft (quick turnaround, high load factors).
(d) Concentration on improving productivity.
(e) Minimise overhead costs.
(f) Get favourable access to sources of supply (fuel discounts).

KoganAir has suffered high fuel costs but these are a common cost in the industry. They affect costs and profit but would not directly affect KoganAir's competitive position. If other costs can be controlled, then rival companies, with less efficient cost structures, are less likely to survive and the survivor companies many pick up their customers.

A significant price increase of 10% is likely to cause confusion about the brand as it would no longer be a low price airline and customers would require additional services for the extra price.

Porter regarded this as a *stuck in the middle* strategy. This means that the firm has sought to attract many segments at different price points and so is seen as not being as differentiated as the market leader but, perhaps because of the costs of serving the differentiated segment, not able to make good profits at the cost leader's prices.

One alternative model to consider this issue is Bowman's Clock

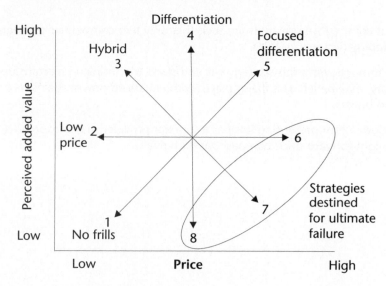

Price-based strategies

Strategies 1 and 2 are price-based strategies.

- A **no frills** strategy (1) has been used by KoganAir aimed at the most price-conscious consumers. This strategy has been used for market entry, to gain experience and to build volume.

- A **low price** strategy (2) offers better value than competitors. This can lead to price war and reduced margins for all. Porter's generic strategy of **cost leadership** is appropriate to a firm adopting this strategy.

If however KoganAir increases its price it is moving more towards a hybrid strategy which may have a valid position in price-quality space, or it may create uncertainty in the minds of consumers.

A similar model is in the diagram below. This diagram shows that a brand can be positioned in a number of ways, eg via a price or emphasis on a particular characteristic or set of characteristics. In other words, positioning means giving a product a place relative to its competitors on factors such as quality, price, image, being exotic, providing status, etc.

Positioning can be facilitated by a graphical technique called perceptual mapping, various survey techniques and statistical techniques like multi-dimensional scaling and factor analysis.

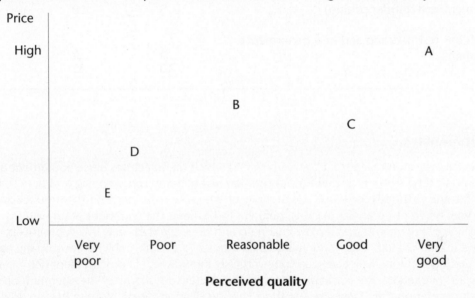

Even such a rather simple product positioning matrix as shown above may give valuable insights in the relative positions of the various brands.

In the case of KoganAir an increase in price without an increase in service would move its positioning upwards vertically. This would make it less competitive in price quality terms compared to its rivals.

The exception would be if rivals also increased prices by a similar amount in order to compensate for common increases in costs. If so, KoganAir's positioning within the industry might be constant, but the competitiveness of the industry compared to alternative forms of consumer expenditure made be reduced (eg consumers may choose to buy a car rather than go on holiday if the prices of flights increase).

Examiner's comments:

Requirement 33.3 requested candidates to evaluate the suggestion of the marketing director to reposition KoganAir upmarket, by referring to Porter's generic strategies and any other appropriate strategic models. There was more or less an equal split between those candidates who only used Porter's generic strategies framework, and those who additionally introduced other frameworks to enhance their analysis eg Bowman's clock; Ansoff; Price-Quality framework.

Those candidates using only Porter's generic strategies framework tended to conclude that the marketing director's suggestion would lead to KoganAir being 'stuck in the middle'. There was however little analysis or use of any other model to justify this conclusion. Where alternative models were offered with reasoned analysis and recommendations, more rounded conclusions were normally drawn.

34 Universal Office Supplies plc (December 2011)

	Knowledge	Skill	Marks
34.1 (a) R&D business strategy	2	4	6
(b) Evaluation of current and proposed structuring and recharging	2	5	7
34.2 Current divisional structure (performance measurement and transfer pricing)	3	10	12
34.3 New divisions restructuring and new performance measurement	3	6	8
	10	25	33

General comments:

The scenario in this question relates to a company (UOS) which manufactures office equipment of two types (1) communication systems (including videoconferencing, audio conferencing and data sharing) and (2) office furniture. The two products sell to many of the same customers but the production technology is very different (ie similar markets, different industries). The communication systems industry and market are dynamic and rapidly changing and dependent on new developments in technology and usage. The office furniture market and industry are more stable. The company has a number of operating divisions which are currently vertically integrated: (1) procurement (2) manufacturing (3) marketing. The company attempts to maintain autonomy of the operating divisions by arm's length transfer pricing. There are also three support divisions: R&D, Human Resources and Finance. The company intends to engage in a restructuring from functional divisional to be product-based divisional. The manner in which the R&D function is charged to divisions will also change.

34.1 (a) R&D can improve products and processes and can be an important element in the strategy of the business. However it is likely to be of greatest value in a dynamic changing environment such as communications, where it can be a source of innovation and competitive advantage, rather than in a lower value, stable environment, such as the manufacture of office furniture.

A key point is that the R&D strategy should be appropriate to the broader corporate strategy.

In the Communications Systems Division, **product innovation** could be a source of differentiation by giving competitive advantage over rivals' products.

Process innovation may enable differentiation or cost leadership. In the Office Furniture division, although it competes on price, it appears not to be a cost leader and does not use R&D. This may be due to the basic and standardised nature of the processes for furniture manufacture, such that the costs of R&D would not be justified by the benefits.

Other strategic aspects of R&D for UOS include:

- **Porter's value chain**: R&D is included within all parts of the value chain including support activities of **technology development**. It can be harnessed in the service of lower costs or improved differentiation.

- **Ansoff matrix**: R&D supports all four strategic quadrants. Strategies of Market Penetration and Market Development can be served by product refinement. Product Development and Diversification will require more significant innovations.

- **Industry and product lifecycles**: the obsolescence of existing products can be accelerated by industry wide product R&D, and so company specific R&D is required to provide the firm with replacements. In UOS's case the communications products are likely to have very short life cycles due to the dynamic nature of the industry hence R&D is essential.

Despite the potential benefits, the new product development process must be carefully controlled. While new products can be a major source of competitive advantage they can cost a great deal to bring to market. A screening process is necessary to ensure that resources are concentrated on projects with a high probability of success.

Examiner's comments:

Requirement 34.1 related to the R&D function and asked candidates to: (a) explain how R&D can contribute to the business strategy of UOS; and (b) compare and evaluate the current and the proposed structuring and recharging arrangements for R&D.

Part 34.1(a) was well answered on the whole. Most answers considered the effect of R&D on product innovation in the context of the Communication Division's differentiation strategy, and also R&D's support for process innovation through the value chain for the Furniture Division in order to deliver a generic strategy of what most candidates considered to be cost leadership. In this respect, there was some excellent knowledge displayed on how R&D was included in value chain analysis and how its relative importance was dependent on where a product was in the product lifecycle.

(b) **Existing R&D structure**

There appear to be two key issues:

- Who initiates and determines the nature of the R&D projects to be undertaken?

- How, if at all, are the costs of R&D to be accounted for in divisional performance measurement?

On the demand side, under the existing structure, R&D is a free good for the communications section, which is the sole internal customer. It therefore has incentives to make excessive demands as it receives the benefits of R&D without incurring any of the costs. Under the current arrangements however it appears that the communications section has limited formal influence over the number or nature of the R&D projects taking place.

On the supply side, the R&D division appears to be setting its own agenda without reference to the communications section (the internal customer) or to those with best knowledge of the needs of the external customers (ie the Marketing Division).

The risk is therefore that new R&D is technology driven by engineers in R&D rather than being driven by customers' needs and desires. This may lead to additional features on the products which incur costs to UOS, but do not give benefits to customers who will not therefore pay a price premium for these new features.

Proposed R&D structure

Under the proposed structure, the R&D projects appear to be demand led because they are initiated by the Communications Systems Division. The fact that the new head of the Communications Systems Division is a marketing person is likely to improve the extent to which new products are market driven, rather than technology driven.

In terms of costs, the R&D Division has no incentives to control costs as these are passed on to the Communications Systems Division. However, it may be that overheads are recharged on a budgeted basis, in which case if there is an insufficient volume of R&D projects demanded by Communications Systems Division then there may be an under-recovery.

The recharging of costs may also act as a disincentive for the Communications Systems Division to demand R&D services, as short-term divisional profit is damaged, while the benefits may only be longer term. This may therefore give incentives only to take on R&D projects which give short-term benefits (eg by enabling short-term cost reduction or immediate and substantial product improvement).

Conclusion

Overall, the new structure seems preferable in terms of how the R&D projects are identified and initiated as it depends on customer needs and benefits in the marketplace.

The recharging of costs, however, needs further consideration in terms of the disincentives for Communications Systems Division to demand R&D services. One alternative may be to amortise the recharge of R&D costs in the divisional budget of Communications Systems Division (eg the current year R&D costs to be spread over (say) the next five years in the divisional accounts of Communications Systems Division). This would enable costs incurred by the Communications Systems Division to be matched against the profile of R&D benefits over time.

Examiner's comments:

Part 34.1(b) answers were highly variable. Many candidates misread the question and provided an evaluation of the existing and proposed structure overall for the whole firm. This was despite the question explicitly stating that the current and proposed structure should be discussed only in respect of the R&D function. The best answers only focused on an evaluation of R&D and recharging arrangements under the current and proposed structures and these candidates tended to perform reasonably well.

34.2 The current structure is a functional structure of vertically integrated operating divisions, with separate support divisions, which are also defined on a functional basis.

Functional structure

A functional structure enables specialisation of skills and economies of scale in coherent groups of: procurement, manufacturing, marketing, R&D, HR and finance. However, where there are significant interdependencies between divisions (eg procurement and manufacturing) then such a structure may lead to bureaucracy as tasks are not always separable.

Conversely, while manufacturing is considered as a single function then the skills needed to produce office furniture are likely to be largely independent of those required to produce communications systems equipment. As a consequence, there may be few benefits of retaining these in the same division.

The combination of functions in manufacturing, without much synergy, seems likely to cause conflict and dispute as it is difficult to allocate costs to each product and thus determine the profitability of each product in order to make pricing and output decisions. It also makes it more difficult to control costs as allocation of responsibility is less clear within a division than it is between divisions given common costs and common tasks.

Transfer pricing

Transfer pricing between procurement and manufacturing divisions

Transfer pricing between procurement and manufacturing divisions provides incentives for the procurement division to minimise purchase costs below budget as much as possible. This has a number of problems:

- Obtaining the lowest cost item may mean lower quality which may damage reputation

- The larger discounts may only be available on older parts and materials. In a rapidly changing environment this many mean less functionality compared to the current industry standard

- If budgets are set at the beginning of the year then, in a rapidly changing environment, they may become irrelevant during the year as prices fall with technological change. This enables the Procurement Division to make profits without much skill or effort

The fact that the nature and quantity of the required purchases are determined by the Manufacturing Division prevents excessive ordering by procurement to obtain quantity discounts. The extent to which the Manufacturing Division can precisely define the type of product required may further limit the ability of procurement to obtain low quality, low cost items and materials.

An additional concern over the transfer price relates to the inclusion of overheads by the Procurement Division in addition to the purchase price. The apportionment of overheads on the basis of purchase price may not reflect the level of effort or achievement by the Procurement Division in making the order. For example, the purchase of wood or metal to make office furniture may be relatively straightforward with a limited number of local suppliers. The sourcing of silicon chips or other small electronic items may however involve a global search of many suppliers requiring significant incremental search costs.

Transfer pricing between manufacturing and marketing divisions

In principle, the setting of transfer prices by negotiation based on market prices preserves autonomy. However there seem to be a number of factors mitigating against the validity of such an approach in the case of UOS:

- Furniture may be an active market, hence the prices of similar items of office furniture can be observed to set transfer prices. However Communications Systems is less likely to be an active market as the products are differentiated, specialised and rapidly changing. The market prices may therefore be a poor guide and it may be expensive to keep up to date information for like-for-like market comparisons.

- The government contract may be a poor guide and the price set is contractual and may be out of date. The price may also not be competitive for the private sector.

- The transfer price is a wholesale price but the gap between wholesale and retail prices may not be justified by the efforts of the Marketing Department. The added value by marketing therefore needs to be questioned.

Divisional performance measurement

To the extent that transfer prices are distorted, the performance measures based on profit centres will also be distorted.

The Marketing Division appears only to be breaking even but it includes installation which is not really a marketing function and it may not therefore possess the necessary core competences.

The profit of the Manufacturing Division does not attempt to distinguish between the profitability of the two separate products. If for instance one of the products was not viable but the other was profitable this would not necessarily be revealed by the profit centre reporting system.

An additional problem is that allocations of overheads with the Manufacturing Division are not required yet may further hide the profitability of each individual product.

The performance of the Procurement Division is as much dependent on the setting of budgeted prices as it is on the actual discounts achieved. Moreover the discounts, as already noted, reflect market movements as much as they reflect effort and searching by the Procurement Division staff.

Examiner's comments:

Requirement 34.2 asked candidates to comment on the merits and problems of the company's current divisional structure in respect of the three operating divisions. Candidates were required to evaluate performance measurement and transfer pricing arrangements.

This requirement was well answered on the whole. Most candidates correctly considered the existing structure to be a functional one and provided discussion of its advantages and disadvantages.

Performance measurement and transfer pricing issues were less well addressed, although many did explicitly recognise the limitations of the existing structure in evaluating the performance of the two separate product lines.

34.3 The new structure is one of product line divisionalisation for the two operating divisions, with support divisions (R&D, HR and Finance) remaining as functional divisions.

Under this system, operating division managers are responsible for products, but also each controls personnel working in a range of functions (procurement, manufacture and marketing).

The advantages of this method of divisionalisation are:

- The focus is on the profitability of individual products

- Managers can be held responsible for product performance

- Product specialisation can be linked to functional specialisation with learning over time (eg marketing of office furniture)

- The different functions involved in making and selling each of the two products can be co-ordinated under a single span of control

- Separation of control over manufacturing of the two products reflects the separate and different nature of the production processes

Disadvantages include:

- Functions are under the control of divisional leaders without expertise in that function (eg Pauline's control over furniture marketing and Andy's control over communications manufacturing).

- The divisions are likely to be larger with a wider span of control for each divisional head.

- Pauline has not previously managed a division and is now in charge of an expanded division with multiple functional activities.

- Change management may cause barriers to change. For example Jim, who previously headed communications systems manufacturing, was not promoted to be communications divisional head, unlike Pauline. This may cause individual demotivation. There may also be group demotivation where functional divisions such as Marketing are split within the new divisional structure with possible loss of security, status or remuneration for some groups or alternatively a change of role.

- The Communications Systems Division shares many of the same customers as the Furniture Division. There may therefore be increased distribution costs and reduced economies of scope if these customers are serviced independently by each division.

Divisional performance measurement

As all the operations for each product now fall within the one division, transfer pricing between operational divisions is no longer necessary. There may be some recharging of support division costs to operational divisions, but this is less of an issue where there is no profit upload (see previous R&D discussion for example).

The absence of transfer prices means that the relevant pricing is with outside parties and is thus market driven. This makes divisional profit more relevant as a measure of divisional performance measurement as there is less need for arbitrary transfer prices. However, there remain some issues:

- The Communications Systems Division shares the same factory as the Office Furniture Division. As a consequence, there are likely to be common overhead costs which need to be shared between the two divisions. As costs are interdependent, then this jointness causes a degree of arbitrariness in divisional profit.

- The Communications Systems Division shares many of the same customers as the Office Furniture Division and there is therefore some interdependence of revenues. If one division treats the customers well (or badly) then there may be benefits (or costs) to the other division.

- The recharging of support division costs (or the absence of such recharging) is also likely to distort profit as an adequate divisional performance measure.

Conclusion

The new structure based on product divisionalisation has many benefits compared to the old functional structure in terms of control, accountability and performance measurement. Most significantly, a clearer idea of the performance of the two products will enable each to be managed more coherently and independently.

Examiner's comments:

Requirement 34.3 asked candidates to evaluate the proposed restructuring of the three operating divisions and suggest the most appropriate method of divisional performance measurement.

This was one of the weakest requirements on the paper for many candidates, although most achieved a pass mark. Often, even with good responses, there tended to be too much focus on change management at the expense of structure, performance measurement and transfer pricing. There was also a tendency to include a fairly lengthy discussion of the use of the Balance Scorecard for performance measurement, but often with little direct relevance to the central issues as depicted in the scenario. Better answers offered very specific observations on the potential splitting of overhead costs and the potential distortion of profits from the absence of recharging.

35 Conchester Theatre (December 2011)

Marking guide

		Knowledge	Skill	Marks
35.1	Ethics	3	6	8
35.2 (a)	Market segmentation	1	4	
(b)	Database	1	4	
(c)	Pricing	3	5	16
		8	19	24

General comments:

This was the smallest question on the paper but includes some basic data about revenue generation. The scenario relates to an independent, regional theatre which is a not-for-profit organisation. It currently has income from three major sources (1) ticket sales (2) membership donations (3) government grants. The mission of the theatre is to promote traditional, high quality drama and musicals in the local community while breaking even financially. Grants have been very significantly reduced by the government this year which has caused a crisis in funding. A rich individual has offered to provide finance to compensate for the loss of government funding, but he requires control over the nature of some performances, which may be contrary to the type of performances in the mission statement. An alternative means of generating revenue would be to use more flexible pricing for tickets using a database of members and those attending the theatre. An ethical issue arises as the trustees would be personally liable if the theatre makes a loss.

35.1 From the perspective of Henry, he is offering a significant sum of money in return for some control over the performances and a role on the board as a trustee. From Henry's point of view this seems an open and transparent offer to the board of trustees which they can accept or reject in accordance with their normal procedures. From Henry's perspective therefore there does not seem to be any major ethical issue based on the information provided.

From the perspective of the board of trustees there is a potential conflict of interest between their role as trustees in protecting the mission and culture of CT and their personal risk in assuming liability for the debts of CT.

Their role of protecting the culture and mission of CT of putting on 'traditional plays and musicals with high artistic merit', may be compromised by the ten plays selected annualy by Henry. This also appears to be contrary to the wishes of at least one stakeholder, the members. It may also be contrary to the wishes of other stakeholders, such as local government, who may be unwilling to offer a subsidised rent to a populist commercial theatre.

The conflicting interest is that if they maintain the culture and refuse the money, the ticket sales may be insufficient to cover costs, debts would accumulate and the trustees may become personally liable. There is therefore the personal incentive to accept the £250,000 to reduce personal risk, even though the mission of CT could be damaged.

There is a further conflict between two objectives within the agreed mission statement – financial break even and the objective of putting on 'traditional plays and musicals with high artistic merit.' In the absence of the government grant, these two objectives may be in conflict and therefore the directors face an ethical dilemma in choosing between them.

However, it may be that the ten plays selected by Henry may fall within this remit of artistic merit, although there is a significant risk that they will not.

The proposed arrangement with Henry would also be a breach of the corporate governance structure as, under the current regime, the board decides which performances take place and the members decide who sits on the board. This would need to be resolved transparently with the members who appear to have the power not to appoint Henry.

Examiner's comments:

Requirement 35.1 asked candidates to discuss the ethical issues for CT's board of Trustees arising from the offer from Henry Strong.

It was reasonably well answered by most candidates. The main structure which candidates adopted in answering this question was to use Transparency, Fairness and Effect. This led candidates to conclude that the Mr Strong was attempting to 'bribe' the trustees and the acceptance of the offer would lead to a breach of the mission for which the theatre was originally established.

Other candidates used ethical language and principles to structure their answers. Some candidates questioned the motives in Mr Strong's offer and therefore questioned his integrity – they concluded that Mr Strong was attempting to make a personal gain by increasing profit from populist theatre productions. This showed that candidates still have a habit of jumping straight to a conclusion and be highly suspicious of any hint of an ethical issue, without reference to the evidence available or analysing the situation from both sides.

Poorer answers tended to ignore the conflict of interest for the trustees regarding their potential personal financial liability and the objectives/mission of the trust, concentrating only on the ethics of Henry Strong.

35.2 (a) Market segmentation is the division of a market into homogenous groups of potential customers. In CT's case it is only information about customers that enables classification into a range of overlapping groups.

The purpose of market segmentation for CT is that it can adjust components of the marketing mix to improve returns from each group according to, for example, spending potential, age, location, needs and tastes.

Thus, for instance, advertising can be targeted at the relevant segment for each performance eg for a drama with appeal to older age groups advertising could be targeted at those who are retired. This may in part come from the database, but could also be widened into magazines and clubs for older people living in the Conchester area.

Similarly, geographical targeting of those living closest to the theatre may be appropriate for performances mid-week when many theatre goers would be unwilling to travel.

Perhaps the most important purpose of segmentation is to set prices according the price elasticity of demand of each segment group. This aspect is dealt with below.

(b) The database retains details of customers' characteristics and their preferences with respected to attending the theatre.

The classification permitted by the database includes:

- **Age** – may give an indication of whether the person is employed and thus available during daytime hours for matinees. It may also give an indication of income and likely preferences in drama and music.

- **Postcode** – may show how far the person has to travel to attend a performance and thus the willingness to attend performances during weekdays. It may also indicate the affluence of the area where they live and thus the degree of price resistance.

- **Profession** – may give an indication of social class and income and thus the degree of price resistance. If, for instance, they are students, this may indicate low income, some daytime availability and youthful tastes.

- **Past attendance** – this indicates the type of performance they are likely to attend, and the frequency of attendance may indicate the extent to which they are worth targeting as a future customer with discounts for regular attendance.

There are however limitations to the database in that only the 'Friends of CT' (including members) are available. Other theatre goers do not appear to have made available their details to CT so only 4,000 of the potential customers can be specifically targeted using this information set. During 20Y1, 100,000 tickets have been sold (£1.5m/£15). While this will include multiple attendances by some individuals, it seems likely that there are many more customers than there are 'Friends of CT'.

Note. Capacity is: 800 × 5 × 50 = 200 000 seats [therefore only 50% utilisation has been achieved]

(c) The current pricing strategy treats all segments as one homogeneous group. Moreover, it treats all seats as homogeneous and all performances as homogeneous.

Segmented customers

A policy of price discrimination involves setting different prices to different groups for the same product/service. To succeed, this pricing policy requires two conditions:

- That segmented groups have different price elasticities of demand.

- There is limited leakage between markets such that tickets intended to be sold to a low income group at a low price, cannot be accessed by high income groups.

Examples of price discrimination arising from market segmentation include:

- Students and senior citizens can obtain discounts when buying tickets if they produce status identification when buying and when attending the performance.

- Discount voucher could be sent to local postcodes or to low income postcodes to encourage attendance.

- High income groups (eg by profession or postcode) could be targeted for sales of premium seats or packages at premium prices.

Differentiated performances

Some performances are likely to be more popular than others (eg with well-known actors or well-known plays). If, in the past, these have filled the theatre with some people unable to obtain tickets, then extra revenue could be raised by increasing price beyond £15 until demand equates to supply.

Conversely, if some performances are poorly attended (eg afternoon matinees) then prices could be lowered if demand is price elastic in order to attract lower income groups and sell more seats.

Also, weekend performances could be priced more highly than weekday ones as there is more demand, and perhaps more demand from lower income groups during the week.

Differentiated seating

All seats at any given performance are currently priced the same. The best seats are therefore obtained by members and early bookers, without any price premium being paid. If the better seats are more highly valued, then this means a price premium could be obtained from these seats and more revenue generated.

Conversely, if £15 is too much for some customers, they may be willing to sit in poorer seats in order to be able to see the performance at all. If these seats would otherwise be empty (eg because nobody would pay £15 to sit in them) then incremental revenue would be generated.

Examiner's comments:

Requirement 35.2 asked candidates to explain: (a) the purposes of market segmentation for CT; (b) how the CT database may be used to segment the market; and (c) how different prices may be set by CT in order to increase revenue.

This part was generally well answered. The knowledge displayed of market segmentation and pricing strategies was good and candidates were very comfortable applying their knowledge to the facts of the scenario. The use of the database produced some very good answers with many candidates recognising both the benefit of being able to segment customers by age, profession, address and attendance type and how this information could be utilised to help Conchester Theatre.

In terms of pricing, answers were well structured and suggestions included: giving discounts for students and retired people; charging lower prices for less popular productions; attempting to do some research into competitive pricing; and using differential pricing throughout the year. Some candidates made calculations from the data given in the question, which showed a good skill in using relevant information.

---

36 Bigville Council (September 2012)

	Knowledge	Skill	Marks
36.1 Key stakeholders	2	6	7
36.2 (a) Breakeven	–	4	4
(b) Implications	–	10	9
36.3 Business case (raise finance, sustainable value and alignment)	3	13	14
36.4 Key risks	2	7	8
	7	40	42

General comments:

This is the mini case and also the data analysis question. Bigville's rugby club is in need of a new stadium with greater capacity as a result of its recent league success (the current stadium is leased from the local council). The local football club is in a similar position. The city council have been approached by the rugby club to consider the creation of a community stadium which could be partly funded by sale of the existing stadium land to a developer for a retail site. The council has undertaken an initial feasibility study and is considering the high level business case for the venture. There is demand for a shared stadium with facilities for rugby, football and athletics, plus a range of additional commercial and community uses on non-match days. Land has been identified which would meet the necessary planning criteria. Either a basic stadium can be constructed, with a shared pitch for rugby and football and community sports facilities, or the Council can spend more on an enhanced stadium with a hotel and conference centre. Additional funding would be available in terms of grants provided certain criteria are fulfilled and a sponsorship deal could be sought with a large credit card company, Finanex, whose HQ is in the city. The stadium is likely to be run by a joint stadium management company (SMC) created by the Council and the two clubs.

Candidates were provided with a range of data concerning the build cost, capacity, forecast revenue and costs for each element of the stadium, and attendance figures for comparable rugby/football clubs.

This question was well attempted by most candidates.

36.1 Stakeholder conflict

The clubs and the Council will have different objectives, which will themselves be linked to their different stakeholders. Key stakeholders for the clubs will include the players, the fans and the governing body. Key stakeholders for the Council will be residents, local businesses, the wider community and central government.

The Council as a Not For Profit (NFP) organisation has a wider range of stakeholders and is likely to have to balance the use of limited resources to ensure it provides the best possible services and maximises benefits for the wider community. The clubs are likely to have two main aims:

- To achieve the best sporting success possible in order to retain/attract new fans
- To generate as much profit as possible in order to be able to acquire better players

In certain cases these aims may coincide with the Council's eg if the clubs achieve sporting success, this will generate additional attendance and income which will increase the wealth of the stadium and facilitate the Council's objectives. However there is also scope for conflict between the individual clubs and between the clubs and the Council:

Construction of the stadium:

The clubs are likely to be predominantly interested in the main stadium and pitch. There may be conflict between them as to the best layout and surface of the pitch for their particular requirements. Each club will be interested in any stipulations or health and safety regulations set out by its ruling league body. Since the football club is contributing more capital, it may expect priority over decisions.

The Council will also be interested in the additional community facilities and there may be conflict between the Council and the clubs if the siting or construction of these is seen to negatively affect anything in relation to the main stadium eg a running track around the pitch may cause the fans to feel separated from the game. Similarly the environmental sustainability of the stadium is of key importance to the Council whereas this may be a low priority for the clubs, particularly if it affects the visibility of fans or anything to do with the playing surface or training/changing facilities. The clubs may also be reluctant to pay additional capital costs for community facilities.

The two clubs may also conflict on the seating capacity if for instance there is little prospect of the rugby club ever being promoted and filling a larger stadium but there are realistic prospects of the football club achieving the new capacity. The clubs may also disagree over the size and nature of the playing surface.

Operation of the stadium:

Again the clubs are likely to have their own interests at heart. Although the clubs typically play matches on different days there may be conflict between them over scheduling of training and cup match scheduling.

Similarly if the rugby club has a big championship match on a Sunday they may not take too kindly to the football club having churned up the pitch on the previous day.

The clubs are likely to want priority over the use of the stadium on match days and for weekday training sessions (unless, like some professional clubs, they have access to separate training pitches). Weekday use may conflict with the Council's desire to make the stadium available for the community. Also the Council may want to use profits generated by the stadium to cross-subsidise the use of the community pitches for example, which may conflict with the clubs' profit motives.

Similarly the Council may want to hire out the stadium for events such as concerts. These may benefit the clubs by attracting a wider audience however the clubs may be concerned about the impact that such events might have in terms of damage to the stadium or the playing surface.

Sharing of joint costs between the Council and the clubs is also likely to be an issue.

Operational Issues for the Council will include: crowd safety and security; noise, lighting, energy, waste management, traffic and transport. In respect of these issues the clubs will be focussed on the needs of the clubs and their fans, whereas the Council will also need to take into account the needs of the wider community which may conflict with those of the fans/clubs.

Clearly the arrangements for the SMC will need to be carefully established and agreements drawn up to minimise the potential for conflict between the parties and to protect the interests of the Council.

Examiner's comments:

Requirement 36.1 requested candidates to assess the potential for conflict between the three key stakeholders (Council, rugby club and football club). On the whole this was very well done. The majority of candidates recognised that the Council was a not-for-profit organisation and were able to discuss the potential for conflict between the clubs – who were likely to be focussed on commercial and league success – and the Council's need to satisfy the wider community (and possibly the stadium sponsor). Better candidates also pointed out that in addition to this conflict, there was also likely to be conflict between the two clubs over the type of pitch, match scheduling etc, and that the football club might expect to have priority given that it was contributing a larger share of the capital. In their desire to apply models, candidates must be selective – a number of weaker candidates had learnt and churned out Mendelow's matrix which tended to result in too much focus on power and interest rather than on conflict between stakeholders. Some weaker candidates also dwelt exclusively on the stakeholders' objectives and did not get round to conflicts at all.

36.2 Break even

(a) **The break even attendance is as follows:**

Contribution per visitor

Football   £640,000/(25 × 3,200) = £8

Rugby   £270,000/(15 × 3,000) = £6

Break even

Football £644,000/£8 = 80,500 visitors p.a which with 25 matches = 3,220 per match

Rugby £214,000/£6 = 35,667 visitors p.a which with 15 matches = 2,378 per match

(b) **Discussion**

Implications of calculations

The BE attendance for the football club is marginally higher (by 20 visitors per match) than the attendance figure used in the forecast, which explains the predicted loss (20 × £8 × 25 = £4,000).

The BE figure is 12.5% higher than the current attendance enjoyed by the football club and 5.6% higher than the average for the league. Thus the projections may be quite optimistic and if the initial attendance is below this figure then the football club will make a bigger loss than predicted. (It can be seen from the appendix that there is a loss of £71,400 based on current attendance and a loss of £34,000 based on the average for the current league.) It would be useful to know what the capacity of the existing football ground is and whether, like the rugby club, it is already at full capacity.

In respect of the rugby club the BE figure is 6.4% higher than the current attendance (which would result in a loss of just under £13k) but 16.3% lower than the average for the league. As the club's existing ground appears to be at capacity there is likely to be an implied waiting list of fans wishing to attend and so the estimated attendance level of 3,000 seems reasonable and provides a margin of safety of 20.7% (3000 – 2378/3000).

Variability of attendance levels

The attendance and financial performance of any sports club is heavily dependent on its team's performance. Thus the financial success of both the football and rugby club will depend on their ability to retain their current league position or the chances of being relegated/promoted, which can be seen from Exhibit 1 to significantly affect attendance levels.

(On average, attendance levels for football clubs are 64% higher in the league above and 41% lower in the league below.)

As the break-even levels of attendance for both clubs are above the average attendance for either club in the lower league, then relegation of a club would lead to significant losses or the need to curtail costs. The financial impact of promotion/relegation is set out in the Appendix, based on the figures for a typical club in the league. These calculations make it clear that the profitability of the football club is much more at risk than the rugby club because of the high level of traceable fixed costs (discussed further below). As a result the potential results for football range from a loss of £284k if relegated to a profit of £356k if promoted, which compares to a loss of £43k and a profit of £146k for the rugby club.

In addition to variations in attendance, success in non-league tournaments during the year would lead to more matches, further increasing profits. Each additional football match would contribute an additional £25,600 on projected attendance levels, with an extra rugby match generating £18,000. Using the expected attendance levels provided, it can be seen from the appendix that 26 football matches and 12 rugby matches would be more than sufficient to break even.

To better assess the accuracy of the forecasts and the likelihood of profitability, it would be useful to know each club's position in the current league to assess the likelihood of promotion/relegation. Also the attendance levels and number of matches for the previous two or three seasons would indicate any trend – in reality the attendance is likely to vary between matches depending on the recent success of the team and who the opposition is.

Revenues and costs

The calculations of break-even attendance depend on assumptions about the average spend per visitor, contribution and traceable fixed costs. If the forecasts have been based on existing ticket prices and spending on merchandise/catering, these may increase with the new stadium, in which case the contribution per visitor might increase and the required attendance would be lower. A breakdown of the average spend per visitor between ticket price and merchandising and details of the different ticket prices, which presumably include concessions for the young and elderly, would be useful.

One of the reasons the football club is predicting a loss is because its traceable fixed costs are significantly higher than those of the rugby club leading to a greater variability of profits if relegated/promoted. This may be because of the level of wages in the market place for footballers but more information is required here.

Appendix: Financial analysis

Estimated profits at various attendance levels: £'000

	Current attendance	If relegated	League average	If promoted	Per forecast
FOOTBALL					
Attendance	2,863	1,800	3,050	5,000	3,200
	£	£	£	£	£
Contribution	572.6	360	610	1,000	640
Fixed costs	644	644	644	644	644
Profit	(71.4)	(284)	(34)	356	(4)
RUGBY					
Attendance	2,234	1,900	2,840	4,000	3,000
	£	£	£	£	£
Contribution	201.06	171	255.6	360	270
Fixed costs	214	214	214	214	214
Profit	(12.94)	(43)	41.6	146	56

Sensitivity to number of matches

	Fixed costs	Forecast contribution per match	BE no of Matches (fixed cost/contribution)
Football	£644,000	640,000/25 = £25,600	25.16
Rugby	£214,000	270,000/15 = £18,000	11.89

Examiner's comments:

Requirement 36.2(a) asked candidates to calculate the breakeven attendance figure per match for both rugby and football and then 36.2(b) to discuss the implications of the variability of attendance on the forecasts, providing supporting calculations.

Answers to 36.2(a) were good with a large number of attempts scoring full marks. The most common mistake was to provide the answer in the form of annual attendance rather than per match. Only a small minority seemed unfamiliar with the breakeven formula or divided fixed costs by revenue instead of contribution.

Answers to 36.2(b) were slightly more disappointing ranging from a discussion with very little use of supporting data, to a set of calculations with no discussion. The key issue here is that the breakeven attendance for football is in excess of that currently forecast, whereas rugby has some margin of safety, although it is not clear how the traceable fixed costs (which are considerably higher for football than they are for rugby) have been arrived at. The calculation also makes assumptions about the number of matches and is based on average spend per visitor which will almost certainly vary. Using the data provided for the 'average' club to estimate attendance, it is evident that the forecast for match profits will not be realised if either club is relegated since they will be loss making, and conversely that league promotion would considerably increase the profits available. Also the risks arising from variability in attendance are higher for football than rugby. This was capably demonstrated numerically by the better candidates. Candidates would be well advised to note that when supporting calculations are asked for, it is very hard to produce a high-scoring discussion without reference to at least some numbers.

36.3 Report

> **To:** Bigville Council
> **From:** A N Consultant
> **Date:** September 20Y2
> **Re:** Community stadium

The council has identified three criteria which it will use to assess the high level business case:

(1) Ability to raise finance
(2) Commercially sustainable venture
(3) Alignment with council's overall strategic priorities

(1) **Ability to raise finance**

The costs of the proposed stadium are as follows:

	£m
Stadium construction	6.75
Community facilities	3.25
Basic stadium	10
Additional level	1.1
Expanded stadium	11.1

Currently the following funding appears to be available:

	£m
Sale of council land	6
Club contributions	3
Finanex payment for naming rights	1
	10

Thus the Council would appear to have sufficient funding in place for the basic stadium, with a shortfall of £1.1m if the additional conference and events facilities are built. The forecasts suggest that an enhanced stadium would increase profits by £250,000 p.a. which means the additional investment would payback in less than 4.5 years (1.1m/250,000) and therefore appears on the face of it to be worthwhile.

It would be useful to know what information the build costs have been based on and whether these make any allowance for potential overruns which are often incurred on this type of project. The amount budgeted and actually spent on comparable stadiums would help assess whether the costs being put forward by the Council fall within the range of other stadiums.

If a 10% allowance was made for overruns and the Council wished to build the enhanced stadium then they would need to find around £2m extra finance. It appears that some grant funding may be available and the Council needs to ascertain the amount that is likely to be forthcoming and the relevant conditions attached (which appear to be quite closely linked to the Council's own priorities in terms of employment, participation in sports and environmental sustainability).

A significant element of the finance is to come from the sale of the land so any uncertainty over the price or timing of this would need to be considered. For example work may need to start on the new stadium before the old one is demolished and the Council will need to ensure sufficient finance is available. In addition the Council is likely to have limited resources and therefore has a duty to consider the opportunity cost of using the money for the stadium in terms of the other projects that require funding.

Overall the initial findings suggest that there is a viable funding proposition provided the Council can find a suitable buyer for the land and receive some grant income. If this is not forthcoming then the Council would need to draw on any existing reserves or use debt finance. An alternative might be to consider the costs of building a smaller stadium since at 6,000 seats the capacity exceeds the maximum attendance for either club if promoted to the league above.

(2) **Commercially sustainable venture**

Basic stadium

	Football £	Rugby £	Non-match £	Total £
Club income				
Current profit/(loss) from clubs	(4,000)	56,000		52,000
Other income				
Community pitches/sports facilities			50,000	
Stadium advertising/sponsorship			200,000	
Revenue from non-match day activities			187,000	
			437,000	
Costs				
Stadium running costs			(375,000)	
				62,000
Overall surplus				114,000

Enhanced stadium
Incremental costs/revenues

Non-match day activities (537 – 187)		350,000	
Advertising (250 – 200)		50,000	
Stadium running costs (525 – 375)		(150,000)	
Additional income generated			250,000
Total surplus (114,000 + 250,000)			364,000

The financial projections suggest that the basic stadium would generate £114,000 of annual surplus, increasing to £364,000 for the enhanced stadium (this is before the interest cost associated with any borrowing requirement, and assumes the forecasts of revenue and costs from the clubs are achieved).

This equates to a ROCE of 1.14% (114k/10m) for the basic stadium and 3.3% for the enhanced (364/11.1m). More importantly the additional tier generates a return of £250,000 on an investment of £1.1m (22.7%) and would therefore seem to be a sensible option.

The commercial viability of the venture is quite heavily dependent on the ongoing sponsorship to be received from Finanex. Without this the basic stadium would generate a loss (ignoring match revenues/costs) of £138k, with the additional commercial activities from the enhanced stadium leading to only a small profit of £62k. If the venture fails however the Council will still be in the position of owning the land on which the stadium is built.

One of the considerations for the Council will be the extent to which it shares in the profits generated by the stadium. Were the clubs to keep their own profits/losses then the predicted income for the Council would be £62,000 from the basic stadium and £312,000 from the advanced. However it appears that the suggested agreement is for the SMC to pay rent to the Council for the stadium and for the members of the SMC (of which the Council is one) to then share the profits/losses from its operation. It is not clear whether the costs of the lease are included in the forecasts provided and what the nature of the profit sharing agreement between the three parties to the SMC will be. To better assess the commercial viability from the Council's perspective it would be useful to compare the Council's share of the incremental costs and revenues of the proposed stadium with the current situation where the Council receives lease payments from the rugby club for its existing ground.

(3) **Alignment with council's overall strategic priorities**

Bigville Council's recently stated strategic priorities are:

- To maintain and develop Bigville's successful economy and provide suitable employment opportunities for residents

- To ensure accessible opportunities for all to engage in culture, leisure and recreational activity

- To promote and provide support for local people to make healthy lifestyle choices

- To create, enhance and maintain cleaner, greener and safer environments

Basic stadium

A shared community stadium should provide job opportunities and if the stadium is used for events on non-match days eg concerts this may attract more visitors to the area, thus stimulating the economy. However the existing football and rugby grounds are likely to employ local people currently and amalgamation of two grounds into one may actually lead to a reduction of jobs in some cases.

Providing a new and improved stadium is consistent with the Council's aims of ensuring accessible leisure and recreational activities and promoting healthy lifestyle choices. The all-weather sports pitches and athletics track will be of benefit to Bigville's clubs, schools and colleges, thus increasing the opportunities available in the area for local people to have a healthy lifestyle. Concerts and other events on non-match days may also increase the cultural activities available.

Finally the design of the stadium appears to focus on environmental sustainability. However, it would be necessary to assess in more detail the impact on the environment of the construction activities and then the ongoing running of the stadium in terms of pollution, noise, use of resources etc.

Enhanced stadium

The extension of the stadium to provide a conference and exhibition centre is likely to significantly increase local employment opportunities, attract more visitors to Bigville, provide opportunities for its businesses and provide more economic benefit than the basic stadium.

In addition it will widen the scope of the activities available in the area. There may also be operating synergies which help the Council to minimise the costs involved in the provision of services or cross-subsidise the community activities from the profits generated by corporate hospitality etc.

Thus the plans for the community stadium do appear to be aligned in overall terms with the Council's four stated priorities and the enhanced stadium is likely to improve rather than worsen the strategic fit.

Conclusion

There does appear to be a positive high level business case for the shared stadium and the preliminary indications are that the enhanced stadium would be the most commercially viable and more likely to help achieve the Council's strategic priorities. The Council should arrange a meeting with the key stakeholders to discuss the project, their requirements and their potential involvement and then create a steering group to take the project forward and undertake a more detailed financial analysis and feasibility study.

Examiner's comments:

In requirement 36.3, candidates were required to write a report to the Council assessing the high level business case for the stadium using the Council's three stated criteria from the scenario: ability to raise finance; commercial sustainability and alignment with strategic priorities. Generally candidates made a good attempt at assessing the ability to raise finance. The vast majority produced calculations showing the estimated costs of construction and the amount of finance already secured, recognising that cash was available to fund the basic stadium but that government grants would be required to build the enhanced version. The better answers pointed out the risk of over-runs and also the fact that there may be some uncertainty associated with the sale of the land to the developer. The evaluation of commercial sustainability was less well done, with the weaker candidates concentrating their discussion on the environmental aspects of the stadium (thereby overlooking the commercial element of sustainability) or merely reiterating their discussion of the variability of match profits, already addressed in 36.2(b). Using the projections in the scenario it is clear that the enhanced stadium increase profits significantly and that the additional £1.1m investment would be worthwhile. The best candidates pointed this out, some producing ROCE or payback calculations which were encouraging, and a number recognising the reliance on income from the sponsor. Only a few candidates pointed out that the Council has a dual role – as lessor of the stadium (which will guarantee a fixed rental income) and as a partner in the SMC (which will entitle them to a share of the profits (losses). Candidates felt more comfortable evaluating whether the stadium met the Councils' strategic priorities, although surprisingly few discussed whether these were better met by the enhanced rather than the basic stadium. The weakest candidates simply made passing reference to the stated priorities and failed to analyse whether and how the stadium would achieve these. Disappointingly some candidates continue to ignore the presentation mark available for formatting their answer appropriately (in this case as a report) and the marks available for further information and a preliminary conclusion (both of which were specifically asked for). Better marks were scored by those candidates who attempted to tailor their request for further information to the scenario.

36.4 Risks

The risks for the Council in relation to the construction of the stadium and its operation by SMC include the following:

Construction

Funding requirement

Risk arises because of the uncertainty regarding the level of capital requirement and the funding available, especially in terms of grants. Should there be a shortfall then the Council may need to find more capital by diverting it from other needs or by borrowing.

The Council may not find a developer willing to buy the land on which the existing stadium is built or one who is prepared to pay the asking price for it. Even if the sale can be arranged there is a risk that it takes time and that construction of the new stadium needs to be started before the finance from the sale of the land is available. Local residents may also decide that the money would be better spent on services such as health and education.

There are uncertainties regarding stakeholder commitment to the project. It is unclear how the football club for example would react to a shared stadium and to the fact that they are contributing more capital than the rugby club. In the current economic climate Finanex may face budget constraints and decide that it has higher priorities to spend its money on.

A major capital cost overrun, which is not uncommon in such projects, would leave the Council with the residual funding risk.

Location and planning

It appears that a site has been earmarked but a potential risk is that it turns out not to be suitable. Planning permission for the new venture is critical. There is a risk that issues arise during the construction period in relation to the environment eg protestors complaining about the impact on the landscape or local residents unhappy about the noise/traffic etc.

Timing

Any delays in construction, as well as increasing costs, could result in adverse publicity for the Council if the clubs do not have a stadium to play in at the start of the season.

Construction company

The council will need to ensure that the building contractor is carefully selected in accordance with policy to avoid the risks associated with the work not being done properly.

Operation by SMC

The current plans are for an SMC jointly controlled by the Council and the clubs. The joint venture potentially reduces risks for the Council (as does the receipt of an annual lease payment) but an agreement will need to be carefully drawn up to minimise the potential for conflict between the parties and to specify profit sharing arrangements, contributions to ongoing costs etc.

Financial

As discussed in 36.2 and 36.3, the financial models are dependent on a number of assumptions and estimates. The Council should undertake more detailed sensitivity analysis/scenario planning to get comfort regarding best and worst case scenarios. Should the venture be loss-making, or Finanex decide to cease their sponsorship, the Council is likely to have to provide further ongoing support/financial assistance.

It appears that the profits of the whole venture will be shared between the three parties but this needs to be clarified. If one or other club starts to perform poorly and/or gets relegated this would cause the stadium to become financially unsustainable and would affect the SMC's ability to make the lease payments.

Alternatively the clubs may be expecting to retain match-day profits in which case the SMC may only share the profits from the rest of the stadium and conferencing. This may reduce the amount of community activities that can be undertaken as the Council is likely to need a share of the profits from the clubs to subsidise such initiatives.

Legal

There is likely to be a range of regulations affecting the Council, its role and powers and, in particular, the Council's legal position if the revenue targets are not achieved.

Changes in regulations of the rugby and football governing bodies may also affect the stadium and/or the number of matches eg there is a risk that increased pitch specifications or health and safety requirements increase the running costs.

Other stakeholders

As commercial entities, the clubs may have more in common with each other than they do with the Council and, if the objectives conflict, the Council may find itself in a minority over certain decisions, resulting in the venture not achieving its strategic priorities.

There is a risk that the clubs fall out or that one of them becomes insolvent and that, as a result, the Council loses one of the parties to the joint venture. Any change in ownership and/or management of the clubs may significantly affect the venture. For example if the football club is acquired by a wealthy investor it may decide that it wants a stadium for its own use.

37 Beauty Soap Ltd (September 2012)

Marking guide

		Knowledge	Skill	Marks
37.1 (a)	Strategic models	3	4	7
(b)	Appropriateness of BS's plans	2	7	8
37.2 Standardisation v adaptation		2	3	5
37.3 Merits of the two options		3	6	8
37.4 Ethical marketing		2	3	5
		12	23	33

General comments:

The scenario in question 2 concerned Beauty Soap (BS), a large UK based company which manufactures and sells personal care products throughout Europe. BS was established over one hundred years ago as a soap producer. It grew organically by investing in research and development to expand its product range, then later by the acquisition of a number of competitors and also a European dental care company. BS wants to reduce its dependence on the European market which is mature and where margins are under pressure. It is keen to expand into Latin America, as forecasts suggest there is considerable growth potential, particularly in countries like Brazil. BS is considering two options: organic expansion using a direct selling model of local workers, or the acquisition of Gomera, a local personal care business with existing product range and supply chain/distribution networks. Preliminary research has suggested that the local market needs smaller products sizes and lower prices than BS's European product model. BS has also recently announced plans to launch an education campaign, in conjunction with the governments in the countries in which it operates, promoting the regular washing of hands with BS soap to reduce infection and disease.

The question provided scope for a limited amount of data analysis as candidates were given brief information about sales revenues in the European personal care industry as a whole, together with those for BS and the market leader.

This question was also well attempted by the majority of candidates.

37.1 (a) Growth strategy

Lynch expansion matrix is a two by two matrix of company growth (internal and external development) and geographic location (home/domestic and international).

Under this model BS's initial growth was carried out internally in its domestic market – the UK. After establishing itself initially as a household soap manufacturer BS used research and development to generate internal organic growth through new products such as shampoos and face creams. BS's growth then continued externally through acquisition. This occurred first domestically with the acquisition of the UK based dental care business and then internationally with the acquisition of other European companies making personal care products.

BS is now proposing further international expansion in respect of Brazil, but has not yet decided whether it will undertake this by internal or external development.

The Ansoff matrix is another two-by-two matrix, of products (existing and new) and markets (existing and new). Relating product opportunities to markets gives rise to four possible strategies:

Market penetration – involves selling more existing products to existing markets. In the case of BS it started as a household soap manufacturer and quickly penetrated the market due to the range of sizes and fragrances on offer.

Product development – selling new products to existing markets. BS did this initially by investing in research and development to expand its product range from soap to shampoos, face creams etc. Later BS further developed its product range in the UK by acquiring a company specialising in dental care products – an area where BS perhaps lacked expertise to develop the product itself internally.

Market development – new markets for existing products, usually requiring an investment in marketing. BS pursued this via acquisitions of personal care product manufacturers in Europe. It is likely that this route offered a faster method of entry to the market and potentially got round barriers to entry. The proposed expansion to Brazil is another example of market development.

Diversification: new products for new markets – BS does not specifically appear to have done this, however an example might be the acquisition of a perfume manufacturer based in America. Since the single-use products proposed for Brazil are already being sold to a European hotel chain this does not really constitute diversification.

(b) Current position and appropriateness of targeting new markets

Current market position

BS is currently operating in Europe, a market which appears to be mature. If we consider the data provided, the overall market for personal care products in Europe has shrunk by 6% between 20Y0 and 20Y1. Since prices are under pressure this could be due to a fall in average selling prices rather than sales volumes. BS's share of that market was maintained at 3.8% in both 20Y0 and 20Y1 but the 6% reduction in the size of the market has led to a 27m euro drop in BS turnover.

Relative to the market leader BS has performed slightly better, generating 30% of their revenue in 20Y0 and 32% in 20Y1.

More information is needed to ascertain the European market trend and exactly where personal care products are in the industry life cycle. At this stage of the life cycle the European market may still offer good profit and cash generating opportunities and it is likely that people will continue to buy personal care products so the market decline may take some time. However for a sustainable future and growth opportunities, BS may need to look elsewhere.

Under the BCG matrix, BS's UK and European business might be deemed a cash cow (or possibly a dog) and its desire to expand in Latin America could be seen as an attempt to create a star.

Appropriateness of targeting emerging market:

- Reduces dependence on core European market and spreads risk given threat to margins

- BS may face less rivalry initially in developing markets such as Brazil compared to mature markets and hence enjoy better margins

- The stage of the industry life cycle will be different in Brazil etc where markets are still developing, which offers opportunities for better cash flow and profits over a longer period

- Western brands may be very attractive in this market so it could be a good opportunity to increase sales volumes

- Economic growth will boost demand and industry forecasts for personal care products are promising

- Expanding internationally outside Europe widens brand and image so BS becomes a more global company – this may also help strengthen its position in Europe

- It may help address any seasonality in terms of revenue and cash flow

- Competitors are doing this elsewhere (eg the three multinational companies already in Brazil)

- There may be financial arguments for setting up eg grants/incentives from local governments

However BS should be aware that there may be some downsides:

- Increased risk of operating in unknown, emerging markets. BS will need to invest time and money to understand the needs of the local market

- Political and legal risk eg as demonstrated by the Brazilian government attitude to foreign owned companies creating value; any quotas/tariffs/restrictions on free trade; any specific regulations to comply with

- Economic and transaction risk – to date BS has only exported to Europe and been exposed to exchange rate risk in terms of the euro

- Existing competition – multinationals will be large with economies of scale; domestic competitors have the advantage of local knowledge. Will BS have any distinct competitive advantage over these players? Also as other markets are predicted to grow other companies may be considering expanding

- Will BS have sufficient resources and management skills to exploit the opportunity eg language skills, ability to recruit local workforce?

- BS needs to consider the extent to which it needs to adapt products/marketing for other markets – these costs, when taken with the additional distribution costs and the exchange movements, may mean the margin is no better but the risk is higher

  If expansion is deemed appropriate, the method of expansion chosen may help to reduce some of the risks/downsides

Examiner's comments:

Requirement 37.1 was split into two parts. Part (a) asked candidates to use relevant models to analyse the ways in which BS has chosen to expand historically and its plans for Brazil. Part (b) went on to request a discussion of the appropriateness of its strategy to move away from the European market and target other international markets. Overall this requirement was answered very well. There were a number of ways to approach an answer to 37.1(a) – as a discussion of organic growth/acquisition; products and markets; or domestic and international expansion. Those candidates who used Lynch's model and/or Ansoff's product/market development matrix to structure their answers tended to achieve higher marks. It was pleasing to see that the majority of answers were very specific to the scenario, identifying how BS had initially used R&D to expand organically through product development and then used acquisition to target other products and markets. In 37.1(b) most candidates used the data in the Exhibit to identify that whilst the European market had declined between 20Y0 and 20Y1, BS has retained its market share, which has increased in relation to the market leader. Whilst further information would be necessary to confirm the trend, this suggests that the European industry may be reaching the mature stage of its lifecycle and that other markets, at an earlier stage of development, might offer more potential for future growth. Quite a lot of candidates identified the scope to use either the BCG matrix or life cycle model here as a starting point for discussion. The better candidates realised that this was not a case of BS immediately leaving the European market, rather that to ensure future prosperity it should continue the expansion strategy discussed in 37.1(a) by finding new markets and/or products offering better potential. Some weaker candidates let themselves down by applying the BCG model very literally and concluding from the data that 'BS should shoot the dog.' Better answers were less categorical, recognising that there is some degree of uncertainty within the BCG categorisation. Sadly, some candidates wasted time here by starting to discuss the methods of expansion being proposed for Brazil, despite a specific instruction to ignore these for this requirement.

37.2 Standardisation v Adaptation

Products can be classified according to their degree of or potential for global marketing:

Local products – suitable in a single market

International products – have the potential to extend to other markets

Multinational products – adapted to the perceived unique characteristics of national markets

Global products – designed to meet the needs of global market segments

The global/local dilemma refers to the extent to which products and services can be standardised across national boundaries or need to be adapted to meet the requirements of specific national markets because of different social and cultural conditions. Adaptation may involve changes to the actual product (involving changes in production) or to the method of promotion (brand, price etc) or some combination of the two.

Whilst standardisation tends to bring benefits in terms of economies of scale it may fail to target the market needs appropriately. Conversely adaptation is likely to involve greater costs, as a minimum in terms of R&D and marketing, but may increase competitive advantage.

The multinational personal care companies have expanded into Brazil using their existing globally branded products. Gomera on the other hand is currently producing a product which is only being sold in a single market – Brazil. It appears that for the market in Brazil, BS believes it has no choice but to adapt its product for financial reasons because its standard European product is not affordable for a significant element of the domestic population. It would be interesting to see how BS products compare in size and cost to the existing products in the market place and to what extent this view is backed up by further market research. BS does however have the advantage that it already produces single-use products for the European hotel chain which should help to reduce the costs involved in adaptation.

The other choice available to BS (and other international companies) is whether to retain its manufacturing in a limited set of locations so as to exploit economies of scale and then distribute a standard product internationally, or whether to set up production facilities in South America.

Examiner's comments:

Requirement 37.2 requested candidates to discuss the need for global companies to consider standardisation/adaptation of products. On the whole this requirement was poorly attempted and answers here were polarised. Some candidates clearly appreciated the nature of the problem and produced good answers discussing the trade-off between economies of scale in production and marketing on the one hand and satisfying the needs of different consumers and market places on the other. Others appeared to confuse this with Porters generic strategies and discussed cost leadership vs differentiation, and some weaker candidates missed this requirement out completely.

37.3 Method of market development

Lynch's expansion method matrix would identify the two options of acquisition vs. direct investment as external development (acquisition) vs internal development (organic growth).

Acquisition of Gomera, the local company, comes with the following advantages:

- Existing knowledge of the environment and local market providing useful initial expertise

- An instant skill base in terms of resources, employees etc is likely to mean faster growth

- It provides access to existing supply chain and distribution networks reaching into remote parts of Brazil

- A locally known established brand and reputation with an existing customer base – this may be viewed more favourably by the Brazilian government and consumers than a foreign owned brand. Once the acquisition has occurred BS can then start to introduce its other products

- Acquisition buys out a potential competitor and better enables BS to compete with the other two domestic companies

- There are likely to be synergies as BS can provide the advertising and product innovation that Gomera is lacking

- Gets round any barriers to entry in terms of resistance from the Brazilian government

- Capitalises on the market opportunity more quickly, which may be important if other European companies are also considering expansion in Brazil

Direct investment offers the following merits:

- Gomera may not be an ideal partner in terms of size or market positioning and there may be a conflict between strategies if BS is seen as a premium producer compared to Gomera. With direct investment BS is free to pursue its own strategy.

- The price BS is required to pay for Gomera may not be appropriate. Organic growth avoids paying for goodwill therefore BS can acquire a larger tangible asset base for the same cost as acquisition.

- May offer a chance for more gradual expansion and an opportunity to test the market by exporting products from Europe to be sold locally under the direct selling model before then investing in production facilities in Brazil.

- Organic growth creates a business with the same culture as BS thereby avoiding any conflict etc on integration.

- The Brazilian government may look favourably on the direct selling model proposed by BS and there may be grants or other incentives available.

- Avoids any hidden or unforeseen losses that do not come out as part of due diligence on Gomera.

On the face of it, it would appear that acquisition is probably preferable, however the final decision as to the most appropriate method of expansion will probably depend on the price that BS is likely to have to pay for Gomera and the premium on acquisition.

Examiner's comments:

Requirement 37.3 asked candidates to discuss the relative merits of the two methods of expansion being considered for Brazil. This was very well done. As usual candidates were well prepared for a discussion of organic growth vs acquisition and the majority undertook this in the context of the scenario. Only the better candidates picked up on BS's proposed use of the direct selling model and questioned where BS was planning to produce the products. Those candidates who attempted to reach a preliminary conclusion as to the better method of expansion attracted higher skills marks.

37.4 Social and Ethical marketing

The marketing concept suggests that a commercial organisation's goals are best fulfilled by identifying customers' needs and providing products which satisfy those needs efficiently and profitably.

The concept of social or ethical marketing extends this idea to see marketing as a social force that reflects and influences cultural values and norms. Thus marketing can extend beyond economic considerations and be used to promote the welfare of society as a whole. Here the social aim of BS's campaign is for improved education and hence better health, thus BS could argue that through marketing it is providing information and helping people make informed choices.

Marketing of BS soap to promote a healthier way of life is designed to instil awareness of the need for hygiene and then to create a behaviour change whereby people wash their hands more often – educating people re standards of hygiene could be argued to eradicate disease and enhance the benefits to society. Thus BS are using the education campaign to promote a global caring image whilst there are clearly additional commercial benefits for BS in terms of getting its brand name and soap products known. There is potentially an even wider benefit for BS in that it will increase awareness of personal hygiene as a concept which will have knock on benefits for the demand and sale of BS's other products such as shampoo.

The concept of responsible marketing suggests that companies should consider the wider social implications of their products and the needs of society at large. Thus BS's decisions to employ a team of direct sellers might be seen to help increase the wealth of local people and alleviate poverty; it will also help reach remote areas.

The BS campaign could be said to link the desire to improve education and welfare with the commercial reality of expanding the business's sales. To this end the interests of the company and the Brazilian government are aligned and soap could be seen as a product that will do social good by meeting people's functional needs.

Critics might argue that such marketing is actually just manipulative selling. The production of soap may involve chemicals which damage the environment, use of soap may pollute local water supplies, and access to clean water and street sanitation is more likely to have a significant influence on health and disease than the use of soap.

They would see BS as wasting the considerable resources needed to engage a Brazilian footballer in the campaign just to convince people to buy products they don't need, and using promotion to convince them that they will be dissatisfied or even unhealthy without them. The motivation might be seen to be to tap into a large potential market in the developing countries, when perhaps the domestic population would be better continuing to use more natural products or the traditional techniques available.

Also ethics could be considered in terms of whether BS is genuinely behind this as a concept – applying it to other countries etc – or whether it is simply a way of getting the Brazilian government to accept the company in the market.

> **Tutorial note:**
>
> Candidates could choose to apply the legality/transparency/fairness/effect model here:
>
> **Legality** – BS does not appear to be doing anything illegal
>
> **Transparency** – BS appears to be being quite open in its plans
>
> **Fairness** – there is nothing to stop other personal care companies doing the same thing (though Gomera for instance may not be able to pay the high fees of the footballer) and indeed there is nothing to stop consumers buying other soap products.
>
> **Effect** – by raising awareness and creating education BS could be said to be having a positive effect on the local community.

Examiner's comments:

Finally part 37.4 asked candidates to assess the ethical implications of the proposed educational marketing campaign. This was poorly done by many candidates. There seems to be a tendency on the part of weaker candidates to approach the ethical requirements with great suspicion and to assume/conclude that what is being proposed is automatically unethical. A high number of candidates thought that the use of the Brazilian footballer was totally inappropriate and that in poorer countries it was unfair to try and influence people into buying anything at all (or indeed to wash their hands), with many focussing on the vulnerability of people in schools and hospitals. Some did apply the transparency, fairness and effect decision making approach, which tended to improve the quality of the answer by at least ensuring they were talking in ethical terms and applying a structured thought process. Only the best candidates provided an initial discussion of ethical marketing principles and concluded that linking marketing with corporate social responsibility is not necessarily unethical (manipulative selling). Some did question however whether the cost and high profile of using the footballer might undermine an otherwise reasonable attempt at CSR and ethical marketing. Answers to the ethics requirement, which is a consistent feature of the exam, continue to be variable and candidates wishing to score well are advised to adopt some form of framework for their answer and to produce a balanced argument rather than a one-sided discussion.

38 Maureen's Motors (September 2012)

Marking guide

	Knowledge	Skill	Marks
38.1 Generic strategy and market positioning	3	4	7
38.2 Service marketing mix	5	8	12
38.3 KPIs	2	4	6
	10	16	25

General comments:

Maureen's Motors is an eponymous insurance company that focuses its product on insurance for female drivers by offering benefits tailored to women that are not offered by most insurers: it provides additional cover for handbags and contents, pushchairs and car seats, and it has a network of female-friendly repairers and a helpline giving advice on all vehicle-related matters. Three famous actresses played the three Maureens in a long-running TV advertising campaign and MM then ran a competition to 'make me a Maureen' for ordinary women to star in their TV and billboard advertising campaign. Because of its brand image the current customer base for primary policy holders is 90% female. Since industry statistics show that women make significantly fewer claims than male counterparts and typically claim for lower amounts, this mix allows MM to make superior profits.

Like questions 1 and 2, this question was well attempted by most candidates.

38.1 Generic strategy and market positioning

Competitive positioning can be viewed in a number of ways but essentially means giving a product or service a place relative to its competitors in terms of factors such as quality, price, image etc. A sustainable competitive advantage can be achieved where there is the ability to outperform competitors in the long run.

Porter identified two distinct generic strategies: cost leadership and differentiation.

A cost leadership strategy attempts to achieve the position of lowest cost producer which facilitates competition on price. Differentiation strategy assumes that competitive advantage can be gained by creating attributes of the product or service which customers value and are prepared to pay a premium for. Such a strategy can be pursued broadly across an industry eg Direct Line insurance which offers a range of cheap telephone/internet based insurance products, or by concentrating attention on one or more segments of the market (focus) eg SAGA who provide insurance and other products for the over 50s.

MM appears to have adopted a focus-based approach within Porter's model, targeting a particular segment of the insurance industry (motor) and within that a specific market niche (female drivers).

The concept of generic strategy has been developed further by considering a possible spectrum of price/quality combinations from low price, low quality/added value (a no frills strategy) through to a high priced, high added value strategy of focussed differentiation.

MM has created differentiation through its product features and also its marketing.

The additional benefits offered by its insurance product suggest that MM has attempted to differentiate its service (through female friendly repairers, helplines, additional cover for handbags and car seats etc). It has also attempted to create a strong lifestyle brand image via use of the 3 Maureens and competitions. Whilst the product attributes may be relatively easy for other insurers to copy, the strong brand image may be harder to replicate.

Another way of looking at the issue of market positioning for MM is through Kotler's 3Cs: cost, customers, competition. This view sees the price/quality trade off in relation to competitors as the key issue. Competition for MM will come from other companies who decide to operate in the same market niche eg Sheila's Wheels and also from the generic motor insurance products offered by the wide range of general insurance companies. Parity pricing would see MM's price and quality as equivalent to competitors – at below parity price sales may be made at the expense of profitability; above parity MM's product will be uncompetitive if identical products are available from competitors at lower prices. This is where the importance of brand comes in to reinforce perceived value, since MM customers who are loyal to the brand may feel they are getting a superior product, even if the basics of the cover are the same, and therefore may be prepared to pay more for it.

Examiner's comments:

Requirement 38.1, which asked candidates to explain the strategy and positioning of MM, was very well attempted. The majority of candidates were well-prepared for a discussion of Porter's generic strategies and almost all identified MM as a differentiator, using appropriate information from the question, such as the provision of handbag cover and replacement car seats, to illustrate this. Some, but not all, recognised that instead of applying differentiation industry-wide, MM has focussed this strategy on a particular market niche resulting in a customer base that was 90% female. Whilst the weaker candidates restricted themselves to Porter, the better candidates also discussed positioning in relation to competitors and price/quality, pointing out that MM was likely to be at the higher end of the market when compared to the large motor insurers. A number also provided a discussion of Bowman's clock. Some weaker candidates spent too long on this requirement for the marks available, leaving themselves short of time for 38.2.

38.2 Marketing strategy

Target market

MM appears to have taken the results of some preliminary market research and used it to identify potential customers that it wants to target: women drivers. It has then tried to address the fact that insurance is seen by many as a 'grudge' purchase and developed a concept of a certain lifestyle to appeal to this target market. Finally it has developed its car insurance service by considering the product benefits that are most likely to appeal to a female market eg handbag cover, female friendly repairers.

MM then needs to develop a marketing strategy to attract this target market, which can be considered using the marketing mix (the set of variables which a firm blends to produce the response it wants from its target market). In MM's case this includes the traditional 4Ps (Product, Price, Place, Promotion) and the additional 3Ps for service industries (People, Processes and Physical evidence). Attracting customers in the first instance is key to market share since industry statistics suggest that women are then less likely to switch insurer.

Product

This refers to the qualities of the product as perceived by potential customers. MM's product offering is made up of three elements:

- The basic or core product which is motor insurance

- The actual product which in MM's case is motor insurance specifically tailored for women and finally this leads to:

- The augmented product consisting of the insurance services that MM believes women particularly value and are prepared to pay for eg female friendly repairers, additional cover for handbags, vehicle advice line etc.

Emphasising the fact that the service is particularly tailored to women will distinguish MM from the general motor insurers and is key to success.

Promotion

The MM brand is critical and promotion must be consistent with this and reinforce the image and alignment of the brand with the 3 Maureens. Advertising is likely to be the most important means of achieving this, hence theTV advertising campaign starring well known actresses has lead to coverage in women's magazines. Using the 'Make me a Maureen' competition strengthens the concept of MM being 'a reassuring brand for real women with real lives'. MM has created a strong brand image at relatively low cost but ongoing promotion will be required to maintain this, particularly if it continues to attract adverse publicity.

Brand recognition can be tested through market research.

Price

MM's pricing policy needs to be appropriate to the wider marketing strategy and consistent with its competitive positioning. The price that potential female customers are prepared to pay for additional benefits can be ascertained through market research. Given the differentiation strategy female customers may be more likely to be attracted to MM for its brand image and benefits its policy offers (perceived value pricing) rather than because it is necessarily the cheapest in price, although MM needs to consider the prices charged by competitors for similar products.

The EU directive means that MM cannot price discriminate between equivalent men and women but elements of the insurance package may be priced separately eg children's car seat cover may not be required by all women. This would also facilitate the product being offered to male drivers who otherwise may not be prepared to pay MM's higher prices for services which they do not value eg additional cover for handbag contents.

The pricing of insurance premiums is a largely risk-based actuarial calculation and so the cost of cover will vary depending on the nature and age of the vehicle, the age of the policy holder etc. The pricing strategy is also likely to include discounts for no claims and MM offers a loyalty bonus which will help retain customers and market share. It also offers discounts through a friend referral scheme.

MM should consider how people pay for their insurance eg it may charge a premium for people who wish to pay by instalments rather than annually. It may also decide to offer a discount for online purchase or for new customers.

Place

Place does not appear to be a key factor in the mix as it is not mentioned in the scenario. MM's products are likely to be sold through remote distribution channels (phone and internet), rather than face to face, and primarily online. MM could consider a possible agreement with certain car manufacturers to promote MM insurance along side new car purchases.

The people involved in this process will be key for MM and so the extension of the 4Ps to the 7Ps model for the marketing of services is relevant.

People

Recruitment of the right staff and training and development will be key to offering good female friendly customer service otherwise the attrition rate will be high.

Customer service staff taking calls and handling claims and those staffing the vehicle advice line will interact with customers and be key to providing a high quality service consistent with the MM brand and its association with the 3 Maureens.

The quality of the service offered by MM will also be heavily reliant on the female friendly repairers and MM will need to have a code of practice, training and monitoring to ensure this is adhered to.

Processes

As part of customer service, efficient administrative processes underpin a high quality provision. Processes need to be female friendly but also efficient. The speed of handling claims and making payments will be critical. If true, the adverse coverage in the newspapers suggests that MM has some work to do to improve in this area.

Technology can be used to ensure efficient processes for taking calls/selling policies/handling claims.

MM also need good processes to hire staff who are perceived by customers to be female friendly and who have the appropriate knowledge if they are manning the vehicle advice line. There will also need to be processes in place to manage the network of repairers and ensure the provision of replacement car seats.

Physical evidence

This is probably of minor importance but refers to items that give substance or evidence of the delivery surrounding MM's service eg tangibles such as the MM logo, claim forms, cover letters and policy documents. MM could also brand the replacement car seats and send out free tax disc holders or key rings to those renewing policies.

Examiner's comments:

Requirement 38.2 asked candidates to discuss the marketing mix adopted by MM. Again the majority of candidates were well-prepared in respect of the knowledge for this question, with most recognising the fact that the service nature of the business meant considering the extra 3Ps (people, processes and physical evidence) in addition to the normal 4Ps of product, price, place and promotion. The aspect that was least well addressed was how to prioritise the 7Ps in relation to the facts in the question. The better answers identified the elements of the mix which were more important to MM and extracted salient information from the scenario to explain how these had been tailored to the target market. Some weaker candidates simply explained what each P represented rather than discussing how MM has chosen to use the various elements of the mix to market its insurance services. A significant minority limited their scores by discussing the 3Ps only, when it was very clear from the scenario that product, price and promotion were also relevant factors.

38.3 KPIs

MM has been criticised for concentrating on new customers rather than existing ones. If this criticism is valid then MM needs to set targets for and measure the improvement in customer service and claims handling. Possible KPIs are as follows:

Note. Candidates were expected to produce 3 KPIS in total, with at least one covering each area – more are however included here for marking purposes.

Customer service KPIs	Explanation
Average score from customer feedback surveys regarding claims handling/use of vehicle advice helpline/speed of response	An increase in this score over time would suggest that customers' satisfaction is increasing
Number of complaints – again split by the different elements of the service	If MM measures the % decrease in complaints received it can assess how effective the steps to improve service have been. By measuring the types of complaint MM can ascertain whether it is their staff or their associates (eg the car repairers) that are the cause of the problem
Number of referrals by customers to friends	An increase in the number of referrals would suggest that more customers are satisfied enough to recommend MM

Claims handling KPIs	
Speed of claim settlement	A reduction in the time taken to process and settle claims would indicate greater efficiency and a higher level of service for customers
Number of claims processed per employee/ case load per employee	Measuring the workload per employee and their productivity would help assess whether MM has allocated sufficient resources to this area
% of claim paid out	Customers will be keen to ensure that they receive the maximum possible amount of their claim and that they do not lose out due to any small print on the policy

Examiner's comments:

Requirement 38.3 asked candidates to explain and justify three KPIs that could be used to assess MM's claims handling and customer service. This was in the light of recent criticisms of both and the suggestion that MM cares more about attracting new customers than retaining existing ones. This part was quite poorly done by some candidates, who were clearly unsure about the distinction between KPIs and goals. For the weaker candidates, KPIs described could have been those for any business and it was not obvious that the candidate was discussing MM or specifically its need to improve claims handling and service to existing customers. Whilst customer satisfaction is relevant to all businesses and therefore customer feedback is vitally important, there was much information in the question, regarding the nature of MMs service and the recent criticisms, which could have been used to produce some high quality answers. The better candidates produced a reasoned justification of their choice of measure and demonstrated clearly how this could be used to track improvement in the relevant areas. Some candidates provided a long list of KPIs, despite the specific request for only three – these additional measures wasted time and did not attract marks.

39 Grassgrind Garden Mowers plc (December 2012)

Marking guide

		Knowledge	Skill	Marks
39.1 (a)	Analysis of performance	–	17	15
(b)	UK market share	2	3	5
(c)	Competitive positioning	2	6	7
(d)	Growth strategy	3	10	12
39.2	Ethical issues	2	4	6
		9	40	45

General comments

This is the mini case and also the data analysis question. The scenario relates to a company manufacturing lawnmowers (GGM). The company manufactures two types of upmarket, petrol-powered mower for use by UK households: tractor mowers and conventional mowers. The company is subject to a take-over bid by BB, which the GGM board is defending. A key issue is the proposed future strategy of BB, in comparison to the defensive strategy of the existing GGM board. The candidate is in the role of a business adviser for the accountants (PP) representing the existing GGM board. PP has been asked to prepare a report evaluating GGM and aspects of the bid strategies.

39.1 (a)

From: Business Adviser
To: GGM independent report to shareholders
Date: XX December 20Y2
Subject: Assessment of strategic plans

| | 20Y1 | | 20Y2 | | 20Y1 | 20Y2 |
	Conventional mowers	Tractor mowers	Conventional mowers	Tractor mowers	Total	Total
INCOME STATEMENT	£	£	£	£	£	£
Revenue	3,240,000	5,400,000	2,952,000	5,076,000	8,640,000	8,028,000
Variable cost	1,944,000	2,700,000	1,771,200	2,820,000	4,644,000	4,591,200
Contribution	1,296,000	2,700,000	1,180,800	2,256,000	3,996,000	3,436,800
Fixed cost	911,250	303,750	885,600	338,400	1,215,000	1,224,000
Profit	384,750	2,396,250	295,200	1,917,600	2,781,000	2,212,800
Profit/revenue %	11.9	44.4	10.0	37.8	32.2	27.6
% change in revenue			−8.9	−6.0		−7.1
% change in vc			−8.9	4.4		−1.1
% change in contribution			−8.9	−16.4		−14.0
% change in FC			−2.8	11.4		0.7
% change in profit			−23.3	−20.0		−20.4
% change in volume			−8.9	4.4		

20Y1

Conventional mowers

In 20Y1 conventional mowers made a contribution per unit of £160, giving a contribution margin ratio of 40%.

The profit per unit after allocating fixed costs was £47.50, giving an operating profit margin (using the method of allocation of fixed costs adopted by GGM) of only 11.9%. This reflects a high proportion of fixed operating costs in the cost structure and therefore a high degree of operating gearing.

In drawing any conclusions about the performance of each product, however, the validity of the operating profit figures depends largely on the validity of the method of fixed cost allocation. While all such allocations are arbitrary (to a greater or lesser extent) the allocation by unit of output seems to be inappropriate in determining a cause and effect relationship between fixed operating costs and production activity. This is particularly the case as the tractor mowers are significantly larger, and probably more time consuming to produce, meaning it is likely they will require more fixed costs.

Based on the information available, it is not possible to produce an accurate allocation (eg using activity based costing) but a better measure might be sales value (as suggested by the CEO), rather than sales volume, as this gives some recognition to the relative scale of productive activity per unit.

On this basis, the following revised data would be produced:

| | 20Y1 | | 20Y2 | | 20Y1 | 20Y2 |
	Conventional mowers	Tractor mowers	Conventional mowers	Tractor mowers	Total	Total
	£	£	£	£	£	£
Contribution	1,296,000	2,700,000	1,180,800	2,256,000	3,996,000	3,436,800
FC by value	455,625	759,375	450,081	773,919	1,215,000	1,224,000
Profit	840,375	1,940,625	730,719	1,482,081	2,781,000	2,212,800
Operating profit/revenue	25.9%	35.9%	24.8%	29.2%	32.2%	27.6%

Compared to the volume based method of allocation, the operating profit of conventional mowers in 20Y1 has more than doubled from £384,750 to £840,375.

In terms of viability, contribution is the most valid measure in the short term, as the issue of allocation of fixed costs is avoided. On this basis, the conventional mower creates a healthy £1,296,000 contribution in 20Y1, making it viable. This generates a reasonable operating profit margin of 25.9%.

Tractor mowers

In 20Y1 tractor mowers made a contribution per unit of £1,000 giving a contribution margin ratio of 50%.

The profit per unit after allocating fixed costs was £887.50 giving an operating profit margin (using the method of allocation of fixed costs adopted by GGM) of 44.4%. As already noted, this reflects the rather favourable treatment of tractor mowers using the original fixed cost per unit allocation method.

Using sales value, rather than sales volume, to allocate fixed costs, this gives a rather less favourable, though still profitable, picture for tractor mowers. Operating profit margin is now somewhat lower at 35.9% than it was under the original allocation method, although it is still higher than the operating profit margin of the conventional mowers.

Other costs

The operating cost and profit figures are only part of the picture in measuring performance. After taking account of finance costs the business may not be profitable at all. More information is needed in this respect.

Overall company profit

While the allocation of fixed operating costs is arbitrary at unit level, the overall cost and profit at company level is the same irrespective of the allocation method. While such costs may not be avoidable in the short term, in the longer term it is essential that they are covered in order to sustain the business.

Nevertheless, overall operating profit of £2,781,000 has been generated on revenue of £8,640,000. This generates a healthy operating profit margin of 32.2% in 20Y1.

20Y2

Conventional mowers

There has been no change in the selling price or in variable cost per unit of conventional mowers between 20Y1 and 20Y2. The key change affecting performance has therefore been a fall in sales volume of 8.9%. As selling prices have not changed, then sales revenue has also fallen by 8.9%.

The impact of fixed operating costs on conventional tractor profitability in 20Y2 is twofold. First, total operating fixed costs have risen by 0.7%, so the pool of costs to be allocated has increased. Second, the volume of conventional mowers sold has decreased, while the number of tractor mowers sold has increased. As a result, the proportion of the fixed overhead pool allocated to conventional mowers has fallen. The net effect of this for conventional mowers (under the existing allocation method) is that while fixed operating cost per unit has increased from £112.50 to £120 (+6.7%), the total fixed operating cost allocated to conventional mowers has decreased from £911,250 to £885,600 (a fall of 2.8%).

As already noted, the method of fixed cost allocation used by the company based on volumes is questionable. The revised sales value based allocation method shows that the overall fixed costs allocated to the conventional product fell from £455,625 in 20Y1 to £450,081 in 20Y2, a reduction of 1.2%.

Using these revised fixed cost allocations the operating profit margin has fallen from 25.9% in 20Y1 to 24.8% in 20Y2. The primary causal factor explaining why this has occurred is the fall in sales volume.

Tractor mowers

In 20Y2 the key factors affecting the change in profitability of tractor mowers were: (1) a 10% reduction in selling price from £2,000 to £1,800; and (2) an increase of 4.4% in sales volume from 2,700 to 2,820. Variable costs per unit were unchanged.

The reduction in selling price may be causally linked to the increase in demand (downward sloping demand curve) but other factors may also have been relevant in that we do not know what would have happened to demand if the price had remained unchanged (see below).

Overall, in consequence of the price decrease and sales volume increase, revenues have fallen by 6% from £5.4m in 20Y1 to £5.076m in 20Y2. To the extent that the volume change was due to the price change, this would imply that demand is inelastic. As a consequence, the price reduction strategy could have significantly contributed to the fall in revenue of the tractor product in 20Y2 compared to 20Y1. The increase in fixed costs of 11.4% has also contributed to the reduction in profit of the tractor range.

Profitability of the tractor mowers has fallen as a result of the reduction in revenues. Using the sales volume basis for fixed cost allocation, operating profit has decreased by 20% from £2,396,250 to £1,917,600. Using the sales value basis for fixed cost allocation, operating profit has decreased by 23.6% from £1,940,625 to £1,482,081.

Comparison of the conventional and tractor range performance

Both conventional and tractor ranges have suffered a significant reduction in profit in 20Y2 compared to 20Y1 under both allocation bases.

In absolute terms, tractor mowers are more profitable than conventional mowers measured by both profit and contribution – although a more detailed review of overhead cost drivers may alter the data significantly.

The cause of the fall in profit for the tractor range may be largely endogenous ie choosing internally a price reduction strategy. It may therefore be within the company's control to reverse this price increase and restore future profitability to 20Y1 levels.

Overall profit

Overall operating profit has fallen by 20.4% from £2,781,000 in 20Y1 to £2,212,800 in 20Y2 (irrespective of the cost allocation method used). While the fall is substantial, the company remains reasonably profitable with an overall operating profit margin on revenue of 27.6%. If the price reduction is reversed, then some of the fall may be recovered in 20Y3.

Examiner's comments:

Requirement 39.1(a) requests candidates to analyse the performance of GGM, and each of its two products, in the financial years 20Y1 and 20Y2.

The majority of candidates answered this question in the report format that was required. The overall analysis of performance varied significantly from candidate to candidate. The higher scoring candidates used a variety of ratios such as change in revenues, profit margins and contribution. These data were used, in part, to explain the impact of the decrease in sales of conventional mowers. Also, the sales price of tractor mowers had reduced and, as a consequence, they had experienced an increase in sales volume. Some extremely good answers were produced in this respect, with candidates using price elasticity of demand to demonstrate the relationship between volume and price and thereby identify causal factors to explain the changes occurring in the data.

Only a minority of candidates developed their answers further and calculated the reallocation of fixed costs on a sales value basis. Most candidates calculated ratios for each of the two types of product separately and for the company as a whole for each year. This gave a structure for them to undertake further analysis.

The key issue which most candidates identified was the fact that tractor mowers were more profitable, but were aimed at a niche market. At the other end of the spectrum, the weaker candidates merely copied out the sales and cost figures from the question and made a vague attempt at analysing profitability. For these candidates there was normally no consideration of the relationship between price and volume, nor of the impact of changing the current method of allocation of fixed costs.

The lowest scoring candidates merely made assertions describing the changes in ratios, with little, if any, attempt at an analysis of causality. Some candidates spent too much time discussing market share in this section, rather than in 39.1(b).

(b)

Market share can be determined in terms of volume of sales or by sales value. Which is selected would depend on the purpose for which the analysis is being used.

A further issue is in defining the market. The broadest useful definition is likely to be the UK mower market. As GGM does not currently produce other powered garden tools and equipment then taking this wider definition does not seem appropriate. Within the mower sector there are various sub-sectors eg type of cutting blade; tractor and conventional; or method of power (petrol, electric, battery and hand-propelled).

The level of sub-analysis which would be appropriate could depend on a number of factors but one key issue would be whether consumers would readily substitute one good for another (eg it carries out the same function and is in the same price range). On this basis one could argue that the tractor mower is different from conventional mowers on the grounds of price and function in its suitability only for large gardens.

Taking the market split of tractor and then conventional mowers, a **sales volume** analysis of market share is as follows:

	20Y1		Forecast 20Y2	
	Conventional mower	Tractor mower	Conventional mower	Tractor mower
GGM (units)	8,100	2,700	7,380	2,820
Market (units)	1.5m	30,000	1.5m	30,600
Market share	0.54%	9%	0.49%	9.2%

In terms of **sales value**, market share is as follows:

	20Y1		Forecast 20Y2	
	Conventional mower	Tractor mower	Conventional mower	Tractor mower
GGM Revenue (£)	3,240,000	5,400,000	2,952,000	5,076,000
UK market at retail prices (£s) (W1)	360,360,000	35,640,000	367,640,000	36,360,000
UK market at wholesale prices (£s) (W2)	288,288,000	28,512,000	294,112,000	29,088,000
Market share at wholesale prices	1.1%	18.9%	1.0%	17.5%
Total market share at wholesale prices	2.7%		2.5%	

WORKINGS

(1) The UK market for mowers, by value, amounted to £396m in 20Y1 and £404m in 20Y2. Tractor mowers make up 9% of this market. However these are retail prices.

(2) Retail prices are reduced to 80% (ie 1/1.25) to obtain wholesale prices.

Thus GGM has a very small share of the conventional mowers market at around 1%, but a reasonably significant share of the tractor mower market.

A further analysis could be of petrol-powered mowers alone but this might not add much to the usefulness of the information if petrol and electric mowers are close substitutes.

Note. The UK mower market share relates to the goods sold in the UK; as opposed to the UK mower industry, which is the goods manufactured in the UK.

Examiner's comments:

Requirement 39.1(b) asks candidates to determine the current UK market share of GGM, highlighting any problems that arise in defining market share in order to produce a useful figure.

Most candidates attempted to determine market share for both products in terms of sales volume and sales value. Only a minority correctly adjusted for differences between wholesale and retail prices, and many ignored this issue altogether. Similarly, only a minority of candidates made a decent attempt at explaining the key problems in defining the market.

(c)

| | 20Y1 | | Forecast 20Y2 | |
	Conventional mowers	Tractor mowers	Conventional mowers	Tractor mowers
GGM				
Average price (per Question)	£400	£2,000	£400	£1,800
Retailer price x 1.25	£500	£2,500	£500	£2,250
UK MARKET				
UK market at retail prices (£s)	360,360,000	35,640,000	367,640,000	36,360,000
Market (units)	1.5m	30,000	1.5m	30,600
Average price	£240	£1,188	£245	£1,188

Conventional mower market

GGM is a minor participant in the UK conventional mower market with a market share of around 1% in both value terms and volume terms. This places it in a weak competitive position in this market.

The fall in conventional mower sales revenue in 20Y2 and the reduction in market share indicates a worsening of GGM's competitive positioning in this market. In volume terms, a decrease from 0.54% to 0.49% implies a worsening in competitiveness.

The fall in conventional mower sales revenue in 20Y2 and the reduction in value-based market share may indicate a worsening of GGM's competitive positioning in this market. Indeed, reduced conventional mower sales volume occurred despite no change in selling price by GGM and with competitors increasing selling price from an average of £240 in 20Y1 to £245 in 20Y2 (2%).

Within the conventional mower market, GGM is placed very much towards the quality end as its price of £400 becomes a retail price of £500 with a 25% mark up, which is more than double the market average of £245 in 20Y2. Its competitive position therefore needs to be considered against rival companies who also operate in the niche up-market sector of the conventional mower product market.

GGM may have suffered with consumers downgrading their purchases to cheaper products in the recession.

Tractor mower market

GGM is a significant player in the UK tractor mower market with a market share of 17.5% in value terms in 20Y2. This places it in a strong competitive position.

The fall in tractor mower sales revenue in 20Y2 and the reduction in value-based market share may indicate a worsening of GGM's competitive positioning in this market. However, in volume terms, an increase from 9% to 9.2% implies an increase in competitiveness on this basis at least.

Within the tractor mower market, GGM is placed very much towards the quality end as its price of £2,000 in 20Y1 is higher than the market average of £1,188 even allowing for differences between retail and wholesale prices. Even in 20Y2 with the price reduction to £1,800 it is still significantly higher than the market average. Its competitive position therefore needs to be considered against rival companies who also operate in the same niche up-market sector of the tractor mower product market.

The tractor mower range has increased sales volume by 4.4% in 20Y2. As already noted, part of this may be due to a price reduction. However there has also been market expansion of 2% in volume terms. So while GGM has increased sales this is partly due to market expansion and partly due to lower prices. Note that the average market price has been constant so GGM has lowered price and has captured more market share but reduced profit in the process.

Note also that as GGM has reduced price and is part of the market, then if the overall average market price has remained constant, on average competitors must have increased prices.

Overall competitive positioning:

In the UK market revenues amounted to £404m in 20Y2.

GGM's revenue is £8.028m, but when adjusted to retail prices it represents £10.035m.

GGM does not export outside the UK, so this is their total revenue. In terms of global sales therefore, GGM may overall be a small participant in the global industry and suffer competitive disadvantage in the UK market against international competitors from relative diseconomies of scale.

Examiner's comments:

In requirement 39.1(c), candidates were asked to explain the competitive positioning of GGM in the UK mower market and to assess how this has changed between 20Y1 and 20Y2.

Most candidates answered this question by starting with Porter's generic strategies then making an attempt to link this with the scenario. Most did this by considering the two products separately.

A significant number of candidates said that the positioning was 'stuck in the middle' with regards to the tractor mower as they were reducing the price, but still trying to promote a quality product. Candidates also used other models such the BCG matrix and Bowman's Clock.

Very few candidates presented decent numerical analysis to this requirement. Most commented on the change in price of the tractor mower, but only stronger candidates commented on the fact that the average market price had also fallen.

(d)

GGM board's strategic plan

The Ansoff matrix is a useful model for identifying growth opportunities. There are four routes to growth in the model's two-by-two matrix of Products (new and existing) and Markets (new and existing).

The expansion strategy proposed by the GGM Board is one of product development in the Ansoff model. This means developing and launching new products into current markets.

The strength of this proposal is that GGM has experience and understanding of buyer and consumer behaviour in this market sector. Customers for the new products (petrol-powered garden tools and equipment including hedge trimmers, strimmers, chainsaws) are likely to be the same garden centres and DIY centres that already purchase the GGM mowers. GGM may therefore have knowledge of the customers, and trust from the customers.

Economies of scope may also occur in distributing goods to common locations, which may reduce common costs.

In terms of manufacturing capability there appear to be common elements and therefore core competencies in production that can be exploited to gain competitive advantage. This is likely to include using a smaller scale version of the petrol engines used on the mowers, but also other aspects such as cutting blades for hedge trimmers and chainsaws.

In terms of the size of market, the UK garden tools and equipment market is larger than the mower market as mower sales make up only 'about 45% of the overall gardening equipment industry.'

Data analysis

	Low demand	Estimated demand	High demand
Volume (units)	20,000	25,000	30,000
Price	£150	£150	£150
	£'000s	£'000s	£'000s
Revenue	3,000	3,750	4,500
Variable cost	(1,800)	(2,250)	(2,700)
Contribution	1,200	1,500	1,800
Fixed cost	(1,400)	(1,400)	(1,400)
Profit	(200)	100	400

Profitability

At the expected level of demand, the GGM board proposal makes a profit. However at only £100,000 this is extremely modest and will only relatively marginally add to the company's current profit for 20Y2 of £2,212,800. Even at the top end of the estimation range it will only add £400,000 a year to profit, and there may be a low probability to this level of demand occurring.

Unless there are synergies with existing production, the new strategy would not add significantly to profit and growth. Indeed, as a measure of the scale of new activity, profit in 20Y1 was £2,781,000 and so profit fell by £568,200 in 20Y2. This fall would not be made good by the new project even at the top end of the range of estimates.

Risk

A key feature of the new project is that it carries risk. In particular, while the contribution margin is high at 40%, there are also high fixed costs, making the operating gearing high. This is illustrated in the above table which shows that, in the worse case scenario, if sales volumes fall by 20% an operating loss of £200,000 will be made.

The break even revenue is:

£1.4m/0.4 = £3.5m

Thus, the margin of safety from the 'most realistic estimate' is only £250,000 of sales. Therefore if sales fall by just 6.7% below the most realistic estimate, no profit will be made. A key issue in assessing risk therefore is how probable it is that sales will fall to this level.

While the market researchers indicate some uncertainty with respect to sales volumes this is only one variable. Other estimates are also likely to be surrounded by some uncertainty (eg price, variable cost, fixed costs).

Conclusion

This project does not look to be sufficiently profitable to improve growth significantly and contains risks which may reduce future profits. While most competitor mower manufacturers also produce petrol-powered garden tools and equipment, and qualitatively it seems a reasonable proposition for GGM, quantitatively, based on the data provided, it does not seem a way forward for GGM. Indeed, had it been so, perhaps the company would have entered this market some time ago.

BB's strategic plan

The expansion strategy proposed by BB is also one of product development in the Ansoff model in respect of UK sales.

However, there is also an element of diversification in the Ansoff model in respect of US sales. This involves moving away from core activities and developing new products for new markets, which involves the greatest risk of all strategies. It requires new skills, new techniques and different ways of operating. This is reinforced as not only has GGM not used battery technology before, but BB has not made mowers before.

A further way of viewing the potential acquisition is from BB's perspective. It is continuing a policy of downstream vertical integration.

In terms of UK sales there are similar advantages as the GGM board proposal (albeit with a different type of new product). There are economies of scope in distribution to the same customers, and there may be some common core competencies (eg the blades) with existing production methods and, although the battery element is new to GGM, it is core to BB.

At a marketing level however there are differences. In the BB case the new products are being separately branded so there is little reputational impact from the existing GGM brand. However BB may not be known in the UK, and consumer recognition in this market needs to be established.

The key advantage is that this proposal gives access to the US market through BB. However while BB operates in the US, it does not sell mowers in the US so the advantage of having BB to exploit its home market may be limited.

Data analysis

	High cost	Est cost	Low cost
Volume	20,000	20,000	20,000
Price	£500	£500	£500
	£'000s	£'000s	£'000s
Revenue	10,000	10,000	10,000
Variable cost	(7,000)	(7,000)	(7,000)
Contribution	3,000	3,000	3,000
Fixed cost	(3,000)	(2,000)	(1,000)
Profit	Nil	1,000	2,000

Taking the data provided at face value, the BB proposal is far more profitable than the GGM board proposal and even at the lower end of the estimation range it does not make a loss, managing to break even. However this data has been provided by BB as part of its take-over bid hence a degree of professional scepticism needs to be applied to these estimates. Due diligence procedures will be needed to ascertain their validity.

The range of variation of fixed costs is considerable and yet only point estimates are given for all the other variables. Additional work is needed to ascertain why the variation is so high for fixed costs and no range of estimates is provided for other variables.

A further note of caution is that, unlike the GGM board's proposal, the BB plan is to produce more mowers. It may therefore be that consumers will buy the battery-powered mowers instead of buying a GGM petrol-powered mower. Due to this substitution, the sales noted above therefore may not be entirely incremental to the company.

Conclusion

Leaving aside these reservations, if the figures are valid, then the BB proposal looks to be a more substantial contribution to growth.

Tutorial note:

Candidates may instead/also use other models such as the Lynch Expansion method matrix. The Lynch model is another two-by-two matrix of company growth (organic growth and external development) and geographical location (home (domestic) and international).

Examiner's comments:

In requirement 39.1(d) candidates were asked to compare the growth strategy of the GGM board with that of BB, make relevant calculations and refer to appropriate strategic models.

Again, the standard of answers here varied significantly between the stronger and weaker candidates. There was data in the question in terms of best case, worst case and estimated demand which could have been used to analyse each strategy. Only the better candidates used the information to compute the profit under the different scenarios and then went on to compute break even and sensitivity analysis.

The majority of candidates tended to use the Ansoff model. The Lynch model was also used in the stronger answers to analyse the difference between the two strategies in terms of discussion of expanding internationally. In terms of the BB strategy, the use of the highest and lowest cost estimates was often ignored in favour of using the expected cost. For the most part, candidates concluded that the BB strategy was the most attractive because of the exposure to overseas markets.

Hardly any candidates expressed any sort of professional scepticism about the data presented by BB.

39.2 Ethics pertains to whether a particular behaviour is deemed acceptable in the context under consideration. Here the issue is that Hetty's government has different laws for health and safety than the UK, but the underlying reasons for having the safety guard remain the same.

In making a decision as to how to proceed, GGM may find it helpful to apply the Institute of Business Ethics three tests:

- Transparency
- Effect
- Fairness

Transparency – would GGM mind people (existing customers, suppliers, employees) knowing that it has manufactured potentially dangerous equipment, even if it were legal . This test is partly about whether GGM's corporate ethics are open and transparent in its actions, rather than just what they claim in ethical statements.

Effect – whom does the decision affect/hurt? GGM stand to gain a major order if they are willing to control costs (by omitting the safety guard) and lower price. In the short term GGM would be making more profit as a consequence of the order.

However GGM risk reputational damage if it came to light it had manufactured unsafe goods and there may be repercussions in terms of lost customers in future.

Other losers would be any customers of Hetty (or other users of mowers) who got hurt in the event of a safety incident.

The ethical issue here is that GGM needs to recognise that, as a business, it has an obligation to the public interest and its wider stakeholders to behave responsibly. The requirement and expectation to make profits need to be constrained by these obligations, but such issues may themselves impact on long term profit.

There may also be certain industry codes of conduct that apply, and consequences from a breach of these, irrespective of where the items are sold.

Fairness – would the decision be considered fair by those affected? The issue for GGM is that they are being asked to manufacture mowers in the knowledge that they might cause harm. Should someone be badly hurt as a result of its actions, it is unlikely that they would perceive GGM's actions as fair, particularly if GGM was seen to have gained financially by winning more business.

Honesty

A final issue is one of honesty and professional scepticism. GGM should take legal advice regarding the legality of the modification being considered in order to substantiate the assertion that any such modification would be legal in Hetty's home country.

Response

GGM may believe that, even if the deal would be in its short term commercial interests, the additional profit is not worthwhile given the breach of corporate ethics that would be involved, even if no safety incident ever transpired from the modification.

One possible course of action would be to insist on fitting the safety guard but to offer a lower price anyway and thereby take a reduced profit per unit. However, GGM may feel that it is not in its interests to do business with a client of this nature even under these conditions.

Examiner's comments:

Requirement 39.2 asked candidates to explain the ethical issues arising from a request to modify its mowers for a potential export contract.

Answers to this requirement varied but were, on the whole, disappointing. Candidates tended to approach this requirement in terms of a transparency, fairness and effect framework. What candidates did not then develop, however, were the next steps or draw any sort of conclusion.

A significant number of candidates mentioned the ICAEW code of ethics, self-interest and integrity. This question did not focus on the code of ethics as the client (from whose perspective the ethical issues are being considered) may not have any ICAEW members. Rather, the question required candidates, in a commercial scenario, to assess the legality and ethics of the proposal and the corporate social responsibility of GGM as a company.

The weakest candidates failed to see the issues at the corporate level and instead presented an answer as though it was an individual's ethical issue. Only some candidates gave sensible business advice, such as providing the mowers with the safety guard but not charging for this feature in the price, in order to break into that market. Instead they just stated that the contract should be refused. Whilst the approach to ethics has improved significantly over the years, there is still an inability of candidates to apply ethical principles to business situations.

40 Care 4U Ltd (December 2012)

	Knowledge	Skill	Marks
40.1 SWOT analysis	3	10	12
40.2 Two strategies			
(a) Operating profit	4	7	
(b) Control and management	–	5	
(c) Incentives for franchieses	–	5	
			19
	7	27	31

General comments

The scenario in this question relates to a private company which owns a large chain of retail pharmacies. It has a good reputation but it has had problems retaining and motivating individual salaried pharmacists.

There are also issues regarding the manner in which the outlets should be controlled and managed. The board has proposed two alternative strategies to expand the chain, to attract pharmacists and increase motivation. These proposed strategies have been identified as: (1) franchising; and (2) shared ownership.

40.1 Strengths

- C4U sells essential products for both prescription items and over-the-counter (OTC) medicines so market demand is likely to be robust to changes in the economy and (for the market as a whole) price inelastic.

- C4U has a significant number of outlets providing scale economies for purchasing (enabling discounts from pharmaceutical suppliers), IT (the centralised system is likely to be mainly a fixed cost enabling additional outlets to benefit at near zero marginal cost) and other central operational services (such as central administration which is likely to have a significant fixed cost element).

- There is a history of sustaining growth through good management which has a track record of competence.

- Funding available for expansion means the company has significant liquidity which lowers financial risk and provides opportunities for growth.

- Good reputation as community pharmacies with free tests, screening and advice increases goodwill and enables a loyal customer base to be established of regular customers/patients.

- Good control through the IT system means the performance of the business is monitored and controlled at the level of each individual pharmacy.

Weaknesses

- There is a shortage of well motivated pharmacists who are good managers which means that, whilst the technical functions may be competently carried out, the same people may not have the key business skills to build revenue and control costs at the pharmacy level of the organisation which is the key interface with customers.

- There are problems retaining pharmacists. This leads to retraining costs and the continued losses of a key human resource. The temporary nature of the employment may mean pharmacists have a low level of long-term commitment to C4U.

- Generous salaries need to be paid to pharmacists which increases the cost base significantly and reduces profit.

Opportunities

- Increases in new drugs becoming available will mean that demand will increase both in terms of volume and, to the extent that new drugs are more expensive, may increase price.

- Pharmacy retailers have exited the industry thereby reducing competition from that source as there are fewer competitors remaining in the industry. There is therefore the opportunity to capture the markets of those leaving the industry.

- Capacity to charge in future for provision of advice, which is currently given free.

- Sell whole business to a large national chain.

- Expand through acquisition.

Threats

- Deregulation has made C4U susceptible to price competition for OTC drugs from supermarkets and other large companies in the industry who have scale economies and common costs with other functions in the store.

- Supermarkets are opening more in-store outlets offering increased non-price competition for all drugs. This competition comes in the form of 24-hour opening, convenience (shopping anyway for other goods), car parking out-of-town, scale of facility (and therefore range of items held in inventory giving choice).

- The prescription drugs market is susceptible to government regulation in terms of contractual conditions. Changes in such regulations are a risk to C4U.

- Government funding cuts will put pressure on prices paid to pharmacies in terms of the products that they will fund and the prices they are willing to pay for drugs and pharmacy services.

- Other goods sold by pharmacies are non-essential and are more susceptible to a sustained economic downturn and to competitive forces from a wider range of competitors outside the pharmacy sector.

- Alternative distribution channels for OTC are likely to be an increasing threat to high street pharmacy retailers (eg on-line sales, drug stores (OTC drug only shops)).

Conclusion

Key factors are:

- Reductions in government expenditure are key as this puts pressure on pharmacies for their main source of income which makes up 80% of revenue and if recoveries from government are reduced, with constant costs, then severe pressure is put on profits. Any cuts are also likely to be sustained as governments continually look to reduce public sector expenditure.

- Competition from supermarkets which: are pervasive in most regions; are instantly recognisable by consumers; have the ability to be low cost providers and tend to be trusted as providers of services (including healthcare).

Examiner's comments:

Requirement 40.1 asks candidates to prepare a SWOT analysis.

Attempts at this requirement were generally good, with candidates demonstrating a strong understanding of the SWOT model and using the information in the question to produce high scoring answers. The key strengths and weaknesses identified centred around the brand name, the established reputation and the good IT control system, together with the problems in staff retention and the lack of management experience from the pharmacists.

The opportunities and threats were not as well identified, although the majority of candidates did manage to identify that the main opportunity was the increase in new drugs, whilst the main threat was government spending cuts. Some candidates attempted to use the PESTEL model, despite the question specifically asking for a SWOT analysis.

It was quite surprising that a number of candidates failed to summarise the key issues from the SWOT analysis despite the requirement specifically requiring a conclusion.

40.2 (a)   Operating profit

Profit shares for average size pharmacy (first five years)

	Total	C4U's profit under franchising	C4U's profit under shared ownership
Revenue	600,000	30,000 (ie 5%)	
Operating costs (80%)	(480,000)		
Operating profit (20%)	120,000		
Management fee (under shared ownership option only)	(20,000)		20,000
Net profit	100,000		50,000
Up-front payment (amortised over 5 years)		5,000	–
Annual profit to C4U		35,000	70,000
Total profit for C4U (over 5 years)		175,000	350,000

Franchising

The up-front cash payment for the franchisee, averaging £25,000, is small by comparison to the shared ownership scheme which averages £40,000. However, with franchising, this payment would be recognised as revenue for C4U (amortised over five years) whereas the initial cash payment under the shared ownership scheme is a capital payment and would never be recognised in C4U's profit.

The up-front payment is small by comparison to the initial cost of opening a pharmacy so there is a small initial stake by the franchisee. This means that C4U has a high capital stake with franchising and may therefore expect a higher absolute level of profit to earn the same % return on investment.

Over the five year period the net cash investment by C4U for an average pharmacy under the franchise arrangement is £175,000 (£200,000 purchase price – £25,000 upfront fee). This is fully recovered according to the above table in terms of C4U's share of profits over the five year term (although this is not the case after tax and interest).

After five years C4U has all rights to the pharmacy business and the full profit stream. Meanwhile however there is an annual interest cost to C4U from providing the funds.

Shared ownership

C4U would receive the management fee in addition to the 50% share in profit, but the profit share is determined after the deduction of the management charge so in effect C4U is incurring half the cost of its own management charge.

As noted above, the additional capital stake is not recognised in C4U's profit.

The profit of the shared ownership scheme is overstated compared to the franchise arrangement as the revenue from intensive support is included but the incremental central costs in providing that support is not included.

The net cash investment by C4U for an average pharmacy under the shared ownership scheme is £160,000 (£200,000 opening cost – £40,000 pharmacist contribution). This is more than fully recovered according to the above table in terms of the C4U's share of profits over the five year term which amounts to £350,000. In this case profit will continue after the five years under the same arrangement unless one party decides to buy out the other.

As with the franchise arrangement, there is an interest cost to C4U in providing the initial funds to set up the pharmacy company. However to the extent that the interest is also a cost to pharmacy companies, it is an income to C4U, half of which is in effect paid by the co-owner.

Comparison

The above table shows that the profit per annum with the shared ownership scheme is double that of the franchise arrangement. At first sight this may suggest that the shared ownership route is better but:

- The start-up period may be a period of low profits as a new pharmacy business tries to become established against incumbents. If some costs are fixed this might mean low (or even zero) profitability in the short term, hence there may be little (or no) profit share for C4U at first with shared ownership. In contrast, under a franchise agreement at least some profit will be earned by C4U from a 5% share of revenue plus the amortised upfront franchise fee.

- The above table assumes that total revenue would be the same under either ownership choice. However if the incentives for the franchisee or the share ownership partner differ between the two options (see section below) then different levels of revenue may be generated from the same pharmacy and thus different levels of profit earned for C4U.

- The franchise profits are only for a period of five years after which full ownership can revert to C4U if it so choses. After the five years the profit stream to C4U would therefore be £120,000 per annum. Thus a lower short term profit will be compensated by higher long term profit with the franchise scheme compared to the shared ownership scheme.

- For both schemes, profits are likely to be overstated as there are likely to be additional central costs, interest and tax which are not reflected in operating profit.

- There may be some depreciation on the pharmacy outlet property.

(b) **Control and management**

Franchising

- Control is exercised loosely by C4U through the franchise agreement contract. This is more on a negative basis in preventing certain courses of action (eg complying with contract terms to avoid damaging the brand) rather than on a positive basis in promoting positive actions.

- Autonomous management. Franchisees appear to be largely autonomous in being able to decide whether to accept or reject advice and support.

- Each pharmacy is separately managed so diversity of approach and management styles may develop between pharmacies.

- Some degree of auditing will be required by C4U in order to gain assurance regarding disclosed revenue figures to verify that the correct 5% franchise payment is being made. This will require direct access, or third party access, to accounting records and accounting systems.

- After five years, ultimate control reverts to C4U at which time it can choose to change or adapt the management style selected by the franchisee.

Shared ownership

- While the day to day management of pharmacies rests with the co-owner (the pharmacist), C4U manages and monitors the performances of individual pharmacies by providing 'intensive support advice, administration and IT facilities' to the company which would be 'a compulsory part of the agreement so C4U can manage the performance of its investment.'

- Thus, while the co-owner takes the day to day decisions, they have a high degree of monitoring by, and accountability to, C4U.

- If performance is poor and interest cannot be paid, ultimate control also rests with C4U, as the holder of the loan can force the company into insolvency.

(c) **Incentives**

Franchising

- The contract is only five years, so franchisees will not have an incentive to build long term reputation.

- Even if a pharmacy performs badly and makes an operating loss, C4U still receives 5% of revenue so there are strong incentives for the franchisee to perform well and increase profit.

- Franchisees have incentives to reduce costs as this will increase profit but C4U will not take any share of this as they only have a share of revenues. This may incentivise franchisees to be efficient, but may also incentivise them to reduce quality.

Shared ownership

- The co-owner earns a salary and retains a half share of profits after management charges and interest. They are therefore incentivised to increase profit.

- The initial contribution by the co-owner pharmacist (£40,000 on average) is at risk if the venture fails and thus this provides an incentive to succeed.

- If the business succeeds then the co-owner pharmacist has an opportunity to buy out the other 50% at a fair value. There is thus the chance of owning his/her own business. However the more successful the pharmacy becomes the greater the cost of the buy-out. This may give a disincentive to over-performing while the pharmacy remains in joint ownership.

Examiner's comments:

Requirement 40.2 requests candidates to compare the two strategies for expansion by considering: operating profit: control and management; and incentives.

Candidates produced few calculations in answering the operating profit part of this requirement, opting to spend more time on the discussion aspects of the question in respect of control and management and incentives. Where calculations were performed, many candidates treated the upfront payment of £25,000 as a cost in the first year and did not amortise it over five years as expected. This led to a computed profit of £5,000 according to the franchising agreement in the first year. Other errors included: not recognising 5% of the revenue; under the shared ownership arrangement attributing C4U 80% of the profit, rather than 50%; and not thinking about 'profit' by recognising the full cost of the PPE as an expense. It was clear from the answers produced, that candidates were familiar with how a franchising agreement operated, but often the comments were general and not applied to the scenario. Also, there was a lack of understanding of the nature and implications of the shared ownership arrangement, with candidates failing to grasp the fact that it gave a significant amount of control and accountability to C4U.

Answers to the incentives part of the question were often relatively brief, with candidates identifying that under the franchising agreement, the pharmacists still received 5% of revenues whereas under the shared ownership, the co-owners would be entitled to a half share of profit.

Overall, the information in the question could have been better used. Many answers to this part were very brief and did not compare the two strategies in sufficient detail or with sufficient insight.

41 The Mealfest Corporation (December 2012)

		Knowledge	Skill	Marks
41.1 (a)	Organisational structure and performance measurement	1	6	
(b)	Pricing strategies	2	7	
				14
41.2 Benchmarking		3	8	10
		6	21	24

General comments

The listed company in question owns a chain of mid-market restaurants controlled from Germany, but also located in France, Switzerland and the UK. The company was originally centrally controlled and had homogeneous prices for all restaurants across Europe. At the beginning of 20Y2 it restructured, forming a separate division for each country. After the restructuring the prices were homogeneous within countries, but not between countries. The Mealfest board now wishes to monitor the success of the new structure and strategy.

41.1 (a) Organisational structure

Pre-20Y2

MC is a multinational corporation. As such, its structure needs to consider not only operational size and diversity, but international variations in culture, taste, economic conditions, currencies, laws and regulations. The centralised nature of the organisational structure prior to January 20Y2 is in danger of ignoring, or minimising the significance of, these cross border variations.

Arising from this, there are a number of detailed issues with this structure and method of performance measurement (aside from the matters relating to foreign exchange rates highlighted by the finance director which are dealt with later below):

- Pre-20Y2 there was a very flat structure with each of 100 restaurants reporting performance directly to head office. This gives a wide span of control where head office staff in Berlin can have little knowledge of all local conditions and the causes behind the changes in the three performance metrics.

- The structure is also highly centralised with the key decisions relating to pricing, food sourcing and staff being taken centrally in Berlin. This may give economies of scale and discounts but narrows variety (eg different national cultures and food type preferences).

- There are differences in laws and regulations with regard to employment and social security law. Apart from Switzerland, the other four countries are in the EU which reduces, but does not remove, employment law differences. Specifically, national regulation issues include the following: the minimum wage differs between countries; social security payments vary; rights of employees from outside the EU to work in the EU differ; employees rights on redundancy or dismissal differ.

- It is unclear whether the performance of (1) the restaurants or (2) the restaurant managers is being evaluated, or both.

- To the extent that it is the restaurant managers that are being evaluated, then they have little control over profit other than the volume of sales/customers. Menu prices, staff allocation, staff pay and sourcing of food are all fixed centrally. Restaurant managers are therefore being held responsible for matters beyond their control if they are being monitored as a profit centre.

- Centralised decisions fail to take account of local conditions. If, in a particular country, there is high unemployment, then staff may be recruited at lower pay than if labour market conditions are competitive.

Post-20Y2

The two key changes post-20Y2 are:

- A change in the degree of centralisation of decision making which is now at national level rather than corporate level (international).

- Additionally measuring performance at divisional level rather than only at restaurant level.

The decentralisation of decision making to national level reduces the issues arising from cultural, economic and legal differences. However, there may still be many of the above differences in cultural taste and prosperity within countries, as well as between countries.

In terms of measuring performance at divisional level, this seems more appropriate as most of the key decisions are now being taken at this level eg pricing (see below) and staffing, so the division is a profit centre (and also a revenue centre) and has control over most of the elements contributing to profit. The exception is food sourcing which remains at corporate level and is therefore an element of performance outside the control of divisional heads.

Other than revenue and profit, a third performance metric is return on assets. To make this a more valid element of performance evaluation, the divisional manager would need control over new investment and divestment (ie an investment centre). This is not the case, even under the post-20Y2 regime.

Exchange rate issues

MC's primary currency appears to be the euro. Germany and France have the euro as their currency so sales in these countries are not directly affected by currency translation. Food purchases from France and local labour in these countries are also payable in euro.

In the UK and Switzerland fluctuations over the year in exchange rates mean that the euro value of sales revenue is likely to change subject to macroeconomic influences, rather than just decisions at restaurant or divisional levels. Wage costs are in the same currency as revenues and so provide some natural hedging.

Given that food costs are in euro, this makes the euro denominated profit in UK and Swiss restaurants even more volatile than their revenues.

Given that performance comparisons are in euro as a common currency, the profit of a division or a restaurant is heavily dependent on the strength of the national currency, as well as the underlying performance of the business.

In measuring the return on assets in the UK and Switzerland, consideration also needs to be given to the exchange rate at which assets are translated.

(b) **Pricing**

Pre-20Y2

Pre-20Y2 pricing exhibits three characteristics:

- The pricing decision is centralised
- Prices are uniform across all four countries
- Prices are only reset once a year

Centralisation

Centralisation means that pricing decisions fail to take account of local information which may be available to restaurant managers, but local conditions are unlikely to be known centrally on an up to date basis for all 100 locations in Europe. As a consequence, pricing decisions are unlikely to take account of local tastes and needs that customers may report back to individual managers.

Uniformity of pricing

Uniform pricing means that MC does not take account of local competitive conditions. This means that the company does not practise price discrimination by taking advantage of variations in price elasticity between either national markets or local restaurant markets.

Reset once a year

Prices are uniform within the year which means they lack inter-temporal flexibility. As an example, if there is seasonality, then prices would not reflect this. This might be particularly relevant where there is large tourist market in summer, but many fewer tourists in winter, generating different demand dynamics.

Post-20Y2

Of the three characteristics noted above, the third point remains the same (ie set only once a year) hence the problems (eg seasonality) are unchanged.

The first two issues (centralisation and uniformity) have changed and the underlying issues may have been moderated, but they have not been removed.

Centralisation

The degree of centralisation has been reduced from being company-wide to each national division. This is an improvement in terms of devolved decision making, but divisional managers might still not be aware of the local competitive conditions facing each restaurant manager.

Uniformity of pricing

There is still uniformity within countries, even though variations are permitted between countries. The issues here relating to a lack of price flexibility are reduced, but variations within a country in terms of competition, prosperity and taste can still be significant, leading to geographical variations in demand and price elasticity and a continued absence of exploiting price discrimination.

Exchange rate issues

Under the pre-20Y2 system of pricing, exchange rate variations have caused volatility in menu prices in the UK and Switzerland. Such exchange rate movements are likely to reflect macroeconomic conditions rather than the conditions in the restaurant market and may thus be distortionary, leading to arbitrary and suboptimal pricing.

Under the post-20Y2 system, there is discretion at national level to set prices and so the impact of exchange rates can be considered by divisional managers. A factor in this would be the relative rates of inflation in the UK and Switzerland compared to eurozone countries.

Examiner's comments:

Requirement 41.1 asks candidates to compare pre and post 20Y2: (a) organisational structure and performance measurement; and (b) pricing strategies.

Answers tended to be brief and concentrated on the fact that pre 20Y2, the structure was highly centralised and flat, whereas post 20Y2, the decentralisation of decision making eliminated some of the cultural differences previously experienced. There was normally little or no reference to the impact of exchange rate fluctuations and resulting issues in terms of revenue differences between countries and the impact on performance assessment. Although candidates acknowledged that within the different structures the performance would be assessed in terms of revenue and profits, very few considered return on assets.

In terms of pricing, candidates did not really seem to know how to approach the question and this often led to brief, unstructured answers which did not focus on the differences between the pre and post 20Y2 position, but instead merely repeated from the question that there had been a move from a centrally fixed pricing system to one now fixed at national level by divisional heads. There was very little analysis of how this would affect the behaviour of managers and customers or of exchange rate risk.

41.2 Benchmarking compares the use of assets across the firm or across the industry and indicates best practice to show where assets might be better used to achieve sustainable competitive advantage (SCA).

One definition of benchmarking is 'The establishment, through data gathering, of targets and comparators, through whose use relative levels of performance (and particularly areas of underperformance) can be identified. By the adoption of identified best practices it is hoped that performance will improve.'

By comparing procedures and performance, internally and externally, MC can understand how to move towards best practice by learning how to reduce costs, improve service delivery in restaurants and thereby improve market positioning to align with market leaders in the sector.

There are four different types of benchmark that can be used: internal; competitive (industry wide); activity (best in class); and generic.

Internal (or historic) – internal benchmarking could be at the level of comparing individual restaurants or divisions with each other to determine those that are under- or over-performing. Comparisons of restaurants could be intra-country or company-wide. It may be however that certain restaurants are best at one function (eg food quality) while other restaurants are better at a different function (eg quality of service or ambience).

Historical comparison also looks at performance over time to ascertain trends/significant changes, etc.

Internal benchmarking is however restrictive as it could be that MC is generally under-performing and the true benchmark of best practice is to be found within external competitors who are out-performing MC.

Competitive (industry-wide) – this benchmark compares the performance of the restaurant or the division with equivalent units in other firms in the same industry or sector. This may assist MC in ascertaining ways to improve performance.

Comparing the performance of a division with a rival restaurant company in the same market sector may be possible if the rival is a company that is restricted to one country. In this case the published financial statements are likely to provide relevant data to compare key financial performance indicators. They may also provide some narrative information to evaluate non-financial performance indicators. Obtaining information about the performance and functions of rivals at the individual restaurant level is more challenging, as there is less information in the public domain. Industry publications and associations could be possible sources alongside informal contacts in the industry and personal visits to rivals.

If the whole national industry is under-performing, international comparisons may be more useful so comparisons could also be made with restaurants in other national markets (eg the US).

Activity (best in class) – compares with best practice in whatever industry can be found eg could compare MC table booking systems with online booking system for hotels or airline seats to ascertain whether there is scope for improved efficiency. Similarly, the levels of service could be benchmarked against other industry service practice (eg first class airline travel; hotel reception); food preparation could be compared to cookery competitions or the best home cooking.

Generic – against a conceptually similar process eg compare food preparation to the treatment of VIPs at visits and events. Food hygiene could be compared to a hospital operating theatre.

Examiner's comments

Requirement 41.2 asked candidates to explain how benchmarking may be used to evaluate performance of divisions and of individual restaurants.

A good knowledge was shown of the nature of internal, competitive, activity and generic benchmarking, with the majority of candidates displaying an understanding of each. However, answers' application to each type to the scenario tended to be very general with insufficient consideration of the circumstances of the scenario. Some candidates went on to use a balanced scorecard approach, identifying CSF's and KPI's. Whilst this identified some reasonable points, this approach was neither necessary nor entirely suitable for this requirement.

	Knowledge	Skill	Marks
42.1 Porter's Five Forces analysis	3	7	9
42.2 (a) Performance evaluation	2	11	
(b) Conclusion	-	6	17
42.3 Advantages/disadvantages	2	4	6
42.4 Critical success factors (CSFs)	3	7	9
	10	35	41

42.1 Five Forces analysis – Filling stations

Threat of new entrants – low

Barriers to entry for fuel retailing are high. As well as needing sites in prime locations, there is the capital required to set up the filling station (underground storage tanks, fuel lines etc) and to comply with ongoing regulatory requirements. In addition the market is dominated by major brands (oil companies and supermarkets) and these larger players have significant cost advantages as a result of scale economies. Entry to the industry is also likely to be unattractive in the current environment given low margins and high levels of competition. As a result of these factors, the threat of new entrants is low although supermarkets may continue to open more filling stations at existing supermarket locations or new out-of-town sites.

Competitive rivalry – high

Because the industry is low margin, high volume, the level of competition is intense.

The supermarkets are keen to compete with each other on the price of fuel since if they can attract customers to the filling station they are also likely to buy other goods. The effect of competition is evidenced by the reduction in the number of filling stations and the failure of a significant number of the smaller independent filling stations.

Power of suppliers – high

Fuel supply is dominated by a few large petrol wholesalers who therefore wield significant power. This is increased by the fact that most are vertically integrated and also control some retail outlets. Suppliers are likely to exert more power in relation to the smaller independent filling stations than the supermarket-owned sites.

Power of customers – varied

Customers are fragmented so in that sense they have relatively low bargaining power in relation to the industry as a whole and the market price will largely be dictated by the petrol wholesaler and government taxes. However switching costs are low and petrol is a homogeneous commodity product so there is little brand loyalty. As a result customers are easily able to transfer business and in this respect they become more important to an individual operator within the industry as they are likely to choose the lowest price filling station in their area. Corporate buyers may have slightly more power because of the higher volume of business they represent.

Threat of substitutes – low

The threat of substitutes is limited although there is some scope for the manufacture and use of bio-fuels from vegetable oils and animal fats. The greater threat for the fuel retailing industry is that as the price of fuel increases people reduce their consumption by driving less, switching to electric cars and/or using alternative means of transport.

Conclusion

This is a highly competitive industry, which is particularly challenging for the smaller independent operators who struggle to compete with the economies of scale and brand loyalty of the supermarkets. With only three sites, Mayhews may lack sufficient throughput to sustain profitability in the fuel retailing industry in the longer term.

Examiner's comments:

Requirement 42.1 requested candidates to prepare a Porter's Five Forces analysis of the UK fuel retailing industry which might help inform Mayhew's discussions regarding the viability of its filling station operations. This requirement was extremely well attempted by the majority of candidates. Whilst many were able to extract salient information from the question and use it to assess the strength of each force, only the better candidates concluded that the industry is extremely competitive, with high supplier power and that the future is relatively bleak for smaller independents such as Mayhews. A minority of candidates discussed only four of the five forces, omitting the need to consider competitive rivalry, which in the context of the scenario was one of the most important issues. A common error by weaker candidates was to discuss supermarket-owned filling stations under the heading substitutes instead of discussing substitutes for the purchase of fuel eg the use of electric cars or public transport.

42.2 Analysis of Mayhews' performance and closure plans

Note. The data to support the following commentary can be found in the Appendix.

Mayhews' overall business performance

Between 20Y1 and 20Y2, despite the total revenue for the business remaining almost static at £4.29 million, there has been a 10.4% increase in gross profit and a 27.1% increase in net profit, resulting in an absolute increase in profit of £125,000. On the face of it therefore the business has done well in a difficult economic climate.

Although the revenue in overall terms has remained static, this masks the fact that the 11% reduction in fuel revenues has been almost exactly compensated for by an 18% increase in repairs revenue.

The movement in fuel revenue is explained by a 5.4% increase in price but a 15.5% reduction in volume. Within the industry fuel volumes are under pressure due to the economic climate and increased engine efficiency but the drop in volume of fuel sold by Mayhews may suggest that they are losing market share to competitors. This is not surprising since their average retail price is 136p/litre, over 2p/litre higher than the 20Y2 UK average and 5p per litre higher than the average supermarket price.

On average Mayhews is selling 1.47 million litres per site which is not only considerably lower than the branded petrol stations but also less than the 1.68 million litres sold by the average independent. The lack of volume will probably result in Mayhews having to pay higher prices to the wholesaler and will also result in higher overhead costs per litre, which may explain the higher prices being charged. This is also reflected in Mayhews' gross margin, which is only 11.3% whereas on average retailers keep 5% of the retail price, equating to a gross margin of 5/40 = 12.5% of the net of tax price.

The repairs revenue has grown by 18%. Given the economic climate it is unlikely that Mayhews will have put its prices up significantly and this is probably due to volume increases as a result of people needing more repairs and servicing as they hold on to their cars longer. It is also likely to reflect a move away from the dealers to local garages as customers attempt to keep their costs down.

Repairs and servicing now accounts for 44% of the total sales (compared to 37% in 20Y1). Since the gross margin on the repairs business is much higher at 52.1% than the margin on fuel (11.3%), this change in sales mix towards repairs has had a positive effect on the company's overall profit.

Operating costs have also remained relatively static at just under 16% of revenue. A breakdown of these would be helpful – since the premises are owned, in addition to the wages and salaries of the owner, filling station staff and garage mechanics, these costs are likely to consist of utilities, marketing and other administrative expenses. More information is required although on the face of it the business appears to have kept these under control.

Individual garages

If we consider the performance of the individual locations, it is clear that some garages are doing better than others. Garage C is performing best of all and contributing 40% of Mayhews' gross profit, which directly reflects its reduced reliance on fuel sales and a greater proportion of high margin servicing.

Garage B is the least successful. It is charging the highest price per litre (£1.38), selling the lowest volume of fuel (1.34m litres) and has lower margins on both fuel and repairs than the other two garages. It is also the most reliant on fuel revenues (over 62% of total revenue).

More information is required about the location of garage B but this may be in one of the less well populated rural areas or alternatively it may face strong competition in the vicinity eg it could be close to a filling station operated by a major supermarket.

Garage A appears to be performing reasonably and accounts for 36% of Mayhews' revenue and gross profit. Comparing the net margins is not particularly useful as the operating costs of garage A include the £45,000 salary cost of Barry which, once removed, shows garage A making a net margin of 14.9%.

If Mayhews is to focus more on repairs it should try and establish what garage C is doing to achieve margins of 55% and replicate that elsewhere (eg considering the procurement policy it has adopted for parts).

Interdependence of revenues and costs

A key issue for Mayhews is the extent to which the fuel and repairs revenue are interdependent. Should Mayhews decide to close one or more of the filling stations then they may lose some customers for repairs and servicing also.

Depending on how closely located the three garages are to each other, the Mayhews brand may be strong enough to close one garage completely but transfer its repair customers to one of the other locations.

Another consideration is the extent to which operating costs at a particular location will be reduced by closing the filling station part of the business.

Preliminary Conclusions and Recommendations

Mayhews has several choices available:

- Continue as it is.

- Close some/all of the filling stations but retain all three repairs and servicing businesses.

- Close one or more garages in their entirety and sell off the sites to help fund investment in the new computer system and the repairs business at the remaining garage(s).

There is intense competition in fuel retailing and the Porters Five Forces analysis in 42.1 suggests that this is a difficult industry for a business the size of Mayhews to make sustainable profits. Thus continuing as it is, Option (i), is unlikely to guarantee long-term future success.

Currently the filling station at each garage is making a positive contribution towards fixed operating costs. However the evidence between 20Y1 and 20Y2 indicates that it would be possible to improve profitability by increasing the proportion of the servicing and repairs business. Barry's comments about reputation indicate that there may be an opportunity to capitalise on the Mayhews brand and their reputation for honesty and reliability.

A preliminary assessment suggests that garage B is underperforming compared to the others and might be considered for closure. However more information is needed about the detailed performance of the individual garages, the likely savings in operating costs and the exit/compliance costs before deciding whether to close individual sites. An important consideration is the extent to which revenue and costs for the filling stations and repairs business are interdependent.

In the event that Mayhews decided to retain some/all filling stations, it could follow competitors and attempt to service local community needs through product diversification (forecourt shops).

In deciding on the future strategic direction of the business, another issue is succession planning, since Barry is 60. It is important to establish his personal aims and objectives for the business, including any exit plans. He may be keen to realise some of the capital tied up within the business, which the sale of one or more sites to a developer would allow him to do.

Further information required

- Details of the locations, markets and customer profiles of each garage

- Previous year's accounts for each garage

- Repairs revenue/margins split between individual and corporate customers

- Breakdown of operating costs between fuel/repairs/other to ascertain the likely savings in operating costs if one or more filling station is closed

- Exit costs associated with closure of one/more filling stations

- Break-even analysis of fuel sales

- Pricing policy for fuel sales

- Likely value of sites to developer

- Industry/sector information re gross margins/average labour costs/overheads

Appendix: Data analysis

Sales volumes and prices:

	Garage A	Garage B	Garage C	Mayhews 20Y2	Mayhews 20Y1
Litres sold (millions)	1.63	1.34	1.43	4.4	5.21
Ave price net of tax/litre	53.9pence	55.1pence	54.3pence	54.4pence	51.6pence
Ave retail price/litre (net of tax price/0.40)	£1.35	£1.38	£1.36	£1.36	£1.29

20Y2	Branded	Independent	Supermarkets	Mayhews
Litres sold per site (millions)	4.04	1.68	10.2	1.47
Ave retail price/litre	UK ave (whole market) = 133.8p		130.9p	136p
Ave price net of tax/litre		53.5p	52.4p	54.4p

Analysis by product/market:

Sales mix (%)

	Garage A	Garage B	Garage C	20Y2	20Y1
Fuel	56	62	51	56	63
Repairs	44	38	49	44	37

Gross margin (%)

	Garage A	Garage B	Garage C	20Y2	20Y1
Fuel	11.7	10.3	11.7	11.3	11.3
Repairs	51.6	48.0	55.0	52.1	52.1
Total	29.2	24.7	33.1	29.3	26.6

Breakdown of 20Y2 revenue by location (%):

	Fuel	Repairs	Total
Garage A	37	36	36
Garage B	31	24	28
Garage C	32	40	36

Breakdown of 20Y2 gross profit by location (%):

	Fuel	Repairs	Total
Garage A	38	36	36
Garage B	28	22	23
Garage C	34	42	41

Gross profit mix (%)

	Garage A	Garage B	Garage C	20Y2	20Y1
Fuel	22	26	18	21	27
Repairs	78	74	82	79	73

Operating costs and net profit

	Garage A	Garage B	Garage C	20Y2	20Y1
Operating costs as % of revenue	17.2 14.3%*	15.4	14.3	15.7	15.8
Net profit margin (%)	12.1 14.9%*	9.2	18.7	13.7	10.7
	(*) = adjusted for Barry's salary				

Mayhews: Overall change in performance 20Y1:20Y2

Decrease in fuel revenue	−10.9%
Increase in repairs revenue	+18.3%
Decrease in total revenue	negligible
Decrease in fuel gross profit	−11.2%
Increase in repairs gross profit	+18.2%
Increase in total gross profit	+10.4%
Reduction in operating costs	−1.0%
Increase in net profit	+27.1%
Decrease in litres sold	−15.5%
Increase in average retail price/litre	+5.4%

Examiner's comments:

Requirement 42.2 asked candidates to evaluate the performance of Mayhew's overall business and the individual garages and to justify a preliminary conclusion as to whether the company should close one or more filling stations to focus on maintenance and repairs. There were some excellent attempts at this requirement with even the weaker candidates typically scoring over half the marks available.

Most candidates produced a range of calculations for Mayhews business as a whole and for each of its garages, typically including margins, sales mix and revenue/profit growth. Better candidates also used the data to assess Mayhews' fuel prices and volumes in relation to the competition/market. At the other end of the spectrum, some weaker candidates produced hardly any numerical analysis and simply copied out absolute figures from the question or only made a vague attempt at analysing increases/decreases.

Most candidates identified the fact that despite falling fuel volumes, Mayhews has performed well, generating a 27% increase in profit from relatively static sales revenue. The key reason for this is that the mix of sales has changed in favour of maintenance and repairs, which has a significantly higher gross margin than fuel.

In relation to the individual garages, most candidates commented that Garage C is performing best of all and that garage B is the least successful. Better answers explained that this reflects C's reduced reliance on fuel sales, whereas B – the most reliant on fuel sales – is charging the highest price per litre and selling the lowest volume of fuel. A pleasing number of candidates identified that comparing the net margins of the three garages is not particularly useful since the operating costs of garage A include the £45,000 salary cost of the owner, which needs to be removed for a more accurate assessment. Better candidates did this calculation and commented on its results.

The strongest candidates identified that more information is required about the location of the garages and that B may be in one of the less well populated rural areas or alternatively face strong local competition. The lowest scoring candidates merely made assertions describing the changes in ratios, with little, if any, attempt at an analysis of causality.

Candidates were requested to make a preliminary conclusion about the closure of one or more filling stations and most did this, recommending that the filling station at either B or C be closed. Only the better candidates went on to qualify their conclusion, pointing out that more information would be required before making a final decision. The very strongest candidates raised the issue of the possible interdependence of costs and revenues, identifying that the filling station business was making a positive contribution at all garage locations and that failure to supply fuel may lead to the loss of customers for repairs.

42.3 Benefits of new information system

There are two aspects to the investment in IT: a new engine diagnostic system which will allow Mayhews to service more modern vehicles and a new computer system which will improve parts management and have marketing benefits.

Advantages

- Mayhews will be able to handle all types of car and therefore attract greater volumes of business. It will also be able to undertake business that has previously had to be referred to the main dealer.

- A customer database will increase marketing opportunities.

- There will be increased revenue opportunities eg online booking of services and repairs, which might attract a different customer profile.

- The system will give Mayhews a competitive advantage. Contacting customers in advance of MOTs and anticipating service needs will improve the quality of the customer experience and enhance service levels. This may increase customer retention and lead to a greater share of their spend.

- The system should provide Barry with better management information and improve decision making – forecasting, customer profitability analysis, assessment of performance by location/product stream.

- A new system may help reduce costs through more efficient work scheduling, parts control etc.

- The system may help with knowledge management and reduce the business' reliance on Barry.

Disadvantages

- The costs of acquiring and installing the system may be prohibitive for a small business like Mayhews.

- Existing staff may lack the skills to use the system and/or to do work on modern cars. Mayhews will need to train staff to use the new systems and may encounter resistance.

- If Mayhews is currently receiving commission on referrals to main dealers it will lose this income.

- Implementation issues with the new system and the risk of system failures/downtime may cause delays/affect customer service levels. Data protection issues will need to be addressed.

- As the technology is likely to change in the future, particularly in relation to engine diagnostics, the system may need replacing or upgrading regularly.

- There is a risk that competitors will do this too – is it competitive advantage or catch up?

Conclusion

As Mayhews currently does not have the facility to carry out repairs to cars with more modern engine management systems, it appears that investing in a new system will be critical to the success of the strategy to increase the focus on the servicing and repairs business.

A detailed cost benefit analysis should be carried out to ensure the new system is commercially viable.

Examiner's comments:

Requirement 42.3 asked candidates to discuss the advantages and disadvantages of the proposed investment in information technology. The key to a good answer here was to identify that there were two aspects to the investment in IT: an engine diagnostic system that would allow Mayhews to service modern cars that they currently had to refer to the main dealers, and a new computer system which would provide a customer database and assist with parts management. Candidates who identified the two aspects tended to score well. Weaker candidates often listed the generic pros and cons of information systems, without applying this to Mayhews. Only the best candidates came to any form of conclusion – pointing out that the investment would be critical to Mayhews proposal to focus on repairs and maintenance and identifying the need for some form of cost/benefit analysis before such investment was undertaken.

42.4 CSFs for Repairs and servicing

CSFs

Johnson, Scholes and Whittington define critical success factors as 'those product features that are particularly valued by a group of customers and therefore, where the organisation must excel to outperform the competition.' Mayhews has both individual and corporate clients and they may value different things eg corporate clients may be more concerned about speed of service whereas individual customers may focus on trust and reliability.

Alternatively a wider definition of CSFs is 'a small number of key goals vital to the success of an organisation – things that must go right.' Thus CSFs can consider not just the actual product/service but other factors vital to commercial success eg availability, competitive knowledge, cost or performance control.

Using CSFs for strategic control

The process of identifying CSFs will help Mayhews' management focus attention on what is important and the things that need controlling/improving. It will also identify areas of little value-added where for example costs could be eliminated.

Mayhews can measure achievement of the CSFs by calculating KPIs for periodic reporting (see below). These KPIs will assist in benchmarking the garages against each other and also against rivals. They can also help to guide the development of the new information system to ensure that Barry and the garage managers receive information about the factors that are critical to the performance of each location.

Possible CSFs for Mayhews repairs and servicing business

Tutorial note:

A number of CSFs have been identified below for marking purposes. Only three were required.

(1) Ability to attract and retain customers – Barry has identified that in this service-based market Mayhews has a reputation for being honest and reliable. Attracting and retaining customers will provide a stable source of income from annual MOTs and servicing and lead to word-of-mouth referrals which should generate growth. Maintaining and winning new corporate contracts will also be important.

(2) Providing top quality service levels – Mayhews wants to differentiate itself by providing dealer quality service. Customers will expect that repairs carried out are of the highest quality and comply with safety regulations and that they are undertaken as quickly as possible.

(3) Offering a competitively priced service – Mayhews has lower overheads and labour costs than the main dealers and its strategy is to capitalise on this by offering the same quality service but at affordable local garage prices. In the difficult economic climate, price may be a key factor for many customers.

(4) Ability to recruit and retain mechanics with appropriate expertise – Mayhews' ability to offer a fast and reliable service will depend on this, particularly if it starts to undertake more complicated engine diagnostics.

(5) Appropriate technology and information systems strategy to support business needs – Without investing in the new engine diagnostic system, Mayhews will struggle to compete with the main dealers. The reliability of the new computer system will also affect online bookings and will enhance the customer experience by predicting service needs.

Performance measures (KPIs) linked to CSFs:

Tutorial note:

A wide range of KPIs has been identified below for marking purposes. Only one relevant KPI was required for each of the three CSFs identified.

(1) **Attraction/Retention of customers:**

Number of cars referred to main dealer (measures Mayhews' ability to carry out work)
Number of contracts for corporate servicing
Average Customer satisfaction scores on post work feedback survey
Level of repeat business for MOTs and annual servicing
Geographical area of customer base
% of enquiries converted to booking for MOT/service

(2) **Quality service levels**

Quality of work undertaken:

% of defects rectified

Warranty costs as a % of revenue

Level of complaints

% of vehicles maintained/repaired which have to be subsequently rechecked

Speed of service

Lead time between customer call and date job scheduled

Availability of parts

Hours taken per repair/service

% of jobs finished on time

(3) **Competitively priced service**

Final price as a % of original Quotation

Hourly labour charge compared to main dealers' labour charges

Price of various work (MOT/routine service etc) compared to competitors

Recovery rates: Hours recharged to customers/Hours worked

(4) **Staffing**

Qualifications undertaken/mechanic

Number of sick/absent days

Staff turnover compared to total number of staff

(5) **Technology and information**

Number of vehicles that Mayhews is unable to diagnose/need referring to main dealer

Number of mechanics trained in the new engine diagnostic system

Number of computer system breakdowns

Examiner's comments:

In requirement 42.4, candidates were asked to explain how the use of critical success factors might assist Mayhews in establishing a strategic control system. Candidates were required to justify three CSFs for the maintenance and repairs business and suggest one appropriate key performance indicator for each. This part was surprisingly quite poorly done. Many candidates restricted their marks by completely ignoring the element of the requirement relating to establishing a strategic control system and simply provided a list of CSFs and KPIs. The weakest candidates were clearly unsure about the distinction between KPIs and targets or goals. For some, the CSFs and KPIs described could have been those for any business and it was not obvious that the candidate was discussing Mayhews' repairs and maintenance business. Whilst customer satisfaction is relevant to all businesses and therefore customer feedback is vitally important, the information in the question could have been used to produce some higher quality answers. The better candidates produced a reasoned justification of their choice of each CSF and then demonstrated clearly how this could be measured. Some candidates provided a long list of KPIs, despite the specific request for only one for each CSF identified – these additional measures wasted time and did not attract marks.

43 Cabezada Ltd (March 2013)

	Knowledge	Skill	Marks
43.1 Business plan			
(a) Strengths and opportunities	1	4	
(b) Weaknesses and threats	1	4	
(c) Benefits of partnership	2	6	
			16
43.2 Additional information	2	7	8
43.3 Market segmentation	3	5	8
	9	26	32

General comments

The scenario in this question relates to a relatively new company which uses steel shipping containers to create short-term living accommodation for events and contract clients. The directors are keen to expand globally and have begun to prepare a business plan to help attract appropriate local partners. Candidates were asked to take the role of a senior in the firm of business advisers which has been appointed to help develop the business plan.

The overall scores on this question were again very good.

43.1 Sections of Business Plan

(a) **Strengths and realistic market opportunities (section 2.2.1)**

Our key strengths:

Innovation – Cabezada are seen as a pioneer within the container accommodation industry and we have built up an extensive database, contact network and team of experienced designers and engineers.

The Cabezada product range is extremely flexible and can be adapted to meet the needs of a wide variety of customers and target markets.

There is a cheap and readily available supply of standardised containers, and with access to worldwide low-cost distribution systems we can quickly, easily and cheaply respond to customer needs.

We have a strong leadership team as a result of the skills and experience acquired in our previous roles as chief executive of a hotel group and operations director of a large construction company.

Realistic market opportunities:

We believe that there are significant opportunities for rapid expansion into global markets via our local partnership model.

Our proven success to date indicates that the container accommodation concept is likely to be successful in a range of other markets eg student accommodation, pop-up retail stores, mobile offices.

The world's population is growing. Land shortages and cost implications mean there is likely to be an increasing need for this type of accommodation.

Similarly the global demand for sustainability and a desire to conserve resources will lead to a growing demand for container accommodation over conventional structures.

Cabezada may be able to further enhance its brand reputation and achieve recognition for corporate social responsibility by working with local governments and charities as potential partners in disaster areas/trouble zones. This and our sustainability ethos may widen market appeal and help attract future customers/investors.

(b) **Weaknesses and threats (section 2.2.2)**

There is limited scope for Cabezada to expand alone due to current size and resources, which is why we have developed a partnership model.

Some of the benefits of container accommodation are a result of the standardisation of containers, the ease of transportation and the readily available supply. These are also downsides as potentially this seems to be an easily replicated idea. Protection of IP in relation to our competitors will therefore be important. However Cabezada also benefits from experience and reputation gained as a result of first mover advantage and establishing a global network should help create barriers to entry.

We recognise that as the business expands the two of us are unlikely to have sufficient time and expertise to manage the wider business. Neither of us has a financial background and we are well aware that many businesses fail because they lack sufficient financial expertise. We currently rely on our accountants to provide this expertise but we plan to appoint a finance director in due course and as the business expands we intend to appoint other directors to the Board.

Projects are heavily reliant on local infrastructure in relation to heat, light, sewerage etc. and delays may occur due to the political nature of certain projects. Cabezada's previous experience can be brought to bear here to ensure such risks are managed and to make sure that appropriate contingency plans are in place.

Legal and regulatory requirements differ between countries but this is mitigated by our use of the local partnership model.

Health and safety issues or accidents could be very damaging to our reputation. We pride ourselves on our unblemished health and safety record. We take this issue very seriously and we expect our partners to do the same.

A successful model will rely on the integrity of a wide range of local partners and we need to ensure goal congruence. Our partnership agreement will be carefully drafted to make clear the obligations on both sides to ensure the Cabezada brand is not diluted by variable standards. Our terms and conditions will also set out restrictive clauses and confidentiality agreements to protect our partners in the event that a local partner chooses to leave the business.

(c) **Benefits of partnership approach for Cabezada and its local partners (section 3)**

Global business using a local model

Working with the right local partners will allow us to capitalise on our brand image as a pioneer in container accommodation, expand rapidly and generate competitive advantage for Cabezada.

It is easier for local customers and governments to do business with local offices, from a language and timing point of view, as well as culturally.

Local teams are better able to identify opportunities in a market and define appropriate price/quality combination.

Since building standards vary from country to country and requirements also change frequently it is better for the local office to work with architects, governments and planning experts.

Support for our local partner

In addition to exclusive rights to operate under the Cabezada brand in your defined area, we will provide you with a range of benefits that result from being part of a global business, and which are unachievable by setting up business alone:

(1) A popular and tested product range suitable for many different uses in many markets and a reference list of successful projects in different countries

(2) Access to an experienced team of designers and engineers dedicated to container accommodation

(3) Marketing support including website, brochures and press articles

(4) Our supplier and customer contact network and our extensive database of technical, financial and marketing information

(5) Assistance with budgets and financial projections for projects

(6) Ongoing support from a committed partner as evidenced by the fact that we are prepared to take a 20% stake in each partner business

Examiner's comments:

Requirement 43.1 asked candidates to prepare three sections of the business plan:

(a) Strengths and realistic market opportunities
(b) Weaknesses and threats
(c) Benefits of partnership for Cabezada and its local partners

This was one of the higher skills elements of the paper and answers were quite polarised. Although candidates were clearly familiar with the knowledge required, which was based on SWOT analysis and methods of business development, weaker candidates struggled to apply this in the context of a business plan to attract potential partners. Candidates who appreciated the need to focus their content on the end user of the document and wrote in an appropriate style, scored very highly. The key here was to (1) emphasise why the company's strengths put it in an ideal position to capitalise on the global opportunities (2) explain any potential weaknesses and threats and how they might be mitigated and (3) highlight how the partnership proposition would be a win-win for both parties. Surprisingly, too many candidates did not produce an answer using the numbered section headings given in the requirement, missing out on an easy format mark. Weaker candidates often provided a bullet point list for each requirement which would not have been suitable for a firm to send to a client. Weak answers were often written as if the focus was on assessing the situation from Cabezada's point of view rather than considering how the information would be received by the partner (ie with a complete failure to consider the marketing/persuasive nature of the document). Another error was for candidates to write in 43.1(a) and 43.1(b)about the strengths and weaknesses of the partnership arrangement, rather than of Cabezada, leaving themselves with little new to say in 43.1(c).

43.2 Additional information requirements

A prospective partner will want sufficient information to be able to undertake appropriate due diligence and decide if the Cabezada business model makes sense given the current and future environment. They will use a range of criteria to assess the proposal and it is important to anticipate what these are likely to be and to cover them in the plan. The assessment criteria are likely to include:

- Viability of business model
- Costs
- Potential returns
- Risks (weaknesses and threats) and how these might be addressed
- Obligations of both parties
- Possible exit route

It would be useful for the plan to start with an executive summary setting out the highlights of the detail contained in the plan. In addition to the current content of the plan, a prospective partner is also likely to want the plan to include the following additional information about:

Owners of Cabezada

Background/track record/qualifications/expertise of owners;

Any other key stakeholders besides the two directors

Details of senior management

Financial security of the company

Recent accounts to indicate the long-term sustainability of the business and its ability to provide partners with on-going support.

Competition

Analysis of existing players in the market place, their USPs and how Cabezada differentiates itself in relation to their products/markets.

Detailed terms and conditions of joint venture

- Terms and conditions of Cabezada's stake
- Obligations of both JV parties
- Details of amount and level of support and training to be provided by Cabezada
- Restrictions on partners eg Regional protection; minimum performance requirements
- Reporting structure for local partners
- Control mechanisms to guarantee quality and performance of other partners
- Restrictions on use of suppliers
- Exit arrangements

Detailed financial information

The required investment level – the amount partners will have to pay for the franchise fee, monthly management charge and % royalty fee on sales.

Annual projections for a typical partner, showing likely profitability and cash flow.

Cabezada's attitude to any continuing financial obligations and the arrangements for financing in the event of expansion.

Evidence of key strategic relationships

- Details of existing projects undertaken
- Supplier contracts
- Quotes/recommendations from existing satisfied customers
- Details of any existing partners/references from them

Other information

Supporting technical detail on the different types of accommodation offered, including photos, plans, diagrams etc.

Examiner's comments:

Requirement 43.2 requested candidates to recommend any further information that should be included in the plan to help potential partners to adequately assess Cabezada's partnership proposition. Candidates who were familiar with the pro-forma contents of a business plan and who then applied this to the scenario tended to score well. Some weaker candidates merely provided a list of information without explaining how this might be useful to a potential partner. Better candidates provided a prioritised discussion, focussing on the fact that the current plan was completely lacking in any financial information – historic results, forecasts and details of the costs of the partnership arrangement – and that this would be vital if partners were to assess the likely returns from their investment. It is likely that partners would also want more information on the key directors with whom they were establishing a relationship.

43.3 Purpose and benefits of market segmentation

Market segmentation is the division of the market into homogeneous groups of potential customers who may be treated similarly for marketing purposes.

The purpose of segmentation is to vary the marketing mix according to the needs of each chosen segment. This is likely to increase the effectiveness of marketing.

For example by dividing the market into events and contract clients Cabezada can tailor its product. Events clients may be more concerned with the appearance of the accommodation and want a range of designs; contract clients may focus on cost and functionality.

Benefits of market segmentation include:

- Identification of new marketing opportunities because it provides Cabezada with an opportunity to spot additional sub-groups or to dominate certain segments of the market (niche).

- Competitive advantage from having a better understanding of customer's needs and attitudes to price in each segment.

- It allows Cabezada to assess returns from each segment and thus assist in performance measurement/provide information for decision making.

Segmentation options for Cabezada:

Cabezada has currently chosen to segment the market by type of buyer: one-off short term events vs contract clients requiring longer term accommodation.

It could also consider segmentation by:

- Geographical location – this may help Cabezada organise its logistical operations and adjust elements of the price/product to local needs

- Type of accommodation: hotel and leisure; key worker; housing; media; temporary disaster recovery

- Quality of accommodation: basic, luxury, environmentally friendly

Examiner's comments:

In requirement 43.3, candidates were required to explain the purpose and benefits of market segmentation and discuss other approaches to segmentation that the company could adopt, besides the current split between contract and events clients.

The majority of candidates were able to define market segmentation and explain how it could be used to focus the marketing mix to specific customer needs. Again better candidates differentiated themselves by illustrating this with examples relating to Cabezada, rather than talking about segmentation in generic terms. Most candidates were able to make alternative suggestions for segmentation according to geography or quality, although a significant minority of suggestions were more appropriate for segmenting consumers than business customers. A small number of candidates discussed divisionalisation, generic strategy or product/market mix rather than segmentation; these answers were not relevant.

44   Chiba (March 2013)

Marking guide

		Knowledge	Skill	Marks
44.1	Ethical issues	2	3	5
44.2	Divestment/growth by acquisition	3	6	8
44.3 (a)	Human resource management	2	3	5
(b)	Change management issues	3	7	9
		10	19	27

44.1 Ethical issues

The issue here is whether it is legal and ethical for the directors to keep the contamination confidential. As well as possibly damaging Malegar's reputation, the contamination will potentially have an effect on the wholesaler(s), the supplier of the bottles, the consumers of the vinegar and the potential purchaser, Chiba.

The directors need to investigate the cause of the problem and consider whether there has been any breach of the law or other regulations that may apply to the industry eg health and safety or food standards. It could be argued that since Malegar takes health and safety and quality control very seriously, there should have been procedures in place to avoid/detect the contamination before the product reached the wholesaler, irrespective of whoever caused the problem.

In the context of the potential acquisition by Chiba, the directors of Malegar have a duty to act in the best interests of the company and to obtain the best value for shareholders. However, since Malegar's parent, VM plc, is a UK listed company it is likely to have certain obligations regarding the disclosure of any information that could materially affect the purchase price. To this effect there may be a conflict of interest between the directors' duty to obtain the best price for their shareholders and their duty to treat Chiba fairly. The directors should therefore seek legal advice as to how much information they are required to disclose to a prospective purchaser and to what extent it is a case of 'buyer beware'. Chiba is likely to undertake due diligence to help understand the risks before taking on ownership and this will almost certainly involve an investigation into potential liabilities and warranties.

Knowingly making statements that are misleading or inaccurate is likely to be considered dishonest and unethical. The omission of information, which is a matter of transparency, is perhaps less clear cut, particularly where it might be argued that this is an acceptable treatment eg if the directors believe that the contamination issue has arisen with the supplier and is likely to be fully compensated.

Malegar's directors need to establish the facts and ascertain the cause of the contamination and then seek legal advice before deciding on the most appropriate course of action which fulfils their ethical obligations but minimises the risk of reputational damage for the company.

Examiner's comments:

Requirement 44.1 asked candidates to explain the ethical issues that arise for Malegar's directors in relation to revealing the possible contamination.

The quality of answers to this requirement varied considerably. The question required candidates to assess the ethical issues arising from the directors' intention to keep the contamination confidential and the responsibility of Malegar to its customers and the potential acquirer, Chiba. Many candidates approached this requirement in terms of a transparency, fairness and effect framework. However only the better candidates went on to develop the next steps or draw any sort of conclusion. The weaker candidates only considered the issue in relation to Chiba, ignoring the other stakeholders in the scenario (namely the wholesaler, glass supplier and end consumers). They often failed to see any grey area and simply stated that Malegar's directors must reveal the potential contamination or risk being sued by Chiba after it had acquired the business. Stronger candidates discussed the fact that the cause of the contamination was uncertain, and that the directors needed first to establish the facts and then decide whether to disclose. The best candidates also discussed whether Malegar would have any legal duty to disclose the issue to its customers or Chiba, which might be expected to undertake its own due diligence, or whether in the context of the acquisition it would be a case of 'buyer beware'.

44.2 Strategy evaluation

As Chiba's marketing director notes, the UK parent may want to sell Malegar because the market is challenging and it is struggling to maintain margins etc. Even so, Malegar may still be worth buying as Chiba may be better placed to exploit benefits due to synergy with its existing brands and the ability to target other markets based on health benefits and alternative uses (eg cleaning).

However it could also be that the Malegar business is viable and that other reasons can be put forward for the divestment by the UK parent:

Reason for sale by UK parent

- Rationalisation of the business as a result of portfolio analysis – here we are told that VM plc wants to focus on a few key food brands (a reversal of diversification strategy). VM plc may have decided that there is a lack of strategic fit between vinegar and its other more profitable brands.

- VM may wish to generate funds for investment in other markets that will generate better growth opportunities. Malegar may be generating insufficient returns for the amount of management time/investment required.

- We are also told that the parent company has incurred significant borrowings. These may be incurring high interest costs and putting a strain on liquidity. A sale would raise funds to reduce this debt burden.

- If exit barriers are high (eg redundancy costs, termination penalties on leases etc) then it is better for VM to sell the business as a going concern rather than just withdraw the product.

- Finally the company may be trying to sell Malegar before the contamination becomes widely known and damages its brand/reputation.

Chiba's growth by acquisition

The Ansoff model is a two-by-two matrix of 'Products' and 'Markets'. In the context of this matrix the acquisition of Malegar would involve market development and, to the extent that malt vinegar is deemed to be different from rice vinegar, product development. The Lynch expansion model is another two-by-two matrix of company growth and geographical location. Under this model, Chiba's proposed acquisition is international external development.

Arguments for growth by acquisition

- Chiba's management has identified a desire to increase its presence in the UK. Chiba has no track record in the UK market and the strong market presence of brand names such as Malegar creates barriers to entry that would make organic growth hard to achieve. Acquisition is likely to be faster than organic growth and potentially less risky.

- Acquisition of the market leader creates instant market dominance for Chiba and at the same time removes a significant player from the market.

- It will provide access to a strong brand name/reputation in the UK market and facilitate a better understanding of the UK market for a Japanese company. This reduces cultural risk and having a 'local image' may also reduce xenophobic tendencies.

- Acquisition gives Chiba instant access to the existing factory location and resources, including employees.

- The acquisition of a business in the UK may give rise to other future opportunities, eg expansion into Europe.

The price of the acquisition will be a major factor in assessing the overall merits of sale or purchase.

Requirement 44.2 asked candidates to discuss the possible reasons why the UK owner might be divesting Malegar (in light of the comments of Chiba's marketing director) and the benefits to Chiba of growing by acquisition in the UK.

Candidates are used to being asked to discuss growth by acquisition and were well-versed in the arguments here, with the majority able to apply their knowledge to the scenario. Some were less prepared for a discussion of reasons for divestment, although most were able to expand on the two reasons given in the question regarding the parent company's desire to reduce borrowings and focus on core brands. Better answers discussed other possible reasons such as product portfolio and life-cycles, liquidity and return. Stronger candidates queried whether the contamination may have had an impact on the decision to sell. Despite the comment in the requirement, relatively few candidates linked their discussion to the marketing director's concerns that Malegar might be loss-making. The best scripts did address this however, often in some form of conclusion, explaining that the fact that Malegar might be making insufficient return for its UK parent did not necessarily mean that it would be an unprofitable acquisition for Chiba, although only the top decile pointed out that the overall benefit of the acquisition might depend on the price to be paid.

44.3 HR strategy and change management

(a) HR management by Malegar

Malegar does not seem to have adopted a strategic approach to HRM. Its approach, which is very authoritarian, treats the staff merely as another resource, rather than as a valued asset. It may have resulted in a high degree of job-related tension, poor working relationships and some manipulation of data by functional managers accountable for their performance. There are likely to be limited prospects for career development.

The disadvantages of such an approach include:

- There is evidence that staff motivation may be a problem as there is a high staff turnover. The loss of staff loses experience and skills for the company with the costs of retraining and learning for new staff.

- There may be dysfunctional behaviour by staff in response to short-term targets instead of focussing on longer-term value-enhancing activities eg this may mean that short-term sales are made at the cost of long-term customer relationships.

- The hierarchical nature of the business and centralised approach to decision making may also have impeded team-working and stifled innovation.

HR management by Chiba

Chiba on the other hand appears to take a more strategic approach with emphasis on the human element. This recognises that collectively the staff are a valued asset and can contribute to competitive advantage.

Chiba is likely to do more to focus on personal and career development, gaining employees' commitment to the organisation's values and goals and creating a more participative environment.

As a result tension and manipulation are reduced and relationships are likely to be better.

The shared approach to decision making is likely to increase goal congruence, although a potential downside of Chiba's approach to HRM is that decision-making may be slower than in Malegar.

(b) Managing the change of culture

It is clear that the two businesses are very different and that acquisition by Chiba will transform the existing structure, culture and values. As a result of the acquisition, Chiba's management will need to develop a strategy for creating and maintaining the necessary culture change, although the fact that the transition will take up to 12 months may help as the changes can be made gradually.

The changes may cause resistance from those wishing to preserve the existing state of affairs and the way that the changes are put forward and implemented will be crucial to Chiba's success. However given Chiba's approach to HRM, the change may be welcomed by many Malegar employees as better than they are used to.

Barrier to change

Barriers to change may be cultural or arise as a result of things which affect individuals and cause them to see the change as a threat (personnel barriers).

Cultural resistance arises as a result of structural inertia, group inertia and power structures.

- Structural inertia – Malegar has operated with a rigid hierarchy and short term targets which will take time to change. Its recruitment and promotion processes are likely to have resulted in certain types of employee who may not fit with Chiba's collective approach and participative decision making.

- Group inertia – this may be less relevant as Malegar's existing structure is unlikely to have led to cohesive teams. However the functional managers may act as a group in resisting change implementation and if employees are in one geographical location this may be a factor in increasing group resistance.

Power structures are threatened by the redistribution of authority or changing communication lines. This will in particular affect higher management in Malegar whose roles may change significantly after the new structure is implemented, as participation and collective responsibility is encouraged. Such management may be reluctant to implement changes which will be against their own interests. For example, managers may have viewed Malegar as having been very successful in the UK, therefore resenting the need to integrate and adopt the new values of a Japanese company.

Other Malegar employees who have been discontented under the existing system may however be supportive at the outset.

Personal barriers

There are also barriers which affect individuals and result in them seeing the change as a threat.

Malegar employees may feel threatened by the changes to their habitual way of working and the lack of familiarity (fear of the unknown). Junior employees may lack the confidence or skills to take on a new challenge and may take time to get used to the participative approach with its emphasis on shared responsibility. It is important that Chiba offers support and training to assist them.

Employees may have concerns over potential income levels and job security, although given the high staff turnover this does not seem to have been a feature of employment with Malegar. Chiba could provide statistics on staff turnover to help reassure employees about employment prospects and their earning capacity.

Selective information processing may cause employees to misinterpret or ignore the arguments for change put forward by Chiba's management.

Change management

Resistance to cultural change can be managed or reduced with genuine and visible support for the change by top management and good communication/participation systems associated with the change.

Chiba's management should identify the key stakeholders and influencers among the Malegar employees and provide communication and appropriate training.

Communication should focus on the benefits of the change to employees. Management needs to communicate Chiba's vision of the future and show how the Malegar employees can contribute to this. Given the gradual nature of the transfer of contracts, a negotiation strategy may be implemented where the process of bargaining leads to a situation of compromise and agreement. The advantage of a negotiation strategy is that Chiba can note possible conflict and deal with it in an orderly fashion, which prevents such problems as industrial action. Also ex-Malegar employees are more likely to support changes made and give positive commitment if they 'own' the change or have a stake in the future of the company.

Lewin suggests that managers should recognise the current state of equilibrium with forces pushing for change on the one hand and, equally, forces resisting change aiming to maintain the present situation. As a result Chiba's management would need to adopt the following process:

- **Unfreezing** – where management convince staff of the undesirability of the present situation, creating the initial motivation to change by emphasising the benefits of Chiba's longer term, participative approach.

- **The change process itself** – which will often involve new information, new attitudes and new concepts. This would involve the communication, negotiation and training outlined above.

- **Refreezing** – which reinforces the new pattern of work or behaviour by rewards, developing the belief that the changed situation satisfies organisational and personal values. Under Chiba's management employees are likely to have more opportunities for career development, staff turnover should reduce and Chiba can also implement non-financial motivators rather than focussing on the achievement of short term targets.

Tutorial note:

This answer includes a wide variety of points for marking purposes and is far more comprehensive than would be expected for the marks available. As an alternative to Lewin, the Gemini's 4Rs framework for planned change could also be applied: Reframe, Restructure, Revitalise, Renew.

Examiner's comments:

In requirement 44.3, candidates were required to (a) contrast Chiba and Malegar's differing approaches to human resource management and (b) explain the change management issues that Chiba is likely to face when integrating the Malegar employees.

Some candidates seemed less well prepared for 44.3(a), with many weaker candidates restricting their answers to a comparison of structure and decision-making, which often was in fact little more than a repetition of points made in the scenario. Better candidates contrasted Malegar's 'hard' approach to HRM which treats employees as a short-term commodity, with Chiba's 'softer', more collective approach where employees are seen as a valued asset, and discussed the impact that this is likely to have on motivation, quality of decision-making and commitment to the organisation.

As usual candidates demonstrated good knowledge of change management in 44.3(b), with most discussing barriers to change and Lewin/Schein's iceberg model (although the Gemini's 4Rs framework could also have been used). It was disappointing that more candidates did not focus on the change in the context of the very different HRM strategy and culture/values of the Japanese company – a point that 44.3(a) had been intended to highlight; weaker candidates instead discussed at length the general change management issues associated with acquisitions. The best candidates recognised that the change will transform the existing culture but is to take place over a gradual period of 12 months and, given some explanation, may be welcomed by most employees as better than their current position. Candidates who went on at length about structural inertia, group norms and job security failed to recognise that these might not be particularly relevant given Malegar's existing high staff turnover.

45 Hire Value Ltd (June 2013)

	Knowledge	Skill	Marks
45.1 Performance and competitive position	2	9	10
45.2 Shortfall in performance and matters requiring further attention	–	18	16
45.3 Risk register	3	7	9
45.4 Ethical issues, and implications of them	3	8	10
	8	42	45

General comments

This is the mini case and also the data analysis question. The scenario relates to a small company (HV) operating in the self-drive, car hire industry. HV decided to expand the business just over a year ago by raising venture capital finance based on a business plan which forecast growth in sales and profits. Whilst there has been some growth, it has not matched the business plan projections and a one-year review has taken place to discover the reasons for this. The review also highlighted some transactions with directors which raised ethical issues. The question also provides information about the market leader, KK.

Data for 45.1 and 45.2

	HV plan	HV Actual	Variance	%	KK
Revenue					
Business £'000s	13,000	7,000	–6,000	–46.15	620,000
Leisure £'000s	17,000	20,000	+3,000	+17.65	580,000
TOTAL REV £'000s	30,000	27,000	–3,000	–10%	1,200,000
Profit £'000s	1,200	1,000	–200	–16.67%	56,000
Vehicles	3,000	2,800	–200	–6.67%	68,000
Days hiring ('000 days)	870	820	–50	–5.74%	21,100
Asset values					
Cars £'000s	20,250	16,800	–3,450	–17.04%	816,000
Other £'000s	10,000	10,000	0	0	664,000
Total assets £'000s	30,250	26,800	–3,450	–11.40%	1,480,000

Analysis

% REVENUE	HV plan	HV Actual			KK
– Business	43.3%	25.9%			51.7%
– Leisure	56.7%	74.1%			48.3%
PROFIT/REV	4%	3.7%			4.7%
REV per car pa	£10,000	£9,642.85			£17,647
REV per day hiring	£34.48	£32.93			£56.87
Days hire per car	290	293			310
Profit/assets	3.97	3.73			3.78
Profit/value of cars	5.93	5.95			6.86
Value of cars/cars	£6,750	£6,000			£12,000
Rev/value of cars	1.48	1.61			1.47

45.1 Key differences between KK and HV which make performance comparisons more difficult are: the larger size of KK; and a different business sector, with KK being upmarket compared to HV's business model. However, both companies operate in a similar product and geographical market, being in the UK.

Competitive position

In assessing market share of KK and HV they are both operating in the short term rental sector which has revenues of £5,000 million. Any assessment of competitive position appears valid in relation to this market sub-sector.

With revenue of £1,200 million this gives KK a substantial 24% share of the short term car hire sector. In contrast, HV has a market share of about 0.5%. With a total industry revenue of about £5,000 million and 100 companies, the average company has a revenue of about £50 million giving it a 1% market share – almost twice that of HV.

As a consequence, HV is very much a niche player in the industry. It appears to adopt a slightly confused business model of a mid-market position in all respects except the key asset of the quality of the vehicles, which is downmarket. Perhaps, as a consequence, it is particularly weak in the business customer sector with only 26% of revenue from business customers.

In contrast, KK generates 52% of its revenue from the business customer sector. It also competes at the upper end of the market with a wide range of large company business customers and a series of partners offering exclusive access to some airlines making it impossible, in the short term at least, for smaller car hire companies, including HV, to compete.

KK's size enables it to have economies of scale and economies of scope for cost advantages and these also provide barriers to entry into this sector of the market making it hard for smaller companies, like HV, to compete.

Performance

In absolute terms, it is clear that KK earns a greater profit than HV. However this is to be expected from a larger company and it does not follow that it has performed better on this basis.

In terms of margins, the data table shows that KK has significantly better operating profit margins at 4.7% compared to 3.7% for HV. This may be due to: better cost control; economies of scale; or premium pricing.

Similarly, revenue per car is much greater for KK at £17,647 per year compared to only £9,643 for HV (83% higher). It would be misleading to conclude however that KK has better revenue generation from its assets on this basis. The table shows that the average value of a KK car is £12,000 while the average value of a HV car is only half that at £6,000. Thus, while KK's car value is 100% greater than that of HV, the revenue per car is only 83% higher. As a consequence, the data table shows that HV's annual revenue per £1 of car value is £1.61, compared to only £1.41 for KK. This may give some support for the HV business model of sourcing two year old used cars.

A key piece of data that indicates market positioning is the price per day of hire. For HV it is only £32.93, whereas KK is able to charge an average of £56.87, although this average may reflect some very high quality vehicles.

In terms of operating efficiency, KK also appears to outperform HV. KK cars are hired out 310 days per year giving a utilisation of 85% (on a 365 day year) compared to that of 80% already noted for HV.

It is clear therefore that in financial and operating terms KK has overall outperformed HV, but nevertheless the strategy of HV may have some favourable aspects and HV may have more potential to grow if it is able to win some large business customer accounts.

Examiner's comments:

Requirement 45.1 requested candidates to compare the performance and competitive position of HV with that of the market leader, KK. Attempts at this part were reasonable with most candidates producing some calculations including operating profit margin, average price per vehicle hired and average number of days hired. However, the interpretation of the data was, in many cases, limited. Candidates struggled with the comparison of a large business with a smaller business with many concluding little more than that KK had greater revenue and profit through its relatively greater size. Some of the reasons for the differences were very general, such as 'KK has economies of scale'. The comparison of competitive position was omitted altogether by a significant minority of candidates.

45.2 Revenue

The above data analysis shows that overall revenues are lower than the business plan by £3m, which is a 10% shortfall on planned sales revenues.

The analysis by sector shows that there is a shortfall of £6m in the business customer sector, but that sales revenue in the leisure sector has exceeded the business plan by £3m. The reason for the shortfall in leisure needs to be investigated further in terms of the assumptions that were expected to lead to growth (eg number of new business customers, new lines of business, pricing policy, one or a few larger business customers expected to be won). It may be that negotiations are continuing on some accounts that are expected to be won in 20Y2/Y3 and that will come to fruition in 20Y3/Y4.

The excess over plan of leisure customer revenues should also be investigated further to continue to exploit any successes in the next period.

The impact of the revenue variances has made the company much more dependent on the leisure sector compared to the business sector (74% v 26%) than was envisaged in the business plan where the relative shares were reasonably equal (57% v 43%).

There is limited additional data on each customer sector but, looking at revenue overall, it can be seen from the above data table that the number of days hiring has fallen short of the plan by 50,000 hire days. In terms of volumes this is a 5.7% shortfall. The fact that sales revenues have fallen by 10% and volumes by only 5.7% implies that the rental charge has been lower than expected. This notion is substantiated by the revenue per vehicle hire day which was £34.48 per hire day in the business plan, but only £32.93 was actually achieved.

This result could be explained by: additional discounting, proportionately more hires of cheaper vehicles or failure to implement intended price increases. The result is, however, inconsistent with the shift in the proportion of business customers to leisure customers as business customers have 'preferential rates' and so one would expect the revenue per hire day to increase with a greater proportion of leisure customers. This matter requires further investigation and analysis by sector.

Profitability

The above data table shows that overall profit before tax is lower than the business plan by £200,000, which is a 16.7% shortfall on profit in the business plan.

The fall of 16.7% in profit based on a 10% fall in revenue may, in part, be due to operating gearing whereby fixed costs still need to be covered and therefore profit falls by a greater amount than revenue.

Profit margins are also lower than planned at 3.7%, compared to the forecast 4%. This also may be due to high operating gearing and lower sales than expected.

Return on assets

Having considered profitability in absolute terms, it is necessary to consider profitability in relation to the asset base generating that profit.

The revenue earning asset base (cars) is smaller than planned, with an actual average count of 2,800 vehicles rather than the 3,000 planned. The reasons for this need to be established. It may have been that with lower demand it was decided to reduce the number of cars held in order not to have surplus underutilised assets. It is possible however that the direction of causation is the other way around ie that it has proved difficult to source the right type of cars at the right price and the shortfall in vehicle capacity has meant that revenues have been affected. This latter explanation seems less likely, but further investigation is needed.

The return on total assets from the data table is 3.7% compared to the level in the business plan of 4%. This has occurred as, even though the asset base is £3.45m (11.4%) lower than expected, the profit is down 16.7% on the planned level.

Further analysis of assets shows that general non-revenue earning assets are constant at £10m. As a result the entire £3.45m fall in the asset base relates to hire cars. This is a 17% reduction. As a consequence, the return on the revenue generating asset base of cars is 5.95% which is slightly higher than the planned rate of 5.93%.

Further analysis shows that the reason for the lower hire car asset base is partly volume with 2,800 cars compared to the planned level of 3,000 (6.7% lower). However the value per car is also lower than planned at £6,000 compared to the planned value of £6,750. This may be due to: a higher proportion of purchases of smaller and cheaper cars than planned; the acquisition of older cars in the period; or a greater than expected fall in the value of the entire vehicle holding due to market conditions. Further investigations would be needed to ascertain the reasons.

Efficiency and utilisation

The number of days per year that cars are out on hire reflects utilisation and is a key factor in determining profitability. The data table shows that cars were out on hire 293 days per year compared to the planned level of 290 days (ie on a 365 day year this is 80% utilization). The most obvious reason for the higher level of utilization is that despite lower sales volumes than expected (ie hire days are 5.7% lower) the number of cars available is 6.7% lower.

The high utilization rates are good in one respect as they reflect high usage of revenue earning assets. In another respect however the high utilization could be seen as excessive. In particular as the business is seasonal then it may be significantly higher than 80% in peak season.

On the basis of the information provided, 30% of annual sales come in each of spring or summer. If there is on average 80% utilization then in summer/spring there is 80% × 30/25 = 96%. At a peak time of the week in peak season there may be 100% utilization for at least some types of vehicle. This may mean lost sales or lack of consumer choice in vehicle selection.

The utilisation and sales loss arguments need to be balanced. Further investigations are therefore needed regarding the number of lost sales from the inability to supply suitable vehicles to customers.

The Business Plan and Professional Scepticism

The shortfall from the business plan may have been due to over-optimistic forecasts in setting the plan rather than poor performance in delivering the plan. In particular, in order to raise finance from the venture capitalists, the HV board may have been incentivised to present the forecasts expected by the venture capitalists.

Examiner's comments:

Requirement 45.2 asked candidates to analyse and explain the shortfall between actual performance and the business plan forecast, then to highlight three matters for further investigation. The weakest candidates produced few or no calculations for this part, thereby providing purely qualitative answers. These types of data analysis and interpretation questions require numerical analysis of data but also explanations of underlying cause and effect relationships indicating why variances may have occurred in order to 'make the numbers speak'.

Many better candidates produced calculations which normally considered days hired, operating profit margins, return on assets and efficiency/utilisation ratios. Better answers also considered the validity of the projections in the business plan itself, questioning whether they were too optimistic in an attempt to obtain venture capital finance. The correct observation was often made that the necessary investment in new vehicles had not taken place hence somewhat diluting the firm's ability to expand the business sector.

Most candidates provided reasonable suggestions for further investigation. For example, some candidates indicated that prior year performance data would be useful in order to assess the reasons for the shortfall.

45.3 (a),(b), (c)

Risk	Impact and likelihood	Risk management
Legal liability from the operation of cars by customers and employees.	• High significance if there is personal injury. • Lower impact as damage will be to only one car. • With many vehicles being operated a reasonably high probability that accidents will occur.	• Insure risk. • Put in place procedures to ensure terms of insurance agreement are complied with. • Implement procedures to minimise the probability of accidents (eg restrict hires to 'clean' licence holders).
Regulation risk which may change the terms of business or the need for compliance costs to be incurred, including tax.	• Increased environment and tax legislation to reduce pollution seems likely. • With so many vehicles owned the impact could be significant.	• Consider acquiring more environmentally friendly vehicles. • Join industry pressure group to influence government.
Strong dependence on airline industry.	• Any problems with airline industry (recession, taxation, strike) are likely to affect the car rental industry.	• Form partnerships and work together with airline industry. • Diversify with partners in other industries (eg insurance).
Competition risk. The internet has made capture of new bookings much easier for smaller companies to compete at the lower end of the market.	Competition may significantly affect price and have a major impact on profits of small companies such as HV. This is likely to occur and at the smaller end of the market there is already significant competition with over 100 UK operators.	• Develop reputation and identity. • Holding slots at airports is one way to restrict competition.
Seasonality means a risk of redundant assets in low season and insufficient capacity in peak season.	If seasonality is pronounced then the effects at the margin may be moderately significant. Highly likely as an established demand pattern.	• Price discrimination according to season. • Rent assets to acquire vehicles to meet short-term peak rather than owning 100% of car pool. • Model seasonality so timings are predictable.
Car prices could change If cars increase in cost then this is the major capital asset and will affect profitability and liquidity.	The car industry is competitive which makes major price changes unlikely. However should it occur it may have significant impact.	• Have portfolio of different types of car of different ages. • Hold cars for longer if car prices temporarily increase.
Second hand values weaken meaning lower residuals at end of car life and greater depreciation and costs of ownership.	Second hand market is competitive but new legislation could mean older cars which are less environmentally friendly may become more costly to run and this reduces their value. Effect possibly significant.	• Lease some cars. • Monitor second hand market and new legislation affecting cars. • Hold cars for longer.

Risk	Impact and likelihood	Risk management
Operating cost increases – eg repairs, petrol, insurance, road tax.	Very likely given past evidence. Cumulative effect likely to be significant, although customers pay for own petrol.	• Review maintenance operations. • Industry wide effect so would not materially impact upon competitive position in the industry which may enable industry wide price increase to offset cost increases.
On-line communication or other computer failure would prevent all bookings for period of problem.	Likely to be short term and isolated but loss of customers to rivals and reputation risk.	IT back up facilities and contingency provisions for disaster recovery.

Note: Only **four** risks were required from candidates.

Examiner's comments:

Requirement 45.3 asked candidates to prepare a risk register. There were some very general answers. For example some candidates merely cited operational or financial risk without being specific as to what these could be. That said, there were some really good answers at the other end of the spectrum which clearly identified very specific risks, their classification (eg financial or strategic), their impact and likelihood and what could be done to mitigate them. The higher scoring answers included the risks of the airline industry and their implications, issues with the online systems, as well as increase in fuel prices, values of vehicles and the ageing and depreciation of cars. Weaker answers typically displayed some or all of the following: covering only three risks; little detail or explanation of each point: highlighting insignificant risks; or identifying unlikely circumstances which were not suggested by the scenario. Most, but far from all, candidates used the columnar format suggested in the question.

45.4 Introduction

In assessing the ethical issues and implications of the three matters raised it is important to assess both whether they are unethical, and the degree of ethical/unethical behaviour. This is particularly the case for the implications of the actions.

In the first instance, it is necessary to establish the full facts in each of the cases highlighted by Gatter LLP. At the moment they are merely accusations which need to be substantiated. An appropriate degree of professional scepticism must be applied to all concerned.

Issue 1 – Private use of company vehicles by executive directors

The company is a separate legal entity from the directors and shareholders, and no-one has rights to use or take the company's assets without due authority. Potentially, the use of company assets by directors, even where there is no loss of revenue, is an illegal act in breach of their statutory duties. In addition, it appears there is a corporate governance problem in that the directors, who are the company's agents, are pursuing their own ends rather than those of the company. It may be necessary to take legal advice. Initially it will be necessary to speak to each director to gather evidence of actions. It will also be necessary to examine director employment contracts with the company to investigate whether they confer rights to use company assets under any conditions. Additionally, it should be established whether there was any direct benefit to the company in directors using the assets in this manner.

The key potential ethical issue is honesty/integrity.

In addition however there is the issue of transparency to shareholders, even if only retrospectively, of the nature and extent of any actions of this kind.

In terms of effect, it needs to be established whether there has been any direct loss to the company (eg lost revenue) or additional cost (eg petrol used) which needs to be made good by the directors concerned.

The fairness of the transaction is in question, in that it may be contrary to the interests of the shareholders. Even where the directors are shareholders it is contrary to the interests of the other shareholders, in particular TopFin.

If any of the directors belong to a professional body, then there may be a code of conduct and guidelines to ensure members behave in an ethical and professional manner, with disciplinary action if they do not. Any director who is a member of the ICAEW for instance would face disciplinary proceedings unless the actions were legitimately within the terms of their employment contract.

There may also be an issue in directors not declaring a taxable benefit.

Issue 2 – The lending of a company vehicle by a director to a third party

The issues are similar to issue 1 except as follows:

- With issue 1, the practice appeared to be at least well known to the other directors. It is not clear whether there was any internal transparency over this incident, other than the one director who was informed.

- It seems implausible that this type of action is part of an employment contract with the director.

- There is potential for the director receiving some benefit from the friend in return for the loan of the car. This would be a key effect and would amount to a personal gain.

- Are there any further undisclosed transactions of this type?

In order to gain transparency internally amongst the directors, as well as externally to shareholders, these facts need to be established in addition to those in issue 1.

Issue 3 – The hiring of a private company vehicle by a director to a third party for personal gain

This is potentially the most serious ethical issue as there is an increased risk of fraud against the company. The distinguishing features from the first two issues are:

- There is a probability of a direct financial gain by a director from deliberate misuse of company property, in breach of her statutory duties as a director

- There is a potential direct effect on the company from loss of revenue on this contract

- Assuming the other directors were unaware of the incident, then there is an issue of internal control and transparency

The facts to be established are:

- Why and how this transaction occurred

- What happened to the proceeds gained? Why were they returned to the company after such a delay?

- Are there any further undisclosed transactions of this type?

Examiner's comments:

In requirement 45.4, candidates were asked to explain the ethical issues and implications arising from a series of transactions by directors.

Candidates' answers to this requirement were the weakest on the paper. Whilst most candidates were familiar with ethical language in terms of transparency, fairness and effect, only a small number of candidates considered honesty/integrity, legality and steps which should be taken to deal with each issue. Moreover, few candidates indicated that the full facts would need to be established prior to forming a firm conclusion. It was apparent in this question that candidates do not adopt a logical, methodical approach, which considers any additional information needed. Instead, many candidates merely concluded that the behaviour is illegal without questioning why or whether they have the legal knowledge or sufficient information to come to this firm conclusion. A significant number believed that Sandra Bevan's conduct amounted to money laundering. More balanced and questioning answers were required that do not assert conclusions without supporting reasoning and evidence. Few candidates questioned the powers and responsibilities of directors in the context of corporate governance or their legal duties.

46 Up 'n' Over plc (June 2013)

		Knowledge	Skill	Marks
46.1 (a)	Expected variable cost	1	4	
(b)	Breakeven level	1	4	
				9
46.2 Report				
(a)	Original strategy	1	6	
(b)	Cost reduction programme	3	6	
(c)	Cease manufacturing	1	6	
				21
		7	26	30

General comments

The scenario in this question relates to a manufacturer of low cost garage doors.

Although attempts had always been made to keep costs low to provide 'best value', losses had been made. As a consequence, a new chief executive was appointed a couple of years ago and pushed costs down further by reducing the quality of the raw materials and freezing all capital expenditure. Initially this had the effect of reducing costs and quality, increasing margins and turning the losses into a profit. More recently, however, there have been increasing customer complaints and falling sales, although profits remain higher than they were before the cost reduction exercise. The board is split between returning to the original strategy or retaining the new low cost strategy. The chairman has suggested a third choice, of ceasing to be a manufacturer and becoming an importer and wholesaler of garage doors from Thailand.

46.1 (a) 20Y3

Sales volume	=	£30m/£400	=	75,000 doors
Variable cost	=	£30m – £14m – £2m	=	£14m
VC per door	=	£14m/75,000	=	**£186.67**

(b) Sales volume = £32m/£400 = 80,000 doors

20Y1

Variable cost	=	£32m – £15m + £1m	=	£18m
VC per door	=	£18m/80,000	=	£225
Contribution per door	=	£400 – £225	=	£175
Break even	=	£15m/£175	=	**85,714.28, ie 85,715 doors**

20Y2

Variable cost	=	£32m – £14m – £3m	=	£15m
VC per door	=	£15m/80,000	=	£187.50
Contribution per door	=	£400 – £187.5	=	£212.50
Break even	=	£14m/£212.50	=	**65,882.35 ie 65,883 doors**

Implications for operating risk

The high level of fixed costs of £15m and £14m in 20Y1 and 20Y2 respectively indicate high operating gearing. This is the seen more clearly when comparing fixed costs with the relative levels of variable costs of £18m and £15m in 20Y1 and 20Y2 respectively, which are only a little higher than fixed costs. The high operating gearing means that profits are volatile when changes in sales occur.

While there was a margin of safety of 14,117 units in 20Y2 (ie 17.6%) the probability of the margin being 'used up' in 20Y3 needs to be considered in the context of increasing customer dissatisfaction and possible cancellation of large orders. The fall in expected sales in 20Y3 from £32m to £30m (6.3%) is indicative of the operating gearing consequences.

Examiner's comments:

Requirement 46.1 asked candidates to compute variable costs and to calculate break even from data provided. For the majority of candidates, the computation of variable cost and the subsequent break even calculations did not pose any problems. There were however some mistakes in calculations, where candidates mixed up the revenue and cost figures or made calculations for the wrong years. The operating risk explanation was not dealt with very well, if at all, by many candidates.

46.2 From: Business Adviser
To: Up 'n' Over Board
Subject: Future Strategy
Date: 12 June 20Y3

(a) **Return to policy of 20Y1 and prior years**

Benefits

Good reputation with customers for best value. The additional costs therefore enhance reputation as a strategic base on which to build, despite recent operating losses.

There is an existing customer base which is partially secured by some long term contracts with larger customers. This ties some major customers into UnO giving the opportunity to restore reputation before the next contract renewal if the cost reductions are reversed.

Problems

An operating loss of £1 million was made in 20Y1, which was the last year of the previous 'best value' policy. The breakeven calculation shows that there is a negative margin of safety of 5,715 units. This means UnO would need to sell another 5,715 doors in order to break even which would be a 7.1% increase in sales volume.

UnO's strategic positioning is unclear. It is neither a differentiator nor a cost leader in accordance with Porter's generic strategies. It therefore runs the risk of pursuing a strategy based on a subjective concept of 'best value' and may be 'stuck in the middle'. At the very least, it needs to be aware of its positioning in terms of price-quality within the industry.

There are 'competitive market conditions' which would make a price increase difficult as a means to increase sales revenues.

Sustainability

A sustainable enterprise is one that generates continuously increasing stakeholder value through the application of sustainable practices through the entire base activity (products and services, workforce, workplace, functions/processes, and management/governance).

The continued operating losses are not sustainable in the longer term as, without profit, the wider stakeholder need cannot be met as the company will not survive. The key question of sustainability is whether the loss in 20Y1 would be typical, or whether it could be reversed by efficiency gains or improvements in sales.

(b) **Cost reduction**

Benefits

A profit is now being achieved of £3m in 20Y2 and there is an expected profit of £2m for 20Y3.

The breakeven calculation shows that there is a margin of safety of 14,117 units for 20Y2. This means UnO would need to sell 14,117 fewer doors at current prices and costs before profit fell to break even, which would be a 17.6% decrease in sales volume.

There has also been a share price increase in 20Y2. It is unclear whether this was entirely due to the cost reduction strategy or whether other factors also had an impact. However, assuming that the strategy was the major factor, this was a 114% increase in share price. While share price then fell to June 20Y3 by 29%, the share price remains above the 20Y1 level. The stock market does not therefore appear to expect UnO to return to losses.

Problems

While there was an initial favourable impact to cost reduction in achieving profit, there appears to be a lagged reputational effect as information gradually becomes available to show that the doors are becoming lower quality and less durable.

There is some evidence, from at least one customer, that they may cease to purchase doors from UnO if this continues.

There is some initial protection from large customers withdrawing arising from the long term contracts but, if they fail to be renewed, the impact may be sudden and substantial from reputational loss.

Moreover, as the large companies hold inventories, they may cease to purchase additional doors near the end of the contract and instead run down inventories.

Sustainability

The benefits of the cost reduction policy appear to be short term and unsustainable. While there is some margin of safety a major and systemic loss of reputation and customer demand from a poor quality product seems likely to push the company into losses fairly quickly.

(c) **Import from Thailand**

Benefits

- Funds generated from closure of manufacturing may enable a return of funds to shareholders or investment and diversification into other distribution activities in the new wholesaler/importer role.

- If a contractual agreement can assure quality control procedures then UnO's reputation may recover.

- Most costs will be variable so the operating gearing will decrease so there is some protection from losses if sales fall.

- The existing distribution competencies of economies of scope and customer relationships can still be exploited.

Problems

- UnO needs to ensure continuity of supply. Given a new supplier and significant geographical distance, some measure of control over failure to supply is required.

- The timing of the supply chain may be more unreliable given the geographical distance, so the lead time may be longer and more variable causing disappointed customers and lack of agility in satisfying their needs unless UnO holds inventory.

- Transport costs may be substantial but appear, even when added to purchase costs, to be less than the current operating costs.

- Exchange rate risk may cause uncertainty over price and profit.

- If the new contract fails then the manufacturing base will be lost so UnO cannot return to the old strategy.

- Are there alternative suppliers at a similar price to diversify risk and maintain security of supply?

- Is there an exclusivity clause to prevent other UK companies importing the same goods from the same supplier?

- Is the contract price fixed for any period?

Sustainability

Continuity of supply in the longer term at a competitive price is key. This may not be from the same suppliers but by changing suppliers over time there may be continuity of supply.

Aside from business sustainability, environmental sustainability may be damaged by transport over such a long distance (eg climate change, pollution, emissions levels, waste, use of natural resources, impacts of product use, compliance with environmental legislation, air quality).

Conclusion

The cost reduction policy and the 20Y1 policy both appear to be unsustainable for different reasons.

The import policy has risks but if a suitable supplier can be found which is reliable then it may be a feasible and desirable strategy to follow.

Examiner's comments:

Requirement 46.2 requested candidates to evaluate the benefits and problems of the three strategies and assess the sustainability of each. Answers to this part varied in standard quite significantly. The better answers addressed all three strategies and all three key areas of each strategy being: benefits, problems and sustainability. Some very good points were made overall, in particularly a return to the old strategy would continue to generate losses and it would leave UnO 'stuck in the middle'. Therefore, in the longer term, the strategy was unsustainable. Discussion of the cost reduction strategy identified the reputational effect and the potential loss of customers. Most candidates opted for the third strategy but recognised that there were significant risks associated with importing from Thailand such as quality control, exchange risks and management of supplier relations. Poorer candidates showed some or all of the following weaknesses: failing to demonstrate an understanding of the differing strategies; failing to comment on sustainability; not providing a conclusion; failure to refer to the numerical analysis calculated in requirement 46.1.

47 Moogle plc (June 2013)

Marking guide

	Knowledge	Skill	Marks
47.1 PESTLE analysis	4	8	11
47.2 Internal/external information	4	11	14
	8	19	25

General comments

The scenario relates to the pet products section of a large supermarket chain. A new executive manager has been appointed to be responsible for UK pet products' profit, pricing and procurement. A key issue is the type of information the manager requires from the IT department to take decisions and control this section of the business.

47.1 Political

Taxation effects of pet food – eg VAT may impact profitability significantly.

Social welfare policy – allowing people to keep pets in government housing, care homes and other regulated environments affects the number of possible pet owners.

Health and safety policies over pet foods may increase costs for suppliers.

Economic

Recession is likely to impact on the number of people who own pets and the amount they are likely to spend on pet products (eg premium foods) if they own an animal.

Exchange rates can affect the price of imported products.

Inflation may cause cost increases for pet food manufactures and increases in prices.

Social

Demographic changes are likely to lead to changes in pet ownership where ownership is concentrated in age groups, social classes or gender.

The total size of the population is likely to lead to changes in total pet ownership.

Trends in housing may affect the number and types of pets owned. For example, a trend towards inner city apartment dwellings is likely to mitigate against owning large dogs, compared to out of town houses with large gardens.

Use of social networking sites for pet owners can alter attitudes and demand by consumers making more informed purchase choices.

Social acceptability of owning some animals may influence market demand.

Social trends in animal accessories may also influence pet owners to purchase more (or fewer) pet products.

Technology

New technological developments may lead to new pet products (such as electronic tags) not previously available.

Information technology, including pet websites enabling purchasing on the Internet, can be a major rival to shopping in supermarkets and other pet stores. This may be particularly the case for bulk purchases of pet food which may not be easily achievable by some people (eg who do not own a car) when visiting a store in person.

Ecological

Animals can have an impact on the environment. Restrictions on behaviour to limit this (eg 'poop scoops') may be positive in providing an additional market for new products or negative in discouraging pet ownership.

Legal

Laws requiring minimum standards of care for animals may be the source of additional markets as owners purchase additional accessories in order to comply (eg kennels).

New onerous laws may however discourage pet ownership and thereby reduce demand.

Health and safety laws with respect to the quality of pet food may increase costs of manufacturers which could be passed on to consumers.

Some elements of the pet market such as pet insurance are heavily regulated, in common with other types of insurance product. This may present a barrier to entry into this sector, which may impact on sales and profits.

Conclusion

The key issues in the industry appear to be:

- Economic factors, and particularly the recession and customers' willingness to purchase premium foods and other luxury pet items

- Social trends determining pet ownership, which define the number and type of pets owned and therefore the scale of the pet market

Examiner's comments:

Requirement 47.1 asked candidates to prepare a PESTEL analysis for the UK pet products industry. Most candidates prepared the PESTEL analysis quite well, although they did struggle for ideas in relation to the political and ecological impacts of the industry. Some weaker candidates did an analysis for Moogle, instead of the pet industry overall, others just gave a list of points from the scenario without explaining the effects on the industry. Few candidates made an attempt to prioritise the points in any way. An overwhelming majority of candidates failed to present any conclusions to their analysis. Often, political and legal issues were addressed together, with candidates identifying that the pet insurance sector was stringently regulated and that government is recently far more conscious of animal welfare and may adopt policies in the future to continue to address this. Better candidates were good at thinking about the wider industry rather than only the points mentioned in the question.

47.2 **Note.** More than three pieces of info are given to guide markers for a range of possible candidate answers

Information	Justification
Internal	
(1) UK sales from each product line compared to (a) the same period last year (b) the previous month	This is important in order to observe overall trends at an early stage but particularly to assess the success or otherwise of new product lines.
	If we change prices of our products generally it will also be necessary to view demand effects. (If prices of individual products change only in some regions, this can be monitored by store managers.)
	The comparison with last year would control for seasonality to make valid comparisons but also predict intra period variations in order to inform purchasing patterns.
	While I would not have time to scrutinise every product, I do need to look at the risk areas where major changes have occurred so I can manage by exception. Please therefore order the data by product according to the size of the variation with the highest variances first and the lowest variances at the bottom of the list.
(2) Shelf space (or floor space) for pet products in total	It is important to see whether allocations of shelf space impact on sales. If shelf space is being reduced then this could be a key factor affecting both sales and the number of items of inventory that can be procured.
	Dividing (1) UK sales by (2) shelf space would give me data to argue for efficient allocation of shelf space across the company if these data are also maintained for other product groupings.
	While I would not have time to scrutinise every store, I do need to look at the risk areas where the ratio of UK sales divided by shelf space is particularly high or low. Could you therefore extract data on a store by store basis but only report to me the top 10% and bottom 10% of stores?

Information	Justification
(3) Price changes by suppliers and notifications of price changes	In order to control costs and monitor the impact of cost changes on profit it is important that I am aware of any proposed or actual change in price by suppliers.
	This information will inform the procurement decision by triggering an investigation of the reasons for the price change, negotiations with the supplier and the possibility of ceasing to purchase from that supplier.
	This is essential in controlling costs.
	Where supplier price increases are accepted then the impact on profit needs to be monitored and the possibility of changing the prices we charge to our customers needs to be considered as a consequence.
(4) New product information	If I introduce new products (eg pet insurance or on-line sales) this may require different types of information and closer monitoring than existing products.
	This is partly because of increased uncertainty and partly because of the different nature of products like insurance where aggregation with general sales would be unhelpful.
(5) Comparisons with our overseas stores	I would like to see key trends from our overseas stores to see if there are lessons to learn in the UK from pet product sales in the rest of the world.
	Key data may include: fastest growing product lines; successfully introduced new products; comparisons of product prices and costs (exchange rate adjusted) where there are large variations (eg same product selling at significantly different prices).
	There may be good reasons for variations but I may need to investigate.
External	
(1) Market trends	I need to know changes in the UK pet market from both market research and market trends.
	This may include our own data gathering (primary data) but also market intelligence (secondary data).
	Examples would be trends for buying:
	• Moist food or dried food • Premium or basic product lines • New product innovations
(2) Competitor pricing	Our prices relative to competitors are a key factor in maintaining competitive advantage and impact on the reputation of the company generally for being good value.
	For branded products these are identical and we need price comparison shopping within the month so we can adjust our prices regularly.
	However I need to know at the month end where our prices have been higher or lower than key competitors. Please report all exceptions beyond a 2% threshold.
	Own brand products are not identical and therefore price comparisons are more difficult. Nevertheless I need to know price differences with our competitors beyond a 5% threshold.

Information	Justification
(3) Innovations and product launches	I need to know in advance any plans by suppliers about new products or changes in products (eg new recipes). We can then plan to purchase them or not at the earliest moment. We can also plan for price changes.

Examiner's comments:

Requirement 47.2 asked candidates to identify three pieces of internal information and three pieces of external information that the pet products manager would need and to explain why this information was needed. Candidates struggled to identify the correct level and type of information required. Often, sales per product from each store were given as relevant information, despite the question flagging that 'the bigger picture' was needed. Candidates did not appear to focus on cost information and discussed revenue, breakdown of sales by store, breakdown of inventory by store and overall store performance. Some candidates did not offer specific information and instead just described the difference between strategic, tactical and operational information and then contrasted information with raw data. In terms of the external information, again, the level of detail requested was too great for someone wanting a strategic picture. Revenue from competitor stores, number of pet owners in the UK and a breakdown of ownership between dogs and cats, were among the types of information discussed. Again, some of these were not relevant for the scenario or suggestion being discussed, and provision of some of the information was not realistic as it would be nearly impossible to get.

48 The Contract Cleaning Corporation Ltd (December 2013)

Marking guide

		Knowledge	Skill	Marks
48.1 (a)	Appropriateness of KPIs	5	6	10
(b)	Data analysis	2	18	18
(c)	Roizer contract	2	8	9
48.2 Ethical issues		2	4	5
		11	36	42

General comments

The scenario in this question relates to a company providing cleaning services to organisations in London. Revenue comes from medium term contracts. Last year CCC lost a major customer. In response, it opened up a new division offering maintenance services alongside the existing cleaning services. Despite this, there are concerns about performance. The company implemented a balanced scorecard system a couple of years ago but it is not well understood by the directors and there is doubt about whether all the measures are appropriate. There is an ethical issue relating to an advert published by CCC which may be misleading to customers. There is also the potential to bid on a new contract for a major company, Roizer, which is an element of a larger contract.

48.1 (a)   Balanced scorecard – general issues

The balanced scorecard (BSC) indicators may be viewed as a vertical hierarchy, with the quality of the skills and processes measured by innovation and learning metrics, leading to improved internal business processes (quality, efficiency and timeliness) and hence customer satisfaction and loyalty; which, in turn, lead to favourable financial outcomes such as profit and ROCE. Conversely, the failure of innovation and internal processes may help explain inefficient operations, lower customer satisfaction and poor financial outcomes.

It is therefore important that CCC links the four quadrants when determining KPIs and using a balanced scorecard considering interdependencies rather than looking at each quadrant in isolation.

In addition, the types of KPIs that were suitable for CCC when it was solely a contract cleaning company may not be appropriate to its Maintenance Services Division. Moreover, even if the KPIs are suitable, the specific targets set may not be appropriate.

When considering performance it may be the target that is at fault, and therefore it might not be an appropriate benchmark by which to judge the actual outcome. It is possible that the targets set could be too ambitious, given the changes arising from the loss of a major customer in the previous year and failure to take into account difficult market conditions. Alternatively, the targets may have been deliberately ambitious, stretch targets in order to motivate employees, in which case some negative variances against target may be acceptable.

Innovation and learning perspective

The % of revenue from new clients seems appropriate, but needs to be judged against other criteria (eg the amount spent on advertising). Similarly, there is a new maintenance division which may better be measured as a separate BSC rather than within the Cleaning Services Division's BSC. Nevertheless, it does represent a new innovation resulting in higher sales. Similarly, the extent to which new customers have been added to the existing customer base is a reasonable objective captured in this metric.

The hours of staff training measure is less appropriate as it measures an input rather than an achievement arising from the training. Merely spending more money on training does not, of itself, promote, or evidence, learning or reflect the benefits from learning. It may be better to measure learning achievements/qualifications by staff on key areas of CCC's activities (eg health and safety; or environmental and green issues).

Internal business perspective

The internal business objective of staff numbers appears inappropriate on its own as, again, it measures an input. Some measure of staff productivity or staff efficiency might be more appropriate. An example may be the number of chargeable hours actually spent working at the client, divided by the total number of paid hours. This might measure unproductive time through travelling between clients, lateness or restricted access by clients, and therefore identify possible areas of inefficiency.

Similarly, the value of cleaning products used is likely to be a poor measure of performance and it is difficult to interpret. A high usage may mean a good quality, diligent service is being provided which will be valued by clients; or it could mean high wastage and a lack of cost control. Perhaps a better measure would relate to the application of quality controls by supervisors, for example the number of satisfactory jobs, as a % of the number of jobs where there was a need to rework or reperform cleaning tasks due to inadequate quality at first attempt.

Customer perspective

The total number of customers may be a reasonable measure as it is indicative of the number of new customers won, net of those lost during the year. A more direct way of capturing similar information would be to measure the gross figures of new customers (eg tenders won); the proportions of customers retained and lost on contract renewal; and the proportions of customers retained and lost on break clause agreements during the year. Further data on whether customers have been lost to competitors, or where cleaning duties have been taken in-house by customers, may identify future threats.

The number of customer complaints is one way of capturing customer satisfaction, but measuring complaints is evaluating only one extreme of the satisfaction spectrum. Moreover, complaints to directors may be only the very worst cases, when it may be difficult to retain the customer if they are unhappy enough to complain at this level. A lower threshold of complaints by customers to supervisors may be a better early warning sign of customer dissatisfaction. Some more positive and comprehensive feedback on customer satisfaction may also be worth measuring (eg a customer survey) with a numbered scaled response to each question.

Financial perspective

Revenue growth is a reasonable KPI but, as already noted, may best be measured separately for each division. Variants on measures of total revenue growth could be revenue growth per customer. ROCE does not appear to be a good measure as this company has few assets and pays out profits as dividends as far as it can with available cash. It has no debt. This means the very low capital base makes ROCE an almost meaningless figure. A measure of operating profit as a % of sales would give a better measure of revenue against the costs needed to generate that revenue.

Examiner's comments:

Requirement 48.1(a) was reasonably well attempted by most candidates. Most candidates identified the use of the balanced scorecard and produced some relevant KPIs. Some candidates supported the use of ROCE, which was not appropriate in this case as CCC has few assets. Knowledge of the balanced scorecard was generally good and candidates were well prepared for this type of question. Answers were generally specific to the scenario. The best responses provided critical reviews of the original measures as well as proposing improved replacements/additions. Weaker candidates tended to suggest that the balanced scorecard and the existing measures were generally appropriate or suggested additional measures without appraising the existing measures.

(b)

	20Y3 Cleaning £	20Y3 Maintenance £	20Y3 Total £	20Y2 Total £	Jarren £	20Y2 total less Jarren £
Revenue	7,200,000	500,000	7,700,000	7,800,000	780,000	7,020,000
Employment costs	4,048,000	324,000	4,372,000	4,128,000		0
Other variable costs	2,024,000	162,000	2,186,000	2,476,800	0	0
Fixed costs	950,000	50,000	1,000,000	1,000,000	0	0
Operating profit	178,000	(36,000)	142,000	195,200	23,424	171,776
Op profit %	2.47%	(7.20)%	1.84%	2.50%	3.00%	2.44%
Revenue growth	(7.69)%		(1.28)%			2.56%
Op profit growth	(8.72)%		(27.18)%			3.73%
Customers	80	5	85	77	1	76
Staff numbers	440	30	470	430		
Wages per emp	9,200	10,800	9,302	9,600		
Rev/customer £	90,000	100,000	90,588	101,299	780,000	92,368
Rev/employee £	16,364	16,667	16,383	18,140		
Op profit/customer £	2,225	(7,200)	1,671	2,532	23,400	2,258
Op profit/emp £	404.55	(1,200)	302.13	453.49		

Overall performance – adjusting the data

In comparing the data for 20Y3 and 20Y2, two significant events have taken place, (one in each year). These are:

- The loss of the Jarren contract during 20Y2

- The commencement of the Maintenance Services Division at the beginning of the 20Y3 financial year

These two events distort underlying data trends and therefore, while recognising their impact on overall performance, need to be stripped out of the raw data provided in order to make like-for-like comparisons of the underlying elements of the business.

Revenue

Total revenue has declined by 1.28% in 20Y3 compared to 20Y2. The decline has been moderated by additional revenues from maintenance services in 20Y3 which did not exist as a division in 20Y2 and therefore made zero revenue in that year.

Stripping out revenues from maintenance services in 20Y3 enables revenues from cleaning activities only to be compared in 20Y2 an 20Y3. This shows a 7.69% decline in 20Y3 compared with 20Y2.

One of the major causal factors for the reduction in revenue has been the loss of the major customer Jarren in June 20Y2. Jarren contributed 10% of total revenue in the year ended 30 September 20Y2, that is £780,000 (even though there were only nine months of revenues from Jarren in the financial year).

Whilst the Jarren contract is a factor in assessing overall performance, it is instructive to assess the performance of the remaining cleaning activities excluding Jarren. The table above shows that in 20Y3 revenue from cleaning activities, excluding Jarren, increased by 2.56% compared to 20Y2 excluding Jarren.

One of the reasons for this increase is that the number of clients for cleaning activities, excluding Jarren, rose by 5.26% from 76 to 80. The revenue growth for this segment of the business can therefore be explained largely in terms of more customers, rather than increased revenue per customer. Indeed, revenue per customer from cleaning activities, excluding Jarren, fell from £92,368 in 20Y2 to £90,000 in 20Y3.

This reduction in revenue per customer may have been due to new contracts being smaller than the existing contracts; or there may have been downward pressure on contract prices generally, such that continuing contracts are generating less revenue on renegotiation.

The number of staff engaged in cleaning activities has increased by 2.3%. One reason for the increase may be the need to service new customers, but the table shows that annual revenue per employee has fallen considerably from £18,140 to £16,364 (9.8% fall). This may be due to the distortion from the loss of the Jarren contract, but separate employee data for this contract is required to carry out further analysis.

Operating profit

Operating profit from cleaning services (excluding Jarren) increased in 20Y3 by 3.73% compared to 20Y2 (ie from £171,600 to £178,000). The figure for operating profit for Cleaning in 20Y3 should be treated with caution, however, as the new Maintenance Services Division has been allocated fixed costs of £50,000. Assuming these fixed costs would have been incurred whether or not the new Maintenance Services Division had been opened, then this is not comparing like with like because in 20Y2 all £1 million of fixed costs were allocated to what is now the Cleaning Services Division.

If an adjustment is made for this, then Cleaning Services Division profits drop to £128,000 (£178,000 – £50,000) giving a decrease of 25.4% from their 20Y2 level of £171,600 (excluding Jarren).

However, such a comparison is not entirely reasonable as there may be an element of fixed costs in the 12% operating profit of Jarren which has been stripped out. This would need to be added back to make a more precise comparison although the data is not currently available.

The operating profit margin is reasonably constant for 20Y3 and 20Y2 for cleaning activities, although it is clear that the Jarren contract was not only large, but had a slightly higher margin than other customers.

Similarly, operating profit per customer for cleaning services (excluding Jarren) is reasonably constant at £2,225 and £2,258 in 20Y3 and 20Y2 respectively. However, the increased number of employees means that operating profit per employee has fallen from £453.49 to £404.55 (down 10.8%), however this also includes Jarren where we do not have separate employee data.

Costs

Employee costs

Cleaning division employee costs have fallen by 1.9% (from £4,128,000 in 20Y2 to £4,048,000 in 20Y3) despite having more employees in 20Y3, and this has contributed to operating profit. The key factor here is the reduction in cost per employee from £9,600 pa to £9,200 pa. This may be the result of shorter working hours for existing employees or new employees on fewer hours. Conversely, there may have been an employee agreement given CCC's financial difficulties following the loss of the Jarren contract. For example, the lower wages and a shorter working week may have been given in return for no redundancies.

Other variable costs

In 20Y3 other variable costs were 50% of employee costs. In 20Y2 they were 60% of employment costs. This marked fall in costs has contributed to operating profit. Possible causes might be greater cost efficiency in perhaps travel and use of materials.

Fixed costs

Fixed costs have remained constant in total between 20Y3 and 20Y2 but, as already noted, the allocation of some of these costs to Maintenance Services Division has boosted Cleaning divisional operating profit in 20Y3 compared to 20Y2. Such an allocation is arbitrary and should not impact upon any assessment of performance of the division over time.

Performance of the new Maintenance Division

The new Maintenance Service Division has incurred an operating loss of £36,000 in its first year of trading in 20Y3. It could therefore be argued that it detracted from the overall performance of CCC compared with 20Y2, when the division did not exist.

However, even in narrow financial terms, this may not be the case. Ignoring the arbitrary allocation of overheads, it generated a positive contribution as follows:

Revenue	500,000
Employment costs	(324,000)
Other variable costs	(162,000)
Contribution	14,000

More generally, performance needs to be assessed strategically rather than in just narrow financial terms. It is difficult to make a profit in the first year of trading as upfront costs are incurred and there is a need to break into new markets. In this vein, the division has performed reasonably well.

Moreover, if customers demand multi-services then the maintenance division may be instrumental in retaining customers for the Cleaning Services Division, and even in winning new joint customers in future. Such interdependencies need to be considered in assessing the overall performance of the Maintenance Services Division.

Conclusion

The loss of the Jarren contract has been a major factor in damaging overall performance in 20Y3 compared with 20Y2. Nevertheless, other aspects of the business appear be performing reasonably well and have shown some improvement in revenue and profits.

It is too early to make a valid assessment of the new Maintenance Services Division but at least it has made a positive contribution in its first year of trading.

Examiner's comments:

In requirement 48.1(b) the main calculations produced tended to focus on revenue and profit. However, the higher scoring answers also used the data in the question more widely and calculated, for instance, revenue per customer and profit per customer. Discussion of the quantitative analysis was varied. The poorer answers restated the ratios, but did not develop the reasons as to why revenue had declined since 20Y2 or the factors which had caused the changes.

Also, the performance of the cleaning and maintenance divisions was often not separated. The better answers presented the calculations in a clear and structured way, and then further analysed the data by removing the maintenance division performance which then resulted in an increased decline in revenue.

While most candidates discussed, or at least referred to, the impact of the loss of the major customer (Jarren), many tended to compare absolute figures without taking account of the fact that the inclusion of Jarren's contribution in the performance data distorted the figures. Very few candidates stripped out the figures relating to Jarren in order to make like-for-like comparisons.

The better candidates provided some good discussion on the positive contribution of the maintenance division and how CCC needed to expand into this area to remain competitive. Weaker candidates just pointed out that the maintenance division made an operating loss, without considering the basis for allocating fixed costs to the two divisions.

Overall, performance on this requirement was good and the data analysis answers are improved from most previous sittings.

(c) **Roizer contract**

Financial assessment

	£
Annual revenue (60,000 × £12)	720,000
Employee costs (Note 1)	(404,800)
Other variable costs (Note 2)	(202,400)
Contribution	112,800

This gives a contribution margin of 15.67%.

Notes.

1 **Employee costs**

   Employee costs, as a variable cost, are based on revenue. The revenue per annum of the Roizer contract is 10% of total cleaning revenues in 20Y3. As a result, the estimated employee cost is 10% of total 20Y3 employee costs (ie 10% × £4,048,000)

2 **Other variable costs**

   Other variable costs are 50% of employee costs in 20Y3.

Tutorial note:

Taking a ratio of other variable costs against revenue would give the same figure.

Benefits

- The contract makes a significant financial contribution

- If employees have been retained, despite the loss of the Jarren contract, then the Roizer contract may more fully utilise them and save potential redundancy costs

- There may be economies of scale so there could be efficiencies, such that variable costs may not increase in a linear fashion

- Coping with a major contact may lead to greater credibility in tendering for other similar contracts

- The contract may be renewed beyond the initial period

Risks

- There are two levels of the risk of termination. (1) GFP may terminate the contract with Roizer and may do so at two year intervals; and (2) Roizer may terminate the contract with CCC annually, even if the header contract with GFP is continuing.

- The contract may be short term (possibly one year) and therefore any initial set-up costs may not be covered.

- Exit costs – if the contract is terminated then there may be exit costs eg redundancy costs for staff specifically recruited for the purpose of this contract.

- Roizer is a rival and promoting its interests may not be in the best interests of CCC. For example it may ease the entry of Roizer into the cleaning sector of the London market.

- Roizer is likely to be earning profit without doing any operational activity. CCC may therefore not be gaining the full potential value of their work.

- Roizer has a problem of recruiting staff quickly enough for this contract and so it has approached CCC. However, in accepting the sub-contract, CCC may have the same problem.

- In the above financial calculations, it is assumed that no incremental fixed costs will be incurred but, given the increase in the scale, fixed costs may be non-linear (eg a step function) and there may therefore be some incremental fixed costs to be incurred.

Examiner's comments:

In requirement 48.1(c) the financial assessment of the Roizer contract for many candidates focussed very simplistically on the increase in annual revenue of £720,000 and the gross profit margin, rather than calculating the contribution margin as directed. Weaker candidates produced no calculations at all.

The risks and benefits were often very generic in terms of the contract making a significant contribution and giving access to new markets; the fact that the contract may be terminated quickly was also frequently referred to. There was information in the question which should have been used to make the answers more detailed and of a far higher standard.

48.2 Ethics pertains to whether a particular behaviour is deemed acceptable in the context under consideration. Sam has become aware of an advert that CCC has published which may be making misleading or untrue statements.

In making any ethical evaluation it is first necessary to establish the facts. In this case, the claims made by CCC in the advert need to be assessed as to their validity.

On the face of it, some statements in the advert claim to be factual while others are less precise or are expressions of opinion.

The issue of legality and compliance with advertising regulations is crucial as any breach of such laws and regulations is unethical.

The four specific claims are:

- 'All of our staff have regular training.' This could be misleading in implying frequent training, rather than regularly every three years

- 'We use environmentally friendly cleaning materials.' This appears to be literally true as it makes no claim as to the extent to which they are used, but may be misleading in implying that it uses only environmentally friendly cleaning materials.

- 'Customer service is our leading priority' this is a vague statement of intent.

- 'We also now offer maintenance services as a major part of our business'. Maintenance services are clearly now part of the business but at only 6.5% of sales it may be misleading to say they are a major part of the business.

In making a decision as to how to proceed, Sam may find it helpful to apply the Institute of Business Ethics three tests:

- Transparency
- Effect
- Fairness

Transparency – would CCC mind people (existing customers, suppliers, employees) knowing that it has made misleading claims?

Effect – whom does the decision to publish the advert affect/hurt? CCC stands to gain new customers at the expense of rivals if misleading claims are believed. New customers obtained on the basis of misleading claims may also be affected.

Fairness – would the claims be considered fair by those affected? The issue for CCC is that they are making claims to attract business on a basis that competitors or new customers may not consider to be fair.

Honesty

A final issue is one of honesty. The claims made may fail the honesty test on the basis of being misleading rather than untrue.

Response

An initial action would be to challenge the CCC board in relation to the claims being made in the advert, asking them to substantiate the assertions made.

If they cannot refute an allegation that the advert is misleading the CCC board could be asked by Sam to withdraw it. Legal advice should be sought in relation to the possible breach of advertising regulations that has occurred.

Examiner's comments:

The answers to requirement 48.2 produced varying results. Some candidates did not apply their answers to the question appropriately and merely restated, in general terms, the main ethical values which an ICAEW Chartered Accountant should uphold. Some candidates approached this requirement from a transparency, fairness and effect viewpoint, but did not always analyse the problems caused by CCC and then recommend a course of action which could be taken.

The higher scoring answers analysed each statement, concluded on whether it accurately reflected the business practice and then considered legality, transparency, fairness, effect and resulting next steps.

49 The Foto Phrame Company (December 2013)

Marking guide

	Knowledge	Skill	Marks
49.1 Product life cyle	2	7	8
49.2 (a) Procurement and supply chain	4	10	13
(b) Two distribution strategies	3	12	14
	9	29	35

General comments

The scenario in this question relates to a manufacturer of cameras which is based in Germany. The question provides a summary of developments in the industry and how changes in technology have affected product life cycles. The company in question, FPC, manufactures mid-market cameras and has global sales. The US is an important market for FPC which has grown in recent years. Distribution to the US currently takes place directly from the German factory. FPC currently has a single local supplier of lenses which is a key component. One of the main products, the MM3 camera, is due to be replaced shortly by the MM4, and FPC is taking the opportunity to review its procurement and supply chain management policies. Specifically, it is examining whether it should continue its single supplier policy or move to a policy of multiple international suppliers. It is also considering cost reduction, part of which involves reviewing the costs of tier 1 and tier 2 suppliers. It is also reviewing its distribution strategy to US customers. Two possible strategies are: to open a distribution centre in the US; or to enter into a joint venture with a Japanese camera manufacturer to develop a US distribution facility.

49.1 The product life cycle (PLC) describes the phases of development that a product goes through. The key stages of the life cycle are:

- **Introduction** – a newly invented product or service is made available for purchase and organisations attempt to develop buyer interest.

- **Growth** – a period of rapid expansion of demand or activity as the product finds a market and competitors are attracted by its potential.

- **Maturity** – a relatively stable period of time where there is little change in sales volumes year to year but competition between firms intensifies as growth slows down.

- **Decline** – a falling off in sales levels as the product becomes less competitive in the face of competition from newer products.

The way in which a product is defined is important in determining the life cycle. It could be defined in terms of the broad technology being used, such as digital cameras. Alternatively, it could be defined in terms of a particular model of camera, such as the MM4 for FPC. Typically, the wider definition of a digital camera would have a much longer life cycle which will only reach maturity when there has been a fundamental shift in industry technology.

From the perspective of FPC's new MM4 camera it is intended to introduce this in one year. It does not however follow from this the MM3 will be replaced immediately. FPC may carrying on producing the MM3 (or at least carry on selling it from existing inventories).

In this way, the PLC for successive products may overlap. As one product is declining, another is simultaneously being introduced. This may be because of continuing product loyalty by consumers for the old MM3. Alternatively, it is common to sell only the new product into key markets (eg Europe and the US) but sell the older product at lower prices into other geographical markets such as developing nations where there is higher price elasticity. This will prevent internal competition between the two products, so long as there is no leakage between the two types of market.

If it is the intention for FPC to extend the PLC of the MM3 then this could be achieved through minor technological improvements and design modifications to the MM3.

Turning to the MM4, its PLC is likely to be uncertain as it is only about to enter its introductory phase and there are many uncertainties about the future. However factors that may affect the life cycle of the MM4 are:

- Success of R&D activities by FPC in developing replacement technology

- Success of R&D activities by FPC's rivals which may reduce MM4 sales and cause it to enter the decline phase sooner than expected

- Changes in customer tastes and preferences

- Pricing policies of FPC and its rivals

- New entrants to the industry

- Developments in competing technologies (eg mobile phones)

- Willingness and ability of FPC to engage in product improvement for the MM4 to extend its product life

49.2 (a)   Issue 1

There are two key issues:

(1) Whether to have one supplier or many suppliers

(2) Whether to continue solely with a current supplier or to engage with new suppliers as well

The current arrangement with Zeegle can be described as one of strategic procurement. This is the development of a partnership between a company and a supplier of strategic value. The arrangement is usually long-term, single-source in nature and addresses not only the buying of parts, products or services, but product design and supplier capacity.

This type of relationship can be beneficial for some organisations which may need to establish close links with companies in the supply chain to meet their own production needs or strategic objectives.

Some of the advantages to FPC from single sourcing with Zeegle may include:

- Consistent lenses (shape, size, quality, clarity) from a single supplier

- Easier to monitor quality

- Zeegle may be dependent on FPC as a major customer, and therefore is more responsive to FPC's needs, if a large amount of its income is being earned from FPC

- More scale economies can be earned by Zeegle to reduce costs which can then be passed on to FPC in reduced prices

- Communication, integration and synchronisation are easier (eg integrated IT systems)

- Collaboration is easier and more mutually beneficial in developing new products because all the benefits come to one supplier

- Zeegle has an existing relationship with FPC and therefore there is less risk and greater awareness

However, there may also be some problems with Zeegle as a single source supplier, some of which have already been experienced by FPC in producing the MM3:

- If there is disruption to output for Zeegle there is disruption to supply for FPC. This may be indicated by the fact that 'there have been occasions when there have been delays in supply' which means FPC has needed to hold inventories

- If there are variations in demand by FPC, a single supplier such as Zeegle may not be able to satisfy these in the short term (which may be another reason for FPC to hold inventory)

- Zeegle might exert upward pressure on prices if it knows FPC is tied into it for a number of years (over the product life cycle) and therefore has no alternative source of supply

If FPC has multiple suppliers (ie five) there are a number of benefits:

- FPC can drive down prices charged to it by encouraging competition between suppliers who know that FPC has a choice of alternative suppliers

- Switching sources of supply is possible by dropping a supplier altogether if it is delivering a poor quality product or service

- FPC can benefit from innovation in future product development from many companies rather than just one

However, if FPC has multiple suppliers there may be a number of problems:

- Each supplier has a smaller income from FPC than a single source supplier and so may lack commitment

- Multiple communications become more difficult and more expensive for FPC (eg more difficult to integrate multiple IT systems)

- Reduced scale economies

- Suppliers are less likely to invest in bespoke equipment and produce a bespoke product for FPC as production volumes may be insufficient

- The lead times and uncertainty of delivery time are greater if the geographical distances are greater, such as with Japan

- Cross-border supply chains may produce regulatory, language, cultural, exchange rate and tax problems. These are reduced because France and Germany are both in the EU, but this does not apply to Japan

- Four of the five potential suppliers would be new and therefore this may create some initial uncertainty and front-end costs in establishing new relationships and communications systems

Advice

The current supplier, Zeegle, has proved reliable and therefore reduces risk and gives assurance over quality. FPC may thus be best continuing with Zeegle as sole supplier but, in negotiations on price and service, the possibility of multiple suppliers could be raised in order to obtain the best possible contract terms.

Issue 2

The integrated supply chain model proposes that it is whole supply chains which compete and not just individual firms. Integration with, and information about, not only FPC's own suppliers (tier 1) but its suppliers' suppliers (tier 2) is consistent with this model.

If tier 2 suppliers can save costs, then this can be passed on to tier 1 suppliers in the form of reduced prices, which in turn can be passed on to FPC. While the integrated supply chain model is about more than cost reduction, this can be a key benefit, particularly where the components are fairly generic. Supply chain management is therefore needed to be able to obtain these benefits.

Supply chain management (SCM) is the management of all supply activities from the suppliers to a business through to delivery to customers. This may also be called demand chain management, reflecting the idea that the customers' requirements and downstream orders should drive activity or end-to-end business (e2e). In essence it refers to managing the value system.

In **Issue 2** the key theme is upstream supply chain management as it does not deal with customers.

The main themes in SCM are Responsiveness, Reliability and Relationships but the focus requested is solely on costs and the reliability aspects of SCM.

While **Issue 2** highlights reliability and cost reduction, responsiveness and building relationships can contribute to this.

While FPC, as the customer, has no legal right to investigate a supplier it can make transparency and openness conditions of FPC doing business with tier 1 suppliers. While such an investigation may appear to be an imposition on a tier 1 supplier (eg a supplier of an electronic component) there may be mutual benefits of greater efficiency and establishing better relationships with a key customer.

The willingness of tier 1 suppliers to do this may depend on how large the supplier is and how important FPC is to it as a customer.

There is no direct contractual relationship between FPC and tier 2 suppliers. As a consequence, at first sight, there may be increased reluctance by tier 2 suppliers to grant access to FPC to investigate cost reduction and reliability of supply. However, a tier 2 supplier (eg the manufacturer of a microchip that is used in an electronic component supplied by a tier 1 supplier to FPC) may be aware of the indirect relationship, and the fact that if FPC ceases to purchase from the tier 1 supplier then the tier 1 supplier may purchase less from the tier 2 supplier.

In terms of who would do the investigation, there may be more certainty if FPC does it itself, but FPC staff may be remote from the industry in which tier 2 suppliers operate and lack, not just the technical knowledge, but the detail of delivery schedules and processes as, unlike tier 1 suppliers, FPC is not a direct user of the output.

Advice

Managing costs down the supply chain seems entirely appropriate and in common with best practice. However, the cost-benefit trade-off from investigating tier 2 suppliers directly may not be favourable, as there is a lower proportion of FPC's costs at stake as we proceed further up the supply chain. Monitoring how tier 1 suppliers review tier 2 suppliers may therefore be the best compromise.

Examiner's comments:

Requirement 49.2(a) produced some very general, and often brief, answers on the difference between a single supplier versus a multiple supplier strategy. Whilst there was some relevant discussion on how supplier management can be seen as a collaborative relationship, it was surprising that the information in the question was not always put to good use.

Quality and cost are issues in any type of supplier relationship and whilst these were mentioned, points were often not developed enough. What was expected was how the quality of the lenses could impact FPC, how lead times may be affected and what the resulting impact on customer goodwill may be if suppliers were not geographically proximate.

It was only a minority of candidates that discussed the Rs model (responsiveness, reliability and relationships) in a structured manner.

A number of candidates surprisingly considered the supplier tiers issue to be equivalent to vertical integration. Also some candidates confused the supply chain with the value chain, without attempting to link these concepts. A surprising number of candidates omitted discussion of the supplier review at all, thereby severely limiting the number of marks they could score on this requirement.

(b) Distribution is a key aspect of marketing. Distribution is also part of the supply chain. It has already been noted that supply chain management is the management of all supply activities through to delivery to customers. Distribution is therefore part of demand chain management, reflecting the idea that the customers' requirements and downstream orders should drive activity or end-to-end business (e2e).

The distribution channel comprises a number of stakeholders including: manufacturer (FPC); wholesalers; retailers; consumers. Either of the proposals shortens the channel between FPC, as manufacturer, and wholesalers/retailers. The local holding of inventory in the US also enables the distribution channel to be shortened in some cases, by cutting out the wholesaler and selling directly from FPC to retailers.

Distribution Strategy 1 – Acquire a US distribution centre

Benefits

- Inventory can be held 'locally' in the US to meet surges in demand more quickly and with less uncertainty for customers than by supplying directly from production output in Germany.

- As a consequence, this strategy is driven by customer need, which is central to the end-to-end business model. The US presence means that FPC is closer to the customers and could perhaps better understand their needs.

- If FPC owns the distribution facility then it has more control over this aspect of operations than with a JV.

- Presence in the US, rather than delivery directly from Germany, means we can use local employees with local knowledge.

- Reputation with customers may improve if they know they are being supplied locally (ie the supply chain is within the US to a greater extent).

- FPC needs to respond to having 30% of its sales in the US and it appears FPC has not kept up with growth. Managing customer service for this extent of sales directly from Germany seems inappropriate, and a distribution facility seems to be a minimum response to satisfy the needs of the US market.

- A more substantial response to US sales growth would be to have a US production facility. However, having a distribution facility holding inventory is a much cheaper alternative than a second manufacturing site in the US which would increase fixed costs and would need an appropriate skills base without any history of production in the US.

Problems

- Mere location within the US still leaves a large geographical distance between the distribution facility and much of the US population. A single distribution facility may therefore only be a partial solution to the need to improve customer service. A network of multiple distribution facilities may be warranted for 30% of FPC's total sales.

- It would appear that little inventory of US-style cameras is currently held in Germany. An intermediate solution, to reduce lead time, would be to hold inventory in Germany rather than in the US.

- The fixed production facility increases fixed costs and therefore increases risk from operating gearing.

Strategy 2

Benefits

- Collaboration with the Japanese manufacturer takes advantage of common aims of both companies and sharing fixed costs from owning a distribution facility. This will give economies of scale.

- Given that both companies have common customers there are economies of scope from deliveries to the same location. Even if this were not the case, there are likely to be economies of scope from deliveries to the similar locations.

- Without a JV there may be insufficient volumes of sales for either company to sustain a feasible distribution network.

- The joint venture means that ownership of vans to make the distribution directly to customers is possible, so there is more control over all aspects of physical distribution without needing to trust third party couriers.

Problems

- There may be a conflict of interest in prioritising deliveries of each company where their needs, or the timing of needs, do not coincide.

- With a JV, one party may wish to terminate the agreement. This may require exit costs and create uncertainty over continuing viability.

- If there is common control between the two companies then issues of governance may arise if a key decision needs to be made that the two parties disagree about (eg a decision to expand or develop).

- Governance could be contractual or through a JV entity. This would impact upon risk sharing, exit costs, control and cost sharing. This would need to be clearly agreed.

- If one party is larger than the other, and therefore gains more benefit from the JV, the issues of sharing costs, sharing benefits and sharing control arise. Unless there are transfer prices from the parent entities, the JV is not revenue generating which may create a range of problems over how the benefits and costs are shared.

Advice

The JV arrangement permits fixed costs to be shared and would facilitate operations in the US and support marketing there. The terms of the contract need to foresee the above potential problems and permit flexibility to enable alternative strategies to be pursued over time as conditions change or sales expand. Alternatively, if a JV partner decides to withdraw from the arrangement, there needs to be protection for FPC from excessive exit costs and options to facilitate alternative distribution strategies.

Examiner's comments:

Answers to requirement 49.2(b) were sometimes very brief. Benefits of acquiring the US distribution centre focussed on access to US customers and use of specialist employees. Risks included exchange rates, but often little else. There was inadequate consideration of the fact that acquisition of an additional distribution centre would increase fixed costs and could therefore impact profit and operating gearing.

The joint venture appeared to be the favoured option as this 'mitigated the risk'. It would have been encouraging to have an analysis of what the 'risks' were as this was not always clear.

Service level agreements were mentioned in this part of the question and marks were awarded for this.

A number of candidates merged their answers for the two distribution strategies. Many of these answers failed to identify the key issues for each of the options.

50 FeedAfrica (December 2013)

Marking guide

	Knowledge	Skill	Marks
50.1 Market research	2	7	8
50.2 Market segmentation	2	6	7
50.3 Measuring and monitoring sustainable development	3	6	8
	7	19	23

General comments

This is the shortest question on the paper. It relates to a NFP charity which raises funds in the UK to support projects which assist communities in Africa to feed themselves more sustainably.

Fundraising has not been successful in recent years and FeedAfrica has appointed a new chief executive to help FeedAfrica market itself more effectively to both individuals and companies. It is believed that marketing expenditure has been wasted in the past by being insufficiently targeted. In order to raise more corporate donations, FeedAfrica believes it needs to measure its performance more clearly to demonstrate how it has contributed to sustainable development.

50.1 Marketing research is the systematic gathering, recording and analysing of information about problems relating to marketing.

Market research can involve looking at all aspects of marketing, including the 7Ps. In this context of marketing for a charity, however, there is no product or service to be sold directly to the donor. Instead, the key issue is to generate donations from people in return for service to be provided to a third party.

Marketing needs to be done effectively to raise income without incurring too many costs to generate that income. It therefore needs to be targeted at the groups of people most likely to give most.

Key objectives for market research for FeedAfrica are therefore to gain information about:

- Who? Which groups of people are most likely to make donations?

- How? How will they prefer to make such donations (ie in what form)?

- When? At what time and in what circumstances would they make donations?

- Why? What motivates people to make donations and therefore how can they best be persuaded, if they are uncertain whether to donate?

- Quantity? How much are the donations likely to be and can people be persuaded to increase donations?

- How often? How frequently does each group of people make charitable donations?

Desk research is the gathering and analysis of existing (or secondary) data from internal and external sources. This may include:

- Accessing an internal database of people who have donated in the past or are currently donating. Analysis of patterns in this behaviour can be useful in targeting the right type of promotional activities at the right people

- Databases of charitable donors to be accessed by FeedAfrica or shared between charitable organisations

- Any publicly available research (ie from psychology) which may help understand what motivates people to donate to charities

- Examination of published surveys/questionnaire about charitable giving (eg by government; universities; charitable bodies)

Field research involves the collection of new (primary) data directly from respondents. This might be in the form of surveys/questionnaires, interviews and focus groups. It is usually more expensive than desk research, so it needs to be clearly focused in its objective of raising charitable contributions with a clear expectation of the benefits to be achieved.

Questionnaire surveys – existing charitable donors could be surveyed to ascertain their reasons for donating. Alternatively (or additionally), they could directly question random members of the public to ascertain: whether they give to charity; the level of recognition of the FeedAfrica name; and whether they are likely to donate to FeedAfrica in future.

In depth interviews – these are similar to a questionnaire, but more detailed responses can be obtained. This may cover general attitudes to charitable giving and a more comprehensive study of attitudes to FeedAfrica.

Examiner's comments:

In requirement 50.1 it was apparent that candidates were well prepared for a 'marketing' type question and were able to identify the difference between desk and field research. The higher scoring answers identified the specific nature of the problem that there is no product or service to sell for a charity and therefore product/service characteristics were not relevant to the market research needed in this case. The type of desk and field research which would be relevant to FeedAfrica in terms of identification of donors was well articulated by the better candidates. Some weaker candidates wasted time by going beyond the boundaries of the requirement by, for instance, discussing the 4 Ps for FeedAfrica in detail.

50.2 **Market segmentation** is the practice of identifying homogeneous sub-groups within a market, to whom promotion can then be targeted in different ways.

In the situation of a charity, no product or service is being sold. Despite this, some people tend to give money, although others do not. Also some people tend to give more than others.

Given that promotional activities are not costless it is important that operations are directed towards those segments of the population who are most likely to make a significant donation. This avoids incurring marketing expenditure on sections of the population who are never likely to make donations to FeedAfrica.

It is also important that promotion is suitable for the sub-group being targeted, as what is likely to persuade one group to give is unlikely to resonate with an alternative group who may be persuaded by a different type of promotional campaign. In this way, the costs of a promotional campaign can be targeted to give the highest donation to cost ratio.

More specifically, examples of segmentation for FeedAfrica could be as follows:

Older people could be targeted with marketing materials that focus on legacies. This is partly because older people are likely to be giving more active consideration to leaving legacies and partly because the time horizon for FeedAfrica receiving such legacies is, on average, shorter than would be the case with younger people.

In terms of more general giving, then the propensity to make donations (subject to the above market research) may be greatest amongst:

- People with a history of making charitable donations
- Higher income groups
- Higher social classes
- People with religious conviction
- Older people
- People in a particular area of the country
- People with experience of living in Africa
- People of a particular political/social persuasion

Examples of how promotional activity could be targeted at these groups would be:

- Email people on a database of making contributions to charities in the past (eg by standing orders)

- Place television adverts for FeedAfrica during a religious television programme

- Place adverts in newspapers and magazine typically read by high income groups or higher social classes

- Advertise legacy giving where older people meet or in the journals they read

Examiner's comments:

In requirement 50.2 most candidates correctly identified the nature of market segmentation and why organisations adopt a strategy of segmentation. Relevant means of segmentation were identified in terms of, for example, high income households, older people and affluent geographical areas. Better candidates took the opportunity offered by data given in the question to consider segmentation on the basis of method of donation (eg direct debit, legacies). Some candidates did not follow the instructions in the question and addressed corporate donors as well as individual donors.

50.3 Sustainability is about maintaining the world's resources rather than depleting or destroying them. This will ensure they support human activity now and in the future.

Sustainable development is the process by which we achieve sustainability.

Sustainability is not limited to the environment. Interpretations of the scope of sustainable development have developed from a narrow interpretation which focuses on 'green issues' to broader interpretations which include concerns such as:

- Extremes of poverty and wealth
- Population growth
- Biodiversity loss
- Deteriorating air and water quality
- Climate change
- Human rights

A commonly employed and useful way of thinking about these issues is under three key headings: **social, environmental** and **economic**. Using these widely-recognised categories will help FeedAfrica demonstrate to its potential corporate donors that the charity is fully aware of all the implications of being involved with sustainable development in Africa.

FeedAfrica's charitable activities appear to be making a contribution to all three of these key aspects. In particular, rather than just donating money and/or food to meet a short-term need, they appear to be facilitating local people to have the means to grow food for themselves in the long term in a sustainable manner.

Measures of sustainable development under each of the headings may therefore include for FeedAfrica:

Economic:

- The increase in the amount of crops grown after projects supported by FeedAfrica have taken effect

- The increase in the value of crops grown as a result of projects supported by FeedAfrica

- Amount of new jobs created

- Number of farms in existence as businesses as a result of projects supported by FeedAfrica

- Number of farms moving from subsistence to profit as a result of projects supported by FeedAfrica

Social:

- Improvements to health by % of illness (eg due to clean water, more and better food)
- Community projects commenced based on wealth generated from FeedAfrica projects
- New employment rights and other local social rights required as a condition of investment

Environmental:

- Use of natural resources eg amount of additional clean water made available
- Use of land – amount of land brought into agricultural use as a result of water made available
- Reduced pollution of water sources – eg size of reduction in water-bourne illnesses

All the above will need to be measured over time to demonstrate that benefits are sustained and not short-lived.

Not all the above are easy to measure and some measures may be required of the situation before any investment by FeedAfrica took place in order to make comparisons with the situation afterwards. This may be available from feasibility studies initially taken to assess the viability of the investment.

When convincing corporate donors, it may also be useful to FeedAfrica to be able to demonstrate the charity's own efficiency, economy and effectiveness. It could therefore present using key NFP indicators such as a low percentage of overheads in relation to funds spent on charitable activities in Africa.

Examiner's comments:

In requirement 50.3 candidates tended to mention sustainability very briefly in their answers without elaborating on what it actually meant. It was extremely rare to see any type of discussion on economic, social and environmental sustainability, or any acknowledgement that it was specifically corporate donors that required FeedAfrica to make measurements. This is a very topical subject so it was surprising that answers were so short.

There were some relevant KPIs suggested, such as the number of new wells introduced, but others were very general and unfeasible, such as 'improvement in population health', with no real consideration of how this could be measured.

With regard to this question as a whole, the best candidates linked their discussion of the separate requirements eg they recognised the need for market research to inform market segmentation.

51 Emelius Ltd (March 2014)

Marking guide

	Knowledge	Skill	Marks
51.1 Risk register	3	10	12
51.2 Value chain drivers	4	8	12
51.3 Emelius Northern franchise	5	12	14
51.4 Letter (benefits of digital data/performance measures)	3	8	10
	15	38	48

General comments

This is the mini case at 48 marks and also the data analysis question. It was the best attempted on the paper.

The scenario relates to a company that offers document storage and management services. Its customers include professional services firms, banks and medical practices which need to archive large volumes of documents. The existing service is paper-based and involves various stages: collection, bar coding, storage, retrieval if required, and end of life destruction. The industry is relatively capital intensive and has high stepped fixed costs. As a result the company runs on a franchise model. Emelius has recently developed a new digital data capture service which its franchisees will have the option to offer to customers. Paper documents will be taken to a central scanning house, converted into digital form and then managed via a web-enabled platform with secure real-time access. A detailed value chain for this service was included in the scenario. One of the franchises, Emelius Northern (EN), is in discussions with a legal client (Swinburne LLP) which has approached EN regarding the physical storage of their paper archive. Swinburne has also expressed an interest in the digital service, which has not yet been introduced by the EN franchisee. Candidates were provided with operating information for the EN franchise for 20Y2 and 20Y3, and some working assumptions for volume, cost and revenue for 20Y4.

Requirements 51.1 and 51.2 relate to Emelius as a whole. Requirements 51.3 and 51.4 both relate to the EN franchise.

51.1 Key risks

Business risk is the variability of returns due to how a business operates, its markets, competitors etc.

It can be sub-divided into:

Strategic – risk relating to the company's strategic position with respect to competitors and environment

Operational – risk arising from how the business is managed and controlled on a day to day business, which also includes compliance issues

Hazard – risk arising from accidents or natural events

Financial – risk associated with how the business is financed

The key risk facing Emelius in each category is set out below:

Risk	Impact and likelihood	Risk management
Strategic: technological change renders the need for a paper-based document service obsolete	Technological developments clearly have a big impact on the nature of storage and the storage systems. Changes in technology may reduce the volume of business but are unlikely to remove the need for paper entirely, which to some extent may be regulatory.	Avoid/reduce risk by developing the digital data capture side of the service so Emelius will retain customers even if they switch archive method. Emelius may actually use this trend in their favour when nearing capacity in a warehouse.
Operational: poor standards of service by a franchisee damage the company's reputation	Emelius works with large organisations, many of which (banks, professional services) are likely to be national businesses expecting consistent standards. The existence of a number of competitors increases the likelihood that customers will go elsewhere if they are dissatisfied, which will have a large impact on Emelius.	Reduce risk by screening franchisees carefully and drawing up strict franchise agreements. Emelius already takes a strict approach to breaches of security and customer complaints which will help.
Hazard: data loss through fire at storage warehouse	Document security is of paramount importance. Loss of a client's records would be very damaging to Emelius' reputation and may result in litigation. The impact would be severe, the likelihood is unknown.	Reduce likelihood by having preventative measures such as advanced smoke detection and sprinkler systems, plus 24-hour monitoring Transfer through insurance Digital back-ups would also reduce this risk

Risk	Impact and likelihood	Risk management
Financial: failure to attract franchisees prevents further expansion	Capital investment requirements to continually open new outlets are significant. Emelius relies on franchise model to fund expansion. High operating gearing means franchise may take time to become profitable so it is not necessarily an attractive proposition. Likelihood: To date Emelius has 10 regional franchises so this does not appear to have presented a problem, although we do not know how this compares to target numbers	Reduce risk of low take-up by ensuring good profit incentives for franchisees Emphasise support offered Need to continually be on look out for prospective partners Again the data capture service may also attract different franchisees

Tutorial note:

Other relevant and important risks were awarded some credit.

Examiner's comments:

Requirement 51.1 asked candidates to prepare a risk register for Emelius' paper-based document storage business, setting out one key risk in each of four categories: strategic, operational, hazard and financial. The standard of answers was generally very good, with almost all candidates following the tabular approach requested. Some candidates did not appear to be clear about the nature of the different types of risk, failing to distinguish the longer term nature of strategic risk from the more day-to-day operational risk, with the financial category being least well understood. That said, there were some really good answers at the other end of the spectrum which clearly identified very specific key risks, their impact and likelihood and what could be done to mitigate them. Weaker answers typically displayed some or all of the following: little detail or explanation of each point; highlighting insignificant risks (or more than one); or failing to discuss both impact and likelihood. A minority identified risks to the digital data capture service which were not relevant.

51.2 Value chain

The value chain is the sequence of business activities by which value is added to the products or services of an entity so that in the end it makes a profit. Value chain analysis can be used to help identify the cost and value drivers behind Emelius' digital data capture strategy and the strategically significant activities of this side of the business. Primary activities are those that create value and are directly concerned with providing the data capture service. The support activities do not create value of themselves, but they enable Emelius' primary activities to take place with maximum efficiency.

Porter's generic strategies suggest that a company should pursue a strategy of either cost leadership or differentiation. Some low cost features are present in the value chain and will help Emelius achieve profitability, although its competitive advantage is more likely to centre on the speed, security and reliability of access to digital information, once captured. As might be expected with digital data, Emelius makes heavy use of technology throughout the chain to address these critical success factors.

Key drivers:

(1) Centralisation of scanning process (Inbound logistics)

Inbound logistics involves converting paper documents to digital form. A key cost driver is Emelius' use of a single centralised facility with large high-tech, high-speed scanners. The central facility can batch-process large volumes and multiple formats, reducing machine set-up costs. The use of relatively low skilled employees at the scanning house with strict targets will also help control costs although this may be counter-productive if it increases error rates, slows down the scanning process or leads to a high number of resubmissions. However Emelius's use of technology to check legibility and errors should prevent this affecting service levels.

(2) Indexing of documents (Operations)

A key value driver is the way in which the documents are indexed (operations). The powerful indexing system supports a multiple search function which should make it easier for users to retrieve a range of documents without knowing the exact title (outbound logistics). It has also built in internal controls to validate the accuracy of indexing which will increase the chance of fast and accurate retrieval. The fact that the system can also generate any linked documents is likely to differentiate Emelius and be something that customers may be prepared to pay a premium for.

(3) Security of documents (Service)

Another key value driver is the security associated with preserving the confidentiality of documents and access to them. Multiple levels of system security exist to prevent unauthorised access but also to ensure records are not created, altered or deleted inappropriately and Emelius is able to offer clients a clear document audit trail. The fact that Emelius keeps copies of digital documents across multiple servers reduces the risk that data will be lost and increases the reliability of the service offered to customers.

(4) Use of outsourcing/extended chain (Procurement)

Linkages between activities in the chain or the wider value system of suppliers and customers also drive costs or value eg the national courier chain has been chosen on the basis of the 24-hour secure service it offers. Centralised purchasing of all equipment and sole supplier agreement for all IT requirements are likely to lead to better prices/discounts. The maintenance of the online platform is outsourced to a specialist provider who is more likely to be an expert in this area than Emelius. Management of these wider linkages will allow Emelius to provide a better service and help to prevent Emelius' competitors from replicating its value chain.

Tutorial note:

Other relevant and important drivers were awarded some credit.

eg **Branding (marketing and sales)**

Limited marketing beyond existing branding will help keep costs down. The existing franchise manager will be responsible for attracting new customers. Since Emelius uses a franchise model, brand image is likely to be important and will be strengthened by the distinctive branding on vans, staff uniforms, website, social media.

Examiner's comments:

Requirement 51.2 requested candidates to explain four key drivers in the value chain for Emelius' new digital data capture service. This was a slightly different take on the normal value chain requirement, as a detailed value chain diagram was already provided in the Exhibit. Weaker candidates had a tendency to merely re-write chunks of the diagram without explaining how the factor they had identified would help Emelius drive value or keep costs down. Better answers: discussed their answer in the context of Emelius' generic strategy using value chain terminology; identified and explained a range of both cost and value drivers; and brought out the importance of linkages in the value chain.

51.3 Data analysis

Expected profit 20Y4 (without Swinburne contract)

	WORKINGS	£
Revenue	90m × 0.036	3,240,000
Variable costs	90m × 0.0115	(1,035,000)
Contribution	90m × 0.0245	2,205,000
Fixed costs		(1,755,000)
Expected profit		450,000

WORKINGS

Revenue per sheet 20Y3 = 2.7m/75m = 0.036 ie 3.6 pence

Comparison of results 20Y2-20Y4

Year	Volume (millions of sheets)	Revenue	Variable costs	Fixed costs	Profit/ (Loss)
		£'000	£'000	£'000	£'000
20Y2 actual	50	1,800	675	1,500	(375)
20Y3 actual	75	2,700	937.5	1,650	112.5
20Y4 forecast	90	3,240	1,035	1,755	450

	20Y2	20Y3	20Y4
% of capacity	50%	75%	90%
Revenue/sheet	3.6p	3.6p	3.6p
Vc/sheet	1.35p	1.25p	1.15p
FC/sheet	3p	2.2p	1.95p
Increase in volume (and revenue)	–	50%	20%
Increase in FC	–	10%	6.4%
Decrease in VC/sheet	–	7.4%	8%

The EN franchise started in 20Y2 and has experienced strong growth in storage volumes (50% in 20Y3 and a further 20% expected in 20Y4), possibly due to a strong brand image and the increasing regulatory requirements requiring customers to store documents securely. Since the selling price charged per sheet has remained constant, all the revenue growth is due to this volume increase. Whilst the selling price has remained constant, the VC per sheet has fallen from 1.35 pence per sheet to 1.15 pence. This is likely to be due to economies of scale being achieved as volumes increase.

Given the high fixed costs of the business, the franchise needs to achieve high capacity in order to be profitable (the break-even volume in 20Y4 is 1,755/(0.036 – 0.0115) = 71.6 million sheets). As utilisation of capacity has increased, so has profitability but EN is now close to maximum and initially, because of the stepped fixed cost model, results are likely to deteriorate if it wants to increase the capacity beyond 100m sheets.

20Y4 forecast with Swinburne contract:

	Workings	£
Revenue	102m × 0.036	3,672,000
Variable costs	102 × 0.0115	1,173,000
Fixed costs	1,755 + 750	2,505,000
Expected loss		(6,000)

This turns EN's profit into a small loss.

Assumptions:

Pricing and variable costs for Swinburne contract would be the same as for the existing business:

Revenue per sheet = 3.6p, VC per sheet = 1.15p (assumes no further economies of scale)

Swinburne contract of 12 million pages requires additional capacity and hence the step in fixed costs will be incurred.

Accept alternative calculations/justifications of impact of contract:

Store 12m additional sheets by increasing capacity

Contribution 12m × (0.0245) = £294,000
Incremental FC = £750,000
Net change in profit = £(456,000)

Store 12m sheets by turning away 2m existing business or destroying 2m documents at end of life to stay within existing capacity

Incremental profit = incremental contribution 10m × (0.0245) = £245,000

Explanation of results and implications

Comparison of Profitability 20Y4:

Year	Volume (millions of sheets)	Revenue	Variable costs	Contribution	Fixed costs	Profit/ (Loss)
		£'000	£'000	£'000	£'000	£'000
Without contract	90	3,240	1,035	2,205	1,755	450
With contract	102	3,672	1,173	2,499	2,505	(6)

Assuming that Emelius Northern achieves its expected volume of 90m sheets in 20Y4, the Swinburne archive would take the storage volumes beyond the capacity of the existing facilities, necessitating a £750k increase in fixed costs. Emelius Northern has enjoyed rapid growth but 20Y4-5 represents the point at which it reaches a step in fixed costs if it is to expand further.

In this case it is perhaps unfair to treat the £750k as an incremental cost of the Swinburne contract. Assuming that demand generally for EN's services continue to grow, the opportunity for the Swinburne business is simply bringing forward the need to expand the business to 20Y4 rather than 20Y5. Even without the Swinburne contract, the expansion point may be reached in 20Y5, since the business has been growing rapidly and it would only require growth of 100/90 = 11.1% before full capacity is reached without the Swinburne contract.

Emelius Northern might be able to avoid or delay expanding the existing warehouse facility and incurring the £750k if it:

(1) Identifies documents still being stored that have reached end-of-life and writes to the relevant clients suggesting destruction

(2) Starts to offer the digital data capture service and persuades existing clients to transfer some/all of their current paper storage to digital – particularly for those clients who need to retrieve documents regularly

Certainly in relation to the Swinburne contract it appears that offering the digital capture service for 40% of the archive (4.8m documents) would delay the required expansion until 20Y5. However before making a decision to implement the digital data service, EN needs to consider the costs involved and the expectations of revenue.

Examiner's comments:

Requirement 51.3 started off by asking candidates to calculate EN's expected profit for 20Y4, ignoring the Swinburne contract, and to analyse the reasons for the improvement in EN's performance since 20Y2. Attempts at the initial profit calculation were normally very good, with most candidates producing the correct figure, although some made errors with variable cost. However the quality of the subsequent analysis was much more variable. The weakest candidates ignored this part of the requirement entirely, or simply used the absolute figures from the question, with no additional calculations, which limited the quality of any discussion. Better candidates spotted that as the selling price has remained constant, the increase in revenue is entirely down to volume growth and that, given the high operating gearing, capacity utilisation is the key to EN's profitability.

Candidates were then asked to quantify the impact on 20Y4 profitability of accepting the Swinburne contract. The ability to tackle this part of the question was extremely varied. The key issue was that the new contract for storing 12 million pages would take EN over its existing capacity, necessitating a £750k step in fixed costs, which would not be covered by the additional £294k contribution. As a result the expected 20Y4 profit would become a loss. Some insightful candidates identified that it might be possible to avoid the incremental costs and accept the Swinburne contract within the current capacity, either by destroying documents at end–of-life or by turning down business from smaller clients. This approach to the calculation, if explained, was awarded full credit.

Finally candidates were asked to consider their results and the implications for EN's decision about whether to introduce digital data capture service. The point here was that if EN could digitally store the 40% of documents that Swinburne need to access regularly it might be able to accept the contract without the increase in capacity.

Better candidates discussed other relevant factors: in light of the business' current growth, other clients would probably be found in 20Y5 to help utilise the additional storage capacity created by the step and that the decision to expand should perhaps be separated from that of accepting the Swinburne contract.

51.4 Emelius Northern
Unit 12,
Weyhill Industrial Park
Waverley
WY4 3XZ

Swinburne LLP
Albany Court
Leeds
L2 6FD

19 March 20Y4

Dear Sirs,

Data Storage and Management

Following our recent discussions, I am writing to you to explain the benefits of outsourcing your data management to Emelius Northern and to recommend the most appropriate data management service for your current needs.

Recommended service package

I recommend that you use a combination of our data management services: paper document management for the 60% of documents that you are unlikely to need to access from the archive, and digital data capture for the remaining 40%.

Why digital?

- Storing paper records reduces your ability to retrieve business critical information quickly, and convenient access to the documents by a wide range of users is limited. Digital data capture allows for rapid distribution of critical information and reduces the inefficiencies of having to handle, copy, distribute, file, store and retrieve paper documents, which slow the execution of tasks and negatively impact the productivity of your employees. Using our web-enabled digital system, solicitors in your five offices will be able to access the same files at the same time, with minimal effort.

- Digital data prevents many of the human errors that occur with manual paper-based procedures, as well as minimising misplaced information, and allows for increased security measures in relation to identity theft and legal liabilities. We have multiple controls to prevent unauthorised access and tampering and this will be of great benefit to you given the confidential nature of your legal documents.

- The immediate availability of files and other data and our comprehensive indexing system will allow you to retrieve the main document quickly plus any linked supporting documents. This may be particularly useful to you in relation to prolonged legal cases or if information is suddenly required in a court case.

- There are many other benefits of capturing documents digitally:

    - It is more efficient and therefore will be cheaper for documents that are to be accessed regularly

    - Back-up files and records will be stored on multiple servers for disaster recovery

    - A certificate of destruction will be issued at end of life in accordance with regulatory requirements

Performance measures

The quality of our data management services can be assured and controlled through a service level agreement, with agreed performance measures. I would suggest the following three key performance indicators (KPIs):

Security of information – this is critical given the nature of your business and the data you hold about clients and cases. An appropriate KPI would be (any **one** of):

- Number of reported security breaches
- Number of unauthorised attempts at access
- Number or % of documents reported lost or unavailable

Speed of retrieval – this will assess the efficiency of the service we provide. An appropriate KPI would be (any **one** of) :

- % of information retrieved within stated target time
- Average time taken to retrieve a document
- % electronic searches resulting in a document being retrieved and opened

Cost-effective service – a key benefit of our digital service is that it should help you reduce costs. An appropriate KPI would be:

- Monthly document storage and access costs

Tutorial note:

Other relevant and important KPIs, with justifications, were awarded some credit, eg:

- Number of documents not removed/destroyed after end of life
- % of documents where end-of-life certificate not issued within an agreed time limit
- % of documents not accessed after more than one year (or other appropriate time period)

We very much look forward to working with you

Yours Sincerely

Lee Gryphon
Emelius Northern

Examiner's comments:

Requirement 51.4 asked for a letter setting out the benefits of digital data capture for Swinburne and three key performance indicators that EN could include in the service level agreement for the new contract. Most candidates were comfortable pointing out the benefits of digital data storage although only the better answers related these to the context of the legal firm in question. Once again not all candidates clearly understand what a KPI is, with some suggesting goals or critical success factors rather than measures that could be applied to service levels. A disappointing number of candidates did not score the mark for laying out the letter properly, either by ignoring it or by setting out their answer as a memorandum.

52 Boom plc (March 2014)

Marking guide

	Knowledge	Skill	Marks
52.1 Directors views and duties	4	10	12
52.2 Commerical and ethical issues	3	9	10
	7	19	22

General comments

At 22 marks, this was the shortest question on the paper. It was reasonably well attempted.

This scenario concerns a large, profitable mining company, Boom plc, which is engaged in extracting shale gas by drilling through underground rock formations at various sites around the world (fracking). Boom has recently discovered a new drill site in a remote but populated area of South America (project SA). The local government is willing to grant Boom a lease to proceed with the drilling and the central government anticipates significant economic benefits in terms of jobs, GDP and tax revenue. An abundant domestic supply of natural gas could also be used to produce cleaner, cheaper electricity and fuel for the region. However there is opposition from environmental groups which claim that the local population have not been sufficiently informed as to the long-term environmental issues associated with fracking. They claim the fracking process would place large demands on already restricted water resources and exacerbate existing environmental concerns about access to drinking water in the region. Boom's mission statement is 'to maximise the investment of our shareholders whilst striving to recognise our corporate responsibility to the wider society.' The finance director (FD) believes the two elements of the mission contradict each other, whilst a non-executive director (NED) believes that, if the directors are to fulfil their legal duties, Boom must consider its impact on the wider community and the environment and the long-term consequences of any decisions.

52.1 Directors' views

Boom's mission states that the company aims 'to maximise the return on investment for our shareholders whilst striving to recognise our corporate responsibility to wider society.'

Finance director

The finance director believes this is contradictory. In the short term any measures taken by Boom to enhance the health and safety of its employees or to protect the local environment, such as spending on recycling water or controlling pollution, may increase costs and reduce profits.

Reduced profits imply reduced shareholder wealth in terms of dividends foregone or lower capital growth. The finance director's view is consistent with the traditional view that it is the duty of the directors, as agents appointed by shareholders, to maximise shareholder wealth. This might suggest that social factors which sacrifice shareholder wealth should not be taken into account. This is the approach that the finance director is taking when he suggests that money spent 'keeping the environmentalists happy' may make certain projects non-viable.

However the mission statement is not necessarily contradictory – it does not say that Boom has to make sure that society is not disadvantaged in any way by its activities; rather it implies that the company will do its best to take society into account in its decision making and operations.

Non-executive director: corporate responsibility

Corporate responsibility is used to describe the duties which a business has to the wider community. It can be defined as the actions, activities and obligations of business in achieving sustainability. A sustainable business is one which is able to generate continuously increasing stakeholder value by applying sustainable practices throughout all its activities.

The last one hundred years has seen a change in society's expectations towards social responsibility and an increased focus on the extent to which a company should exceed its minimum obligations to stakeholders and society. The modification of the Companies Act has shifted the focus for directors from looking solely at shareholders' interests to taking account of other stakeholders as well when fulfilling their statutory duty to promote the success of the company. The aim is to promote an 'inclusive' approach towards the interests of stakeholders and to encourage a long term view to be taken of corporate investment.

This is more the approach that the NED is referring to when he quotes the statement from the conference that 'the directors have a legal duty to run the company for the benefits of its members as a whole.'

Boom's shareholders, as owners of the company, will be primarily interested in the long term profitability of the various mining projects undertaken. However mining is also likely to bring benefits to a wider group of stakeholders than just Boom's shareholders. For example, employees will benefit from pay, job security and employment prospects. There are benefits too for the local governments of the countries in which Boom mines, which need to be seen to satisfy the demands of their electorate. They may argue that they are doing so by attracting foreign investment, thereby creating employment, increasing the wealth of the economy and collecting additional tax revenues. Boom's activities will also financially benefit the suppliers of its materials and equipment, and mining will also benefit those customers who use the gas that Boom produces.

Nevertheless, whilst wider society might indeed benefit from drilling and mining, the local community and environment in which any of Boom's mining activities take place might be adversely affected through pollution or the use of scarce water resources.

If Boom is to be true to its mission statement, it must recognise its responsibility here and this is perhaps where the potential for conflict arises:

Corporate governance and directors' duties

Corporate governance is concerned with the direction and control of the company, and helps determine the structure of an organisation, its objectives and the relationship between the organisation's management, its board of directors and its shareholders.

Responsibilities fall on the Board collectively and there is no legal distinction between the duties of executive and non-executive directors, but they do have differing roles. The executive directors are more involved in the day-to-day running of the business, whilst the NEDs bring an independent view and help facilitate the strategic decision-making process, by providing objective challenge and criticism. Good corporate governance requires the directors to put in place a risk management strategy and the NED refers to this.

Risk management

If Boom is merely paying lip-service to corporate responsibility in its mission statement, then it is much more likely to be subject to risks resulting from the diverse range of issues relevant to external stakeholders. Therefore the possibility of corporate risk failure and potential financial volatility is increased.

Transparent and accountable governance structures should incorporate the highest standards of ethics. Sustainable business practices will help to manage and minimise Boom's exposure to a broad range of risks relating to the environment, and social and workplace issues. Minimising risk ultimately places Boom in a stronger, more sustainable market position than an unengaged competitor who is likely to be exposed to a greater number of external variables.

If Boom undertakes active and responsive engagement with a broad range of stakeholder groups, this will improve its relationships with stakeholders and give it a better understanding of the environment in which it operates. Such procedures will equip Boom to anticipate the inclinations of those who prescribe regulations and sharpen its response to third party pressures.

Conclusion

The link between social engagement and financial performance ultimately suggests that companies should be motivated to implement socially responsible strategies since this will reduce risk and aid long term profitability, maximising the value of shareholder investments.

On this basis, there would appear to be no inherent conflict in Boom's mission statement. Given that the directors' duties are owed to the members as a whole, any actions which foster long term profitability appear to be in the company's best interests and therefore both elements of Boom's mission statement are achievable simultaneously.

If Boom engages sincerely in social, environmental and other sustainability issues, it is, for example, more likely to secure future access to government controlled natural resources and therefore more likely to achieve superior profit maximisation for its shareholders.

Examiner's comments:

Requirement 52.1 asked candidates to discuss the views of the two directors in relation to Boom's mission statement. They were also asked to explain the directors' duties in respect of corporate governance and corporate responsibility. Attempts at this requirement were quite polarised. Many weaker candidates chose to apply the models of Ashridge and Mendelow, but in doing so failed to address the requirement to discuss directors' duties and corporate governance. Most candidates were confident discussing the concept of corporate responsibility, wider stakeholders and sustainability. A surprising number were however unable to distinguish adequately between corporate responsibility (the activities and obligations of a business in achieving sustainability) and corporate governance (the rules governing the structure and objectives of the organisation and the relationship between management, the board and the shareholders). Better candidates discussed the fact that the roles of the FD and the NED might influence their viewpoint and highlighted the latter's responsibility to bring an independent viewpoint to strategy and standards of conduct. Risk management was mentioned in the scenario but only the better candidates discussed the duties of the Board in ensuring an appropriate risk management framework – particularly relevant in the context of fracking and the danger that decisions might be taken to increase profits without having due regard to the risks involved.

52.2 Commercial and ethical issues

Commercial issues

Boom needs to evaluate the costs and benefits of the proposed SA project to assess what level of return the company is likely to make for its shareholders.

However the decision to invest should not be made without considering non-financial aspects or those who might be disadvantaged by the project.

Financial projections can be prepared, incorporating estimates of the production volumes of gas, the price that it will be able to sell it at, the costs of leasing the land, and mining and distributing the gas.

Non-financial or indirect benefits include the number of jobs created in the local economy, the tax revenues paid to the local government, and the environmental benefits from the reduction in the use of coal and other fossil fuels.

Boom also needs to establish the likely costs to society – for example it needs to assess the likelihood of environmental damage from hazardous chemicals and take all steps possible to reduce the risk of contamination. This could increase the operating costs of the project.

Commercially however, as explained by the FD, if the costs of protecting the environment are too great the project may become non-viable which, given the potential benefits to the local community, would not necessarily be in anyone's interests. Therefore Boom would not be expected to incur costs to eliminate all environmental risks, just those that are deemed most likely and most significant, which it would seem reasonable to address.

Ethical issues

Boom needs to consider whether there are any legal or regulatory issues in relation to the project. Given the nature of Boom's business there may be voluntary industry codes of conduct which should be adhered to.

The project appears to have the support of the local government who are willing to grant the lease, and the central government who believe that there will be considerable economic benefits. Provided the government is prepared to grant Boom a lease to mine the land then there would not appear to be a legality issue. However the shale gas is presumably non-replaceable so the government/local region needs to be compensated for Boom's use of the limited resource – presumably this will be reflected in the price of the lease for the land.

Regulatory issues may also relate to health and safety and the working conditions of employees, who have the right to be safe and to be treated fairly. It is important that Boom acts with integrity to maintain its reputation for the highest standards of health and safety and does not exploit lower standards or the lack of regulation that may exist in the region.

From a sustainability point of view the project is expected to have long term environmental benefits. However Boom and the local government must balance the need to find alternative fuel sources with the need to conserve local water supplies. They need to consult the local population, farmers etc. and take their views into account. Consideration should be given to the alternative sources to using freshwater that exist (eg salt water or non-drinking water) and the extent to which any waste water can be treated and recycled. This may result in slightly higher costs but will increase the sustainability of the project.

There is an issue of transparency. The environmental groups are claiming that the local population is not fully informed in relation to the impact of the fracking. This claim needs to be investigated and the facts established. Boom must ensure that it has been open and honest in its negotiations with the local government to obtain the lease. It also needs to consider the extent to which the environmentalists have genuine concerns which are backed up by evidence or whether these are merely overreactions or scaremongering claims. Meetings should be held with representatives of the government, the local community and the environmental groups to exchange information and to help address their concerns. One possible issue in relation to environmental damage is the fact that the long-term detrimental effects of fracking, which is a relatively new technique, are not yet known.

In relation to integrity, Boom must ensure that its dealings with the local government and others are honest and above board, that the local community is in no way misled about the development and its long term effects, and that it is not involved in any financial attempts to induce or persuade people to act in its favour.

Conclusion

Boom needs to weigh up the benefits of project SA for its shareholders and the wider stakeholders who benefit from the shale gas production, with the disadvantages to the local environment. Provided Boom has been transparent with the government and the local community and its consultations/negotiations are genuine then the company is probably likely to be deemed to act ethically.

Examiner's comments:

Requirement 52.2 requested candidates to discuss the commercial and ethical issues for Boom which are involved in the decision to extract shale gas in South America.

A wide number of points could be made in relation to the commercial issues and the better candidates covered a number of these. Only a very few explained that in undertaking an assessment of the viability of the project Boom would need to consider both financial and non-financial costs and benefits, including where relevant the costs to society. A minority of candidates missed this element of the requirement out altogether and concentrated on ethical issues only.

Candidates' answers to the ethics element were quite mixed. Better candidates considered both the negative and positive sides of the problem, identifying that although fracking may bring some environmental problems locally, it will also reduce the need for fossil fuels, Boom has the support of local and central government, and there will be considerable benefits to the area, all of which are consistent with acting sustainably. Some weaker candidates failed to use any ethical language or principles such as transparency and integrity in their answers. Others applied the transparency/effect/fairness framework, but took a simplistic view, asserting that the farmers and local people would be badly affected, that Boom would not want people to find out about this and that as a result the project was probably not ethical. This approach failed to consider the need to assess the facts and evidence before assuming the environmentalists' claims are accurate. It also overlooked the wide range of benefits that fracking is expected to generate for the region. As has been stated before, the ethics issues are not always clear-cut and weaker candidates need to take note that more balanced and questioning answers are required that do not assert conclusions without supporting reasoning and evidence.

An overwhelming majority of candidates failed to present any sort of conclusion to their analysis, which is disappointing. Commercially, if the costs for Boom of protecting the environment are too great the project might become non-viable, which would cause the wider community to miss out on the possible benefits. Thus a balance needs to be found between the interests of the shareholders and the benefits to wider society on the one hand and those that will be affected by damage to the local environment on the other. Provided Boom is transparent and genuine with all parties and addresses the most significant environmental issues then it may well be acting ethically.

53   Tai Ltd and Jelk plc (March 2014)

Marking guide

	Knowledge	Skill	Marks
53.1 Product portfolio	3	8	10
53.2 Other key benefits	2	5	7
53.3 Strategic disasdvantages and management issues	3	7	9
53.4 Preliminary conclusions	–	4	4
	8	24	30

General comments

The third question, worth 30 marks, was the least well attempted. The scenario concerns two companies considering a merger. Tai Ltd is a well-established Chinese company that manufactures travelators. It uses high quality materials and prides itself on customer service and post-installation maintenance. Jelk Ltd is a UK listed company which manufactures elevators for commercial use. It has contracts to supply and service lifts in office developments, railway stations, airports etc. It also designs, manufactures and installs stairlifts for domestic use, of which about 40% are exported, predominantly to Eurozone countries.

The products of both companies go through a similar life cycle of installation, maintenance and replacement, although the lengths of the cycles are different. Jelk's CEO believes that a merger will be of great benefit to both parties in terms of product portfolio and market coverage and that integration can be successfully managed.

Candidates were required to discuss whether the merger should proceed and were provided with the following headings to structure their answer: product portfolio benefits; other key benefits; key strategic disadvantages and management issues; and preliminary conclusions. As no particular addressee had been specified, candidates were expected to consider the merger from the point of view of both parties where relevant.

53.1 Product portfolio

The BCG and product life cycle models can help assess the balance of a product portfolio. Typically a wider portfolio of products helps spread risk and improve financial performance.

BCG matrix

The BCG matrix is a way of analysing a portfolio of products by considering their relative market share and market growth:

Considering the companies individually:

	Jelk Sales	Largest competitor	Market share: Jelk sales/ Largest Competitor	UK market growth rate	BCG analysis
Elevators	£54m	£260m	20.8%	–2%	Dog
Stairlifts	£96m	£80m	120%	8%	Cash cow
Total sales	150m				

	Tai Sales	Largest competitor	Tai sales/ Largest competitor	Chinese market growth rate	BCG analysis
Travelators	$19.6m	$342m	5.7%	15%	Problem child or ?
In £ at $1 = £0.65	£12.74m	£222m			

Jelk's stairlift product in the UK market might be considered to be a Cash cow or money earner. Jelk is well-established and the market leader in a market that is growing steadily, but slower than in the emerging markets of Asia. The presence of three large competitors should prevent new players entering the UK market. This is likely to mean Jelk has cash flows available for investment to develop new products/markets.

Jelk's elevators are however in a more challenging position, with a relatively low share and little market growth potential. The market is dominated by four global companies and due to the depressed construction sector has experienced a decline of 2%. Stairlifts are likely to generate sufficient funding to allow Jelk to maintain this position until the market regenerates, or Jelk might benefit from finding new markets.

However neither of its established products offers Jelk significant future growth potential. A major competitor has been taken over and further consolidation is likely in a mature market.

In China, Tai has just under a 6% share of an elevator market that is an emerging market, growing at 15%. This would probably put it as a question mark or problem child – a product where the market is growing but share is still limited. Tai is probably not operating at full efficiency, plus its share is likely to need defending against competitors.

Since the two companies have products in different BCG categories, the merger will result in a better balanced portfolio, with products in three quadrants of the matrix. The funds generated from sales of stairlifts can be used to help develop Tai's competitive position in the elevator market.

Product life cycle

The product life cycle concept can be used in conjunction with the BCG:

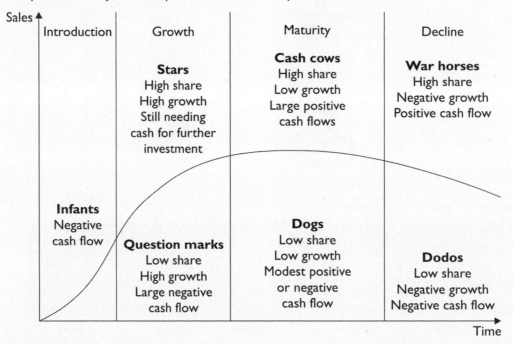

Most businesses would not want to risk having a single product or group of closely related products all at the same stage in their life cycle as they may all decline together. The life of a product can be extended and the balance of a product portfolio improved by considering markets at different stages in the life cycle and this is a key benefit of the proposed merger for Jelk Ltd. Its traditional UK market appears to have reached maturity whereas the Chinese market offers rapid growth potential for both stairlifts and elevators. From Tai's point of view Jelk's size and funding is likely to help it improve its competitive position.

Conclusion

As Jelk's CEO states, the merger will create a more comprehensive and better balanced portfolio for the new company and help sustain funds to support future needs. It will allow Jelk to access a new geographic market for stairlifts and allow Tai to benefit from the size and funding of a market leading company.

53.2 Other benefits/reasons for merger

Synergies

Both companies are independent manufacturers and leaders in their specialist markets. They both focus on product safety. Jelk pays great attentions to quality and aftersales care, and it also has a reputation for post-installation maintenance. Tai has very strong R&D. There is likely to be synergy from having strengths in different areas that are however complementary and can be used to increase competitive advantage.

Marketing advantages

As has been seen in 53.1 the combined businesses will have a more balanced product portfolio. This is likely to improve their success rates when tendering eg Jelk recently lost a tender in Poland to a competitor because of its inability to offer travelators. The merger is likely to help strengthen Tai's chances of winning the railways contract as it can take advantage of Jelk's reputation for post-installation service and use the increased size of the merged company to point to its ability to manage the contract.

Production advantages

It may be possible for the businesses to consider centralising the production of all products in China if this were to reduce manufacturing costs. Alternatively each could start manufacturing the other's product in their local market ie travelators in UK and elevators/stairlifts in China, which would reduce the distribution costs incurred.

R&D advantages

Tai has R&D expertise, in particular in relation to energy efficiency. This may help Jelk to improve its position in the elevator market place by developing new, more efficient systems.

Risk spreading – diversification

The merged company will have less reliance on a single product (Tai) or a single geographic market (Jelk) and therefore the risk of the combined entity will be lower than that of each individual company.

Overcome barriers to entry

The barriers to entry for either company attempting to expand geographically are high. This would probably be more difficult for Jelk to achieve in China without some sort of JV partner than it would be for Tai. Tai will however benefit from Jelk's strong brand.

Outplay rivals

Since the European (and therefore probably the US markets) are mature, most of the big companies will be looking for expansion in South America or Asia and so Jelk would be advised to get ahead of the crowd in this respect if it wants to establish its brand quickly ahead of other competitors.

Finance and management

Certainly as far as Tai is concerned, the merged entity is likely to benefit from better access to funding and Tai may benefit from the experience and skills of the Jelk team in managing global operations.

Examiner's comments:

In requirement 53.2 candidates were asked to consider other key benefits of the merger. Some weaker candidates simply reiterated the product arguments they had already discussed in 53.1, missing the opportunity to consider possible synergies that might arise from the merger. Alternatively they made generic points which were not always relevant here given the geographical dispersion of the two businesses. Better candidates applied their knowledge to the scenario and were able to cite a range of points including geographical diversification, risk reduction, strategic fit, the ability to overcome barriers to entry and possible production and research advantages. Weaker candidates tended to consider benefits from Jelk's perspective only whereas stronger candidates took a more balanced view.

53.3 Strategic disadvantages and management issues

Strategic disadvantages of the merger stem from the following:

Jelk is significantly bigger than Tai so in one sense it is more likely to be a takeover than a merger.

Most of the growth opportunities seem to be in China so Jelk may stand to benefit more than Tai from the combination.

Aside from the language difference, the cultural differences between Jelk and Tai are likely to be large and bridging this gap will pose a significant challenge and business risk.

Cultural differences are likely to arise between the two firms in relation to:

- Values and attitudes eg individualism vs collectivism, diversity and gender stereotypes, work ethics

- Methods of managing staff eg unionisation, hierarchies and status systems, motivation and reward systems

- Methods of doing business eg conventions of negotiations and tenders, need to ensure self-respect and status, hospitality

- Expectations of business conduct eg in relation to CSR, short term vs long term time horizon of investments, government involvement

There will also be regulatory differences and the merged entity will need to ensure compliance with all legal requirements, especially in respect of employment terms and conditions.

Management issues

If the merger goes ahead, there would be significant integration challenges in relation to HR and culture. A key issue in assessing the people and cultural challenges will be understanding the level and depth of integration anticipated — from minimal integration, where Jelk and Tai continue to be run as stand-alone subsidiaries, to full integration, which since Jelk is the bigger player (£150m sales compared to Tai's £12.7m) is likely in this case to mean Tai relinquishing its identity and being subsumed into Jelk's operations. A further complication is that different parts of the organisation may be integrated at different levels, for example, minimal integration of the sales function but full integration of the supporting IT and finance function.

Understanding the similarities and differences in the way Jelk and Tai do business will enable the merged company to focus more sharply on what needs to change (in Jelk or Tai), who needs to change, and how and when these changes should take place.

A major strategic decision needs to be made in relation to how the merged firm will be managed and the shape of the new structure, and who will fill the key jobs. The eventual structure of the merged entity may not necessarily reflect the prior structure of either business.

If the merger proceeds, the change is likely to be transformational. A dedicated change management team will need to be established to manage the integration across the business units and geographies and to address a wide range of global integration challenges, including clearly defining the new organisation structure and its responsibilities, managing relevant stakeholders through clear and frequent communications, and addressing cultural differences between the two companies.

Examiner's comments:

Requirement 53.3 requested candidates to discuss strategic disadvantages and management issues. Whilst Jelk's CEO has been very upbeat about the merger, it is not without its issues, not least the fact that Jelk is considerably bigger than Tai and on the face of it stands to gain more. There will also be a large language and cultural gap to breach, which will present significant integration challenges if the merger goes ahead. Better candidates discussed these and other points, distinguishing between strategic disadvantages and management issues. Weaker candidates tended to limit the scope of their answers by merging their discussion of disadvantages and management issues, and rehearsed their knowledge of change management in a generic fashion, instead of applying this to the specific issues in the scenario.

53.4 Preliminary conclusions

As Jelk's CEO states, it appears that the merger would be beneficial to both parties. The combined product portfolio will be more balanced than either of the companies individually and this is likely to increase their competitive advantage when it comes to tendering. The business risk of the combined company entity will be lower as the merger will reduce Tai's reliance on a single product and Jelk's reliance on a single market. There are likely to be some cultural issues associated with the integration, but these may be at a strategic rather than operational level, if Tai operates in China and Jelk in the UK, each distributing the other's products.

Clearly the benefits to the respective shareholders will depend on the financial structure of the transaction but, on the face of it, strategically the merger appears viable.

Examiner's comments:

Requirement 53.4, the preliminary conclusion was generally well done. Those who briefly summarised the key points from each section and produced a conclusion which was consistent with their earlier discussion tended to score highly. A minority of candidates who had mismanaged their time on earlier sections or questions omitted this requirement entirely.

54 Albatross Golf Equipment plc (June 2014)

Marking guide

	Knowledge	Skill	Marks
54.1 Data analysis	2	18	18
54.2 Supply chain management and market positioning	4	11	14
54.3 Ethics	2	7	8
	8	36	40

General comments

The scenario in this question relates to a company (AGE), which manufactures good quality golf clubs from its factory in the UK under the LazySwing brand. Sales have declined in recent years, partly due to competition from larger rival manufacturers with greater R&D expenditure. AGE has recently been acquired by a private equity firm, FF, which has appointed a new chief executive.

The chief executive undertook a strategic review, but he would like more analysis to determine the underlying causes of the decline in performance. The chief executive has also proposed to reposition the LazySwing brand from up-market to mid-market.

A further proposed strategy is to import a new range of lower-cost golf clubs from China, with two sub strategies: (1) sell these clubs through existing distribution channels with the existing LazySwing brand name; or (2) sell them through downmarket sports retailers under a new 'Eagle' brand.

An ethical issue has arisen whereby the chief executive was told in confidence by a professional golfer that the professional golfer used by AGE to promote its products is taking performance-enhancing drugs.

54.1

	AGE			Galdo		
	20Y1	*20Y2*	*20Y3*	*20Y1*	*20Y2*	*20Y3*
Number of clubs sold	250	240	234	556	519	484
% decrease		4%	2.5%		6.7%	6.7%
UK market	380,000	365,000	350,000			
% decrease		3.9%	4.1%			
Gross profit margin %	20%	18%	16%	30%	30%	30%
Operating profit margin %	6.8%	3.5%	0.2%	20.0%	19.6%	19.1%
% sales UK	80%	82%	84%	40%	40%	40%
% sales export	20%	18%	16%	60%	60%	60%
Sales revenue decrease						
UK		6.8%	5.8%		4.0%	4.2%
Export		18.2%	18.2%		4.0%	4.2%
Total revenue		9.1%	8.0%		4.0%	4.2%
Revenue per club	£88.00	£83.33	£78.63	£179.86	£184.97	£190.08
AGE/market leader						
Sales	22.0%	20.8%	20.0%			
Op profit	7.5%	3.7%	0.3%			
Market share (golf equipment market)	4.63%	4.49%	4.42%	10.53%	10.52%	10.51%
Market share (golf club market)	6.62%	6.41%	6.31%	15.04%	15.03%	15.01%

(1) **Revenues**

Total revenues of AGE have declined in 20Y2 and 20Y3 by 9.1% and 8% respectively. Part of the decline can be attributed to the shrinkage of the UK golf equipment market which is beyond the control of AGE management. However, UK market revenues only fell by 3.9% and 4.1% in 20Y2 and 20Y3 respectively. The decline in revenues for AGE has therefore been more than double the market average. More information is needed on changes in the UK golf clubs market.

To examine how this decline in AGE's revenues arose, a sub analysis of the UK market sales and export sales provides some insight. In 20Y1, AGE's UK sales were 80% of its total sales, with exports being only 20%. By 20Y3, however, these figures had changed to 84% and 16% respectively, thereby indicating an increasing relative reliance on the UK market, despite the absolute fall in sales in that market.

Indeed, there has been a decline in AGE's sales revenues in the UK of 6.8% and 5.8% in 20Y2 and 20Y3 respectively, which is still in excess of the overall decline in UK market sales for golf equipment and represents a poor performance.

The export sales performance is however far worse with a reduction in sales of 18.2% in each of the years 20Y2 and 20Y3.

In order to explore further the underlying causes for the decline, it is necessary to examine changes in sales prices and sales volumes. This detail is not analysed separately for UK and exports in the data provided, but it would be required as further information to make a more complete analysis.

Nevertheless, using the data provided, sales volumes have declined by 4% and 2.5% in 20Y2 and 20Y3 respectively. This is a smaller decrease than that in sales revenues, but the difference can be explained in lower prices.

Price can be determined by using revenue divided by volumes, thus average price changed from £88.00 in 20Y1 to £83.33 in 20Y2 (a 5.3% reduction) and then to £78.63 in 20Y3 (a further 5.6% reduction).

It is possible that there has been a change in sales mix between high value and lower value clubs to explain some of the fall in average price. More information is needed on sales volumes of different clubs within the LazySwing range.

Overall therefore, ignoring a possible change in sales mix, the decline in revenue is due to a combination of price decreases and sales volume decreases. This is indicative of weak demand as the price reductions may have been expected to have had a positive effect on sales volumes given a negatively sloped demand function.

Profit

The decline in profit over the period is even more severe than the decline in sales. The reduction of the gross profit margin from 20% in 20Y1 to 16% in 20Y3 is indicative that manufacturing costs comprise an increasing proportion of sales revenues. This is likely to be because some manufacturing costs are fixed costs and do not decline linearly with falling sales volumes, thereby forming a greater proportion of revenues.

The administrative and other fixed costs mean the operating profits are even more volatile than gross profits. As a consequence, operating profit margins have fallen from 6.8% in 20Y1 to near zero in 20Y3.

Trends

There is a clear decline over the period for which information is available, but this period is too short to establish any reliable trends. Moreover, markets can be cyclical and the poor recent performance may be reversed if there is a general upturn in the market. It would be inappropriate to ignore this possibility, but complacent to rely on it as a future strategy for growth.

Conclusion

Over the period 20Y1 to 20Y3, the performance of AGE has declined significantly, even after allowing for the overall decline in UK market sales of golf equipment. More information is needed to determine the extent to which the poor performance in export markets is attributable to a decline in those markets.

(2) **Comparison with Galdo**

The market leader provides a benchmark against which to judge performance of other companies in the industry.

In many respects it provides a better benchmark than the UK market average as it includes export markets and judges performance for a UK manufacturing base.

The relative size of a company compared to the market leader is important in making valid comparisons. In 20Y1 AGE's sales were only 22% that of Galdo and this had fallen to 20% by 20Y3. Comparisons therefore need to be relative (eg in % terms) rather than in absolute terms.

Although Galdo is the market leader, it only has a market share of just over 10%. This implies there are many participants in the industry, or it could suggest the significance of imports to the UK market. AGE has a smaller and declining market share at 4.63% in 20Y1; falling to 4.42% in 20Y3.

Revenues

Sales revenues of Galdo have declined by 4% and 4.2% in 20Y2 and 20Y3 respectively. This is the case in both the UK market and the export market and therefore for overall revenue. This is broadly in line with the average decline in the UK market over this period of 3.9% and 4.1%. In this respect Galdo has withstood the UK market decline rather better than AGE.

The underlying causes of the sales revenue change can be better understood by examining price and sales volume changes. In sales volume terms, AGE has actually performed better than Galdo which has suffered declines of 6.7% in 20Y2 and 20Y3 compared to 4% and 2.5% for AGE. However, the changes in selling prices are causally linked to these volume changes. In 20Y1, Galdo was charging £179.86 per club compared to £88.00 charged by AGE. This is a significant difference, but by 20Y3 it had widened further, with Galdo charging £190.08 per club compared to £78.63 charged by AGE. Thus, the difference in sales volumes can be partially attributed to a shift along the demand curve caused by price changes, rather than a shift of the demand curve which would have suggested changes in underlying demand conditions.

The combined effects of price and volume are reflected in sales revenues which, as already noted, strongly favour the performance of Galdo over AGE.

In terms of export markets, Galdo is rather more dependent than AGE as 60% of sales come from export markets and, unlike AGE, this figure has remained steady throughout the period in question. Further information would be required on price, quantity and sales mix in to make more valid comparisons. Also, the specific countries to which exports are being made by the two companies would need to be known.

Market positioning

Based on price, it would appear that Galdo is in a significantly higher sector of the market than AGE and this is likely to have had an influence on performance as there is a different set of competitors.

Based on the above data, Galdo charges more than double per club than AGE and this gap has widened over the period 20Y1-20Y3 as AGE has reduced selling prices, while Galdo has increased them.

Given that Galdo's sales revenues have only fallen in line with the UK market average in this period despite the price increase, it appears that demand is more robust than for AGE, where sales revenues and volumes have fallen despite a price decrease.

These data provide some support for the chief executive's argument that the LazySwing brand can no longer compete at the high end of the market.

Profits

Whilst AGE's profits have declined severely to near zero, Galdo's operating profits have only suffered a more modest decline from £20 million to £17.6 million (12%). This is reflected in gross profit margins remaining at 30% and operating profit margins only falling from 20% in 20Y1 to 19.1% in 20Y3.

While AGE's revenues were 22% that of Galdo in 20Y1 its operating profit was only 7.5% that of Galdo indicating that Galdo is a more profitable company even after controlling for the size difference between the two companies. By 20Y3 AGE's operating profit has nearly fallen to zero and was only 0.3% that of Galdo.

Examiner's comments:

The data analysis section was generally well answered, with most candidates making appropriate calculations in order to support sensible conclusions regarding relative performance. The majority of candidates examined both profit and revenue. Some also considered non-financial aspects such as R&D.

Concerning layout, whilst most candidates set out their calculations in an initial table, a minority mixed calculations within their discussion and this sometimes caused them to lose flow and structure. Some candidates looked at each year separately, while others looked only at the entire period.

Narrative explanations of relative performance over time, and in comparison to a larger competitor, Galdo, tended to be variable, depending partly on which calculations had been attempted. For example, those candidates who did not calculate revenue per club were less able to explain the overall decline in revenue for AGE.

The best answers compared and contrasted the performance of AGE and Galdo in terms of their relative positions/strategies in the industry, focusing, for example, on Galdo's ability to raise prices in a declining market and AGE's decline in revenue and sales volumes, despite a falling price per club.

The poorer answers made little attempt at identifying cause and effect relationships or key trends, for the most part simply re-stating the calculated numbers in terms of ups and downs.

54.2 Supply chain management

Supply chain management (SCM) is the management of all supply activities from the suppliers to a business through to delivery to customers. This may also be called demand chain management reflecting the idea that the customers' requirements and downstream orders should drive activity, based on the concept of end-to-end business (e2e). In essence it refers to managing the value system. SCM relates to the new products imported from China rather than the existing LazySwing products.

Key themes in SCM are Responsiveness, Reliability, Relationships. This raises important issues for AGE, but they appear to be the same for both strategies. Consideration of SCM is therefore important in determining if either strategy involving the Chinese imports is viable, but seems unlikely to be helpful in distinguishing between the two strategies.

- **Responsiveness** – the ability to supply customers quickly. This has led to the development of Just in Time (JIT) systems to keep raw materials acquisition, production and distribution as flexible as possible.

  Given the geographical distance between the UK and China then there are likely to be long lead times for orders. It is therefore essential that demand can be predicted throughout the year in order to avoid shortages and surpluses. The seasonal nature of outdoor sports could add to the difficulty of forecasting demand.

- **Reliability** – the ability to supply customers reliably. Service level agreements about the reliability of supplies should be made to enforce reliability.

- **Relationships** – the use of single sourcing and long-term contracts to better integrate the buyer and supplier. JiangGolf would appear to be a single source supplier which would assist in building relationships. However, it also builds dependency and there is a risk that if this supplier fails to deliver, for whatever reason, then AGE may be unable to supply its own customers.

A key further element is cost. It is clear that JiangGolf is cheaper than any European manufacturer of equivalent quality. This lower purchase cost needs to be balanced however with length and uncertainty over lead times.

The minimum of 100,000 golf clubs is an important constraint as it represents a high proportion of AGE's existing sales volumes. There needs to be a degree of confidence about demand volumes reaching this level before accepting this contract term. In this respect, Strategy 2 may be preferable as the lower price and the distribution through general sports equipment retailers may have a better chance of achieving higher sales volumes.

Market positioning

Market positioning relates to both the existing LazySwing products and the new products imported from China.

LazySwing products

Regarding the existing product, Lee has suggested that it may be trying to compete at too high a market position. Evidence to support this proposition is that price has been reduced but sales volumes have still fallen. While adverse market conditions are also a factor, Galdo was increasing its price over the same period, indicating it is moving upmarket.

In the absence of being able to set aside a large R&D budget, it appears likely that AGE does not have the resources to keep pace with its competitors at the high end of the market. Charging high prices without the corresponding quality is not offering customers a reasonable value proposition.

Price

High   A

                              B

                                        C

              D

            E

Low

                    Perceived quality

    very poor   poor   reasonable   good   very good

Thus in the above diagram the LazySwing brand on existing products manufactured in the UK, might be perceived to be at B. This would be dominated by product C which offers higher quality for a lower price.

In order to reposition the price would need to be reduced.

The suggestion of Lee to reduce the price to £55, from its current level of £78.63 (see table in 54.1) appears to be a move in this direction. The benefits might be increased sales volumes as LazySwing is now competing against mid-market competitors. There may also be a cost saving in R&D if there is a consumer expectation that LazySwing is not at the cutting edge of technology, but instead offers good value.

Tutorial note:

Other models such as Bowman's Clock could also have been used.

Imported goods from China

Regarding the market positioning of the imported clubs, this appears to have two possible market positions which are based on two different prices. At first sight, this might seem unusual in the context of the above diagram as the quality is the same no matter what the price and the market it is sold in. However, price can be a signal of perceived quality, as can the distribution channel used.

With Strategy 1, the imported clubs will be sold at an average price of £30 and distributed to high end specialist outlets. The price and the distribution channel might signal some degree of quality and thereby raise the market positioning as high as possible for the physical attributes of this product.

In Strategy 2 the same physical product will be sold at the lower price of £25 and distributed through channels which are further downmarket. The advantage of this is that sales volumes may increase as they are seen as better value and exposed to more potential customers.

Branding

It has already been noted that the two strategies for imported clubs involve the same physical product, but are distinguished by different prices and different distribution channels. A further distinction between the two products is their different branding.

With Strategy 1, the imported clubs use the upmarket LazySwing brand. In terms of creating a perception of quality and added value this is likely to help sales and support the higher price of £30 compared to Strategy 2. It also offers economies of scope in delivering through existing distribution channels. The downside is it might damage the perceived quality of the existing LazySwing clubs manufactured in the UK. In other words there may be confusion in the minds of consumers as to what the LazySwing brand stands for.

In balancing these propositions, the scope for damaging the sales of existing UK manufactured clubs is considerable as sales volumes are higher, at 234,000 per year, than the imported clubs as indicated by the minimum level of 100,000 (although it is recognised they could sell well beyond this level).

With Strategy 2, the use of the Eagle brand is unlikely to help sales at first as it is a new brand where consumers will be unaware of what it stands for. Over time however there is the opportunity to develop a separate brand message through marketing (eg good value, low to mid-market, for occasional golfers). The brand will be initially perceived through the price of £25 and the distribution channel where consumers would not expect to see high quality equipment.

The main advantage with Strategy 2 might appear to be that the perceived quality of the existing LazySwing brand is protected. Even here however there is a risk in the sense that the AGE company name may itself be a brand. If consumers perceive that both Eagle and LazySwing are from the same company, there may be some reputational effect. In particular, the reputation as a manufacturer of golf clubs may be damaged once it becomes known that AGE is also an importer and wholesaler.

An additional brand risk for both strategies might be that JiangGolf sells to other UK manufacturers and wholesalers (or directly into the UK) and therefore the same golf clubs can be obtained elsewhere, under an alternative brand, perhaps at lower prices to consumers.

Conclusion

Careful consideration should be given to the business case for importing golf clubs. The clear downsides for both strategies are:

- If it will not be possible to sell 100,000 units, then losses could be made from unsold inventories.

- There will be reputational damage to the LazySwing brand if there is brand confusion by customers.

Conversely, however, the existing strategy is failing and this would be an attempt to enter a different section of the market, whilst maintaining the existing products, having repositioned them.

Strategy 2 is recommended as more favourable as it has a greater probability of reaching 100,000 units with a lower price and it goes further towards protecting the existing LazySwing brand name by using a new brand. Nevertheless, significant market research is required before committing to either strategy.

Examiner's comments:

Differences in candidate performance normally related to whether or not both strategies were fully evaluated in terms of both SCM, and also market positioning and branding. Poorer answers either only concentrated on one of the proposals, or mainly on either market positioning or SCM. Often, a sub-heading would be provided (eg SCM) but then the following discussion focused mainly on market positioning, and vice versa.

Only a minority of candidates made explicit reference to the RRR framework under SCM, and some of these did not use the framework very well to inform discussion.

A majority considered adopting a mid-market position by AGE to be an example of pursuing Porter's 'stuck in the middle' strategy, with only a few referring to Bowman's clock or the price/quality trade-off matrix.

Under branding, the majority recognised the possible risk, with Strategy 1, of damage to the perceived quality of existing LazySwing products.

A majority of those who provided conclusions recommended Strategy 2 for the imported clubs.

54.3 Ethics pertains to whether a particular behaviour is deemed acceptable in the context under consideration.

In making any ethical evaluation it is first necessary to establish the facts. In this case, it needs to be established whether the disclosure about Gary is true and whether his behaviour is in fact against the law. Since the information came from a fellow professional golfer, who may be Gary's rival, it is very possible that it is false information given to damage Gary's reputation, and therefore must be carefully checked.

A key ethical principle is illegality ie whether there is a legal duty for Lee to disclose Gary's conduct (eg if any crime had only been committed in another country this might not be the case). If there is a legal duty there is a clear ethical imperative for Lee to obey the law.

A second ethical principle is self-interest. If there is a disclosure then AGE would lose value and Lee would also lose income. If disclosure is made on ethical grounds, then this would therefore be at a personal cost to Lee and a corporate cost to AGE.

A third ethical issue is that Lee was told 'in confidence' and therefore any public disclosure could be deemed a breach of that confidence.

A fourth ethical issue relates to honesty. Gary is being held out as a golfer with integrity, when Lee at least knows this may not be true and is therefore knowingly deceiving customers.

A key final ethical issue is the distinction between the ethics of the individual (Lee) and the corporate ethics of AGE.

In making a decision as to how to proceed, it may be helpful to apply the Institute of Business Ethics three tests:

- Transparency
- Effect
- Fairness

Transparency – at the moment Lee is the only person in AGE management who knows of the allegations. If the AGE board is to make an ethical choice then it needs to be informed of what is known, albeit that it may want to ascertain the facts. Lee has a duty to his fellow directors and to the company to disclose to them and thereby aid transparency, as there may be consequences for AGE and its stakeholders.

Effect – whom does the decision affect/hurt? Almost everyone directly concerned with the issue (Lee, AGE and Gary) stands to lose from disclosure. However, there is a wider public interest and a question of honesty to wider customers. There is also an ethical principle of 'doing the right thing' irrespective of the consequences.

Fairness – would maintaining secrecy of what could have occurred be considered fair by those affected? The issue for AGE and Lee is that they may be condoning the actions of Gary by continuing to support him and promote the brand while knowing that the image of integrity is false.

Response

An initial action would be for Lee to challenge Gary in relation to the claims being made about him and obtain any evidence.

Unless the evidence is conclusive that the claims about Gary are untrue, Lee has a duty to report the facts to the other board members, as the interests of AGE may be affected.

Lee and AGE may also take legal advice whether they have a duty to disclose the illegal act to the police and the right to disclose it to the public.

If there is evidence to support the allegation, the contract should be terminated or there should be public disclosure of what is known, so an honest position is presented to the public and to customers.

If there is not to be immediate public disclosure then the issue of transparency to other stakeholders should also be considered (existing customers, suppliers, employees).

Examiner's comments:

Too many candidates failed to use appropriate ethical language or apply relevant ethical principles. Many candidates failed to identify the necessary actions that should be taken as required by the question. Many candidates also failed to recognise the key point that it is necessary to establish the facts, and not to act on rumours concerning the alleged drug-taking. Those who identified that fact-finding needed to take place and then gave options for actions, including disclosure to the authorities if illegal activities had taken place, scored well. Weaker candidates tended to describe the commercial risks to the company presented by the scenario, rather than the ethical issues.

55 Best Fresh Bakeries Ltd (June 2014)

Marking guide

	Knowledge	Skill	Marks
55.1 Risks (Best Fresh Bakeries and Stakeholders)	3	10	12
55.2 Transfer pricing	2	8	9
55.3 Governance	2	6	7
	7	24	28

General comments

The scenario in this question relates to a family company with five shops, each baking and retailing food. The company is owned by Henry, who owns 80% of the shares, and his two sons, who own the remaining shares. The three family members comprise the board of directors.

The sons want to expand by building a central baking facility to transfer internally to the shops and to sell to third parties. Henry has different risk preferences to his sons and does not wish to incur the cost and risk of expansion. Brief biographies of the board members are provided.

A governance issue has arisen whereby the two sons are attempting to push the expansion decision through the board by outvoting their father. Henry is considering appointing two friends as non-executive directors so he effectively has the majority of board votes.

55.1 (a) Risks for BFB

The plan for expansion has significant strategic, operating and financial risks for BFB.

Strategic risks

These are the risks associated with the long term strategic objectives of the business.

The new investment in a centralised baking facility risks departing from the core marketing slogan of the business which is: 'Baked and sold on the premises on the same day.'

Whilst it will still be on the 'same day' it will not be baked on the individual shop premises and hence the change will be visible to customers. Even if there is no change in quality, this may be perceived by customers to be the case, given the overt change in the scale of baking.

More particularly, quality assurance for large scale production is more difficult than for small scale production and the brand being associated with 'high quality' may suffer from a strategy of 'high volume'.

Pricing strategy may also need to change if actual, or perceived, quality changes.

An additional strategic risk is that BFB products from the new bakery will be available to third parties who may then compete with BFB's shops, thereby reducing its sales directly to the public.

It may be that the new strategy of higher volumes will be successful and the additional sales will compensate for any lost sales from reduced quality. However, a change in strategy is a risk as this is a different market sector to the current core market.

Operating risks

The scale of the new baking facility is significant at £2 million, relative to existing operations with net assets of £3 million.

The operating gearing will be increased significantly by the new baking facility. The initial cost is £2 million, but also manufacturing is likely to have high fixed operating costs relative to variable costs. The means that profits will be volatile relative to changes in sales.

The high fixed costs are also likely to raise the breakeven point. One measure of risk would be whether the breakeven point is significantly above the level of internal sales, which would require significant external sales to make it viable.

Exit costs are likely to be significant if the venture fails, as there is likely to be a large financial commitment to specialist baking equipment which is likely to have a low realisable value.

Further operational risk arises from the management of a centralised baking facility and dealing with commercial customers, both of which may be outside the core competences of a management team that has experience only in managing small-scale shops with individual retail customers.

There would be a distribution risk in transporting fresh produce from the bakery to the shops. In the past this did not arise as baking was carried out on the premises. There are also health and safety risks arising from distribution.

Financial risks

The additional borrowing generates additional financial gearing which raises financial risks. This means that residual earnings after interest payments will be more volatile and there is increased risk of insolvency if repayments on the loan cannot be made.

This means that cash flows may be at risk, and therefore going concern could be questionable, if sales do not match expectations.

In dealing with commercial customers, rather than only retail customers, there is increased credit risk from bad debts.

(b) **Shareholder-director risks**

Henry

Henry's potential exposure if the business fails as a result of the new venture is the value of his shareholding of £4 million (£5m × 80%). There would also be the loss of some future income although, as he is nearing retirement, this may not be substantial.

It may also be that Henry might need to make personal guarantees for the new lending.

If the new venture fails (even if BFB survives) the value of BFB shares will fall, so Henry will be at risk from a reduced payment for his shares on retirement. Given he is risk averse, then Henry would be accepting significant risk from the new venture and it may not therefore be desirable for him.

Ralph and Nigel (common risks)

Their 10% shareholdings are at risk if the company fails (£500,000 each)

If the company fails completely, their future income as directors over many years is also at risk.

If the project succeeds, then there is a risk that the value of BFB shares will rise and the brothers may not then be able to afford to acquire Henry's shares when he retires.

There is also the risk of board conflict and loss of Henry's support. This may mean that they are removed from the board by Henry and not offered the opportunity to acquire Henry's shares on his retirement.

Ralph

Other than his shares, Ralph has few personal assets for creditors to attack, even if he has given personal guarantees.

The risky nature of the project is not inconsistent with his attitude of being willing to take 'reasonably high risks'.

For Ralph, the project may be acceptable as he will share in the upside potential and the risks are both limited by his low asset ownership and appropriate to his risk preferences.

Nigel

Nigel is risk neutral so may be less accepting of the common risks than Ralph. Also he has personal assets which would be at risk if personal guarantees have been given.

Overall it may be questionable that Nigel should accept the risks. His supportive attitude to the project may mean he has high expectations that the project will succeed and therefore accepts the associated risks. Alternatively, it could mean that he has not fully considered, or fully comprehended, all the risks.

Examiner's comments:

This was generally well answered. The better answers considered strategic, financial and operating risks for BFB as a whole. However, some candidates tended to concentrate too much on financial risks at the expense of other risks. Weaker candidates did not identify different types of risks and merely listed risks randomly.

Most candidates considered the three different stakeholder perspectives, but explicit discussion of overlapping risks was only provided by a small minority.

55.2 A transfer price is the price at which one division in a group sells its products or services to another division in the same group.

The transfer prices will be important for BFB as they have a number of implications:

- They determine the profits of divisions. If the baking facility division charges a high transfer price, then most of the total profit from company sales will be attributed to it, with less to the individual shops. This will give a false measure of performance for both divisions.

- If high transfer prices are passed on to ultimate customers then sales volumes may fall and overall profits may be distorted.

- Inappropriate transfer prices can lead to dysfunctional decisions. If either division believes it can get a better deal from outside markets it may take it. For example, if the shop managers could obtain supplies of equal quality at lower cost from third parties then they may, if permitted, choose to purchase outside the company, leaving the baking facility division with reduced sales. Conversely, if transfer prices are too low, then the baking facility division management might supply to alternative channels at a higher price and leave the shops without an internal supply of produce.

The likelihood of these implications being realised depends on the way in which the transfer prices are set and imposed. There are a number of choices:

(1) **Cost-based methods of setting transfer prices**

This method leads to the inevitable problem of deciding which cost to use:

- **Full cost**: The variable costs plus an amount to cover the baking facility's overheads. This leaves the baking facility division in a break-even situation from internal sales if based on actual full cost. There may be some surplus/deficit arising from efficiencies or overruns if based on budgeted full cost. The baking facility division may make profit from its external sales.

- **Variable cost** (or marginal cost): This leaves the baking facility division making nil contribution and so enduring losses equal to its fixed costs from internal sales.

- **Opportunity cost**: The revenue forgone by not selling the item to the highest bidder.

In terms of cost-based transfer prices, optimal transfer pricing requires that divisions sell components at the higher of variable cost and opportunity cost.

(2) **Other methods of setting transfer prices**

The following methods of transfer pricing enable the baking facility division to record a profit.

- **Negotiated prices**: The transfer price is established by discussions between the baking facility division managers and shop managers in a bargaining process.

- **Two-part transfer prices**: The transfer price is set at variable cost to ensure corporate optimality but, in addition to this price, the baking facility division records an extra amount in its sales to arrive at a profit figure for evaluation purposes.

- **Dual pricing**: The shops record the transfer at the baking facility's standard variable cost which may aid decision making. The baking facility division reports the transfer at a higher value (eg cost plus) to give a profit incentive. This should lead to goal congruence but may lead to poor cost control as profits are made more easily. The accounting problem makes this method unpopular.

- **Market prices**: transfer prices are set according to market prices to external customers. In this case the baking facility division charges the same price internally to BFB shops as to its external customers.

Conclusion

Transfer prices could be set by negotiation where the outcome is influenced strongly by market prices charged to third party customers by the baking facility division. This would recognise the opportunity of either division to buy from or sell into external markets on an arm's length basis.

Examiner's comments:

This was reasonably well answered, on the whole. Most candidates understood the key issues involved in setting transfer prices between the divisions, and provided possible methods for setting the prices. Better answers also gave due consideration to motivation/incentives and goal congruence.

The best candidates, a very small minority, also outlined the correct principles for transfer prices – set the price at the opportunity cost of the supplying division which will be variable cost if the division has spare capacity, or variable cost plus lost contribution on external sales if at full capacity.

The vast majority of candidates failed to recommend how transfer prices should be set but instead gave a number of different options.

55.3 Governance

At its broadest, governance covers all aspects of operating and controlling the organisation including its structure and systems. Governance affects the organisational structure, determines objectives of an organisation and influences the relationship between the organisation's management, its board of directors and its shareholders.

BFB is a small private company so it has a simple structure with family-based ownership and control around three individuals. As a private company, BFB is not bound by the UK Corporate Governance Code. Nevertheless, aspects of the Code may act as guidance to best practice.

Nigel's and Ralph's voting intentions

Henry's position as the 80% shareholder gives him control over the votes in shareholder meetings.

This would generate a total contribution of:

IT services	£1.60m
Electrical	£1.32m
Total	**£2.92m**

Discussion

Feasibility

There would appear to be few problems of feasibility in charging different prices for the two types of service in terms of operationalising the policy. The two services are carried out by different employees and all that is required is appropriate time keeping records.

In terms of the feasibility in the market place of being able to charge different prices for the two types of service, this will depend on whether such differential pricing is acceptable to customers.

Benefits

This policy is not price discrimination as they are different types of service. The pricing policy that EIL has followed appears to be a cost based pricing policy, in that it would appear (based on the finance director's quote) that the company believes that if costs are the same, then prices should be the same.

An alternative view would be to let markets dictate optimal prices and therefore, if the two types of service are valued differently in the marketplace, they should be priced differently.

If the two services are priced according to their own markets then the above table shows that this policy gives a higher overall contribution than uniform pricing for both types of service, as it optimises the price in each of the two separate markets, rather than merely in total.

Using the above data, the price for IT services should be increased by £4 from the current level of £32 per hour to £36 per hour. The IT services market appears more resilient to higher prices than electrical services. This may be because they are more highly valued by customers or because of the pricing policies and availability of competitors. This higher price is advantageous to EIL as although it leads to a fall in demand for IT services of 16.7% (from 120,000 hours to 100,000 hours), the 12.5% price increase (from £32 to £36) more than compensates for this in terms of additional contribution from this group (contribution increases by 11.1% (£1,440,000 to £1,600,000)).

The table also shows that the current price of £32 per hour is optimal for electrical services. As a result, the contribution from electrical services would be unchanged.

Overall contribution from differential pricing of the two types of service is that contribution increases from £2.76m to £2.92m (ie 5.8%).

As already noted, even if there was homogeneous pricing for both services, an additional contribution can be gained, compared to the current situation, by increasing the price from £32 to £34 per hour. This will increase total contribution from £2.76m to £2.8m.

Examiner's comments:

Similar points regarding the use of revenue, rather than contribution, as were made in requirement 56.1 above, also apply here.

The majority concluded that considering price variation based on services, rather than incomes, was an improvement and did not suffer from many of the problems associated with the latter.

Many candidates incorrectly referred to the service approach as price discrimination, with only a small minority pointing out that it differs in principle from price discrimination.

56.3 (1)   **Evaluation**

The market analysis above examines only a limited range of the factors that need to be considered in pricing. Namely:

- A narrow range of specified prices
- Demand according to incomes
- Demand according to type of service
- Variable costs

In order to achieve a more robust overall pricing strategy other factors need to be considered.

In so doing, there are two alternatives to the chief executive's suggestion of local pricing:

(a)   The centre sets prices that apply to all depots.
(b)   Separate prices are set for each depot based on local conditions.

Further information is required in this respect to clarify the alternative benchmark against which the local pricing policy is being judged.

In evaluating the chief executive's suggestion two key issues arise:

(1)   The way in which prices are set (eg who, when, how, why)
(2)   The factors to be considered in setting prices

(1)   **The way prices are set**

The above data analysis is static (ie at a point in time). Market conditions are likely to change and therefore a method of setting prices according to changing markets over time is required, not just a decision on a revision of existing prices on a one-time basis. Consideration therefore needs to be given to how frequently they are reset and this requires a degree of agility in decision making which would be more appropriate at local depot level than for the company as a whole.

There is therefore some support for the CE's suggestion that local determination of prices by depot managers is a more responsive method of setting prices which can take account of local conditions and indeed, price based on individual transactions, rather than for groups of customers or types of service.

(2)   **Factors to be considered in setting prices**

There are a range of factors that need to be considered in setting prices. The key question in this context is whether depot managers are better positioned to consider these factors than the centre.

Leakage – as the depots are 50km apart and the range for each depot is 25km then there is no leakage between markets if differential prices are set between depots (ie there is no internal competition).

Variable costs – the average variable cost is £20 per hour across the company. However this is an average and may vary both (1) between depots and (2) within depots for different jobs. For example, there may be a variation between depots due to a need to pay higher wages for depots nearer London. Within depots, a job 25km away may be more expensive than a job 1km from the depot. These variations are almost impossible to accommodate centrally, but could be allowed for at local level with local knowledge.

Fixed costs – information is not provided on fixed costs so this is required. However, it seems likely that fixed costs will vary between depots. For example, there may be a variation between property costs, such as rentals, between depots nearer London and those further away from London. Whilst not relevant to short term pricing, the level of fixed costs would be relevant to a long term pricing strategy in order to make a reasonable return on investment.

Price discrimination – local knowledge of housing and individuals could enable a series of prices, based on a series of income levels, rather than just the two suggested by the market survey.

Competition – the industry is quite diverse between smaller sole proprietors and larger IT/electrics companies. The nature and intensity of the competition is therefore likely to vary between depots. Even if the centre is aware of this variation in local competition, it is not easy to set prices centrally for each depot as local conditions may change rapidly.

Employee level price variation – it appears there is uniform remuneration of operational employees. Notwithstanding this, the level of skill and experience is likely to vary between employees which may enable differential prices to be charged for their services based on local knowledge. Thus, for example, higher prices can be charged for more skilled or more popular employees (eg based on customer requests).

The counter-argument

The above arguments tend to support the CE's view of a local pricing policy based on local knowledge of markets and operating conditions. However the counter view may include a few issues:

- By surrendering price control to depot managers there is a loss of control and more uncertainty at the centre.

- Depot managers may lack the experience of setting appropriate prices.

- Customers may in the long run prefer more certainty over prices and thus prefer uniform and stable prices over variable and varying prices.

(2) Implementation

In order to be able to implement the policy of local pricing at depot level, the degree of autonomy of depot managers needs to increase significantly and this raises a series of questions relating to implementation including decision making authority, accountability, the role and competence of depot managers, and internal reporting mechanisms.

Decision making authority – Giving depot managers additional autonomy in setting prices raises the question of whether this should be the only devolution of authority from the centre. For example, it may be difficult to uncouple the pricing decision from other issues surrounding pricing and which arise from a change in price, such as a change in demand. In the above table, the decision to raise the price of IT services by £4 per hour to £36 causes demand to fall from 120,000 hours pa to 100,000 hours pa. The human resource operations of this consequence therefore need to be considered alongside, and possibly in advance of, the pricing decision. To best achieve this, the local manager would also need autonomy over staffing as a consequence of having autonomy over pricing.

Accountability – In devolving decision making there is a corresponding duty of accountability on a depot manager in being responsible for those decisions and their consequences. This is likely to have consequences for internal reporting mechanisms as they report back to the centre.

Training and competence – Depot managers would need the appropriate level of training in order to be competent in their wider role and to enable them to make appropriate pricing and related operating decisions.

Conclusion

Greater flexibility is needed in pricing. One conclusion would be to adopt both the policies of price discrimination based on estimated household incomes and differential pricing of IT and electrical services, but at depot level.

Further analysis of existing information from the market survey at depot level is required to be able to do this. It will require analysing responses for each of the two services according to the two income groupings.

Overall, making prices respond more flexibility to market conditions, service types and customer characteristics will present a more complex pricing structure, but there is significant scope to increase profits if this can be implemented at local level by competent managers with local knowledge and the consequences controlled at central level.

This part was the weakest part of the question for most candidates. Many referred to goal congruence issues, but often without providing examples of a lack of goal congruence.

A few candidates made the point that the geographical boundaries between depots may be unclear, thereby questioning the quality of any relative performance data.

Many candidates talked about customers going to another depot – they were failing to notice the point that this is a home service where an engineer comes to your house and you will be served by a specific depot. Those who discussed implementation issues arising from the change in structure for decision making scored well, but many ignored this element of the question.

57 Forsi Ltd (September 2014)

Marking guide

	Knowledge	Skill	Marks
57.1 Performance analysis/non-financial information	2	16	16
57.2 Exisiting structure	2	5	7
57.3 Knowledge management/implementation	3	6	8
57.4 (a) Subsidiary/forensic science division	3	6	
(b) Change management recommendations	2	5	
			14
	12	38	45

General comments

This is the mini case at 45 marks and also the data analysis question. It was the best attempted question on the paper.

The scenario relates to a company – Forsi Ltd – which provides forensic science services to both public organisations (police, HMRC) and private clients. It was created when the UK government closed its inefficient state forensic science service and four of its leading scientists set up on their own. Forsi experienced rapid growth and quickly had to employ more scientists but over the last two years competition in the market has increased. The company has operated with an informal structure, wanting to minimise bureaucracy and focus on technical expertise. Most support tasks (payroll, accounting etc) are outsourced. Work is organised on a project basis, with an appropriate team created for each specific client request. Recently Forsi's loose structure has started to inhibit growth. There has been a lack of collaboration, with scientists preferring to work independently on each project and with delays because all discussions with clients are still handled by the four initial founders. Forsi has experienced cost overruns as there is little in-house financial control. As a result it has started to lose some contracts to competitors or has had to accept lower margins as a result of fixed price agreements. Forsi has been approached by an Australian multi-national (Aussi) which offers a range of scientific services to global private and public clients. Its forensic science division is the Australian market leader. Aussi wants to buy Forsi but does not want to destroy Forsi's research-centred culture and acknowledges its success to date has been dependent on the founders' knowledge and contacts. Aussi is not sure whether to operate Forsi as a separate subsidiary or a division but whatever the structure selected, Forsi will be required to comply with more stringent targets on price, margins and ROCE. Candidates were provided with a balanced scorecard of financial and non-financial data on Forsi and basic operating data for Aussi.

57.1 Data Analysis

Appendix of calculations

Tutorial note:

A wide range of calculations is provided here for marking purposes. Candidates were not expected to produce all of these for the marks available

Note. Figures in red were given in question.

	Forsi 20Y2	Forsi 20Y3	Aussi Forensic science division 20Y3
Sales revenue £million	5.4	5.088 (2.3% of Aussi)	220.3
Direct Costs £million	4.175	4.165 (2.5% of Aussi)	165.225
Gross profit £million	1.225	0.923 (1.7% of Aussi)	55.075
R&D £million	0.254	0.260 (5.9% of Aussi)	4.4
Marketing £million	0.108	0.090 (1.0% of Aussi)	9.000
Other operating expenses £million	0.268	0.270 (3.1% of Aussi)	8.645
Operating profit £million	0.595	0.303 (1.0% of Aussi)	33.03
Asset value £million	4.02	3.91 (2.1% of Aussi)	183.5
Gross margin	22.7%	18.1%	25.0%
Operating margin	11.2%	6.0%	15.0%
ROCE	14.8%	7.7%	18.0%
R&D as % of sales	4.7%	5.1%	2.0%
Marketing as % of sales	2.0%	1.8%	4.1%
Other operating expenses as % of sales	5.0%	5.3%	3.9%
Order Book as % of revenue	25%	16.8%	29.5%
Order Book (months)	3	2	3.5
No of employees	45	45 (2.25% of Aussi)	2,000
Revenue per employee	120,000	113,067	110,150

	Forsi 20Y2	Forsi 20Y3	Aussi Forensic science division 20Y3
Per project			
Average value of project	50,000	48,000	89,992
Direct cost per project	38,657	39,292	67,494
GP per project	11,343	8,708	22,498
No of projects	108	106 (4.3% of Aussi)	2,448
No of projects completed on time	90 (83%)	81 (76%)	2,179 (89%)
No of projects completed late	18 (17%)	25 (24%)	269 (11%)
No of projects completed in budget	78 (72%)	69 (65%)	2,252 (92%)

Forsi: Year on year change	%
Sales revenue	−5.8
Direct costs	−0.2
Gross profit	−24.7
R&D	+0.2
Marketing	−16.7
Other operating expenses	+0.7
Operating profit	−49.1
Net asset value	−2.7%
No of employees	No change

Forsi: Year on year change	%
No of projects	−1.9
Order book	−36.7

Analysis of performance

Whilst still profitable, Forsi's performance has deteriorated significantly between 20Y2 and 20Y3, with a £312,000 drop in sales revenue (5.8%) and a £292,000 drop in operating profit. As a result, operating profit at £303,000 is only just over half the previous year's figure.

Sales:

Sales revenue has fallen by just under 6%. The number of projects undertaken in the year was broadly similar (106 compared to 108) but the average project value has fallen from £50,000 to £48,000 which may reflect the price pressure that Forsi has been experiencing and the fact that it has had to agree lower prices to avoid losing clients. Forsi is very small in relation to Aussi's forensic science division – its revenue is only 2.3% of Aussi's. At £89,992 Aussi's revenue per project is almost twice that of Forsi's which could be a result of different pricing strategies or projects of a different size/nature.

In addition by the end of 20Y3, the value of Forsi's order book represents two months' worth of sales, compared to three months at the end of 20Y2. This suggests that order levels are falling and could either represent a lack of demand or an increased failure to win client tenders. More information is needed in this area (see below).

Forsi spent £18,000 less on marketing in 20Y3, a drop of 16.7% compared to the previous year, which could have had a negative effect on revenue, given the increasingly competitive environment. Its marketing expenditure as a % of sales is only 1.8% compared to Aussi's 4.1%. It is possible that awareness of the founders' expertise through word-of-mouth recommendations or existing contacts is diminishing and that more marketing needs to be undertaken to raise awareness of the company's services.

Given the increasing number of specialist providers, Forsi may be losing projects in particular areas of forensic science, so an analysis of revenue by field of expertise would be useful.

Revenue per employee is above that for Aussi (£110,150) although it has fallen from £120,000 to £113,067 which could reflect a lack of productivity due to delays experienced when project requirements are being re-negotiated, or an increase in the amount of scientists' time that is non-chargeable. Alternatively it could reflect the pressure on prices that has been discussed previously or the increased number of fixed price projects. Aussi's figure may be lower if it has more administrative staff – the statistic would be more meaningful if information were available to calculate it based on the number of fee earning employees.

Gross margin

The gross margin has fallen from 22.7% to 18.1%. This is below the 25% achieved by Aussi and less than the 20% target that would be required if Forsi was acquired.

Whilst revenue per project has fallen by 4%, direct costs per project have increased by 1.6%. The deterioration in gross margin could reflect a drop in recovery rates – compared to 20Y2, 7 more projects over-ran on time and/or budgeted cost. If clients are increasingly dissatisfied they may be refusing to pay for the over-runs and Forsi may be having to write off time/money spent on the project.

Expenses

With the exception of marketing (discussed above), expenditure on R&D and other operating costs has not changed significantly. As a % of revenue, Forsi spends more on R&D than Aussi, possibly because the latter has greater efficiencies/economies of scale.

ROCE

The halving of operating profit has resulted in a similar drop in ROCE, falling from 14.8% to 7.7%. This is considerably below Aussi's ROCE of 18% and the 15% target that Forsi would need to achieve if it were owned by Forsi.

Lack of management control

The fact that the number of projects over-running on time and/or budget has increased and is considerably worse than that achieved by Aussi suggests that Forsi's founders are not exerting sufficient control over costs and scheduling or that budgets are overly optimistic, perhaps in an attempt to win tenders. In some cases these over-runs may be unavoidable (eg due to additional client demands) but in this case Forsi needs to ensure it has renegotiated passing these on to the client.

Other non-financial information that would be useful:

- Statistics on the number of tenders won vs the number actually submitted, including an analysis of which fields of forensic science these related to

- Details of the number of new clients won and existing clients lost during the year and the split of new projects/repeat business

- Breakdown of projects by private/public sector

- Amount of hours recharged to clients/hours actually spent on projects

- Breakdown of hours worked by scientists between client work and R&D

- Typical project length to establish average size of project team

Examiner's comments:

In requirement 57.1, candidates were asked to analyse the performance of Forsi, contrasting it with Aussi's where appropriate and to suggest other non-financial information that may be useful.

The data analysis section was generally very well answered. Most candidates made some appropriate initial calculations based on the balance scorecard provided, in order to support sensible comments regarding Forsi's deteriorating performance. The majority of candidates examined revenue, margins and return on capital, and attempted to use the non-financial aspects, such as the increase in delays to project completion and the cost overruns, to explain the financial results. Whilst most candidates set out their calculations in an initial table, a minority mixed calculations within their discussion and this sometimes caused them to lose flow and structure or fail to address certain aspects. Some weaker candidates limited their analysis to the movement in figures across the two-year period.

Narrative explanations of relative performance in comparison to Aussi tended to be variable, depending partly on which calculations had been attempted. For example, those candidates who did not calculate ROCE were less able to discuss the shortfall between Forsi's current ROCE and gross margin and the targets that Aussi would require. The best answers compared and contrasted the performance of Aussi and Forsi, highlighting the vast difference in their size and market, and considering their relative performance in respect of the average size of the projects undertaken and their ability to complete on time and to budget.

The poorer answers made little attempt at identifying cause and effect relationships or key trends, for the most part simply re-stating the calculated numbers in terms of ups and downs. Weaker candidates also produced a generic list of additional information required, which was often financial, failing to address the specifics of the requirement which asked for non-financial information.

57.2 Existing structure:

Forsi undertakes specialised work based on expert knowledge. To some extent its structure has not really evolved from that of a simple entrepreneurial one, with the four original founders exerting total control over the running of the business.

One way of analysing Forsi's structure is with reference to Mintzberg's organisational configurations.

The key component (or building block) within Forsi appears to be the operating core, with scientists working directly on providing the technical forensic science service to clients.

Forsi's structure has developed incrementally and reflects the values and behaviour of the four original founders, who form the strategic apex of the organisation and currently control all client relationships.

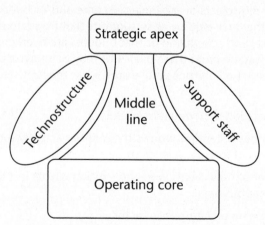

Its existing structure might be seen as Mintzberg's adhocracy or innovative configuration, suitable for a complex dynamic environment.

Key features of Forsi's structure are:

- Research and innovation are key objectives and scientists (operating core) carry out their work independently.

- There is little formalisation (an absence of technostructure) and no layer of middle management (middle line). Staff are likely to be intelligent and self-motivated, with the expertise and knowledge to make the appropriate decisions whilst working in a project.

- Such a structure avoids the trappings of bureaucracy and remains flexible to encourage innovation.

- The number of support staff is limited as these functions (HR, accounting) are largely outsourced.

An alternative model might be Handy's shamrock organisation or flexible firm – with Forsi being seen as a lean organisation comprising a core of essential workers (scientists) providing specialist services to customers and supported by a contractual fringe of outside contractors, whose services are bought in as required.

Whilst the simple, flexible structure promotes innovation and allows Forsi to focus on the activities important for competitive advantage, there are some disadvantages and the informality and lack of control appear to be causing Forsi some difficulties now that it is a bigger organisation:

- The structure is lacking in coordination mechanisms:

- Teams and scientists have a tendency to work in isolation rather than sharing knowledge. Such independence may result in a lack of goal congruence with personal interests being put before shared company ones

- Loose control and lack of financial awareness has led to cost overruns and impact on margins

- The founders acting as a go-between between scientists and clients has led to delays and client complaints

Recommendation:

- It may be better to have project managers responsible for liaison with the client

- Senior management could monitor projects and liaise externally to ensure Forsi is keeping abreast of industry developments, changes in competition/market. However this would necessitate an improved management information system to allow monitoring

Examiner's comments:

Requirement 57.2 requested candidates to discuss the appropriateness of Forsi's existing structure, referring to relevant models. It was well attempted by the vast majority of candidates, who were clearly very well-prepared for this topic. The majority of candidates identified that the informal, largely entrepreneurial structure had initially fostered successful innovation and flexibility in a dynamic environment but was no longer suitable for the growing size of the company and was, at least in part, to blame for Forsi's deteriorating performance discussed in 57.1. Candidates were asked to refer to relevant models and those who discussed Forsi's structure with reference to Mintzberg's organisational forms and/or Handy's shamrock structure produced answers that had more depth than those who limited their discussion to functional, divisional and matrix structures.

57.3 Why knowledge management is important

Knowledge is a key strategic asset for an organisation such as Forsi which is providing a highly technical scientific service. It may have limited tangible assets other than the technical expertise of its people.

As an organisation grows it needs more formal processes to ensure that the wealth of knowledge within the business is being captured and shared. Eg knowledge gleaned by scientists on a project for one police force may assist scientists working on a similar project for another force, thereby reducing the learning curve and cutting time or costs.

It is important that the founders recognise that a formal strategy is required and that knowledge does not just flow round the organisation of its own accord.

Forsi's knowledge management (KM) strategy needs to capture the knowledge that is critical to its competitive advantage and then disseminate and use that knowledge in the decision-making process. Eg KM could help Forsi to identify ways to meet client needs that are better than competitors or to improve processes or develop new and innovative forensic science techniques.

Implementing a knowledge management strategy

Implementing a knowledge management strategy would involve the following steps:

(1) Identifying the knowledge that exists within Forsi

- Human capital eg specific scientific knowledge held by a particular scientist in a particular field or discipline

- Intellectual property (the result of innovation) eg patents over any new techniques developed

- Client data eg lists of client contacts held by founders, details of projects undertaken by client

- Organisational infrastructure (processes and policies) eg the negotiating skills and relationship management tools used by the founders when dealing with clients

(2) Capture/document the knowledge to create some form of knowledge base. This may include capturing knowledge from outside Forsi (eg intelligence on competitors, renowned experts in a particular scientific field, the police's in-house labs)

(3) Disseminate the knowledge to the appropriate people so it can be harnessed to:

- Improve efficiency and performance
- Identify opportunities to provide a better service for customers than competitors
- Innovate new forensic science techniques

(4) Determine ways in which Forsi's knowledge can be developed and tracked. KM also requires an organisation to identify any knowledge it lacks and to spend time investing in improving the knowledge of its employees (eg technical training or update courses) or helping them to use it more effectively (organisational learning)

(5) Ensure that key strategic knowledge is kept secure and confidential within Forsi and does not leak to competitors or is not lost when staff leave eg ensuring all scientists have confidentiality clauses in their contracts, protecting IP wherever possible

Some knowledge will be explicit eg particular forensic science procedures or protocols. Other knowledge may be tacit (in the heads of the scientists and/or founders and therefore invisible).

It is more difficult to harness the tacit knowledge and the informal networks and communities or practices that exist within an organisation. However encouraging increased collaboration between scientists would help Forsi to transform tacit knowledge into explicit knowledge.

Forsi needs to try and break down the barriers to sharing eg scientists may be protective of their knowledge and feel reluctant to give away their value or feel that they are losing their position of influence or professional respect if they share their expertise with everyone.

Encouraging increased collaboration between scientists and creating a culture of openness where knowledge sharing is rewarded, would help Forsi to transform tacit knowledge into explicit knowledge.

In a field such as forensic science negative knowledge is also important. A company with an effective knowledge management process will be able to build a permanent body of awareness of 'negative knowledge' which provides information to improve on – those approaches that didn't work out as hoped or anticipated, or the reasons why a particular tender was lost.

A KM strategy is likely to place significant reliance on information technology and systems and Forsi may need to invest more money in this area.

Electronic tools such as online bulletin boards, blogs, intranets and wikis may all facilitate knowledge sharing.

Examiner's comments:

Requirement 57.3 asked candidates, on the assumption that the business was not taken over, to explain why knowledge management is important to Forsi and recommend steps to implement a knowledge management strategy. Answers to this requirement, which was the least well done of all the paper, were very polarised and only a small minority of candidates scored the maximum marks. The weakest candidates knew very little about knowledge management or misinterpreted the requirement and wrote about the need for a management information system. Better candidates identified that scientific knowledge was a key strategic asset for Forsi and a source of competitive advantage. They went on to discuss how IP might be protected and the steps Forsi could take to capture and disseminate the knowledge that its scientists and founders possess.

57.4 (a) **Choice of operating structure**

Irrespective of the structure chosen, ownership by Aussi is likely to provide Forsi with additional administrative support and may reduce the need for outsourcing.

Forsi will also have greater access to funding.

Better financial controls and a focus on efficiency and returns may prevent acceptance of unprofitable or unacceptable projects.

Combined organisational knowledge is likely to increase as the businesses differ in geography, culture and operating practices, so sharing experience and best practice may enhance activities for both Aussi and Forsi.

However:

The need for central sign-off of projects by Australia may delay the speed of response so Forsi could lose tenders to competition

Rejection of a project purely on financial grounds may overlook the fact that it leads to repeat business or other more profitable work

Ownership by a larger global company inevitably brings more bureaucracy which could stifle Forsi's innovation and research culture.

Specific issues relating to the two different options for structuring the management of Forsi:

Integration of Forsi within the existing division of Aussi

If Forsi is fully incorporated into Aussi as part of its forensic science operating division, then its strategy and operations will be formalised centrally.

This may help with knowledge sharing etc – Aussi is likely to have procedures in place.

Forsi may be able to increase efficiency by benchmarking its activities against the rest of the division.

Integration may also generate economies of scale. The parts of the business will be geographically separate but there may be economies in areas like procurement.

However, having too great a technostructure would seem to run counter to the needs of an innovative business and direct supervision is unlikely to be welcomed by scientists, who are used to working independently.

Decision making could become slower and inflexible and barriers between scientists and clients may increase.

Some UK clients may have a negative attitude to Australian ownership, especially those in the public sector. Conversely being part of the acknowledged market leader in Australia/Asia may give Forsi credibility at tenders and help win more business/public sector projects.

Aussi's forensic division may be more conservative in their attitude to risk which might affect the nature of projects undertaken.

Aussi's main activities are in Australia and Asia so it may not make sense to have European activities integrated in the same area when markets, regulations etc may be quite different.

It will be harder for Aussi to assess how Forsi is doing if its activities are subsumed within the existing division – Forsi will only be a very small part of the existing activities.

Separate subsidiary company

Forsi would have more freedom to operate as it has done before, retaining its research-centred culture.

Forsi's founders may continue to negotiate its own projects and have more flexibility re pricing and margins, although it will still be subject to Aussi's project screening procedures so will not be completely autonomous.

Objectives of the subsidiary may become more determined by financial considerations and the need to meet Aussi's targets.

Forsi's culture could change and this may affect the behaviour of the workforce who appear happy with the current loose informal structure.

Australian ownership may be less visible to clients if Forsi continues to operate as a separate subsidiary.

Forsi would be a very small subsidiary compared to Aussi's existing division.

Recommendation:

Forsi should be operated as a subsidiary. Aussi needs to create some overarching management principles to guide activities but not overemphasise rules, regulations and procedures, otherwise research and innovation will be stifled.

ROCE and margin targets may need to be different than for the existing division to take account of the different market place, clients etc.

(b) **Change management**

The acquisition will involve rapid one-off change to the culture and structure of the organisation and is likely to be viewed by Forsi's employees as transformational. It is likely to involve changes to the way activities are carried out, new management structures and new reward systems.

The change is likely to be greater if Forsi is to be incorporated within the division of Aussi than if it is to continue as a stand-alone subsidiary. The way in which Aussi manages the change will affect the future success of the business.

Integration will require a careful change management programme.

If the founders have agreed to sell then they may encourage and support the change programme, particularly if they are involved in any sort of earn-out. The founders may therefore be able to help break down any forces resisting change.

Intelligent staff such as the scientists employed by Forsi will want to feel like they are being offered the chance to participate in the change process. One danger of consultation however is that should they provide input which is ignored they might become demotivated. Thus some careful negotiation and trade-offs may be required to accommodate the wishes of all parties involved in the change.

Open communication as to the reasons for the change in structure may help Forsi's staff to accept it, although care needs to be taken that such education is not done in a patronising way. Power, coercion or manipulation are unlikely to work with the majority of the scientists and may result in the loss of key staff.

Examiner's comments:

The assumption in requirement 57.4 was that Forsi's founders did agree to be taken over by Aussi. Candidates needed to discuss whether Forsi should be operated as a subsidiary or as part of Aussi's forensic science division, and to recommend how Aussi should manage the change when the takeover is announced. Again this requirement was well attempted.

Most were comfortable discussing the choice of operating structure, in the light of Aussi's desire to retain Forsi's research-centred culture. Better candidates discussed the impact the choice might have on performance monitoring, given Aussi's project screening process and requirements for target returns, and provided a preliminary recommendation as to the best option. However some weaker candidates seemed to overlook the fact that the two businesses were very dissimilar in size and geographic location. As in previous sittings, candidates were well versed in the technical knowledge for the change management requirement but an inability to apply this knowledge was again evident on the part of the weaker candidates. A key issue here was that the nature of the change, the likely barriers and the appropriate change management practice were dependent on the choice of structure, a fact that the better candidates identified.

58 ToyL Ltd (September 2014)

	Knowledge	Skill	Marks
58.1 Appraisal of business plan/recommendations	5	12	15
58.2 Benefits of outsourcing	2	4	6
58.3 Information requirements	2	8	9
	9	24	30

General comments

This question was also well attempted. The scenario concerns ToyL, a provider of educational toys which will be sold to individual customers (parents, grandparents, children) and wholesale purchasers (schools and daycare centres/nurseries). ToyL is a start-up business which has developed three distinct educational toys that use interactive technology to teach young children number skills, alphabet skills and phonics. The company has been founded by Pavel and Rosemary, a team of husband (IT specialist) and wife (educational consultant). The toys are in prototype form but functionally complete. The product line is expected to grow over time as new ideas are generated. While prototypes will be designed and manufactured in-house, production will be outsourced. A website will be used as the key marketing tool. ToyL hopes to be profitable by the end of year one and expects a steep increase in sales for the next few years. ToyL is in the process of producing a business plan to attract funding and a draft version is included in the scenario.

58.1 Report on draft Business Plan

To: Rosemary and Pavel Bochev
From: AN Accountant
Date: September 20Y4

This analysis is done in two parts:

- The quality and completeness of the existing sections of the plan
- Additional sections or information that would be relevant

The current plan is lacking in critical financial detail and this is discussed further below.

Quality and completeness of existing plan

(1) *Executive summary*

One of the most important sections of a business plan is the executive summary. The executive summary should grab the attention of potential investors, help them understand what ToyL is about and the implications for their investment, and make them want to read the plan in more detail.

Pavel and Rosemary have correctly identified that although it is the first thing that will appear in the plan, it should be the last thing to be written.

It will need to highlight the key points from the other sections:

- Overview of the business
- Why it will be successful
- What finance is being sought
- What financial performance an investor can expect
- Any major risks and how they can be mitigated

(2) *Introduction and management team*

This section should introduce the business and the owners' vision for its future. Anyone investing in ToyL needs to have faith in Pavel and Rosemary's management skills and commitment to the business.

There is insufficient detail about the management team. The business is clearly going to be very dependent on the two directors and a prospective investor is likely to want more information to assess the risk that this creates:

- Ages

- Personal objectives

- Financial management experience

- CVs (include in an Appendix)

- Other personnel that the business is planning to employ to address any skills gaps – a key concern for any investor would be Rosemary and Pavel's apparent lack of financial expertise

(3) *Products*

This section clearly explains ToyL's products. However since the business is at a very early stage, it will be important to provide evidence about how realistic the idea is:

- USPs compared to existing products on the market
- Evidence of field testing
- Feedback on prototypes and modifications required
- Cost and time required to get product ready for market
- Details of who will manufacture the products
- Details of toy safety regulations and ToyL's compliance
- Outline of ideas for future products

(4) *Marketing*

The target market is clear but the language used to describe its nature and size ('we think', 'about 3.3 million', 'around 8% pa') is vague and does not inspire confidence. Evidence to show that it is a viable market is required; as it stands some of the figures seem optimistic, especially in relation to growth in the target market. The plan needs to describe the factors that drive this growth.

A more detailed marketing plan is necessary. It seems unlikely that reliance on the website will be sufficient.

More information is needed on pricing:

- What is the pricing strategy?
- How will prices compare to competitors?
- What level of price discount will be offered to/expected by wholesale clients?

Details of any market research undertaken should be included in the Appendix.

(5) *Competition*

This section should explain how ToyL believes it is going to compete effectively.

The information about competitors is not sufficiently detailed. It is not clear whether ToyL intends to take on the global market leaders or the regional manufacturers.

More information about the customer base and market share of main rivals would be helpful.

Evidence is required to support the superiority claimed for ToyL's products.

(6)   *Strategy and operations*

The title of this section does not really match the content which is a mixture of strategy and financial information. In relation to strategy, this section could include the business' overall mission and objectives. It should also evaluate the alternative strategies open to the business in terms of market positioning. More information could be included on supply chain management and the plans to outsource production.

The figures include projected revenue but there is no information on costs or prospective margins. The expectation that the business will break-even in the first year seems quite optimistic and more evidence is required to substantiate the projected sales of £367,000 in year two and £475,000 in year three (see below).

Additional sections or information that would be relevant :

- *Financial information*

   As this is primarily a plan to attract additional finance this is a critical section and needs to be comprehensive. It should clearly identify:

   –   What the finance needs are

      How much money is being sought from investor(s) and in what format? How has any initial capital been spent (eg what is the breakdown of the £24,000 set-up costs) and how will any new funds be used?

   –   What the financial future of the business might look like

      The plan needs to include detailed profit projections and cash flow forecasts covering a period of at least three years.

   –   The business plan should have a clear statement of underlying assumptions

      An investor will be keen to assess the realism of the business plan and forecasts. It is important not to be over-optimistic.

Since the future is uncertain, it is important to include here anything that might change the forecasts or mean that things don't quite go to plan. A prospective investor will ask 'What if?' questions. Eg: What will happen to the expected profit if sales fall by 5%? What sales will need to be achieved to break even?

- *Risks and mitigation/contingency plans*

   Some business owners are reluctant to include information on the business' weaknesses or on business threats. However, a prospective investor will want to know that the owner has considered the risks facing the business and that there is a plan to manage them. Risks facing ToyL include:

   –   Reliance on two owner directors

   –   Toys aimed at young children – onerous health and safety requirements

   –   Highly competitive market, lots of substitutes, easily copied

   –   Products rely on technology which is rapidly changing, so they are likely to have a short life and need to be updated/amended frequently

   –   Environmental/industry issues (PESTEL/Five Forces analysis)

- *Appendix of supporting documentation*

   So that the plan is concise and focussed, any detailed information should be included here, rather than in the main body of the plan.

   This section should also include any other information necessary to present a full picture of the business/its owners:

   –   Statement of owners' personal wealth
   –   Copies of personal tax returns
   –   CVs of Pavel and Rosemary
   –   Details of any market research undertaken
   –   Copies of any patents/product safety certificates
   –   Letters of intent or contracts with suppliers/wholesalers

Requirement 58.1 asked candidates to critically assess the content of the draft business plan and make recommendations as to how the document may be improved in order to attract the necessary investors. Although many candidates were clearly familiar with the knowledge required (the pro-forma contents of a business plan), weaker candidates struggled to apply this in the context of a plan to attract potential investment. Candidates who appreciated the need to focus their content on the end user of the document, and who wrote in an appropriate style, structuring their answer using the headings from the draft plan, scored very highly. The key here was to appreciate that the draft plan made a number of claims about the superiority of the proposed products but that the lack of substantive data/evidence in relation to the products/markets, and the absence of any real detail about the amount of finance or the expected future performance needed, would be of major concern to a prospective investor. This needed to be addressed as a priority. It is likely that an investor might also want more information on the directors with whom they were establishing a relationship, and on how Rosemary and Pavel intend to handle their lack of financial expertise. Weak answers often spent far too long appraising the existing sections of the plan, sometimes with little structure, and then identified the need for more financial information almost as an after-thought at the end. Key elements which should have been included in the business plan, such as a focused executive summary plus financial forecasts, were ignored by many candidates.

58.2 An outsourcing model is likely to be appropriate for ToyL for a number of reasons.

(1) Neither Pavel nor Rosemary has any experience of manufacturing operations/supply chain. An outsource company may provide greater expertise.

(2) Outsourcing will keep overhead costs to a minimum, making all production costs variable and reducing operating gearing.

(3) This will allow the management team to focus on marketing and new product development which makes best use of their skills.

(4) Financial risks will be reduced by not committing to the expense of a manufacturing facility. An outsourcing model will allow greater flexibility.

(5) Outsourcing will increase the scalability of the business model, which will be particularly important if ToyL succeeds in attracting a number of wholesale clients.

On the face of it outsourcing would seem sensible, however ToyL will need to consider:

- The impact on variable costs of production
- Control over quality
- Bargaining power as ToyL may be small relative to suppliers

Examiner's comments:

In requirement 58.2, candidates were requested to explain the benefits of outsourcing as a production model for ToyL. The majority of candidates were clearly well prepared for and scored very highly on this requirement.

58.3 The information requirements will depend on the purpose for which the information is required.

Management team

Pavel and Rosemary will be managing the business on a day-to-day basis. As a result they will require information for planning, control and decision making.

Internal information

Quite a lot of the information for control purposes is likely to be operational in nature. They have identified that the implementation of strict financial controls is a critical success factor – they will need to monitor the company's performance in terms of profitability, cost control and working capital management

This means that typically they will find management accounting information more relevant than financial reporting information as they will require:

- Detailed analysis of costs and revenues
- Reports comparing actual performance and budget, showing variances
- Detailed monthly information, analysed by product and type of customer
- Development costs incurred on various products

External information

Pavel and Rosemary will need to decide which product lines to pursue and how to price them, what distribution channels to use, and how to promote the products.

To do this they will need to analyse information on the market they are operating in: competitors, market share, new products launched, educational trends etc.

They will need to collect data on the effectiveness of different marketing initiatives.

Non-financial information

Information should also focus on non-financial measures and the CSF's identified eg customer feedback.

Equity investors

Private investors will be focussed on the quality of their investment and the returns they can expect.

The extent of the information they require may depend on the size of their stake and the nature of the role they decide to take eg whether they are involved in some non-executive capacity.

They are likely to want information about the performance achieved by ToyL in summary or overview form. Typically this will be more like financial reporting information.

It will also relate to the longer term strategic picture, including future expected returns and value on exit. An investor will want to monitor the overall profitability, liquidity and gearing of the business.

They will also want to assess the quality of the management team (Pavel and Rosemary), their strategy and their ability to manage the risks attached to the investment.

Data about Toyl is likely to be benchmarked against other investments/sector/economy norms._

Examiner's comments:

Requirement 58.3 asked candidates to explain how the information requirements of Pavel and Rosemary as managers will be different from the information requirements of the additional private investors, once the business is operational. Surprisingly this was one of the least well attempted requirements. The key here was to identify the purpose for which any information was to be used. Most candidates appreciated that whilst Rosemary and Pavel would be interested in information to manage the day-to-day operations, private investors would probably be more interested in evaluating the return on their investment. Having done so however, weaker candidates talked in generic terms and did not go on to give sufficiently detailed examples of the type of information that would be useful to each party. Only the best candidates identified that the exact requirements of the investor(s) may depend on the size and nature of their investment and therefore risk, and the extent to which they are involved in the business eg in a non-executive capacity. Some candidates started by applying Mendelow's stakeholder matrix, but often, having identified the likely interest and power of the investor, were unsure of the implications for the information needs of managers and investors.

Marking guide

	Knowledge	Skill	Marks
59.1 Sustainable enterprise	2	5	7
59.2 Ethics of marketing	3	6	8
59.3 Two proposals	3	9	10
	8	20	25

General comments

The third question, worth 25 marks, was the least well attempted overall, largely as a result of requirement 59.2. The scenario relates to a social enterprise 'Ontap'. Its founder, Nala, is a keen athlete who was fed up with the amount she was spending on bottled water and the level of plastic bottle waste. The Ontap concept involves a water bottle, made from recycled aluminium foil for use by athletes, commuters and students. Once purchased from Ontap, the bottle can be taken to a range of participating cafes and shops (currently only in central London) and re-filled with tap-water for free. The Ontap website provides a list of tap locations and there is also a free mobile app showing refill sites, all of which prominently display the Ontap logo. 70% of the business' profits are donated to fund clean water projects in India and used to raise awareness of the damaging effects of bottled water on the environment. The business has been successful and is keen to expand. Two options are being considered: (1) a corporate scheme whereby companies will purchase co-branded Ontap bottles to replace the water cooler and plastic cups typically found in most offices; and (2) geographical expansion outside London. Information was also provided in the scenario about the marketing activities of the bottled water companies and supermarkets.

59.1 Sustainable enterprise

A sustainable enterprise is one that takes account of social and environmental returns as well as financial ones. As a social enterprise, on the face of it Ontap would appear to be such a business.

A key issue is the concept that a sustainable organisation is one that has a long term orientation and does not just focus on short-term results and measures when making decisions. As a social enterprise, Ontap's objectives will be wider than just financial. Its goals will be externally as well as internally focussed and will include taking account of customers'/partners' business objectives and meeting the needs of the Indian communities it is serving. Ontap will want to optimise its profits (rather than maximise them), in order to give more money away to fund water projects and raise educational awareness.

To be financially sustainable (ie to survive in the long term), a business needs an understanding of the changing external environment so that it can respond and adapt to the opportunities and threats presented by it. So for example Nala has developed a product in response to society's changing attitudes to bottled water and environmental waste.

Sustainability is therefore an issue for any business in relation to risk mitigation, innovation and the development of new skills and capabilities to create and sustain competitive advantage over rivals. One question over Ontap's financial sustainability will be whether refillable bottles prove to be a fad and/or whether other businesses copy the idea, although in a sense this would help Ontap in its desire to persuade individuals to move away from bottled water in order to protect the environment.

In the context of environmental sustainability, an organisation should only use resources at a rate that allows them to be replenished in order to ensure they will continue to be available.

Ontap's whole concept is aiming to protect the environment by persuading individuals to move away from bottled water, thereby reducing the volume of bottles that end up in landfill. It donates profits to education campaigns and clean water projects and its own bottle is made from recycled

A socially sustainable organisation is one where decision making is linked to respect for people, communities and the environment. An increased focus on sustainability should support investment in human capital, engaging in innovation and establishing more reliable supply chains even if these do not maximise short-term financial performance. A key issue for Ontap will be ensuring that the supplier(s) of its bottles and the cafes and restaurants it partners with also act in a socially responsible manner.

Conclusion

In social and environmental terms, Ontap would appear to constitute a sustainable enterprise. The steps Nala is proposing to capitalise on the success of the business may help ensure it is also a financially sustainable one.

Examiner's comments:

In requirement 59.1 candidates were asked to discuss the extent to which Ontap is a sustainable enterprise. A significant number of candidates started their discussion with the Brundtland definition of sustainability but did not necessarily explore how this related to the concept of a sustainable enterprise. Many candidates then limited their discussion by concentrating on either the environmental aspects or the financial aspects of Ontap's sustainability and it was extremely rare to see a discussion of all three aspects of sustainability: economic, social and environmental. Clearly, Ontap is striving for environmental sustainability, but the extent to which it is financially sustainable as a model may be more questionable. Disappointingly, despite having been asked to assess the extent of Ontap's sustainability, candidates often failed to reach a conclusion on this matter.

59.2 Ethics of marketing

Bottled water manufacturers

An ethical argument sometimes raised against marketing is that it wastes resources by selling people things that they don't want or using promotional techniques to persuade people that they are dissatisfied without them.

This criticism could perhaps be levied at the bottled water manufacturers, who have spent significant resources on advertising to create brand/lifestyle images (eg Evian roller babies) in order to persuade consumers to buy water which they could otherwise choose to get free from our taps.

Some would argue that charging money for something that is freely available or certainly cheap to obtain in order to make a profit for shareholders is unethical and does not demonstrate corporate responsibility. However marketing is undertaken by most organisations so is a reality in the commercial world.

One aspect of the marketing mix is 'Product'. The bottled water product itself could also be argued to lead to environmental pollution. The financial costs to both the consumer and the environment are high:

- The cost of the actual product
- Energy required in production
- Pollution created as a result of the production process
- Transportation costs
- Packaging material that has to be discarded (75% of the 18bn bottles end up in landfill)

The way marketing is carried out may also sometimes cause ethical concerns. Information about the content and effects of products needs to be clear otherwise there is an issue of transparency, particularly if the manufacturers, either deliberately or by omission, suggest their product is something that it is not. Hence the example given in the scenario of the UK supermarkets being criticised when it became apparent that some of their own-brand bottled water was simply filtered, purified tap water.

However most businesses will abide by industry and voluntary codes of practice in how they promote their products and would argue therefore that they are behaving responsibly in marketing their products.

The bottled water companies might also argue that consumers have a free choice and, provided they are given clear information, it is up to the buyer to decide whether to buy or to choose not to buy if they think the product is unethical.

Such companies might also argue that there is an ethical good that comes from the marketing of their product in the form of creating employment and jobs. Some of the bottled water companies have also started to try and address ethical criticisms by donating funds to promote clean drinking water in the developing world or selling more ecologically responsible products, using recycled bottles eg Volvic's Drink 1 give 10 campaign or the One Foundation.

Ontap

Marketing will be undertaken by Ontap in relation to:

- Sale of water bottles
- Promotion of business in order to attract cafes and restaurants as partners
- Education relating to environmental impact of buying and drinking bottled water

Ontap's product is not a luxury good – it is aiming to fill a distinct need, saving customers money and protecting the environment at the same time, so it is unlikely to be subject to the same degree of criticism.

In promoting a more ecologically responsible product, aimed at persuading its target audience to voluntarily change behaviour and revert to tap water, Ontap's marketing could be argued to reduce waste and save resources. Also it is aimed at steering people to products that are helpful to them and to society.

However Ontap will face a conflict between spending resources on marketing and generating more profits to donate to good causes. By harnessing social media, the use of logos in cafés and restaurants and on bottles to build its brand image, Ontap may be able to keep its marketing spend to a minimum.

A possible criticism of Ontap might be that, like the bottled water companies, it is also trying to sell consumers a product (in this case a bottle) when they could just ask for free tap water. Also if Ontap's business model proves not to be sustainable, customers will have wasted £8 on a bottle that they may not then be able to refill for free if there are no longer participating cafes.

Overall Ontap's marketing is likely to be seen as more ethical and transparent than some other companies in the bottled water industry. Certainly, since Ontap is a not–for–profit organisation, society is likely to be less cynical about its motives compared to the for-profit bottled water companies.

Examiner's comments:

Part 59.2 asked candidates to compare and contrast the ethics of the marketing activities of Ontap with its competitors in the bottled water industry. This is only the second time that ethical marketing has been specifically examined (it was last set in September 2012) and the requirement was poorly done by many candidates. Some did apply the transparency, fairness and effect decision-making approach, which tended to at least ensure they were talking in ethical terms and applying a structured thought process. Only the best candidates provided an initial discussion of ethical marketing principles and the arguments for and against marketing in the context of the activities of Ontap and the bottled water companies (providing choice/ raising awareness/ promoting responsible products vs wasting resources/persuading consumers to buy products they don't need/attempting to portray products as something they are not). Better answers pointed out that, whilst attempting to sell tap water as bottled mineral water lacked transparency, attempts to strengthen brand image through marketing is common place and legal and not necessarily unethical, providing industry advertising standards are adhered to. A small minority did question whether Ontap's own marketing activities were in reality that different, since under the umbrella of corporate social responsibility they were also hoping to make money by marketing a product that in theory people could obtain for free, and that if their business model is not financially sustainable, people will have wasted £8 on a bottle they cannot then use for its intended purpose. Answers to the ethics requirement, which is a consistent feature of the exam, continue to be variable and – as has been said before – candidates wishing to score well are advised to adopt some form of framework for their answer and to produce a balanced argument rather than a one-sided discussion.

59.3 Expansion strategies

Nala's desire to expand – general factors to consider

- Expansion will require finance which may not be available given that a significant proportion of Ontap's profits are donated

- It is likely to be harder for Nala to control a bigger business

- Ontap will need to be sure it can source sufficient supply of water bottles from ethical suppliers

- The business is likely to need to expand by taking on more staff

- There is a limited market – once a consumer has bought a bottle they don't need to replace it

- Will the Ontap concept prove to be a passing fad?

- Product concept is very easy for others to copy

- If you are an existing customer in the restaurant/café/bar you don't need a water bottle. Also Ontap cannot prevent people refilling their own bottles and containers.

- Ontap may face reaction/competition from bottled water companies

Corporate sales scheme

- This will generate significant volumes from persuading one company to buy (less time, cost and effort) although fulfilling the order may be problematic.

- Ontap needs to target businesses which want to be more environmentally responsible. Companies who are keen to improve their image may be prepared to sign up

- A partnership with a large blue chip company will enhance Ontap's reputation and co-branded bottles will raise awareness

- This idea may be popular with staff – Ontap could get existing customers to lobby their employers on Ontap's behalf

- The downside is that Ontap will be relatively small in relation to a large corporate buyer, which may insist on a substantial volume discount. Ontap's image and reputation could be badly affected if the wrong 'partner' is chosen, and Ontap's ability to source sufficient bottles may be a problem

- Perhaps Ontap could offer a corporate customer a trial scheme to start with

Geographical expansion

- It would be easiest achieved by targetting national and regional chains eg pizza restaurants

- Getting first mover advantage and wider national coverage may create barriers to entry for the competition

- Cafes can also act as sales outlets for the bottles which would increase the potential market

- Ontap should be able to find appropriate partners as the cafes benefit from a page on the Ontap website, increased footfall, free marketing via Ontap's app. They can also attract additional customers rather than replacement ones as they will still also be selling bottled water to other consumers

- Again Ontap will need to be careful about the image/ethics of the cafes and restaurants it chooses to partner with.

- This option is likely to be harder for Nala to control than the corporate option and would result in slower growth, at least initially.

Recommendation:

The options may not both be mutually exclusive – Nala's ability to pursue them will be limited by Ontap's resources in terms of people and finance, and its ability to source bottles.

Both are probably sensible ways of expanding.

60 Confo plc (December 2014)

Marking guide

	Knowledge	Skill	Marks
60.1 Transfer price	3	7	9
60.2 Perfromance	2	15	15
60.3 Recovery plan	4	12	15
60.4 Ethics	3	5	7
	12	39	46

General comments

This is the mini case worth 46 marks and also the main data analysis question.

The scenario is based on a manufacturer of confectionery products, Confo, which also owns and franchises retail outlets, which sell the company's products. Following a period of difficult trading, Confo implemented a three-year recovery plan which: closed a number of owned outlets, reopening some of these as franchised outlets; opened a new commercial division; and opened a new export division. There was also a change in the way the manufacturing division priced transfers to owned and franchised outlets. The change was from cost plus 20% to full cost, with franchisees also paying an increased fixed annual fee. One year into the recovery plan, the board undertook a review of progress. This review showed that the overall performance of the company had deteriorated. An additional ethical issue has arisen whereby the procurement manager of a major customer had been asking for gifts of sweets from a Confo sales manager. These requests were small in value at first, but increased in amount and frequency over time. Their eventual cessation by Confo led to the customer withdrawing its custom.

60.1 Transfer prices

A transfer price (TP) is the price at which one division in a group sells its products or services to another division in the same group.

The transfer prices will be important for Confo as they have a number of implications:

- They determine the profits of divisions. If the Manufacturing Division charges a high transfer price then most of the total profit from company sales will be attributed to it, with less to the other divisions. This will give a false measure of performance for all divisions.

- As the price to franchisees is the same as the transfer price to the owned shops, this may impact upon the willingness of third parties (favourably or unfavourably) to take up franchises and the volume of goods they purchase whilst a franchisee.

- If high transfer prices are passed on to ultimate customers then sales volumes may fall and overall profits may be distorted.

- Inappropriate transfer prices can lead to internal conflict between divisions. As shops only sell Confo's confectionery, the Retail Division cannot access outside markets to obtain lower cost products from third parties. The Manufacturing Division is therefore a monopoly supplier to owned shops and to franchisees and, from 1 October 20Y3, to the Commercial and Export Divisions.

Pre-1 October 20Y3 transfer pricing system

The transfer pricing system pre-1 October 20Y3 was on a full cost plus 20% basis.

The Manufacturing Division

From the perspective of the Manufacturing Division, the cost-plus formula guaranteed an operating profit margin of 20%. This meant that any cost inefficiencies could be passed on to the Retail Division with an additional mark-up. Perversely, this could mean that the more inefficient the Manufacturing Division was, the more profit it made.

There does not appear to be any rationale for the 20% and this figure appears to be arbitrary. More meaningful is the mark-up overall for the company.

A further concern is that, although fixed costs are not as large as variable costs, they are significant. In attempting to recover fixed costs per unit then an estimate needed to be made at the beginning of the year, not just of total fixed costs to be incurred, but also of the output volume to be achieved in order to determine budgeted fixed cost per unit and hence price. Any error would result in an under- or over-recovery of fixed costs.

A related problem is that costs (fixed and variable) need to be allocated to each type of product to set each transfer price. Given that production is likely to be interdependent between different products, costs are incurred jointly on different products and it can be difficult to identify cost drivers to separate them in order to be able to calculate each product's transfer price.

Conversely, however, there are a number of positive points that could be made for Confo's former transfer pricing system:

- The same prices were being successfully charged commercially to franchisees which may imply it was at (or below) the market rate. However, in this case, franchisees were also paying a fixed fee which needs to be considered alongside the transfer price to determine viability for the franchisees.

- The full cost may be budgeted costs rather than actual so any cost overrun would be incurred by the Manufacturing Division rather than the Retail Division (although the data shows 20% related to actual cost, it could be that the budget equalled actual).

The Retail Division

The Retail Division had no control over the transfer price it paid to the Manufacturing Division and there was no alternative supplier of confectionery it could use. The transfer prices therefore had significant implications for the validity of its status as a profit centre. Being a profit centre would imply that divisional managers had significant control over costs and revenues, but this appears not to have been the case. As a consequence, the divisional loss of £400,000 for the Retail Division had little meaning.

In favour of the transfer prices, it could be that the Confo board had set cost plus 20% as their best estimate of the wholesale market value of the confectionery. The fact that there are no identical confectionery products being sold by rival companies makes this difficult to substantiate.

Post-1 October 20Y3 transfer pricing system

The transfer pricing system post-1 October 20Y3 is on a full cost basis. This treats the Manufacturing Division as a cost centre and the other divisions (Retail, Commercial and Export) therefore recognise the full profit to be made from the sale by the company.

The Manufacturing Division

The Manufacturing Division is now a cost centre and so its performance cannot be measured on profit, but rather on its ability to control costs (eg against budget). An example of how well it has performed in this respect is the reduction in fixed costs compared with the previous year (see below).

Given the franchisees are also acquiring the goods at the same full cost, manufacturing has few incentives to promotes sales to franchisees as there is no profit. The only advantage for the Manufacturing Division of more sales to franchisees is that fixed costs are being spread over more units of output thereby increasing its cost efficiency.

The Retail, Commercial and Export Divisions

These divisions are profit centres and have the advantage of acquiring inventories at cost price, whereas rivals would need to pay outside suppliers wholesale market rates including a mark-up for profit.

In terms of incentives, these divisions may be motivated to over-order from Manufacturing Division or under-price to consumers/customers compared to rivals as they can acquire confectionery more cheaply.

Alternative methods of transfer pricing

There may be distortions in incentives given that internal transfer prices and prices to franchisees are unlikely to be at wholesale market rates.

An alternative system of transfer pricing would be to make transfers at market rates.

This could be done by estimating the wholesale market value of each type of sweet by comparison to rivals' products (albeit there are no identical products).

A further alternative would be to let divisional directors negotiate the transfer prices by discussion in a bargaining process. This may cause conflict, but would result in an agreed set of transfer prices, rather than a centrally imposed set. It may also tend towards market prices over time. However, the problem with this is that the strongest negotiator may dominate, possibly providing a sub-optimal outcome overall.

Conclusion

Transfer prices should be set by negotiation where the outcome is influenced strongly by market prices charged to third party customers (or to franchisees) in a competitive market.

Examiner's comments

Answers were variable in quality. A significant minority failed to explain the motivational aspects of transfer pricing, particularly for the manufacturing division. For example, some considered the revised transfer pricing approach as not motivating managers in this division to control costs. Only a few candidates appreciated that any revised performance management/reward approach would incorporate success in cost control for the Manufacturing Division, as opposed to success in generating profits. Even fewer made the point that the downside could be a reduction in product quality in pursuit of lower costs.

Of those who referred to goal congruence, many did not explain this in the context of the question. The same observation applies to discussion of alternative transfer pricing approaches. With reference to transfer prices at opportunity cost, there appeared to be no appreciation of the fact that the manufacturing division only supplies internally and is a monopoly supplier to the shops. Better answers did refer to the use of market prices in this context, but normally did not consider that these may be difficult to determine, given the unique nature of the firm's products. Weaker candidates did not justify the alternative methods of transfer pricing and instead just listed various methods (such as variable cost plus, fixed cost plus, market prices, negotiated prices) without any explanation or discussion. A small minority of candidates discussed methods of pricing in general rather than of transfer pricing.

	20Y3 Owned shops	20Y4 Owned shops	20Y3 Manufacturing	20Y4 Manufacturing
Revenue per shop £	160,000	180,000		
Operating profit per shop £	–2,667	16,500		
Revenue per product £	2	2	1.50	1.25
Operating profit per product £	–0.033	0.183	0.25	0
Total cost per product £			1.25	1.25
Operating profit margin (profit/revenue %)	–1.67%	9.17%	16.67%	0%

Profit from franchisees:

	20Y3 £'000	20Y4 £'000
Profit on transfers from manufacturing (8,100*20/120)	1,350	0
Fees	1,200	2,500
	2,550	2,500
Profit per franchisee shop £'000	28,333	20,833

Manufacturing costs

	20Y3	20Y4
Fixed costs per unit	50p	50p
Variable costs per unit	75p	75p
Transfer price	£1.50	£1.25

Total profit for Retail and Manufacturing

	20Y3 £'000	20Y4 £'000
Manufacturing	4,350	0
Retail	(400)	1,320
Fees	1,200	2,500
Total operating profit	5,150	3,820

Overall performance of Retail and Manufacturing

In comparing the data for 20Y3 and 20Y4 for Retail and Manufacturing Divisions, four significant elements of the recovery plan have occurred. These are:

- The closure of 70 owned shops to scale down the owned network significantly

- Opening 30 new franchised shops in replacement of some owned shops

- Transfers from Manufacturing Division at full cost in 20Y4, rather than full cost plus 20% in 20Y3

- More than doubling, in total, of the fixed franchise fee from £1.2m to £2.5m

These decisions distort underlying data trends and therefore impact on any comparable assessment of overall performance. This makes like-for-like comparisons difficult for the underlying elements of the business.

Note: The Commercial and Export Divisions are new lines of business and are analysed separately.

Revenue – owned outlets

Total revenue for owned shops has declined by 40% from £24m in 20Y3 to £14.4m in 20Y4. Similarly, the volume of sales (number of items sold) has declined by 40% from 12 million in 20Y3 to 7.2 million in 20Y4. The average selling price has remained the same at £2, so this does not appear to be a factor in the change in revenue or volume of sales.

A key causal factor in this decline has been the scaling down of the number of owned shops by 46.7% from 150 in 20Y3, to 80 in 20Y4.

Thus, rather than reflecting poor performance, the change in revenue has been a deliberate rescaling within the recovery strategy.

Revenue per owned shop has increased from £160,000 in 20Y3 to £180,000 in 20Y4 (12.5%). This is indicative, in revenue terms at least, that the worst performing shops have been closed and the shops with higher revenue generation have remained open.

Thus, while there has been a downscaling of the number of owned shops in the network, the average sales generation performance per owned shop has improved.

Operating profit – owned outlets

Total operating profit for owned shops has improved from an operating loss of £400,000 in 20Y3 to an operating profit of £1.32 million in 20Y4.

At first sight, this appears to indicate improved performance, particularly as it has been generated by a scaled down network of owned shops.

Further analysis indicates, however, that a key causal factor in this improvement has been the reduced transfer price from the manufacturing division. Adjusting the data to show the operating profit/loss if the previous transfer pricing policy in 20Y3, of full cost plus 20%, had been maintained for 20Y4 reveals the following:

	£'000
External sales	14,400
Internal & franchisee transfers (9,000 × 1.2)	(10,800)
Variable costs	(1,080)
Fixed costs	(3,000)
Operating (Loss)	(480)

> **Tutorial note:**
>
> A comparable analysis could be carried out by scaling down the 20Y3 data.

Thus, rather than operating profit of the owned shops improving, had the transfer pricing policy remained at full cost plus 20%, then the operating losses would have increased from £400,000 to £480,000.

This has occurred, despite the improvement in revenue generation per shop, because the smaller network has meant that fixed costs of owned shops have decreased by only 25% (from £4m to £3m) while volumes of sales have decreased by 40% (see above) thereby increasing fixed costs per unit.

Franchised shops

The recovery strategy has been to favour franchised shops rather than owned shops. In this respect there has been some operational success in opening a further 30 franchised shops in replacement of owned shops.

Overall, the profit from franchising has decreased by 2% from £2.55m to £2.5m. This is in the context of an increase in the number franchised shops of 33.3% from 90 to 120.

As a consequence, the operating profit to Confo per franchised shop has fallen by 26.5% from £28,333 in 20Y3, to £20,833 in 20Y4. This may be indicative of poorer performance, but it could also reflect a short term policy to expand the network by offering improved conditions for the franchisee contract.

It may also reflect the fact that the newer franchisees may take some time to become established. More information would be needed on the relative performance of new and existing franchisees.

Manufacturing

The key factor affecting the 'profit' generated by the manufacturing division has been the change in transfer pricing policy from a profit centre (cost plus 20%) to a cost centre. This is a corporate level decision and is not indicative of the underlying performance of the Manufacturing Division itself.

Basing performance on its ability to control costs, it has performed well. The overall output has reduced by 5.7% from 17.4 million units to 16.4 million units. This is a reflection of reduced sales but additional information would be needed to confirm that sales were not constrained by reduced production capacity.

Variable cost per unit has remained at 75p so any reduced scale economies have not been a factor.

More significantly, the fixed cost per unit has remained constant despite the fall in sales and production output. This reflects a good performance in reducing fixed costs.

Examiner's comments

Generally, this requirement was fairly well answered, with most candidates providing up-front calculations in a reasonably well structured table. Analysis often endeavoured to explain changes and results for the two years in terms of cause and effect. Weaker candidates were poor in this regard, merely reiterating the percentage changes. Weaker candidates also provided occasional calculations within their narrative, rather than in an initial structured table.

Calculations most commonly focussed on gross and net profit margins and commented on changes year on year. Only the better candidates calculated specific ratios such as revenue per shop, operating profit per shop and cost per shop. There was some good discussion of the differences in results between the franchised outlets and owned outlets.

Better responses recognised problems in comparisons between the two years, particularly due to the change in the transfer pricing system and organisational structure changes. A very small minority adjusted the data to take out this distortion, normally by adjusting the 20Y3 data by removing the 20% mark-up on internal transfers, thus arriving at more sensible comments regarding the relative performance of the manufacturing and retail divisions. Weaker candidates omitted to comment on problems in making comparisons, or to suggest additional information that would assist analysis, despite these being required in the question.

60.3 (a)

To: The Confo plc board
From: A Student
Date: 10 December 20Y4
Subject: Strategy review

Both divisions are in the start-up phase of their life cycle so it is difficult to make judgements about the success of the performance or strategy at this stage. Nevertheless, there are some early indicators.

Using the Ansoff matrix these are both examples of market development whereby existing products are being sold in new markets.

Export Division

In the case of the Export Division the new markets in the Ansoff matrix are new geographical markets.

In terms of the Lynch Expansion Method it would be regarded as growth through internal development abroad (ie exporting).

These sales are likely to all be incremental with minimal leakage between home and export markets. While this is positive in terms of generating more revenue, the strategy has a number of problems in relation to costs and risks:

1. The costs incurred in penetrating new markets may be significant compared to the revenues earned

2. The downstream supply chain is lengthened significantly, thereby increasing costs of getting goods to customers

3. There may be different tastes in different countries such that products developed for the UK market tastes may be unsuitable (eg some sweets may be unsuitable in hot climates)

4. Additional risks apply (eg international physical distribution and foreign exchange rate risk on settlement)

The Export Division has made a small profit of £200,000 for the year. Whilst this is unlikely to be sufficient in the long run to justify the investment, this is the start-up phase to penetrate markets.

The profit is small but, based on the above argument; it is all incremental, with little or no damage to the existing business. Indeed, as an international brand it may enhance the existing business in the UK in terms of reputation.

Commercial Division

In the case of the Commercial Division, the new markets in the Ansoff matrix are new distribution channels.

In terms of the Lynch Expansion Method it would be regarded as growth through internal domestic development.

The key strategic issue in this case is that there may be competition between Confo's existing markets and the new commercial market. If consumers become aware that the supermarkets are selling the same products as Confo's owned shops and franchisees, but at a lower price, then this strategy may reduce contribution and destroy value for Confo overall.

The Commercial Division has made a small profit of £300,000 for the year. Unlike the Export Division, we cannot be certain that this is entirely incremental. Indeed, the lost contribution on existing sales (if consumers perceive it is the same product but own-labelled) may be greater than £300,000.

(b) **Evaluation of success of the recovery plan**

In pure financial terms Confo has generated less profit in the year following the introduction of the recovery plan (£4.32m) than in the year before the plan (£5.15m). This is a reduction in operating profit of 16.1%.

However as the marking director pointed out, it would be unwise to judge performance on one year's data. This is particularly the case as it is a transitional period and only the first year of the three year recovery plan.

Positive signs included:

(1) The willingness of 30 franchisees to take up new franchises
(2) Profit in first year for Export Division
(3) Profit in first year for Commercial Division

Negative signs include:

(1) Overall reduction in volume of sales
(2) Significant fall in operating profit per franchisee shop

Given that several simultaneous changes have been made by Confo, it is difficult to determine precisely which changes have impacted performance most in the short term. Given that the planning horizon is three years, it is appropriate to review progress after one year, but unreasonable to draw firm conclusions as to whether the changes will be successful when the three year planning horizon is reached.

Examiner's comments

The main weakness in this requirement was inadequate evaluation of the overall recovery plan, which was unsatisfactory in nature and in the level of detail in the answers of most candidates.

The majority of candidates incorporated analytical frameworks, and most who used models made use of Ansoff's matrix. A smaller number also referred to Lynch.

Only a small minority recognised potential cannibalisation of the Retail Division's sales by the Commercial Division, combined with consumer awareness that the products are identical apart from packaging. More saw the revised packaging as a protection against this.

In terms of the overall recovery plan for the company, of those who considered this, most concluded it to be favourable, on balance, as time is needed for it to come to fruition. Better candidates included calculations to support this conclusion. A few explicitly referred to the three-year time horizon.

60.4 Ethical issues

Ethics pertains to whether a particular behaviour is deemed acceptable in the context under consideration. In short, it is 'doing the right thing'.

In making any ethical evaluation it is first necessary to establish the facts. In this case, it would seem that the facts are reasonably clear in terms of what has happened, although the lack of documentary evidence to support the facts may limit the actions that can be taken.

The issue of legality and compliance with the Bribery Act needs to be considered and legal advice taken by Confo. If a crime has been committed there may be a duty to disclose in the public interest.

Both the offering, and the receiving, of an inappropriate inducement may be considered illegal and/or unethical.

In making a decision as to how to proceed, it is helpful to apply the Institute of Business Ethics three tests:

- Transparency
- Effect
- Fairness

Transparency – would CCC mind people (existing customers, suppliers, employees) knowing that these transactions have taken place. In the first instance, there appears to be a degree of internal transparency as Kirsty reported the initial Christmas gift to the commercial director. It is not known whether John reported the gift within Lenton but, given his subsequent behaviour, this seems unlikely. At this stage Kirsty may be deemed to have taken actions which are not inappropriate give the scale, context and disclosure.

Subsequent gifts made by Kirsty were not disclosed and hence the ethical test of openness does not appear to have been met. Since March 20Y4 Kirsty has made gifts of company property without notification, consultation or authority, which appears both fraudulent and unethical. The question of how she obtained the goods needs to be asked and who knew about this (as opposed to the purpose for which they were being used), if anyone.

Her refusal to make undisclosed gifts beyond £100 is appropriate, but does not compensate for her earlier actions.

Effect – whom does the decision to make the ever larger transfers of sweets affect or hurt? The initial Christmas gift may be appropriate based on its scale (small amount of £10), context (seasonal gift and industry norm) and expected frequency (annual at Christmas) in that it would be unlikely to be of sufficient size to affect John's commercial decisions about the Confo contract. However, subsequent larger gifts may have had the effect of John choosing to make purchases from Confo, rather than a rival company which might be offering preferential commercial terms to Lenton, but with no personal inducement for John. The effect in this case would be that Lenton shareholders are suffering due to John receiving inappropriate personal inducements. Conversely, Confo may be the best commercial provider and the ceasing of gifts may have made John choose an inferior provider, to the detriment of Lenton shareholders.

In this context, sweets with a relatively small financial value (even at £100) could trigger decisions on a commercial contract worth many thousands of pounds.

Fairness – would the transfers be considered fair by those affected? Confo may be obtaining an unfair commercial advantage over rivals through paying inappropriate (and possibly illegal) inducements. Similarly, John has gained a significant and unfair benefit compared to more honest colleagues who would not have engaged in such actions. Whilst the benefit is in kind, rather than cash, this is not the key issue if it amounts to an inducement. Moreover, it is possible that the confectionery could be sold by John to convert to cash.

Honesty and integrity

Further issues are those of honesty and integrity. The inducements may fail the honesty test as they are not earned, authorised or disclosed by, or on behalf of, the giver or the recipient.

Actions

An initial action for Kirsty would be now to act honestly and make transparent what has occurred to the commercial director by full disclosure of all the facts, with any supporting evidence to which she has access. The matter is likely to be of sufficient seriousness that she may offer her resignation in anticipation of possible legal action against her for misappropriating goods belonging to the company to a third party without authority.

Kirsty should co-operate in all investigations made by the company or the police.

The fact she received no direct financial benefit may mitigate, but not remove, her culpability. Indirectly, in making more sales, she may have benefited in the long run by achieving promotion or more job security.

Confo may have benefited initially from Kirsty's action and may suffer reputational damage by external disclosure, but nevertheless there is a public interest disclosure requirement if, on the basis of legal advice, a crime has been committed. The Confo board should therefore inform the Lenton board of what has occurred in order that it can make its own investigations. If the Lenton board does not make disclosure to the police then the Confo board should consider doing so, notwithstanding that documentary evidence is limited.

Examiner's comments

This requirement was well answered, on the whole, with most candidates making use of ethical principles and language to assist their balanced discussion, and recognising the potential adverse effects to be much greater than a few boxes of chocolates as it could have impacted on the cessation of the supply contract between the two companies. Legal aspects were also often referred to, including bribery, though a worrying minority dismissed the idea of there being any legal ramifications out of hand. Some considered the culpability to be only with John Drake, rather than also relating to Kirsty at Confo.

Only a minority recognised the need for a clear formulation of a company policy on the issue of gifts to business contacts. Poorer candidates failed to deal with required actions and instead just analysed the scenario in general terms using transparency, fairness and effect.

---

61 Radar Traditional Radios Ltd (December 2014)

Marking guide

	Knowledge	Skill	Marks
61.1 Porter's 5 Forces	3	8	10
61.2 Segmentation	4	9	12
61.3 Abandon	2	8	9
	9	25	31

General comments

RTR is a family-owned company which is an upmarket manufacturer of radios with retro styling. It operates in the UK market.

RTR makes both digital and analogue radios, but it is concerned about the impact of the transfer of radio broadcasting in the UK from analogue to digital, which has been much slower than expected. As the broadcasting industry moves increasingly to digital, RTR is concerned about the increasing competition from the variety of devices that can receive digital radio broadcasting. There is also significant competition from larger global radio manufacturers which have large R&D and marketing budgets compared to RTR. Some disagreement has arisen on the RTR board as to how the R&D and marketing budgets should be targeted and focused to give maximum benefit.

61.1 Porter's Five Forces

Substitutes

A substitute product is a product or service produced by another industry which satisfies the same customer needs as the industry under consideration.

Where there are readily available substitutes accessible to consumers at reasonable cost, then this acts as additional competition and competes away industry profitability.

In the radio manufacturing industry, close substitutes exist in a range of other devices which can receive digital audio transmissions to replicate the function of radios. These include digital televisions, internet devices and smart phones.

The growth in the use of internet and mobile phones for listening to radio between 20X9 and 20Y3 (see table) indicates that they are relatively close substitutes.

Moreover, while some of the other devices are more expensive than buying a radio, they also perform other functions, so consumers are, for example, already likely to have a television and there is no incremental cost to listening to the radio. In addition, switching costs are minimal if other devices are already owned.

While the other products noted above are close substitutes, they are not perfect substitutes. For example:

- The other devices do not receive analogue broadcasts

- The sound quality (eg from many smart phones) may not be as good as a radio

- A radio is portable unlike some other devices (eg a television)

Nevertheless, these substitutes affect the profitability of the radio manufacturing industry through:

- Putting a ceiling on prices eg it is unlikely very high prices could be charged, even for high quality radios

- Affecting volumes of demand as the market is split not only between rivals in the industry, but with manufacturers of substitute products

- Forcing expensive investments and technology improvements to keep pace with technology changes outside the industry

Defining the industry as radio manufacturing is quite narrow. Many of the larger consumer electronics manufacturers are also likely to make the substitute products noted above and hence are internally diversified. The companies most exposed to the threat of substitutes in the industry are those (like RTR) who only make radios.

Conclusion

Overall the threat from substitutes is significant and could, in the longer run, be industry destroying.

Competitive rivalry amongst existing firms

The intensity of competition amongst existing rival firms in the industry will tend to compete away the collective profitability of participants in the industry.

Competition in radio manufacture is global, even if some companies in the industry are focused, like RTR, on one national market. There are major international companies which, although not based in the UK, can distribute efficiently to the UK.

The level of competitive rivalry in radio manufacturing will depend on the following factors.

Digital radios

- Rate of market growth – the market for digital radios is changing:

  - It may be rising as fewer people buy analogue radios, which will reduce competitiveness and make the industry more profitable; or

  - It may be falling as the overall market for listening to radio is fairly constant (in listening hours) and the availability of substitutes means that the remaining demand for radios is falling, leaving the incumbent manufacturers chasing a smaller market.

- Ease of switching for buyers – buyers of digital radios can easily switch to rival products when a radio is replaced thus competition is intense in relation to every product cycle.

- Degree of uncertainty over the actions of rival firms – new digital technology could emerge on a regular basis meaning that profits could fall away for many firms in the industry. This requires high R&D budgets which reduce industry profitability.

Analogue radios

- Level of fixed costs – if there is a smaller market for analogue radios in future and as volumes fall across the industry then fixed costs per unit increase and industry profitability therefore falls

- Importance of capacity utilisation/economies of scale – a shrinking market means fewer economies of scale and more spare capacity thereby reducing industry profit

- Exit barriers – these may be high (non-current assets with a low break-up value; redundancy payments, costs of withdrawal) due to the specialised nature of the equipment which means competition remains in the industry much longer than would otherwise be the case (zombie companies)

Conclusion

Overall, the threat from competitive rivalry amongst existing firms is significant and could cause less efficient companies to exit the industry.

Examiner's comments

This requirement was generally very well answered. Most recognised the relevance of substitutes and competitive rivalry to industry competitiveness and concluded that both forces are relatively strong, hence tending towards an increasingly unattractive competitive environment. Fewer candidates emphasised the fact that analogue radio faces less of a threat from substitutes than digital.

The competitive rivalry section was less well done than substitutes, with candidates often failing to recognise that the market for radios was changing. Candidates tended to conclude that competitive rivalry was high, but often without really justifying why.

Weaker efforts tended to confuse substitutes with competitive rivalry and spent a lot of time discussing how digital radios are substitutes for analogue.

61.2 Market segmentation

Market segmentation is the division of the market into homogeneous groups of potential customers who may be treated similarly for marketing purposes.

Focus players like RTR may only be able to use market segmentation in a limited way as one segment might be their sole consumer group. Broader market players may use market segmentation to market in different ways to different groups.

RTR has a premium pricing strategy. Necessarily, there are fewer people that can afford expensive radios than can afford cheaper radios, which limits the size of the market, but also changes the characteristics of the consumer group (see pricing section below).

Market segmentation is therefore a tool of marketing strategy that can help RTR management to focus on relevant customer groups, and to use a marketing mix to arrive at a desirable marketing proposition. This enables RTR to customise its marketing mix to make it appropriate to likely customers.

The market can be segmented in a number of general different ways. For example:

- Age
- Income
- Gender

More specific segmentation might refer to the number of hours listening to the radio, or technology spending of consumers (eg identified by purchasing technology magazines or other technology products purchased).

Different types of market segmentation can be combined in order to refine the sub group which is most likely to appeal as potential consumers of RTR radios. Thus, for instance, a particular type of radio programme might appeal to higher income groups with an age group of around 55, perhaps with more females in the audience. These can be targeted for radio advertising during these programmes.

There are a number of problems in doing this type of market segmentation:

- The groupings are crude (eg 55% female buyers for RTR is only just above half and there is therefore little benefit above mass marketing to the population generally).

- Obtaining the information to target these groups may be difficult. It may be necessary to use databases which tend to be typical of the market segments identified, rather than use the characteristics (age, income, gender) directly. The best such database is RTR's historic customer list, as these have chosen to buy RTR radios before. Other companies' customer lists, with similar customer characteristics to RTR (where they can be legally and ethically obtained) may also be a useful means of segmentation.

The marketing mix

Following market segmentation, targeting involves selecting the most appropriate market segments.

Target marketing tailors a marketing mix for one or more segments identified by market segmentation.

Promotion

Advertising is the most obvious form of promotion, and it should be appropriate to the targeted market segment.

Radio manufacturing is related to the media industry, so advertising through this means seems one of the most obvious channels to use. This may include transmissions through other rival devices such as TV, mobiles and the internet.

The internet may take target marketing down to very small groups who have shown an interest in radios and radio broadcasting through their choice of websites.

In terms of broader radio audiences, data may be available by audience characteristics for particular programmes and placing adverts adjacent to these programmes would stand the best opportunity of reaching the RTR target customer base and gain best value for its advertising spending.

Other media might include journals and magazines used by older, high income age groups, ideally with some radio listening theme.

Price

RTR has a premium pricing strategy. Necessarily, there are fewer people that can afford expensive radios than can afford cheaper radios, which limits the size of the market, but it also changes the characteristics of the consumer group willing to pay more for radios, compared with the mass market of radio purchasing consumers.

Even within the high income group who buy RTR's radios, more customers could be created by lowering the price, but this has some disadvantages:

- Lowers the profit per unit

- Demand is likely to be inelastic in this market niche thus sales volumes may not increase significantly even if prices are substantially lower

- It sends the wrong marketing signal where this is a luxury good and the quality cannot be readily observed, thus price is a signal of quality

A key factor in assessing price is the prices being charged by the closest competitors, which should be identified in market research of competitors. In this case, however, as a signal of quality, a virtue is being made of setting prices above competitors.

Product

A product is not just the physical item with features, but the perception of the item to the customer and the package of benefits that it provides.

The technology features used by RTR are good quality, but the styling of the goods is important and is distinctive, being part of the brand image.

The brand name is key in representing these qualities and making the RTR radios distinct from other brands.

In the case of RTR, the company name is the brand name.

Thus, for example, the 'retro' old fashioned style may particularly appeal to the older age market segment who can remember when all radios were styled in that way.

Place

Given RTR currently only sells through retail outlets in the UK, this limits the geographical market. The distribution network should be reviewed to make sure that the shops where RTR radios are being sold are consistent in image with the high income, middle age market segmentation strategy.

However, there may also be scope for widening the perception of the attainable geographic market by marketing to similar high income, middle aged groups overseas. Further market research could reveal whether the same segmentation groups apply in other countries as they do in the UK.

In terms of distribution, a radio is small and portable so the costs of transporting them may be low and this would enhance the opportunity to open up international markets through on-line sales without damaging the relationship with UK retailers, as there is likely to be little leakage between markets.

Examiner's comments

This requirement was well answered on the whole. Most began with definitions of segmentation and applied this to the question.

A minority wasted time discussing in detail market research approaches to segmentation, but then often proceeded to ignore the data which had been provided in the question.

The best answers related each different type of segmentation to the marketing mix. Weaker efforts only discussed the latter in generic terms.

There was little discussion by most candidates of the problems of applying market segmentation.

Virtually no candidate attempted to discuss the marketing mix in the broader context of an overall marketing strategy for the firm.

61.3 Factors to consider

RTR currently makes both digital and analogue radios. Analogue still makes up most of the sales of RTR by volume at 60%, although by value it is less than this at 53% (see below) as digital radios are more expensive.

In sales value terms at retail prices:

	20Y3 £'000	
Analogue radios (60,000 x £150)	9,000	53%
Digital radios (40,000 x £200)	8,000	47%

While analogue radios are the more important product in terms of sales volumes, they are declining as they near the end of their product life cycle, due to both technology and regulation. In terms of a BCG matrix analysis of its product portfolio, RTR's analogue radios are the company's key 'cash cows' as they still generate significant cash flows which can be used to fund increased marketing and/or investment in R&D for the 'problem child' digital products. Cash flows are likely to decline soon however, as analogue radios head towards 'dog' status. In contrast, digital radios are in the growth phase of their product life cycle, but at a slow rate of only 1,000 radios per year on average.

The immediate abandonment of the major product seems implausible, and this is not being suggested. Rather, the suggestion is that RTR should no longer invest in analogue R&D and marketing and thus gradually let sales decline (perhaps over two to three years) to the point where they will then be abandoned.

If the process of decline in analogue is rapid (as two to three years may seem to be), this is very risky as the major product may be in its decline stage of the product life cycle but is still generating most of the major cash flows for RTR. Indeed, any R&D and marketing costs may be self-financing in terms of additional sales.

Despite the above, it seems clear that the UK government intends to abandon analogue broadcasting eventually, thereby ending sales of analogue radios in the UK. Whilst there may be overseas markets to sell analogue radios to (eg developing nations) it seems clear this market will disappear over time in favour of digital radios.

In essence therefore, the key decision for RTR is not *whether* to abandon producing analogue radios, but *when*.

In making this decision the key factors are as follows.

In favour of abandoning analogue sooner and investing in digital radios

- Analogue is to cease being broadcast. In anticipation of this, consumers will cease to buy analogue radios some time before the switch-off date

- Industry support appears to be in favour of digital, so working with broadcasters in digital research may be more fruitful than analogue research

- Only 40% households own digital radios, but in total 90% of people listen to radio programmes, so there is a big potential first time buyer market

- As technology develops rapidly, consumers will wish to replace their radios more frequently with the new features

- Distribution outlets for analogue radios may shrink as retail chains stop selling them

- New features like Bluetooth are needed to keep pace with changes in technology in order to compete and R&D is needed for this

Against abandoning analogue sooner and continuing to invest in it for longer

- Digital reception is only available to 90% of the UK population. This not only restricts the market but makes it less likely in the short term that government will switch off analogue

- Uncertainty arises from the intensity of future competition in digital communications (within the industry and with substitutes)

- Analogue is still a larger market than digital by current sales volumes and current listeners

- Digital may fail to take hold in the global market and therefore fail commercially as a technology

- Analogue may continue for many years, perhaps due to the greater sound quality.

- If other companies exit the analogue market, but RTR remain in it, then it may be less competitive for RTR

Conclusion

There are significant uncertainties about the nature and timing of the relative popularity of digital and analogue. It may be appropriate to keep the real option and continue with both technologies until it is clearer about the pace of change in market preferences and the timing and certainty of the analogue switch off.

Examiner's comments

The responses to this question were mixed. The best answers were well balanced and often explicitly introduced either the product life cycle or the BCG matrix, or both. Many were implicitly aware of the relevance of these frameworks, so some credit was given.

Only a few referred to the uncertainty of the analogue switch-off date, with most assuming that this will happen in 20Y9. The weakest answers concluded that the firm should quit analogue production as soon as possible, with little consideration of the adverse cash flow impact this would have. Weaker answers also failed to make any reference to the data provided.

The higher scoring answers recognised that if other companies exited the analogue market, then RTR could benefit from this as the industry supply would be reduced to offset, to some degree, falling industry demand for analogue devices.

Additionally they tended to spend a lot of time discussing partially relevant issues such as redundancies, with little focus on the timing, product portfolio and cash flow issues.

Very few referred to the real option characteristics of the choices faced by the firm.

62 The Norgate Bank plc (December 2014)

Marking guide

	Knowledge	Skill	Marks
62.1 KPISs	2	11	12
62.2 Benchmarking	4	8	11
	6	19	23

General comments

The Norgate Bank (NB) has both business customers and individual customers who are based in the UK and France. It has no branches but communicates with customers entirely through internet and telephone banking. Historically, NB had one telephone call centre near London, but last year it opened a new call centre in Vietnam to service all its French-speaking customers. At each centre, employees are divided into two separate groups which service business and individual customers. In the first year of operation, three key KPIs were used to measure and monitor performance being: time to answer a call; length of a call; and customer satisfaction survey results. Concern has been raised about the suitability of these measures. The company also wants to use benchmarking to evaluate performance and improve efficiency. Data on performance is provided.

62.1 KPIs

KPIs are metrics in relation to a target that will deliver the organisation's objectives in the area to which they relate.

KPIs should therefore be related to the relevant critical success factor. In the case of the call centres this means dealing with customer enquiries to satisfy customer expectations, build relationships and achieve this as efficiently as possible in terms of time and cost.

The actual KPIs achieved are given in the Exhibit but there is no target measure against which to judge these metrics in order to determine whether performance has been at an appropriate level. The idea of benchmarks to determine an appropriate target is examined below.

Dealing with the nature of the KPI's used by Ron:

Average time taken to answer a customer call

This is measure of efficiency, but also it is a measure of capacity to take calls. If the KPI achieved is not at an appropriate level of efficiency (eg customers are ringing off before the call is answered) then this may damage relationships with customers and cause dissatisfaction leaving customer enquiries unsatisfied.

There is therefore a trade-off between efficiency, capacity and cost. If sufficient resources are dedicated to call centres then all calls could be answered immediately, but this may not meet the objective of cost efficiency as too many staff may be idle waiting when call volumes are low.

Being efficient would be trying to meet customer expectations, including unexpected peaks and troughs in call volumes, without undue idle time and therefore excessive cost.

Overall this seems to be a reasonable measure in that long waiting times are likely to be viewed unfavourably by customers. What is not clear is how to determine the target for the optimal time that customers should wait to balance service delivery with cost.

Average length of a customer call

This KPI is, to a degree, ambiguous. If the average call is long then it could be sign of quality in meeting customer needs by giving due time to resolve all the issues raised and make the customer feel in receipt of a good service.

Conversely, it could be a sign of inefficiency in being unable to deal with customer enquiries quickly and efficiently and so wastes customer time as well as NB staff time and costs.

A further alternative may be that the length of the call is dependent on the subject matter. Thus business customer calls may deal with more complex issues than calls from private individuals and may therefore take longer on average.

Overall, therefore, this seems a difficult measure to determine, not just the level of the KPI, but the direction relative to target. In this respect many of the relevant factors may be captured in the final KPI which is:

Scores from customer satisfaction surveys

Scores from customer satisfaction surveys are a good measure of whether objectives are being achieved in relation to building customer relationships and offering appropriate service.

On their own however crude measures of how satisfied customers are with a call does not of itself indicate why they are satisfied. Further questions may therefore add detail (eg whether it is the length of the call, ability to resolve issue quickly, friendliness). It also leaves open the question of satisfaction relative to cost.

Conclusion

The KPIs selected emphasise effective service delivery by omitting measures of the efficiency with which that service is delivered.

Additional measures of efficiency (eg meeting peaks and troughs with the right scheduling of staff hours to meet demand at key times in the day, and for key days of the week) and capacity (idle hours to total hours ie utilisation) would be useful.

Also there are no financial KPIs which is key to call centre financial efficiency. Cost per call could be one such measure. In this case, the costs of the Vietnam centre per call may be much lower than the London centre, even if operational efficiency is lower in Vietnam.

Examiner's comments

The quality of responses was mixed for this requirement. The best answers provided critical evaluation of each of the three KPIs after an introduction defining KPIs, their role and their relationship to critical success factors or goals. Alternatives were suggested during the course of the evaluations and, often, afterwards. Weaker candidates failed to link the KPIs with CSFs.

Relatively few candidates explicitly or implicitly discussed the trade-offs between efficiency, capacity and costs. Likewise, only a significant minority considered the issue of different types of customers and/or locations.

Additionally, a few referred to direct sample monitoring of calls as well as using the 'mystery shopper' approach to direct quality evaluation.

In order to consider critical success factors, some attempted to use the Balanced Scorecard framework, but in many instances suggested goals and measures which were largely unrelated to the performance of the call centres.

Some candidates redefined the entire requirement in terms of the Balanced Scorecard, which tended to lead to poor marks.

62.2 Benchmarking

Benchmarking is: 'The establishment, through data gathering, of targets and comparators, through whose use relative levels of performance (and particularly areas of underperformance) can be identified. By the adoption of identified best practices it is hoped that performance will improve.'

Benchmarking compares the use of assets and activities across the firm, or across the industry, and indicates where they might be used better or where they are already a source of superior performance. Once a business has identified its CSFs and core competences, it must identify performance standards which need to be achieved to outperform rivals and achieve sustainable competitive advantage. These standards are sometimes called key performance indicators (KPIs).

Benchmarks can therefore provide a means of determining target KPIs which, if achieved, will match the best standards in the industry. Such benchmarks not only set targets for existing KPIs, but may suggest different types of KPI to measure new CSFs.

In so doing, by comparing performance with other entities, NB can learn how to reduce costs and improve customer service quality. Additionally, benchmarking may help NB better understand whether it is achieving competitive advantage and superior performance in the call centre operations area of its activities.

Different types of benchmarks may provide different types of guidance:

Historic or internal benchmarking – internal benchmarking would be at the level of comparing individual units (for businesses and individuals) at each call centre (London and Vietnam) with each other to determine those that are under- or over-performing when considering the different demands and circumstances. At the moment however this is the first year of operation of Vietnam and learning may still be taking place. Conversely London may still be adjusting to losing the French customer calls. Nevertheless, internal benchmarking attempts to raise performance to the standard of the best internal unit and demonstrates to other units that this level of performance is achievable.

Historical comparison looks at performance over time to ascertain trends/significant changes, but the danger is that performance against competitors is ignored and long-standing internal inefficiencies are not highlighted. Note. For the first year of operation this is not possible in Vietnam.

In the Exhibit, it would appear that data could be used (for example) to compare the number of hours of calls handled per annum for each member of staff. In the UK call centre for individuals this is 800 hours pa ((1,200,000 x 4/60)/100) but in the other three functions (UK individuals, Vietnam business and Vietnam individuals) it is 1,000 hours pa. This would at least raise some questions. The differences in satisfaction also vary between centre and between types of customer, but there is no obvious pattern.

Competitive benchmarking – compares performance with other firms in the same industry or sector. This may assist NB in ascertaining ways to improve performance – eg comparing the performance with other banks' call centres. An alternative is to widen the definition of the industry from banks to financial services and include the experience of Ron's deputy who has worked in the related industry of insurance. The differences may be accounted for in the differences in the types of calls received by banks and insurance companies but questions may be asked to improve performance even though the comparisons are not identical.

This may involve the use of league tables, but more detailed information may be difficult to achieve as competitors may be reluctant to share data with rivals. Partnerships or industry groupings or a benchmarking centre may help overcome this lack of information.

Activity (best in class) benchmarking – compare with best practice in whatever industry can be found eg could compare with a hotel telephone booking system, or ticket booking or emergency telephone system, whichever is 'best in class' for the function dealing with telephone calls efficiently. This has the advantage that a firm may share operations in common with non-competitor external organisations, which might be 'best in the class' for a particular function, more readily than with a rival firm in the same industry.

Generic benchmarking – This is benchmarking against a conceptually similar process eg compare an online system of banking compared to telephone calls which can achieve the same outcome (eg simple transactions online or by telephone). It is unlikely that this will result in comparison of detailed measures but it could identify conceptual areas for improvement.

Disadvantages

There are disadvantages to benchmarking. A full programme can overload managers with demands for information, restrict their attention to the factors that are to be benchmarked and affect their motivation by seeming to reduce their role to copying others. It can also undermine competitive advantage by revealing trade secrets. Strategically, it can divert attention away from innovation and the future by focussing it on the efficiency of current operations.

Since benchmarking is about processes rather than results, measures would have to be linked to outcomes at some stage.

Examiner's comments

Most candidates discussed three or four types of benchmarking and many also provided an introduction to the purpose of benchmarking in the performance management process of identifying critical success factors and related KPIs.

A significant minority described the approaches with little or no evaluation of advantages and problems in their application in this particular scenario. Many did mention, in general terms, the difficulties involved in obtaining competitor/comparator data. Additionally, there was a tendency to evaluate internal benchmarking only, tending to ignore the other types of benchmarking, beyond an initial description.

Good answers also related their discussion to their previous consideration of KPIs. However, a minority of weaker candidates displayed a lack of awareness of the benchmarking process and simply carried on evaluating KPIs.

63 Rocket Co (March 2015)

Marking guide

	Knowledge	Skill	Marks
63.1 Performance	2	18	18
63.2 Consideration of factors	3	9	10
63.3 Change management	4	7	10
63.4 Ethics	3	6	8
	12	40	46

63.1 **Performance analysis**

Appendix: **Further analysis**

Tutorial note:

A wide range of possible calculations have been given here for marking purposes and to illustrate the scope for additional numerical analysis.

Analysis of income

	20Y4	20Y3
Fee income F'000 (given)	7,091	6,653
Mix of fee income:		
Accounting:Tax	47:53	45:55
Absolute fee income:		
Accounting F'000	3,333 (increase 11.3%)	2,994
Tax F'000	3,758 (increase 2.7%)	3,659
Average fee charged		
Accounting	F335 (increase 11.7%)	F300
Tax	F415 (increase 15.3%)	F360
Premium charged for tax (tax rate/accountancy rate)	23.9%	20%
Hours billed		
Accounting	9,949	9,980
Tax	9,055	10,164
	Total 19,004	Total 20,144
Change in total hours:	-5.7%	
Accounting	-0.3%	
Tax	-10.9%	

Market information

	20Y4	20Y3
Fee income F'000 (given)	7,091	6,653
Market share (given)	12%	14%
Hence market size F'000	59,092 (increase 24.3%)	47,521

Profitability

	20Y4	20Y3
Fee income F'000 (given)	7,091	6,653
Net profit margin	20.8%	23.1%
Net profit F'000	1,475 (decrease 4.0%)	1,537
Total costs F'000	5,616 (increase 9.8%)	5,116
Fee income per partner F'000 (given)	1,773	1,663
No. of partners	4	4
Average profit per partner	368.75 (4% decrease)	384.25

Variances on non-financial indicators

	20Y4	20Y3	Variance
Market share	12%	14%	2% decrease
%Satisfied clients	75%	85%	10% decrease
Total staff turnover	23.5%	17.6%	5.9% increase
Error rates	10%	8%	2% increase
Utilisation rate	70.5%	66.5%	4% increase

Rocket uses a balanced scorecard approach to performance measurement which combines financial and non-financial information. Some of the non-financial factors in the scorecard can be used to help explain the financial performance of and the prospects for the business and give much greater insight into key operational issues within the business.

Income and market share

Fee income is up by 6.6% compared to an increase of 9.2% the previous year which suggests that growth is slowing and may explain Rocket's desire to consider new products.

However referring to the market share information (customer perspective), it is clear that Rocket has underperformed the market, losing 2% of its share at a time when the market for services (measured by revenue) has increased by 24.3%. It would be helpful to have the market share information analysed between tax and accounting to consider both lines of service separately and assess whether one is out-performing the other. The sales mix has altered with the more lucrative tax work representing only 53% of income (F3.758million), compared to 55% in 20Y3 (F3.659million), so it may be that Rocket is falling behind in this market. Since tax services command a premium rate compared to accounting, the change in sales mix will have an adverse effect on income.

The cause of the growth in fee income needs to be analysed between price and volume:

Rocket increased the fees charged for both services – accounting by 11.7% and tax by 15.3%. As a result the hours billed have fallen by 5.6% in total, from 20,144 to 19,004. This is consistent with a drop in market share. One possible reason for the increase in price would be to cover the pay rise that Rocket has had to offer staff to keep its salaries more in line with competitors.

It can be seen from the analysis that the tax services seem to have been more sensitive to the change in price, with chargeable tax hours reducing by 10.9% and thus only a 2.7% increase in overall tax revenue (compared to 11.3% for accounting). It would be useful to know to what extent the level of WIP (work done not yet billed) is comparable across the years and to try to ascertain whether the loss of chargeable hours is a timing issue or symptomatic of a loss of clients. It would also be useful to obtain competitor charge-out rates for the sports and leisure sector to see whether Rocket's fees are reasonable, although as discussed above the fact that Rocket has lost market share may be in part due to over-pricing.

Another reason for the drop in hours billed may be to do with loss of clients due to client dissatisfaction. The 20Y4 customer survey has revealed that only 75% of clients are satisfied, compared to 85% in 20Y3 – a 10% adverse variance. The cause of the dissatisfaction needs to be investigated. It may be linked to an increase in error rates from 8% to 10% of jobs (internal business) or to staffing issues – see below. Certainly if clients are being asked to pay higher fees they are likely to expect standards and quality of service to be at least maintained, so a 25% increase in the error rate is unlikely to be acceptable. It would be useful to know the reasons for the dissatisfaction and to ascertain whether one service has been affected more than the other.

Rocket has not been paying staff the appropriate market premium and this has probably led to demotivation and dissatisfaction, as evidenced by the increase in staff turnover (17.6% to 23.5% - innovation and learning). This represents one more fee-earner (5.9% x 17 fee earners) leaving and needing to be replaced. The pay rise offered may have come too late for some staff and more may choose to leave given the increasing employment opportunities in the marketplace. Continuity of staff is important as clients may resent revealing personal financial details to a variety of different people each year. Recruiting replacement staff costs the business money and there is then a learning curve period, during which perhaps errors may be made. In addition the business does not appear to be investing much in training, with qualified staff only receiving two days per year. In a specialist sector this may not be sufficient to keep abreast of developments and may be an additional cause of the error rates.

Profitability

Despite the 6.6% increase in fee income, Rocket's net profit for 20Y4 of F1.475million is 4% lower than in 20Y3.

The net profit margin has fallen from 23.1% to 20.8% as a result of the total cost increase (9.8%) exceeding that of the revenue increase. A number of factors have caused Rocket's costs to increase in 20Y4:

- Rent review

- Increased PII premiums

- Pay rise for staff (it would be useful to know how much this was and at what point in the year it was made as it does not yet appear to have stemmed the staff turnover)

One factor which will be adversely affecting profitability is the poor staff utilisation rate. Although this has improved from 66.5% to 70.5% it still means that staff are spending a considerable amount of time engaged in activities that are not billed to clients. This may be due to having to incur write-offs of time e.g. on fixed fee jobs or because staff are spending time on business development, or too much time on administrative issues. Assuming staff work 7 hours a day, 5 days a week for 48 weeks, there are 1,680 hours available per fee earner. Assuming utilisation rates were between 85% and 90%, Rocket would only need 13 staff to achieve the 20Y4 billed hours. In the change management memo the partners identify the need for qualified staff to consider delegating more tasks to concentrate on higher value activities which would increase profitability.

Summary

In conclusion, although the revenue has grown and margins are still reasonable, the financial results do not show the full picture. Rocket appears to have some fundamental weaknesses in its core business that need to be addressed, if it is to continue to grow into the future. The success of the MDP proposal will be dependent on existing clients' willingness to buy additional legal services from Rocket, which they will not do if they are dissatisfied with the existing services and perceive staff to be inadequately trained.

Examiner's comments

Candidates were asked to analyse and evaluate the performance of Rocket between 20Y3 and 20Y4, using the balanced scorecard.

The data analysis requirement was reasonably attempted but certainly not as well answered as in recent sittings. The fact that a balanced scorecard of performance indicators was provided in the Exhibit seemed to discourage a surprising number of candidates from undertaking any further numerical analysis. Better candidates provided some additional up-front calculations in a reasonably well structured table to help explain some of the changes in the scorecard (fee income per service stream, billable hours, market size, profit per partner). Weaker candidates were very poor in this regard, merely reiterating the KPIs that had been given or at most providing occasional calculations of changes in figures, within their narrative.

Most candidates structured their narrative explanation using the four headings from the scorecard and made good links between the different sections, successfully drawing conclusions from the non-financial information to explain the reasons behind the financial performance.

Only the stronger candidates suggested additional information that would assist their analysis and concluded that Rocket would need to address some of its internal issues relating to client and staff dissatisfaction before becoming an MDP.

63.2 Factors affecting ability to create MDP

Human resource capabilities

Rocket's existing partners and staff are all experienced in accountancy and taxation, not law, so it does not currently have the HR capability to implement this strategy. It would appear that it intends to use its existing support staff but will need to employ new 'fee-earners'.

It is critical to the venture's success that the legal staff have appropriate specialist expertise, otherwise there will be no incentive for existing clients to switch their legal services to Rocket. The MDP will take longer to set up if Rocket recruits piecemeal rather than acquires an existing team. However the advantage of the former is that Rocket may be more likely to integrate individuals into its own culture and may experience less resistance from staff.

From a cost point of view, Rocket may have to offer higher pay/rewards to induce staff to move, particularly if it has a reputation for poor pay and high staff turnover. The upside of recruiting an existing team however is that they may bring some clients with them.

Increasingly law firms are employing para-legal/non-lawyers to do routine work such as document processing, so Rocket will need to consider how many staff are required and what the appropriate mix is. This will depend on the expected demand for its legal services.

Legal and regulatory issues

These forces may relate to/be affected by government policies and be politically driven. They are largely outside Rocket's control.

Changes in the regulations affecting the legal services market appear to be an attempt by government to increase competition in the market. However this could change.

The new MDP will need a licence to operate and will be monitored by the new regulatory authority. It is not clear how easy it will be for Rocket to acquire the licence, the time and cost involved, what terms and conditions will apply eg in relation to the mix of partners, governance requirements etc. and what the costs of compliance are likely to be. Rocket is presumably used to being accountable to the relevant accountancy and tax regulators so it has some experience in this area.

It will also need to consider the prospect of further regulations affecting MDPs/law/accountancy firms and also in relation to the sports sector where there are likely to be rules and regulations of different sports governing bodies, disciplinary matters etc.

Competitors and market structure

The reduction of barriers to entry is likely to increase competition and give rise to a number of alternative professional services providers.

Other accountancy firms may also decide to create MDPs.

Alternatively legal firms could develop their own accountancy and tax businesses so Rocket may lose referrals that it is currently getting from these firms.

Possible consolidation in the market place is likely to increase the size of the various players and if they are able to reduce costs, this may result in lower prices for services which will affect margins.

Rocket's advantage is that it specialises in sports and leisure, so it may face less competition in this niche than if it were targeting the whole market.

Candidates were required to analyse various factors that might influence Rocket's ability to create an MDP.

Requirement 63.2 was very well answered on the whole. The majority of candidates identified that Rocket does not currently have any legal expertise and that recruiting the necessary staff and obtaining the licence would be critical success factors for the creation of an MDP. Better candidates discussed the two different approaches to resourcing suggested in the question, in light of Rocket's current staffing issues. They also highlighted the uncertainty surrounding the MDP licence and rules given that the regulatory framework is new and designed to increase competition. Weaker candidates typically found it more difficult to discuss competition and market structure, although candidates who used their knowledge of rivalry and barriers to entry from the Porter's 5 forces model had more to say.

63.3 Change management

The change to an MDP is a major transformational change for Rocket, which is being made in response to changes in the external environment. As the internal memo points out, it may have a significant effect on the staffing and management structure of the firm.

The Gemini 4Rs framework to change involves reframing, restructuring, revitalising and renewal. To an extent, in advance of the memo, Rocket's partners have already addressed the first three of these:

- Reframing – Rocket has asked fundamental questions about what the organisation is about, decided to become an MDP and created a vision of what it will stand for: a mid-market professional services practice offering one-stop legal, tax and accounting advice for its existing wealthy sporting clients.

- Restructuring – the alignment of the physical organisation with the plan. Again the partners have addressed this by identifying the need to recruit resources, creating a central administration function and setting up appropriate account teams.

- Revitalising – this is the process of securing a good fit with the environment and explains the motivation for the change – here the partners of Rocket have quickly decided to adopt a new business model in response to the deregulation of the legal services market and are one of the early adopters in the hope of gaining competitive advantage.

This leaves the critical element – renewal - which is ensuring that people in the organisation support the change process and have the necessary skills to contribute to it.

Here the partners appear to have left the major change of culture and structure to be announced to staff in a memo. This is a coercive change approach, with little attempt at participation. As a result they have possibly underestimated the forces of resistance to change and do not appear to have attempted to harness support in favour of the new structure.

The problem with this is that change affects individuals in different ways and that the way change is introduced can influence the degree of resistance to it. Staff are likely to have lots of questions about the MDP and there will be a great deal of uncertainty surrounding the impact that the new legal staff will have on the firm's culture, structure and systems. The fact that the partners state they will 'be examining the potential for cost savings and efficiencies across the firm' is likely to cause staff to worry about earnings and job security.

Existing staff may see the change as a threat for a variety of reasons: administrative staff in particular are being told to increase efficiency and informed that there will be target staffing ratios. Qualified staff may fear that in delegating work to juniors they lose their power base or may become redundant. Junior staff may feel ill-prepared to take on the additional work that is expected of them and worry about their lack of appropriate skills and training.

Such an approach can lead to low staff morale, which may already be a problem given that Rocket is not paying the market premium for specialist staff and has experienced an increase in staff turnover.

Instead of presenting staff with a fait accompli, Rocket would have been better undertaking some consultation process in advance of the announcement, allowing discussion about individual needs and creating opportunities for staff to contribute to the changes. This would have given staff time to get used to the idea and reduced the resentment and feelings of helplessness.

Thus whilst Rocket is taking a proactive approach to changes in its environment, its chosen method of communicating the change falls short of best practice. In the aftermath of the email, Rocket would be well advised to hold meetings to address any concerns and offer staff the chance to become involved in the implementation phase of the change process.

Examiner's comments

Candidates were asked to discuss, in light of the partners' email, the extent to which Rocket's approach meets best practice in change management, referring to an appropriate change model such as Gemini 4Rs.

The main difference in the answers to this requirement related to whether candidates were familiar with the specific model suggested for use. Candidates are normally well versed in the technical knowledge for the change management requirement but the Gemini 4Rs model proved to be an exception. A significant number of candidates, clearly unable to recall the Gemini model, made comments along the lines of 'whilst Gemini 4Rs is useful, so is Lewin Schein's iceberg model' and then went on to use that as an alternative.

Candidates are advised that if the examiner recommends an approach, there is usually a good reason for doing so. Whilst credit was awarded to candidates who used an alternative model, the use of the recommended Gemini model would have created scope to make a wider variety of points. Faced with changes in the external environment, Rocket appears to have **reframed** what the practice should stand for, is **restructuring** (recruiting lawyers and creating a central admin team) and attempting to **revitalise** by being an early adopter of the MDP model. However this is a major transformational change and staff are already unhappy, yet Rocket appears to have adopted a coercive change approach with little consultation. Thus the critical element of **renewal**, ensuring people in the organisation support the change, is lacking. Better answers were produced by the very few candidates who understood the model and recognised this.

As usual, weaker candidates failed to apply their knowledge to the question, simply discussing the type of change and the likely barriers rather than evaluating Rocket's decision to announce the change via email.

63.4 Ethics issue

This situation gives rise to a number of different potential ethical issues:

- Facilitation by the manager of unethical behaviour or even possibly illegal actions by the client

- Conflict between Alina's obligations as an ICAEW professional accountant and her obligations to Rocket, her employer

- Possible issues with the tone at the top within Rocket.

Every employee has a duty of loyalty to their employer and in this case Alina owes a duty to Rocket Co. As a result Alina must not just turn blind eye to suspected wrongful behaviour because saying something might put her in an uncomfortable position with colleagues or because of self-interest in relation to her job or career. Thus if there is evidence of wrongdoing then keeping quiet should not be an option. Instead she needs to consider morally and ethically what the right thing to do is in relation to her suspicions.

A longstanding personal relationship with a client may have given rise to a familiarity threat to the manager's fundamental principles of objectivity. However it is important that Alina does not automatically assume that the manager has done something wrong. She needs to try and ascertain the facts. An effective relationship with superiors needs to be open, honest and trusting – the culture of Rocket should be such that Alina feels able to go to the managers and partners she works for and discuss opinions/ask questions/even challenge. It is not clear to what extent Alina has already done this with the manager concerned in relation to the statement of wealth and what evidence she has that the client's personal wealth has been misstated. If Alina has felt unable to raise her concerns then there may be a cultural issue to be addressed here by Rocket (the manner in which the change management was handled may suggest that this is the case).

Alina also needs to consider whether there is any statutory duty here and what legislation applies. Professional accountants need to be mindful of their responsibilities to their clients and employers to keep any information they learn confidential. Certainly Alina needs to avoid spreading news of the potentially dishonest activity by discussing it with colleagues or others who do not have responsibility over the matter. However there may be anti-fraud and/or anti-money laundering legislation that might govern reporting requirements. Whistle-blower protection provisions are common in most of Europe so she also needs to consider what legislation exists in the country to protect whistle-blowers, particularly for example in relation to the disclosure of confidential information about the client concerned.

In determining the appropriate action, Alina should consider whether there is any guidance in her employment contract, staff handbook, Rocket's code of conduct, or any internal guidance on whistleblowing. She also needs to consider her professional responsibility as a qualified accountant and the IESBA code of ethics (which is likely to apply to her manager and Rocket's partners to the extent that they are qualified accountants). Alina may be able to contact the firm's HR representative for assistance and/or seek legal advice.

Discussing her concerns with superiors in Rocket may be key as a means of preventing/detecting possible fraud. It would also highlight the inadequacies in Rocket's systems and culture which have allowed this to happen. Were Alina not to take any action, this would be allowed to perpetuate.

Examiner's comments

Candidates were requested to discuss the ethical issues associated with Alina's concerns and advise her on appropriate actions to take.

This requirement was well answered, presumably because the ethical issues (the suspected provision of misleading information to the bank and the need for internal/external disclosure) were reasonably easy for most candidates to identify. The vast majority of candidates recognised that there is likely to be a legal issue here - possibly fraud or money laundering. Most candidates made good use of ICAEW ethical principles and ethical language to assist their discussion and were able to identify the potential actions open to Alina. Some weaker candidates did apply the transparency, fairness and effect decision-making approach, although this is often more relevant in relation to a business dilemma and was much less useful here.

64 The Scottish Woodlands Commission (March 2015)

Marking guide

	Knowledge	Skill	Marks
64.1 Strategic fit	3	7	9
64.2 Financial benefits	2	8	10
64.3 Risks	2	6	7
64.4 Governance issues	3	7	8
	10	28	34

64.1 Strategic fit

To: SWC's Trustees
From: Business adviser
Date: March 20Y5
Re: Woodsaway LLP

Strategic fit

SWC's mission is to 'manage, protect and expand the public woodlands in Scotland and to increase their value to society and the environment'. In order to achieve this, it is authorised to undertake woodland management, nature conservation and provide facilities for public recreation

The Woodsaway venture is likely to increase the number of people who are able to enjoy Campbell Forest and assist SWC in fulfilling one of its subsidiary objectives, of providing the general public with widespread access to the natural woodlands environment, and to promote woodlands as a location for sports and leisure activities.

It would not appear to directly assist with woodland management or nature conservation. Indeed construction of the log cabins may have a negative impact on the habitat for local wildlife, the maintenance of which is the other of SWC's subsidiary objectives.

However if the LLP generates additional income for SWC (see financial benefits below), then it may indirectly allow it to better achieve its primary and secondary objectives by providing more financial resources. Also woodland activities undertaken by Woodsaway's customers may have educational benefits by raising awareness and, if paid for, could also generate funds for conservation.

For the venture to be a success the two members of the LLP need to have complementary and aligned objectives.

CabinCo's mission is 'to be one of the UK's leading providers of luxury short breaks in natural surroundings'. It has created a strong brand and is seeking competitive advantage from having access to Campbell forest to develop a holiday village, and first option on the development of future villages on SWC woodlands in Scotland. As a private commercial company, CabinCo's aims are likely to involve growth and profits. Its primary objectives are more likely to be financial rather than non-financial, with a probable focus on cost control and margins. However the sustainable tourism market it is targeting may be more in line with SWC's environmental aims. Also the benefit to SWC is that CabinCo brings commercial experience to the venture, which may help increase profits and hence SWC's share.

There may be possible conflicts of interest about the strategy and activities of Woodsaway, between CabinCo as a private entity and SWC as a public body, since they have very different stakeholders and different planning horizons. CabinCo as a company accountable to its shareholders is likely to have a shorter term focus than the 20 year planning horizon that woodland management entails. A balance will need to be struck between financial return and delivering a service to customers and the general public.

Also conflicts may arise between the interests of the LLP and the separate interests of the two participating members. For instance CabinCo's desire to increase the profitability of the Woodsaway venture may conflict with SWC's mission to protect the woodlands and increase their value to society.

This is further discussed under the governance heading below.

Examiner's comments

In the first section of the report, candidates had to assess the strategic fit of the proposed venture. It was well answered. Most candidates were comfortable discussing the extent to which the venture is aligned with SWC's mission and secondary aims, recognising that construction of the log cabins might be inconsistent with the achievement of some of these aims (e.g. protection of the woodland and nature conservation) but might facilitate others (increasing access and education). The better candidates also highlighted the very different nature of the two organisations involved in the LLP and questioned the conflict that may arise as a result. Most, but surprisingly not all candidates, scored an easy format mark for setting out their answer in the report format required. Some candidates created a time management issue for themselves by using all three headings from the suitability, feasibility, acceptability model when in fact 'suitability' is sufficient to assess strategic fit.

64.2 Financial benefits

The public/private partnership reduces the need for investment from SWC which would have to come from central government and SWC's limited commercial funds.

CabinCo (and possibly Woodsaway) will be able to raise funds privately from banks etc as it is not under the same restrictions regarding borrowing as SWC. The access to finance could provide opportunities for SWC, which would be unlikely to be able to find the £2m building costs. In the future it would also allow extension of the concept to other sites.

The venture provides SWC as landlord with a guaranteed income stream in the form of the lease rentals of £30,000pa. Depending on the occupancy levels, SWC, as a member of the LLP, will also receive a 50% share of the profits. Provided Woodsaway does not make a loss of more than £60,000 then SWC will avoid any financial loss.

Looking at the figures in the exhibit, the financial returns to SWC are highly sensitive to occupancy, which is likely to be lower in the early years:

Occupancy rate	40%	65%	90%
	£'000	£'000	£'000
Rental	30	30	30
Share of Woodsaway (loss)/profit	(153)	118	372
Net return to SWC	(123)	148	402
Annual return on £2m land value invested	-6.15%	7.4%	20.1%
Occupancy rate	40%	65%	90%

	£'000	£'000	£'000
Cabin revenue	1,752	2,847	3,942
Contribution	1,226	1,993	2,759
Fixed costs incl rent	(1,532)	(1,757)	(2,015)
Loss/Profit	(306)	236	744

The cabins are projected to generate a gross profit of £84 per night (eg £1,226,000/(365 x 40)). There are 36,500 available cabin nights (365 x 100 cabins). If operating costs were £1,532,000 including rent then for the Woodsaway venture to break-even it needs to sell £1,532,000/84 = 18,238 cabin nights which equates to 50% occupancy.

Were operating costs to be £1,757,000 including rent then it would need 20,917 cabin nights or 57% occupancy. In reality it appears that some operating costs are stepped (14.7% increase in operating costs for 25% increase in occupancy), so break-even occupancy is somewhere between 50% and 57%.

It would be useful to know what occupancy CabinCo currently achieves in its other holiday villages, which is said to be 'high', but if Woodsaway achieves anything over 65%, it would appear to be providing SWC with a decent return.

It is not clear who has supplied the figures and how these compare to other CabinCo ventures. More detail on the breakdown of operating costs would be useful and the assumption of 365 days availability may be over-optimistic.

As discussed above, money from Woodsaway can be used to fulfil SWC's other objectives and is a useful source of income given its reliance on government funds.

Examiner's comments

Answers to this section on financial benefits were varied and there were a considerable number of poor answers, resulting in this section having the lowest overall mark. Once again a surprising number of candidates made no reference to the numbers provided in the question, despite the fact that this was the obvious place to do so. Weaker candidates simply discussed the fact that SWC is limited in its ability to raise finance and that the venture may help with this, without considering the financial returns.

The key to evaluating the financial benefits was to identify the two separate roles of SWC in relation to the Woodsaway venture:

- As landlord in receipt of annual rental
- As a member of the LLP, sharing in 50% of the profits or losses

Better candidates recognised this and used the various projections to calculate SWC's profit share for the different occupancy levels. The best candidates used the financial projections provided to give some indication of the likely return on SWC's £2m land investment and examined the sensitivity of the venture (eg by calculating a break-even occupancy).

64.3 Risks

A key issue for SWC is risk and who will take responsibility for managing those risks.

Compared to SWC operating a holiday village on its own, the risk of the Woodsaway venture is reduced because it is structured as an LLP and risk is shared with CabinCo, an experienced partner in the holiday sector. The public/private partnership integrates the complementary resources of the two parties. However as discussed in 64.1 above, a conflict of interest may arise between the interests of the LLP and the separate interests of the two participating members.

The Woodsaway venture brings its own additional risks:

Economic risk– financial events that would affect the management of the holiday village and/or the forest. This might include the volatility of revenue streams and profit share due to the state of the economy. Also any impact that operating the holiday site may have on revenues from the sale of timber. The construction of the cabins may require tree felling which could generate revenue initially but may then reduce the areas available for replanting, adversely impacting SWC's future revenue.

Reputational risk – the possible negative impact of the LLP and the holiday site on the image of SWC in the minds of other organisations it deals with, the general public and the government. If Woodsaway is very profitable it may not be appropriate for SWC to be seen to be associated with this, conversely the same may be true with a financially unsuccessful venture. There may also be reputational issues if Woodsaway is seen to pay high salaries/bonuses or alternatively if it treats staff poorly or causes environmental damage (see below).

Environmental risk – the creation of a holiday site exposes the woodland estate to possible additional threats in relation to damage and disease. There is a possible risk of urbanisation of forest through construction of cabins, which might destroy natural habitats, and there may be ongoing issues relating to damage due to footfall, more vehicles, creation of waste etc.

Hazard risk - similar to the environmental risk above, there is an increased risk of fire damage from the use of the forest as a holiday site.

Social risk – the holiday site may open the woodland up to more people but if CabinCo's customers are largely in England and Wales, these may not necessarily be from the community which SWC serves. Also the luxury cabins may only be affordable by a small minority and could be seen to be elitist.

SWC will need to ensure that appropriate risk management processes are put in place to address the additional risks that arise as a result of the Woodsaway venture. It needs to insist on controls in relation to woodland management, protection of habitat and leisure.

Examiner's comments

The majority of candidates were clearly well prepared to discuss the risks associated with the proposed venture and scored very highly on this section of the report. Most candidates identified a range of risks and discussed their potential impact. Better candidates also discussed their likelihood and suggested how they might be mitigated/managed if SWC is to go ahead with the proposal, pointing out that the risks are reduced by the creation of the LLP to operate the venture.

64.4 Governance issues

Applicability of corporate governance

Corporate governance generally refers to the system by which companies are directed and controlled. The aim of corporate governance is to facilitate effective, prudent management in order to deliver long term success. It is underpinned by the principles of accountability, transparency, probity (honesty) and focus on long term sustainable success.

Whilst the second SWC trustee is correct that the UK Corporate Governance Code applies to listed companies only, good governance is essential not just for companies but to any organisation, irrespective of whether it is private or public, if that organisation is to be well led and high performing.

It could be argued that good governance is even more important in the context of a public sector body, like SWC, which needs to ensure that public funds are wisely spent and that resources such as Scotland's woodlands are properly safeguarded and are used economically, efficiently, and effectively. This is the view expressed by the first trustee.

More generally therefore, governance relates to the framework of accountability to users, stakeholders and the wider community, within which organisations take decisions, and lead and control their functions, to achieve their objectives. As such it would apply to both SWC and Woodsaway. Without effective governance, the proposed public/private partnership is unlikely to be successful.

Nolan principles

Governance in the public sector has much in common with corporate governance for companies. As a publicly funded body, SWC's management board needs to act in accordance with the Nolan principles, which include the principles of integrity, accountability, openness (transparency) and honesty (probity). These are very similar to the core corporate governance principles. In addition, holders of public office are expected to comply with the additional principles of selflessness, objectivity and leadership.

Of particular relevance in the context of the Woodsaway venture are:

Selflessness: holders of public office should take decisions solely in terms of the public interest. They should not do so in order to gain financial or other materials benefits for themselves, their family, or other friends. Thus SWC needs to balance its different responsibilities and ensure that its involvement in Woodsaway does not give rise to the risk of appearing to act in a manner contrary to public interest.

Objectivity: in carrying out public business, including making public appointments, awarding contracts, or recommending individuals for rewards and benefits, holders of public office should make choices on merit. The trustees need to be seen to have considered alternative partners as well as CabinCo, which has been selected because it is the best option

Public sector organisations operate in complex legislative, political and local contexts, in which they have to make difficult decisions. Well-governed organisations balance their different responsibilities and use information to decide where to allocate effort and resources to meet competing demands.

Governance of Woodsaway

The principles of governance will apply to Woodsaway, as an LLP. A key part of good governance is risk management and this will be particularly important to SWC given the additional risks that arise as a result of the Woodsaway venture (discussed in 64.3 above).

CabinCo and SWC will each be entitled to appoint three representatives on Woodsaway's senior management committee so neither party would appear able to dictate decisions.

SWC needs to insist on controls to ensure Woodsaway LLP does not undermine SWC's objectives in relation to woodland management and the protection of habitat and nature. It will also need to agree on the methods for resolving any disputes and the exit arrangements should either party want to terminate the venture.

Conclusion

Overall the project appears likely to generate financial returns and would appear to help SWC further some of its aims. It seems to have the support of government, which has granted preliminary approval for the formation of the LLP. More work should be done on the financial projections and SWC could engage in stakeholder consultations to assess the public perception of the proposals. The LLP will need to be set up carefully to ensure that the risks and governance issues identified are properly addressed.

Examiner's comments

Answers to the governance section were very variable in quality. There were really two issues here: addressing the trustees' comments in relation to governance and considering the governance of the proposed LLP. A significant minority failed to appreciate the distinction between the UK Corporate Governance Code that applies only to listed companies and corporate governance, which is the system by which companies are directed and controlled. The better candidates recognised that the principles of good governance (accountability, transparency etc) are very similar to those enshrined in the Nolan principles and are best practice for the prudent and effective management of any organisation. Thus governance may be more, rather than less, relevant for a public sector organisation such as SWC with a wider group of stakeholders to account to and a need to act in the public interest.

Having discussed this in the light of the trustees' comments, better candidates also went on to consider governance in relation to the LLP as a critical factor in the likely success of the venture, and discussed the proposals for the structure of Woodsaway's senior management committee.

Recognising that the overall purpose of the report was to evaluate the proposed venture, most candidates provided reasoned advice at the end as to whether SWC should go ahead with the Woodsaway venture. This was pleasing to see.

	Knowledge	Skill	Marks
65.1 Strategic options	3	12	14
65.2 Decision tree	2	5	6
	5	17	20

General comments

The third question, worth only 20 marks, was also well attempted overall, with good scores on requirement 65.1 making up for poorer answers to requirement 65.2.

The scenario relates to a company which produces high-performance thermal drysuits for scuba diving. The drysuits are very expensive and are typically bought by professional divers, although WeDive also distributes its drysuits to diving retailers for recreational users who want a high quality product. The directors are keen to expand and are considering two mutually exclusive strategies:

Option 1: Expand the range of products for the UK market by sourcing lifestyle clothing and selling it under WeDive's own brand, through existing distribution channels (diving retailers). Due to limited funds, WeDive intends to use social media to market this option.

Option 2: Produce drysuits for export markets. This would involve finding and partnering with new distributors. Since a key aspect of WeDive's high-performance drysuit is the fit, the product may need some redesigning to fit the local population in each export market. Some basic financial information is provided in the form of possible outcomes, and their probabilities, for one possible market being considered - New Zealand.

65.1 Evaluation of options

Option 1: expand the range of products for the UK market

Option 1 in terms of the Ansoff matrix constitutes product development.

Advantages

- It may be less risky than targeting overseas markets as there are no language/cultural barriers

- WeDive's brand name is already known to the UK market and seen as high-quality, so it can easily capitalise on it

- Casual lifestyle clothing is related to the existing product range so there is some strategic fit and it may appeal to existing recreational dive customers.

- These products can probably sell through the existing distribution channels which facilitates implementation of the strategy.

- The new products may also appeal to other market segments, so this strategy could involve an element of market development too.

- The marketing of the product via social media may fit with the appeal of lifestyle clothing to a younger market.

Disadvantages

- From a generic strategy point of view, WeDive's existing product is very differentiated and it protects itself from competition by operating in a market niche. There are high levels of competition in the lifestyle clothing market already and the products are more homogeneous.

- Margins on casual clothing may be lower than on existing drysuit products and will be affected by the level of competition and the fact that there are low-cost producers outside the UK.

- There is likely to be a short product life cycle as typically these lifestyle brands come and go as far as fashion is concerned

- 65% of sales are to professional divers and these products may be less attractive to them than the recreational divers

- WeDive will need to source a supplier(s) as it has no experience in manufacturing

- There is little scope for using WeDive's existing expertise

- The new strategy will require marketing expenditure and social media may be insufficient to attract a wide customer base

- This strategy is still UK focussed and may offer limited scope for growth

Option 2: focus on core product but expand market overseas

Option 2 in terms of the Ansoff matrix constitutes market development.

Advantages

- Exporting drysuits builds on existing competences and is consistent with WeDive's differentiation strategy

- WeDive already have a tried and tested product that has been well received by the market

- It may be possible to achieve better expansion by targeting contracts with professional divers rather than recreational ones, using existing links with police, armed forces etc

- Overseas markets may be more price sensitive/have different price elasticities which could increase their profitability

- It may be sensible to try out one or two markets initially that are more close to the UK in terms of the size, fit and climate requirements.

Disadvantages

- WeDive's brand name may not be recognised in export markets although once established, this strategy will help to create a global brand

- The nature of the product may not work in some countries – eg different fabric may be required for tropical rather than cold water diving

- The product may require amendments to the fit to suit different population sizes and characteristics

- Risk arises due to the lack of familiarity with overseas markets although this will be reduced if WeDive find the right distribution partner

- WeDive is likely to face competition from existing players in these markets

- A factor to consider is where the suits will be made and whether WeDive has the production capacity to cater for the increased volumes.

Preliminary conclusions

- The existing product has a three year warranty and may not involve frequent repeat purchases so it seems sensible to consider opportunities to expand revenue

- Either option will help reduce dependence on the existing UK market and on professional dive contracts in particular

- Market research of either strategy offers the opportunity to reduce the risk of expansion

- WeDive needs to consider financial projections before making a decision

- Option 2 is probably more likely to be successful in the longer term as it makes use of existing expertise and builds on WeDive's differentiation strategy. The company could consider selling online initially as a means of export then find distributors if it becomes clear that there is demand.

Examiner's comments

The requirement to evaluate the two alternative strategies was straightforward and well done by most candidates. A significant number of candidates identified that WeDive is currently a differentiator, focussed on a niche market. Many started their discussion by positioning the proposed strategies within the Ansoff matrix as product development and market development respectively. Most candidates produced sensible answers setting out the advantages and disadvantages of the two strategies and showed good knowledge of the specific issues relating to overseas expansion. Some used the 'suitability, feasibility, acceptability' approach to good effect to generate a range of points. The better candidates went on to reach a conclusion as to which of the strategies might be more appropriate for WeDive, recognising the need to obtain more detailed financial projections before making a final decision.

65.2 Decision Tree

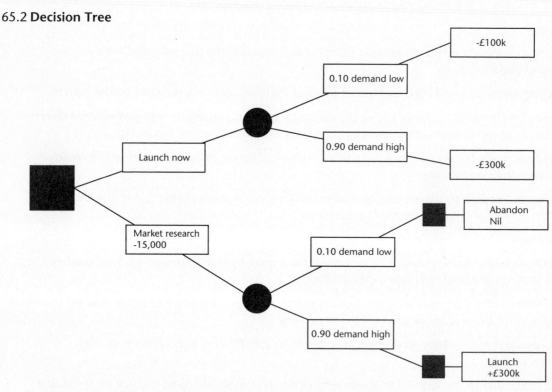

Launch now without MR: (0.9 × 300k) + (0.1 × (100k)) = 260k

With MR: (0.9 × 300k) + (0.1 × 0) = 270k less 15k research cost = 255k

Hence financially it is better not to undertake MR but this is based on EV which is a long term average and not necessarily applicable to a one-off decision. It also ignores risk:

Without MR, actual outcomes are +300 or -100, spread of 400k in potential return

With MR, actual outcomes become +300 or zero. Therefore depending on WeDive's attitude to risk it may be worth paying £15k for the ability to minimise downside risk despite the lower expected outcome.

Examiner's comments

This was the first time that a decision tree has been examined and answers were very variable. For candidates who knew how to draw the tree, and then do the simple expected value calculations, this requirement was a source of easy marks. Many lacked the required technical knowledge however which resulted in some non-attempts. Sensible candidates who used the numbers in the scenario to produce an expected value calculation and then went on to make some relevant comments were still able to score a pass however.

66 Reyel plc (June 2015)

	Knowledge	Skill	Marks
66.1 (a) Quarter data analysis	1	11	
(b) Comparative data analysis	1	8	18
66.2 Capacity management and pricing	4	7	10
66.3 Estimated loss	1	7	7
66.4 Ethics	3	4	7
	10	37	42

General comments

This is the mini case worth 42 marks and also the main data analysis question.

The scenario is based on an international company, Reyel, which owns and operates mid-market hotels. A new division, 'The Extended Stay Hotel Division' (the ESH), was set up to enter the extended stay hotel market. The initial strategy, to test the market, was to establish one hotel, The Clarre, in London. Quarterly management accounts are produced to measure performance, where seasonality is an issue. The performance of The Clarre is also benchmarked against one of Reyel's traditional hotels in London, The Zoy.

Two issues that have arisen with respect to the management of The Clarre are: managing capacity and pricing.

An ethical issue has arisen whereby the manager of The Clarre has offered regular business customers discount vouchers for private holidays if they agree to a premium over the standard price for a guestroom, at their employer's expense.

66.1 (a)   Quarterly data analysis: The Clarre

			The Clarre			The Zoy
	Quarter to 30 June 20Y4	Quarter to 30 September 20Y4	Quarter to 31 December 20Y4	Quarter to 31 March 20Y5	Year ending 31 March 20Y5	Year ending 31 March 20Y5
Capacity (nights)	21,600	21,600	21,600	21,600	86,400	108,000
Number of nights actually occupied	15,552	17,280	16,848	15,120	64,800	62,640
Operating profit % (based on guestroom revenue)	18.3%	28.1%	28.1%	16.6%	23.3%	*21.7%
% of annual revenue	22.8%	27.5%	27.5%	22.1%	100%	–
% of annual nights	24.0%	26.7%	26.0%	23.3%	100%	–
% of annual operating profit	17.9%	33.1%	33.2%	15.8%	100%	–

*   18.2% If based on total revenue

Revenue

The Clarre was a new start-up on 1 April 20Y4, which is the beginning of the current financial year. As such, it is likely to take some time to establish a customer base and grow, particularly as this is a new type of hotel for the Reyel group. The first year of operations is therefore probably atypical and there is likely to be growth in future years. Similarly, there is likely to be growth between quarters as the hotel becomes established during the year. Some of the underlying quarterly variation may therefore be due to early growth, rather than just seasonal variation.

Revenue in each of the two quarters ending 30 September 20Y4 and 31 December 20Y4 (Q2 and Q3) was greater than in each of the other two quarters (Q1 and Q4). In terms of revenue generated 55% of annual revenue occurred in Q2 and Q3, being equally split between these two quarters.

It terms of volumes (ie number of guest nights) the seasonal variation is less pronounced with only 52.7% of guest nights occurring in Q2 and Q3 (being 26.7% and 26% respectively). This variation however understates the variability in seasonal demand as the lowest occupancy rates in Q1 and Q4 were incurred despite the lowest average prices of £68 per night, compared with averages of £74 and £76 per night respectively for Q2 and Q3. Had the same prices been charged throughout the year then a much more pronounced seasonal variation is likely to have occurred.

In summary, the highest demand occurred in Q2 and Q3 despite these quarters having the higher average prices. Whilst Q1 may have been disadvantaged as the start-up quarter, the same cannot be said for Q4 which had longer to establish a customer base than Q2 and Q3.

Additional information, which would be an indicator of the Q1 start-up effect, can be found by comparing revenue for Q1 with the quarter ended 30 June 20Y5, which is near completion.

Additional useful information would be:

- Seasonal variation of any other extended stay hotels in the London area to use as a benchmark to strip out industry average seasonality in the geographical area (though this information may be difficult to obtain)

- Variations in prices and occupancy within each quarter.

Operating profit

The quarterly operating profit margins for Q2 and Q3 (28.1% for each) show that they are much more profitable than Q1 and Q4 which had margins of only 18.3% and 16.6% respectively.

A similar picture can be seen from analysing the percentage of total operating profit for the year earned in each quarter. Almost two thirds (66.3%) of total operating profit for the year was earned in Q2 and Q3, being 33.1% and 33.2% respectively. This trend is far more pronounced than that for revenue, discussed above, which amounted to only 55% in Q2 and Q3.

There are number of causal factors which are likely to have given rise to this:

- The average price per night is higher in Q2 and Q3 so the margins are higher.

- There will be a large element of fixed operating costs in running a hotel. These will have an operating gearing effect, such that variations in revenue are magnified in operating profit as the fixed costs must still be covered when revenue falls. This means the lower demand in Q1 and Q4 gives rise to a disproportionate decrease in operating profit.

- The average length of a stay is greater in Q2 and Q3 (at 15 and 18 nights respectively, against 14 and 13 nights in Q1 and Q4), so the costs of room change-overs are reduced.

(b) **Comparison of The Clarre and The Zoy**

Difficulties in making valid comparisons should be recognised. These include:

- A different business model, although both are in the same industry
- The Clarre is a start-up whereas The Zoy is well established

Despite this, the two hotels are operating in the mid-market hotel sector, are of similar size and are in similar locations. Reasonable comparisons are therefore possible.

A key distinction is that The Zoy has two sources of revenue: room revenues and other revenues (from the restaurant and bar). The operating costs provided are not divided between these two revenue streams and this would be useful additional information in identifying the source of the performance. The interdependence of revenues and costs between these two revenue streams would however need to be recognised, even if this cost analysis information were to be available.

Guestroom revenues

Guestroom revenues generated by The Zoy are 34.9% higher than those of The Clarre. In analysing the underlying causes of why the revenue is greater there are three key factors:

- Capacity (number of room nights available)
- Occupancy
- Price

It can be seen from the above table that the number of nights occupancy (ie volume) is similar for the two hotels, with The Clarre and The Zoy being 64,800 and 62,640 respectively for the year ended 31 March 20Y5. These figures are determined as a function of capacity and occupancy.

Despite the volume of room nights being similar, this is achieved in a different way with The Zoy having a much higher capacity (108,000 room nights compared to 86,400), but a lower occupancy (58% compared to 75%).

Given the similar volumes sold (ie the number of room nights) the fact that The Zoy has revenue that is 34.9% higher than The Clarre is caused by an average price of £100 for The Zoy per night, compared with £71.70 per night for The Clarre (ie 39.5% higher).

Data could meaningfully be calculated based on revenue per guest if comparing two traditional hotels or two extended stay hotels. However, given that the relative business models create very different average stays, such a comparison would be almost meaningless in comparing The Clarre with The Zoy as it would not compare like with like.

Other revenue

'Other revenue' for The Zoy is £1.2 million, which is 16.1% of the total revenue of £7.464 million for The Zoy. This is therefore reasonably substantial and makes the total revenue for The Zoy 60.7% higher than that of The Clarre. (However, the operating costs of the restaurant and bar are not separately provided so it is difficult to draw conclusions about the profitability of The Zoy restaurant.)

Operating costs

Additional information is needed analysing operating costs into the component accounts.

Overall, however, The Zoy has operating costs which are 71.5% higher than those of The Clarre. The underlying causes of this are likely to be:

- Costs of the restaurant and bar
- Greater levels of service (eg daily cleaning)
- More frequent change-overs (as average stay is 3 days rather than 15 days for The Zoy)

Note however that the volume of room nights actually used is similar for both hotels.

Further information indicating the breakdown of fixed and variable costs may be useful to determine how costs relate to volumes and how operating costs are likely to change in future.

Operating profit

As already noted, The Zoy has revenue 60.7% higher than The Clarre, but operating costs 71.5% higher. Despite this, in absolute terms, The Zoy has made more profit than The Clarre in the year ended 31 March 20Y5, as revenue is greater than operating costs. Indeed, the operating profit of The Zoy is 25.3% higher than The Clarre.

Conclusion

The Zoy has outperformed The Clarre but this is not unexpected given this is the latter's first year of trading. Greater sales in future, as The Clarre generates a more established customer base, seem likely to close the gap and perhaps permit the performance of The Clarre to exceed that of The Zoy.

Examiner's comments

(a) Candidates' answers were generally reasonably good on this requirement. For most candidates, there was an improvement over previous sittings on the presentation of the data analysis by using an initial table of calculations, followed by a qualitative analysis of the results.

The majority recognised the seasonality evident in the data. Many also identified the need for a breakdown of costs into fixed and variable after recognising that there had been a more than proportional increase in operating profit relative to the increases in revenue.

The better scoring scripts analysed occupancy rates per quarter and the overall impact of occupancy on profitability. The discussion part of the question was done quite well with candidates linking seasonality, location and hotel type back to the scenario. However, only a small number identified that the data presented was from a start-up business and could be subject to major variations in the future.

Weaker candidates merely copied data from the question, often without calculating any new ratios. Where new ratios were calculated, weaker candidates tended to provide only very general ratios such as operating profit margins, without considering any indicators of performance specific to the scenario. In their narrative, weaker candidates tended to merely describe what had happened, rather than providing an analysis determining causal factors and explaining how and why a movement in the data had occurred.

(b) Calculations were mostly limited to percentage changes and basic margins. In terms of analysis, only the strong candidates highlighted the difficulties in making comparisons due to the differences in the business models of the two hotels and the fact that the Clarre was a start-up. While trying to make similar comparisons, candidates wanted to 'strip out' the restaurant but, in doing so, often deducted the revenue while not recognising some of the operating costs would be attributable to the restaurant. Conclusions were not always offered.

66.2 Capacity management and pricing

Capacity planning

Capacity planning is the process of determining the capacity needed by an organisation to satisfy changing demands for its products or services.

Effective capacity in the hotel industry is the maximum number of guests that a hotel is capable of accommodating in a given period, due to constraints such as physical resources (guestroom capacity), human resources, quality threshold issues (guestrooms in good repair and cleaned) and delays (room turnaround).

A difference between the capacity of a hotel and the demand from its guests results either in under-utilised resources (eg available guestrooms unoccupied) or unsatisfied demand (guests turned away when the hotel is full). The goal of capacity planning is to manage this difference.

Capacity can be increased through introducing new techniques, processes or assets, or varying the number of employee hours.

Capacity management in the hotel industry can be short-term or long-term. Within each of these time frames, capacity management can also be viewed from the supply side or the demand side.

Long-term capacity management

Supply side

In the context of a hotel, the number of guestrooms sets an upper limit on physical capacity in the medium to long term. Whilst it may be possible, from the company perspective, to build new extended stay hotels, from the perspective of the manager of The Clarre, an extension of physical capacity is difficult as there are limitations of building in a city such as London. Possibilities in the longer term to raise physical capacity might be to: change common areas into more guestrooms; build additional floors; reconfigure the guestrooms to make them smaller, but more plentiful; use an overflow venue.

It would be a mistake however to consider capacity solely in terms of either (1) physical capacity or (2) only increasing capacity.

Capacity could have a number of aspects. For example, the need may be to reduce capacity in order to reduce costs, rather than increase capacity. The average utilisation of The Clarre is 75%. Maintaining the ability to service 100% occupancy, if long-term demand remains at 75% occupancy, would be an inefficient use of resources and would involve the provision of expensive and unutilised capacity.

Demand side

Demand management might involve increasing demand in order to utilise surplus capacity. This might include, in terms of long-term demand management: improving facilities to attract more people to stay at the hotel (eg business centre, bar); improve guestroom quality; recruit more staff; reduce standard prices.

Short-term capacity management

Supply side

Flexibility in short-term capacity is needed as hotel bookings may vary unpredictably, so the need to match variations in demand with variations in capacity reduces underutilised resources or lost sales.

Labour is a key aspect of planning short-term capacity. For example, flexible contracts (eg staff might be required to work overtime or shifts at short notice) to meet changes in demand from bookings will enable resources to be acquired quickly to match demand changes in the short term.

Short-term closure of a section of rooms, or a floor, may reduce short-term capacity (eg from the data provided, demand is seasonal for The Clarre). This would save costs such as heating a floor.

Demand side

The use of IT and marketing models to predict variations in demand will help give management more time to manage capacity.

Demand management capacity planning may be used to reduce peak demand by switching it to the off-peak periods, such as by offering relatively lower off-peak prices. This is a form of price discrimination which is discussed below. The utilisation of the advertising budget may also be applied disproportionately to attract demand in the low season.

Pricing

Flexible prices, taking the form of price discrimination, can include charging customers different amounts to reflect their individual price elasticities. To be able to do this, there needs to be separation of markets.

Examples of effective separation of markets can include businesses which make a large number of bookings compared to individuals who may only make a single booking. The individual cannot access the business price as he/she does not normally require as many hotel stays as a business.

The objective of the pricing strategy needs to be clear. Setting prices to maximise utilisation is not necessarily a good idea if revenues can be maximised by a higher price with less than 100% utilisation.

Even revenue maximisation may not be appropriate as it may not equate to profit maximisation.

The data in the exhibit shows that demand varies between quarters, but will also vary within quarters (eg if a major event is on in London, higher prices can be charged and yet there may still be full utilisation). These demand peaks can generate higher prices in order to reduce demand (in terms of guest nights) to the capacity level of the hotel.

Conclusion

Where there is a strict physical limit on the number of guestrooms (at least in the short term) then pricing can be one of the most effective means of capacity planning. If capacity management is aligning capacity and demand then, where capacity is upwardly inflexible, pricing is the primary means in the short term of adjusting effective demand to match available capacity.

Examiner's comments

Most candidates only considered the short term when discussing capacity management. However a range of interesting suggestions were provided. Good quality candidates tried to link capacity management and pricing policy. Few candidates distinguished supply-side and demand-side aspects of capacity management.

The treatment of pricing was variable in quality. A high proportion of candidates used the 4Cs approach to structure their answers. Many candidates recognised that varying prices could be charged due to the seasonality of the business, but many failed to recognise key issues such as price discrimination or price elasticity.

Some candidates conflated the issues of capacity management and pricing within a single narrative, which usually limited the clarity and scope of their answers.

66.3 Estimate of lost revenue

The impact of opening The Clarre on the revenues of The Zoy is the difference between the following two figures:

(1) The revenues actually generated by The Zoy

(2) The revenues that would have been generated by The Zoy had The Clarre not been opened (the counter factual).

Whilst figure (1) is known, figure (2) needs to be estimated.

The starting point is that if The Clarre had not been opened it may have been the case that The Zoy's revenues may have changed over the past year anyway, due to other factors. These other factors need to be evaluated in order to make an assessment of the figure in (2) above.

Macro and industry factors

In estimating the change in The Zoy's revenue from last year, industry trends and macroeconomic trends need to be considered, particularly in the context of the London market. Thus, if London hotels generally suffered a fall in revenues compared to last year, then this factor could be stripped out of last year's The Zoy revenue in estimating (2) above.

Internal changes

Any changes that Zoy management has made this year compared to last year need to be considered. Price changes may have had an effect on demand, as may other factors including staffing, refurbishment (or lack of it), customer service policy and advertising. These factors need to be stripped out in estimating (2) above.

Data analysis

An analysis of data might reveal more information.

For instance, if there has been a sharp fall in the number of long stays at The Zoy (of over 8 days) then this seems more likely to have been caused by the opening of The Clarre than if there had been a fall in the number of short stays, which are not the same market sector as The Clarre.

If there is a Reyel loyalty card, or company credit card, then specific evidence could be gathered on individual customers who stayed at The Zoy last year but transferred over to The Clarre this year.

Examiner's comments

The answers to this requirement were the weakest on the entire paper, and formed the highest rate of non-attempts. Many candidates failed to grasp the key issue of what would have happened to the revenue of The Zoy if The Clarre had not opened. Weaker candidates, implicitly or explicitly, assumed it would have remained at the level of the previous year.

Many candidates did not give due consideration to external factors, in addition to the internal ones, relevant to the possible impact on The Zoy arising from opening The Clarre. Few focussed on what had happened specifically to the longer stay customers of the Zoy.

66.4 Ethical issues

Ethics pertains to whether a particular behaviour is deemed acceptable in the context under consideration. In short it is 'doing the right thing'.

In making any ethical evaluation it is first necessary to establish the facts. In this case, the claims made against Kevin need to be established to assess their validity. This may include establishing the use of vouchers by The Clarre customers and tracing these back to the prices they have paid for staying at The Clarre.

The issue of legality applies; where an inducement has been given then this may come under the Bribery Act. It may also be fraud. Legal advice should be taken.

The offering of vouchers may not, of itself, be unethical and may be common practice in the industry. However, two other factors to consider are:

- The value of the vouchers and whether they are sufficiently significant to amount to a material inducement; and

- The fact that vouchers are not being offered for booking a guestroom on normal commercial terms but, rather, for individual business guests agreeing that their employers should pay in excess of the standard price set for other guests, with no clear commercial cause or benefit to the employer. There is a clear and possibly substantial benefit to the employee as an individual.

In making a decision as to how to act, it may be helpful to apply the Institute of Business Ethics three tests:

- Transparency
- Effect
- Fairness

Transparency – would the Reyel board mind people (existing customers, suppliers, employees) knowing what has happened? In particular, the issue of transparency will apply to the employers who have paid inflated amounts. This is likely to have consequences in refunding money to employers.

Effect – whom does the decision to provide inducements affect/hurt? Clearly this includes the employers who have paid more than the market rate. Other rival hotels, who were offering lower prices to employers but without additional inducements, may also have suffered.

Fairness – would the inducement be considered fair by those affected? The issue for Reyel's board is that the company may have benefited from the action of the manager, even though the board did not itself instigate the particular actions nor was even aware of them at the time.

Honesty – A final issue is one of honesty. The inducements fail the honesty test on the basis of Rexel making an improper gain. There is now the onus to make other parties (eg employers) aware and return the excess amounts received.

Response

Where there is appropriate evidence an initial action would be to inform the employers and return any excess amounts charged. The manager's continued employment should be reviewed. The operation of the discount voucher scheme company-wide should also be reviewed

If there is suspicion there has been a crime then disclosure to the police, based on legal advice, may be appropriate.

Examiner's comments

On the whole, this requirement was reasonably well answered. Most candidates considered the legality issue, although many then immediately dismissed it as not relevant in this case.

Many candidates adopted the transparency, effect, fairness framework. Only better students went on to identify other ethical issues outside this framework. Actions to be taken by management were often ignored. Frustratingly, this included some students who produced excellent commentary on the ethical issues, but then failed to identify any subsequent actions.

---

67 Home of Leather plc (June 2015)

Marking guide

	Knowledge	Skill	Marks
67.1 Break-even/ volume of sales	3	6	9
67.2 Three strategies	2	10	10
67.3 Mendelow's matrix	3	4	7
67.4 Change management	3	6	8
	11	26	34

General comments

HoL is a company which manufactures good quality leather furniture. The company is located in Puddington, where its site comprises a factory, distribution centre and office.

In order to remain competitive, HoL needs to reduce costs by making fundamental changes to its business. Three potential strategies have been identified: relocate within the UK; relocate manufacturing overseas; or cease manufacturing then import as a wholesaler. All strategies would involve redundancies to varying degrees.

The board has set a target annual profit of £7.2 million, but prices and costs vary between the three strategies. Data on costs and revenues are provided.

67.1 (a)   Break-even and sales volume

To: Home of Leather plc Board
From: A Business Advisor
Date: 10 June 20Y5
Subject: Proposed reorganisation strategies

Break-even price

Strategy 1

B/E contribution	$=£14.4m/120,000$	$= £120$
B/E price	$=£200 + £120$	$= £320$

Strategy 2

B/E contribution	$=£10.8m/120,000$	$= £90$
B/E price	$=£160 + £90$	$= £250$

Strategy 3

B/E contribution	$=£1.8m/120,000$	$= £15$
B/E price	$=£280 + £15$	$= £295$

(b) **Sales volume to achieve a profit of £7.2m**

Strategy 1

(£14.4m + £7.2m)/(360 − 200) =   135,000 units

Strategy 2

(£10.8m + £7.2m)/(324 − 160) =   109,756 units

Strategy 3

(£1.8m + £7.2m)/(324 − 280)   =   204,545 units

Examiner's comments

The performance on this requirement was generally good, although it did tend to polarise between the many candidates who managed to arrive at the correct calculations, thereby scoring full marks, and the minority who scored nominal marks. Weaker candidates often provided break-even sales volumes, rather than the volumes necessary to achieve an annual profit of £7.2 million. Others determined break-even volumes, instead of break-even prices.

Many candidates failed to achieve the mark available for presenting their answer to this question in report format.

67.2 Evaluation of proposals

	Strategy 1 £'000	Strategy 2 £'000	Strategy 3 £'000
Sales	43,200	38,880	38,880
Variable cost	(24,000)	(19,200)	(33,600)
Annual fixed costs	(14,400)	(10,800)	(1,800)
Profit	4,800	8,880	3,480

Strategy 1

While this strategy involves some downsizing, it is the least transformational change and therefore has fewer transition costs. Nevertheless, there would be a loss of 60% of the employees who have skills which may be difficult to replicate with a new workforce.

In terms of ongoing production, the product quality is maintained and therefore the risk of alienating existing customers in the hope of attracting new customers through a lower price-quality mix is avoided.

In terms of the data offered Strategy 1 is not as profitable as Strategy 2 (see above), but more profitable than Strategy 3.

There is however less risk with Strategy 1 than the other two strategies in a number of respects:

- There is currency matching between the currency of 70% of sales and the currency in which costs are incurred. There is therefore less risk from currency fluctuations.

- As the proposal is based on existing production there is more certainty surrounding estimates

- There is no change in market positioning

This strategy however has greater risk than the other two in having more fixed costs and therefore higher operating gearing. As an example, if the Grint contract is lost then the high fixed costs still need to be incurred and a large loss will be made.

Also, in respect of the Grint contract, the break-even price of £320 is only £40 less than the price indicated by the Grint board as a maximum, making profits only marginal on this contract.

Strategy 2

Based on the data provided, this is the most profitable contract, with an estimated annual profit of £8.88 million.

There are, however, a number of operating and financial factors which increase risk and mitigate against the higher return.

In the first instance, this strategy is likely to be the greatest transformational change and therefore have the highest initial costs from change. It is unclear whether these initial costs have been annualised into the fixed costs in the table or whether they have been treated separately.

The supply chain is lengthened significantly which may cause operational uncertainty in meeting customer delivery needs.

The break-even price at £250 is £70 lower than the break-even price for Strategy 1 at £320. However, the quality of the output is better with Strategy 1, making any given price easier to achieve. Nevertheless, if the quality differential in relation to price is correct, then Strategy 2 remains more competitive than Strategy 1 in price-quality terms.

That said, the market positioning in Strategy 2 is different from the existing market positioning and there is a risk that it may take time to adjust to a new customer base which prefers a lower price-quality mix.

Looking at the break-even data in (67.1) above there appears to be a greater margin of safety for Strategy 2 than the other two strategies. This indicates lower risk in terms of variation of price and demand.

Strategy 3

On the basis of the data presented, Strategy 3 looks to be the least favourable option as it has the lowest expected profit and the least favourable margins of safety in terms of price and volumes demanded.

The issues of price-quality mix and currency risk are the same as for Strategy 2.

The key area where outsourcing in Strategy 3 has an advantage however is that it has the lowest fixed costs and therefore the lowest operating gearing. If the Grint contract were to be lost then high fixed costs would not need to continue to be incurred. There is more financial agility with Strategy 3, even though the expected return is lower. There is therefore downside protection. Exit costs are also likely to be lower as there is only a supply contract to exit and a warehouse to sell, rather than an entire factory.

Conclusion

For the renewal of the Grint contract, it would seem that Strategy 2 and Strategy 3 offer the potential to make a more competitive bid on price than Strategy 1. However much will depend on how significant quality is to Grint in the tender process.

Examiner's comments

Generally, there was a good performance by most candidates. Not all made use of financial data in their commentary. Others made good use of the data, for example determining profits and margins of safety, but then provided limited narrative (eg on supply chain issues). Some candidates drifted into a discussion of change management, despite being explicitly told they were not to do so. Those who used the suitability/acceptability/feasibility framework often wrote too much, yet missed key points, and were not normally helped by structuring their answers in this way. Most candidates provided a reasoned conclusion as to which strategy appeared best.

67.3 Mendelow

Strategy 1

Current employees

Power – Low
Interest – High negative

The current employees have high negative interest as they are under immediate threat of losing their jobs. The power of current employees to stop or moderate any relocation decision is limited. If the entire UK workforce is united against the move then significant costs to HoL can arise from disruption.

Given however that not all jobs are under threat, there may be limited co-operation in industrial action from the 40% of employees who are willing to relocate 150 kilometres away. This may be particularly the case if HoL pays generous removal expenses to relocate employees.

Even amongst the employees losing their jobs some may be happy with redundancy as they intend to retire or move jobs anyway.

Despite the above, it is likely that most employees have a strong negative interest in the relocation, particularly as the company is a key part of the town and perhaps families and friends are located there, who may suffer from a decline in the local economy following the closure of the factory. This may also make it harder for redundant employees to find new employment locally and therefore reinforce their negative interest.

One final qualification is employees may have a strong negative interest compared to the status quo of the factory in Puddington. If however there is an acceptance of the board's decision of the commercial need to make a change then, in relative terms, compared with the other two strategies, employees could favour Strategy 1 as there are fewer redundancies.

Grint

Power – High
Interest – Moderate

Given that 35% of HoL's sales are from Grint, it has considerable power over HoL and is likely to be in a position to influence the decision to relocate production. The cost savings from transferring production are likely to be a factor in the next tender, but also the level of quality of the products that HoL can provide is dependent on which of the three strategies is selected.

Grint may however be only moderately interested in the relocation as furniture manufacture is a competitive industry, with a range of alternative suppliers being available if HoL fails to deliver the required quality at the required price. Nevertheless, HoL is presumably currently Grint's preferred supplier for good reasons, so there may be a moderate wish to continue the relationship, despite the concerns over price expressed in their communication.

Examiner's comments

This requirement was very well answered by the majority of candidates and was, on average, the best answered requirement on the paper. Relatively comprehensive rationales were usually provided to support the positioning of current employees and Grint on Mendelow's matrix.

67.4 Change management

The change management process needs to be appropriate to the nature of the change.

In this case, the change is fundamental and transformational for either Strategy 1 or Strategy 2.

The transformational and reactive nature of the change classifies it as 'Forced Change' in the sense that the company will be unable to continue to compete if it does not reduce costs by making major changes.

Whilst there are commonalities between the two strategies which may require similar change management procedures, there are also differences which suggest a different change management approach for each strategy.

In terms of managing the impact of change, then there are very different effects for employees staying with the company and those being made redundant.

While there is a major effect on those being made redundant, in the longer term they will not be employees so, while the leaving process needs to be managed, there may be limited long-term effects on motivation if the change is well-managed. For Strategy 2 the change impacts on nearly all employees.

However, in the shorter term, following announcement the employees may not know which of the two groups they will fall into, and thus all employees may be demotivated by the uncertainty in this period. This may have adverse effects on quality of work and reputation.

There is also a danger of focusing only on change with respect to employees. Other stakeholders should also be considered in change management including:

(1) Continuing customers – who need to be reassured that they will continue to be supplied quality goods and that the delivery will continue to be reliable, particularly with Strategy 2 where the supply chain is geographically extended.

(2) Suppliers – to manage the continuing relationship with Strategy 1 and the issues that may arise from the change in geographical location. With Strategy 2 there is a need to ensure reliability of supply in the closing months when UK suppliers will be aware that contracts are to be terminated.

However, change does not only involve people but also:

(a) Changes in management structure due to the change in the nature of the business (eg automation with Strategy 1) and the location of the business (with Strategy 2).

(b) Change in culture. There is likely to be a change in culture particularly in Strategy 2 where employees will have a different national culture as well as management having the opportunity to work with employees to set up a new corporate culture.

Much more than Strategy 2, Strategy 1 has the change management issue of managing employees who are continuing in employment with HoL, but who may need to adapt to new practices in an automated environment and deal with a new culture.

In this context, for continuing employees, Lewin and Schein's Iceberg model has three stages in managing change:

- Unfreeze
- Move
- Refreeze

Unfreezing involves a trigger, a challenge of existing behaviour, involvement of outsiders, alterations to power structures.

Moving means making the changes, and communicating and encouraging adoption of the new situation.

Refreezing means consolidation and reinforcement of the new situation.

While these phases may be appropriate to employees moving or changing roles within the company, the changes to the factory are absolute (ie closure) and thus there is no concept of refreezing a new situation for employees who are leaving.

The model's application is therefore limited in the context of this factory closure, as some employees are lost to the company rather than having to accept a new structure or culture.

The **coercive change** approach is where change is forced without participation. This requires the ability to push through the change without co-operation but it may be appropriate in these circumstances as there is no requirement to maintain the goodwill of most of the factory workforce post changes, as they will no longer be working for HoL.

The **Gemini 4Rs** model of reframing, restructuring, revitalising and renewal is, like the Lewin model, largely based on the needs, not just of getting rid of the old structure, but also of reformulating the new structure. In the case of factory closure and for Strategy 2, the latter part of the model is largely redundant as there is little scope for renewal for employees who are leaving.

There are likely to be barriers to change, particularly from employees, which need to be managed as part of the change management process.

(!) **Cultural barriers**

Strategy 1 is more difficult to manage as it involves maintaining elements of the existing culture/structure/ workforce despite closing the factory. In contrast, Strategy 2 is more about managing closure and a new start up than managing a continuing process.

Strategy 1 puts forward fundamental changes that will affect the culture of the organisation. Power structures within the company may be threatened by the redistribution of decision-making authority or resources, or the changing of lines of communication.

For example, this will affect management and thus management may be reluctant to implement changes which will be contrary to their own interests.

(2) **Stakeholder groups**

Group inertia may block change where the changes are inconsistent with the norms of teams and departments, or where they threaten their interests.

Examples might include:

- Strikes and other forms of resistance to change implementation by staff who are to be made redundant

- UK raw material suppliers taking legal action for contract termination if the business is now to be switched to overseas suppliers under Strategy 2

- Shareholders selling shares as a result of the changes.

(3) **Individuals**

There are also barriers which affect individuals and result in them seeing the change as a threat to earnings and job security.

Conclusion

The transfer overseas in Strategy 2 is operationally more difficult as it involves setting up in a new country and almost starting the manufacturing process again. However, managing employees who are to move from the old factory to the new factory in Strategy 1 also presents challenges and a greater opportunity for resistance to change from those involved in that change. Each will require elements of common change management and differences in change management.

Examiner's comments

Answers were variable in quality. Weaker candidates' answers were unstructured and often did not refer to models at all, but merely discussed common sense issues such as uncertainty, redundancy and a lack of buy-in by the employees.

For those candidates that did use change management models, such as Lewin's iceberg model, answers were mixed. Where models were used, the weaker candidates did not apply the model to the scenario, while stronger candidates tended to analyse each strategy separately and conclude how best to manage change in each case.

68 Zuccini plc (June 2015)

	Knowledge	Skill	Marks
68.1 Typhoon	3	10	12
68.2 Hurricane	3	10	12
	6	20	24

General comments

Zuccini plc (Zuccini) is a niche manufacturer of motorbikes which is small in the context of the industry. It has an R&D centre in Italy and two factories, one in Italy and one in the UK. Product life cycles are a key feature of the industry and, as Zuccini is having liquidity issues, the product portfolio needs to be considered using models such as the product life cycle and the BCG matrix.

One of Zuccini's motorbikes, the Typhoon4, is nearing the end of its product life cycle and consideration is being given either: (1) to replacing the Typhoon4 with a completely new model, the Typhoon5; or (2) to modifying the Typhoon4 to produce a slightly updated version, the Typhoon4A, to extend the existing life cycle.

Another motorbike, 'the Hurricane', is currently in its R&D phase, but technical difficulties have caused delays and some uncertainties. Consideration is being given whether to: (1) launch 'the Hurricane' next year as a low-price, basic model; or (2) delay the launch and continue R&D for three years, then launch as a higher price, mid-market product.

68.1 The product life cycle

The product life cycle (PLC) describes the phases of development that a product goes through. The key stages of the life cycle are:

- **Introduction** – a new product or service is made available for purchase and organisations attempt to develop buyer interest.

- **Growth** – a period of rapid expansion of demand or activity as the product finds a market and the product demonstrates its potential.

- **Maturity** – a relatively stable period of time where there is little change in sales volumes year to year but competition between firms intensifies as growth slows down.

- **Decline** – a falling off in sales levels as the product becomes less competitive in the face of competition from newer products.

The PLC can be viewed in conjunction with the BCG Matrix in determining the impact on the company's cash flow from a portfolio of products at various stages in their life cycles. The BCG Matrix portfolio analysis is useful because it provides a framework to consider and forecast potential market growth and to evaluate the competitive dimension through an evaluation of market share. (Note. as Zuccini is a niche player then, in one sense, all of its products have a small market share in relation to the largest companies in motorbike industry. Zuccini's relative market share therefore needs to be considered in comparison to the other niche players.)

The Typhoon4 appears to be in its decline phase with sales falling, and may be viewed as a 'Dog' product (or perhaps a Dodo) within the BCG Matrix with low market share, low or negative growth, and modest or negative cash flow.

The StormRaider appears to be in the growth phase with replacement not due until 20Y9. It may therefore be viewed as a 'Star' within the BCG Matrix.

The Hurricane is in its R&D phase. It will not enter its introduction phase until either 20Y6 or 20Y8 (see below). It may therefore be viewed as an infant in the BCG Matrix with negative cash flow.

Overall, the benefit of the BCG Matrix is to view Zuccini's portfolio of products as impacting cash flows and liquidity in different ways at different points in their life cycles. Thus, for example, established or growth products are financing the development of new products.

When to end Typhoon4 production

In deciding on the timing of change for the Typhoon4 it is necessary to consider it in the context of the wider company product portfolio.

Whilst Typhoon4 sales are declining, the product is not necessarily unprofitable. As it is made in a separate factory in Italy, most of the costs associated with the Typhoon4 should be readily identifiable in order to make an assessment of product profitability.

In order to determine how long the production of the Typhoon4 should be allowed to continue in its decline phase, the following factors should be considered:

- How much inventory of the Typhoon4 exists (ie how many months' sales). If inventory is significant, then production will need to cease some time prior to sales ceasing.

- Evaluate the exit barriers to determine the optimum time to cease production (eg at the end of a lease agreement on machinery specific to the manufacture of the Typhoon4 or at the end of the useful life of machinery for making the Typhoon4).

- Potential response of competitors to any change.

- Need for new updates (eg a change in regulations on emissions with which the Typhoon4 does not comply, but with which the Typhoon4A and Typhoon5 do comply)

- Availability of cash to replace or modify. Even though its sales are declining, the Typhoon4 may still be cash generative. In contrast, the introduction of the Typhoon4A or the Typhoon5 would be likely initially to consume cash at a time it may be needed on R&D projects, eg for the Hurricane (see below).

Whether to produce the Typhoon4A or the Typhoon5

At this stage, there is insufficient information to make a firm decision as to whether the Typhoon4 should be replaced or modified. There are however a number of indicative factors which can be considered.

In terms of the product life cycle (PLC) replacing the Typhoon4 with the Typhoon4A will provide an extra two years of product life, effectively pushing it back into the maturity phase, and extending its life before the replacement of the Typhoon4A is needed with the Typhoon5 in 20Y7.

Replacing the Typhoon4 with the Typhoon5 on the other hand will, in PLC terms, in effect commence a new introduction phase with a much longer extended life cycle.

One of the problems of replacing the Typhoon4 with the Typhoon4A is that it is a two-stage process, as the Typhoon4A will then need to be replaced with the Typhoon5 two years later.

This raises two key questions:

- Will the transition costs of converting from the Typhoon4 to the Typhoon5 in one step be significantly different from the transition costs of converting from the Typhoon4 to the Typhoon4A, and then later from the Typhoon4A to the Typhoon5, as a two-step process?

- If the Typhoon5 starts production two years later, will its life cycle finish two years later, or at the same time for both options, irrespective of its introduction date?

The cash needed to replace a product is much greater than the amount needed to modify one, therefore the introduction of the Typhoon5 is likely initially to consume much more cash than the modification to the Typhoon4A. This may be at a time it is needed on R&D projects, eg for the Hurricane (see below).

Turning to marketing aspects, in trying to compete in a difficult external market it is important that Zuccini's product reputation is maintained and improved. This would indicate that the best product should be launched as soon as possible, which would be the Typhoon5. Prolonging the introduction of the Typhoon5 with the Typhoon4A may damage reputation and make future sales of all Zuccini's products more difficult.

Conclusion

Subject to more detailed information becoming available, based on the current information the Typhoon5 should be introduced as soon as possible. This will save a double change of product type and ensure that the best product is available to customers as soon as possible. The life cycles are driven by market conditions and so could well be coterminous for the Typhoon5 under either option. It may be that sales of the Typhoon4 continue to be made from inventory but, in this case, a short period of overlapping life cycles, where the old product price is discounted, is likely to be more acceptable than forcing customers into buying Typhoon4A technology which is not the best that Zuccini can offer.

Examiner's comments

Candidates appeared to be comfortable in the application of the product life cycle and the BCG matrix, identifying that the Typhoon 4 was in decline and could be classified as a dog product. The higher scoring answers also identified capital investment and the resulting liquidity position as key factors in making the decision. Disappointingly, most answers did not discuss the wider product portfolio context that in order to manage a product range, it is a sensible strategy to have a range of products all at different stages of the life cycle. Many candidates did not make sufficient distinction between types 4A and 5.

68.2 Factors

The launch of the Hurricane would introduce an extra model to the product portfolio, making it three in all. It would sit at the bottom end of the Zuccini quality range whether introduced in June 20Y6 as a basic product, or in June 20Y8 as a mid-market product.

Strategic factors

The StormRaider is an upmarket motorbike and the Typhoon4 is a mid to upmarket motorbike. The introduction of the Hurricane as a basic motorbike extends the product portfolio down the quality spectrum, which may cause brand confusion and damage reputation for the two other products in the portfolio.

There will be a significant delay of three years (until 20Y8) before the mid-market version of the Hurricane can be launched. There is significant uncertainty here as competitors are likely to launch new models during this period so the degree of competition by 20Y8 is difficult to estimate, causing additional uncertainty.

R&D plays a key role in product strategy and a number of strategic models are relevant in this context.

Porter's generic strategies: Product innovation could be a source of differentiation. Process innovation may enable differentiation for the £9,000 motorbike or cost leadership for the £6,000 motorbike.

Porter's value chain: R&D is included within the support activities of technology development. It can be harnessed in the service of lower costs or improved differentiation for the £6,000 motorbike.

Ansoff matrix: R&D supports all four strategic quadrants. Strategies of market penetration and product development are relevant to Zuccini in this context.

Industry and product life cycles: The obsolescence of existing products can be accelerated by R&D by other companies and so R&D is required to provide Zuccini with replacements to compete.

Operational factors

There appear to have been uncertainties relating to technical factors in the R&D process. In this sense R&D is key to determining the nature of the product and the way it is positioned in the market. However, the very nature of R&D means that it has uncertainty of operational outcomes. The mid-market product appears to present more difficulties and therefore more delay and more uncertainty. This would favour the earlier launch of the basic product in order to reduce uncertainty.

The R&D process may have unintended externalities. In other words, R&D may discover processes and products which may be of use, not just on the Hurricane, but also on the other two models, even though this was not the original purpose of the R&D.

Financial factors

Given that the company may have liquidity issues over the next few years then this may be a key factor in deciding between the 20Y6 launch and the 20Y8 launch.

Comparing the two choices, the 20Y8 launch is cash negative in the next few years. R&D tends to be expensive and over the next three years the mid-market motorbike R&D project will be consuming cash in its R&D efforts whilst delaying the product launch and therefore the future cash inflows. Even after the 20Y8 launch, the Hurricane would be in the introductory phase of its PLC and it may take a while before it will be any more than cash neutral.

In contrast the basic model will complete the R&D outflows in 20Y6 and launch thereafter with the ability to generate cash as it comes out of its introductory phase.

More information is needed to decide which alternative will ultimately generate the greater NPV over its life cycle but if short-term liquidity is an issue this points towards the basic model.

In pure undiscounted cash terms (ie zero discount rate) the cash flows from one unit of each product (in the absence of information on volumes) would be generated as follows:

20Y6 launch: £6,000 × 7 years = £42,000
20Y8 launch £9,000 × 6 years = £54,000

Whilst the 20Y8 mid-market product generates more revenue, there are several financial factors which mitigate against this, in favour of the 20Y6 launch of the basic product:

- The 20Y6 launch generates cash flows earlier and so will have a higher present value on average per £1 generated

- Additional R&D costs will be incurred for the 20Y8 mid-market product

- It seems likely that for the 20Y8 launch there will be greater operational costs in producing a mid-market product rather than a basic product

Conclusion

More information is needed on costs and volumes. However, based on the information available there seem too much delay and too much uncertainty to favour the 20Y8 mid-market product. Moreover, in financial terms the 20Y6 basic product generates more cash earlier. This may support the development of other products.

Rather than damage reputation it may be considered that the 20Y6 basic product could be launched under a different brand name.

Examiner's comments

This part was attempted reasonably well, with better candidates structuring their discussion using the headings provided in the question of strategic, operational and financial factors. In this part of the answer, most candidates did think about the overall strategy of where to position the product in the market and how a delayed launch would be perceived. The majority also identified the generic strategy issue in launching the low cost model, given the firm's differentiated niche focus. Conclusions were not always offered and, if they were, they were usually not fully explained or justified.

69   Kentish Fruit Farms (September 2015)

Marking guide

	Knowledge	Skill	Marks
69.1 PESTEL factors	3	6	9
69.2 Evaluation of two strategies	2	18	18
69.3 Ethical issues	3	6	8
69.4 Control procedures	3	6	8
	11	36	43

General comments

This is the mini case at 43 marks and also the data analysis question. It was well attempted.

The scenario relates to an organic fruit farm, KFF Ltd, which grows apples that are either sold to retailers or used in producing its own brand of organic apple juice. To increase capacity, KFF has planted some additional land with a new variety of apple trees and has also started to buy in apples from other organic farmers to use to produce juice. KFF's board is keen to evaluate the success of these strategies against its medium-term business objectives for revenue and profit. A supply chain issue has however arisen as a recent batch of KFF's organic apple juice, made using fruit from one of the new suppliers, was tested by the Food Standards Agency and found to contain artificial pesticides. 20% of the production run has already been distributed to a major retailer and KFF is considering whether to issue a public recall of these bottles, and what it can do to identify such quality problems in future.

Tutorial note:

Only 3 forces need to be analysed but these need to be justified as Key. There was plenty of obvious information in the scenario to discuss Social/Technological/Ecological/Legal. There was less in the scenario to support Political/ Economic.

69.1 *The key forces are:*

Social – consumers' attitudes to organic food are changing because of concerns about health and the environment. Organic food is seen to be more socially responsible – it helps address issues around global warming and the environment and reduces concerns about the consumption of harmful pesticide and fertiliser residues. These factors will work to increase industry demand. The accountability of farmers as a result of organic certification is also likely to increase consumer confidence in what they are buying. A focus on the procurement of local goods will benefit organic farmers in their region, as will public sentiment against genetically-modified crops.

Technological – the industry relies on the use of technology to avoid using harmful fertilisers and pesticides. As a result it has developed sophisticated weather management systems and atmospherically controlled growing and storage tunnels. These factors will help increase yields and also reduce the seasonality impact and perishability problems by extending the life of the product through storage, thus benefiting cashflow. Further technical advances may help the industry reduce costs and hence prices, making the products accessible to more consumers.

Ecological (Environmental) – a key factor in the growth of the organic farming industry has been a drive for more environmentally friendly products. Organic farming is seen to be more ecologically sound – the farming methods reduce harmful waste from the manufacture and use of agrochemicals and, since it is often also more local, there is less carbon footprint associated with its distribution. However the need for environmentally friendly farming methods may mean the industry struggles to compete on price with traditional farming methods. The latter may be more pest-resistant due to the use of fertilisers or may be able to achieve greater yields through artificial growth methods. A further environmental issue is the weather which can have a significant impact on crop quality and yields and which the industry attempts to manage through technology (discussed above).

Legal (Regulatory) – there is significant regulation in the food industry generally and particularly for organic produce. As well as complying with FSA and EU regulations regarding production, packaging and labelling, organic farmers also need to comply with regulations specifying organic farming methods. In addition they need to be approved for and obtain certification, then comply with its terms. There are severe sanctions for breaching regulations, and as a result compliance is critical and costs are likely to be high. Any changes in standards in the future will have an impact on the industry – also different countries have different standards which can be an issue for exports.

Political (there is much less in the scenario to go on for this)

Political factors refer to the attitude and approaches of the government and other parties to the organic farming movement. Any change in government may affect future regulations. The Green Party for example supports changes in the farming industry to make food production more sustainable and protect the environment and its resources; they are also in favour of local food production. Government initiatives to promote sustainability and healthy eating are likely to increase demand for organic products and hence benefit the industry. Inevitably these are links between political factors and legal factors such as consumer protection regulations and the certification of organic farmers.

Economic –(there is much less information to go on in the scenario for this)

Historically organic produce has been seen as a luxury product and is therefore less in demand when disposable incomes fall. However the move towards organic as a lifestyle choice reduces this risk for the industry, which appears to be in a growth phase. As demand increases there may be pressure to intensify farming operations which may not be consistent with organic methods. Many smaller organic farmers may find it challenging to deal with the size and bargaining power of large retail buyers, which could dictate prices and hence margins. From a financial point of view organic farmers, like traditional ones, are at risk due to seasonality of cashflows and unpredictability of weather.

Examiner's comments

This requirement was very well answered and was, on average, the best answered requirement on the paper. Most candidates used relevant information from the scenario to justify the importance of their selected PESTEL factor and explain its likely impact on the industry. A common mistake among weaker candidates was to treat PESTEL as if it were a company rather than industry model and/or to discuss relatively unimportant factors. A minority of candidates wasted time by completing a full PESTEL analysis when only three factors were required.

69.2 Data Analysis

Table 1:

	20Y3	20Y4
Hectares of KFF orchards yielding fruit	40	55
Tonnes of apples harvested	480	720
Yield (tonnes produced /hectare)	12.0	13.1
Tonnes of apples sold as fresh fruit	288	468
Tonnes of own apples used for juice	192	252
Crop Mix: fruit:juice	60:40	65:35
Tonnes of own apples used for juice production	192	252
Tonnes of apples bought in	-	48
Total tonnes of apples used for juice production	192	300
1 litre bottles of juice produced and sold	96,000	150,000
Bottles produced per tonne	500	500
Revenue: fresh fruit £'000	576	889
Tonnes of apples sold as fresh fruit	288	468
Fresh fruit: Revenue per tonne	2,000	1,900
Revenue: juice £'000	336	525
Total tonnes of apples used for juice production	192	300
Juice: revenue per tonne £'000	1,750	1,750
Juice: revenue per 1 litre bottle £	3.50	3.50
Sales revenue mix: Fruit : juice	63:37	63:37
Cost of sales £'000	540	812
Tonnes of apples sold as fruit/juice	480	768
Cost per tonne used £	1,125	1,057
Gross profit £'000	372	602
Gross profit per tonne £	775	784

Table 2:

	20Y3	20Y4
Gross profit margin	41%	43%
Operating margin	12%	10%
Operating costs as % of sales	28%	32%
Interest cover	2.13	1.97

Table 3: Analysis of yield from new trees

Incremental land	15 hectares
Incremental apple crop	240 tonnes
Yield (tonnes produced per hectare)	16 tonnes/hectare
15 hectares at standard yield of 12 tonnes	180 tonnes
Increased yield due to efficiency of new planting	60 tonnes

Table 4: Analysis of changes in revenue 20Y3-20Y4

	£
Revenue generated from additional trees: Strategy 1	
Incremental fruit crop: (468 - 288) x £1,900	342,000
Incremental juice crop (252 - 192) x £1,750	105,000
	447,000
Revenue generated from fruit bought in: Strategy 2	
48 × £1,750	84,000
	531,000
Revenue lost due to reduction in market price of fresh fruit:	
288 × £(2,000 – 1,900)	(28,800)
Total incremental revenue (Note. £1,414 – £912k = £502k)	**502,200**

Commentary:

KFF's profitability is limited by its capacity to meet all the demand for its products. To generate additional capacity, KFF have implemented two new strategies that impact on 20Y4 results:

(1) The purchase of land and intense planting of new trees to increase apple production and also improve yields per hectare. The first crop from this was produced in 20Y4.

(2) The decision from 20Y4 to purchase apples from local farmers to increase juice production. This will increase sales volumes of juice but is likely to reduce the margin if it is more expensive to buy in apples than to home grow them.

It is not clear whether these strategies will have had a 12 month impact or only affected results for part of the year, and more information would be useful to assess the timing of the change.

The overall performance of the business in relation to the objectives set is as follows:

	Objective	Actual 20Y4	Comment
Annual revenue growth	15%	55%	Achieved
Gross margin	45%	43%	Not achieved

On the face of it therefore the new strategies have achieved the required revenue growth, although since this is the first year of impact, the growth achieved may not be sustainable. The gross margin target has not been met, although gross margin has increased from 41% to 43% so it is moving in the right direction.

However further analysis is required, of each strategy, of performance overall and of performance in relation to the objectives.

Strategy 1: New trees:

The purpose of acquiring the land is twofold:

- To increase supply of apples
- To improve profitability by increasing the yield per hectare

The supply of apples has increased as the new orchard has come on stream, providing an additional 15 acres which in terms of land base increases the capacity of the farm by 37.5%. Ordinarily at KFF's 20Y3 yield the new land would have produced 12 tonnes per hectare or 180 tonnes of apples in total. The new farming method was expected to increase yields by 30%. In 20Y4 the new trees actually generated an additional crop of 240 tonnes, 60 tonnes above standard output, which is an increase in yield of 33.33% and resulted in a yield of 16 tonnes per hectare.

As a result the purchase of the land and the switch to more intensive planting appears to have been successful in increasing capacity. Table 4 shows that the fruit grown on the new trees increased revenue by £447,000 in 20Y4, although as we have no detail on costs we do not know how profitable this was.

A greater proportion of the crop was sold as fresh fruit (65% compared to the previous year's 60%) which perhaps suggests better quality output, but the revenue per tonne fell which, as KFF is a price-taker, is likely to be due to market factors.

Strategy 2: Purchase of other fruit:

During the year KFF acquired 48 tonnes of fruit from neighbouring farms, which it turned into juice and from which it generated £84,000 extra revenue. The additional volume of bottles did not have any impact on the price per bottle, which remained constant at £3.50 and therefore suggests strong demand. Again more information on the costs of buying in and processing the fruit would be useful. Also there is now some doubt about whether all fruit bought in met the required organic standards, and this may give rise to concerns over this strategy in the future.

Success of strategies:

No breakdown is given of the costs of either strategy. In total, they have allowed KFF to increase revenue by £531,000 in 20Y4 (58% of 20Y3 revenue). The actual revenue increase of 55% (or £502,000) is lower because the market price for fresh fruit has fallen from £2,000 to £1,900 per tonne in 20Y4.

Overall the revenue mix of fresh fruit and juice has not changed.

The increase in revenue of 55% exceeds the objective of 15%. However this type of growth would be expected in the first year of the capacity increase. The objective is for annual revenue growth of 15% but it is not clear whether that is expected to be each year or on an average basis. In 20Y5 KFF will only be able to generate more revenue by purchasing additional apples for juice or adopting more new farming methods to increase yields.

Profitability

The gross profit margin has increased overall. Purchasing fruit is likely to have reduced margin on the bottles of juice which incorporate it. The increased yield per hectare will have an upward effect on margin, although this may depend on how expensive the new farming method is. The fact that the cost of sales per tonne has fallen from £1,125 to £1,057 implies that the net effect has been positive.

In order to assess the profitability of the decisions, it would be useful to know:

- the cost per hectare of farming the new trees on the new land compared to the existing trees on the existing land

- the cost per tonne that KFF has had to pay to buy in the fruit

Although the gross margin has increased, the operating margin has fallen from 12% to 10% which is due to increased operating costs. Thus £502,000 of additional revenue has generated £230,000 of additional gross profit but only £33,000 of extra operating profit. More information is needed about the increase in operating costs.

Cash flow

Interest cover has fallen from 2.13 times to 1.97 times because of the 40% increase in interest costs. The customer mix may have changed and the additional sales may have come from retailers who have dictated longer credit terms. Thus the business' cash position has deteriorated and interest charges have increased. More information on cash flows, and on KFF's capital structure, would be useful.

Further details:

To better explain performance, the business needs to analyse costs between the old and the new trees and also separately analyse the profitability of the two product lines, juice and fresh fruit. Management accounts for 20Y4 showing monthly statement of profit or loss and cash flow would help better assess the seasonality of the business and also the impact of the new strategies.

Examiner's comments

The data analysis requirement was well attempted by the majority of candidates. Most were well practised at providing a table of up-front calculations and a list of additional information, although this was not always tailored to the scenario. The key to a good answer was to identify appropriate financial and operational calculations which would help determine the impact of each strategy separately: both the planting of the additional trees and the purchase of apples from other farmers. The better candidates did this, providing calculations to assess the impact of the additional land capacity and the change in yield, and structuring their evaluation under two separate headings. Weaker candidates were poor in this regard, merely providing calculations of changes in financial figures, within their narrative, and evaluating the performance of the company overall, rather than the impact of each strategy against the objectives that had been set. The best candidates recognised that there was sufficient information to assess the revenue impact of the strategies but not their overall profitability.

69.3 Ethical issues

Ethics pertains to whether a particular behaviour is deemed acceptable in the context under consideration. In short, it is 'doing the right thing'.

In making any ethical evaluation it is first necessary to establish the facts. In this case, it would seem that the facts are reasonably clear in terms of a batch of KFF juice being identified as containing non-organic pesticides and the fruit having been traced to a supplier. What is uncertain is how KFF should react to this.

Given the extensive regulations affecting the organic food industry, the issue of legality needs to be considered and legal advice taken by KFF as to its responsibility. Although the fruit concerned may have come from another farm, the juice is sold under the KFF brand and KFF are likely to be held responsible for the breach by the FSA, which may apply sanctions. KFF may face losing their organic certification, which may require that everything they sell should be 100% organic.

Joe Fielding appears to be prepared to behave ethically in relation to the undistributed product, which would be relabelled and sold as non-organic, presumably at a lower price. It is the action suggested in relation to the bottles that have already been distributed which raises ethical issues.

In making a decision as to how to proceed, it is helpful to apply the Institute of Business Ethics three tests:

- Transparency
- Effect
- Fairness

Transparency – a public recall of the juice already distributed would be transparent and in the public interest. It would be consistent with the reputation KFF has built as an ethical farm. Keeping quiet about the bottles that have already been distributed and only addressing the remaining inventory is less transparent and KFF should consider whether it would mind people (existing customers, regulators, employees) knowing that it has taken this action. Lack of full disclosure may in fact not be an option as it may be imposed by the regulator as a matter of public interest.

Effect –A full recall may embarrass KFF and the retailer but would prevent harm to the end-consumers. The effect of a partial action would be to keep information from the retailer, and consumers who have already bought the juice would suffer due to KFF acting in its own and not the public interest. As a minimum this would be because consumers pay higher prices for organic juice which is in fact non-organic. More serious, although perhaps less likely, is the fact that their health may be affected by the consumption of pesticide residues.

Fairness – It is likely that competitors, the retailer and consumers would not take kindly to the fact that KFF has knowingly deceived them and mis-represented its product.

Actions

KFF should be guided by legal advice and its discussions with FSA, and should co-operate in all investigations made by the FSA. The matter may be of sufficient seriousness for FSA to apply sanctions. The best action would be for KFF to act honestly and with integrity, making a full disclosure of all the facts. Even if the FSA does not require disclosure, KFF should consider doing so, to avoid further damage to its reputation. KFF should then have discussions with the supplier concerned to establish how the use of non-organic pesticides has arisen and why it was not detected. It may have recourse against the supplier depending on the contractual terms.

Having made the suggestion that the company should be dishonest, the board should consider discussing with Joe Fielding the importance of ethical behaviour, and should review the company's overall culture to ensure that all staff are in line with the importance of maintaining ethics and also the organic status of the company's produce.

Examiner's comments

This requirement was well answered. The ethical issues relating to the possible production and sale of non-organic juice were reasonably easy for most candidates to identify. The vast majority of candidates also recognised that there was a legal/regulatory issue here given the FSA and the need for organic certification. Some candidates restricted their marks by not providing clear actions. Better answers distinguished between the actions that might be appropriate in respect of the contaminated juice that has already been distributed and the action that the company should take regarding the remaining bottles.

69.4 Control procedures and information systems

Given the nature of KFF's business, quality is a critical success factor. Quality assurance and quality control are critical to standardise the quality of fruit and juice products and also ensure that they are safe to consume.

Even if KFF was not an organic farm, the requirement to produce safe foods in a hygienic way is part of the law and there are serious penalties for contravening hygiene and food safety legislation.

In creating a new relationship with suppliers, KFF should establish a service level agreement, agreeing not just on the financial terms of supply but also on key targets/standards that need to be met and the consequence of not doing. Any expectations that KFF has in relation to ethics and sustainability and the need for suppliers to conform to KFF's policies in these areas would need to be set out.

Suppliers should be selected based on their experience and the quality of their products. Clearly verifying a supplier's organic certification and credentials would be a critical step in early due diligence, before contracts are agreed. KFF should carry out an annual inspection visit where the supplier is required to confirm that organic standards have been met. If suppliers are local then occasional drop-in visits may be feasible.

Once a supplier has been contracted then a key control procedure is to measure and monitor supplier performance. Joe is correct that early detection of problems is desirable but costs (both financial and reputational) are generally lower if KFF is able to prevent defective output rather than simply detecting it.

KFF should go through each stage of processing, from purchase of apples and other ingredients/packaging products to the bottling of the final juice, to identify where factors exist that could influence either product quality or safety and then devise procedures that control those factors.

Quality assurance focuses on procedures and standards that will ensure product problems are eliminated or minimised during the production process. In KFF's case this might include inspecting or sample testing fruit that is bought in, before using it in production, in the hope that any poor quality fruit is identified and rejected or that any traces of pesticides would be identified.

Fruit that is to be stored before use might need testing on arrival at KFF and then inspecting again after storage but before use. Any bottles, caps or other items involved in the juice production should also be inspected and tested, since these may cause quality issues.

Quality control is associated with checking a product after it has been produced and this might involve sample testing bottles of juice from every batch of production. Even if there are no pesticide issues, this may be a good idea to ensure consistency of the product over time in relation to flavour, appearance etc.

Given the importance of local reputation, the need for certification and the high level of regulation in the industry, KFF would be advised to apply quality control procedures to all its own fruit and juice production, as well as to suppliers' fruit, if it is not already doing so.

If it is unable to expand its own capacity, then for long-term sustainability of the farm, KFF needs to establish partnerships with local farmers which are transparent and add strategic value. An information system can be used to enhance this, not just from the point of view of supplier control and monitoring but also for measuring KFF's own performance, by capturing a range of data.

An information system can track performance overtime, and may be useful in identifying trends or detecting early warning signs of future problems. It also provides KFF with evidence for its own organic certification and in relation to supplier performance when discussing or renewing contracts with suppliers.

Appropriate operational measures (KPIs) to monitor supplier performance might include:

Quality assurance

Rejection rate of apples per tonne purchased – this could be compared against KFF's own achievement and also across suppliers and harvests

The reasons for reject could then also be broken down as this will help identify and address the cause of the problem eg:

Level of pesticide/fertiliser detected on apple crop

% of apples contaminated eg by insects

% of apples that were mouldy/physically damaged

These would need to be considered in relation to any agreed tolerances that have been established with the supplier but also in relation to organic standard requirements.

Quality control

Rejection rate of bottles per batch of juice

Level of wastage during production process

% of bottles not meeting specifications (weight, volume, appearance, labelling etc)

Other measures useful for supplier monitoring might include:

Tonnes delivered vs tonnes promised

Number of disruptions to production caused due to late delivery/apple shortages

Price per tonne

Examiner's comments

This was one of the worst attempted requirements on the paper but answers were quite polarised. The main difference in the standard of answers to this requirement related to whether candidates were familiar with the concept of quality assurance and control procedures. Weaker answers simply listed brief checks that KFF could undertake in relation to suppliers. Stronger candidates identified procedures and processes that could be used to prevent and detect quality issues and monitor performance. A significant number of candidates ignored the requirement to suggest some specific KPIs.

70 Premier Paper Products plc (September 2015)

Marking guide

	Knowledge	Skill	Marks
70.1 Business development and CSFs	3	8	10
70.2 Risk register	3	6	9
70.3 Memorandum	3	10	11
	9	24	30

General comments

Overall this question was also well attempted.

The scenario concerns Premier Paper Products plc (PPP) a company which prints banknotes and identity documents for a variety of central banks and governments. New technology means that some central banks have recently decided to change from using paper banknotes to polymer notes and PPP's board is unsure whether to invest in the new technology, which has already been adopted by one of its competitors.

70.1 CSFs for PPP

PPP's growth

Ansoff

The Ansoff model is a two-by-two matrix of Products (new and existing) and Markets (new and existing).

PPP started out as a manufacturer of banknotes (existing product) for its country's central bank (existing market). The growth of its business has then come from both geographical expansion and the development of new products.

Market development – existing products and new markets.

The expansion of the banknote production into over 100 countries across Europe and Asia is market development on a geographical basis, as is the sale of security paper to the state-owned printing works which use it to produce their own banknotes. In terms of CSFs, PPP's design skills and innovative security features are likely to have helped it build market share.

Product development – new products and existing markets.

PPP realised that its existing customer base of central banks would benefit from other products. As a result, 60 years ago, it capitalised on one of its CSFs - its existing customer relationships and contracts - by expanding its product range and moving into the related area of banknote sorting and counting machines and inspection equipment.

Further product development or Diversification - new product, new market

Growth continued with the establishment of a new product range: passports and identity cards. PPP continued to leverage its expertise in designing and printing security paper and its reputation for maintaining security and confidentiality by extending this to government identity schemes. In 20X0 PPP won its first contract to print passports and driving licences for its own government and now produces documents for 65 countries.

Although closely related to central bank clients, governments might be said to be a different market and hence this strategy might be deemed diversification.

Lynch Expansion method matrix

The Lynch model is another two-by-two matrix of method of company growth (organic growth and external development) and geographical location (home (domestic) and international). Under this model, the primary focus for PPP's growth has been through organic growth and international development. Both banknote and identity card production started with the domestic market, but because the size of this is limited, to achieve economies of scale PPP had to expand internationally, targeting a variety of global central bank and government clients.

PPP's CSFs have allowed it to grow organically rather than through acquisition. It has achieved this by continuing innovation through in-house research and development and also by leveraging its client base.

Critical success factors are the product features that are particularly valued by customers and/or the activities that an organisation must excel at to outperform the competition.

In the case of PPP, a summary of the key critical success factors discussed above that have facilitated its development are:

- Innovation - expertise in evolving innovative and sophisticated security features for paper, notes and identity documents

- Reputation - for the design of high quality, elegant banknotes and for maintaining security/confidentiality

- Relationships and partnerships/contracts with central banks and governments

- Operational excellence in relation to quality, accuracy, reliability

70.2 Risk register

A variety of key business risks facing PPP's banknote division are set out below:

Nature of business risk	Impact and likelihood	Risk management
Strategic: technological change renders the need for banknotes obsolete	Technological developments clearly have a big impact on the industry and are changing the nature of the product and market as the demand for cash reduces and it is replaced by cards and other contactless payment methods. Changes in technology may reduce the volume of business but for the present time it seems unlikely that it will remove the need for banknotes entirely. Also the technology is likely to be adopted at different rates in different markets.	Reduce risk in short term by developing different technologies eg polymer notes so PPP will retain central bank customers even if they switch from paper. May have to accept this as a risk in longer term PPP as a whole has reduced risk by diversifying product range eg identity cards and passports
Strategic: failure to produce technologically advanced and competitive banknote products	Industry standards and security features are continually evolving. Failure to innovate would likely result in lost market share and lower margins.	Reduce risk through: continued investment in R&D and design, and employment of skilled designers. Consider JV with universities/scientists
Strategic: failure to win or renew key contracts	Contracts are often long-term so timing of renewal may be predictable. The loss of contracts is likely as this is a competitive environment and contracts are awarded by central banks which can be affected by political factors outside PPP's control. Failure to win contracts may result in PPP operating below optimal capacity, restricting growth and profitability	Reduce risk by maintaining close, trusted relationships with customers. Monitor sales pipeline and undertake production planning to ensure critical mass. Monitor activities of competitors where possible. Maintain brand and reputation for design and operational excellence. Implement/maintain a CRM system and focus on key contracts as they come due for renewal.

Nature of business risk	Impact and likelihood	Risk management
Operational: poor quality product or standards of service damage the company's reputation	Highly technical contracts with very detailed specifications mean this is a key risk. The very public nature of the product and the high profile central bank customer mean that if a problem does occur reputational damage is quite likely, with a serious impact including possible loss of contracts. Poor quality banknotes or errors would require re-working or perhaps contract penalty payments.	Reduce risk through quality assurance/total quality management and operational excellence programmes.
Operational: product security. A breakdown in security procedures resulting in theft of products from a site or loss of notes in transit	Likelihood: PPP's past history suggests this is reasonably unlikely Impact: PPP may be contractually liable	Reduce risk by: Security screening for all staff. Physical controls regarding site access, material stores etc would reduce the risk on site. Use of stringent controls for personnel and carriers involved in distribution. Transfer risk through Insurance.
Hazard: loss of a key manufacturing site or inventory at a site eg through fire	Depending on the details of the contract, this may result in litigation. The impact would be severe, the likelihood is unknown.	Reduce likelihood by having preventative measures such as advanced smoke detection and sprinkler systems, plus 24 hour monitoring. Transfer through insurance. Contingency plan for other sites to operate as back-up.
Compliance: failure to comply with legal or regulatory requirements	Value and nature of product means there is some likelihood here and reputational impact would be high	Avoid/reduce by: Implementing code of conduct and ethics Screening and security clearance for all employees Disciplinary procedures Training in rules and procedures

Tutorial note:

Other relevant key risks were awarded credit. Only THREE were required.

Examiner's comments

The majority of candidates produced a well-structured table, identifying three risks facing PPP's banknote division, although weaker candidates did not always concentrate on the key ones. Some candidates limited their marks by not addressing all elements of the requirement comprehensively eg focussing on the impact of the risk and its management, without considering its nature and likelihood. The strongest answers identified a range of key risks and used the TARA model to identify appropriate risk management strategies. A number of candidates wasted time and marks discussing risks facing PPP as a whole rather than the banknote division.

70.3 Memorandum

To: PPP Board
From: A Manager, Banknote division
Date: September 20Y5
Re: Polymer bank notes

Factors to consider in deciding whether to invest in the technology to produce polymer banknotes include the following:

Competition

Uniquel is currently the only competitor producing polymer notes, but if these are deemed by central banks to be the way forward, then other printing companies are likely to follow suit. This will have an impact on

(1) The demand for PPP's paper product
(2) The number of contracts that PPP can retain on renewal

Likely buyers and their preferences

Potential customers for polymer notes include:

- Central banks who already outsource production to PPP

- Central banks who outsource production to PPP's competitors (private companies or other in-house printers)

- Central banks who currently print in-house

Since a major issue for the industry is security it appears likely that more central banks will move to polymer or alternatively demand increasingly expensive security features for paper notes. A way of ensuring optimal production is to approach other in-house state printing works that do not have PPP's economies of scale and may increasingly find it too costly to keep up with security developments for a small volume of notes.

Environmental considerations

The desire on the part of governments, businesses and consumers to be more environmentally friendly and to promote sustainability may influence the move away from paper to polymer.

Timing of any adoption of new technology

PPP could wait and see to what extent central banks move to polymer as their contracts come up for renewal and make a decision once it has more information. However this will allow Uniquel and any other competitors which enter the market to steal market share. Since banknote contracts are long-term (10 years on average) and this may increase, given the seven year lifetime of the new notes, it could be locked out of the market for a long time. PPP must also consider the impact on its reputation for innovation of being seen not to adopt new technology.

Resources and competences

New machinery is required which may necessitate more factory space. In addition it will take time to recruit the appropriate workforce and source suppliers of polymer. PPP is an expert in producing security paper products – it may not currently have in-house expertise to develop, design and print polymer banknotes. Any errors or issues of quality in the early stages of the process may affect its reputation and position in the paper banknote market.

Costs

A contract for paper notes requires production of notes every three years, compared to every seven for polymer. Thus PPP will need to tender for and win new contracts every year or persuade existing customers to switch to ensure efficient utilisation of production facilities.

Other issues to consider if a decision is taken to introduce polymer are:

- Whether to run the two technologies side by side or cease paper production and switch to polymer

- Whether eventually demand for banknotes will cease altogether as payments move to electronic systems in the longer term

Product portfolio

Paper notes appear to be a cash cow product for PPP currently. The question is to what extent demand will decline and to what extent PPP, as a major industry player, might influence this decline by making the move to polymer. The immediate abandonment of PPP's major product seems implausible, however over the next few years sales may decline to the point where paper notes might then be abandoned.

The adoption of polymer notes is at an early stage in the lifecycle. PPP could aim to stay in the paper notes market all the time it is making sufficient returns and as one of the biggest players it has economies of scale which will probably allow it to outlast smaller competitors. However whether in the long term there will be a dual market for both paper and polymer, or whether eventually paper notes will disappear over time in favour of polymer, needs to be considered.

The future of the banknote

The lifecycle of the banknote industry appears uncertain. Changing consumer preferences appear to have reduced demand for traditional cash payment. Thus the banknote division faces a long-term threat posed by phone, card and other digital payment mechanisms. Scenario planning may help to identify future risks and possible strategic responses. However although demand for cash is reduced, it appears likely that it will not disappear altogether and that there may be more demand for cash in some parts of the world than others, because different countries are at different stages in the lifecycle of cash and electronic payment mechanisms.

Conclusion

On balance it appears that there is a sound strategic argument for the introduction of the new technology. However forecasts need to be prepared and a detailed cost benefit analysis/investment appraisal undertaken to assess the incremental effect of introducing polymer.

Examiner's comments

Most, but surprisingly not all candidates, scored an easy format mark for setting out their answer in the memo format required. Candidates who used sub-headings to structure their answer tended to produce a wider range of points than those who merely listed a range of unconnected factors. Better candidates provided a balanced argument regarding the benefits and problems associated with investing in the polymer technology, linking their answers to the risks identified in 70.2. Most candidates provided an initial recommendation as to whether the investment was advisable and the best candidates identified the steps that should be taken to reach a decision.

---

71 Taxi Tracker (September 2015)

Marking guide

		Knowledge	Skill	Marks
71.1	Cost and value drivers	3	6	8
71.2	Benefits of dynamic demand-based pricing	3	6	8
71.3	Calculations and evaluation	1	11	11
		7	23	27

General comments

The third question had the lowest average mark, which was influenced by a number of poor answers to requirement (71.3).

The scenario relates to a company, TT, which has launched a free smartphone app that allows it to act as an intermediary between private hire taxi drivers and their potential customers in a major capital city. Private hire drivers who pass TT's screening process are issued with a TT smartphone which allows them to be registered and tracked on the TT system. Customers can use the TT app to get a fare quote, book a driver and track their arrival. Fares are set using a dynamic demand-based pricing model and increase when vehicles are in short supply. TT currently retains 20% of the fare as commission. There are rumours that a rival firm is planning to launch its own taxi booking app in the city, and TT is considering cutting its fares by 25% for a limited period of four weeks but is unsure whether to alter its commission.

71.1 Cost and value drivers

An organisation's value chain is the sequence of activities by which value is added to its service. This influences the margin a customer is prepared to pay over the costs the organisation incurs in delivering the service.

Within the value chain there can be both cost and value drivers. Whilst cost drivers influence the cost of a given activity, value drivers help an organisation to differentiate itself from competitors. TT's success has been built around its smartphone app which facilitates ease of booking, cashless payment, and improved customer service compared to both Citicabs and existing PHVs. As a result it appears to be following a differentiation strategy.

In the case of TT, the key drivers include:

Tutorial note:

Only **three** were required.

Technology as a value driver of customer service – TT makes widespread use of existing technology (GPS, phone, electronic payments) to add value by making it easier for customers to book a car, track it and pay for it. Using the phone as a meter makes prices more transparent for customers and the payment system is also more secure as drivers do not handle money.

- Technology as a cost driver - The use of the smartphone app reduces the costs to TT of matching drivers and customers since this largely happens without any need for intervention by TT. It means that TT can provide a very high level of customer service at a low cost to itself, connecting customers with the nearest available driver at the touch of a button.

- Procurement (cost driver) – TT's HR model is one of independent contractors rather than employees. While this reduces cost the dynamic demand-based pricing model would also ensure that there is flexibility of supply, as drivers are incentivised to make themselves available when more cars are needed.

- After sales (value driver) - Asking customers to rate journeys and drivers creates a perception that TT cares about the customer experience. The fact that drivers have to score at least 4 out of 5 to be able to continue is likely to give the customer confidence in the quality of the service.

- Customer service (value driver) - Fast booking and reduced waiting times for cars, the ability to track cars and the ease of payment all create an enhanced customer service experience.

- Firm infrastructure (cost driver) - TT operates a low-cost, flexible model. It has little in the way of infrastructure costs (no requirement for investment in non-current assets such as cars) or employment costs of drivers.

Examiner's comments

This requirement was well done by most candidates, who as usual demonstrated good knowledge of Porter's value chain analysis. The better candidates linked their discussion to TT's generic strategy, identified whether each key driver selected was a cost or value driver, linked it with the relevant aspect of the value chain, and explained how it gave TT a competitive advantage.

71.2 Benefits of dynamic demand-based pricing

Dynamic demand-based pricing is an attempt by TT to find a price at which supply and demand are equal and hence could be argued to be a market-driven approach. TT increases the price in periods of peak demand, when the supply of available PHVs is lower than the number of customers. This has the effect of attracting more drivers because the journeys are more lucrative, hence increasing supply, whilst potentially reducing demand temporarily as the more price-sensitive customers decide to make alternative arrangements for their journey or wait until prices fall again. The extent to which this happens will depend on the price elasticity of demand.

Essentially this strategy is similar to one of price discrimination, used for example by railways or cinemas, where prices vary according to the time of day, or dynamic pricing used by airlines, where prices vary according to the actual level of demand compared to what is deemed a normal level.

The model allows TT to extract the maximum possible revenue by charging higher prices to people who are willing to pay more. Whilst some may argue this is unfair to customers, TT is transparent about their approach to pricing and customers have alternative forms of transport and other PHVs/Citicabs available so are making a free choice.

It could be argued that customers benefit as this approach to pricing is not just about exploiting demand but also about incentivising drivers to work at peak times in order to increase supply, thereby offering the customer a better service. Also drivers benefit as they earn more money and are therefore compensated for having to work at times that are perhaps less sociable eg public holidays.

To some extent it is a matter of perception as to which price (the high or low fare) is seen as the norm and therefore whether TT are seen to exploit customers by increasing the price in busy periods, or considered to be offering a discount at quieter times.

Unlike Citicabs, whose prices are fixed by the regulator, TT is free to set its own prices. It would be interesting to see how the maximum prices charged by TT compare to those of Citicabs.

Examiner's comments

The discussion of the benefits of demand-based pricing was well done by the majority of candidates, with many identifying both demand and supply side factors. The requirement to consider whether this was unfair to customers was less well done and some weak candidates ignored it altogether. Better answers identified that the use of price discrimination is common in many industries. They pointed out that TT's demand-based pricing model will serve to balance supply and demand, facilitate its promise to make cars available in five minutes, and be transparent so customers can choose rivals such as Citicabs if they are cheaper.

71.3 Calculations and evaluation

(a) Evaluation of fare reduction strategy:

Current fares received	£
130,000 x 4 x £10	5,200,000
Split:	
Drivers 80%	4,160,000
TT 20%	1,040,000

Fares reduced by 25%, demand unaffected	£
130,000 x 4 x £7.50	3,900,000
Split as now:	
Drivers 80%	3,120,000
TT 20%	780,000

TT would lose £260,000 (£780,000 compared to £1,040,000) and drivers would be £1,040,000 worse off (£3,120,000 compared to £4,160,000).

Fares reduced by 25%, demand increases 15%

	£
130,000 x 1.15 x 4 x £7.50	4,485,000
Split to maintain drivers' income:	
Drivers	4,160,000
TT	325,000

TT is £715,000 worse off (£325,000 compared to £1,040,000 previously).

Drivers are unaffected.

(b) For neither TT nor the drivers to be worse off, and there to be no change in the 20% commission structure, revenue would need to be maintained at £5,200,000 still.

Where n is the number of journeys: n x 4 x £7.5 = £5,200,000

Hence n = 173,333 (£5,200,000/£30)

This requires an increase in demand of 33.3% for the month.

(c) Evaluation of fare reduction strategy

	TT	Drivers
	£'000	£'000
Current strategy	1,040	4,160
25% reduction, no change in demand, 20% commission	780	3,120
25% reduction, 15% increase in demand, maintain driver income	325	4,160
25% reduction, 20% commission, 33.3% increase in demand	1,040	4,160

If fares are reduced by 25%, with no corresponding increase in demand, the total fares received are £3,900,000 and under the 20% commission, both TT and the drivers are worse off: TT would lose £260,000 and drivers £1,040,000.

This is likely to cause drivers to move away from TT and contract with other PHV operators in an attempt to maintain their income levels. A lack of availability of drivers may then affect TT's customer service levels or cause higher demand-based prices.

If fares are reduced and demand increases by 15%, the new fares received are £4,485,000.

If TT guarantees that drivers will receive the same income, then TT suffers all the impact of the fare reduction and would be £715,000 worse off than in a normal four week period.

However if the increase in demand is permanent as customers stay loyal to TT, then in future months TT's income will increase. Also TT would be able to advertise this to drivers as a reduction in its commission to 7% (£325k/£4,485k) and may actually attract more drivers as a result. This seems a sensible strategy.

For neither TT nor the drivers to be affected by the fare reduction, an increase in demand of 33.3% for the month is required, which seems an ambitious target and may depend on the elasticity of demand as well as the reactions of competitors.

Other factors to consider:

Although the fare reduction may be attractive, in peak periods when the demand-based pricing model kicks in, the reduction may not be obvious to customers and hence may not have the desired effect.

TT's price reduction may lead to a price war in the PHV market, which will end up permanently reducing every operator's prices and hence margins.

The level of demand will be stimulated if demand for TT's product is price-sensitive, but the customer's decision to use TT may be more about ease of use, service, age of customer – in which case the price reduction may not stimulate demand.

Ultimately TT may be prepared to suffer a short-term reduction in income in the hope of strengthening its loyal customer base and ensuring it retains its drivers before the entry of a new rival.

Examiner's comments

This was the worst attempted requirement on the paper. Candidates seemed to score very well or very poorly. Common mistakes in the calculations included not considering the impact for a 4 week period, confusing the percentage commission with the percentage price reduction and ignoring the constraint of maintaining the driver's income in the second calculation. Many weaker candidates ignored either the calculation element or the discussion element of the requirement completely, limiting the marks available. Better candidates used their calculations as a starting point to discuss whether the strategy was sensible, identifying that the numbers are based on certain limiting assumptions and that wider issues may be relevant.